STAR WARS

HEROES FOR A NEW HOPE

STAR WARS

HEROES FOR A NEW HOPE

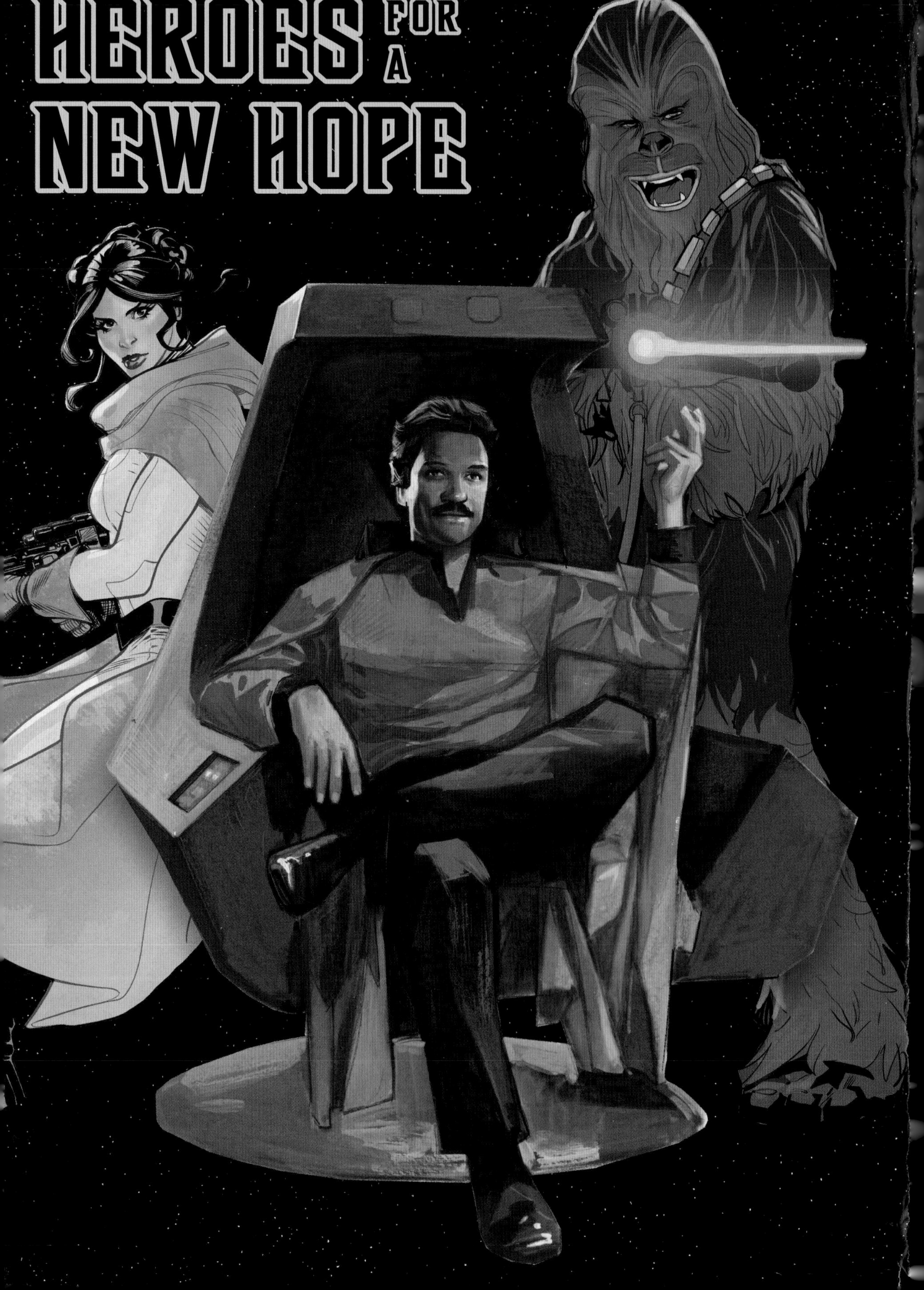

PRINCESS LEIA

Writer	**MARK WAID**
Penciler	**TERRY DODSON**
Inker	**RACHEL DODSON**
Colorist	**JORDIE BELLAIRE**
Letterer	**VC's JOE CARAMAGNA**
Cover Art	**TERRY DODSON & RACHEL DODSON**

LANDO

Writer	**CHARLES SOULE**
Artist	**ALEX MALEEV**
Color Artist	**PAUL MOUNTS**
Letterer	**VC's JOE CARAMAGNA**
Cover Art	**ALEX MALEEV** WITH EDGAR DELGADO (#1)

CHEWBACCA

Writer	**GERRY DUGGAN**
Artist	**PHIL NOTO**
Letterer	**VC's JOE CARAMAGNA**
Cover Art	**PHIL NOTO**

Assistant Editors	**HEATHER ANTOS & CHARLES BEACHAM**
Editor	**JORDAN D. WHITE**
Executive Editors	**C.B. CEBULSKI & MIKE MARTS**

Editor in Chief	**AXEL ALONSO**
Chief Creative Officer	**JOE QUESADA**
Publisher	**DAN BUCKLEY**

For Lucasfilm:

Creative Director	**MICHAEL SIGLAIN**
Senior Editors	**JENNIFER HEDDLE, FRANK PARISI**
Lucasfilm Story Group	**RAYNE ROBERTS, PABLO HIDALGO, LELAND CHEE**

Collection Editor	**JENNIFER GRÜNWALD**
Associate Editor	**SARAH BRUNSTAD**
Editor, Special Projects	**MARK D. BEAZLEY**
VP, Production & Special Projects	**JEFF YOUNGQUIST**
SVP Print, Sales & Marketing	**DAVID GABRIEL**
Book Designer	**ADAM DEL RE**

STAR WARS: HEROES FOR A NEW HOPE. Contains material originally published in magazine form as PRINCESS LEIA #1-5, LANDO #1-5 and CHEWBACCA #1-5. First printing 2016. ISBN# 978-1-302-90223-0. Published by MARVEL WORLDWIDE, INC., a subsidiary of MARVEL ENTERTAINMENT, LLC. OFFICE OF PUBLICATION: 135 West 50th Street, New York, NY 10020. STAR WARS and related text and illustrations are trademarks and/or copyrights, in the United States and other countries, of Lucasfilm Ltd. and/or its affiliates. © & TM Lucasfilm Ltd. No similarity between any of the names, characters, persons, and/or institutions in this magazine with those of any living or dead person or institution is intended, and any such similarity which may exist is purely coincidental. Marvel and its logos are TM Marvel Characters, Inc. **Printed in China.** ALAN FINE, President, Marvel Entertainment; DAN BUCKLEY, President, TV, Publishing & Brand Management; JOE QUESADA, Chief Creative Officer; TOM BREVOORT, SVP of Publishing; DAVID BOGART, SVP of Business Affairs & Operations, Publishing & Partnership; C.B. CEBULSKI, VP of Brand Management & Development, Asia; DAVID GABRIEL, SVP of Sales & Marketing, Publishing; JEFF YOUNGQUIST, VP of Production & Special Projects; DAN CARR, Executive Director of Publishing Technology; ALEX MORALES, Director of Publishing Operations; SUSAN CRESPI, Production Manager; STAN LEE, Chairman Emeritus. For information regarding advertising in Marvel Comics or on Marvel.com, please contact Vit DeBellis, Integrated Sales Manager, at vdebellis@marvel.com. For Marvel subscription inquiries, please call 888-511-5480. **Manufactured between 6/24/2016 and 9/12/2016 by R.R. DONNELLEY ASIA PRINTING SOLUTIONS, CHINA.**

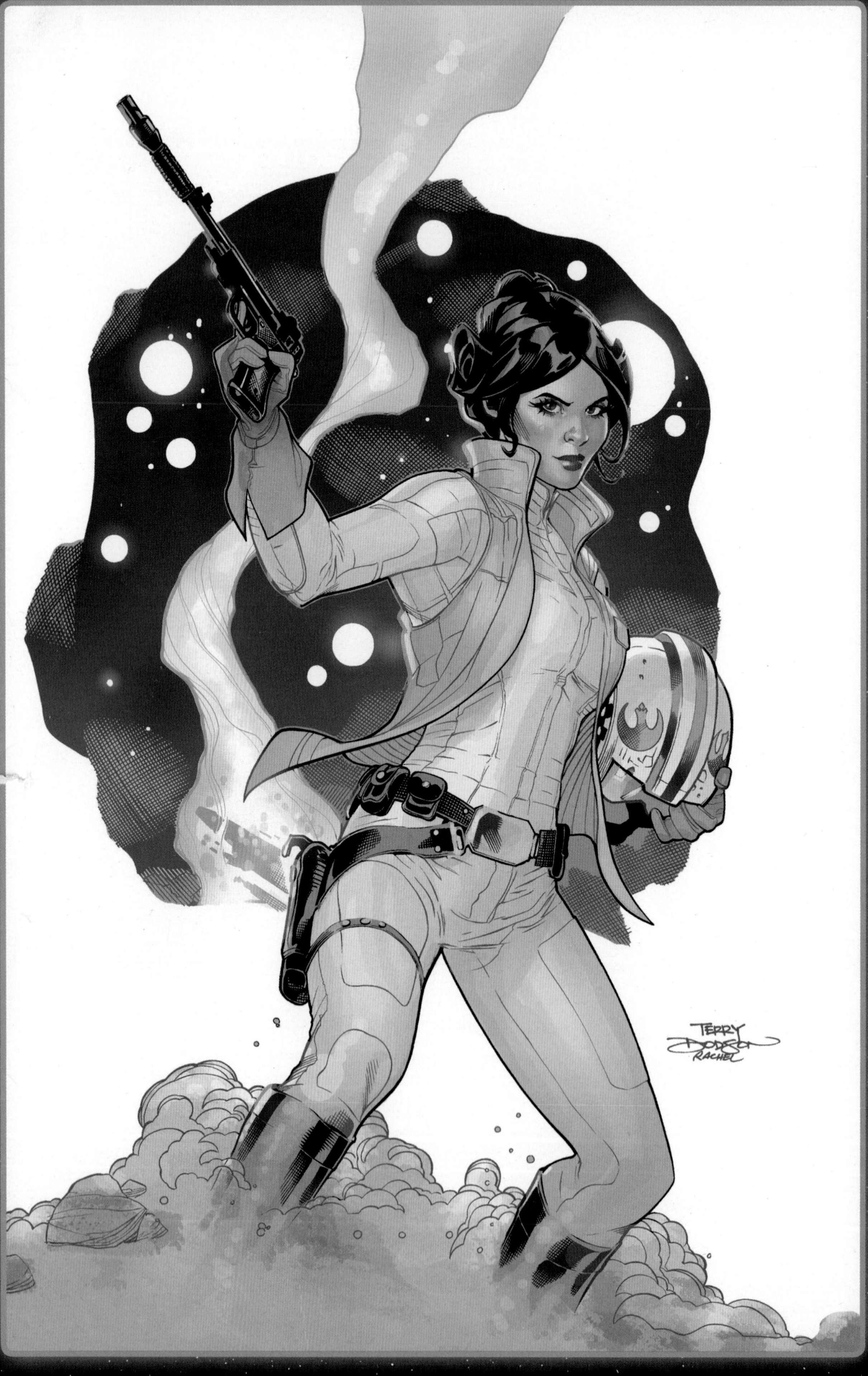
TERRY
DODSON
RACHEL

PRINCESS LEIA 1

PRINCESS LEIA

It is a time of both hope and mourning within the Rebellion. While on a secret mission to deliver stolen plans for the Death Star to the Rebel Alliance, PRINCESS LEIA ORGANA was captured by the Galactic Empire and forced to witness the battle station's power as it destroyed her home planet of Alderaan.

With the help of a farmboy pilot and a fast-talking smuggler, Leia escaped her captors and completed her mission. Using the plans, the Alliance was able to destroy the Empire's ultimate weapon.

Having proven themselves a formidable enemy to the Empire, the rebels are in more danger now than ever, leaving them with little time to celebrate their triumph, or lament their loss....

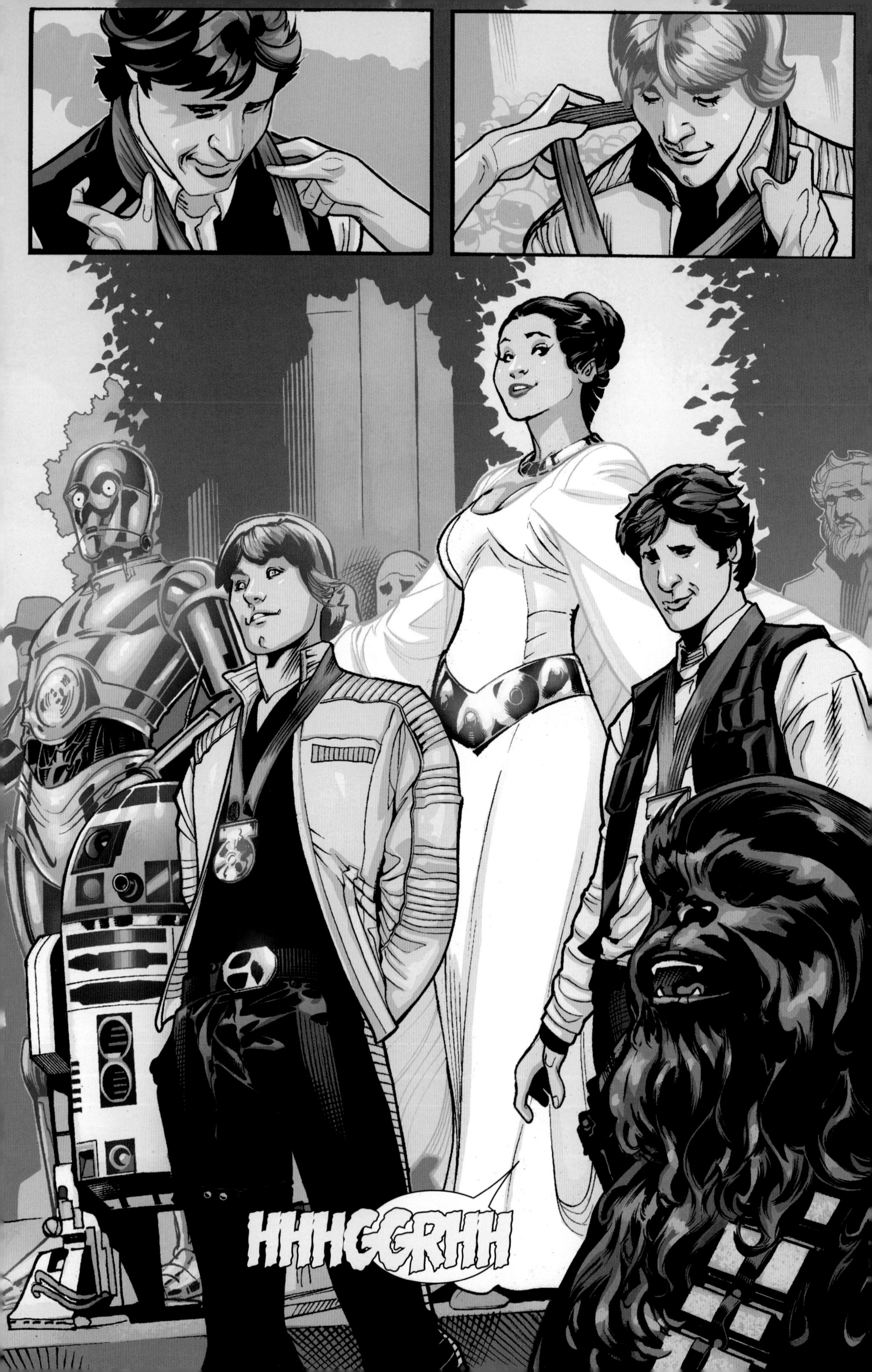
HHHGGRHH

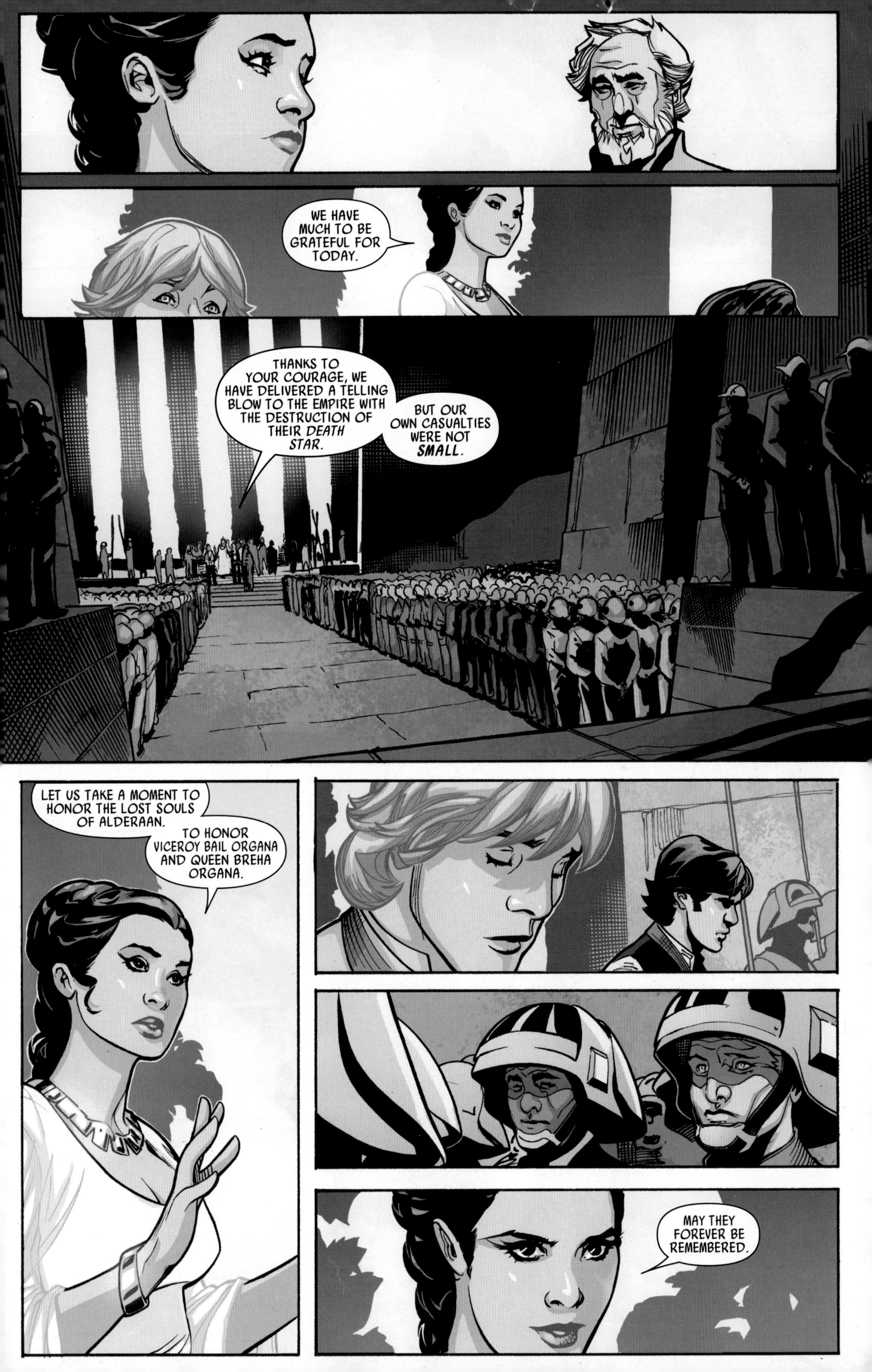
WE HAVE MUCH TO BE GRATEFUL FOR TODAY.
THANKS TO YOUR COURAGE, WE HAVE DELIVERED A TELLING BLOW TO THE EMPIRE WITH THE DESTRUCTION OF THEIR *DEATH STAR*.
BUT OUR OWN CASUALTIES WERE NOT ***SMALL***.
LET US TAKE A MOMENT TO HONOR THE LOST SOULS OF ALDERAAN.
TO HONOR VICEROY BAIL ORGANA AND QUEEN BREHA ORGANA.
MAY THEY FOREVER BE REMEMBERED.

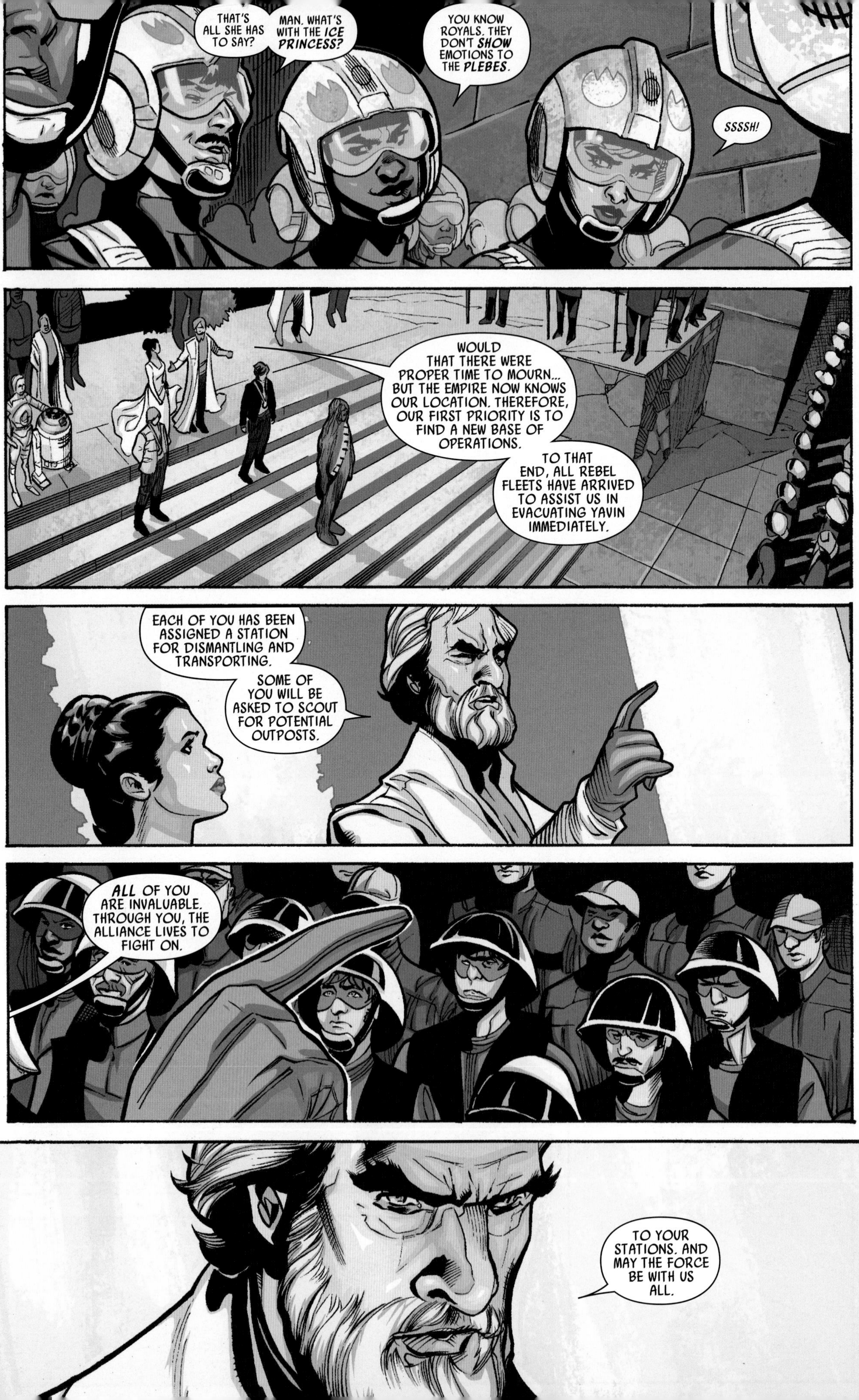

THAT'S ALL SHE HAS TO SAY?
MAN. WHAT'S WITH THE *ICE PRINCESS?*
YOU KNOW ROYALS. THEY DON'T *SHOW* EMOTIONS TO THE *PLEBES*.
SSSSH!
WOULD THAT THERE WERE PROPER TIME TO MOURN... BUT THE EMPIRE NOW KNOWS OUR LOCATION. THEREFORE, OUR FIRST PRIORITY IS TO FIND A NEW BASE OF OPERATIONS.
TO THAT END, ALL REBEL FLEETS HAVE ARRIVED TO ASSIST US IN EVACUATING YAVIN IMMEDIATELY.
EACH OF YOU HAS BEEN ASSIGNED A STATION FOR DISMANTLING AND TRANSPORTING.
SOME OF YOU WILL BE ASKED TO SCOUT FOR POTENTIAL OUTPOSTS.
ALL OF YOU ARE INVALUABLE. THROUGH YOU, THE ALLIANCE LIVES TO FIGHT ON.
TO YOUR STATIONS. AND MAY THE FORCE BE WITH US ALL.

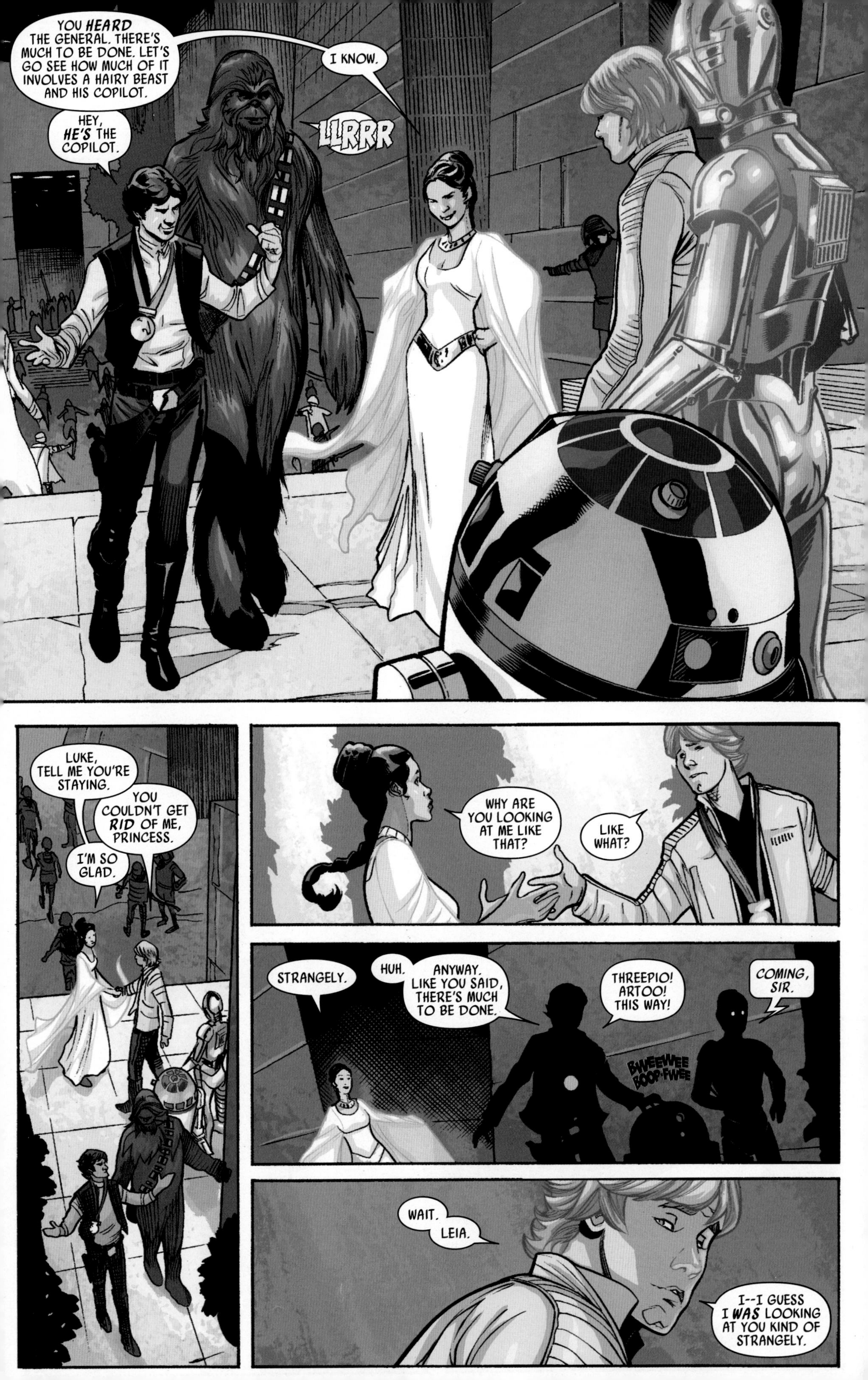
YOU HEARD THE GENERAL. THERE'S MUCH TO BE DONE. LET'S GO SEE HOW MUCH OF IT INVOLVES A HAIRY BEAST AND HIS COPILOT.
I KNOW.
HEY, HE'S THE COPILOT.
LLRRR
LUKE, TELL ME YOU'RE STAYING.
YOU COULDN'T GET RID OF ME, PRINCESS.
I'M SO GLAD.
WHY ARE YOU LOOKING AT ME LIKE THAT?
LIKE WHAT?
STRANGELY.
HUH.
ANYWAY. LIKE YOU SAID, THERE'S MUCH TO BE DONE.
THREEPIO! ARTOO! THIS WAY!
COMING, SIR.
BWEEWEE BOOP-FWEE
WAIT.
LEIA.
I--I GUESS I WAS LOOKING AT YOU KIND OF STRANGELY.

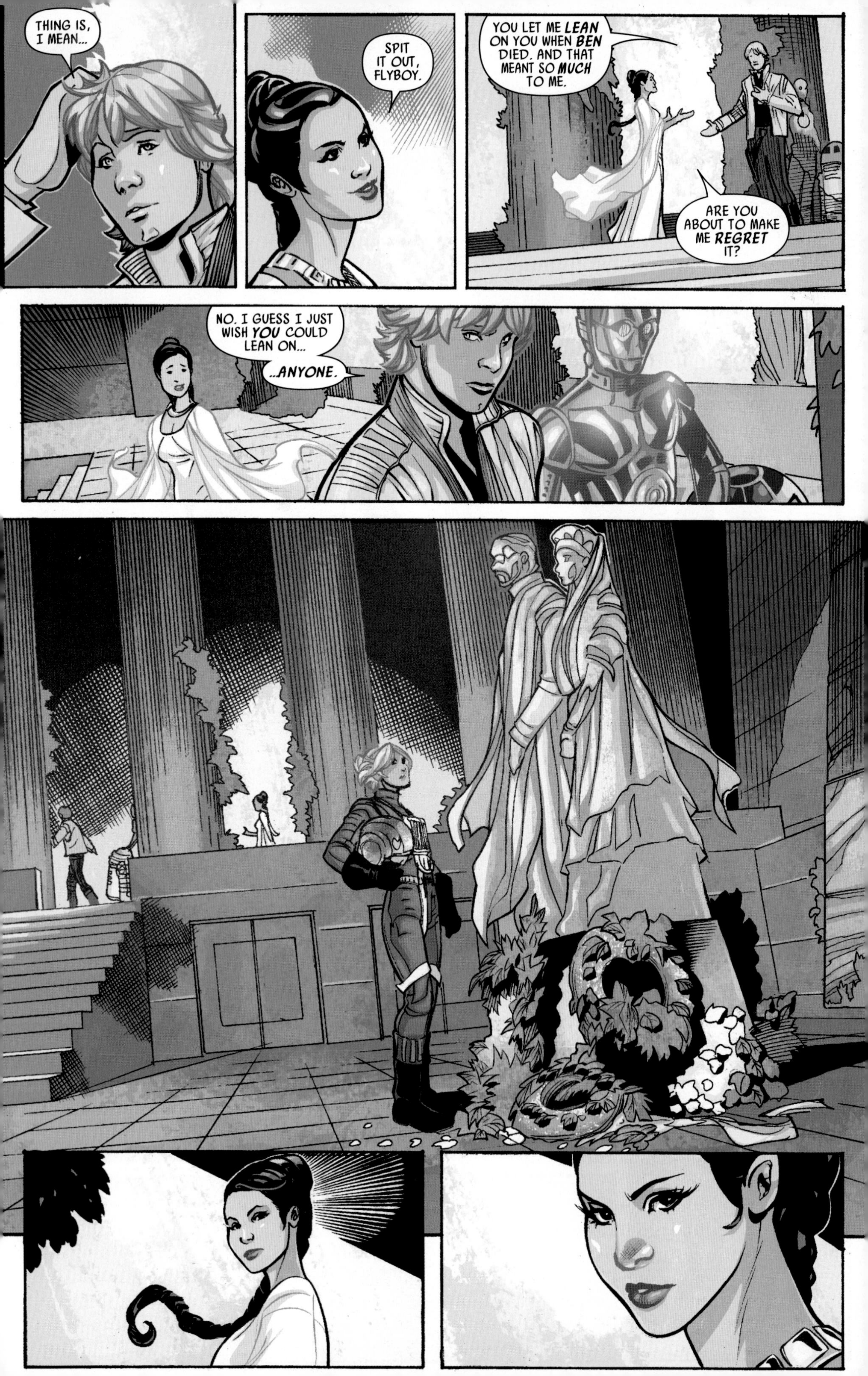
THING IS, I MEAN...
SPIT IT OUT, FLYBOY.
YOU LET ME LEAN ON YOU WHEN BEN DIED. AND THAT MEANT SO MUCH TO ME.
ARE YOU ABOUT TO MAKE ME REGRET IT?
NO. I GUESS I JUST WISH YOU COULD LEAN ON...
...ANYONE.

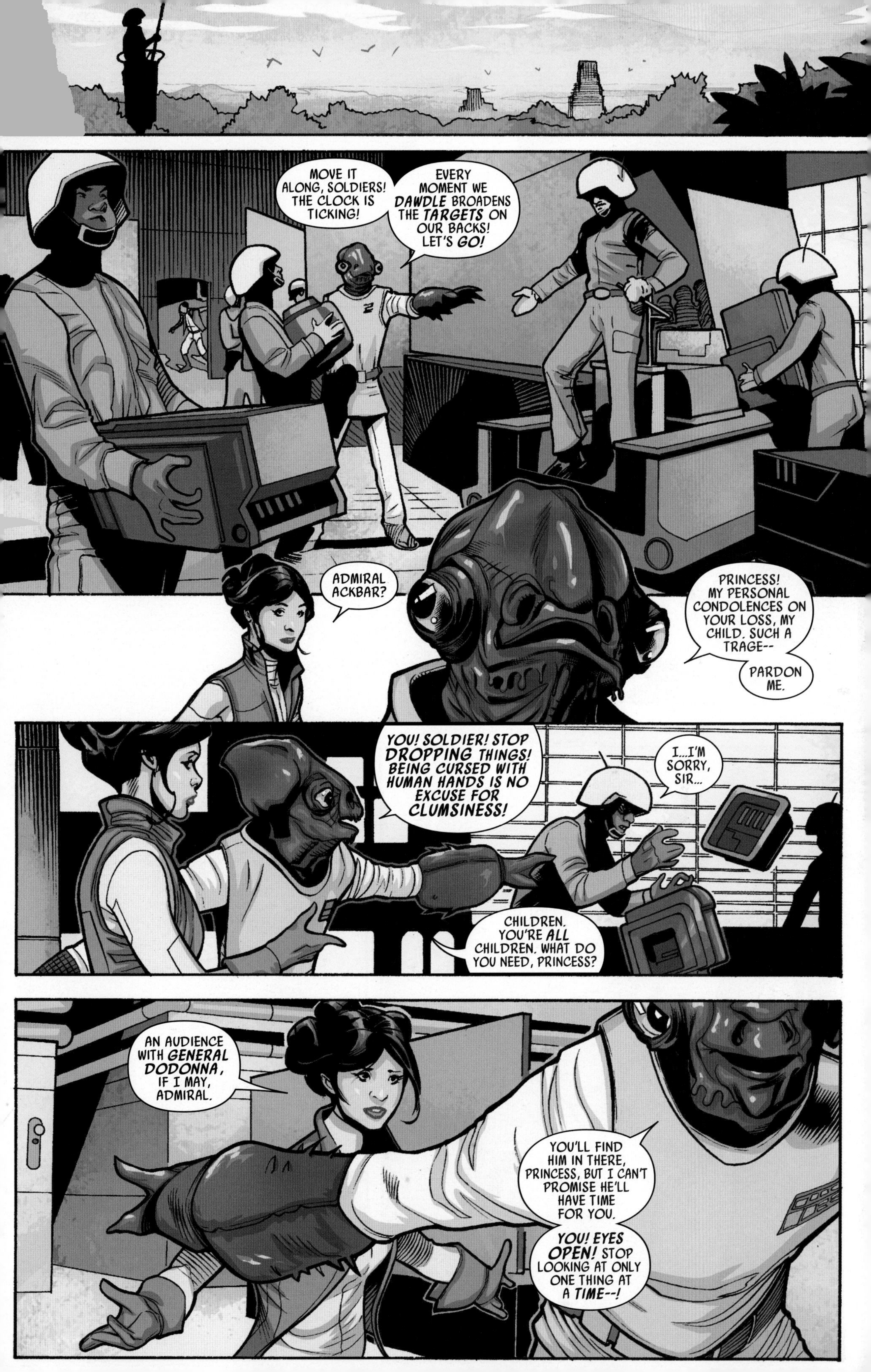
MOVE IT ALONG, SOLDIERS! THE CLOCK IS TICKING!
EVERY MOMENT WE DAWDLE BROADENS THE TARGETS ON OUR BACKS! LET'S GO!
ADMIRAL ACKBAR?
PRINCESS! MY PERSONAL CONDOLENCES ON YOUR LOSS, MY CHILD. SUCH A TRAGE--
PARDON ME.
YOU! SOLDIER! STOP DROPPING THINGS! BEING CURSED WITH HUMAN HANDS IS NO EXCUSE FOR CLUMSINESS!
I...I'M SORRY, SIR...
CHILDREN. YOU'RE ALL CHILDREN. WHAT DO YOU NEED, PRINCESS?
AN AUDIENCE WITH GENERAL DODONNA, IF I MAY, ADMIRAL.
YOU'LL FIND HIM IN THERE, PRINCESS, BUT I CAN'T PROMISE HE'LL HAVE TIME FOR YOU.
YOU! EYES OPEN! STOP LOOKING AT ONLY ONE THING AT A TIME--!

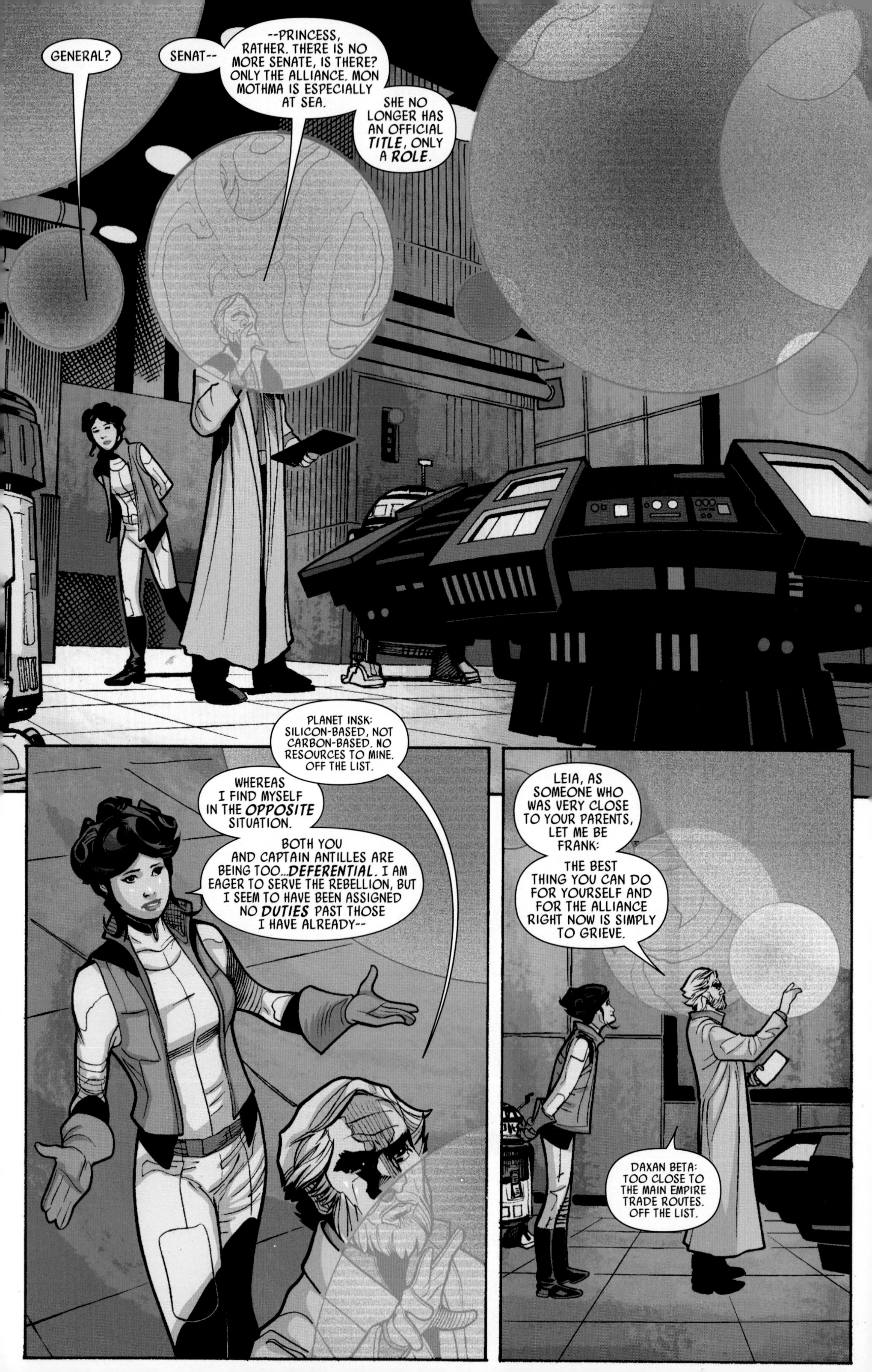
GENERAL?
SENAT--
--PRINCESS, RATHER. THERE IS NO MORE SENATE, IS THERE? ONLY THE ALLIANCE. MON MOTHMA IS ESPECIALLY AT SEA.
SHE NO LONGER HAS AN OFFICIAL TITLE, ONLY A ROLE.
PLANET INSK: SILICON-BASED, NOT CARBON-BASED. NO RESOURCES TO MINE. OFF THE LIST.
WHEREAS I FIND MYSELF IN THE OPPOSITE SITUATION.
BOTH YOU AND CAPTAIN ANTILLES ARE BEING TOO...DEFERENTIAL. I AM EAGER TO SERVE THE REBELLION, BUT I SEEM TO HAVE BEEN ASSIGNED NO DUTIES PAST THOSE I HAVE ALREADY--
LEIA, AS SOMEONE WHO WAS VERY CLOSE TO YOUR PARENTS, LET ME BE FRANK:
THE BEST THING YOU CAN DO FOR YOURSELF AND FOR THE ALLIANCE RIGHT NOW IS SIMPLY TO GRIEVE.
DAXAN BETA: TOO CLOSE TO THE MAIN EMPIRE TRADE ROUTES. OFF THE LIST.

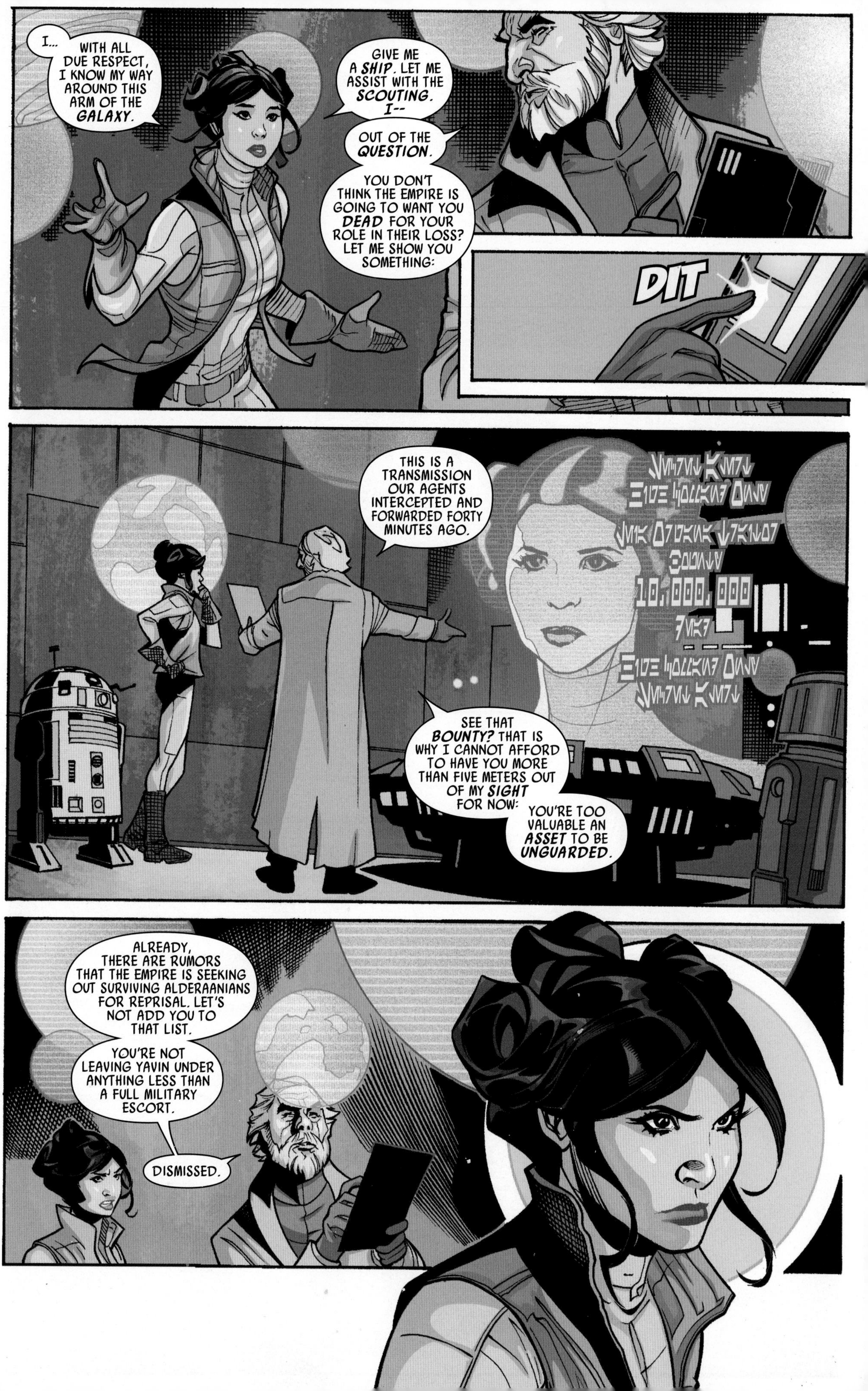
I...
WITH ALL DUE RESPECT, I KNOW MY WAY AROUND THIS ARM OF THE GALAXY.
GIVE ME A SHIP. LET ME ASSIST WITH THE SCOUTING. I--
OUT OF THE QUESTION.
YOU DON'T THINK THE EMPIRE IS GOING TO WANT YOU DEAD FOR YOUR ROLE IN THEIR LOSS? LET ME SHOW YOU SOMETHING:
DIT
THIS IS A TRANSMISSION OUR AGENTS INTERCEPTED AND FORWARDED FORTY MINUTES AGO.
10,000,000
SEE THAT BOUNTY? THAT IS WHY I CANNOT AFFORD TO HAVE YOU MORE THAN FIVE METERS OUT OF MY SIGHT FOR NOW:
YOU'RE TOO VALUABLE AN ASSET TO BE UNGUARDED.
ALREADY, THERE ARE RUMORS THAT THE EMPIRE IS SEEKING OUT SURVIVING ALDERAANIANS FOR REPRISAL. LET'S NOT ADD YOU TO THAT LIST.
YOU'RE NOT LEAVING YAVIN UNDER ANYTHING LESS THAN A FULL MILITARY ESCORT.
DISMISSED.

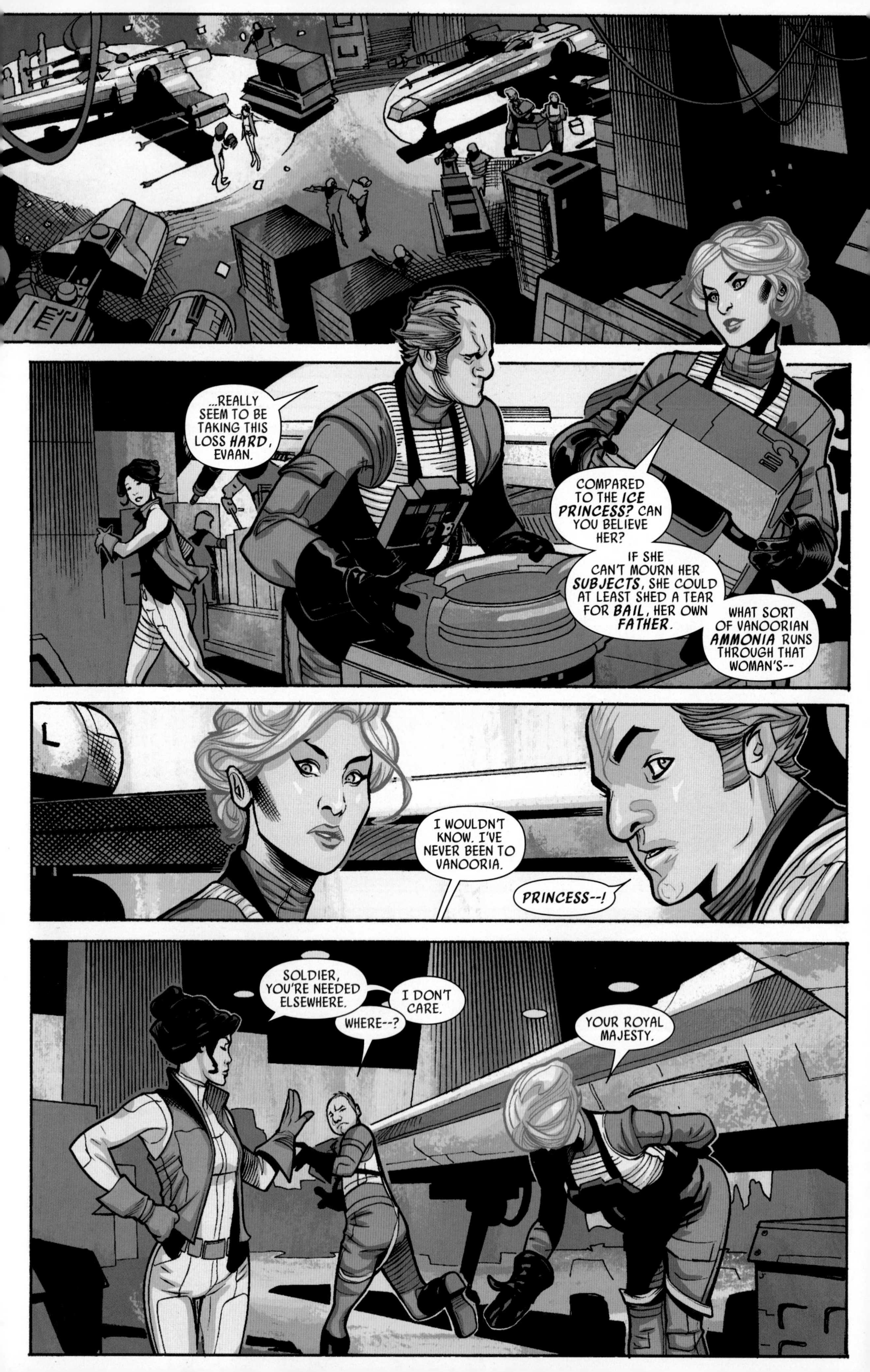
...REALLY SEEM TO BE TAKING THIS LOSS HARD, EVAAN.
COMPARED TO THE ICE PRINCESS? CAN YOU BELIEVE HER?
IF SHE CAN'T MOURN HER SUBJECTS, SHE COULD AT LEAST SHED A TEAR FOR BAIL, HER OWN FATHER.
WHAT SORT OF VANOORIAN AMMONIA RUNS THROUGH THAT WOMAN'S--
I WOULDN'T KNOW. I'VE NEVER BEEN TO VANOORIA.
PRINCESS--!
SOLDIER, YOU'RE NEEDED ELSEWHERE.
WHERE--?
I DON'T CARE.
YOUR ROYAL MAJESTY.

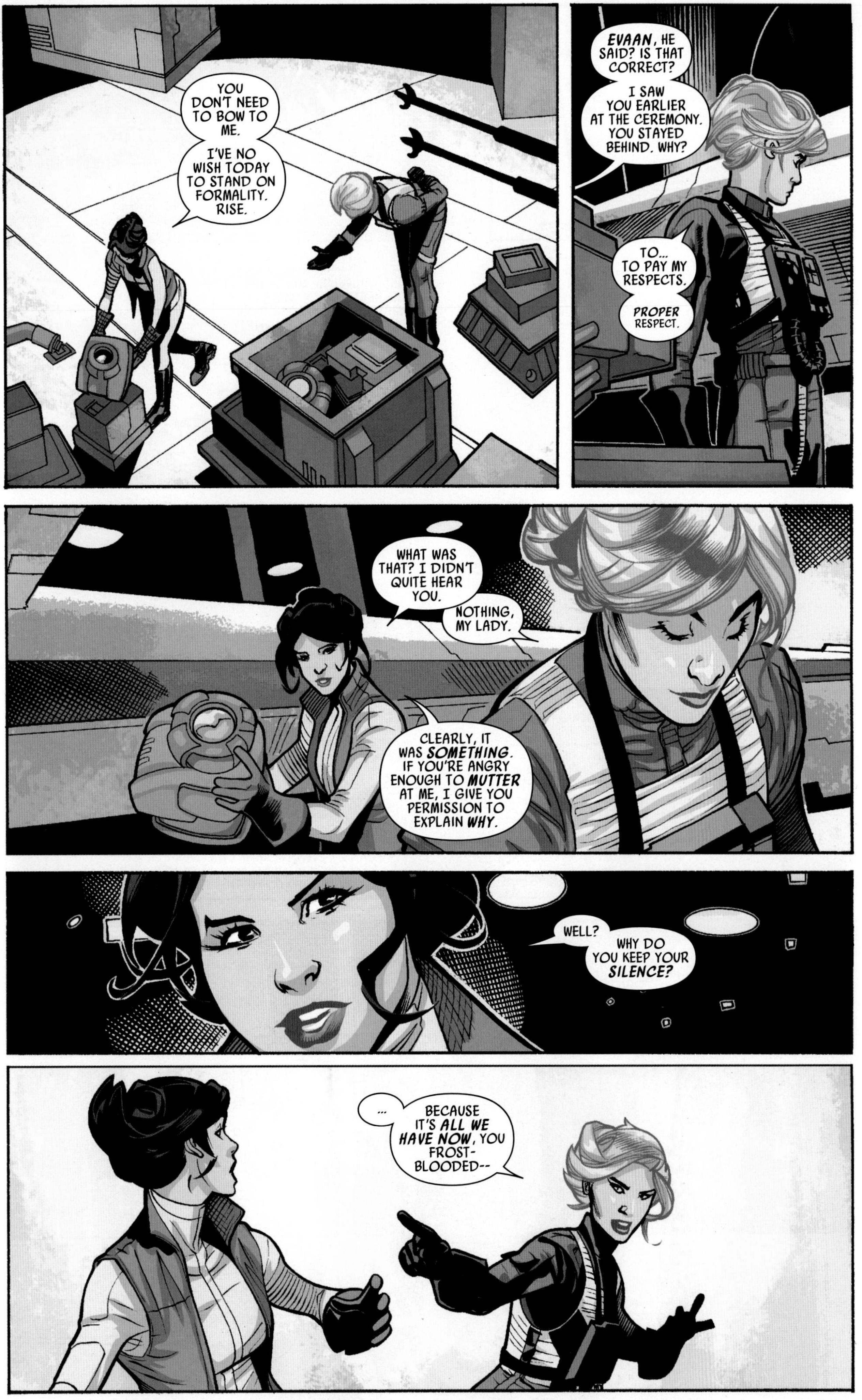
YOU DON'T NEED TO BOW TO ME.
I'VE NO WISH TODAY TO STAND ON FORMALITY. RISE.
EVAAN, HE SAID? IS THAT CORRECT?
I SAW YOU EARLIER AT THE CEREMONY. YOU STAYED BEHIND. WHY?
TO... TO PAY MY RESPECTS.
PROPER RESPECT.
WHAT WAS THAT? I DIDN'T QUITE HEAR YOU.
NOTHING, MY LADY.
CLEARLY, IT WAS SOMETHING. IF YOU'RE ANGRY ENOUGH TO MUTTER AT ME, I GIVE YOU PERMISSION TO EXPLAIN WHY.
WELL?
WHY DO YOU KEEP YOUR SILENCE?
...
BECAUSE IT'S ALL WE HAVE NOW, YOU FROST-BLOODED--

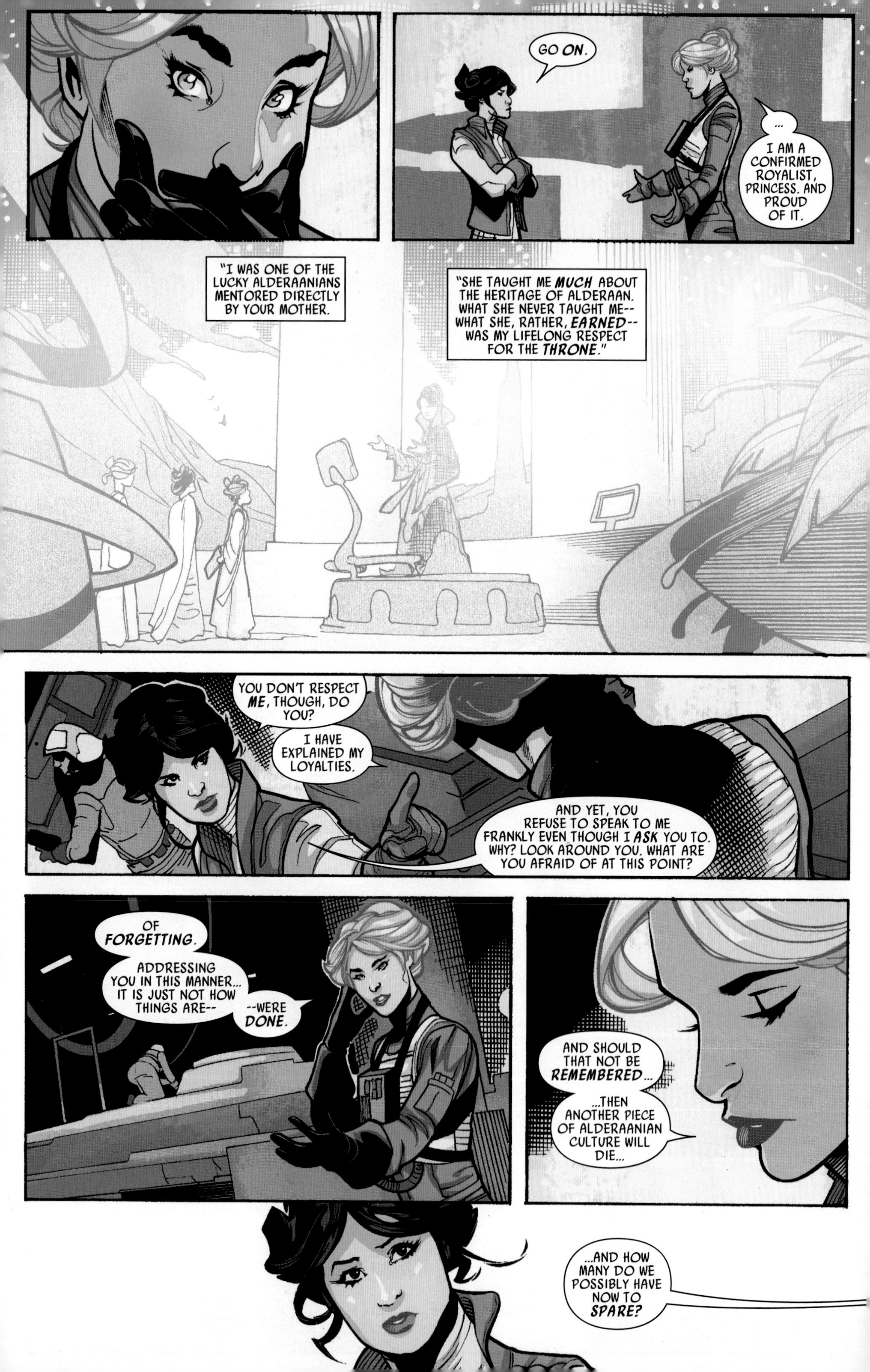
GO ON.
...
I AM A CONFIRMED ROYALIST, PRINCESS. AND PROUD OF IT.
"I WAS ONE OF THE LUCKY ALDERAANIANS MENTORED DIRECTLY BY YOUR MOTHER.
"SHE TAUGHT ME MUCH ABOUT THE HERITAGE OF ALDERAAN. WHAT SHE NEVER TAUGHT ME--WHAT SHE, RATHER, EARNED--WAS MY LIFELONG RESPECT FOR THE THRONE."
YOU DON'T RESPECT ME, THOUGH, DO YOU?
I HAVE EXPLAINED MY LOYALTIES.
AND YET, YOU REFUSE TO SPEAK TO ME FRANKLY EVEN THOUGH I ASK YOU TO. WHY? LOOK AROUND YOU. WHAT ARE YOU AFRAID OF AT THIS POINT?
OF FORGETTING.
ADDRESSING YOU IN THIS MANNER... IT IS JUST NOT HOW THINGS ARE--
--WERE DONE.
AND SHOULD THAT NOT BE REMEMBERED...
...THEN ANOTHER PIECE OF ALDERAANIAN CULTURE WILL DIE...
...AND HOW MANY DO WE POSSIBLY HAVE NOW TO SPARE?

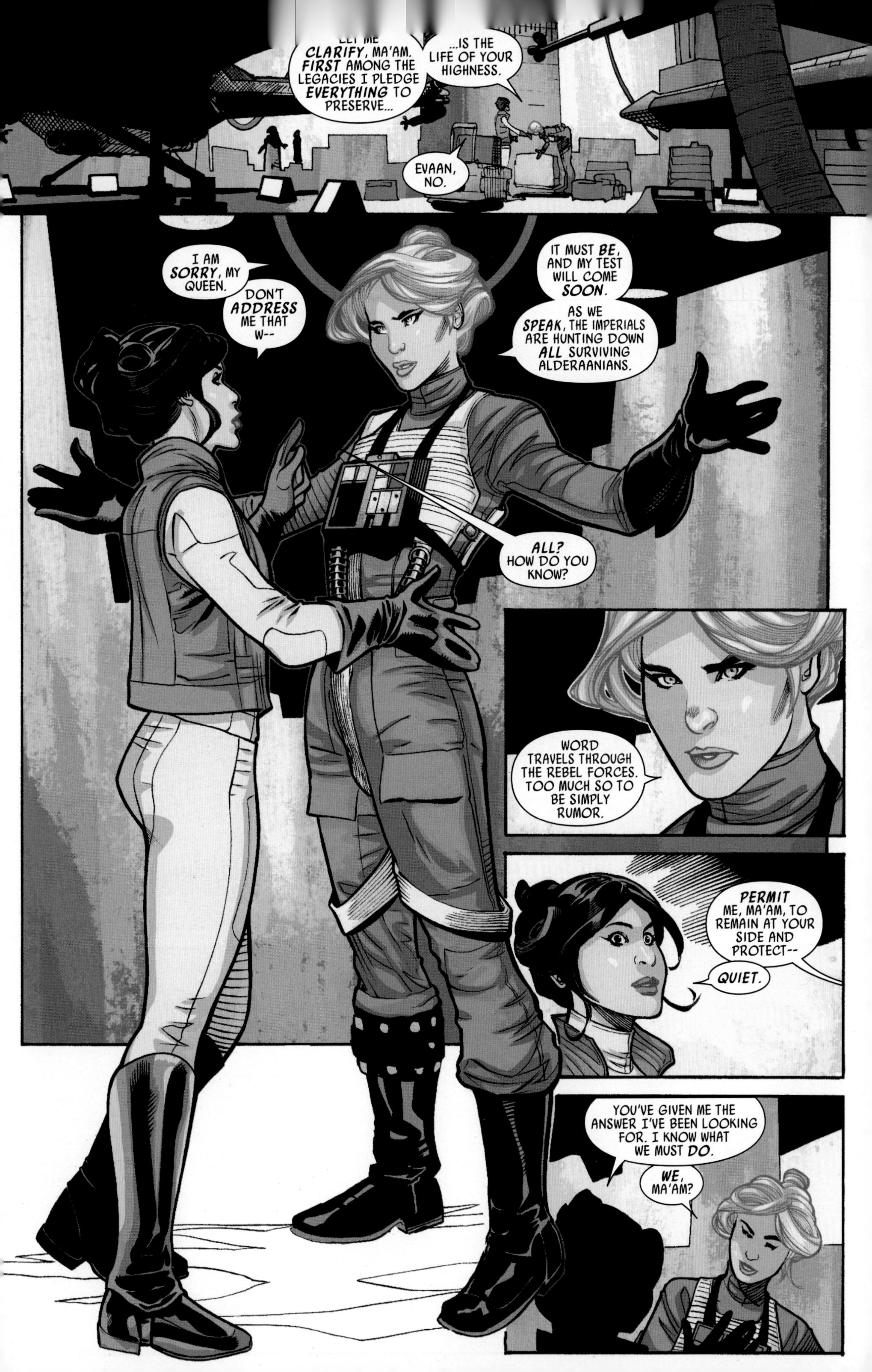

...LET ME CLARIFY, MA'AM. FIRST AMONG THE LEGACIES I PLEDGE EVERYTHING TO PRESERVE...
...IS THE LIFE OF YOUR HIGHNESS.
EVAAN, NO.
I AM SORRY, MY QUEEN.
DON'T ADDRESS ME THAT W--
IT MUST BE, AND MY TEST WILL COME SOON.
AS WE SPEAK, THE IMPERIALS ARE HUNTING DOWN ALL SURVIVING ALDERAANIANS.
ALL? HOW DO YOU KNOW?
WORD TRAVELS THROUGH THE REBEL FORCES. TOO MUCH SO TO BE SIMPLY RUMOR.
PERMIT ME, MA'AM, TO REMAIN AT YOUR SIDE AND PROTECT--
QUIET.
YOU'VE GIVEN ME THE ANSWER I'VE BEEN LOOKING FOR. I KNOW WHAT WE MUST DO.
WE, MA'AM?

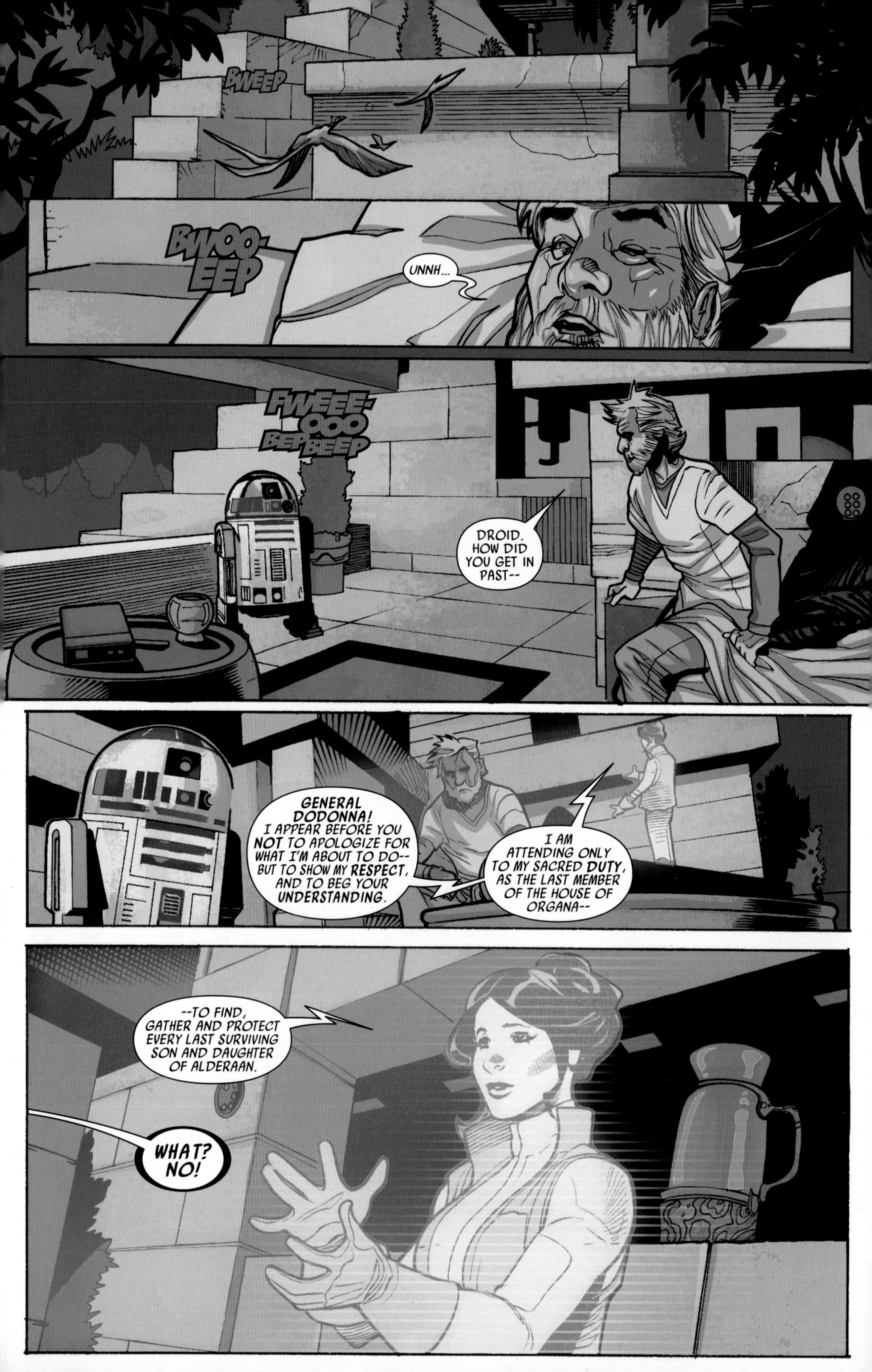
BWEEP
BWOO-EEP
UNNH...
FWEEE-OOO BEP BEEP
DROID. HOW DID YOU GET IN PAST--
GENERAL DODONNA! I APPEAR BEFORE YOU NOT TO APOLOGIZE FOR WHAT I'M ABOUT TO DO-- BUT TO SHOW MY RESPECT, AND TO BEG YOUR UNDERSTANDING.
I AM ATTENDING ONLY TO MY SACRED DUTY, AS THE LAST MEMBER OF THE HOUSE OF ORGANA--
--TO FIND, GATHER AND PROTECT EVERY LAST SURVIVING SON AND DAUGHTER OF ALDERAAN.
WHAT? NO!

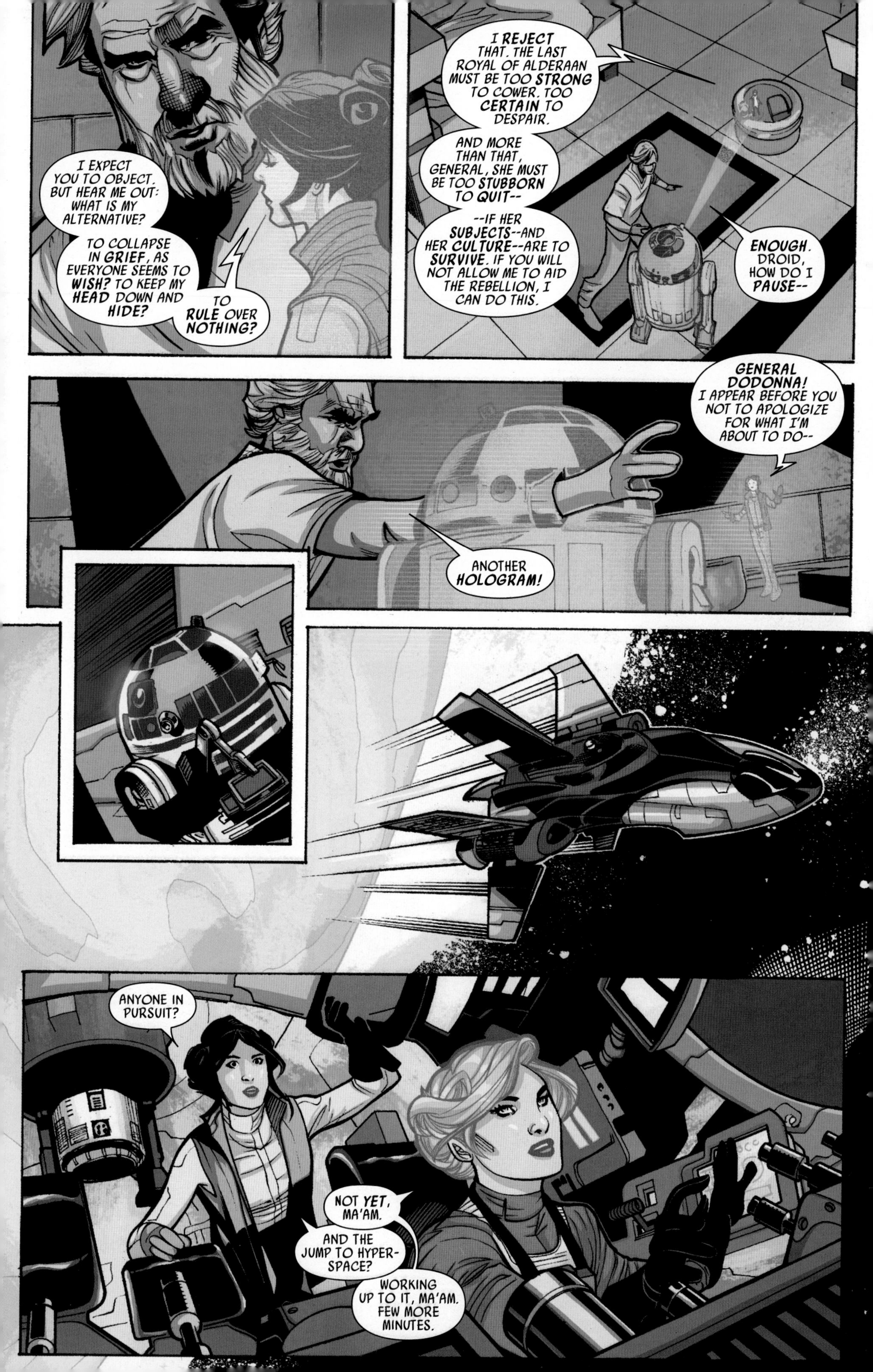
I EXPECT YOU TO OBJECT. BUT HEAR ME OUT: WHAT IS MY ALTERNATIVE?
TO COLLAPSE IN GRIEF, AS EVERYONE SEEMS TO WISH? TO KEEP MY HEAD DOWN AND HIDE?
TO RULE OVER NOTHING?
I REJECT THAT. THE LAST ROYAL OF ALDERAAN MUST BE TOO STRONG TO COWER. TOO CERTAIN TO DESPAIR.
AND MORE THAN THAT, GENERAL, SHE MUST BE TOO STUBBORN TO QUIT--
--IF HER SUBJECTS--AND HER CULTURE--ARE TO SURVIVE. IF YOU WILL NOT ALLOW ME TO AID THE REBELLION, I CAN DO THIS.
ENOUGH. DROID, HOW DO I PAUSE--
GENERAL DODONNA! I APPEAR BEFORE YOU NOT TO APOLOGIZE FOR WHAT I'M ABOUT TO DO--
ANOTHER HOLOGRAM!
ANYONE IN PURSUIT?
NOT YET, MA'AM.
AND THE JUMP TO HYPER-SPACE?
WORKING UP TO IT, MA'AM. FEW MORE MINUTES.

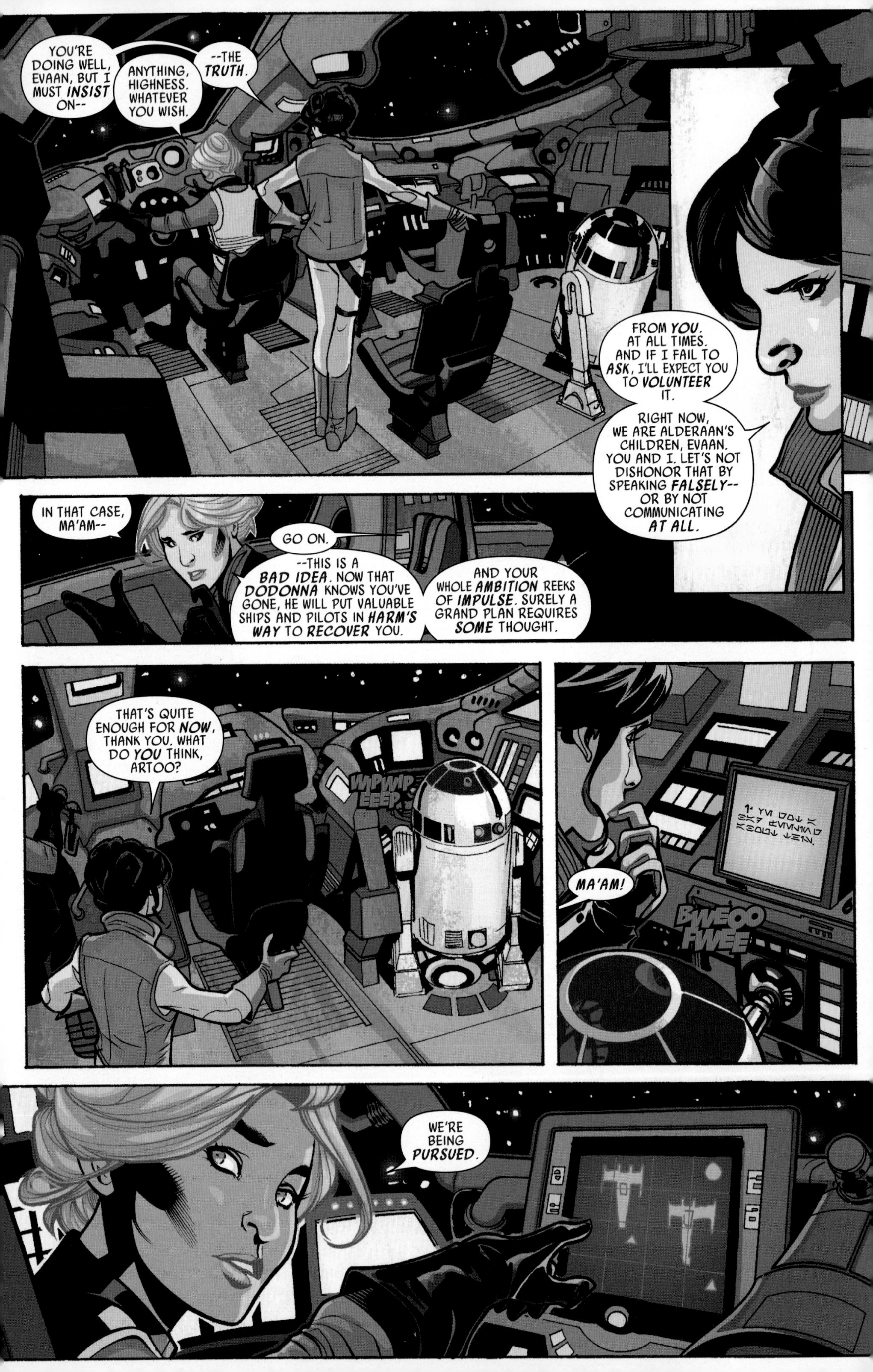

YOU'RE DOING WELL, EVAAN, BUT I MUST INSIST ON--
ANYTHING, HIGHNESS. WHATEVER YOU WISH.
--THE TRUTH.
FROM YOU. AT ALL TIMES. AND IF I FAIL TO ASK, I'LL EXPECT YOU TO VOLUNTEER IT.
RIGHT NOW, WE ARE ALDERAAN'S CHILDREN, EVAAN. YOU AND I. LET'S NOT DISHONOR THAT BY SPEAKING FALSELY-- OR BY NOT COMMUNICATING AT ALL.
IN THAT CASE, MA'AM--
GO ON.
--THIS IS A BAD IDEA. NOW THAT DODONNA KNOWS YOU'VE GONE, HE WILL PUT VALUABLE SHIPS AND PILOTS IN HARM'S WAY TO RECOVER YOU.
AND YOUR WHOLE AMBITION REEKS OF IMPULSE. SURELY A GRAND PLAN REQUIRES SOME THOUGHT.
THAT'S QUITE ENOUGH FOR NOW, THANK YOU. WHAT DO YOU THINK, ARTOO?
WIPWIP EEEP
MA'AM!
BWEOO FWEE
WE'RE BEING PURSUED.

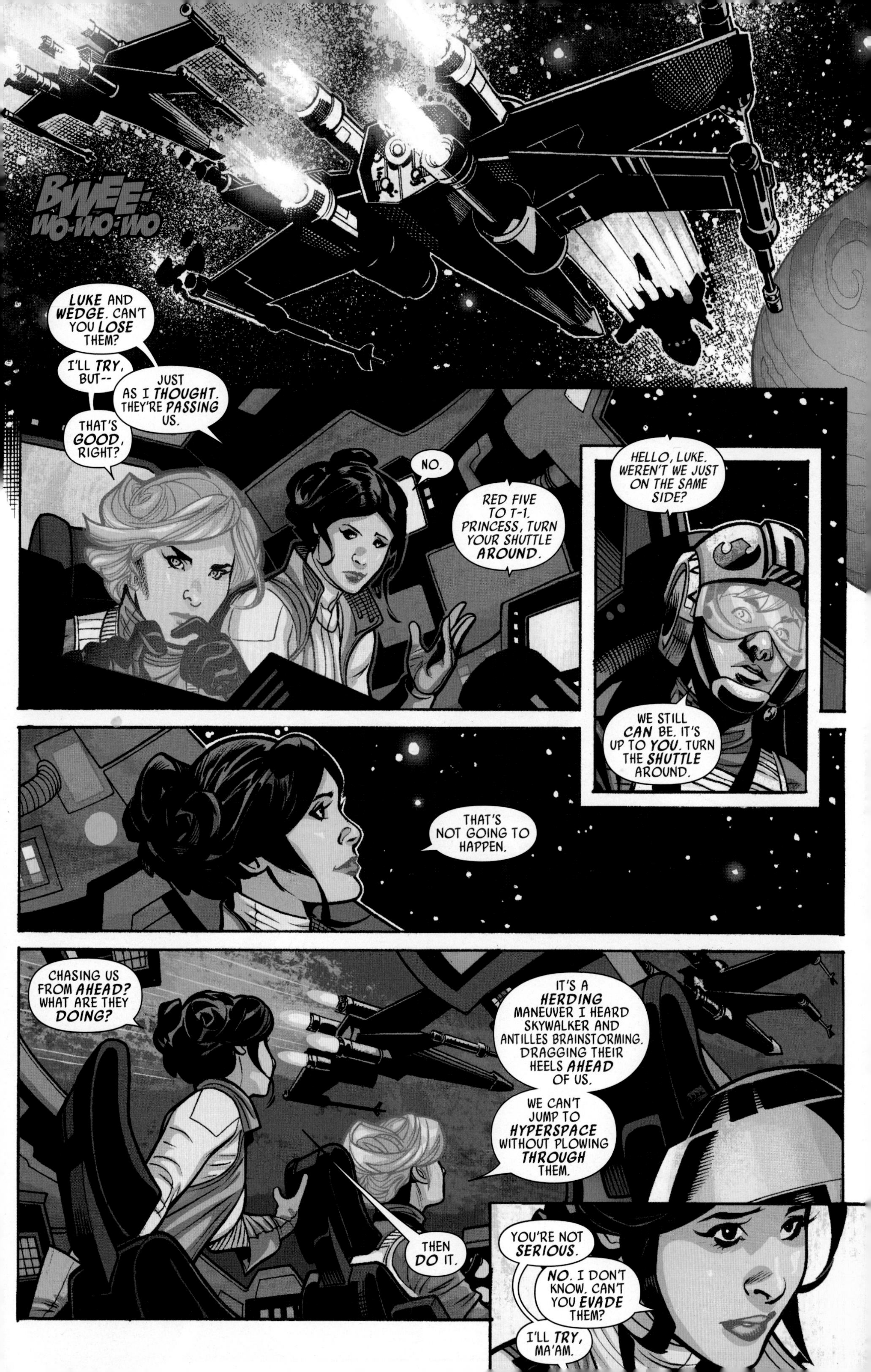
BWEE-WO-WO-WO
LUKE AND WEDGE. CAN'T YOU LOSE THEM?
I'LL TRY, BUT--
JUST AS I THOUGHT. THEY'RE PASSING US.
THAT'S GOOD, RIGHT?
NO.
RED FIVE TO T-1. PRINCESS, TURN YOUR SHUTTLE AROUND.
HELLO, LUKE. WEREN'T WE JUST ON THE SAME SIDE?
WE STILL CAN BE. IT'S UP TO YOU. TURN THE SHUTTLE AROUND.
THAT'S NOT GOING TO HAPPEN.
CHASING US FROM AHEAD? WHAT ARE THEY DOING?
IT'S A HERDING MANEUVER I HEARD SKYWALKER AND ANTILLES BRAINSTORMING. DRAGGING THEIR HEELS AHEAD OF US.
WE CAN'T JUMP TO HYPERSPACE WITHOUT PLOWING THROUGH THEM.
THEN DO IT.
YOU'RE NOT SERIOUS.
NO. I DON'T KNOW. CAN'T YOU EVADE THEM?
I'LL TRY, MA'AM.

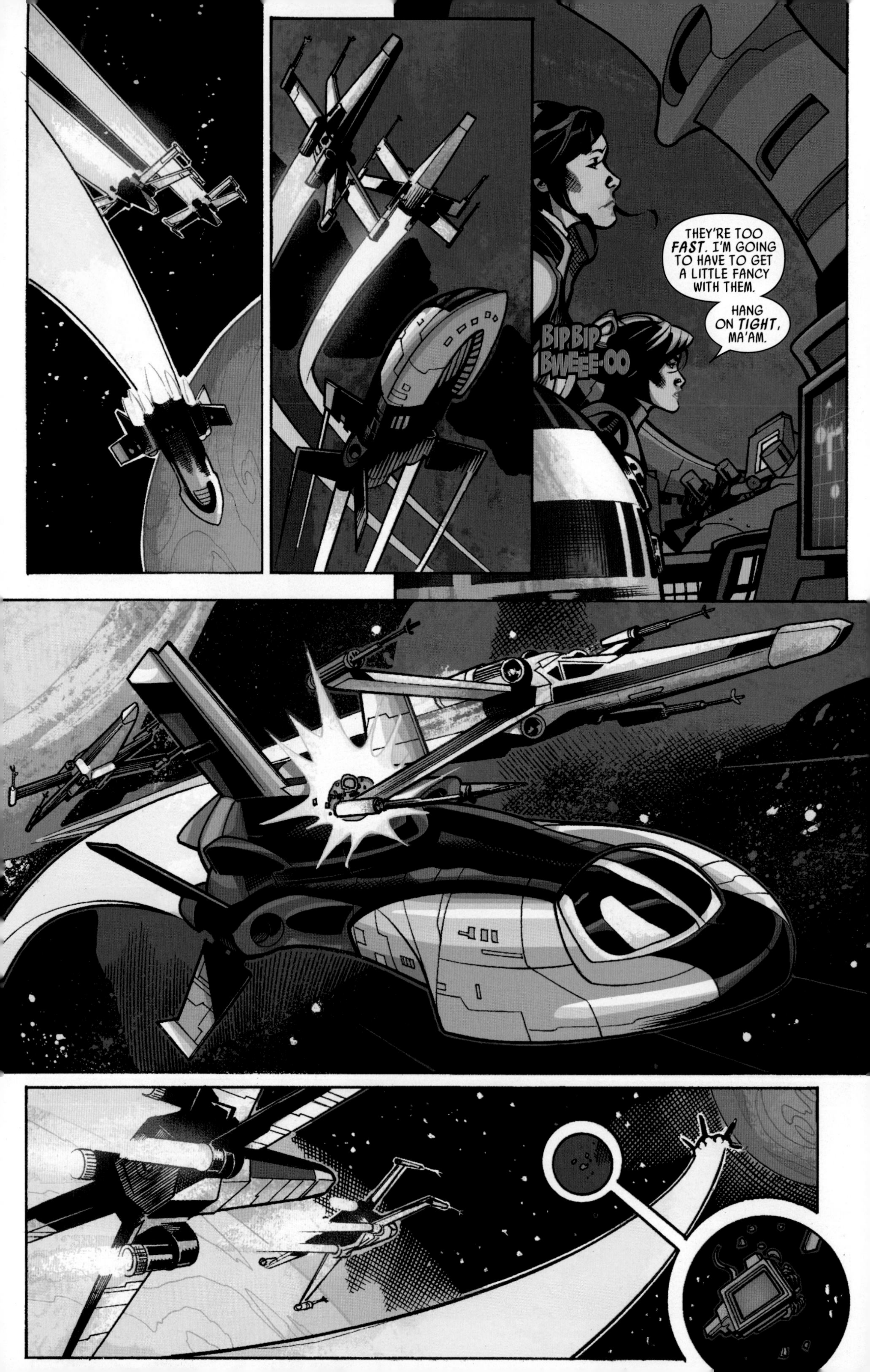

THEY'RE TOO FAST. I'M GOING TO HAVE TO GET A LITTLE FANCY WITH THEM.
HANG ON TIGHT, MA'AM.
BIPBIP BWEEE-OO

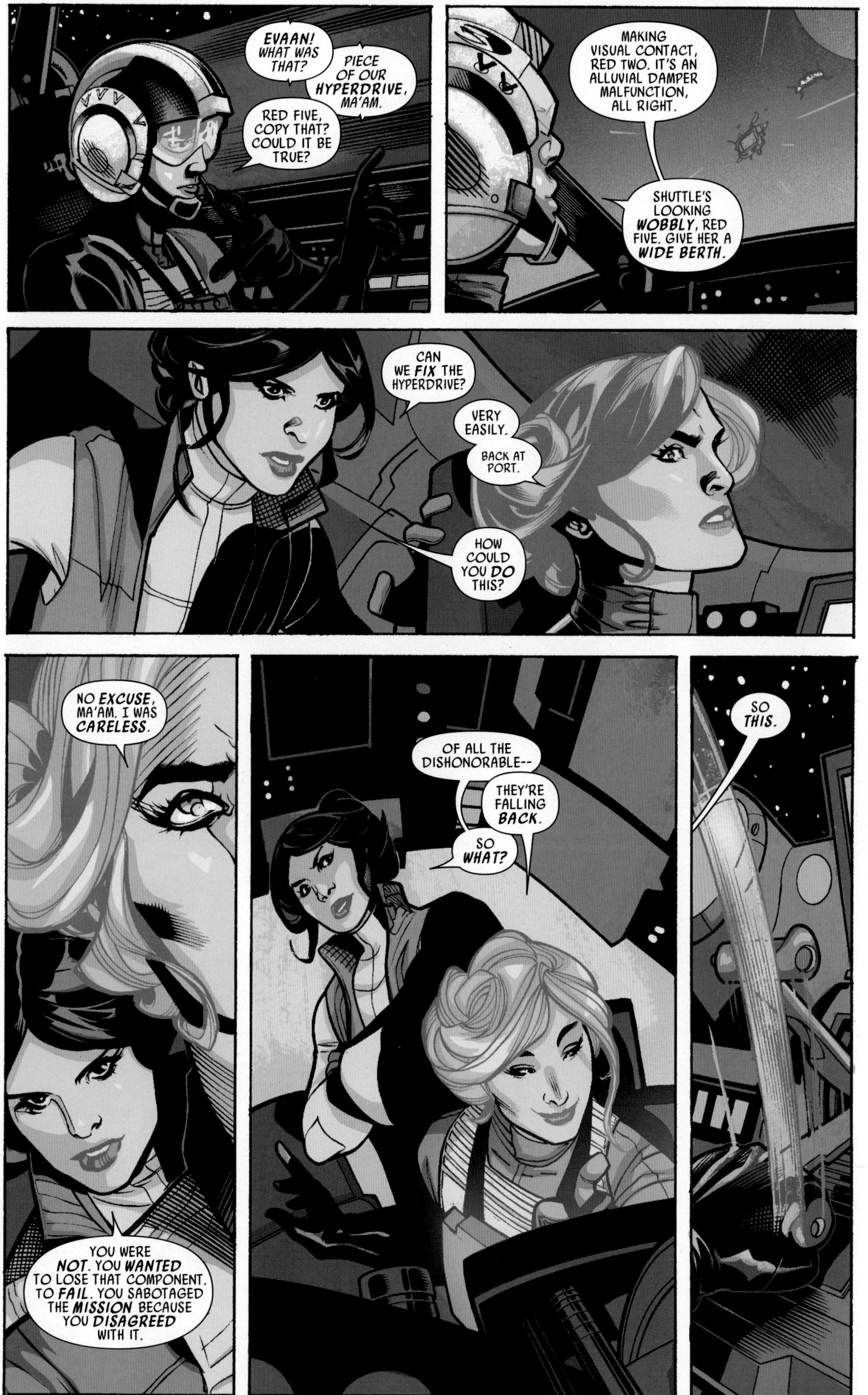
EVAAN! WHAT WAS THAT?
PIECE OF OUR HYPERDRIVE, MA'AM.
RED FIVE, COPY THAT? COULD IT BE TRUE?
MAKING VISUAL CONTACT, RED TWO. IT'S AN ALLUVIAL DAMPER MALFUNCTION, ALL RIGHT.
SHUTTLE'S LOOKING WOBBLY, RED FIVE. GIVE HER A WIDE BERTH.
CAN WE FIX THE HYPERDRIVE?
VERY EASILY.
BACK AT PORT.
HOW COULD YOU DO THIS?
NO EXCUSE, MA'AM. I WAS CARELESS.
YOU WERE NOT. YOU WANTED TO LOSE THAT COMPONENT. TO FAIL. YOU SABOTAGED THE MISSION BECAUSE YOU DISAGREED WITH IT.
OF ALL THE DISHONORABLE--
THEY'RE FALLING BACK.
SO WHAT?
SO THIS.

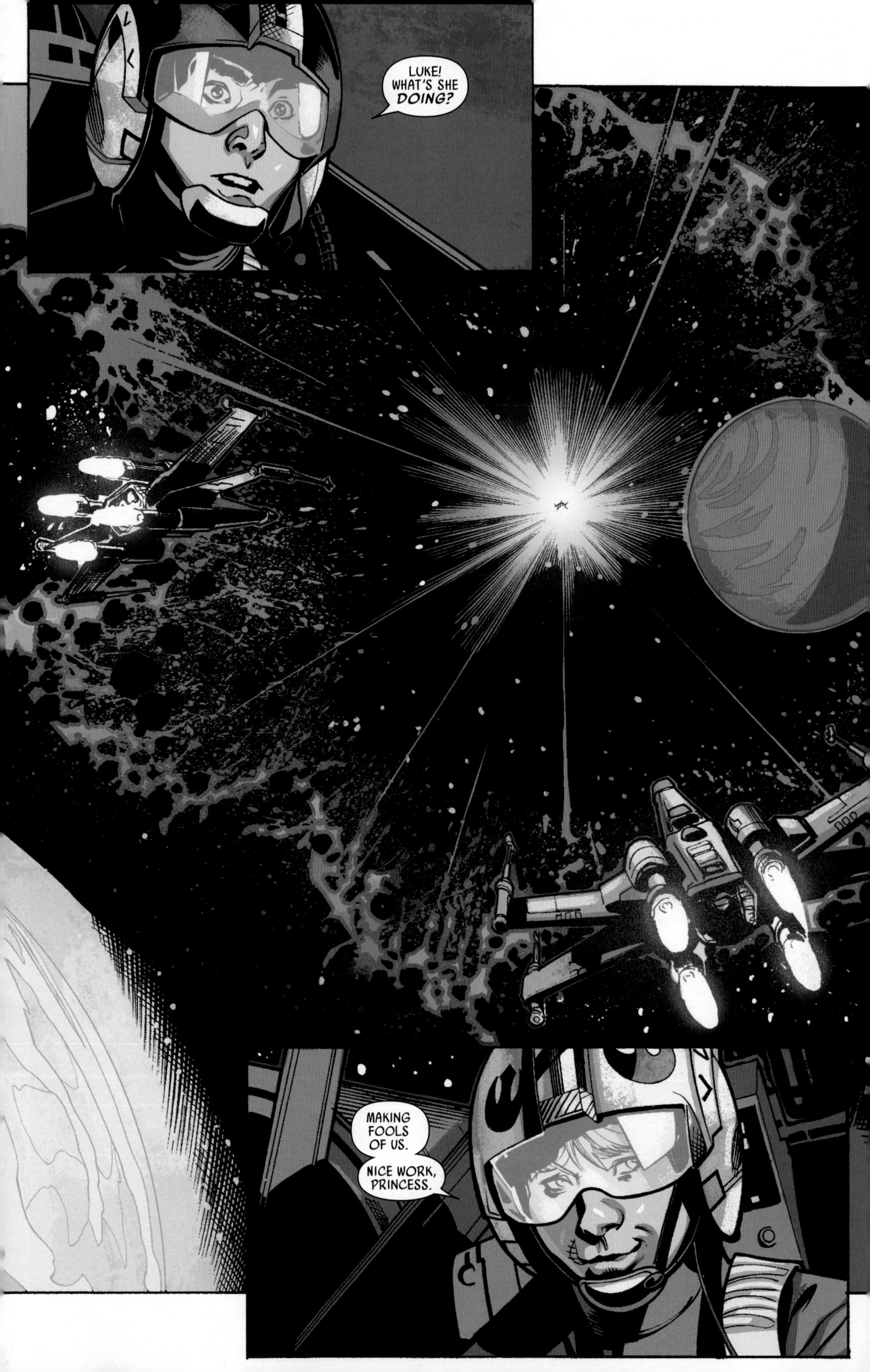
LUKE! WHAT'S SHE DOING?
MAKING FOOLS OF US.
NICE WORK, PRINCESS.

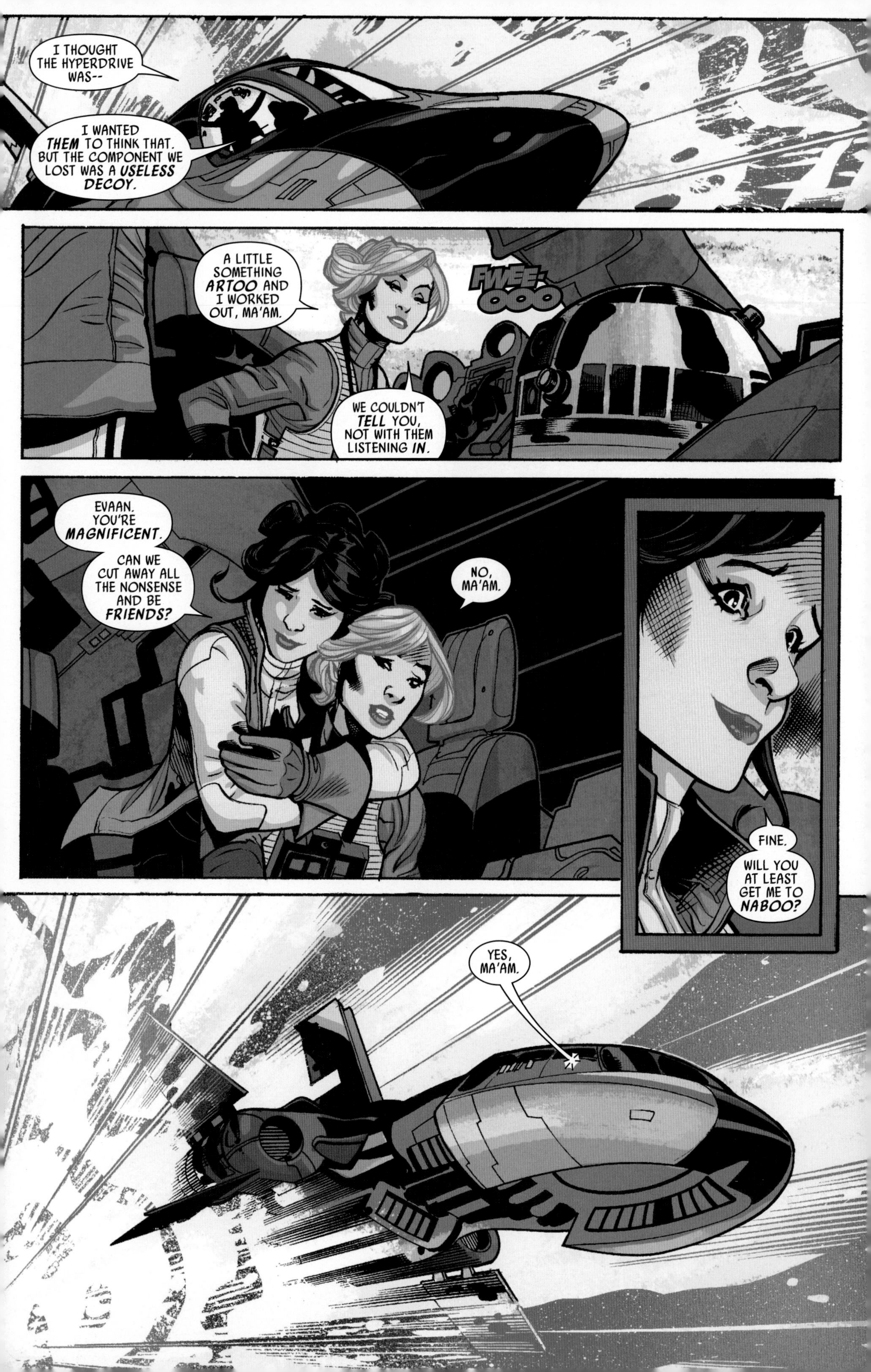
I THOUGHT THE HYPERDRIVE WAS--
I WANTED THEM TO THINK THAT. BUT THE COMPONENT WE LOST WAS A USELESS DECOY.
A LITTLE SOMETHING ARTOO AND I WORKED OUT, MA'AM.
FWEE-OOO
WE COULDN'T TELL YOU, NOT WITH THEM LISTENING IN.
EVAAN. YOU'RE MAGNIFICENT.
CAN WE CUT AWAY ALL THE NONSENSE AND BE FRIENDS?
NO, MA'AM.
FINE.
WILL YOU AT LEAST GET ME TO NABOO?
YES, MA'AM.

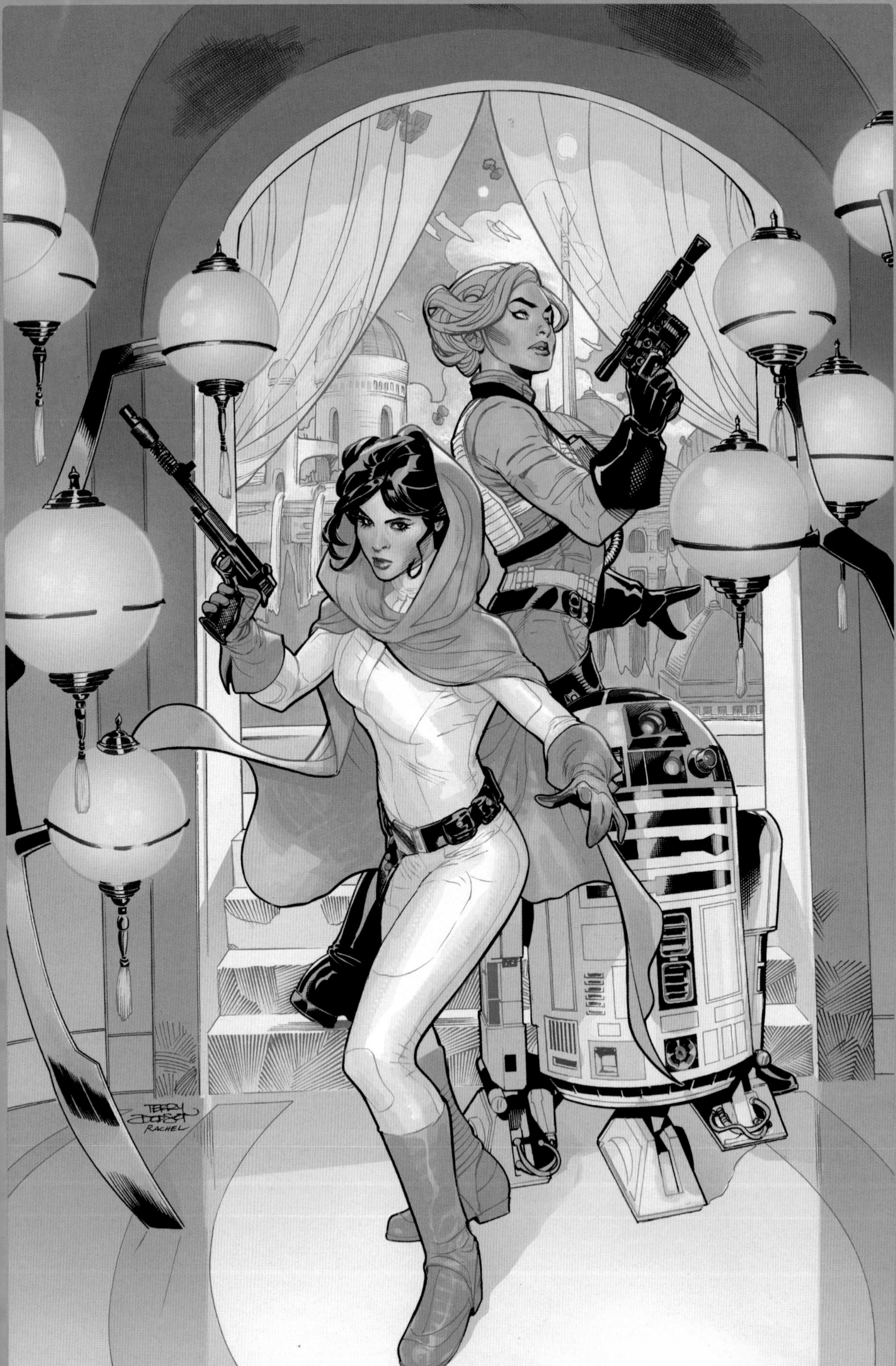
TERRY DODSON
RACHEL

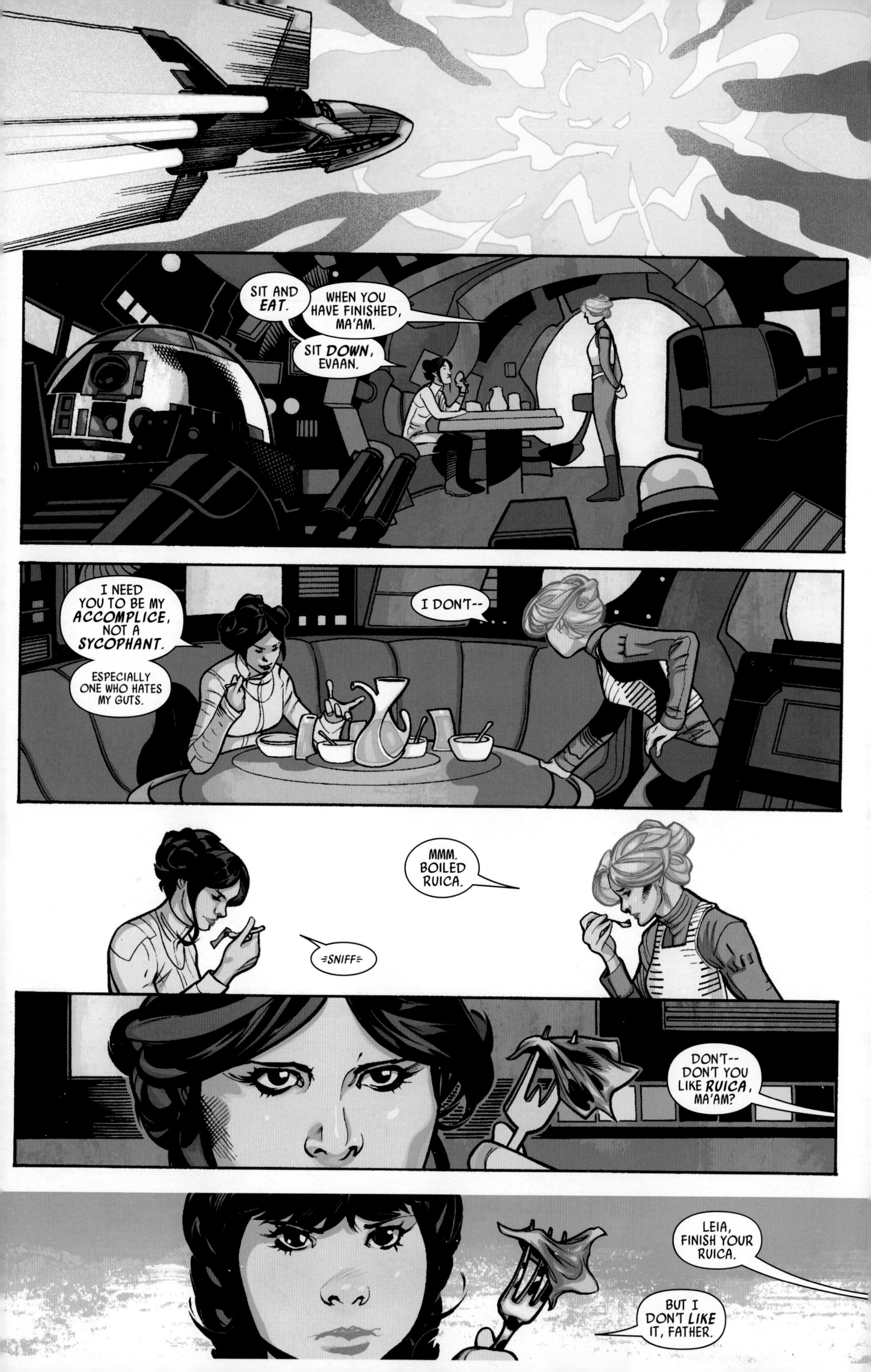
SIT AND EAT.
WHEN YOU HAVE FINISHED, MA'AM.
SIT DOWN, EVAAN.
I NEED YOU TO BE MY ACCOMPLICE, NOT A SYCOPHANT.
ESPECIALLY ONE WHO HATES MY GUTS.
I DON'T--
MMM. BOILED RUICA.
=SNIFF=
DON'T-- DON'T YOU LIKE RUICA, MA'AM?
LEIA, FINISH YOUR RUICA.
BUT I DON'T LIKE IT, FATHER.

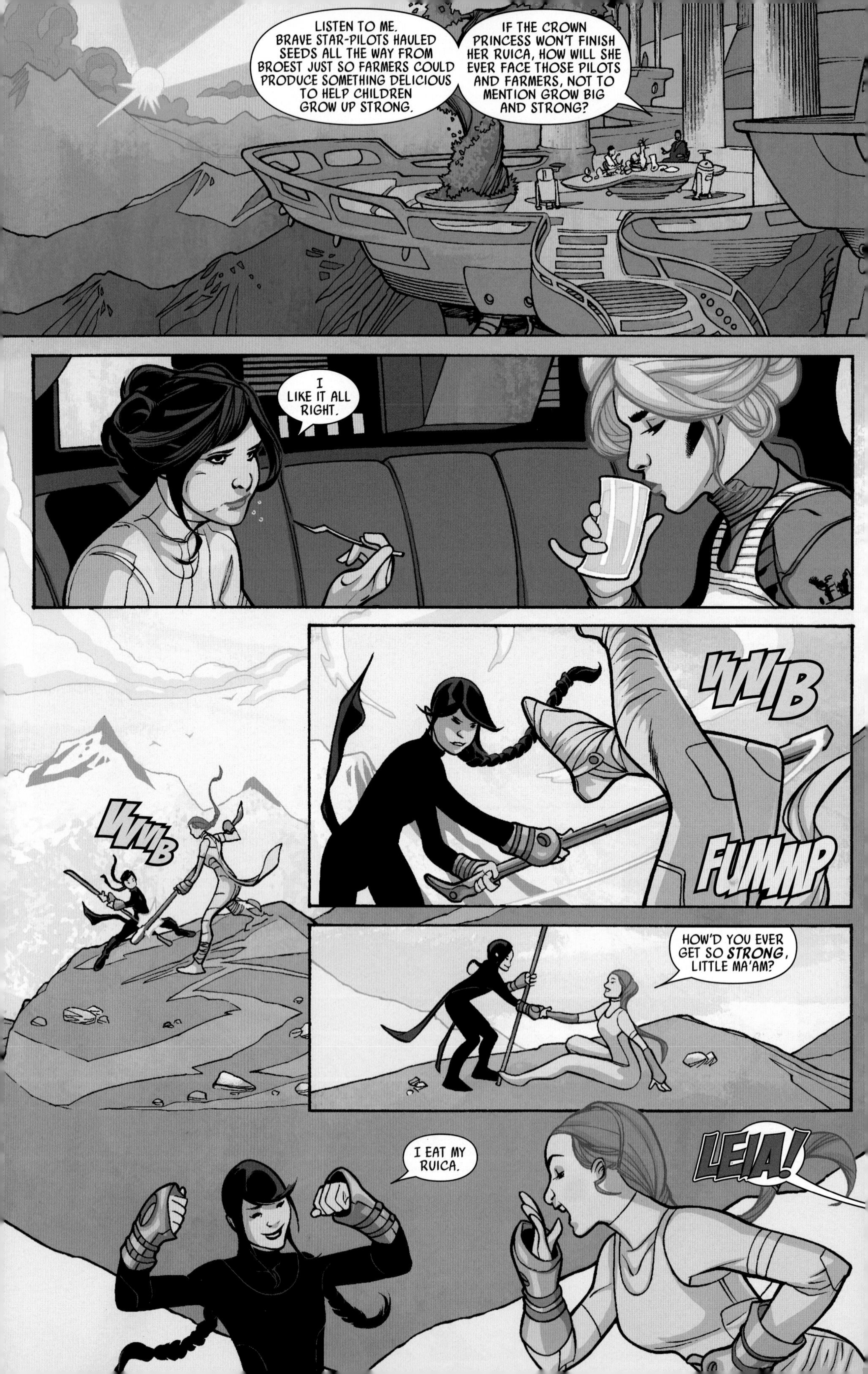
LISTEN TO ME. BRAVE STAR-PILOTS HAULED SEEDS ALL THE WAY FROM BROEST JUST SO FARMERS COULD PRODUCE SOMETHING DELICIOUS TO HELP CHILDREN GROW UP STRONG.
IF THE CROWN PRINCESS WON'T FINISH HER RUICA, HOW WILL SHE EVER FACE THOSE PILOTS AND FARMERS, NOT TO MENTION GROW BIG AND STRONG?
I LIKE IT ALL RIGHT.
WVIB
WVIB
FUMMP
HOW'D YOU EVER GET SO STRONG, LITTLE MA'AM?
I EAT MY RUICA.
LEIA!

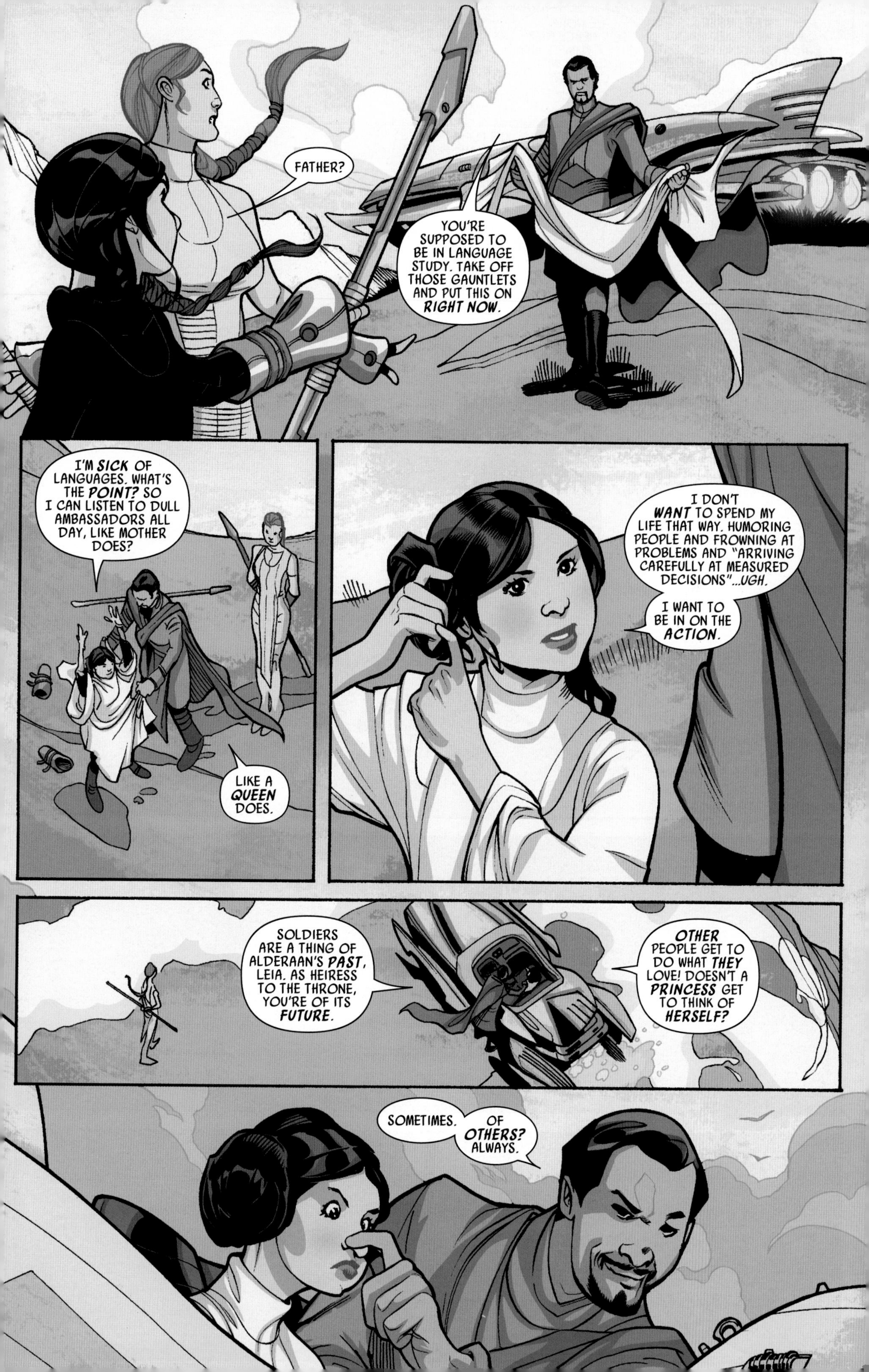
FATHER?
YOU'RE SUPPOSED TO BE IN LANGUAGE STUDY. TAKE OFF THOSE GAUNTLETS AND PUT THIS ON RIGHT NOW.
I'M SICK OF LANGUAGES. WHAT'S THE POINT? SO I CAN LISTEN TO DULL AMBASSADORS ALL DAY, LIKE MOTHER DOES?
LIKE A QUEEN DOES.
I DON'T WANT TO SPEND MY LIFE THAT WAY. HUMORING PEOPLE AND FROWNING AT PROBLEMS AND "ARRIVING CAREFULLY AT MEASURED DECISIONS"...UGH.
I WANT TO BE IN ON THE ACTION.
SOLDIERS ARE A THING OF ALDERAAN'S PAST, LEIA. AS HEIRESS TO THE THRONE, YOU'RE OF ITS FUTURE.
OTHER PEOPLE GET TO DO WHAT THEY LOVE! DOESN'T A PRINCESS GET TO THINK OF HERSELF?
SOMETIMES.
OF OTHERS? ALWAYS.

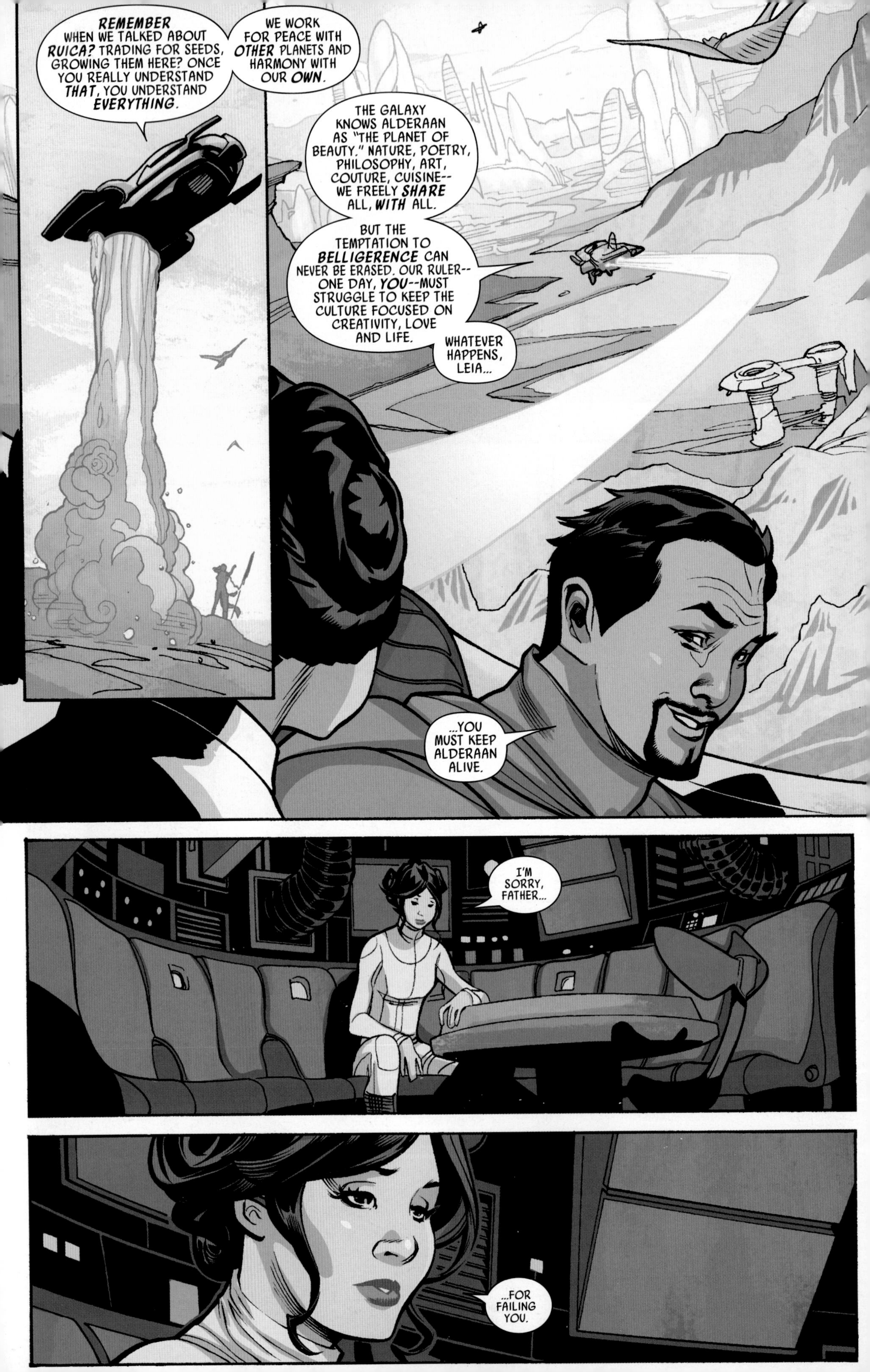
REMEMBER WHEN WE TALKED ABOUT RUICA? TRADING FOR SEEDS, GROWING THEM HERE? ONCE YOU REALLY UNDERSTAND THAT, YOU UNDERSTAND EVERYTHING.
WE WORK FOR PEACE WITH OTHER PLANETS AND HARMONY WITH OUR OWN.
THE GALAXY KNOWS ALDERAAN AS "THE PLANET OF BEAUTY." NATURE, POETRY, PHILOSOPHY, ART, COUTURE, CUISINE-- WE FREELY SHARE ALL, WITH ALL.
BUT THE TEMPTATION TO BELLIGERENCE CAN NEVER BE ERASED. OUR RULER-- ONE DAY, YOU--MUST STRUGGLE TO KEEP THE CULTURE FOCUSED ON CREATIVITY, LOVE AND LIFE.
WHATEVER HAPPENS, LEIA...
...YOU MUST KEEP ALDERAAN ALIVE.
I'M SORRY, FATHER...
...FOR FAILING YOU.

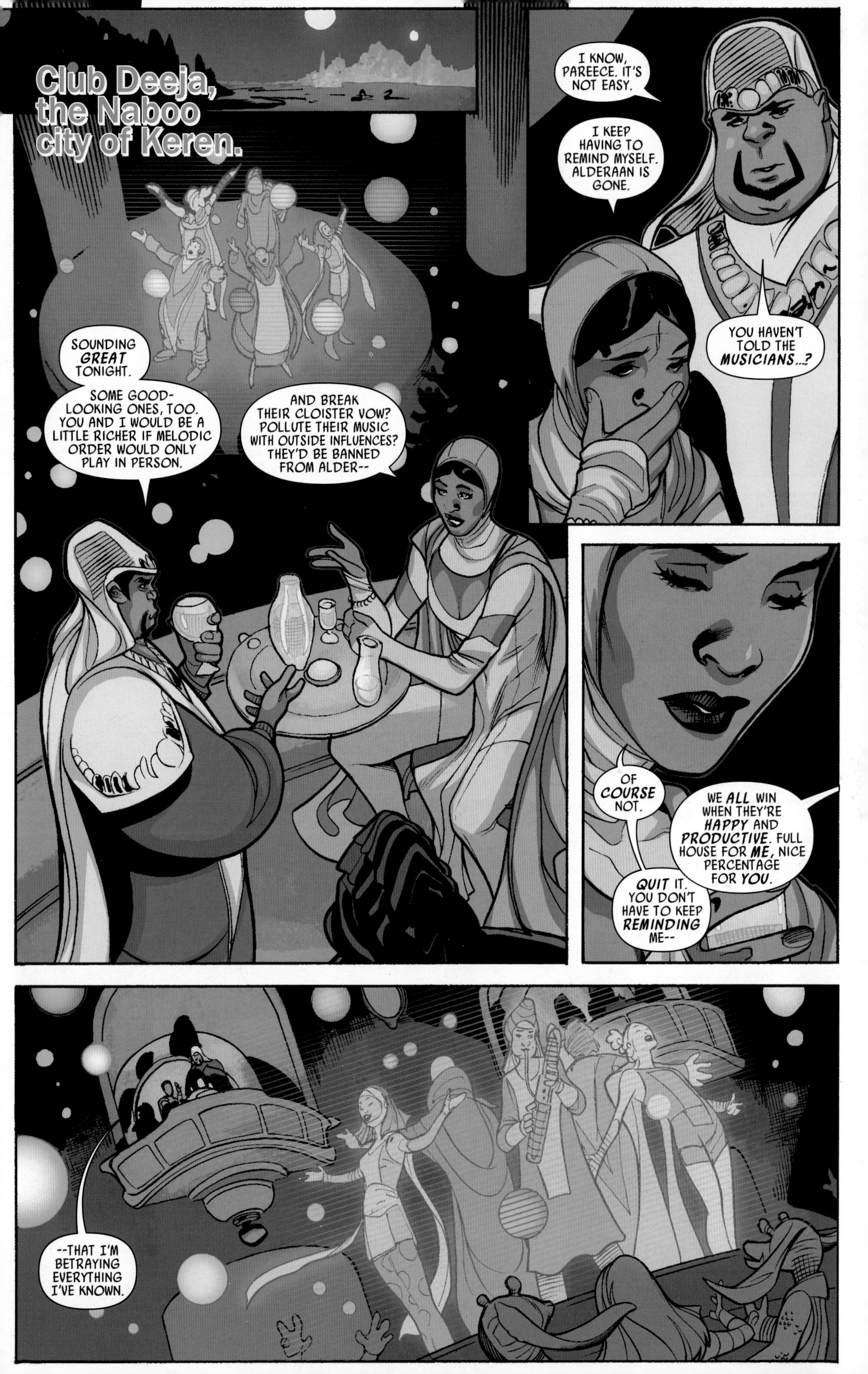
Club Deeja, the Naboo city of Keren.
SOUNDING GREAT TONIGHT.
SOME GOOD-LOOKING ONES, TOO. YOU AND I WOULD BE A LITTLE RICHER IF MELODIC ORDER WOULD ONLY PLAY IN PERSON.
AND BREAK THEIR CLOISTER VOW? POLLUTE THEIR MUSIC WITH OUTSIDE INFLUENCES? THEY'D BE BANNED FROM ALDER--
I KNOW, PAREECE. IT'S NOT EASY.
I KEEP HAVING TO REMIND MYSELF. ALDERAAN IS GONE.
YOU HAVEN'T TOLD THE MUSICIANS...?
OF COURSE NOT.
WE ALL WIN WHEN THEY'RE HAPPY AND PRODUCTIVE. FULL HOUSE FOR ME, NICE PERCENTAGE FOR YOU.
QUIT IT. YOU DON'T HAVE TO KEEP REMINDING ME--
--THAT I'M BETRAYING EVERYTHING I'VE KNOWN.

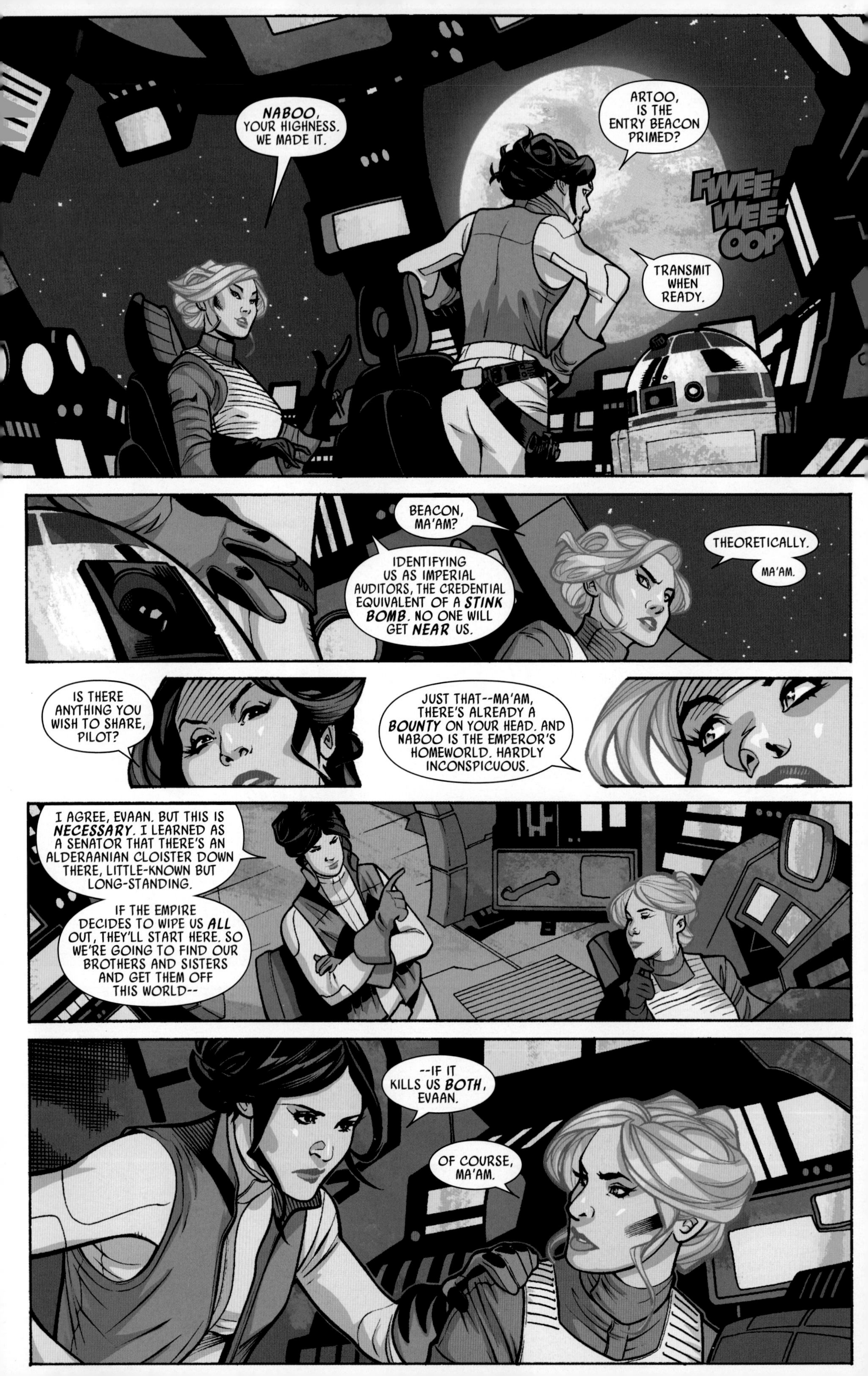
NABOO, YOUR HIGHNESS. WE MADE IT.
ARTOO, IS THE ENTRY BEACON PRIMED?
FWEE-WEE-OOP
TRANSMIT WHEN READY.
BEACON, MA'AM?
IDENTIFYING US AS IMPERIAL AUDITORS, THE CREDENTIAL EQUIVALENT OF A STINK BOMB. NO ONE WILL GET NEAR US.
THEORETICALLY.
MA'AM.
IS THERE ANYTHING YOU WISH TO SHARE, PILOT?
JUST THAT--MA'AM, THERE'S ALREADY A BOUNTY ON YOUR HEAD. AND NABOO IS THE EMPEROR'S HOMEWORLD. HARDLY INCONSPICUOUS.
I AGREE, EVAAN. BUT THIS IS NECESSARY. I LEARNED AS A SENATOR THAT THERE'S AN ALDERAANIAN CLOISTER DOWN THERE, LITTLE-KNOWN BUT LONG-STANDING.
IF THE EMPIRE DECIDES TO WIPE US ALL OUT, THEY'LL START HERE. SO WE'RE GOING TO FIND OUR BROTHERS AND SISTERS AND GET THEM OFF THIS WORLD--
--IF IT KILLS US BOTH, EVAAN.
OF COURSE, MA'AM.

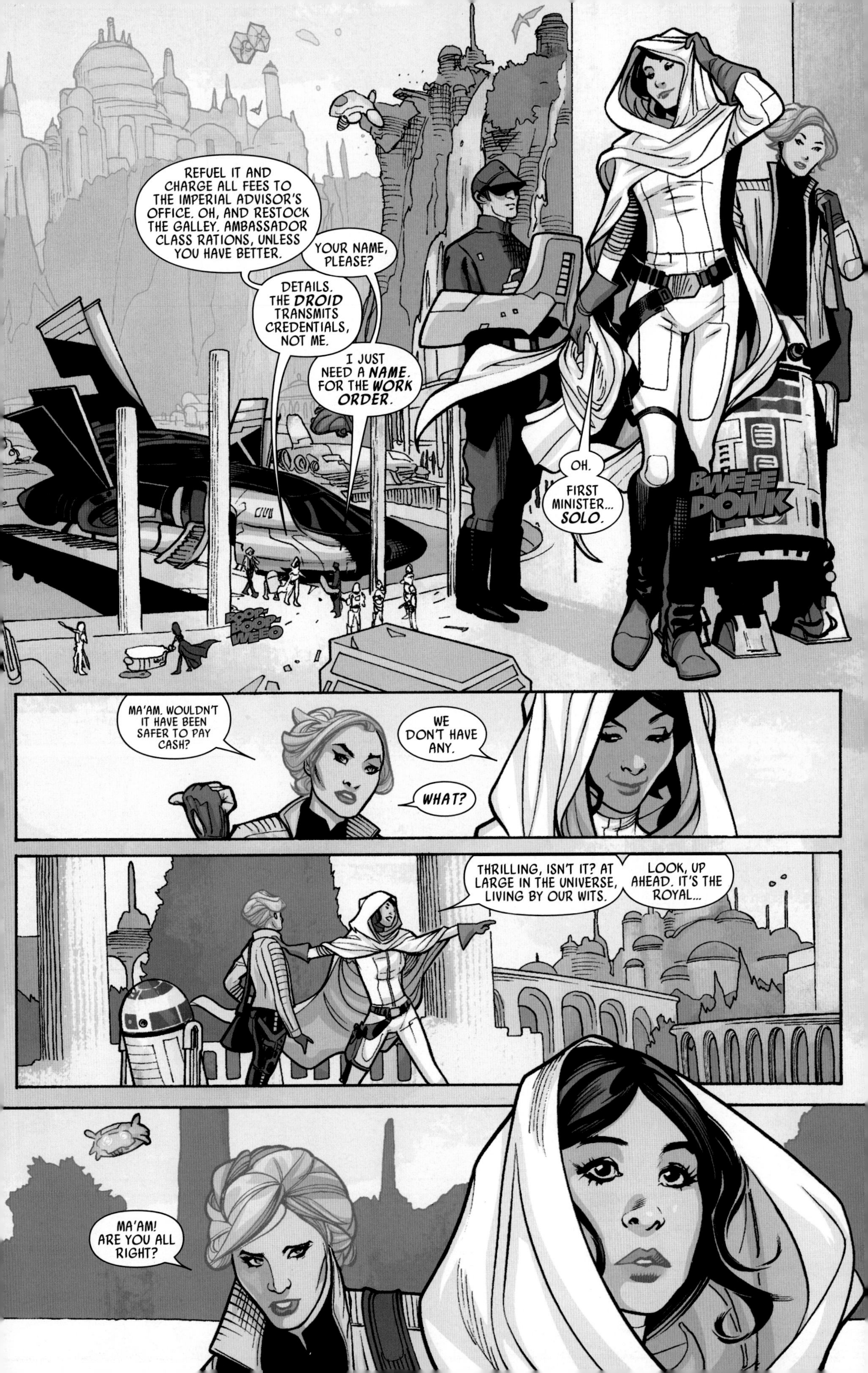
REFUEL IT AND CHARGE ALL FEES TO THE IMPERIAL ADVISOR'S OFFICE. OH, AND RESTOCK THE GALLEY. AMBASSADOR CLASS RATIONS, UNLESS YOU HAVE BETTER.
YOUR NAME, PLEASE?
DETAILS. THE DROID TRANSMITS CREDENTIALS, NOT ME.
I JUST NEED A NAME. FOR THE WORK ORDER.
OH.
FIRST MINISTER... SOLO.
BWEEE DONK
BOOP-BOOP-WEEO
MA'AM. WOULDN'T IT HAVE BEEN SAFER TO PAY CASH?
WE DON'T HAVE ANY.
WHAT?
THRILLING, ISN'T IT? AT LARGE IN THE UNIVERSE, LIVING BY OUR WITS.
LOOK, UP AHEAD. IT'S THE ROYAL...
MA'AM! ARE YOU ALL RIGHT?

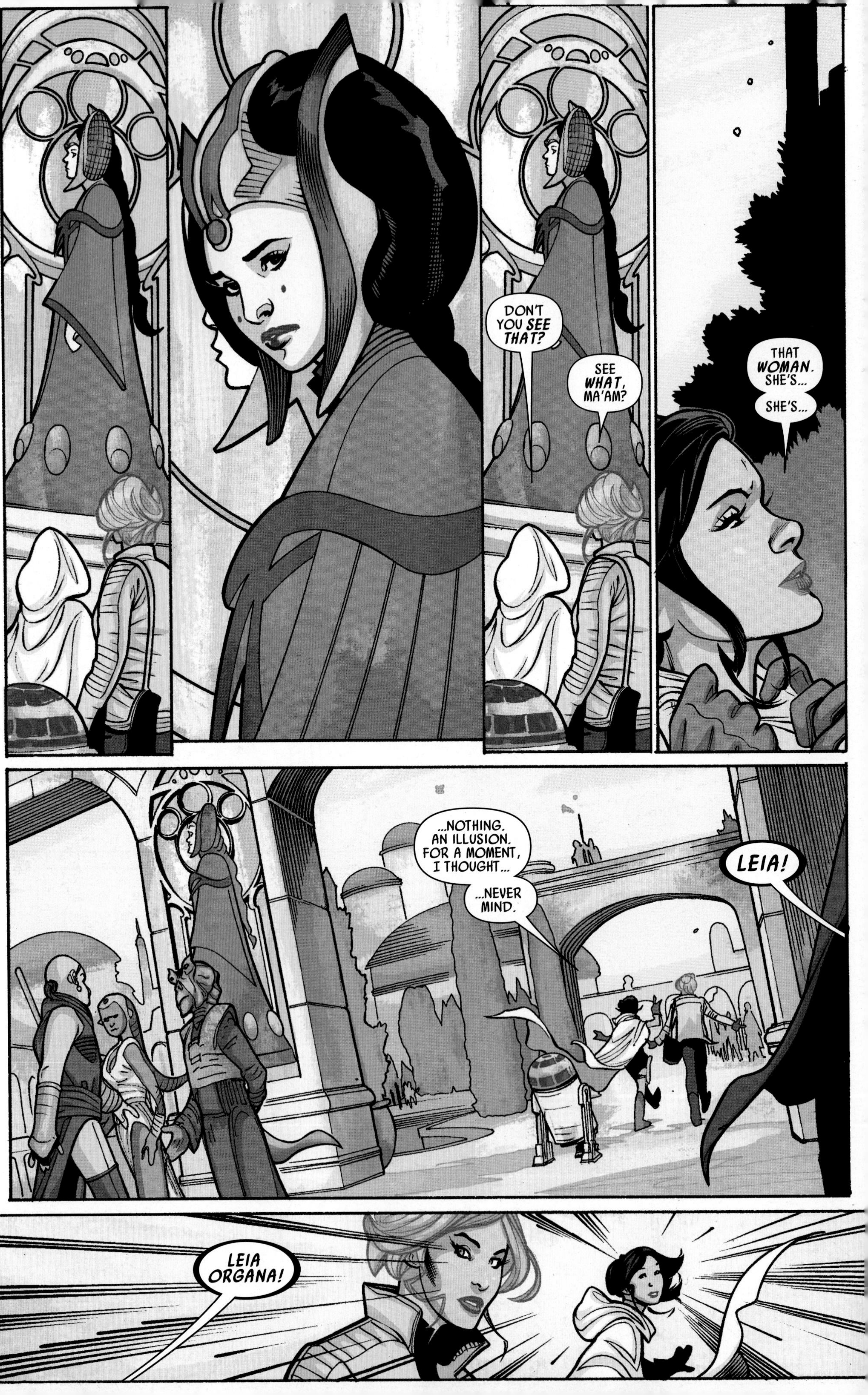
DON'T YOU SEE THAT?
SEE WHAT, MA'AM?
THAT WOMAN. SHE'S...
SHE'S...
...NOTHING. AN ILLUSION. FOR A MOMENT, I THOUGHT...
...NEVER MIND.
LEIA!
LEIA ORGANA!

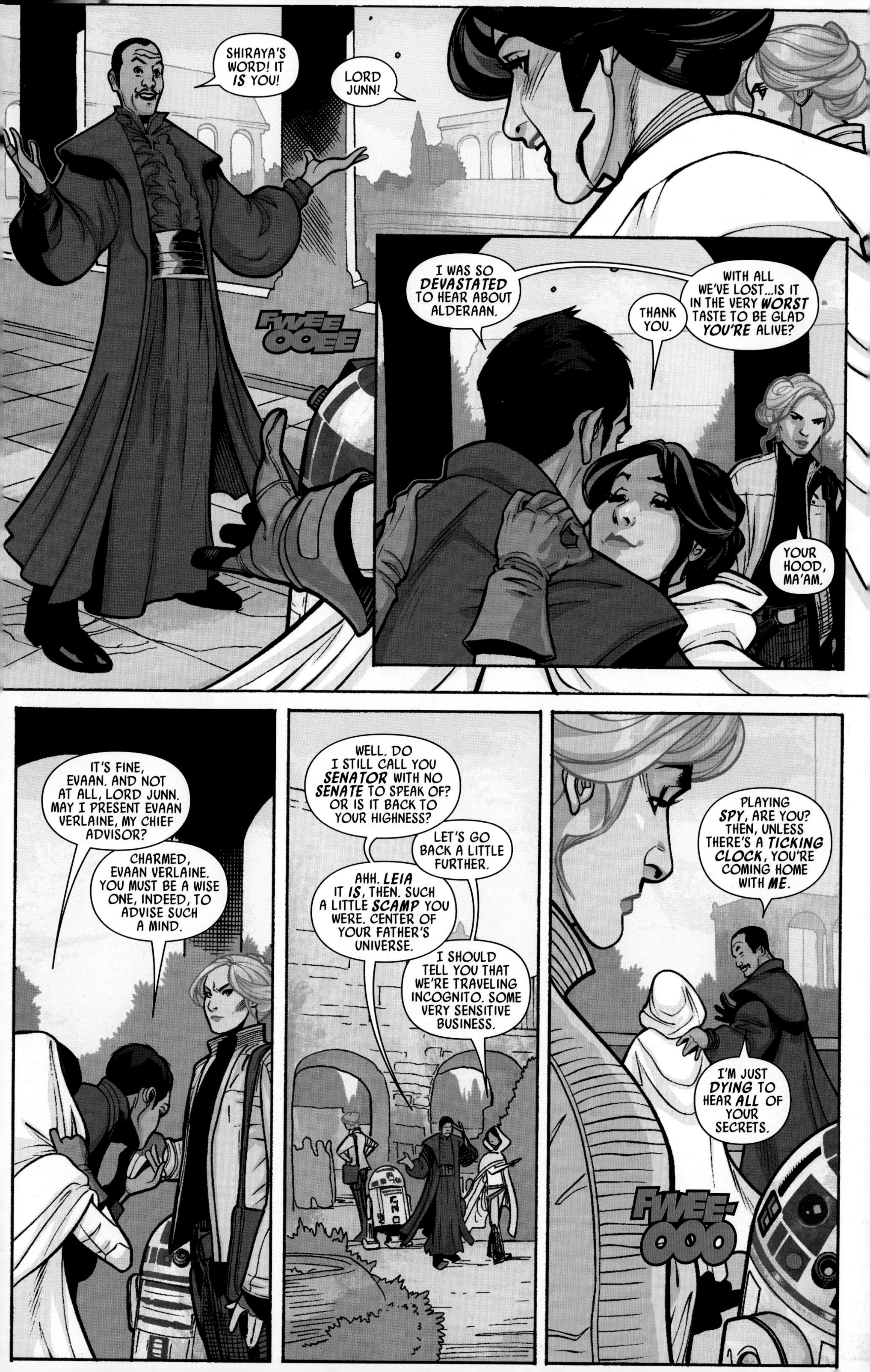
SHIRAYA'S WORD! IT IS YOU!
LORD JUNN!
FWEE OOEE
I WAS SO DEVASTATED TO HEAR ABOUT ALDERAAN.
WITH ALL WE'VE LOST...IS IT IN THE VERY WORST TASTE TO BE GLAD YOU'RE ALIVE?
THANK YOU.
YOUR HOOD, MA'AM.
IT'S FINE, EVAAN. AND NOT AT ALL, LORD JUNN. MAY I PRESENT EVAAN VERLAINE, MY CHIEF ADVISOR?
CHARMED, EVAAN VERLAINE. YOU MUST BE A WISE ONE, INDEED, TO ADVISE SUCH A MIND.
WELL. DO I STILL CALL YOU SENATOR WITH NO SENATE TO SPEAK OF? OR IS IT BACK TO YOUR HIGHNESS?
LET'S GO BACK A LITTLE FURTHER.
AHH. LEIA IT IS, THEN. SUCH A LITTLE SCAMP YOU WERE. CENTER OF YOUR FATHER'S UNIVERSE.
I SHOULD TELL YOU THAT WE'RE TRAVELING INCOGNITO. SOME VERY SENSITIVE BUSINESS.
PLAYING SPY, ARE YOU? THEN, UNLESS THERE'S A TICKING CLOCK, YOU'RE COMING HOME WITH ME.
I'M JUST DYING TO HEAR ALL OF YOUR SECRETS.
FWEE-OOO

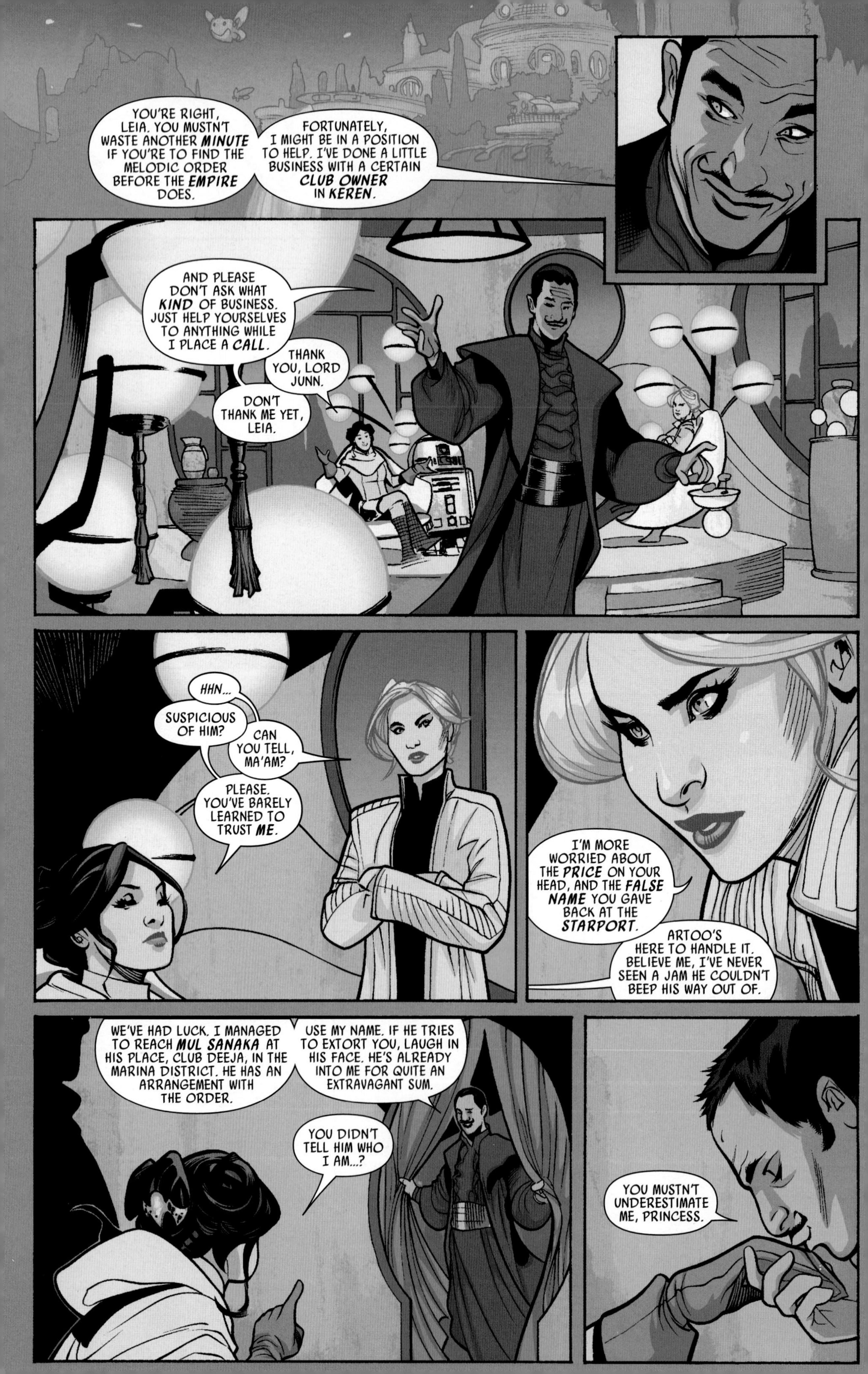
YOU'RE RIGHT, LEIA. YOU MUSTN'T WASTE ANOTHER MINUTE IF YOU'RE TO FIND THE MELODIC ORDER BEFORE THE EMPIRE DOES.
FORTUNATELY, I MIGHT BE IN A POSITION TO HELP. I'VE DONE A LITTLE BUSINESS WITH A CERTAIN CLUB OWNER IN KEREN.
AND PLEASE DON'T ASK WHAT KIND OF BUSINESS. JUST HELP YOURSELVES TO ANYTHING WHILE I PLACE A CALL.
THANK YOU, LORD JUNN.
DON'T THANK ME YET, LEIA.
HHN...
SUSPICIOUS OF HIM?
CAN YOU TELL, MA'AM?
PLEASE. YOU'VE BARELY LEARNED TO TRUST ME.
I'M MORE WORRIED ABOUT THE PRICE ON YOUR HEAD, AND THE FALSE NAME YOU GAVE BACK AT THE STARPORT.
ARTOO'S HERE TO HANDLE IT. BELIEVE ME, I'VE NEVER SEEN A JAM HE COULDN'T BEEP HIS WAY OUT OF.
WE'VE HAD LUCK. I MANAGED TO REACH MUL SANAKA AT HIS PLACE, CLUB DEEJA, IN THE MARINA DISTRICT. HE HAS AN ARRANGEMENT WITH THE ORDER.
USE MY NAME. IF HE TRIES TO EXTORT YOU, LAUGH IN HIS FACE. HE'S ALREADY INTO ME FOR QUITE AN EXTRAVAGANT SUM.
YOU DIDN'T TELL HIM WHO I AM...?
YOU MUSTN'T UNDERESTIMATE ME, PRINCESS.

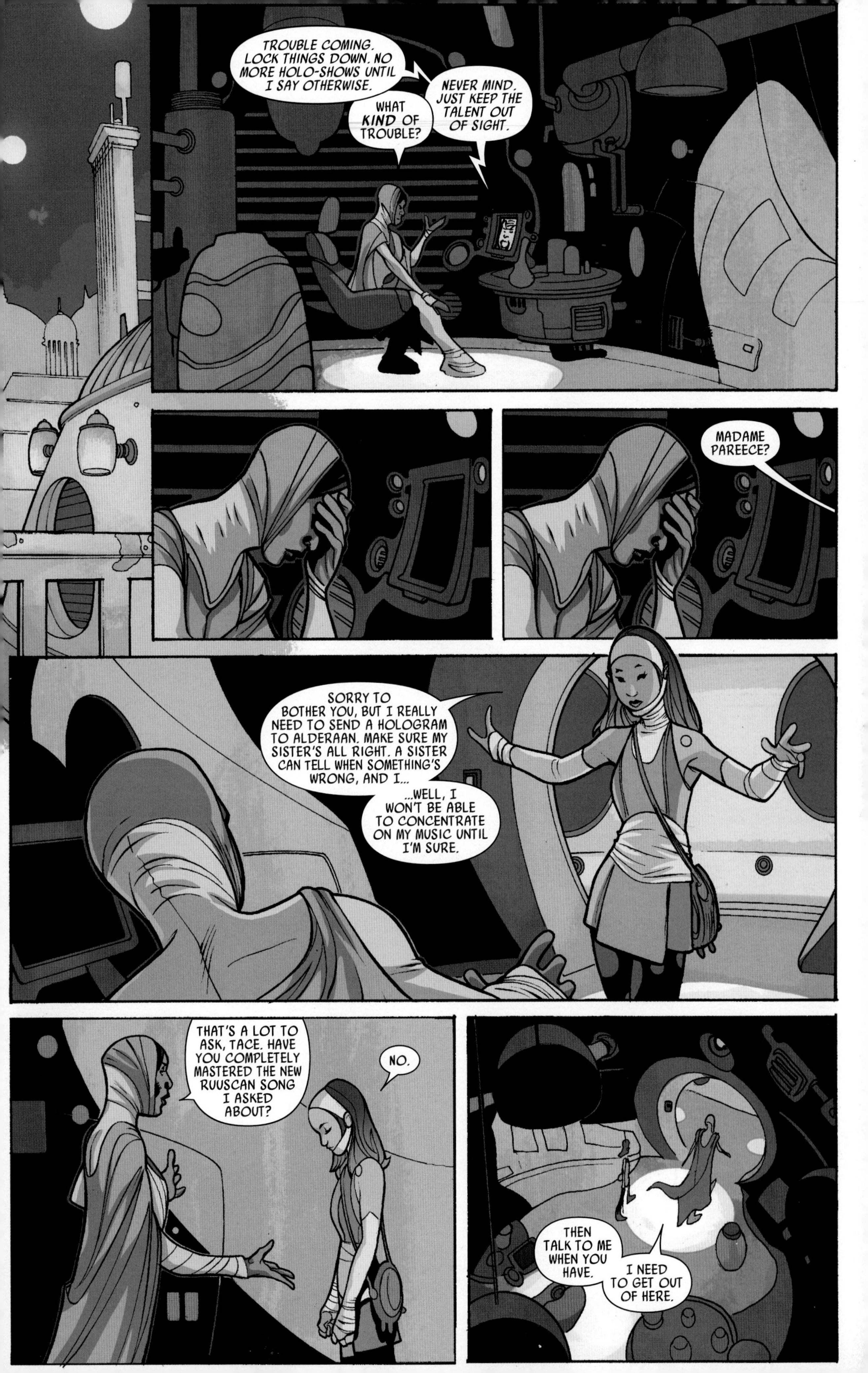
TROUBLE COMING. LOCK THINGS DOWN. NO MORE HOLO-SHOWS UNTIL I SAY OTHERWISE.
WHAT KIND OF TROUBLE?
NEVER MIND. JUST KEEP THE TALENT OUT OF SIGHT.
MADAME PAREECE?
SORRY TO BOTHER YOU, BUT I REALLY NEED TO SEND A HOLOGRAM TO ALDERAAN. MAKE SURE MY SISTER'S ALL RIGHT. A SISTER CAN TELL WHEN SOMETHING'S WRONG, AND I...
...WELL, I WON'T BE ABLE TO CONCENTRATE ON MY MUSIC UNTIL I'M SURE.
THAT'S A LOT TO ASK, TACE. HAVE YOU COMPLETELY MASTERED THE NEW RUUSCAN SONG I ASKED ABOUT?
NO.
THEN TALK TO ME WHEN YOU HAVE.
I NEED TO GET OUT OF HERE.

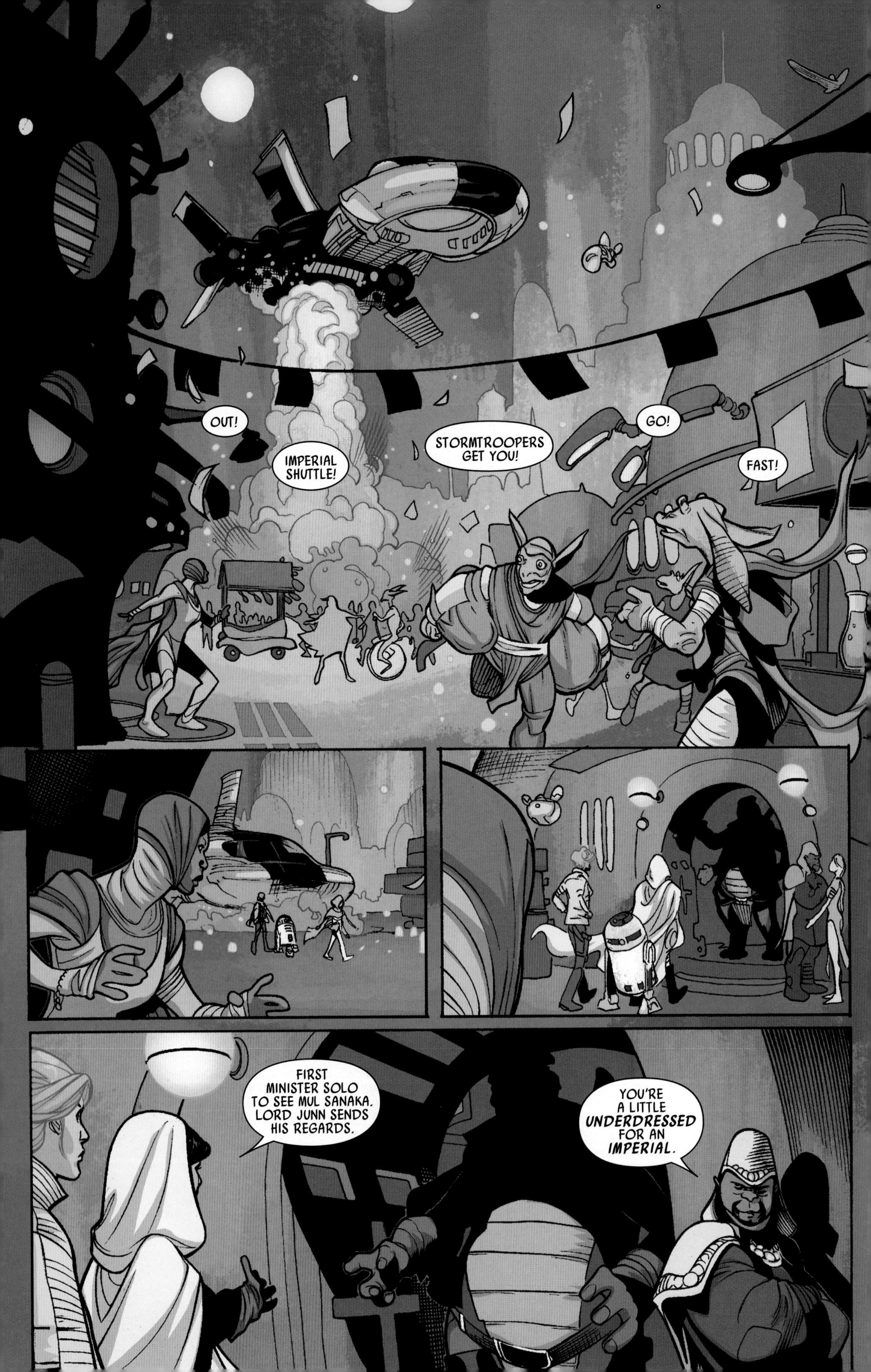
OUT!
IMPERIAL SHUTTLE!
STORMTROOPERS GET YOU!
GO!
FAST!
FIRST MINISTER SOLO TO SEE MUL SANAKA. LORD JUNN SENDS HIS REGARDS.
YOU'RE A LITTLE UNDERDRESSED FOR AN IMPERIAL.

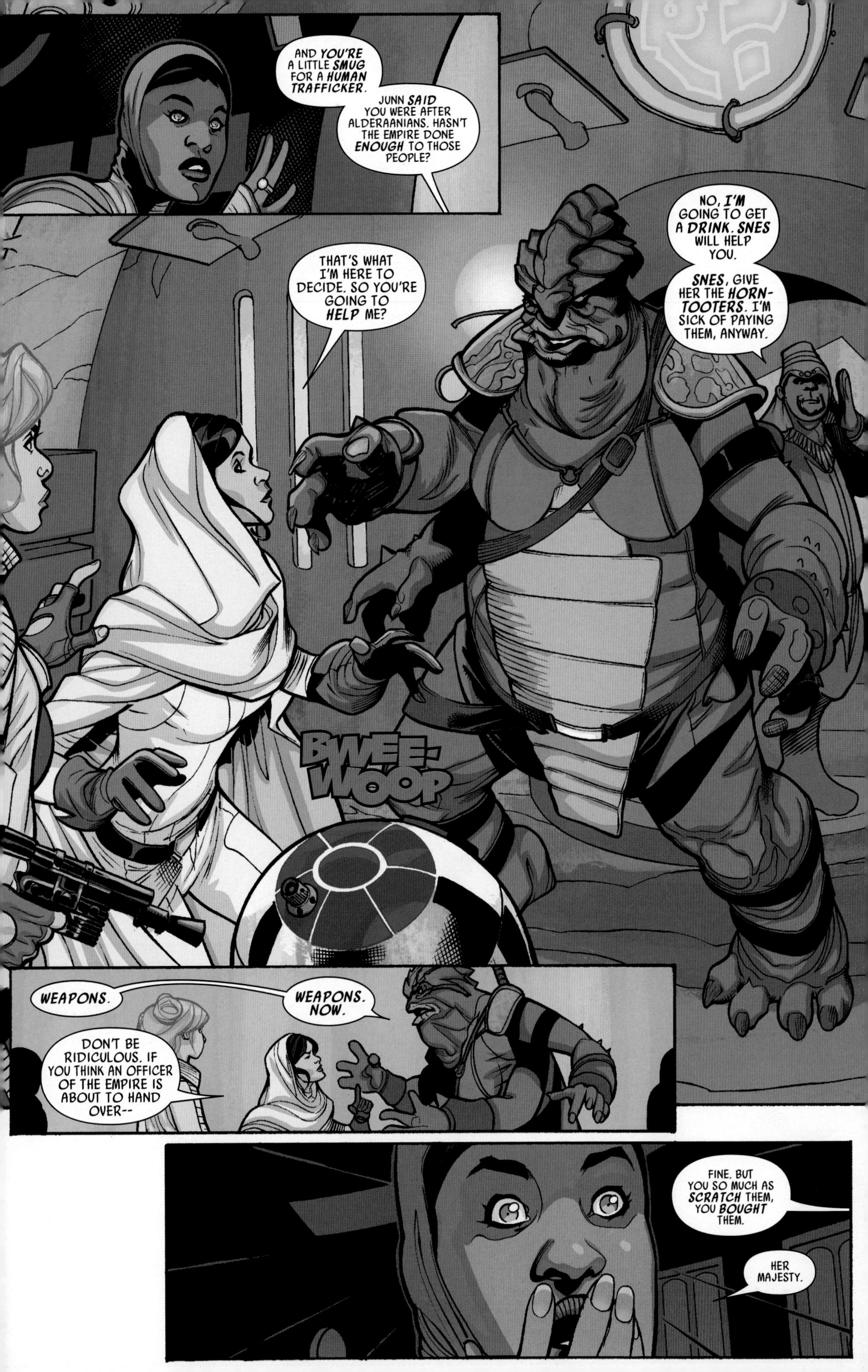
AND YOU'RE A LITTLE SMUG FOR A HUMAN TRAFFICKER.
JUNN SAID YOU WERE AFTER ALDERAANIANS. HASN'T THE EMPIRE DONE ENOUGH TO THOSE PEOPLE?
THAT'S WHAT I'M HERE TO DECIDE. SO YOU'RE GOING TO HELP ME?
NO, I'M GOING TO GET A DRINK. SNES WILL HELP YOU.
SNES, GIVE HER THE HORN-TOOTERS. I'M SICK OF PAYING THEM, ANYWAY.
BWEE-WOOP
WEAPONS.
WEAPONS. NOW.
DON'T BE RIDICULOUS. IF YOU THINK AN OFFICER OF THE EMPIRE IS ABOUT TO HAND OVER--
FINE. BUT YOU SO MUCH AS SCRATCH THEM, YOU BOUGHT THEM.
HER MAJESTY.

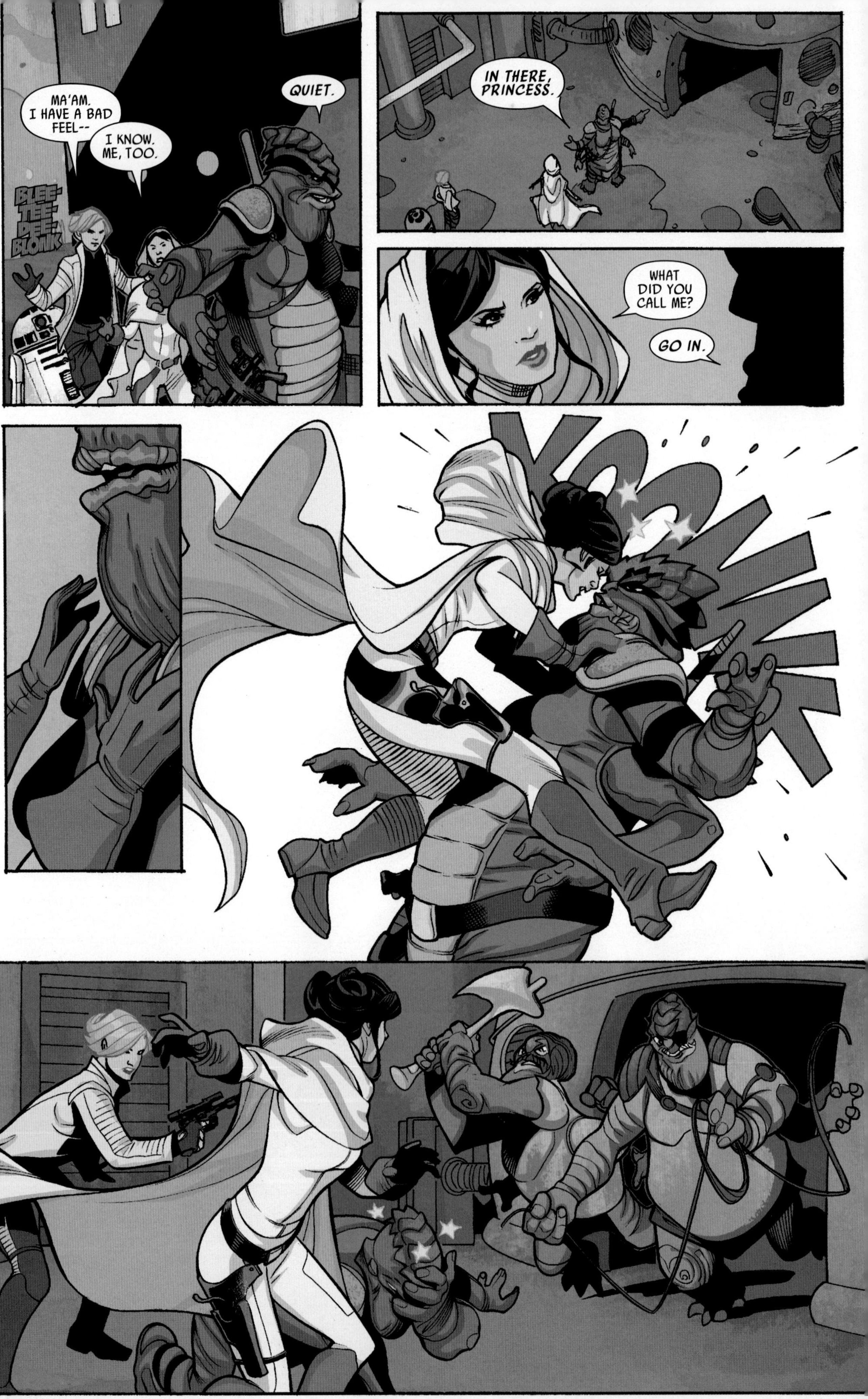
MA'AM. I HAVE A BAD FEEL--
I KNOW. ME, TOO.
QUIET.
BLEE-TEE-DEE-BLONK
IN THERE, PRINCESS.
WHAT DID YOU CALL ME?
GO IN.

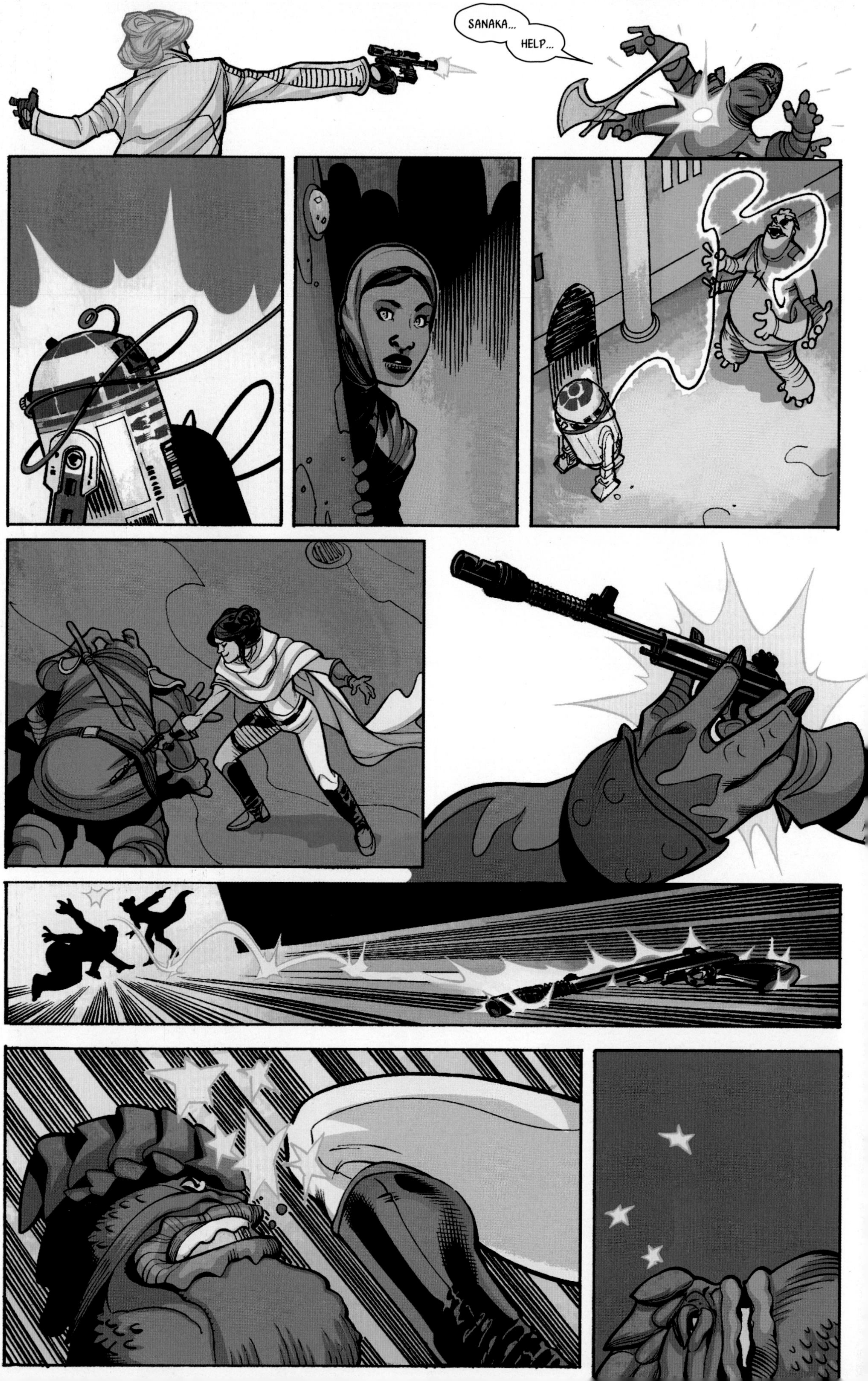
SANAKA...
HELP...

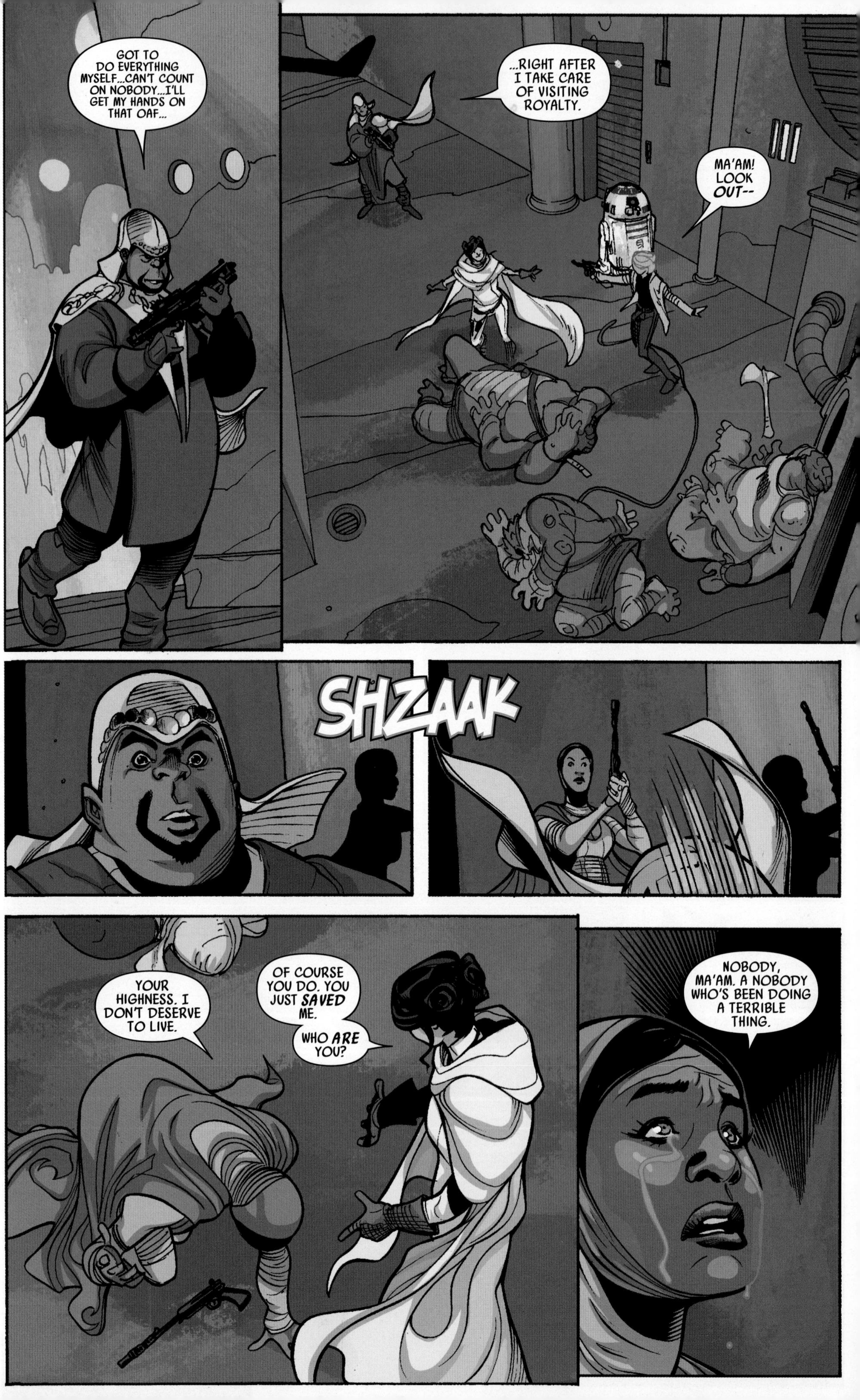
GOT TO DO EVERYTHING MYSELF...CAN'T COUNT ON NOBODY...I'LL GET MY HANDS ON THAT OAF...
...RIGHT AFTER I TAKE CARE OF VISITING ROYALTY.
MA'AM! LOOK OUT--
SHZAAK
YOUR HIGHNESS. I DON'T DESERVE TO LIVE.
OF COURSE YOU DO. YOU JUST SAVED ME.
WHO ARE YOU?
NOBODY, MA'AM. A NOBODY WHO'S BEEN DOING A TERRIBLE THING.

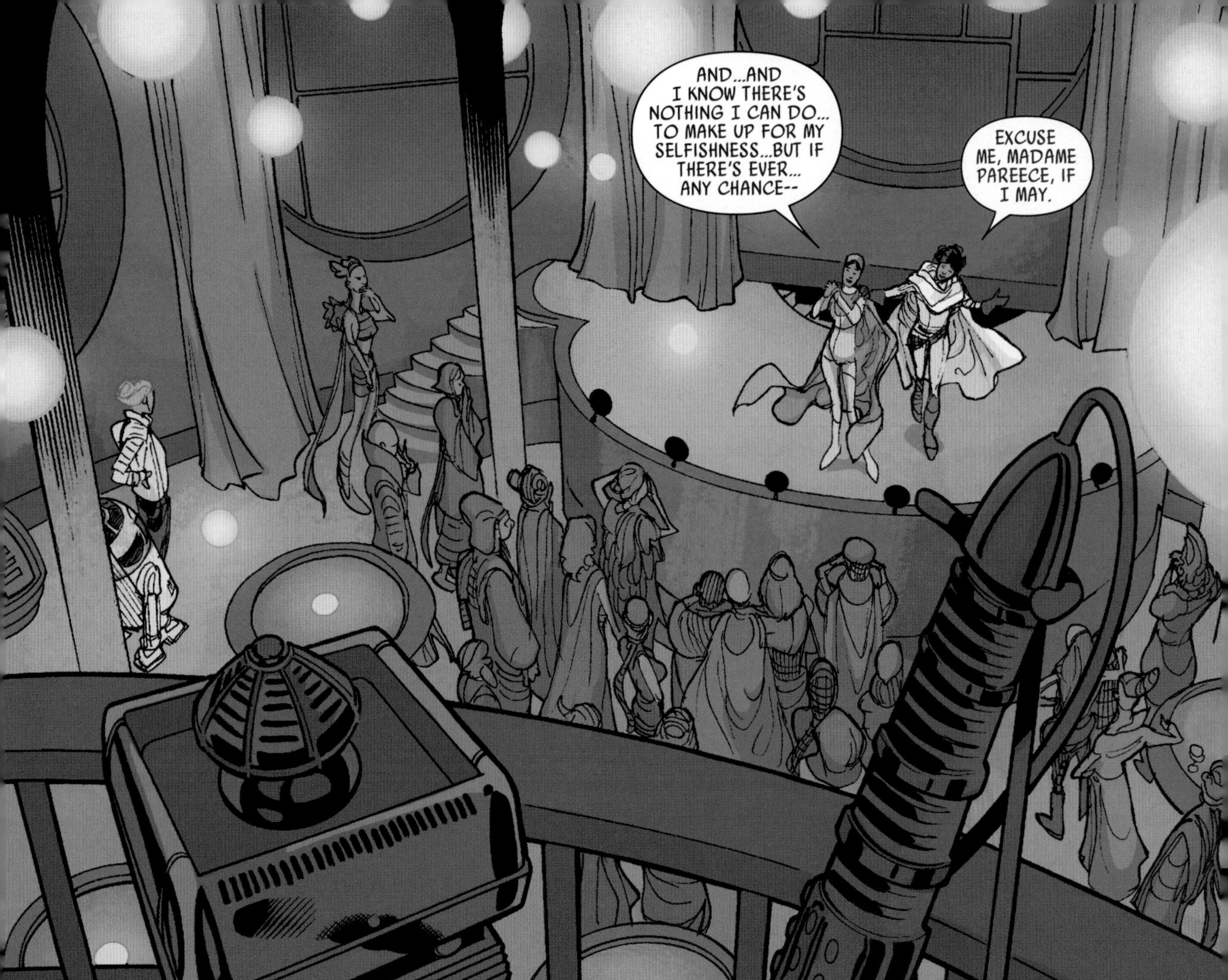
AND...AND I KNOW THERE'S NOTHING I CAN DO... TO MAKE UP FOR MY SELFISHNESS...BUT IF THERE'S EVER... ANY CHANCE--
EXCUSE ME, MADAME PAREECE, IF I MAY.

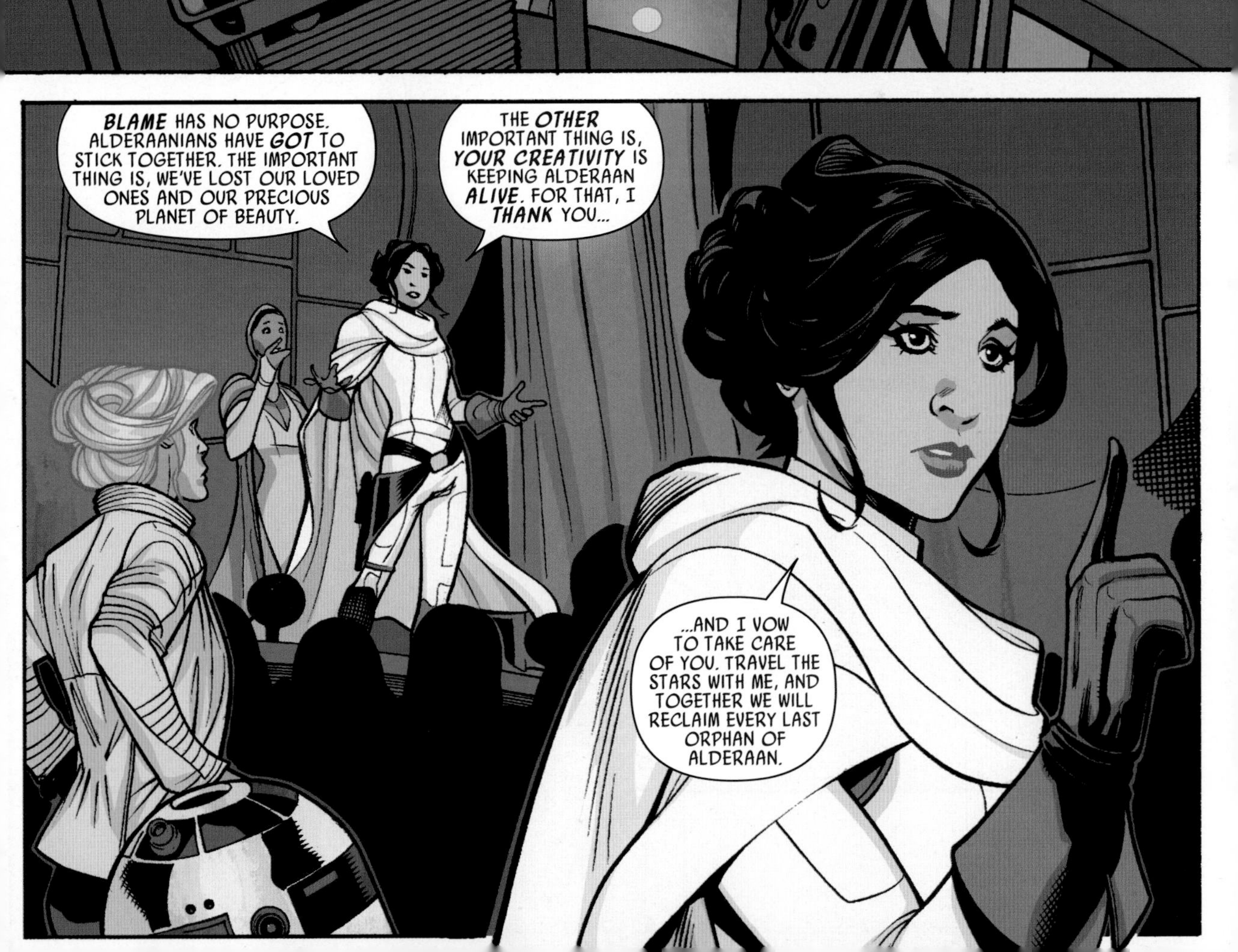
BLAME HAS NO PURPOSE. ALDERAANIANS HAVE GOT TO STICK TOGETHER. THE IMPORTANT THING IS, WE'VE LOST OUR LOVED ONES AND OUR PRECIOUS PLANET OF BEAUTY.
THE OTHER IMPORTANT THING IS, YOUR CREATIVITY IS KEEPING ALDERAAN ALIVE. FOR THAT, I THANK YOU...
...AND I VOW TO TAKE CARE OF YOU. TRAVEL THE STARS WITH ME, AND TOGETHER WE WILL RECLAIM EVERY LAST ORPHAN OF ALDERAAN.

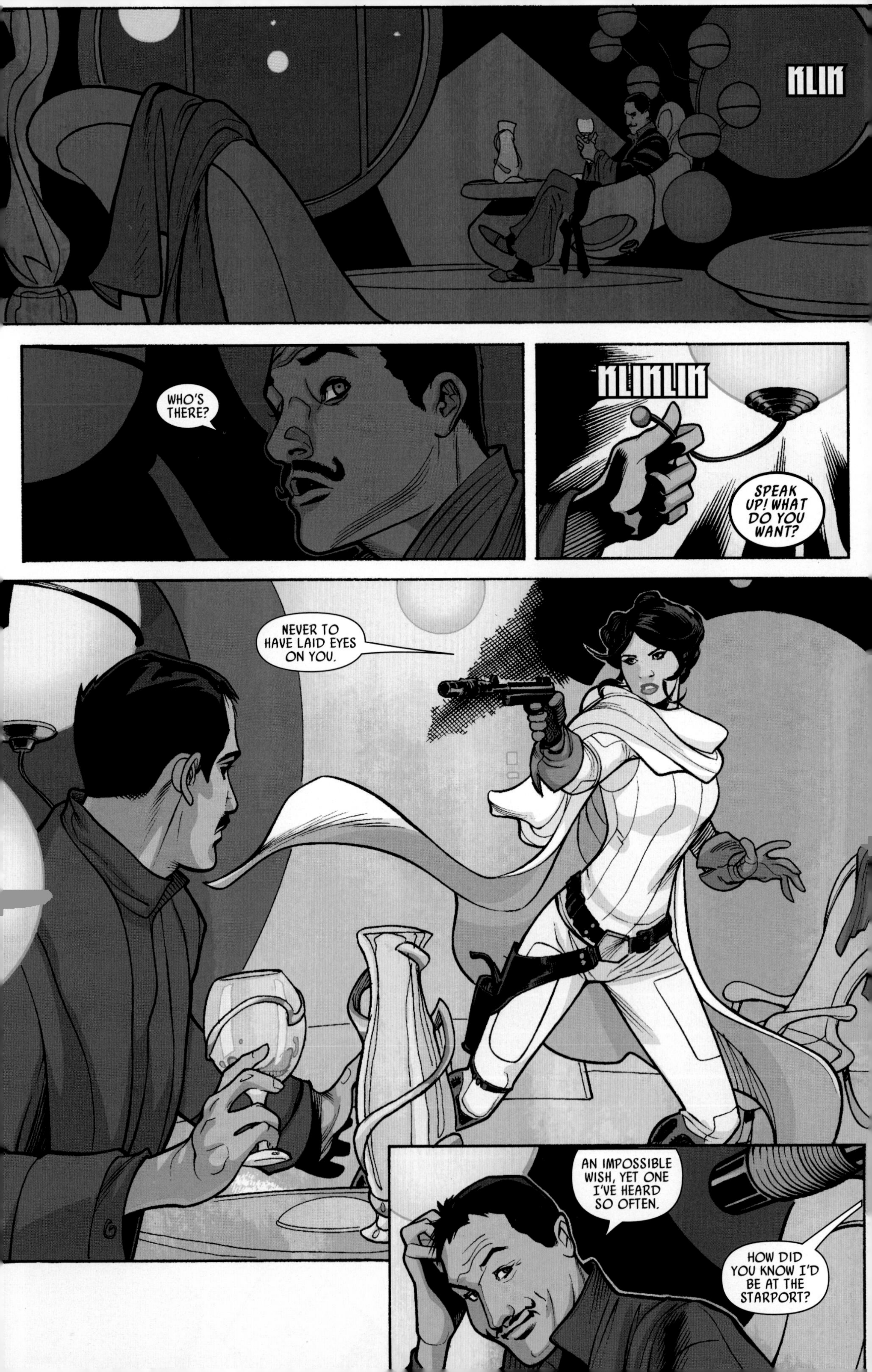
KLIK
WHO'S THERE?
KLIKLIK
SPEAK UP! WHAT DO YOU WANT?
NEVER TO HAVE LAID EYES ON YOU.
AN IMPOSSIBLE WISH, YET ONE I'VE HEARD SO OFTEN.
HOW DID YOU KNOW I'D BE AT THE STARPORT?

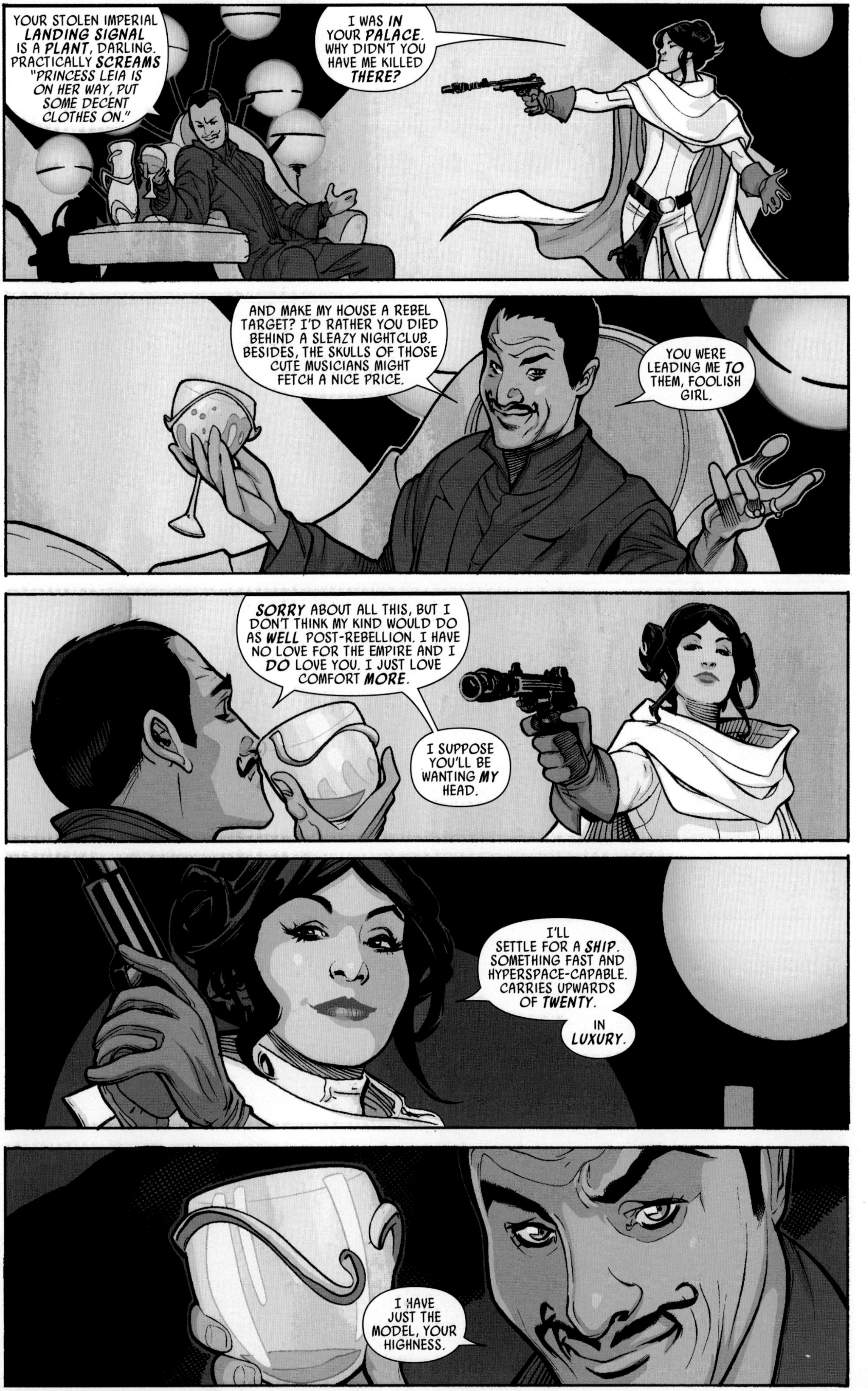
YOUR STOLEN IMPERIAL LANDING SIGNAL IS A PLANT, DARLING. PRACTICALLY SCREAMS "PRINCESS LEIA IS ON HER WAY, PUT SOME DECENT CLOTHES ON."
I WAS IN YOUR PALACE. WHY DIDN'T YOU HAVE ME KILLED THERE?
AND MAKE MY HOUSE A REBEL TARGET? I'D RATHER YOU DIED BEHIND A SLEAZY NIGHTCLUB. BESIDES, THE SKULLS OF THOSE CUTE MUSICIANS MIGHT FETCH A NICE PRICE.
YOU WERE LEADING ME TO THEM, FOOLISH GIRL.
SORRY ABOUT ALL THIS, BUT I DON'T THINK MY KIND WOULD DO AS WELL POST-REBELLION. I HAVE NO LOVE FOR THE EMPIRE AND I DO LOVE YOU. I JUST LOVE COMFORT MORE.
I SUPPOSE YOU'LL BE WANTING MY HEAD.
I'LL SETTLE FOR A SHIP. SOMETHING FAST AND HYPERSPACE-CAPABLE. CARRIES UPWARDS OF TWENTY.
IN LUXURY.
I HAVE JUST THE MODEL, YOUR HIGHNESS.

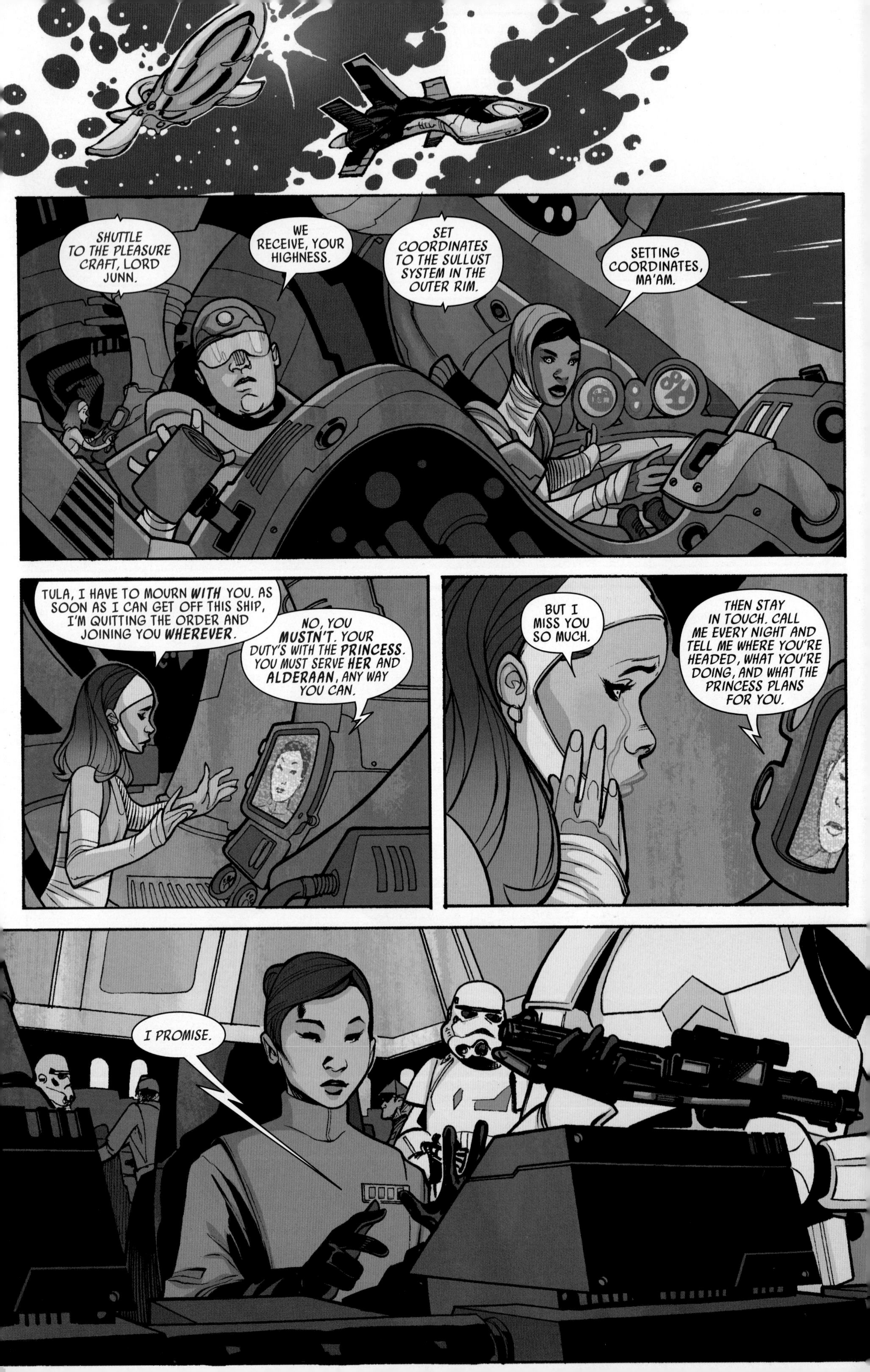
SHUTTLE TO THE PLEASURE CRAFT, LORD JUNN.
WE RECEIVE, YOUR HIGHNESS.
SET COORDINATES TO THE SULLUST SYSTEM IN THE OUTER RIM.
SETTING COORDINATES, MA'AM.
TULA, I HAVE TO MOURN WITH YOU. AS SOON AS I CAN GET OFF THIS SHIP, I'M QUITTING THE ORDER AND JOINING YOU WHEREVER.
NO, YOU MUSTN'T. YOUR DUTY'S WITH THE PRINCESS. YOU MUST SERVE HER AND ALDERAAN, ANY WAY YOU CAN.
BUT I MISS YOU SO MUCH.
THEN STAY IN TOUCH. CALL ME EVERY NIGHT AND TELL ME WHERE YOU'RE HEADED, WHAT YOU'RE DOING, AND WHAT THE PRINCESS PLANS FOR YOU.
I PROMISE.

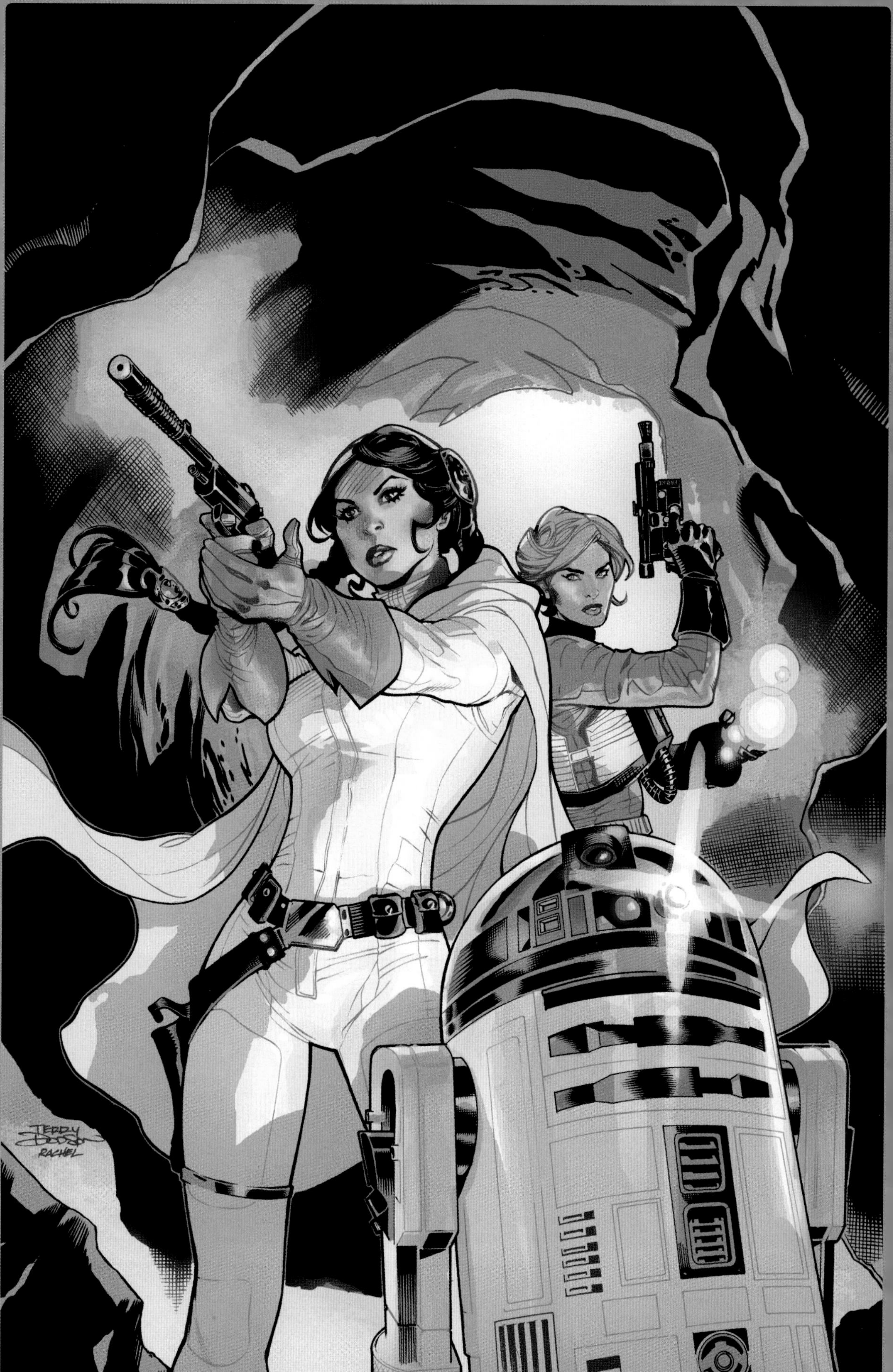

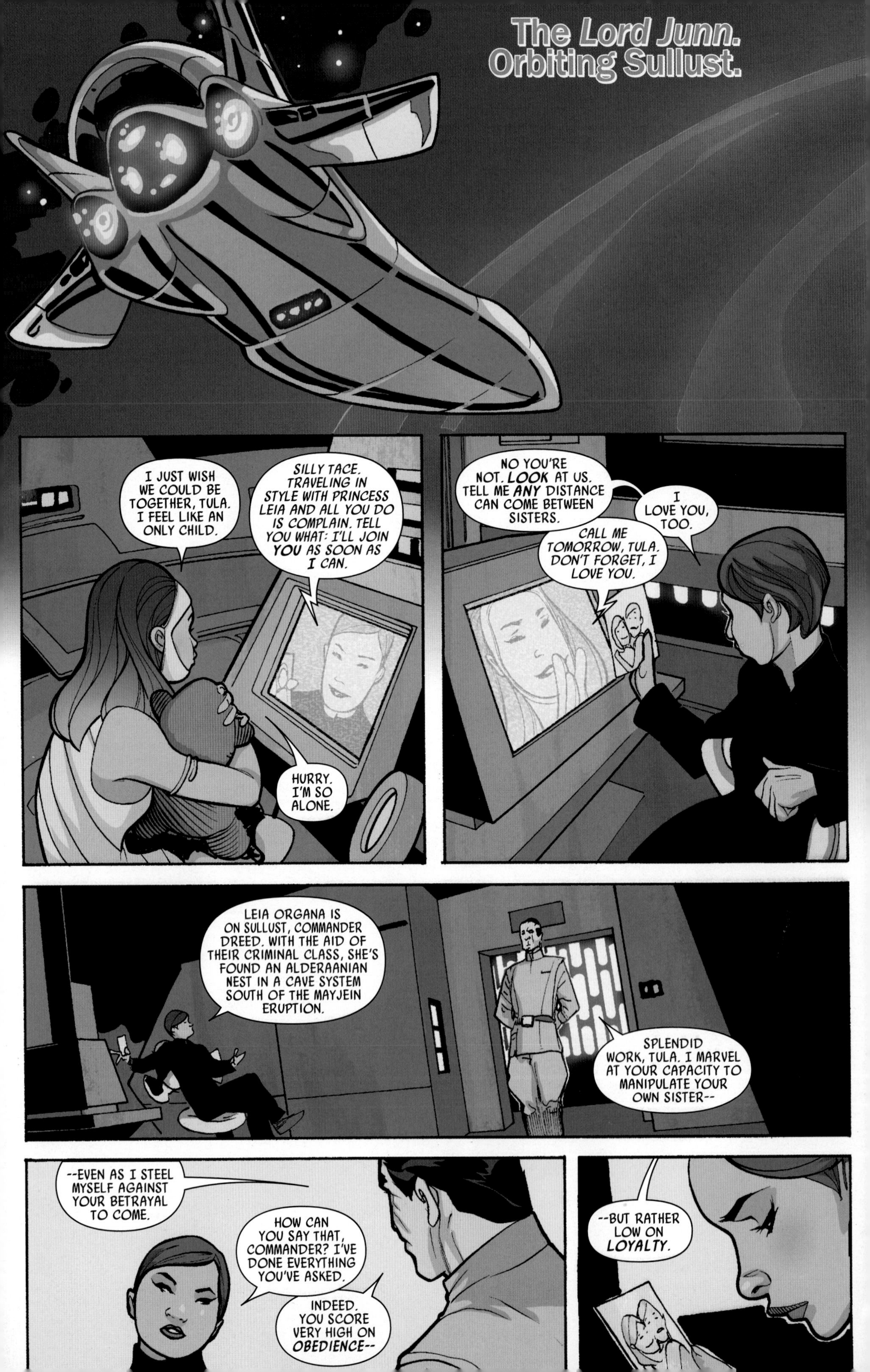

The Lord Junn. Orbiting Sullust.
I JUST WISH WE COULD BE TOGETHER, TULA. I FEEL LIKE AN ONLY CHILD.
SILLY TACE. TRAVELING IN STYLE WITH PRINCESS LEIA AND ALL YOU DO IS COMPLAIN. TELL YOU WHAT: I'LL JOIN YOU AS SOON AS I CAN.
HURRY. I'M SO ALONE.
NO YOU'RE NOT. LOOK AT US. TELL ME ANY DISTANCE CAN COME BETWEEN SISTERS.
I LOVE YOU, TOO.
CALL ME TOMORROW, TULA. DON'T FORGET, I LOVE YOU.
LEIA ORGANA IS ON SULLUST, COMMANDER DREED. WITH THE AID OF THEIR CRIMINAL CLASS, SHE'S FOUND AN ALDERAANIAN NEST IN A CAVE SYSTEM SOUTH OF THE MAYJEIN ERUPTION.
SPLENDID WORK, TULA. I MARVEL AT YOUR CAPACITY TO MANIPULATE YOUR OWN SISTER--
--EVEN AS I STEEL MYSELF AGAINST YOUR BETRAYAL TO COME.
HOW CAN YOU SAY THAT, COMMANDER? I'VE DONE EVERYTHING YOU'VE ASKED.
INDEED. YOU SCORE VERY HIGH ON OBEDIENCE--
--BUT RATHER LOW ON LOYALTY.

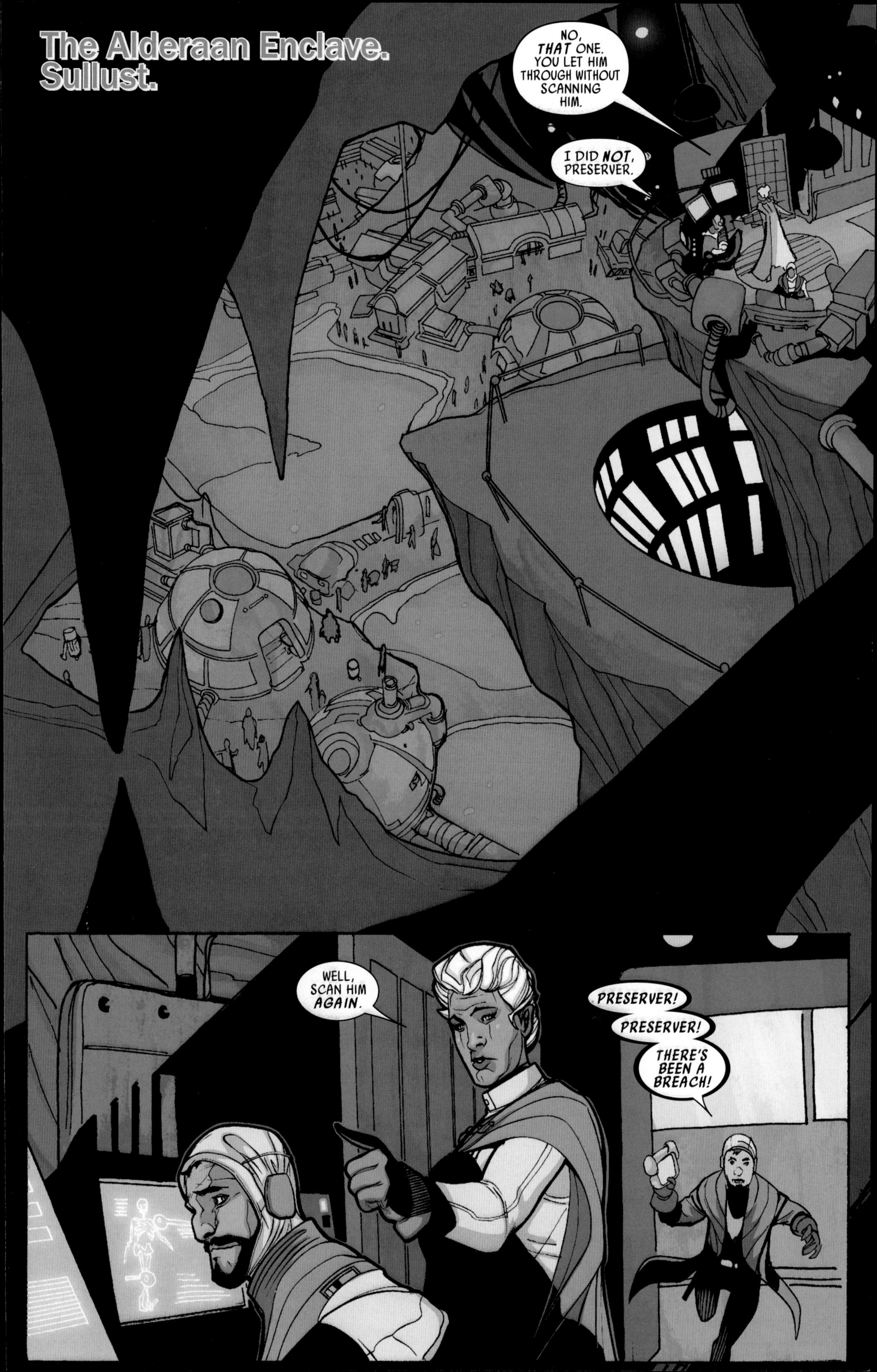
The Alderaan Enclave.
Sullust.
NO, THAT ONE. YOU LET HIM THROUGH WITHOUT SCANNING HIM.
I DID NOT, PRESERVER.
WELL, SCAN HIM AGAIN.
PRESERVER!
PRESERVER!
THERE'S BEEN A BREACH!

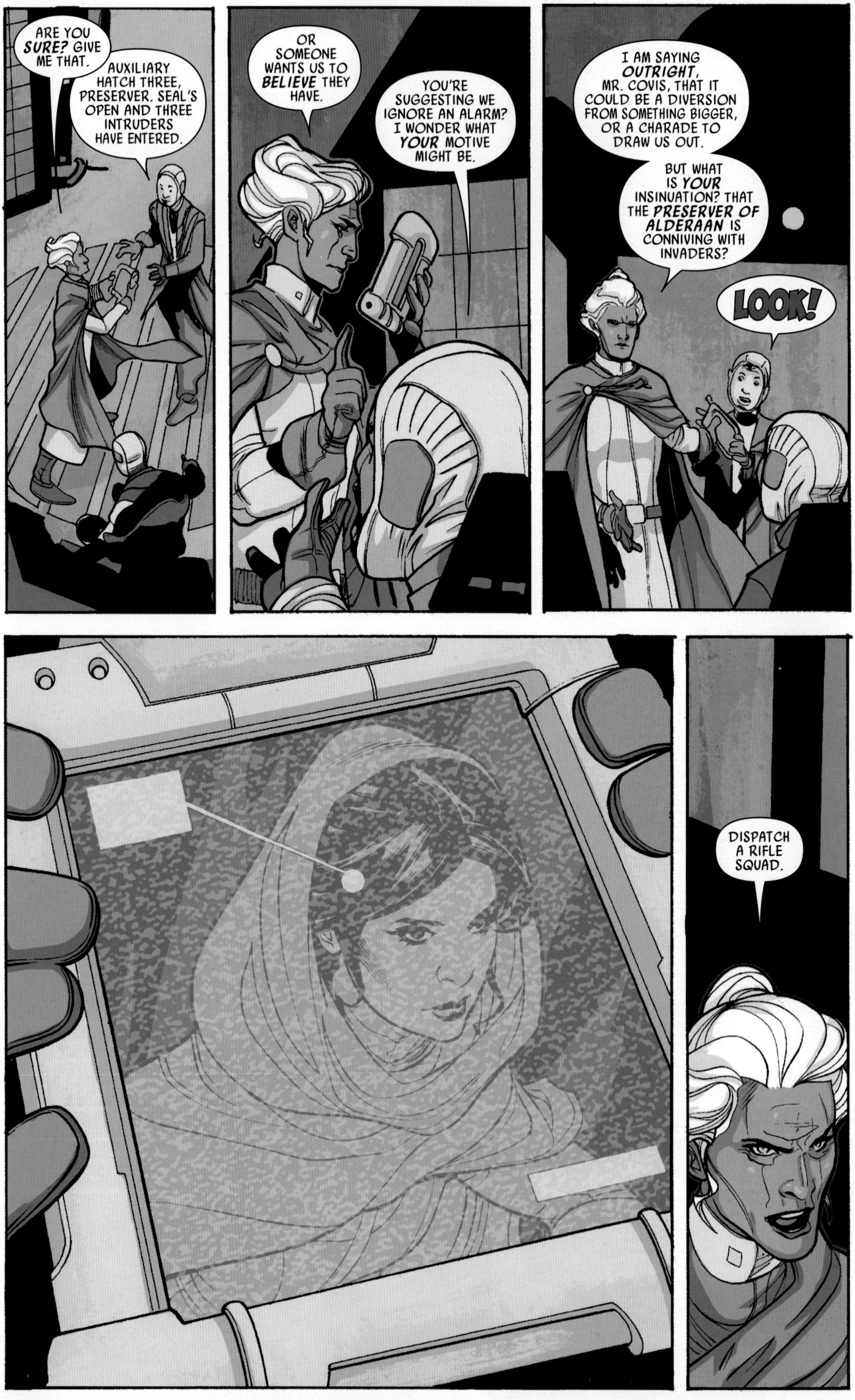
ARE YOU *SURE?* GIVE ME THAT.
AUXILIARY HATCH THREE, PRESERVER. SEAL'S OPEN AND THREE INTRUDERS HAVE ENTERED.
OR SOMEONE WANTS US TO *BELIEVE* THEY HAVE.
YOU'RE SUGGESTING WE IGNORE AN ALARM? I WONDER WHAT *YOUR* MOTIVE MIGHT BE.
I AM SAYING *OUTRIGHT*, MR. COVIS, THAT IT COULD BE A DIVERSION FROM SOMETHING BIGGER, OR A CHARADE TO DRAW US OUT.
BUT WHAT IS *YOUR* INSINUATION? THAT THE *PRESERVER OF ALDERAAN* IS CONNIVING WITH INVADERS?
LOOK!
DISPATCH A RIFLE SQUAD.

PՐԾ⅃Ƨ Pռ̇ò

He's trying to say it nicely, ma'am, but...he thinks the local Alderaanians here have gone insane.

Can you blame them? They lost their entire world.

Ma'am, it was our world, too.

Then don't get too confident about *our* mental health.

Pᒪ∩PPƧ ⅃ȯ̇ȯ̇⅃

He says they've cut off communication with anyone outside the compound. Which is fine with the Sullustans if it cuts the risk of Imperial attention.

Ask Mr. Tivvy how a handful of Alderaanians managed to seize this land.

ᑭᔑ⅃�∩⅃ᔑᑎꝀ⅃ ⅃ȯ̇ȯ̇ᑭ⅃.

P⅂ᒪ⅃Ƨ Pռ̇ò⅃

They *bought* it, ma'am. Pooled their wealth.

Gained from *smuggling*, no doubt--the cornerstone of Sullust's economy. I won't ask what your friend *Tivvy* does for a--

Hand over your weapons.

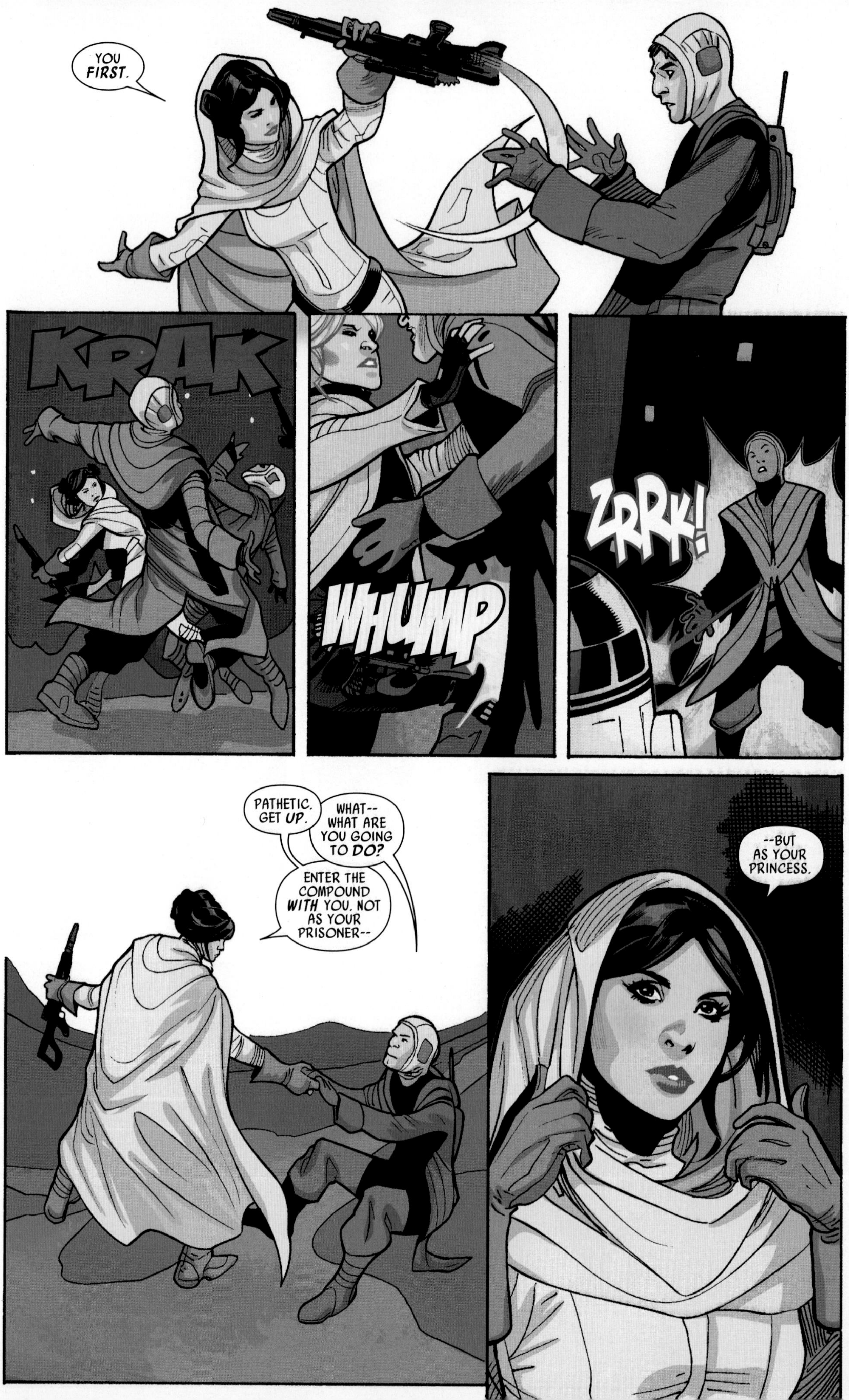

YOU FIRST.
KRAK
WHUMP
ZRRK!
PATHETIC. GET UP.
WHAT-- WHAT ARE YOU GOING TO DO?
ENTER THE COMPOUND WITH YOU. NOT AS YOUR PRISONER--
--BUT AS YOUR PRINCESS.

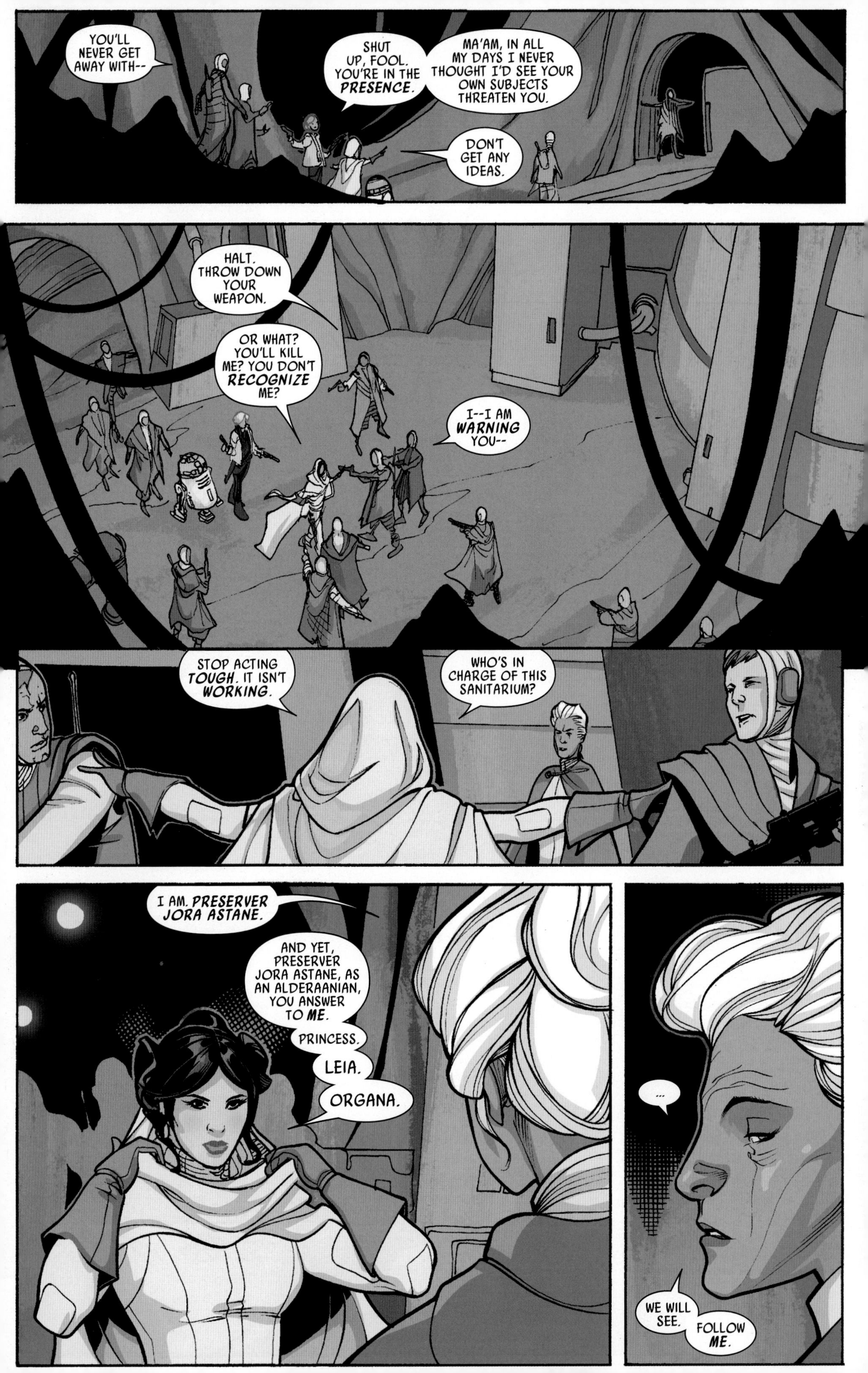
YOU'LL NEVER GET AWAY WITH--
SHUT UP, FOOL. YOU'RE IN THE PRESENCE.
MA'AM, IN ALL MY DAYS I NEVER THOUGHT I'D SEE YOUR OWN SUBJECTS THREATEN YOU.
DON'T GET ANY IDEAS.
HALT. THROW DOWN YOUR WEAPON.
OR WHAT? YOU'LL KILL ME? YOU DON'T RECOGNIZE ME?
I--I AM WARNING YOU--
STOP ACTING TOUGH. IT ISN'T WORKING.
WHO'S IN CHARGE OF THIS SANITARIUM?
I AM. PRESERVER JORA ASTANE.
AND YET, PRESERVER JORA ASTANE, AS AN ALDERAANIAN, YOU ANSWER TO ME.
PRINCESS.
LEIA.
ORGANA.
...
WE WILL SEE.
FOLLOW ME.

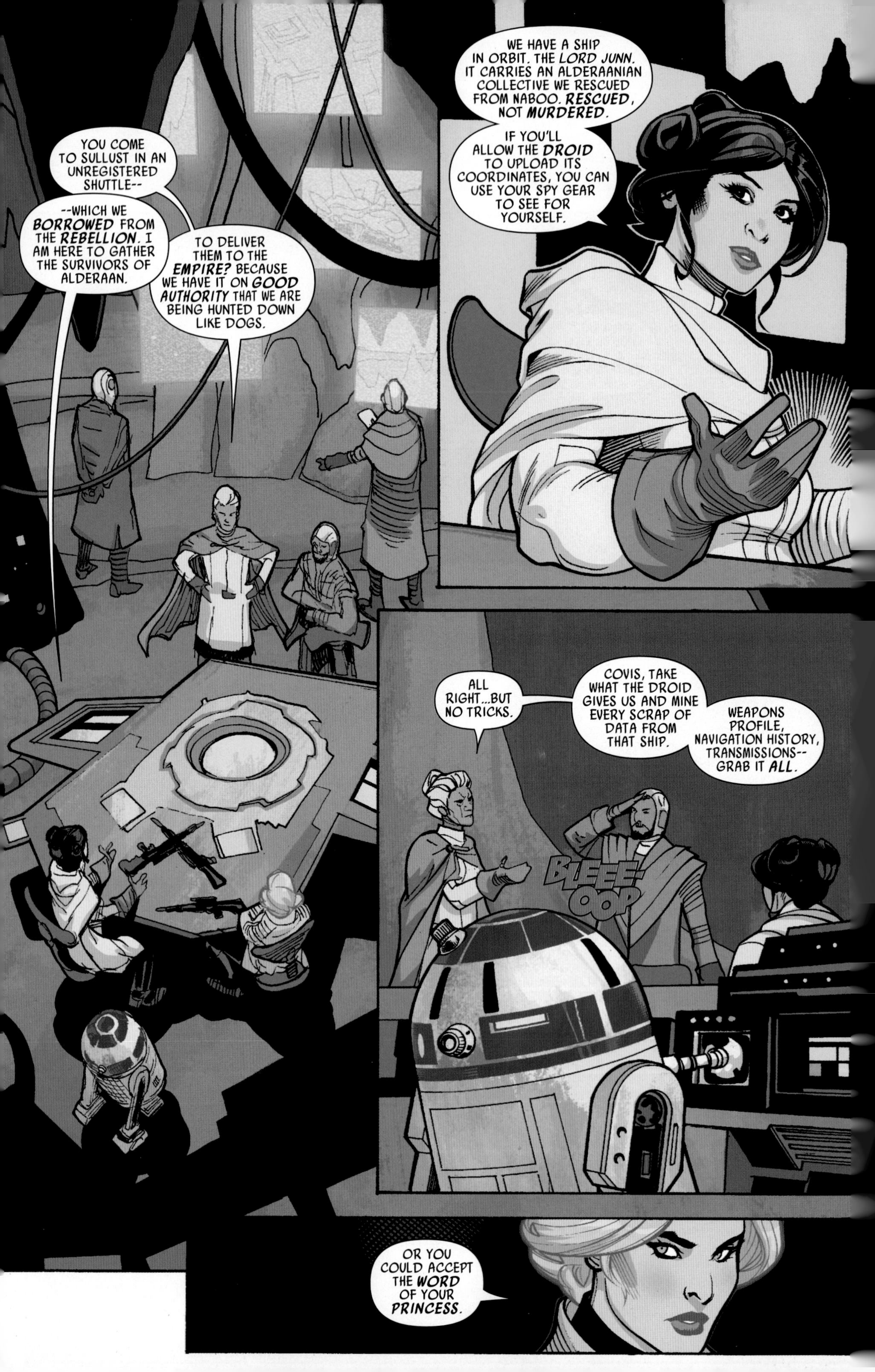
YOU COME TO SULLUST IN AN UNREGISTERED SHUTTLE--
--WHICH WE BORROWED FROM THE REBELLION. I AM HERE TO GATHER THE SURVIVORS OF ALDERAAN.
TO DELIVER THEM TO THE EMPIRE? BECAUSE WE HAVE IT ON GOOD AUTHORITY THAT WE ARE BEING HUNTED DOWN LIKE DOGS.
WE HAVE A SHIP IN ORBIT. THE LORD JUNN. IT CARRIES AN ALDERAANIAN COLLECTIVE WE RESCUED FROM NABOO. RESCUED, NOT MURDERED.
IF YOU'LL ALLOW THE DROID TO UPLOAD ITS COORDINATES, YOU CAN USE YOUR SPY GEAR TO SEE FOR YOURSELF.
ALL RIGHT...BUT NO TRICKS.
COVIS, TAKE WHAT THE DROID GIVES US AND MINE EVERY SCRAP OF DATA FROM THAT SHIP.
WEAPONS PROFILE, NAVIGATION HISTORY, TRANSMISSIONS-- GRAB IT ALL.
BLEEE-OOP
OR YOU COULD ACCEPT THE WORD OF YOUR PRINCESS.

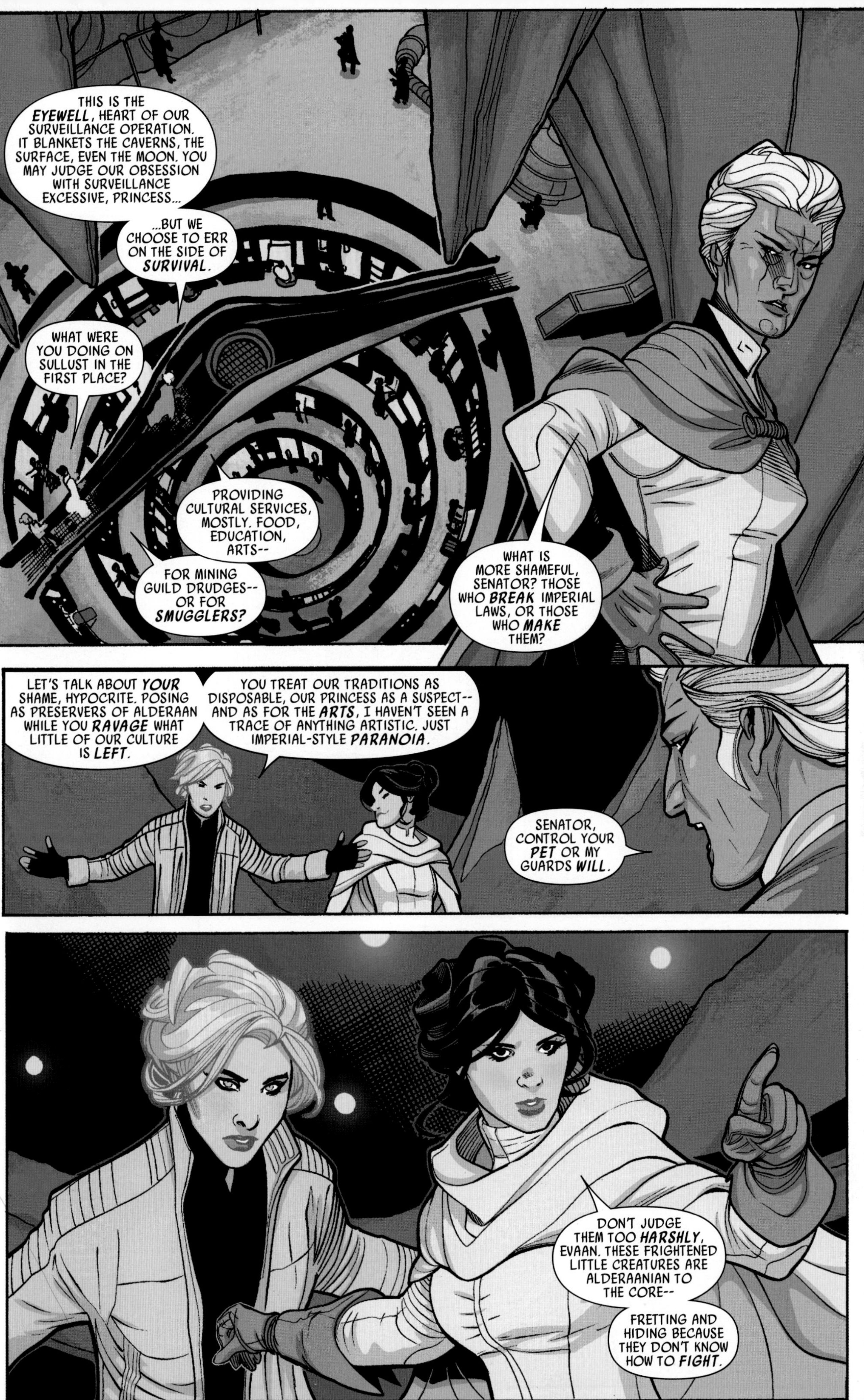
THIS IS THE EYEWELL, HEART OF OUR SURVEILLANCE OPERATION. IT BLANKETS THE CAVERNS, THE SURFACE, EVEN THE MOON. YOU MAY JUDGE OUR OBSESSION WITH SURVEILLANCE EXCESSIVE, PRINCESS...
...BUT WE CHOOSE TO ERR ON THE SIDE OF SURVIVAL.
WHAT WERE YOU DOING ON SULLUST IN THE FIRST PLACE?
PROVIDING CULTURAL SERVICES, MOSTLY. FOOD, EDUCATION, ARTS--
FOR MINING GUILD DRUDGES-- OR FOR SMUGGLERS?
WHAT IS MORE SHAMEFUL, SENATOR? THOSE WHO BREAK IMPERIAL LAWS, OR THOSE WHO MAKE THEM?
LET'S TALK ABOUT YOUR SHAME, HYPOCRITE. POSING AS PRESERVERS OF ALDERAAN WHILE YOU RAVAGE WHAT LITTLE OF OUR CULTURE IS LEFT.
YOU TREAT OUR TRADITIONS AS DISPOSABLE, OUR PRINCESS AS A SUSPECT-- AND AS FOR THE ARTS, I HAVEN'T SEEN A TRACE OF ANYTHING ARTISTIC. JUST IMPERIAL-STYLE PARANOIA.
SENATOR, CONTROL YOUR PET OR MY GUARDS WILL.
DON'T JUDGE THEM TOO HARSHLY, EVAAN. THESE FRIGHTENED LITTLE CREATURES ARE ALDERAANIAN TO THE CORE--
FRETTING AND HIDING BECAUSE THEY DON'T KNOW HOW TO FIGHT.

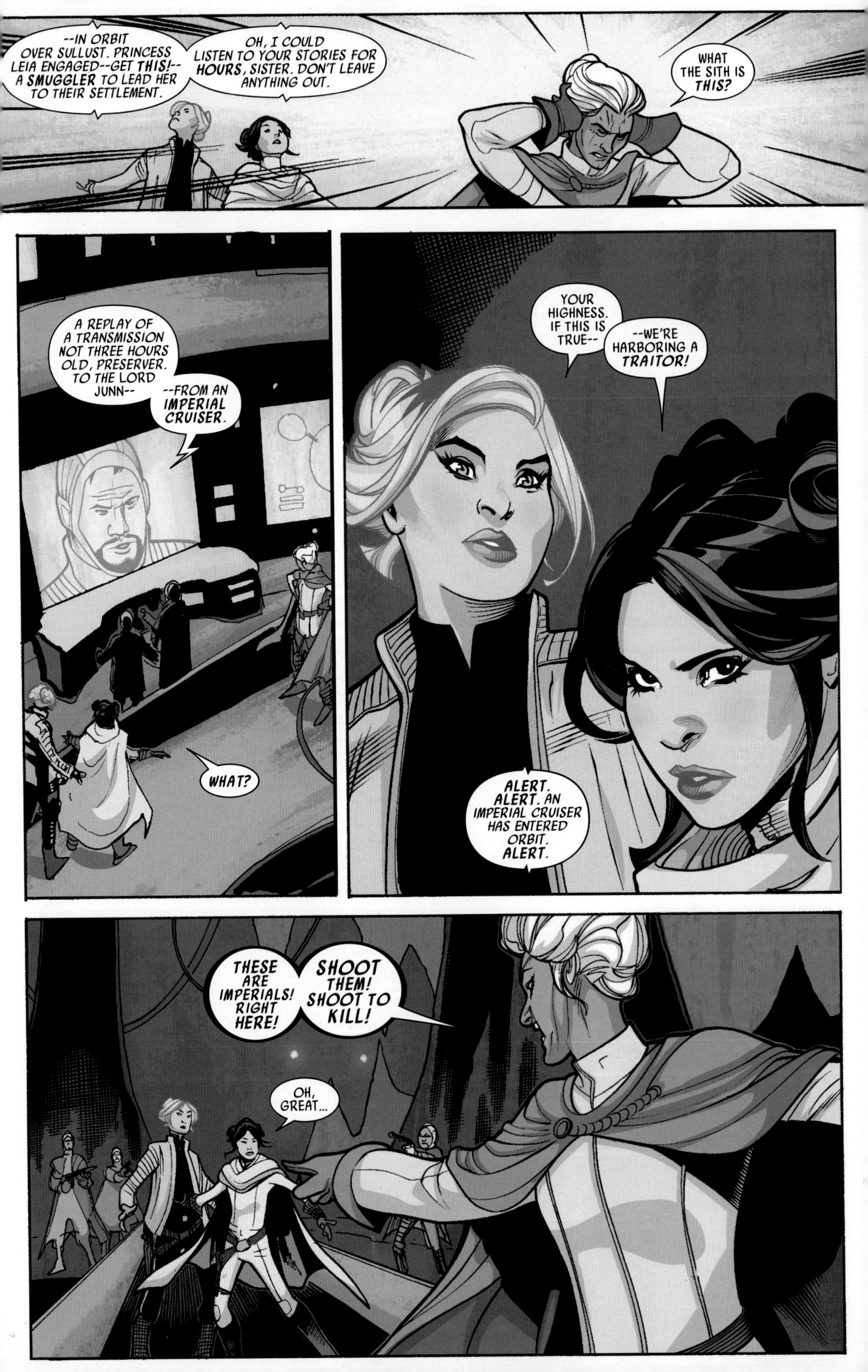
--IN ORBIT OVER SULLUST. PRINCESS LEIA ENGAGED--GET THIS!--A SMUGGLER TO LEAD HER TO THEIR SETTLEMENT.
OH, I COULD LISTEN TO YOUR STORIES FOR HOURS, SISTER. DON'T LEAVE ANYTHING OUT.
WHAT THE SITH IS THIS?
A REPLAY OF A TRANSMISSION NOT THREE HOURS OLD, PRESERVER. TO THE LORD JUNN--
--FROM AN IMPERIAL CRUISER.
WHAT?
YOUR HIGHNESS. IF THIS IS TRUE--
--WE'RE HARBORING A TRAITOR!
ALERT. ALERT. AN IMPERIAL CRUISER HAS ENTERED ORBIT. ALERT.
THESE ARE IMPERIALS! RIGHT HERE!
SHOOT THEM! SHOOT TO KILL!
OH, GREAT...

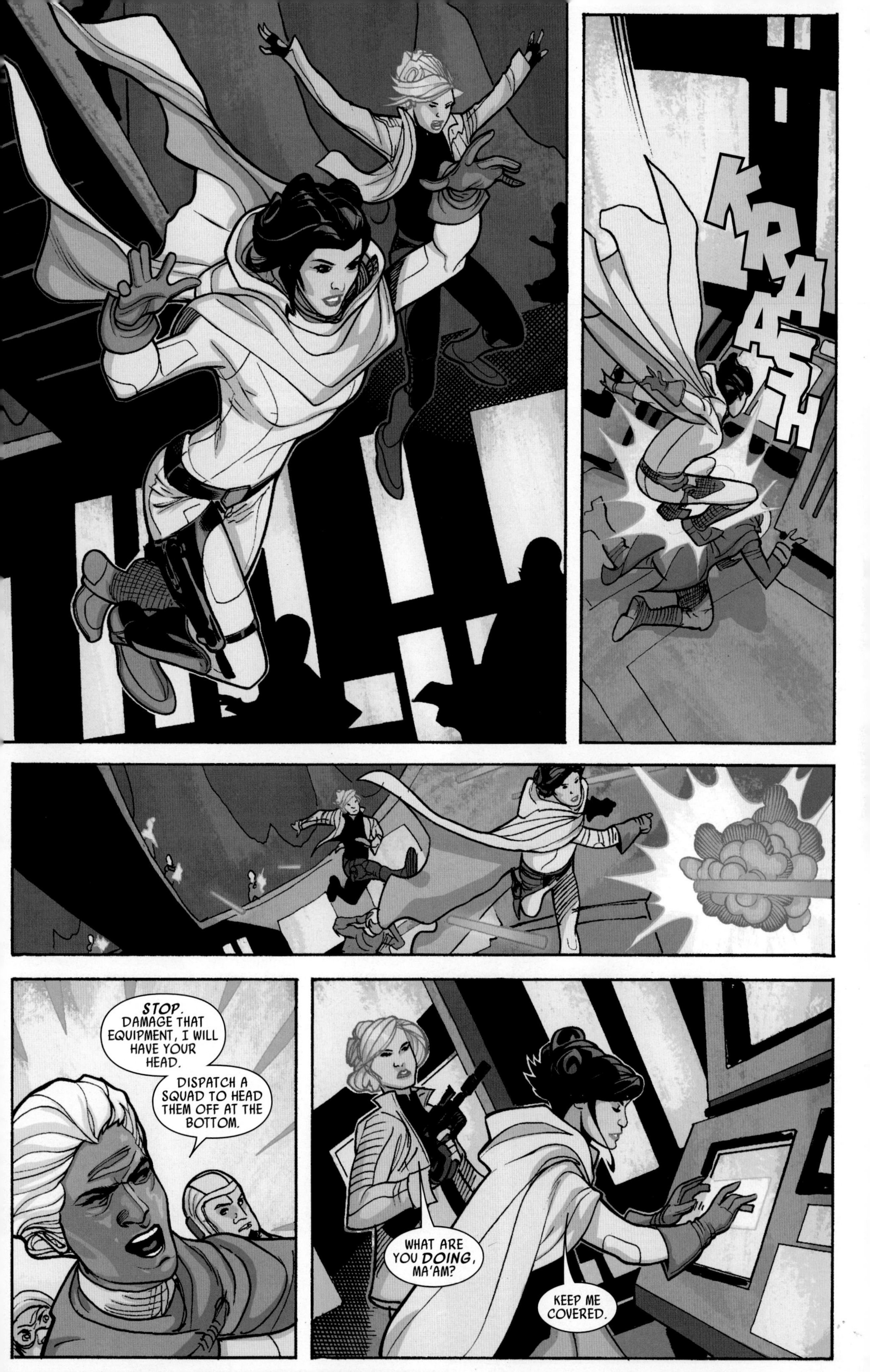
KRAASH
STOP. DAMAGE THAT EQUIPMENT, I WILL HAVE YOUR HEAD.
DISPATCH A SQUAD TO HEAD THEM OFF AT THE BOTTOM.
WHAT ARE YOU DOING, MA'AM?
KEEP ME COVERED.

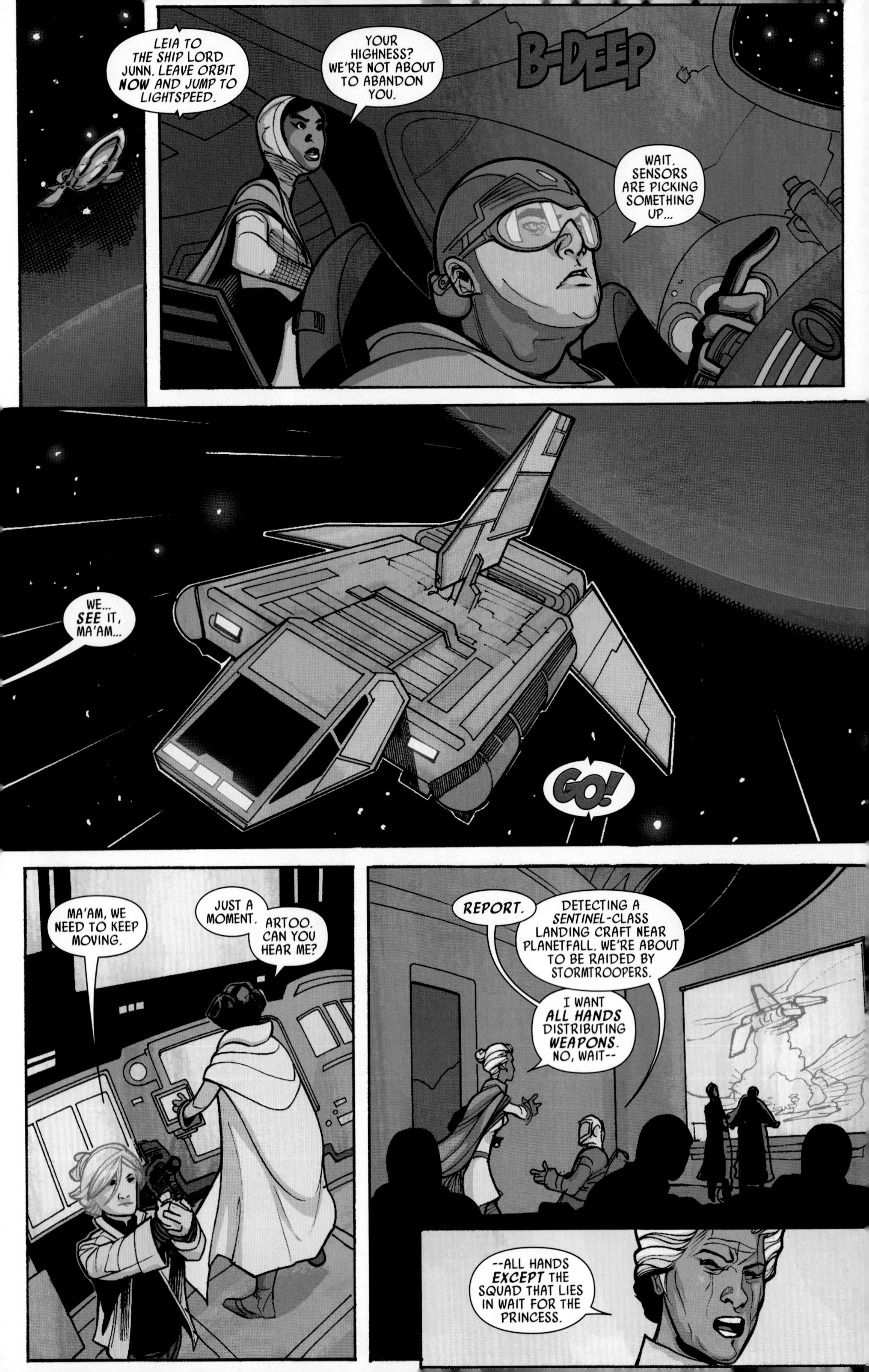
LEIA TO THE SHIP LORD JUNN. LEAVE ORBIT NOW AND JUMP TO LIGHTSPEED.
YOUR HIGHNESS? WE'RE NOT ABOUT TO ABANDON YOU.
B-DEEP
WAIT. SENSORS ARE PICKING SOMETHING UP...
WE... SEE IT, MA'AM...
GO!
MA'AM, WE NEED TO KEEP MOVING.
JUST A MOMENT.
ARTOO. CAN YOU HEAR ME?
REPORT.
DETECTING A SENTINEL-CLASS LANDING CRAFT NEAR PLANETFALL. WE'RE ABOUT TO BE RAIDED BY STORMTROOPERS.
I WANT ALL HANDS DISTRIBUTING WEAPONS. NO, WAIT--
--ALL HANDS EXCEPT THE SQUAD THAT LIES IN WAIT FOR THE PRINCESS.

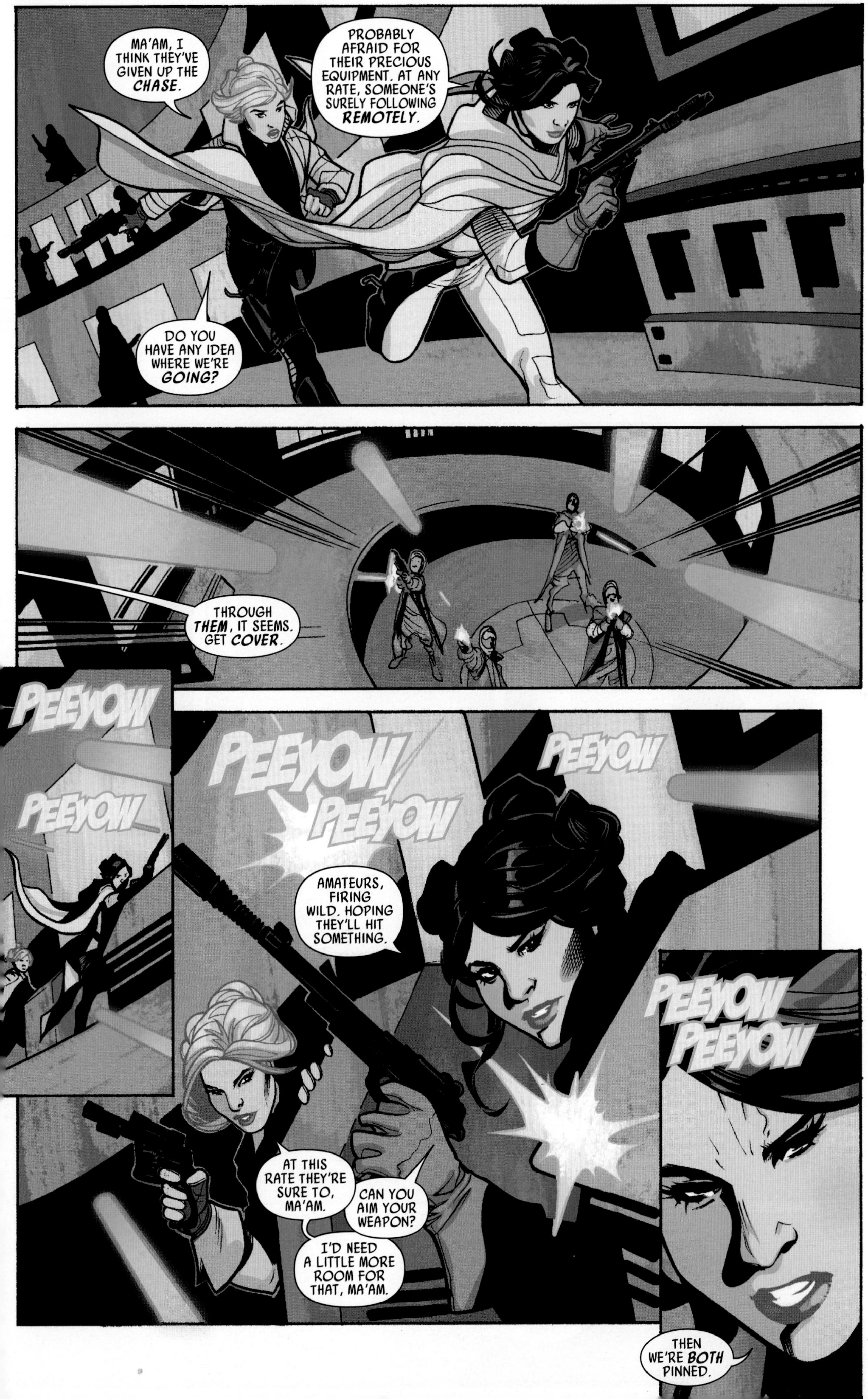
MA'AM, I THINK THEY'VE GIVEN UP THE CHASE.
PROBABLY AFRAID FOR THEIR PRECIOUS EQUIPMENT. AT ANY RATE, SOMEONE'S SURELY FOLLOWING REMOTELY.
DO YOU HAVE ANY IDEA WHERE WE'RE GOING?
THROUGH THEM, IT SEEMS. GET COVER.
PEEYOW
PEEYOW
PEEYOW
PEEYOW
PEEYOW
AMATEURS, FIRING WILD, HOPING THEY'LL HIT SOMETHING.
PEEYOW
PEEYOW
AT THIS RATE THEY'RE SURE TO, MA'AM.
CAN YOU AIM YOUR WEAPON?
I'D NEED A LITTLE MORE ROOM FOR THAT, MA'AM.
THEN WE'RE BOTH PINNED.

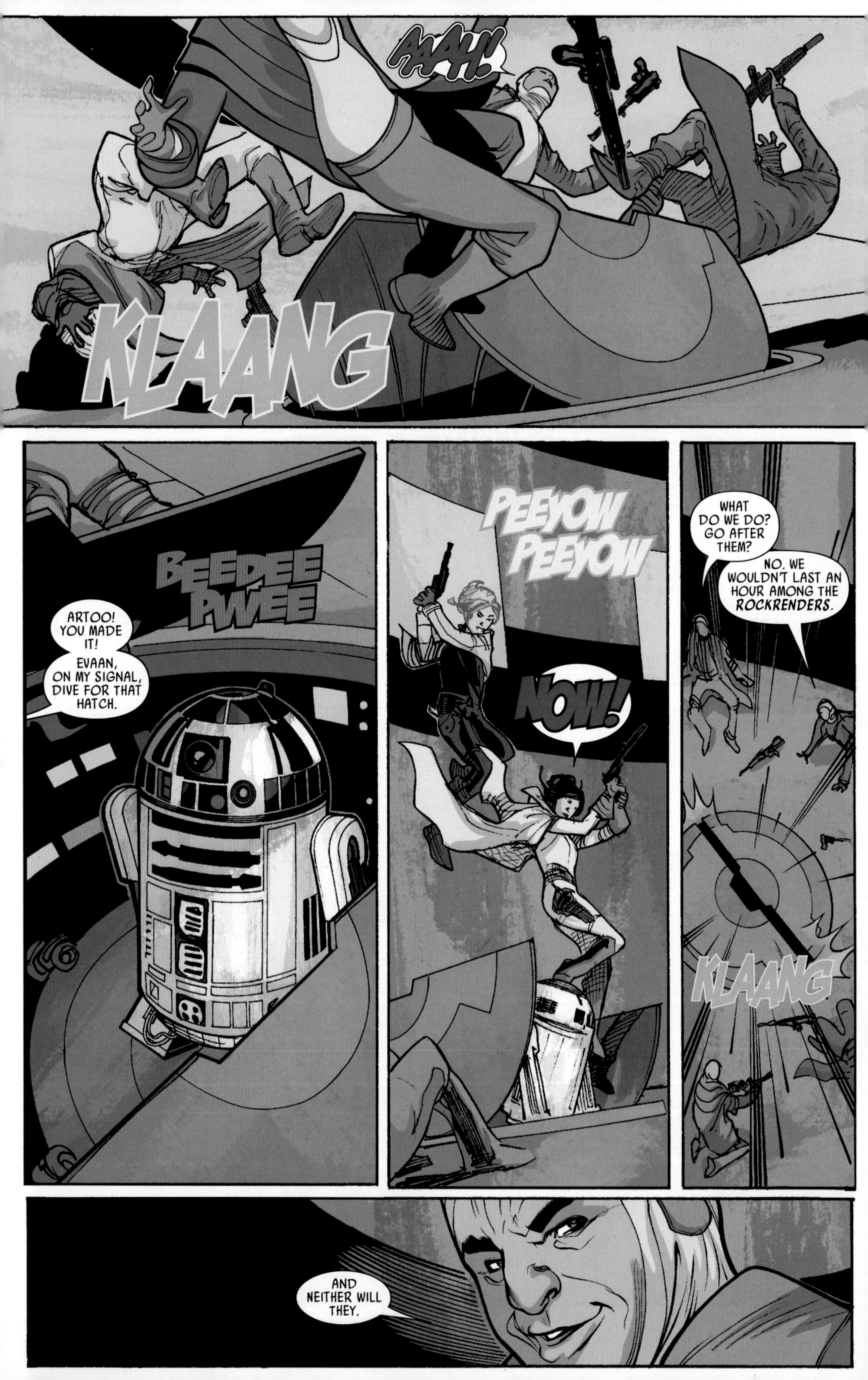
AAAH!
KLAANG
BEEDEE PWEE
ARTOO! YOU MADE IT!
EVAAN, ON MY SIGNAL, DIVE FOR THAT HATCH.
PEEYOW PEEYOW
NOW!
WHAT DO WE DO? GO AFTER THEM?
NO. WE WOULDN'T LAST AN HOUR AMONG THE ROCKRENDERS.
KLAANG
AND NEITHER WILL THEY.

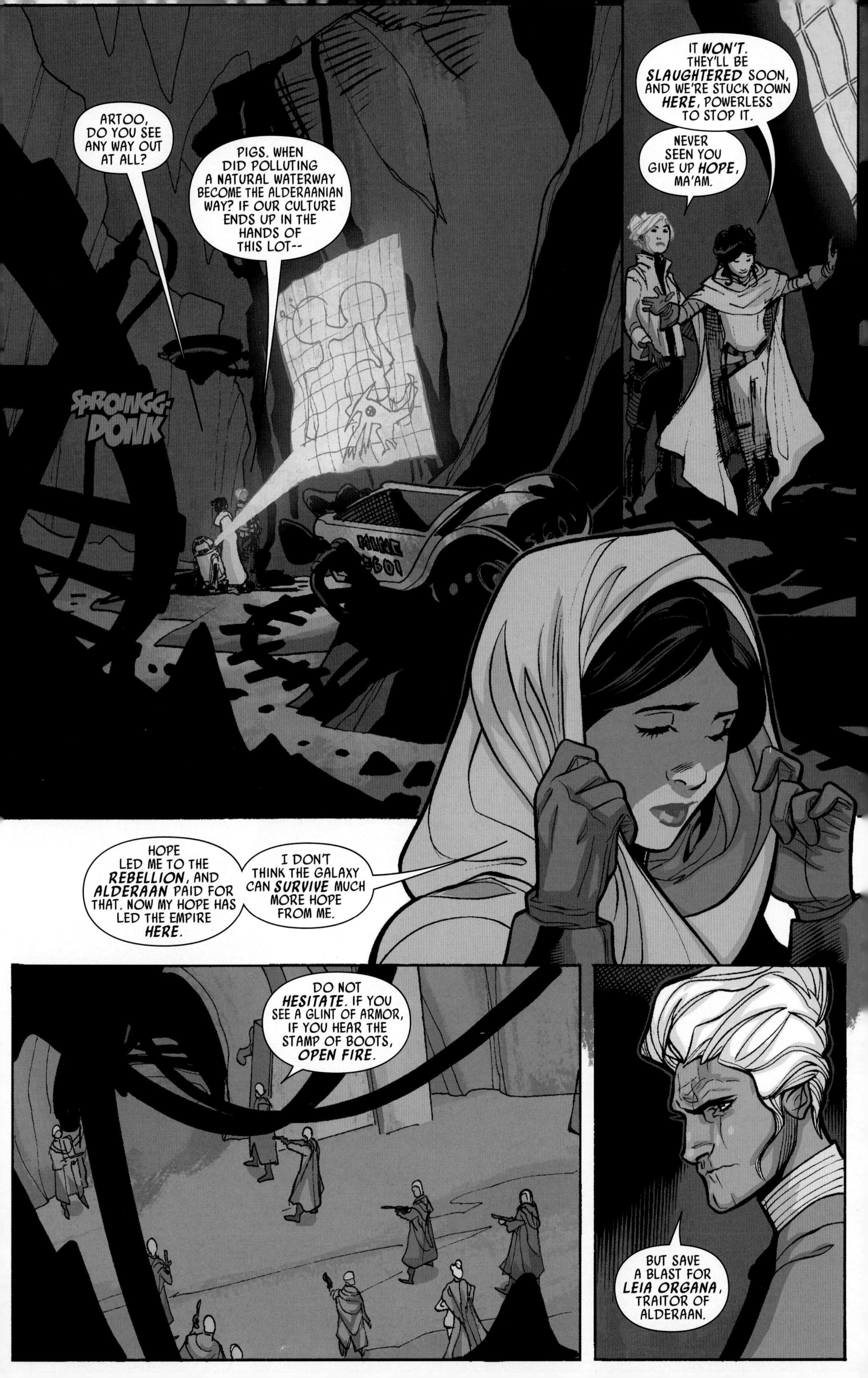

ARTOO, DO YOU SEE ANY WAY OUT AT ALL?
PIGS. WHEN DID POLLUTING A NATURAL WATERWAY BECOME THE ALDERAANIAN WAY? IF OUR CULTURE ENDS UP IN THE HANDS OF THIS LOT--
SPROINGG-DONK
IT WON'T. THEY'LL BE SLAUGHTERED SOON, AND WE'RE STUCK DOWN HERE, POWERLESS TO STOP IT.
NEVER SEEN YOU GIVE UP HOPE, MA'AM.
HOPE LED ME TO THE REBELLION, AND ALDERAAN PAID FOR THAT. NOW MY HOPE HAS LED THE EMPIRE HERE.
I DON'T THINK THE GALAXY CAN SURVIVE MUCH MORE HOPE FROM ME.
DO NOT HESITATE. IF YOU SEE A GLINT OF ARMOR, IF YOU HEAR THE STAMP OF BOOTS, OPEN FIRE.
BUT SAVE A BLAST FOR LEIA ORGANA, TRAITOR OF ALDERAAN.

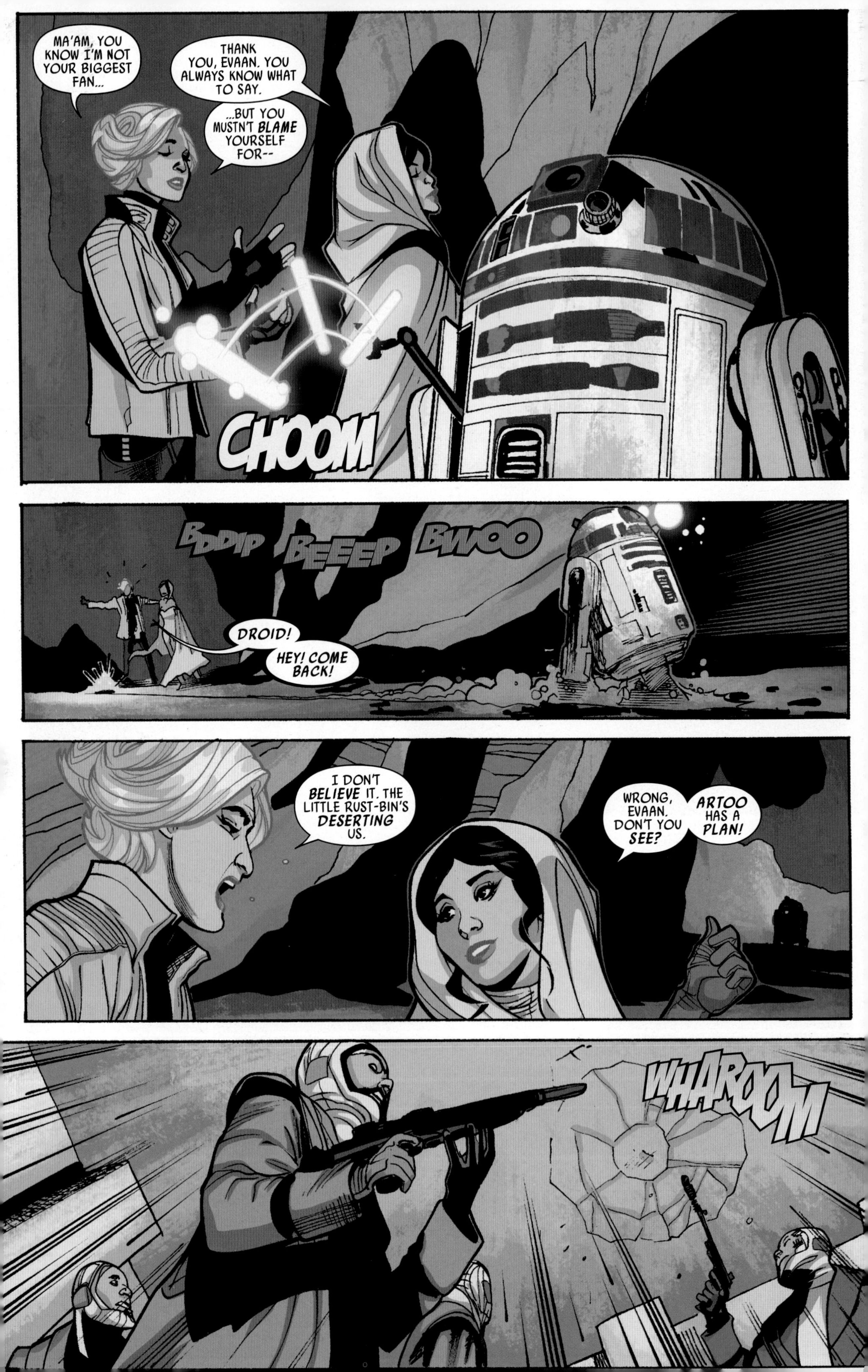
MA'AM, YOU KNOW I'M NOT YOUR BIGGEST FAN...
THANK YOU, EVAAN. YOU ALWAYS KNOW WHAT TO SAY.
...BUT YOU MUSTN'T BLAME YOURSELF FOR--
CHOOM
BDDIP
BEEEEP
BWOO
DROID!
HEY! COME BACK!
I DON'T BELIEVE IT. THE LITTLE RUST-BIN'S DESERTING US.
WRONG, EVAAN. DON'T YOU SEE?
ARTOO HAS A PLAN!
WHAROOM

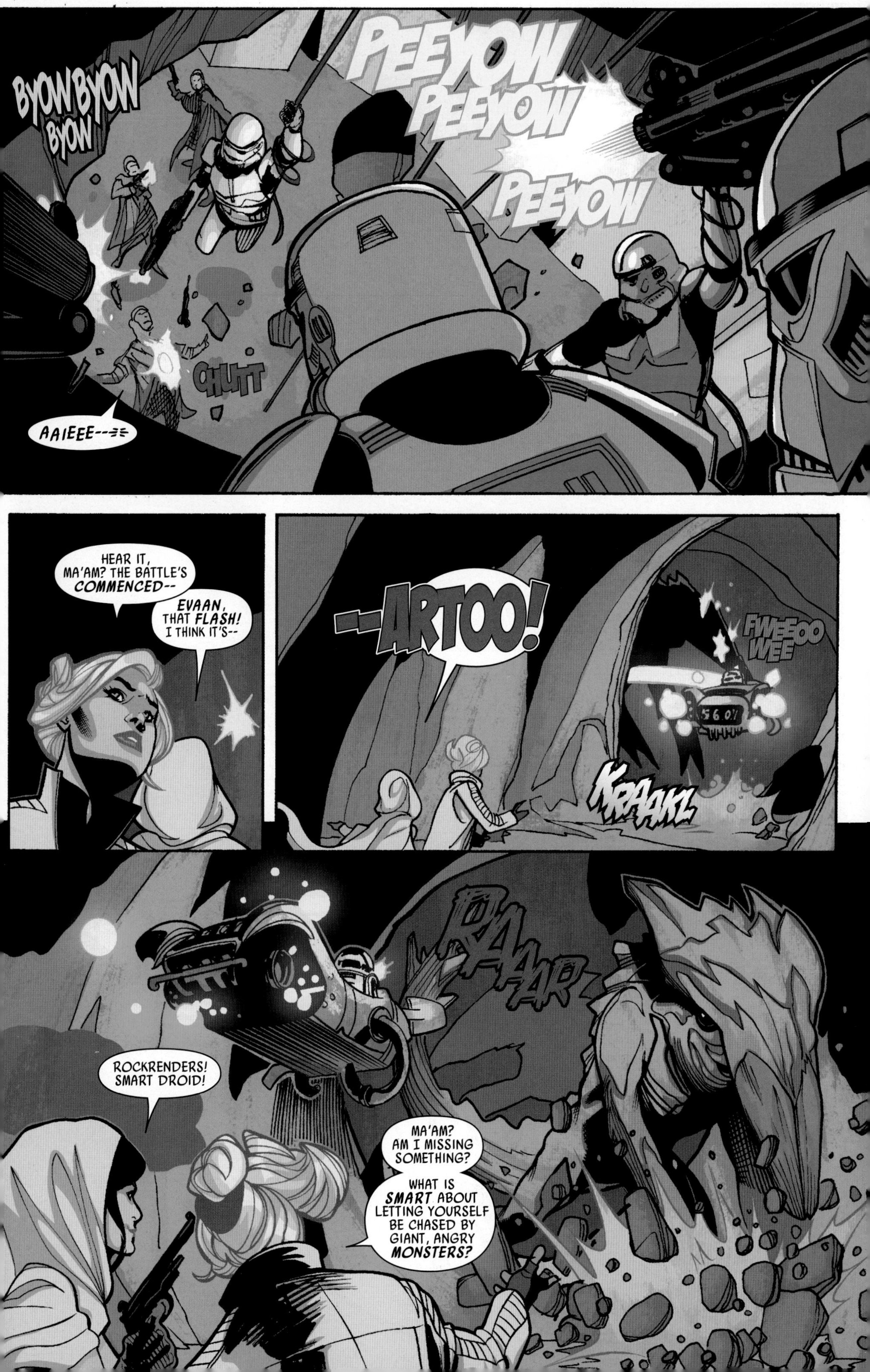
BYOW BYOW BYOW
PEEYOW PEEYOW
PEEYOW
CHUTT
AAIEEE--
HEAR IT, MA'AM? THE BATTLE'S COMMENCED--
EVAAN, THAT FLASH! I THINK IT'S--
--ARTOO!
FWEEOO WEE
KRAAKL
RAAAR
ROCKRENDERS! SMART DROID!
MA'AM? AM I MISSING SOMETHING?
WHAT IS SMART ABOUT LETTING YOURSELF BE CHASED BY GIANT, ANGRY MONSTERS?

HE'S NOT BEING CHASED. HE'S *HERDING* THEM.

HELP ME STEER THEM TOWARDS THE WALL.

PEEYOW PEEYOW

KRAAASH

WHOOSH

RAAAR

FWEE-FO-WOOOP

KRAAADASH

MA'AM, I'M NOT SURE ABOUT THIS. AREN'T THE BEASTS A DANGER TO ALL OF US?

THEY'RE *ROCKRENDERS*, NOT FLESH EATERS. THEY CAN'T RESIST THE MOUTHFEEL OF DENSE MINERALS... SUCH AS *STORMTROOPER* ARMOR.

AAH. GOOD PLAN.

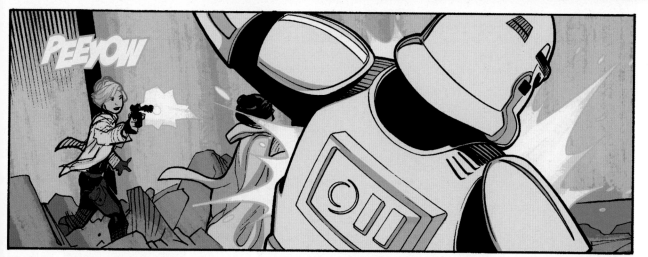

PEEYOW

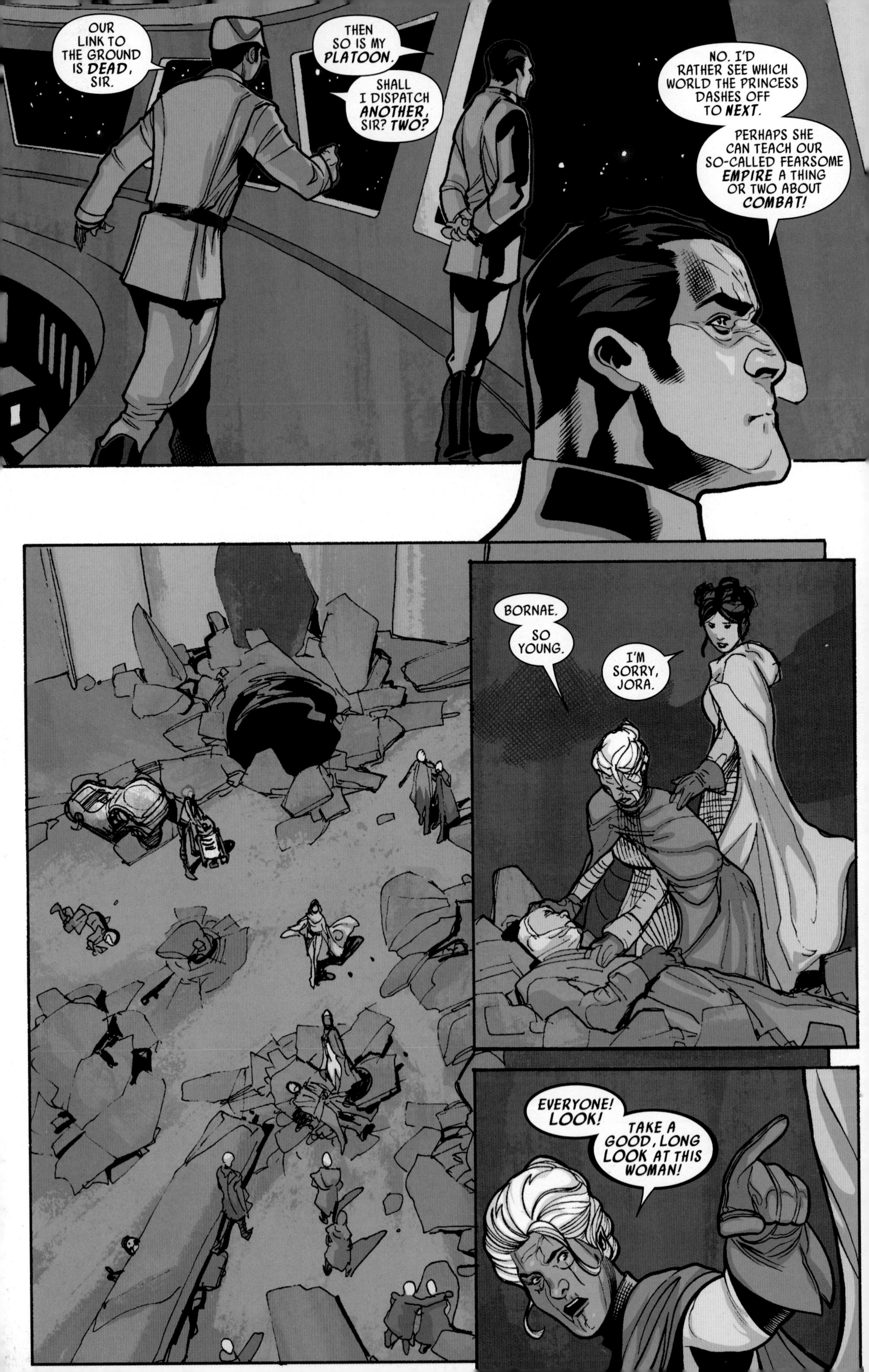

OUR LINK TO THE GROUND IS DEAD, SIR.
THEN SO IS MY PLATOON.
SHALL I DISPATCH ANOTHER, SIR? TWO?
NO. I'D RATHER SEE WHICH WORLD THE PRINCESS DASHES OFF TO NEXT.
PERHAPS SHE CAN TEACH OUR SO-CALLED FEARSOME EMPIRE A THING OR TWO ABOUT COMBAT!
BORNAE.
SO YOUNG.
I'M SORRY, JORA.
EVERYONE! LOOK!
TAKE A GOOD, LONG LOOK AT THIS WOMAN!

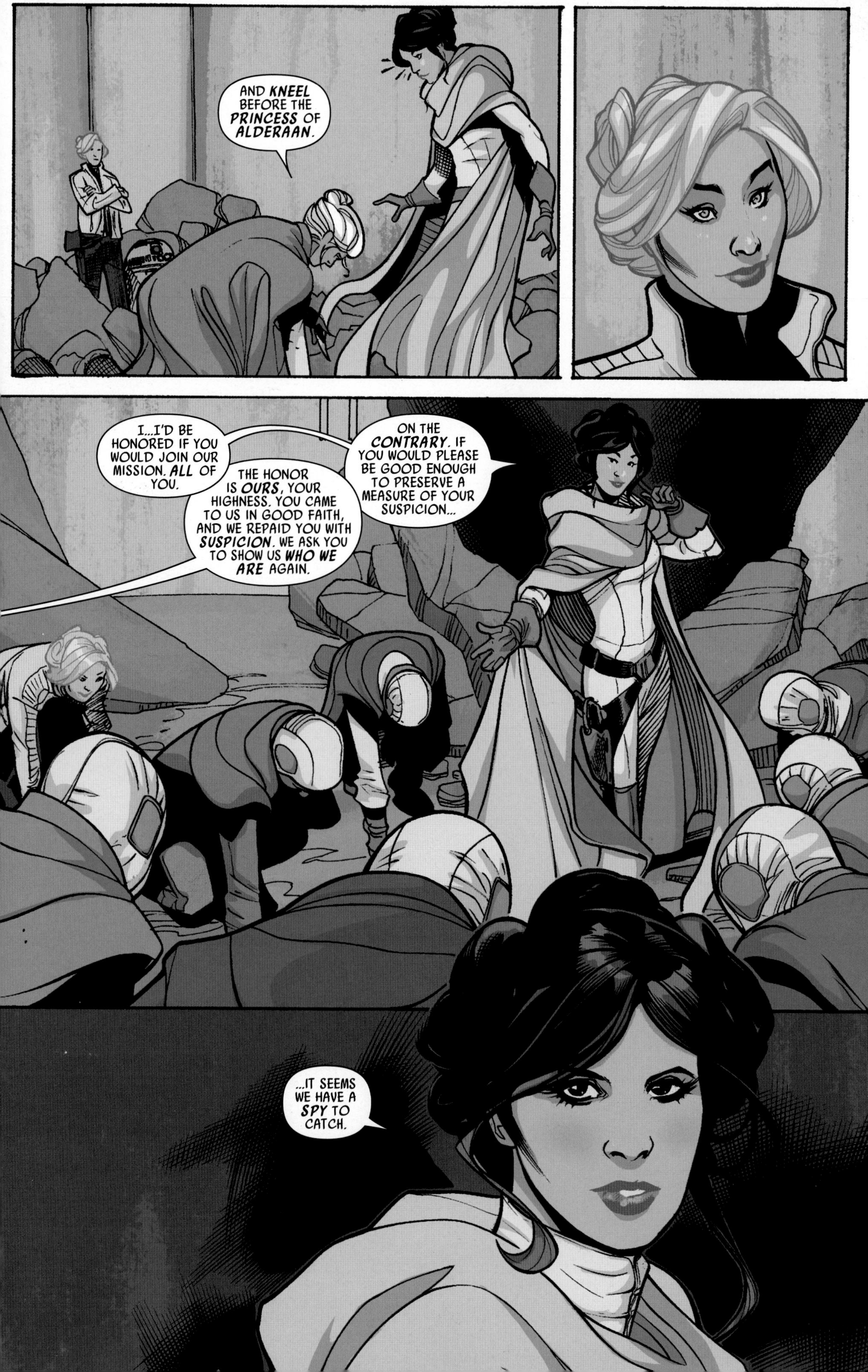
AND KNEEL BEFORE THE PRINCESS OF ALDERAAN.
I...I'D BE HONORED IF YOU WOULD JOIN OUR MISSION. ALL OF YOU.
THE HONOR IS OURS, YOUR HIGHNESS. YOU CAME TO US IN GOOD FAITH, AND WE REPAID YOU WITH SUSPICION. WE ASK YOU TO SHOW US WHO WE ARE AGAIN.
ON THE CONTRARY. IF YOU WOULD PLEASE BE GOOD ENOUGH TO PRESERVE A MEASURE OF YOUR SUSPICION...
...IT SEEMS WE HAVE A SPY TO CATCH.

"You're my only hope."

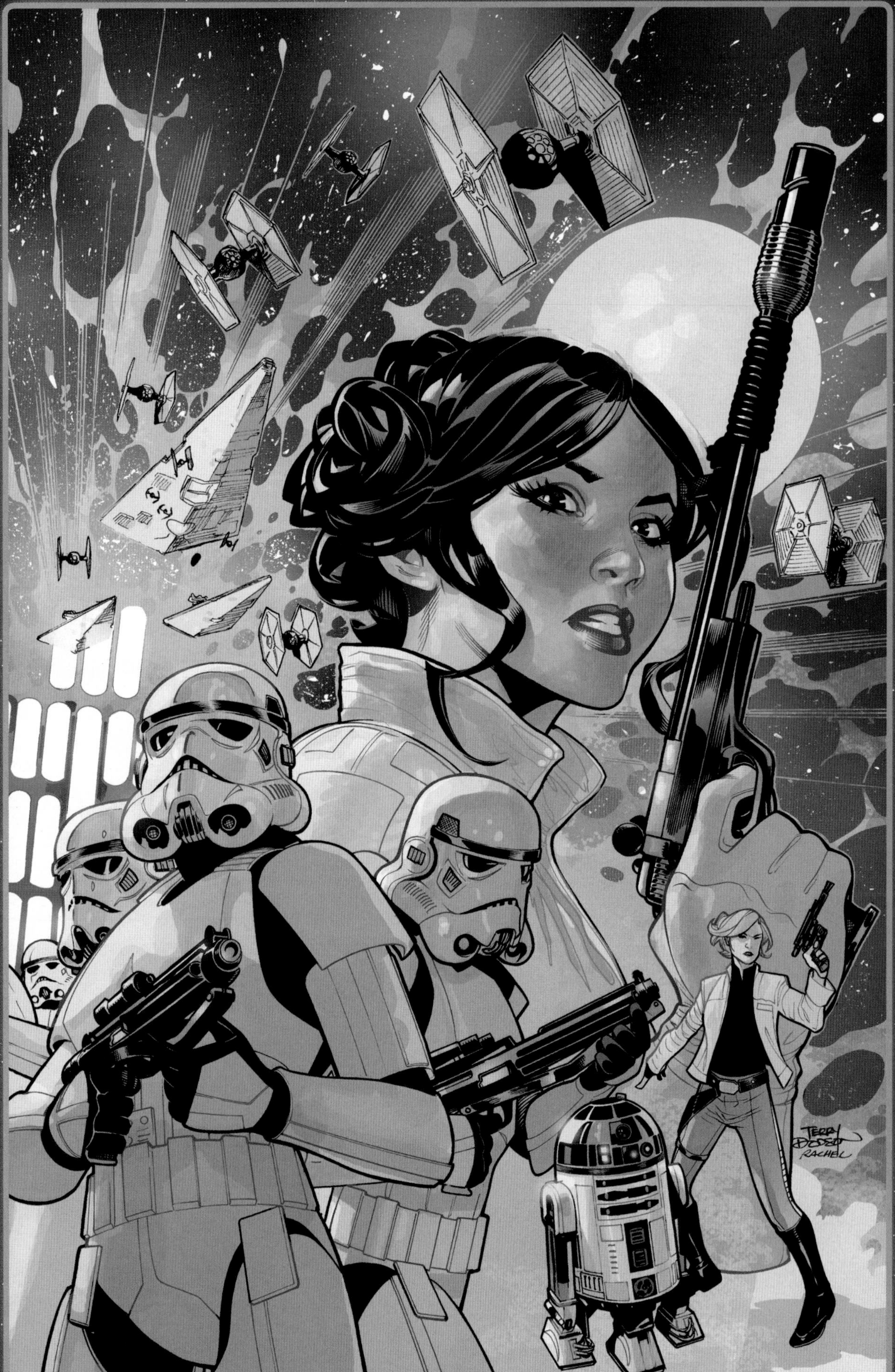
TERRY DODSON RACHEL

PRINCESS LEIA 4

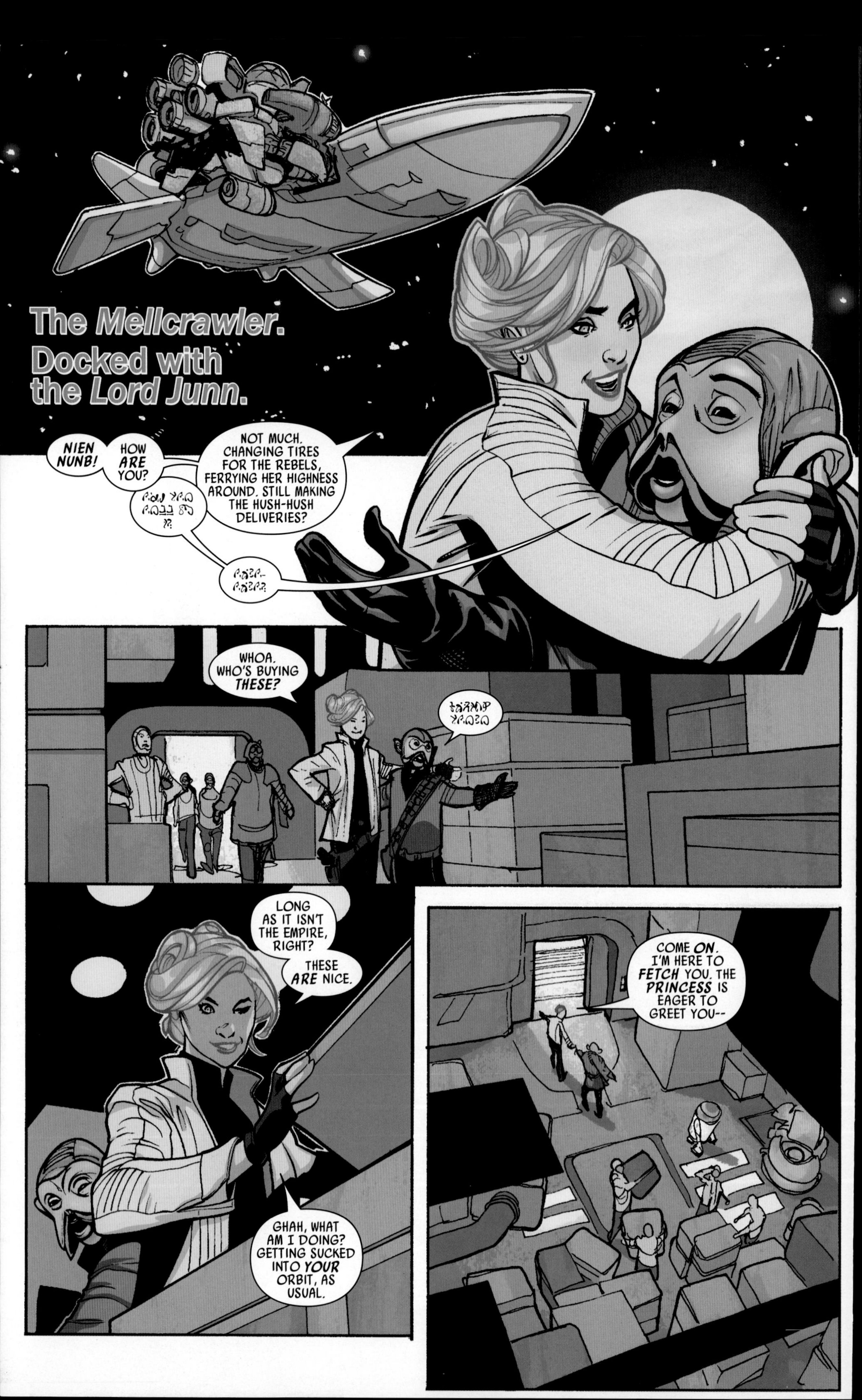
The Mellcrawler.
Docked with the Lord Junn.
NIEN NUNB!
HOW ARE YOU?
NOT MUCH. CHANGING TIRES FOR THE REBELS, FERRYING HER HIGHNESS AROUND. STILL MAKING THE HUSH-HUSH DELIVERIES?
WHOA. WHO'S BUYING THESE?
LONG AS IT ISN'T THE EMPIRE, RIGHT?
THESE ARE NICE.
GHAH, WHAT AM I DOING? GETTING SUCKED INTO YOUR ORBIT, AS USUAL.
COME ON. I'M HERE TO FETCH YOU. THE PRINCESS IS EAGER TO GREET YOU--

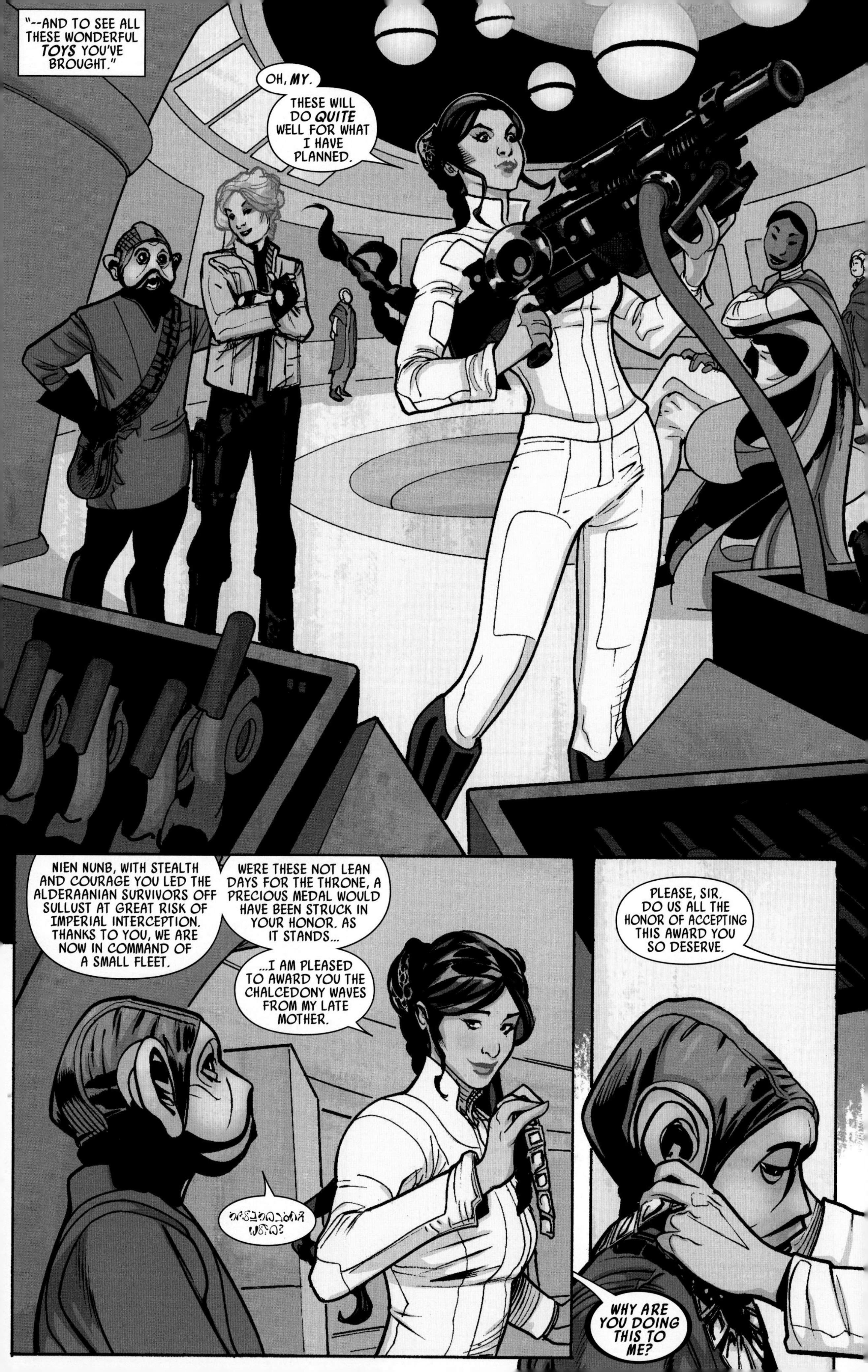
"--AND TO SEE ALL THESE WONDERFUL *TOYS* YOU'VE BROUGHT."
OH, *MY*.
THESE WILL DO *QUITE* WELL FOR WHAT I HAVE PLANNED.
NIEN NUNB, WITH STEALTH AND COURAGE YOU LED THE ALDERAANIAN SURVIVORS OFF SULLUST AT GREAT RISK OF IMPERIAL INTERCEPTION. THANKS TO YOU, WE ARE NOW IN COMMAND OF A SMALL FLEET.
WERE THESE NOT LEAN DAYS FOR THE THRONE, A PRECIOUS MEDAL WOULD HAVE BEEN STRUCK IN YOUR HONOR. AS IT STANDS...
...I AM PLEASED TO AWARD YOU THE CHALCEDONY WAVES FROM MY LATE MOTHER.
PLEASE, SIR. DO US ALL THE HONOR OF ACCEPTING THIS AWARD YOU SO DESERVE.
WHY ARE YOU DOING THIS TO ME?

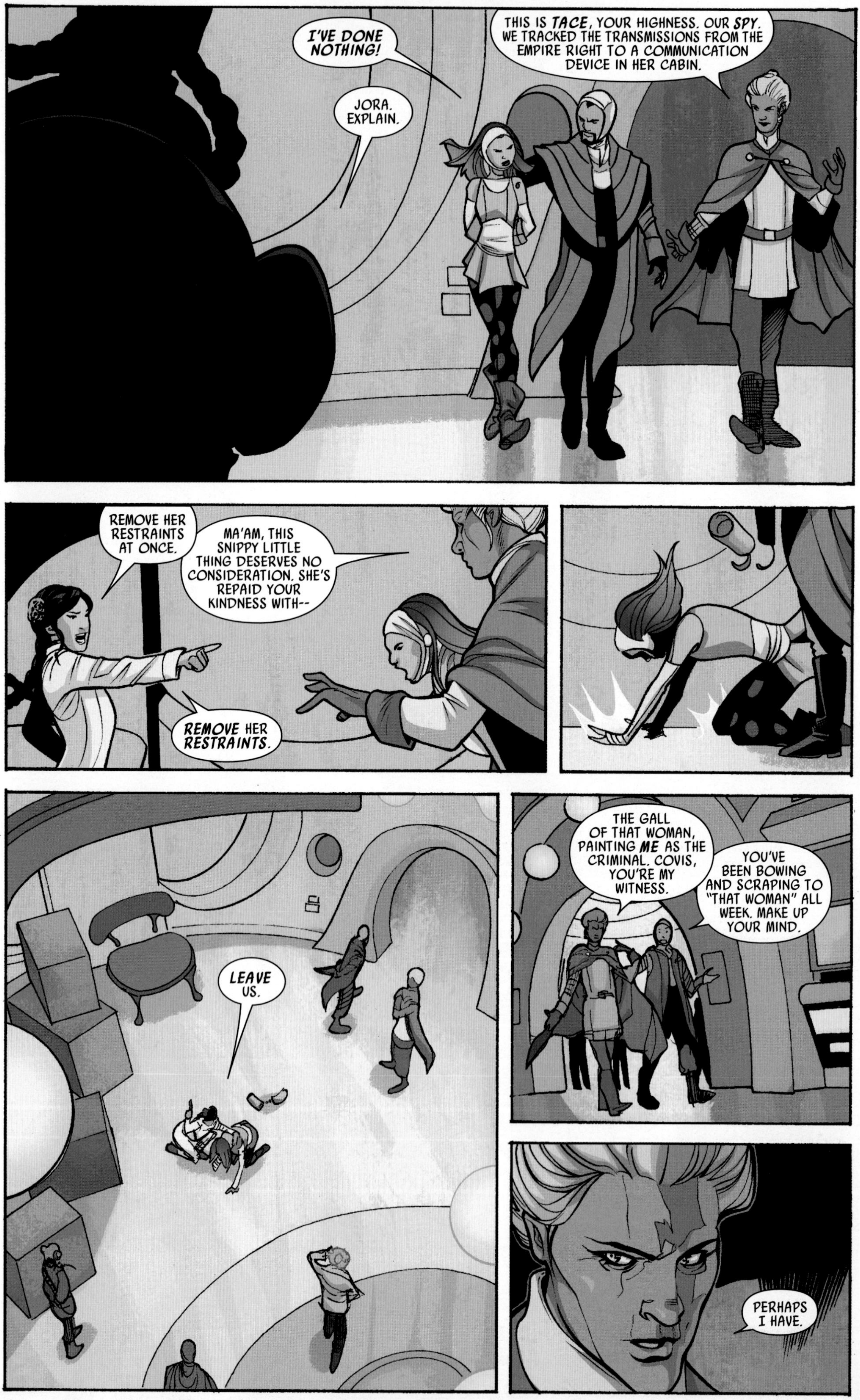

I'VE DONE NOTHING!
THIS IS TACE, YOUR HIGHNESS. OUR SPY. WE TRACKED THE TRANSMISSIONS FROM THE EMPIRE RIGHT TO A COMMUNICATION DEVICE IN HER CABIN.
JORA. EXPLAIN.
REMOVE HER RESTRAINTS AT ONCE.
MA'AM, THIS SNIPPY LITTLE THING DESERVES NO CONSIDERATION. SHE'S REPAID YOUR KINDNESS WITH--
REMOVE HER RESTRAINTS.
LEAVE US.
THE GALL OF THAT WOMAN, PAINTING ME AS THE CRIMINAL. COVIS, YOU'RE MY WITNESS.
YOU'VE BEEN BOWING AND SCRAPING TO "THAT WOMAN" ALL WEEK. MAKE UP YOUR MIND.
PERHAPS I HAVE.

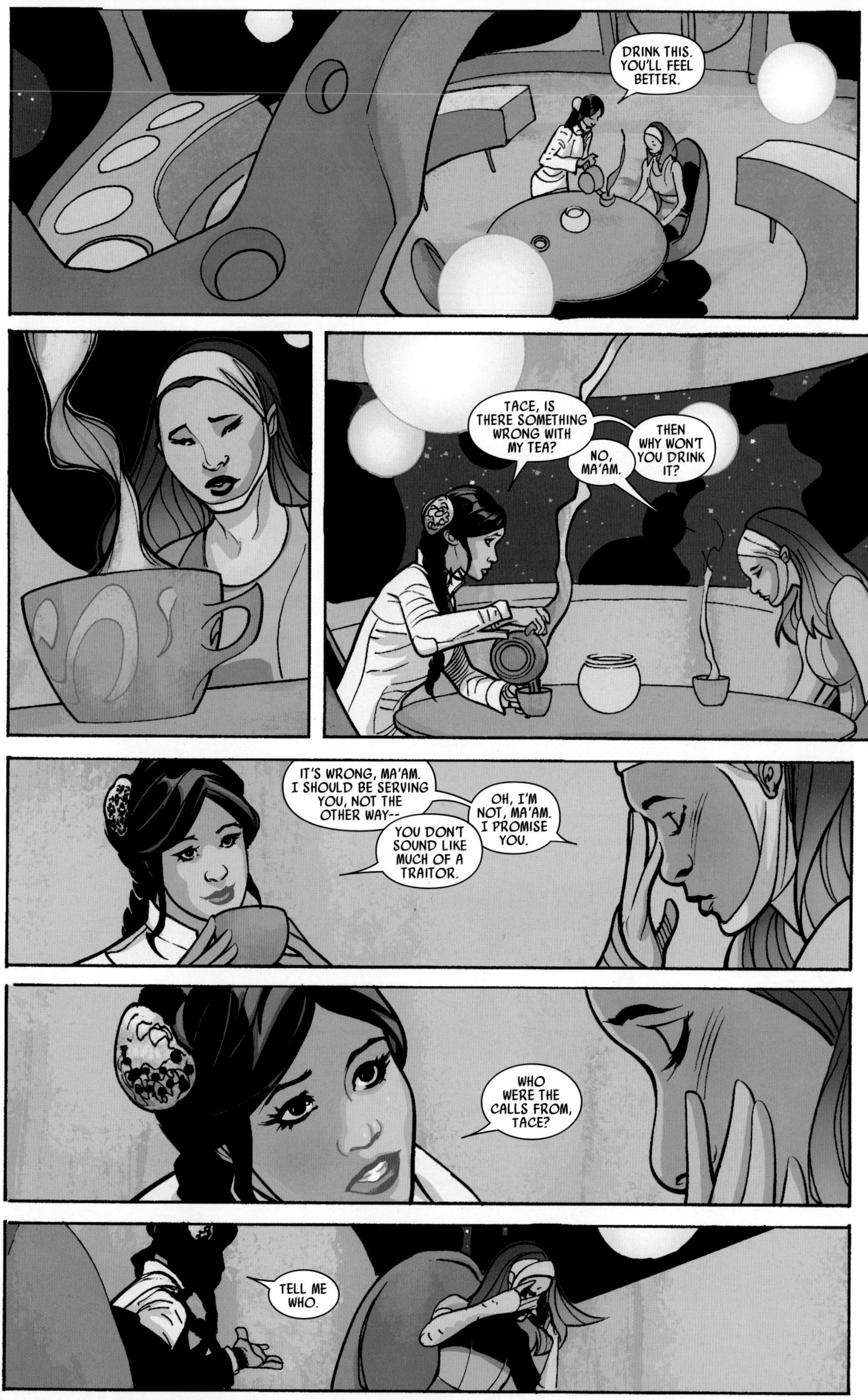
DRINK THIS. YOU'LL FEEL BETTER.
TACE, IS THERE SOMETHING WRONG WITH MY TEA?
NO, MA'AM.
THEN WHY WON'T YOU DRINK IT?
IT'S WRONG, MA'AM. I SHOULD BE SERVING YOU, NOT THE OTHER WAY--
YOU DON'T SOUND LIKE MUCH OF A TRAITOR.
OH, I'M NOT, MA'AM. I PROMISE YOU.
WHO WERE THE CALLS FROM, TACE?
TELL ME WHO.

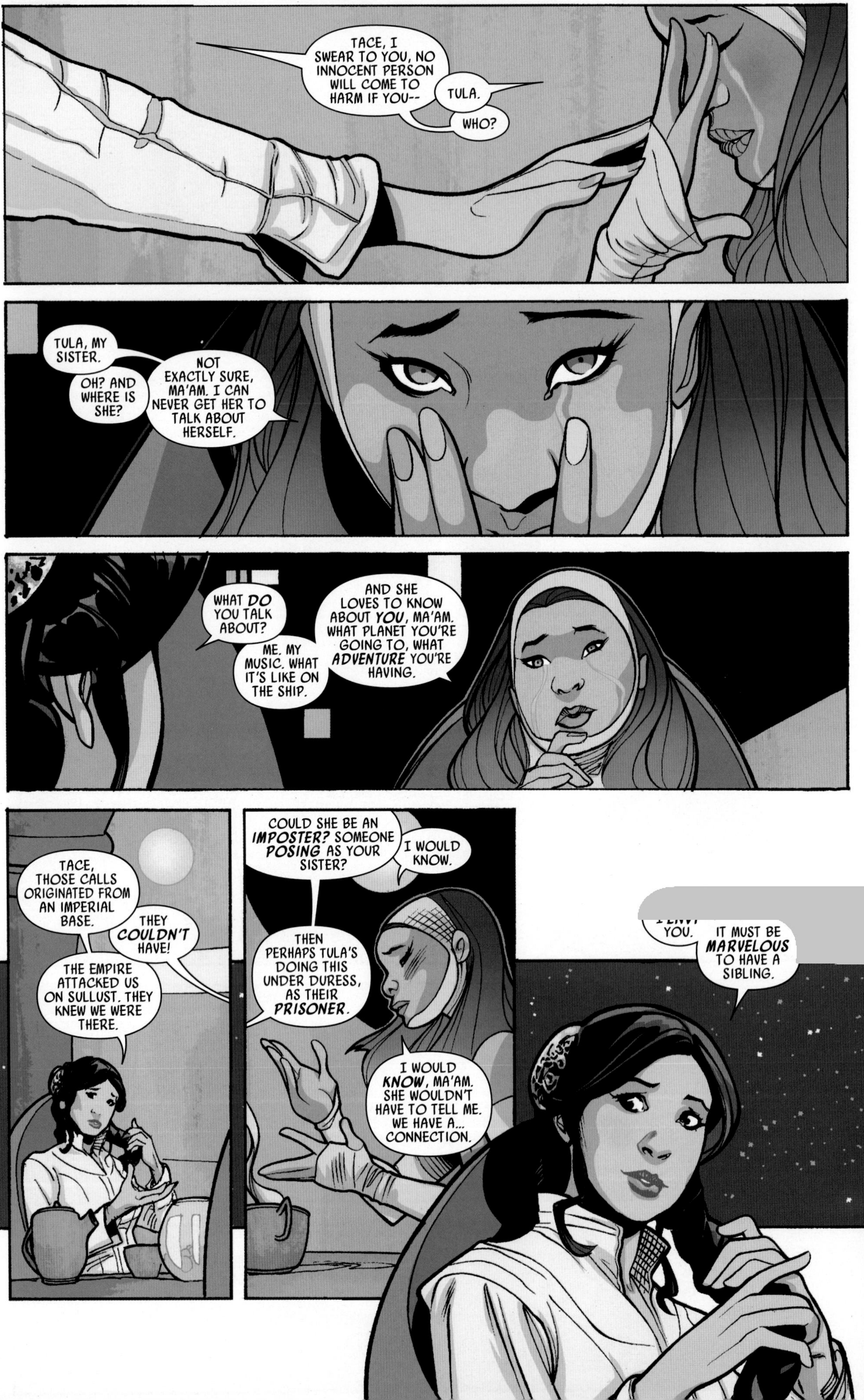
TACE, I SWEAR TO YOU, NO INNOCENT PERSON WILL COME TO HARM IF YOU--
TULA.
WHO?
TULA, MY SISTER.
OH? AND WHERE IS SHE?
NOT EXACTLY SURE, MA'AM. I CAN NEVER GET HER TO TALK ABOUT HERSELF.
WHAT DO YOU TALK ABOUT?
ME. MY MUSIC. WHAT IT'S LIKE ON THE SHIP.
AND SHE LOVES TO KNOW ABOUT YOU, MA'AM. WHAT PLANET YOU'RE GOING TO, WHAT ADVENTURE YOU'RE HAVING.
TACE, THOSE CALLS ORIGINATED FROM AN IMPERIAL BASE.
THEY COULDN'T HAVE!
THE EMPIRE ATTACKED US ON SULLUST. THEY KNEW WE WERE THERE.
COULD SHE BE AN IMPOSTER? SOMEONE POSING AS YOUR SISTER?
I WOULD KNOW.
THEN PERHAPS TULA'S DOING THIS UNDER DURESS, AS THEIR PRISONER.
I WOULD KNOW, MA'AM. SHE WOULDN'T HAVE TO TELL ME. WE HAVE A... CONNECTION.
YOU.
IT MUST BE MARVELOUS TO HAVE A SIBLING.

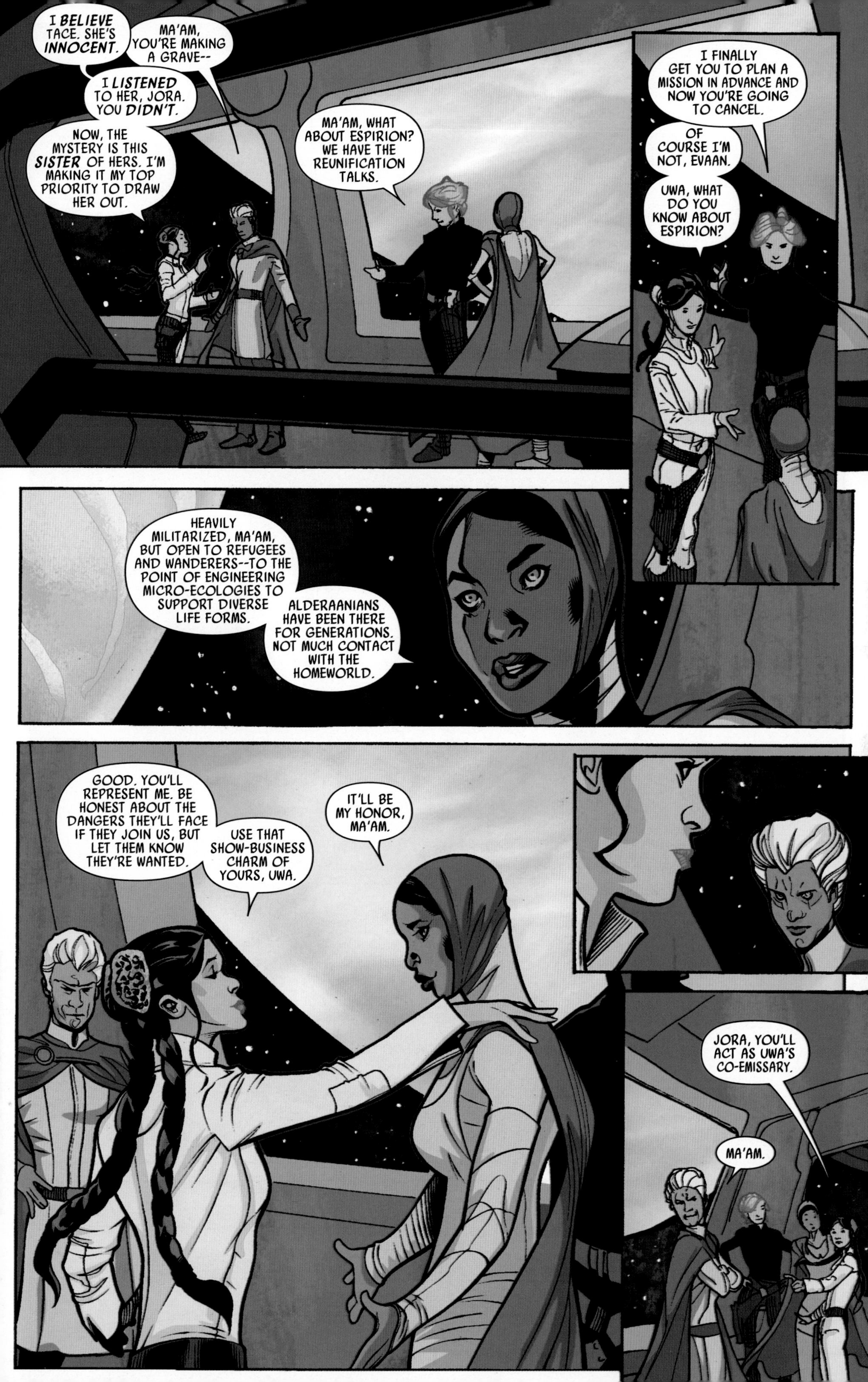
I BELIEVE TACE. SHE'S INNOCENT.
MA'AM, YOU'RE MAKING A GRAVE--
I LISTENED TO HER, JORA. YOU DIDN'T.
NOW, THE MYSTERY IS THIS SISTER OF HERS. I'M MAKING IT MY TOP PRIORITY TO DRAW HER OUT.
MA'AM, WHAT ABOUT ESPIRION? WE HAVE THE REUNIFICATION TALKS.
I FINALLY GET YOU TO PLAN A MISSION IN ADVANCE AND NOW YOU'RE GOING TO CANCEL.
OF COURSE I'M NOT, EVAAN.
UWA, WHAT DO YOU KNOW ABOUT ESPIRION?
HEAVILY MILITARIZED, MA'AM, BUT OPEN TO REFUGEES AND WANDERERS--TO THE POINT OF ENGINEERING MICRO-ECOLOGIES TO SUPPORT DIVERSE LIFE FORMS.
ALDERAANIANS HAVE BEEN THERE FOR GENERATIONS. NOT MUCH CONTACT WITH THE HOMEWORLD.
GOOD. YOU'LL REPRESENT ME. BE HONEST ABOUT THE DANGERS THEY'LL FACE IF THEY JOIN US, BUT LET THEM KNOW THEY'RE WANTED.
USE THAT SHOW-BUSINESS CHARM OF YOURS, UWA.
IT'LL BE MY HONOR, MA'AM.
JORA, YOU'LL ACT AS UWA'S CO-EMISSARY.
MA'AM.

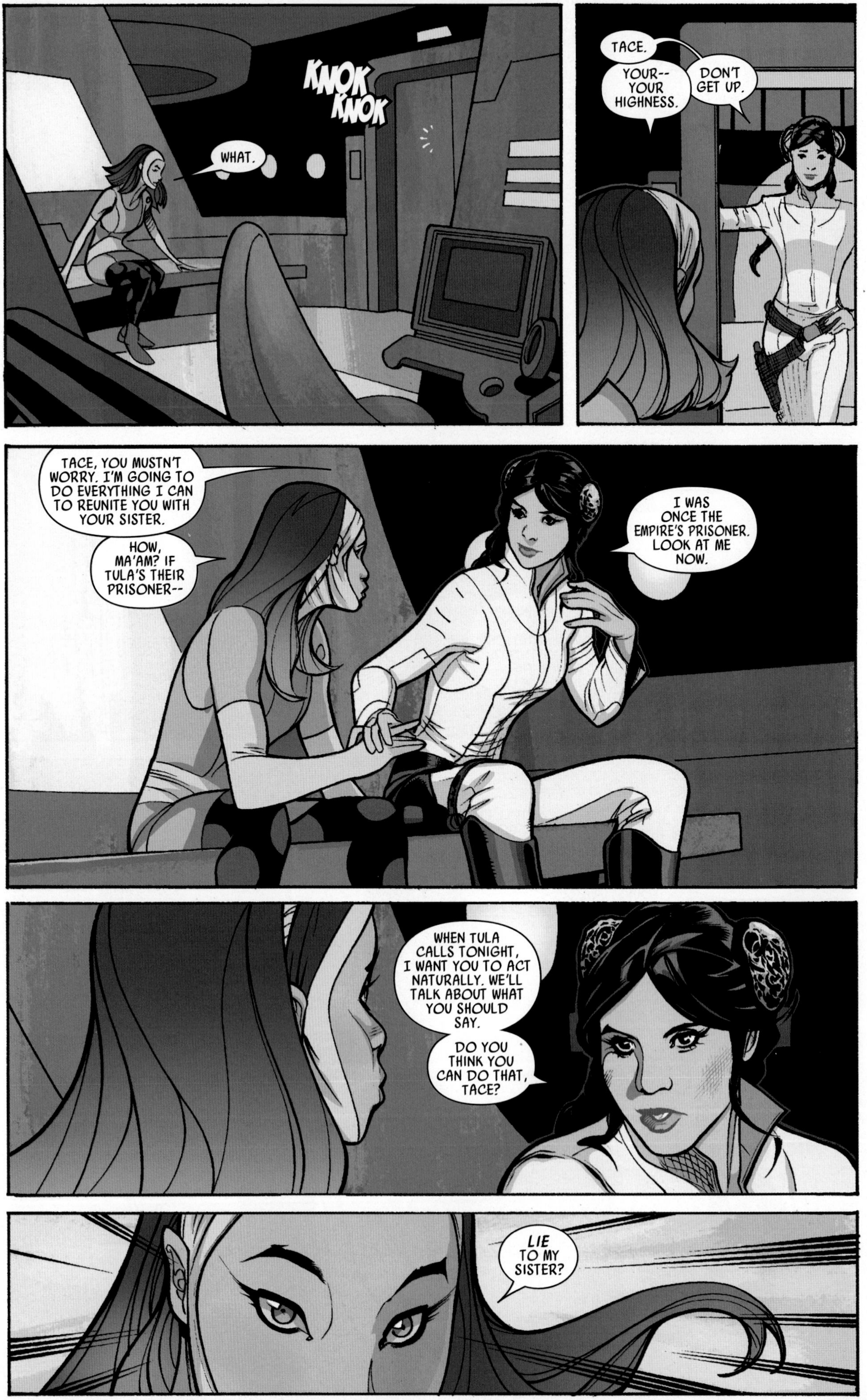
KNOK KNOK
WHAT.
TACE.
YOUR-- YOUR HIGHNESS.
DON'T GET UP.
TACE, YOU MUSTN'T WORRY. I'M GOING TO DO EVERYTHING I CAN TO REUNITE YOU WITH YOUR SISTER.
HOW, MA'AM? IF TULA'S THEIR PRISONER--
I WAS ONCE THE EMPIRE'S PRISONER. LOOK AT ME NOW.
WHEN TULA CALLS TONIGHT, I WANT YOU TO ACT NATURALLY. WE'LL TALK ABOUT WHAT YOU SHOULD SAY.
DO YOU THINK YOU CAN DO THAT, TACE?
LIE TO MY SISTER?

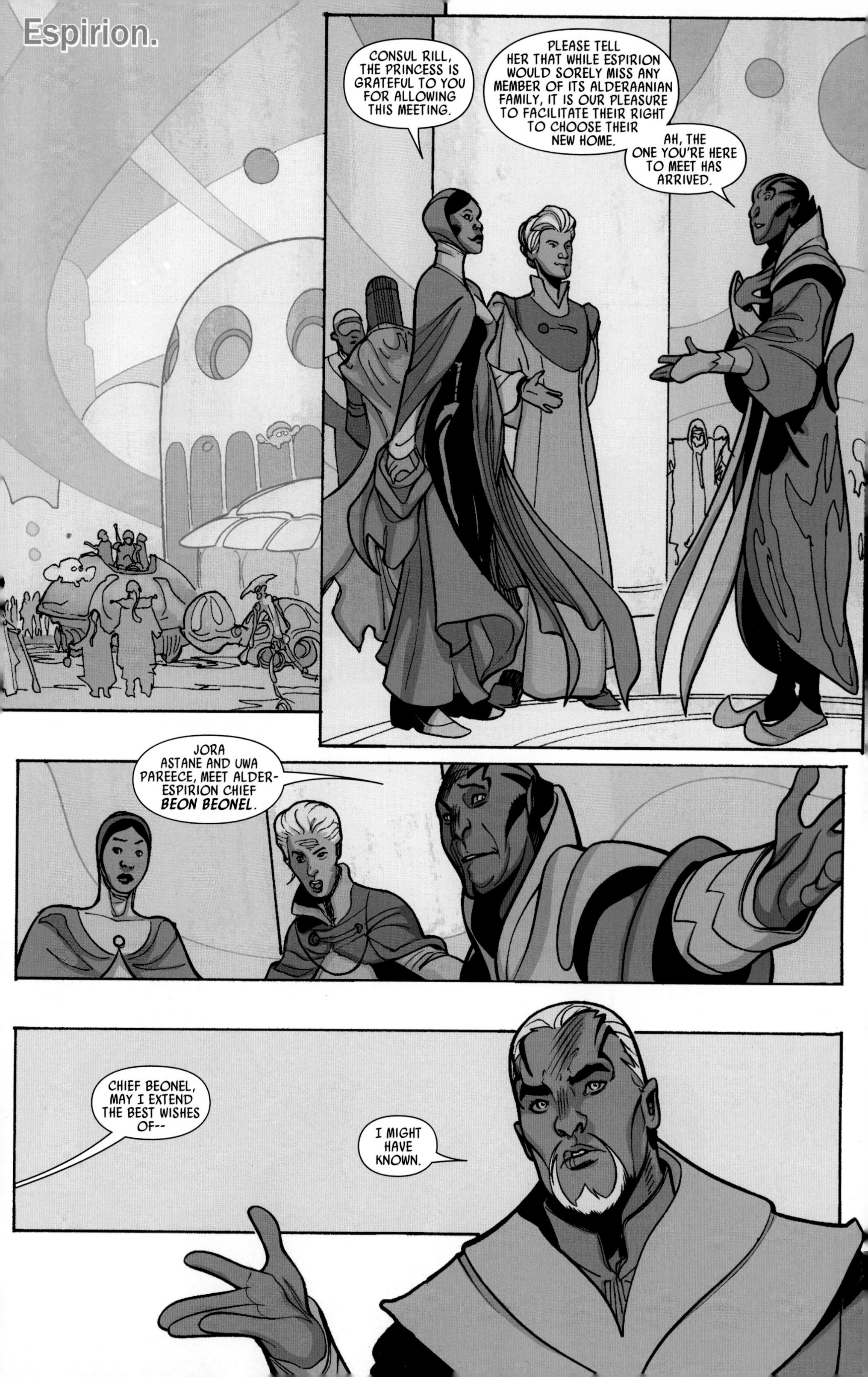
Espirion.
CONSUL RILL, THE PRINCESS IS GRATEFUL TO YOU FOR ALLOWING THIS MEETING.
PLEASE TELL HER THAT WHILE ESPIRION WOULD SORELY MISS ANY MEMBER OF ITS ALDERAANIAN FAMILY, IT IS OUR PLEASURE TO FACILITATE THEIR RIGHT TO CHOOSE THEIR NEW HOME.
AH, THE ONE YOU'RE HERE TO MEET HAS ARRIVED.
JORA ASTANE AND UWA PAREECE, MEET ALDER-ESPIRION CHIEF BEON BEONEL.
CHIEF BEONEL, MAY I EXTEND THE BEST WISHES OF--
I MIGHT HAVE KNOWN.

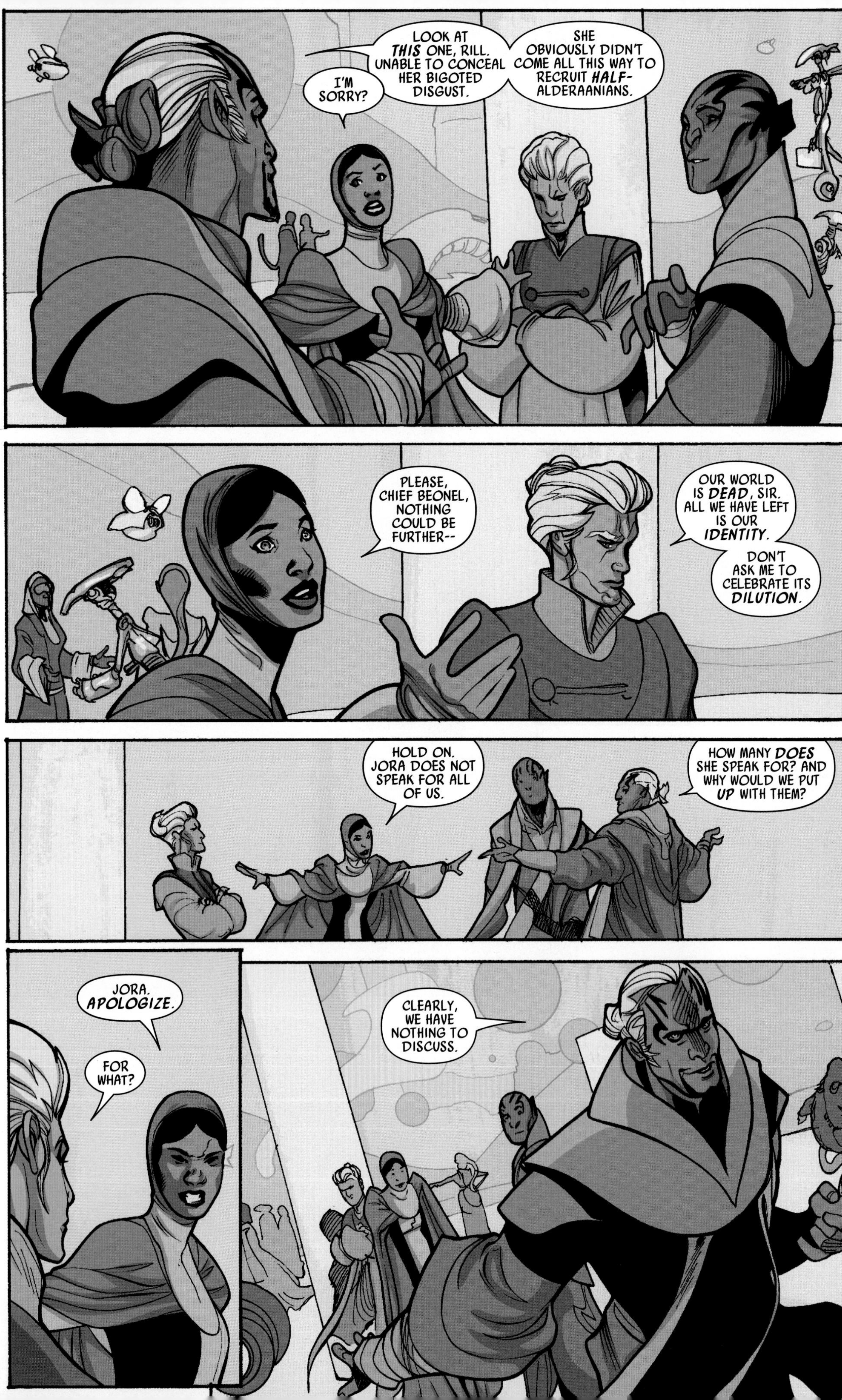
LOOK AT THIS ONE, RILL. UNABLE TO CONCEAL HER BIGOTED DISGUST.
SHE OBVIOUSLY DIDN'T COME ALL THIS WAY TO RECRUIT HALF-ALDERAANIANS.
I'M SORRY?
PLEASE, CHIEF BEONEL, NOTHING COULD BE FURTHER--
OUR WORLD IS DEAD, SIR. ALL WE HAVE LEFT IS OUR IDENTITY.
DON'T ASK ME TO CELEBRATE ITS DILUTION.
HOLD ON. JORA DOES NOT SPEAK FOR ALL OF US.
HOW MANY DOES SHE SPEAK FOR? AND WHY WOULD WE PUT UP WITH THEM?
JORA. APOLOGIZE.
FOR WHAT?
CLEARLY, WE HAVE NOTHING TO DISCUSS.

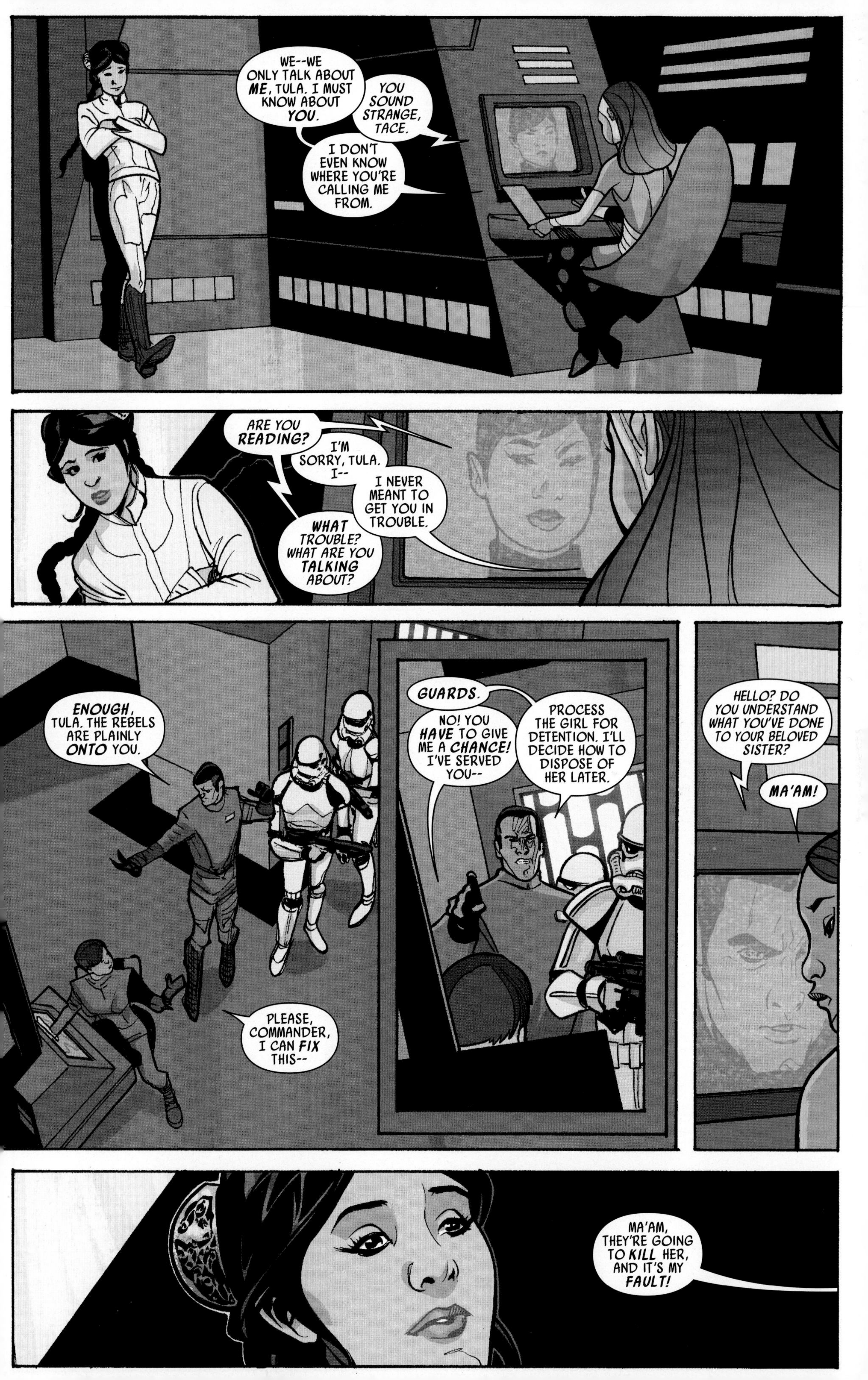
WE--WE ONLY TALK ABOUT ME, TULA. I MUST KNOW ABOUT YOU.
YOU SOUND STRANGE, TACE.
I DON'T EVEN KNOW WHERE YOU'RE CALLING ME FROM.
ARE YOU READING?
I'M SORRY, TULA. I--
I NEVER MEANT TO GET YOU IN TROUBLE.
WHAT TROUBLE? WHAT ARE YOU TALKING ABOUT?
ENOUGH, TULA. THE REBELS ARE PLAINLY ONTO YOU.
PLEASE, COMMANDER, I CAN FIX THIS--
GUARDS.
NO! YOU HAVE TO GIVE ME A CHANCE! I'VE SERVED YOU--
PROCESS THE GIRL FOR DETENTION. I'LL DECIDE HOW TO DISPOSE OF HER LATER.
HELLO? DO YOU UNDERSTAND WHAT YOU'VE DONE TO YOUR BELOVED SISTER?
MA'AM!
MA'AM, THEY'RE GOING TO KILL HER, AND IT'S MY FAULT!

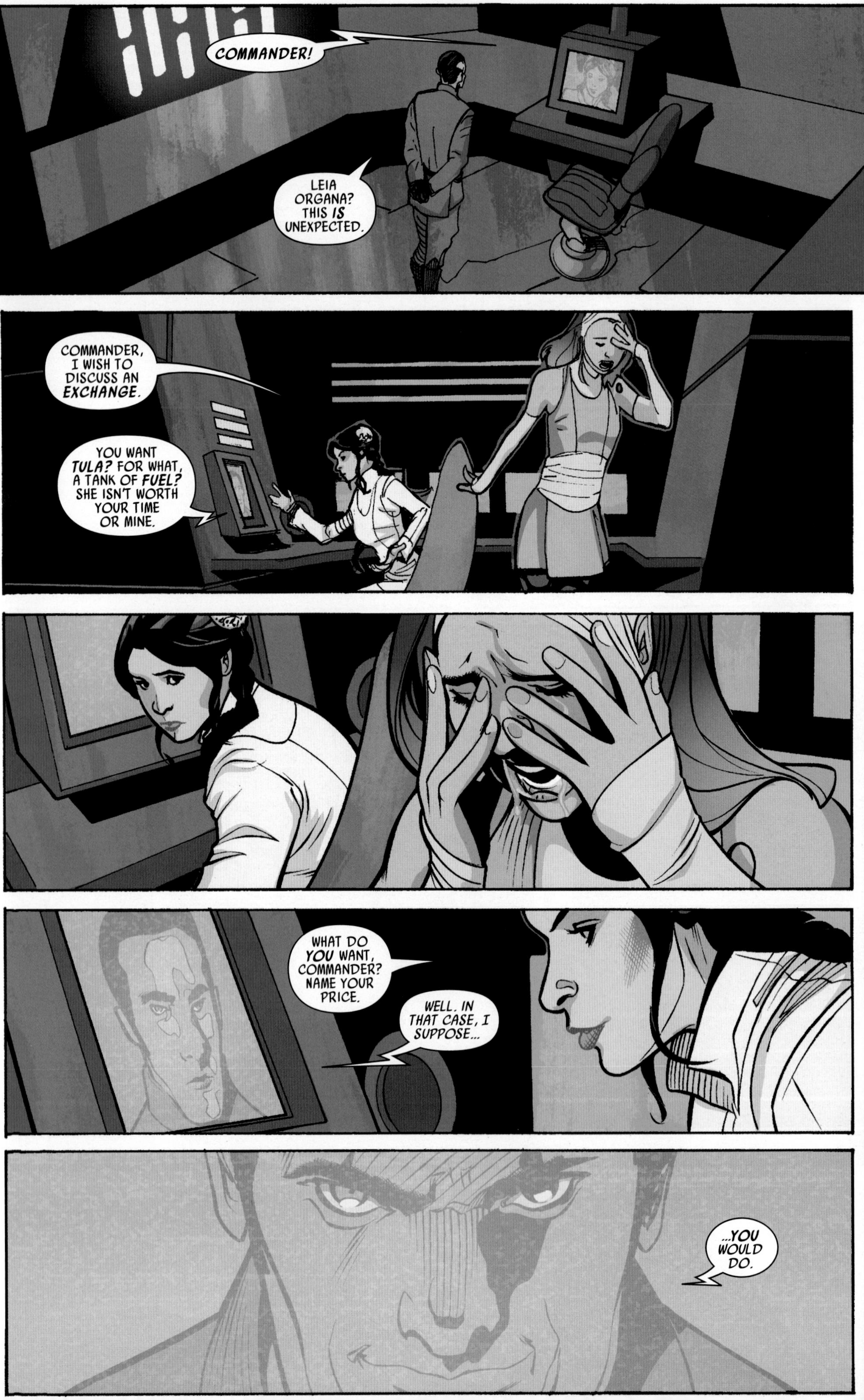
COMMANDER!
LEIA ORGANA? THIS IS UNEXPECTED.
COMMANDER, I WISH TO DISCUSS AN EXCHANGE.
YOU WANT TULA? FOR WHAT, A TANK OF FUEL? SHE ISN'T WORTH YOUR TIME OR MINE.
WHAT DO YOU WANT, COMMANDER? NAME YOUR PRICE.
WELL. IN THAT CASE, I SUPPOSE...
...YOU WOULD DO.

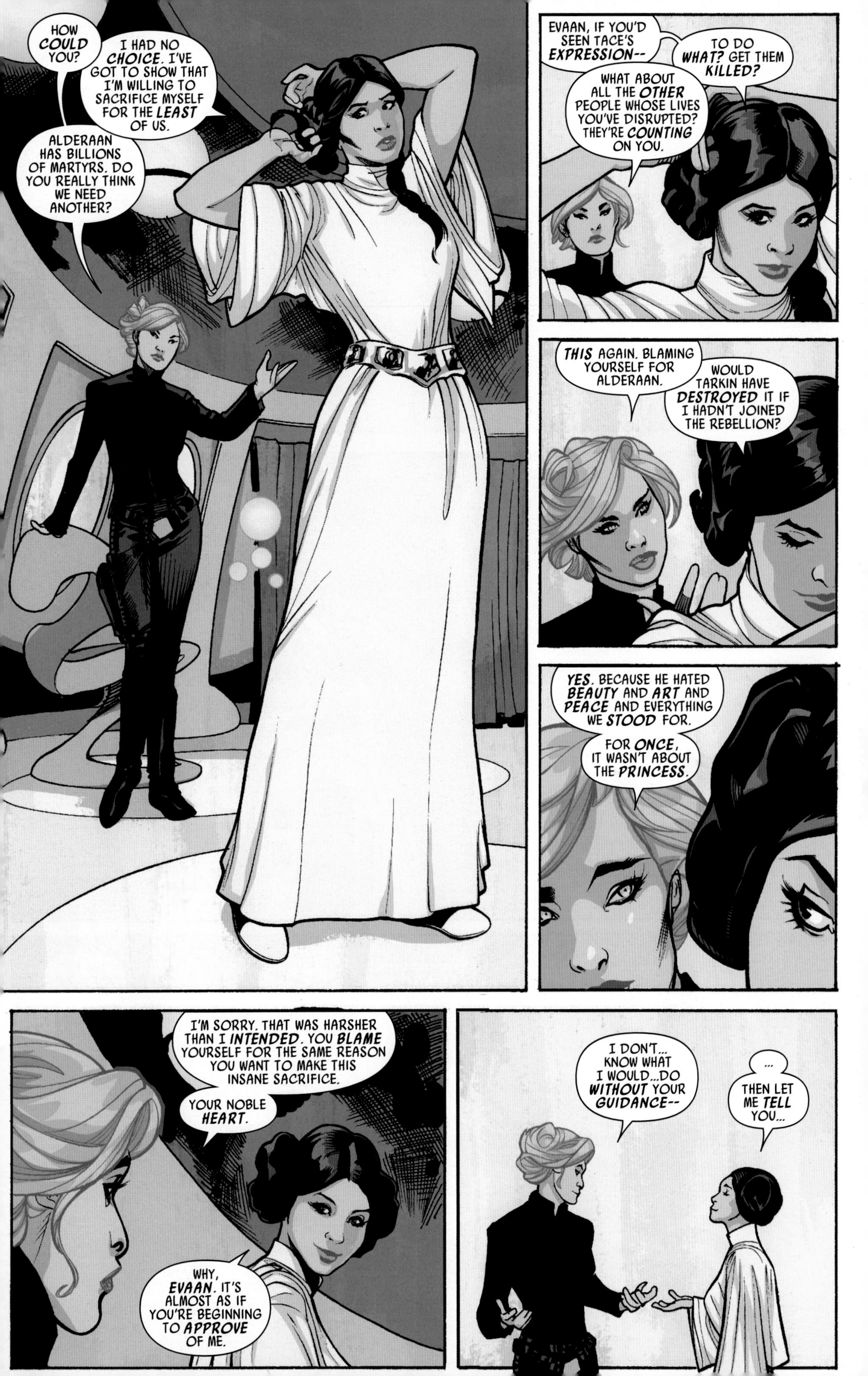
HOW COULD YOU?
I HAD NO CHOICE. I'VE GOT TO SHOW THAT I'M WILLING TO SACRIFICE MYSELF FOR THE LEAST OF US.
ALDERAAN HAS BILLIONS OF MARTYRS. DO YOU REALLY THINK WE NEED ANOTHER?
EVAAN, IF YOU'D SEEN TACE'S EXPRESSION--
TO DO WHAT? GET THEM KILLED?
WHAT ABOUT ALL THE OTHER PEOPLE WHOSE LIVES YOU'VE DISRUPTED? THEY'RE COUNTING ON YOU.
THIS AGAIN. BLAMING YOURSELF FOR ALDERAAN.
WOULD TARKIN HAVE DESTROYED IT IF I HADN'T JOINED THE REBELLION?
YES. BECAUSE HE HATED BEAUTY AND ART AND PEACE AND EVERYTHING WE STOOD FOR.
FOR ONCE, IT WASN'T ABOUT THE PRINCESS.
I'M SORRY. THAT WAS HARSHER THAN I INTENDED. YOU BLAME YOURSELF FOR THE SAME REASON YOU WANT TO MAKE THIS INSANE SACRIFICE.
YOUR NOBLE HEART.
WHY, EVAAN. IT'S ALMOST AS IF YOU'RE BEGINNING TO APPROVE OF ME.
I DON'T... KNOW WHAT I WOULD...DO WITHOUT YOUR GUIDANCE--
...
THEN LET ME TELL YOU...

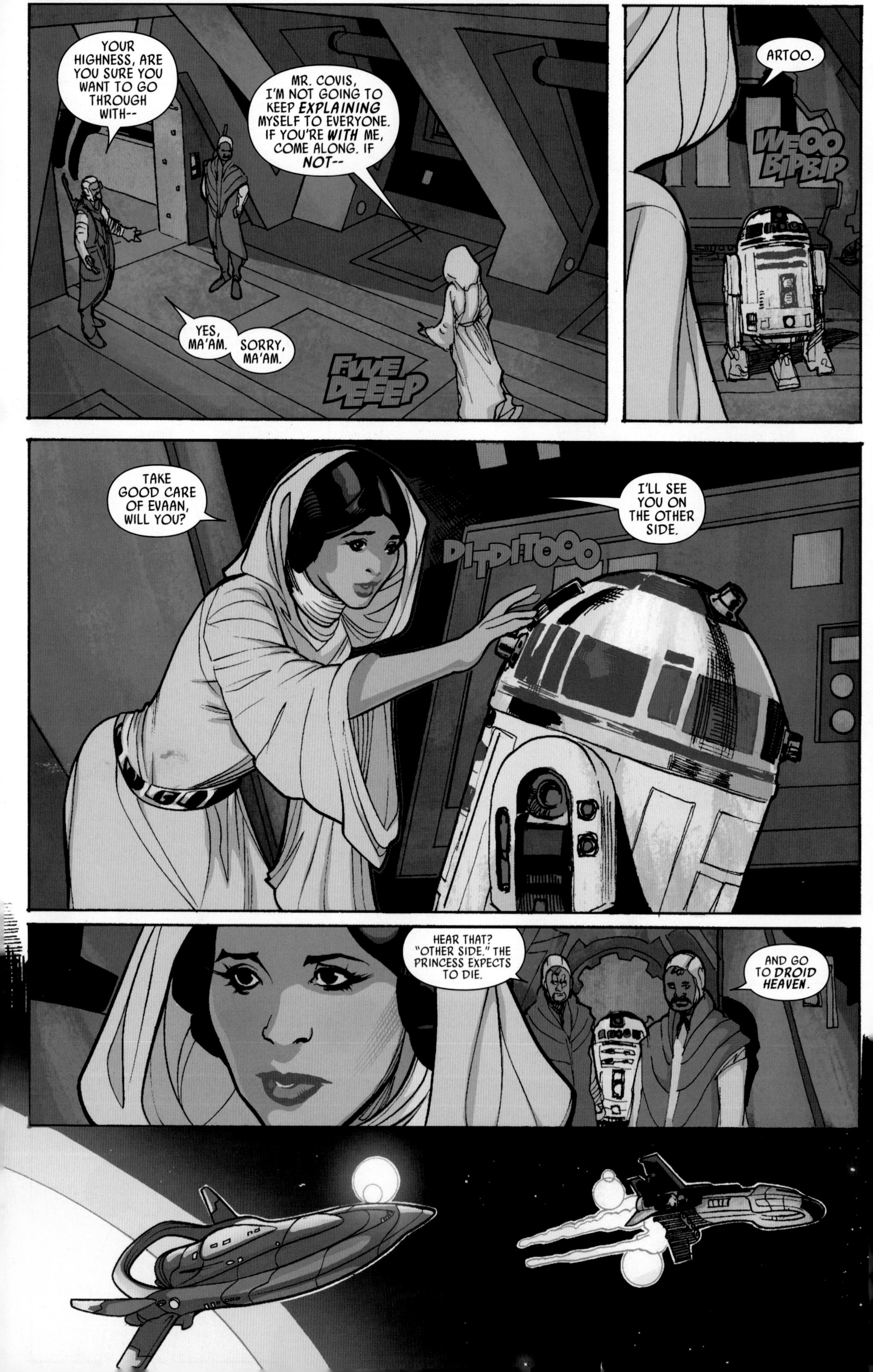
YOUR HIGHNESS, ARE YOU SURE YOU WANT TO GO THROUGH WITH--
MR. COVIS, I'M NOT GOING TO KEEP EXPLAINING MYSELF TO EVERYONE. IF YOU'RE WITH ME, COME ALONG. IF NOT--
YES, MA'AM.
SORRY, MA'AM.
FWE DEEEP
ARTOO.
WEOO BIPBIP
TAKE GOOD CARE OF EVAAN, WILL YOU?
DI-DI-TOOO
I'LL SEE YOU ON THE OTHER SIDE.
HEAR THAT? "OTHER SIDE." THE PRINCESS EXPECTS TO DIE.
AND GO TO DROID HEAVEN.

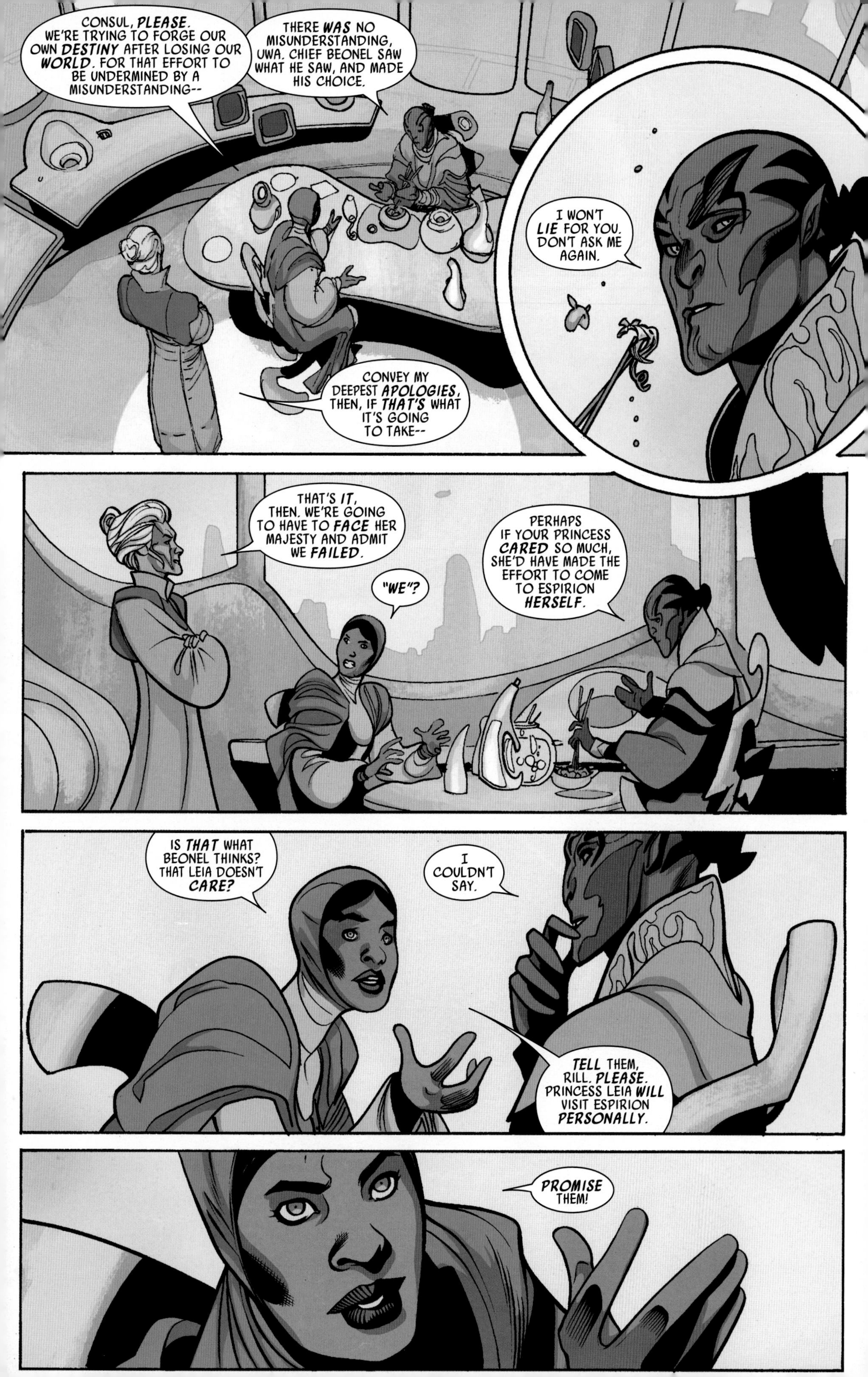
CONSUL, PLEASE. WE'RE TRYING TO FORGE OUR OWN DESTINY AFTER LOSING OUR WORLD. FOR THAT EFFORT TO BE UNDERMINED BY A MISUNDERSTANDING--
THERE WAS NO MISUNDERSTANDING, UWA. CHIEF BEONEL SAW WHAT HE SAW, AND MADE HIS CHOICE.
CONVEY MY DEEPEST APOLOGIES, THEN, IF THAT'S WHAT IT'S GOING TO TAKE--
I WON'T LIE FOR YOU. DON'T ASK ME AGAIN.
THAT'S IT, THEN. WE'RE GOING TO HAVE TO FACE HER MAJESTY AND ADMIT WE FAILED.
"WE"?
PERHAPS IF YOUR PRINCESS CARED SO MUCH, SHE'D HAVE MADE THE EFFORT TO COME TO ESPIRION HERSELF.
IS THAT WHAT BEONEL THINKS? THAT LEIA DOESN'T CARE?
I COULDN'T SAY.
TELL THEM, RILL. PLEASE. PRINCESS LEIA WILL VISIT ESPIRION PERSONALLY.
PROMISE THEM!

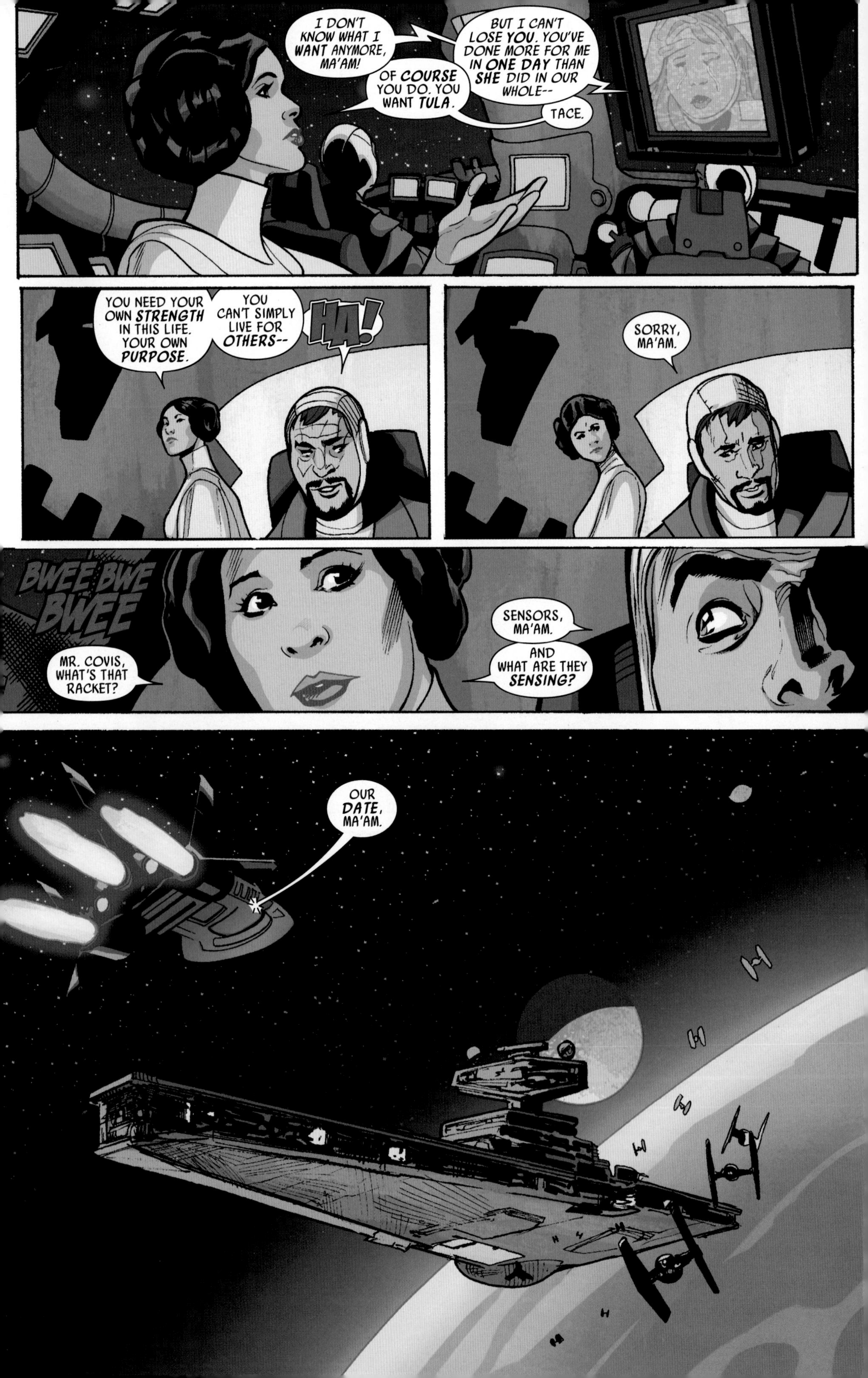

I DON'T KNOW WHAT I WANT ANYMORE, MA'AM!
OF COURSE YOU DO. YOU WANT TULA.
BUT I CAN'T LOSE YOU. YOU'VE DONE MORE FOR ME IN ONE DAY THAN SHE DID IN OUR WHOLE--
TACE.
YOU NEED YOUR OWN STRENGTH IN THIS LIFE. YOUR OWN PURPOSE.
YOU CAN'T SIMPLY LIVE FOR OTHERS--
HA!
SORRY, MA'AM.
BWEE BWE BWEE
MR. COVIS, WHAT'S THAT RACKET?
SENSORS, MA'AM.
AND WHAT ARE THEY SENSING?
OUR DATE, MA'AM.

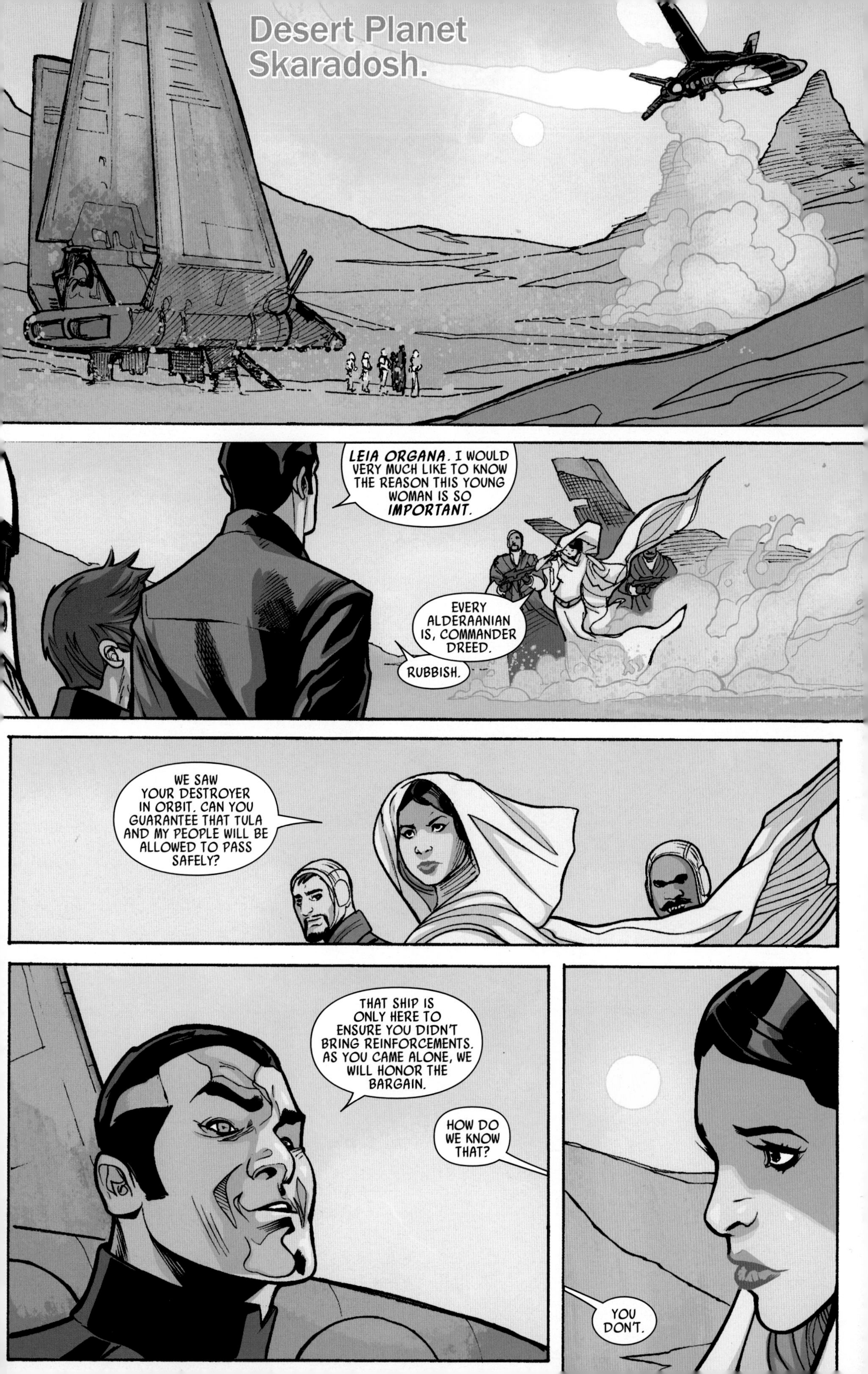
Desert Planet Skaradosh.
LEIA ORGANA. I WOULD VERY MUCH LIKE TO KNOW THE REASON THIS YOUNG WOMAN IS SO IMPORTANT.
EVERY ALDERAANIAN IS, COMMANDER DREED.
RUBBISH.
WE SAW YOUR DESTROYER IN ORBIT. CAN YOU GUARANTEE THAT TULA AND MY PEOPLE WILL BE ALLOWED TO PASS SAFELY?
THAT SHIP IS ONLY HERE TO ENSURE YOU DIDN'T BRING REINFORCEMENTS. AS YOU CAME ALONE, WE WILL HONOR THE BARGAIN.
HOW DO WE KNOW THAT?
YOU DON'T.

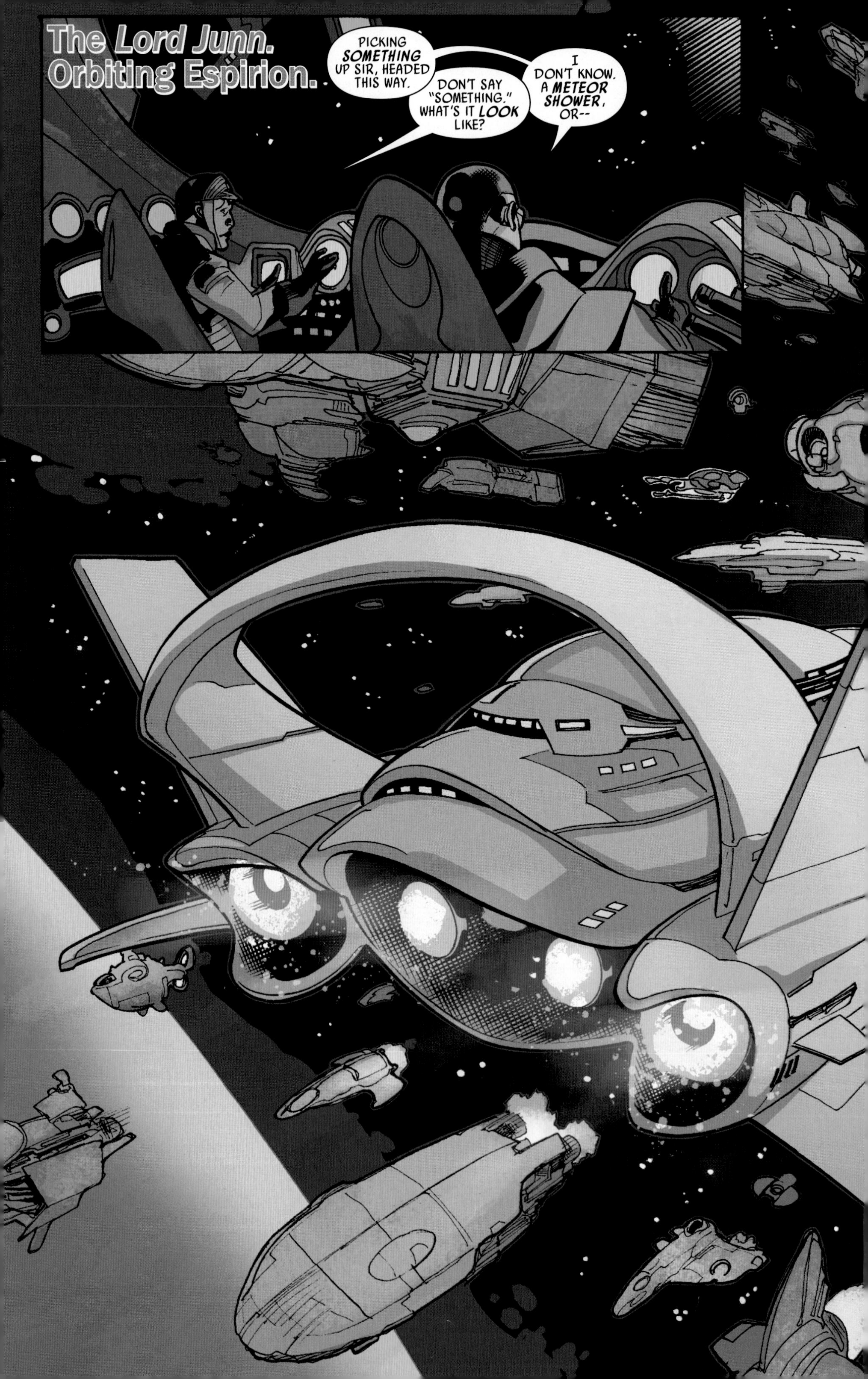

The Lord Junn. Orbiting Espirion.
PICKING SOMETHING UP SIR, HEADED THIS WAY.
DON'T SAY "SOMETHING." WHAT'S IT LOOK LIKE?
I DON'T KNOW. A METEOR SHOWER, OR--

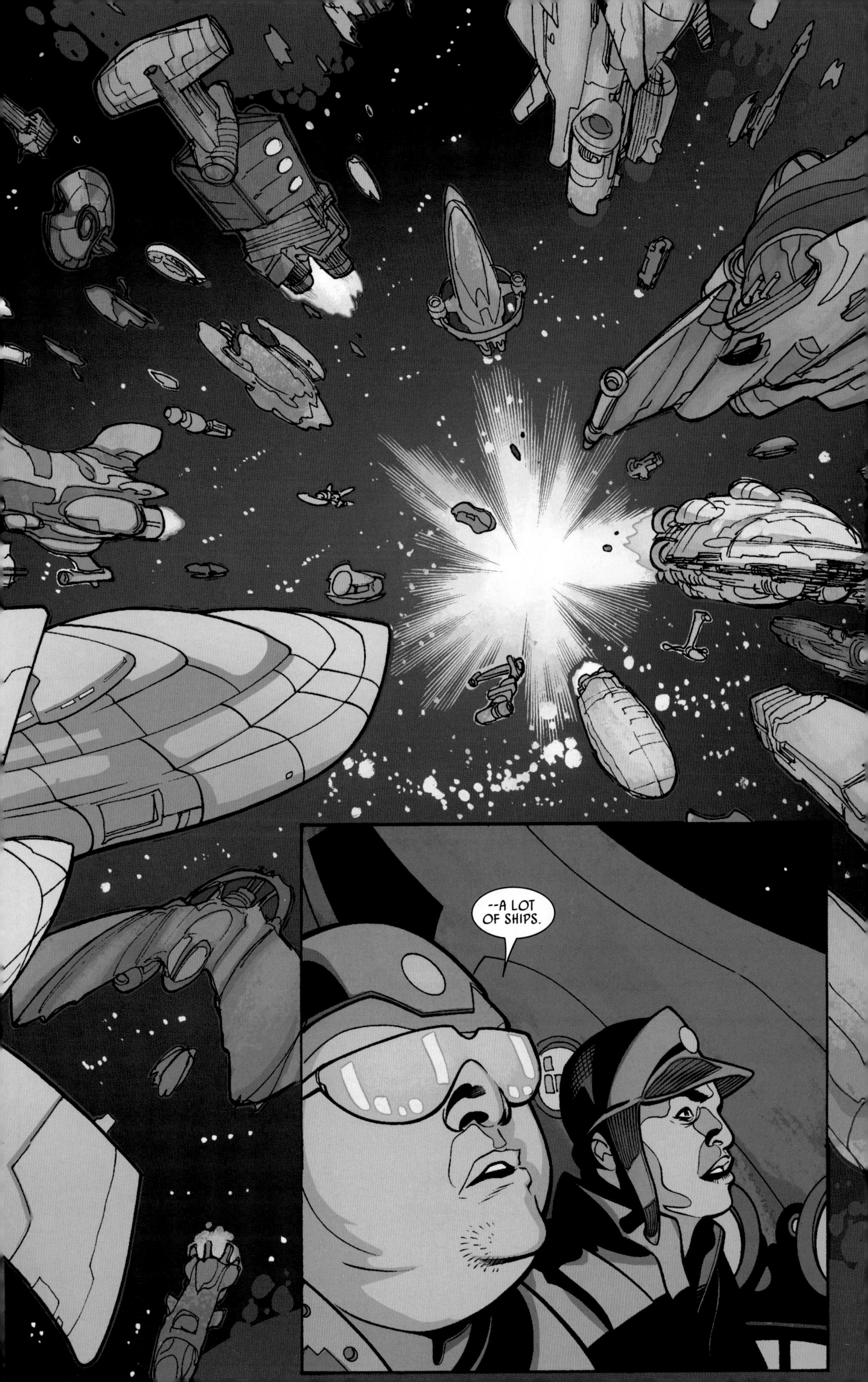
--A LOT OF SHIPS.

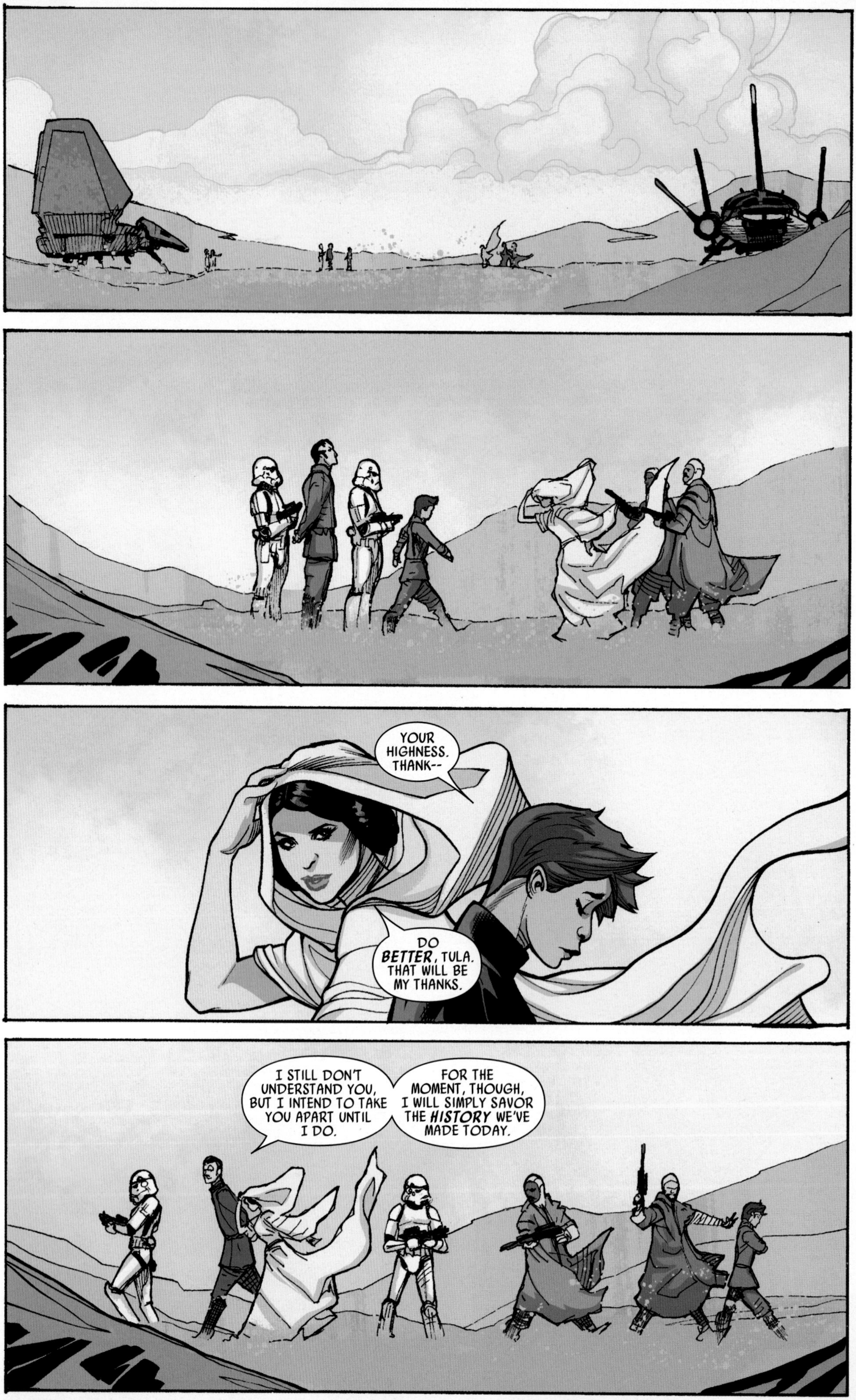
YOUR HIGHNESS. THANK--
DO BETTER, TULA. THAT WILL BE MY THANKS.
I STILL DON'T UNDERSTAND YOU, BUT I INTEND TO TAKE YOU APART UNTIL I DO.
FOR THE MOMENT, THOUGH, I WILL SIMPLY SAVOR THE HISTORY WE'VE MADE TODAY.

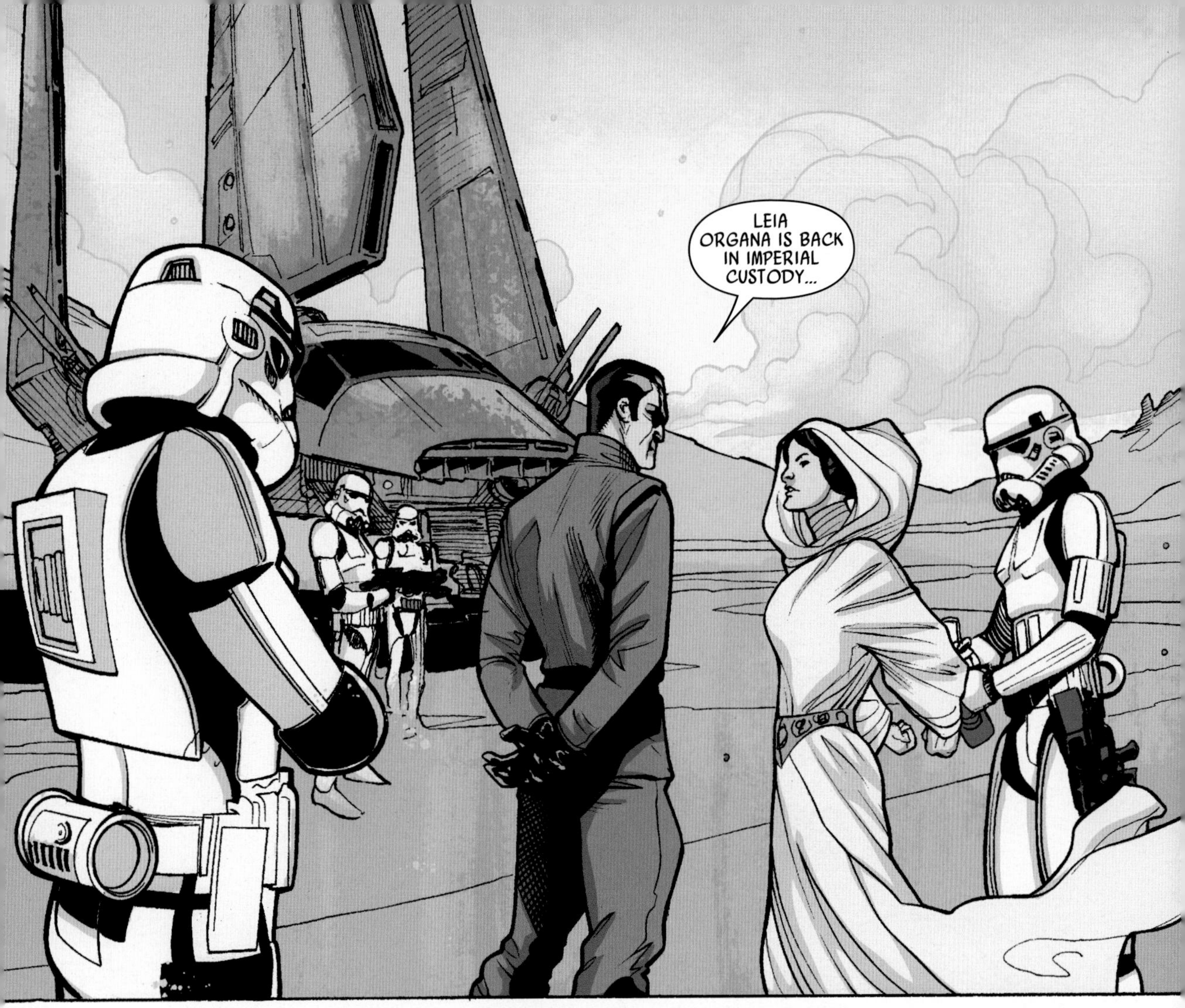
LEIA ORGANA IS BACK IN IMPERIAL CUSTODY...

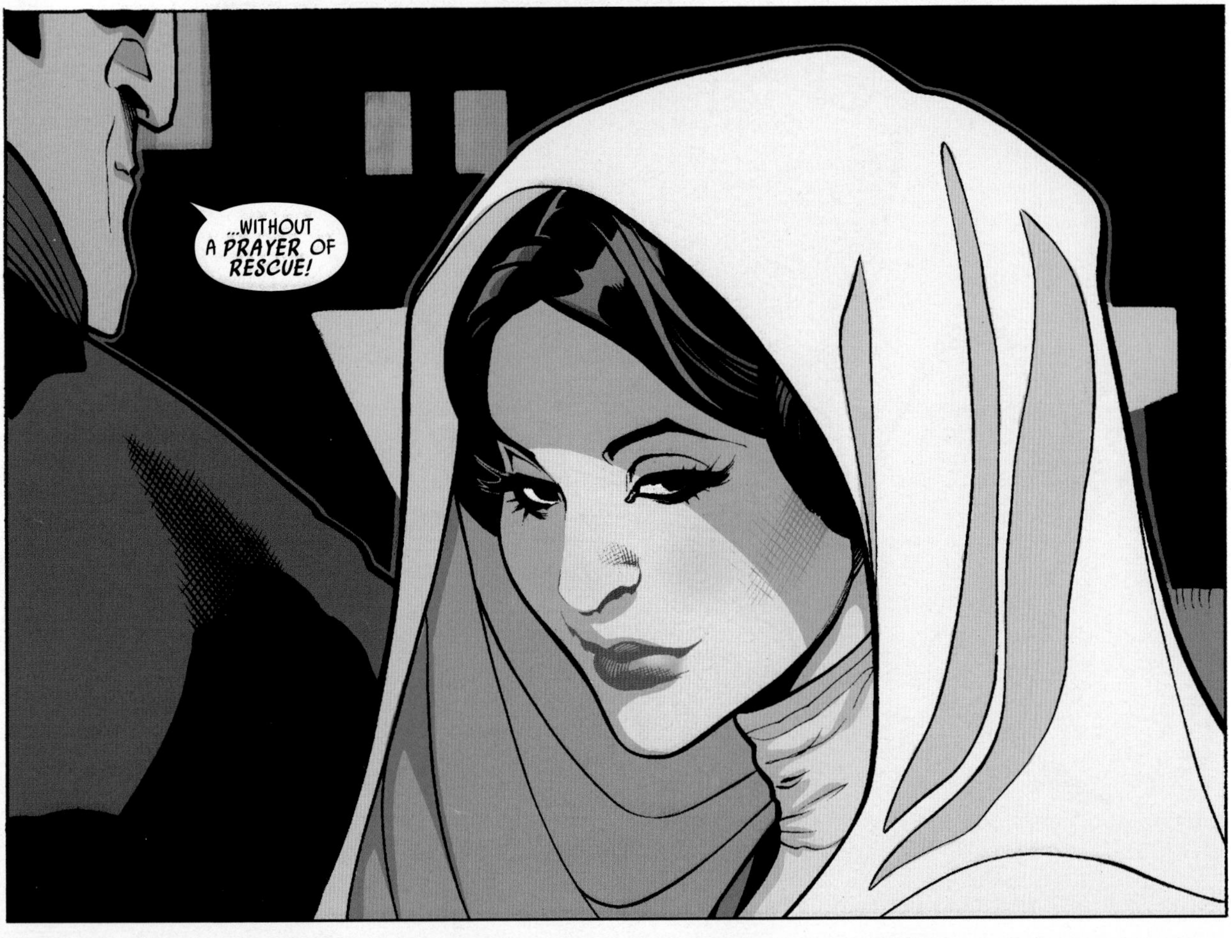
...WITHOUT A PRAYER OF RESCUE!

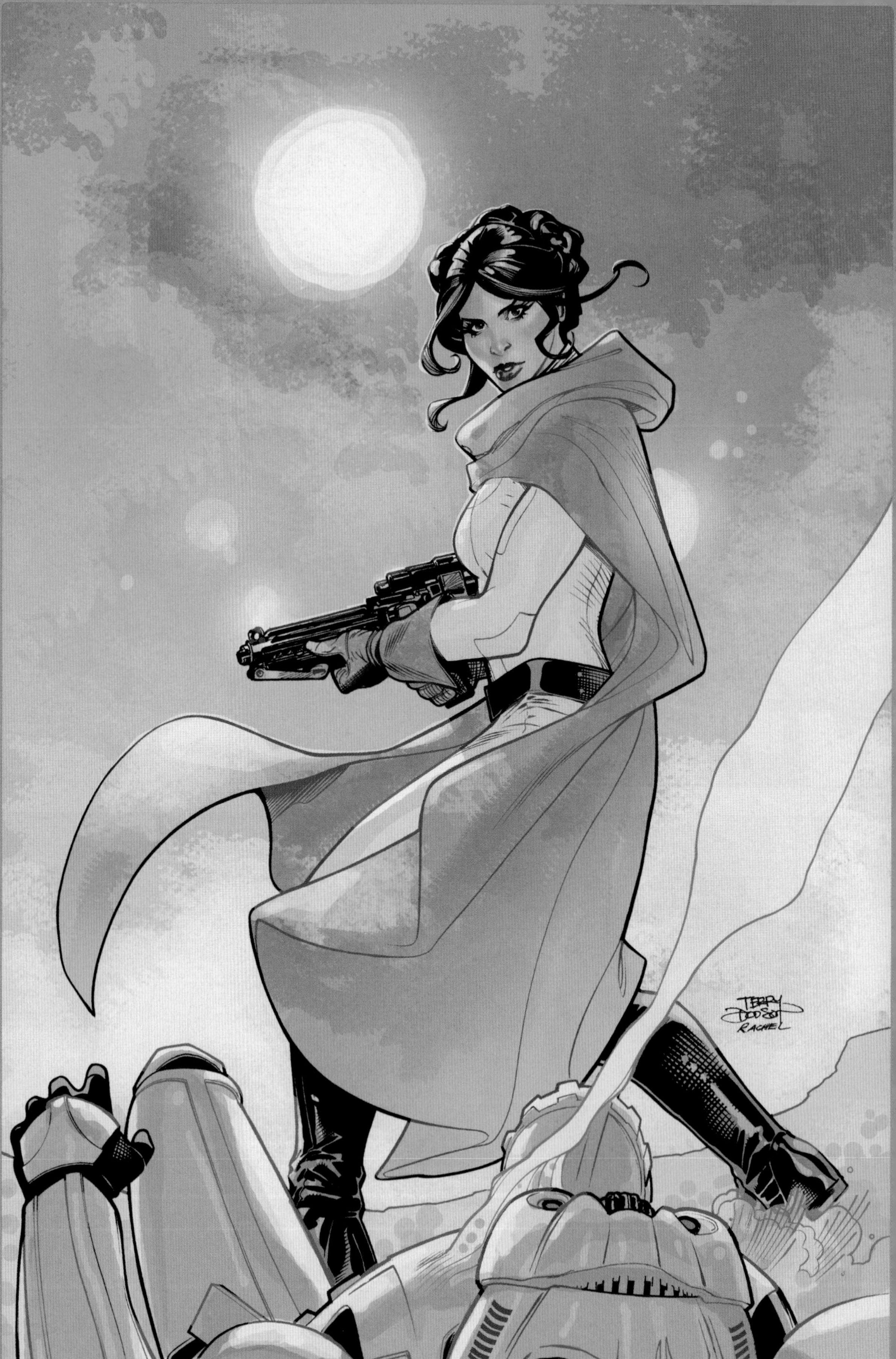
TERRY DODSON
RACHEL

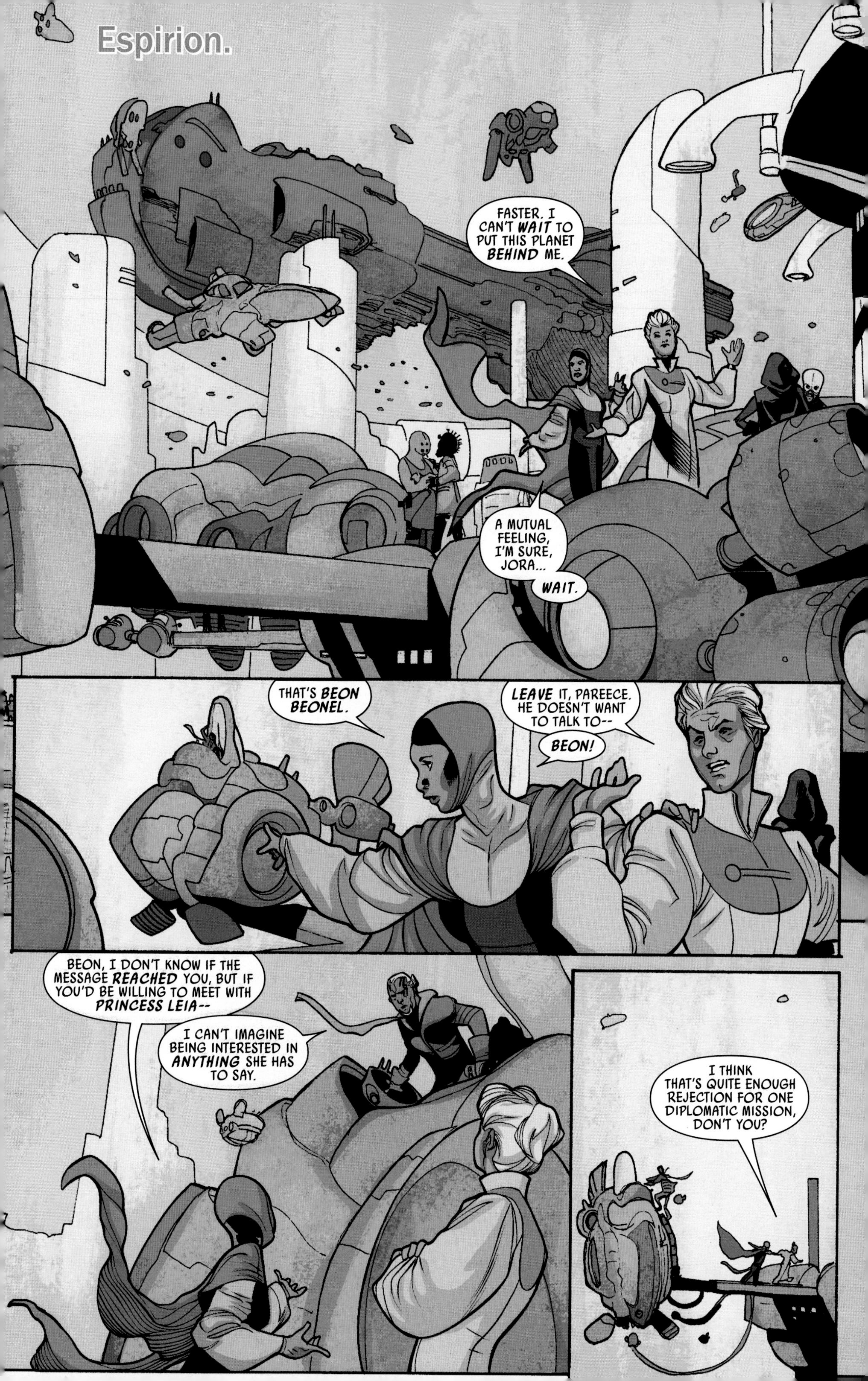
Espirion.
FASTER. I CAN'T WAIT TO PUT THIS PLANET BEHIND ME.
A MUTUAL FEELING, I'M SURE, JORA...
WAIT.
THAT'S BEON BEONEL.
LEAVE IT, PAREECE. HE DOESN'T WANT TO TALK TO--
BEON!
BEON, I DON'T KNOW IF THE MESSAGE REACHED YOU, BUT IF YOU'D BE WILLING TO MEET WITH PRINCESS LEIA--
I CAN'T IMAGINE BEING INTERESTED IN ANYTHING SHE HAS TO SAY.
I THINK THAT'S QUITE ENOUGH REJECTION FOR ONE DIPLOMATIC MISSION, DON'T YOU?

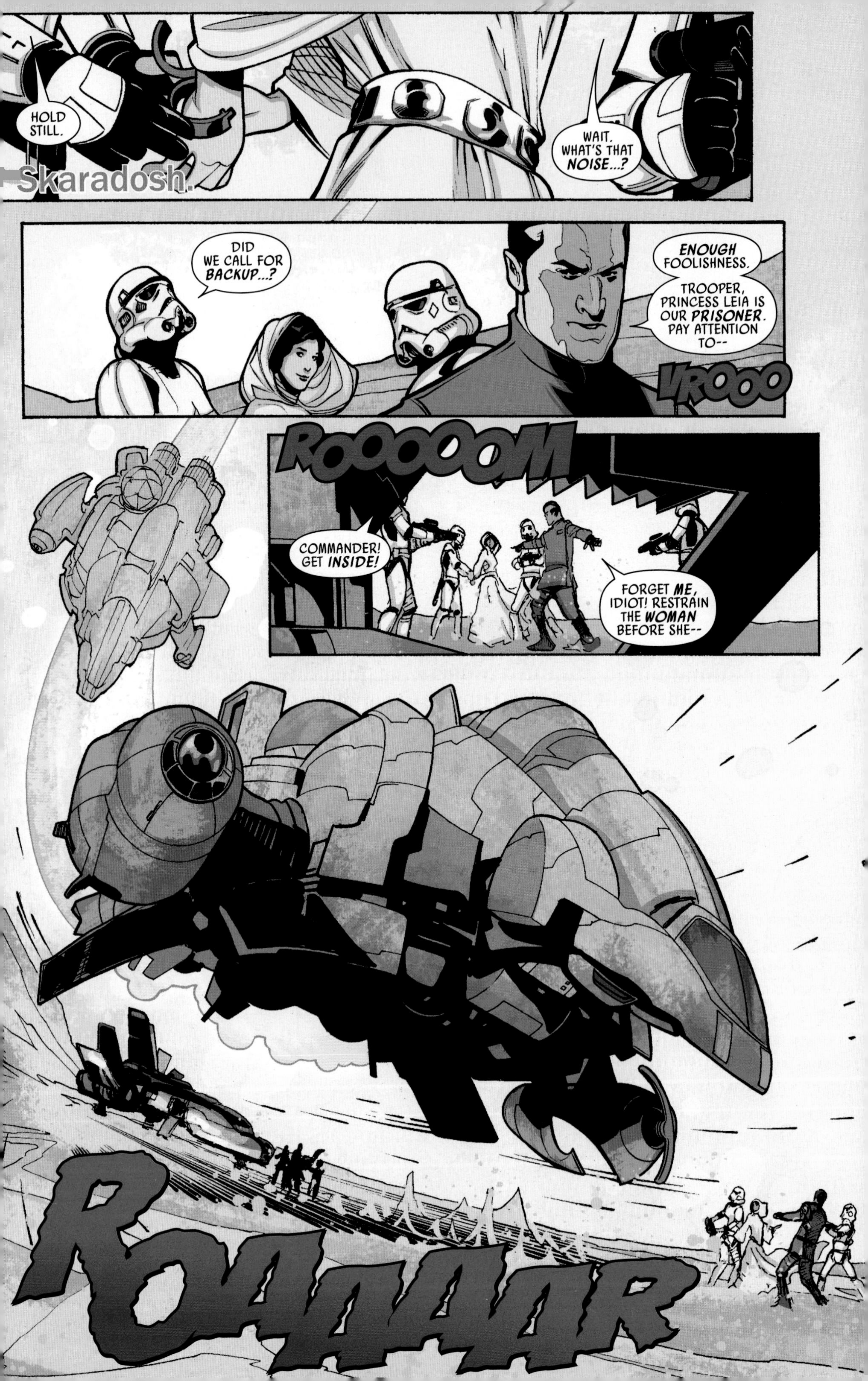
HOLD STILL.
Skaradosh.
WAIT. WHAT'S THAT NOISE...?
DID WE CALL FOR BACKUP...?
ENOUGH FOOLISHNESS.
TROOPER, PRINCESS LEIA IS OUR PRISONER. PAY ATTENTION TO--
VROOO
ROOOOOOM
COMMANDER! GET INSIDE!
FORGET ME, IDIOT! RESTRAIN THE WOMAN BEFORE SHE--
ROAAAAR

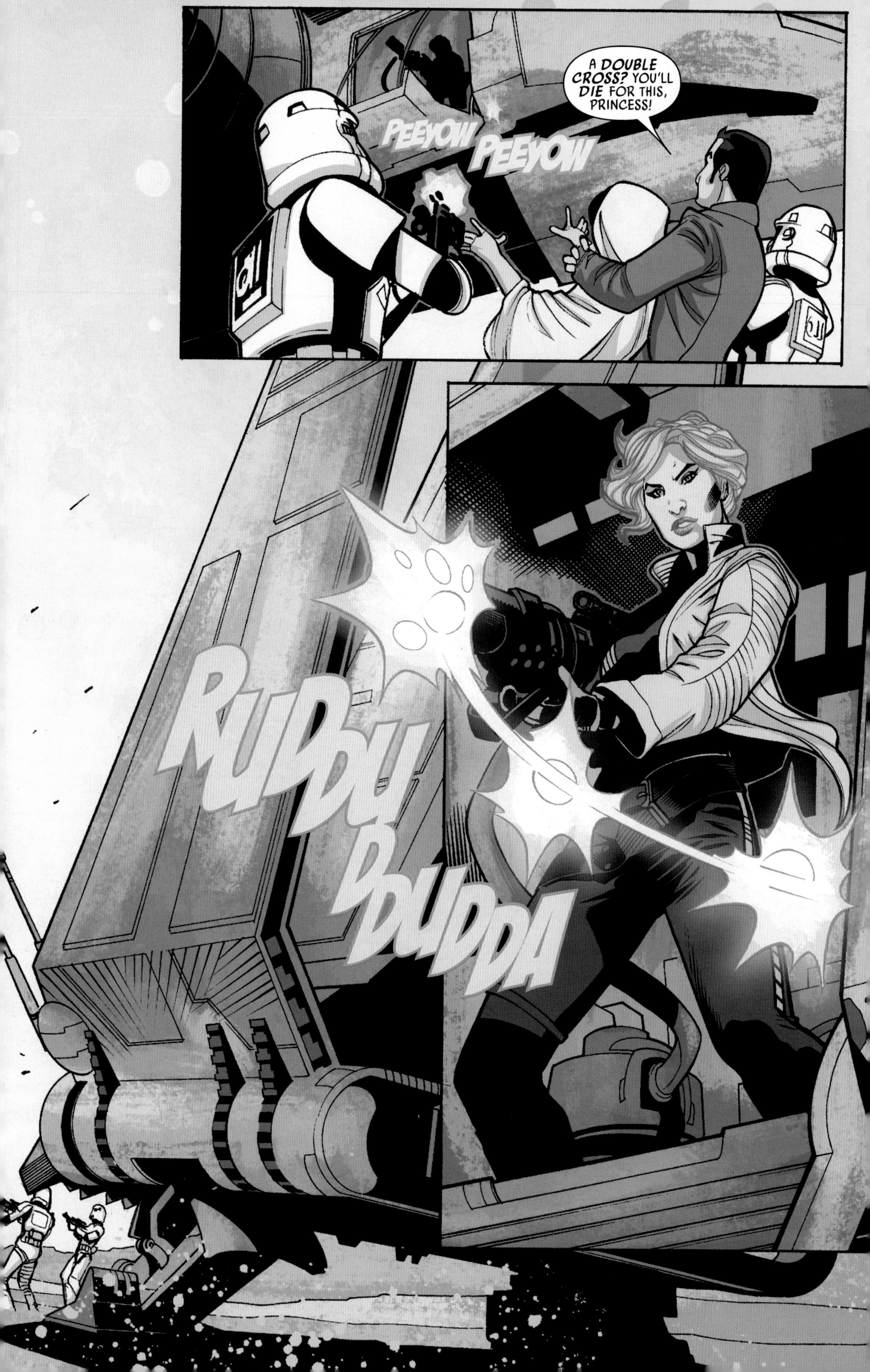
A DOUBLE CROSS? YOU'LL DIE FOR THIS, PRINCESS!
PEEYOW PEEYOW
RUDDU DDUDDA

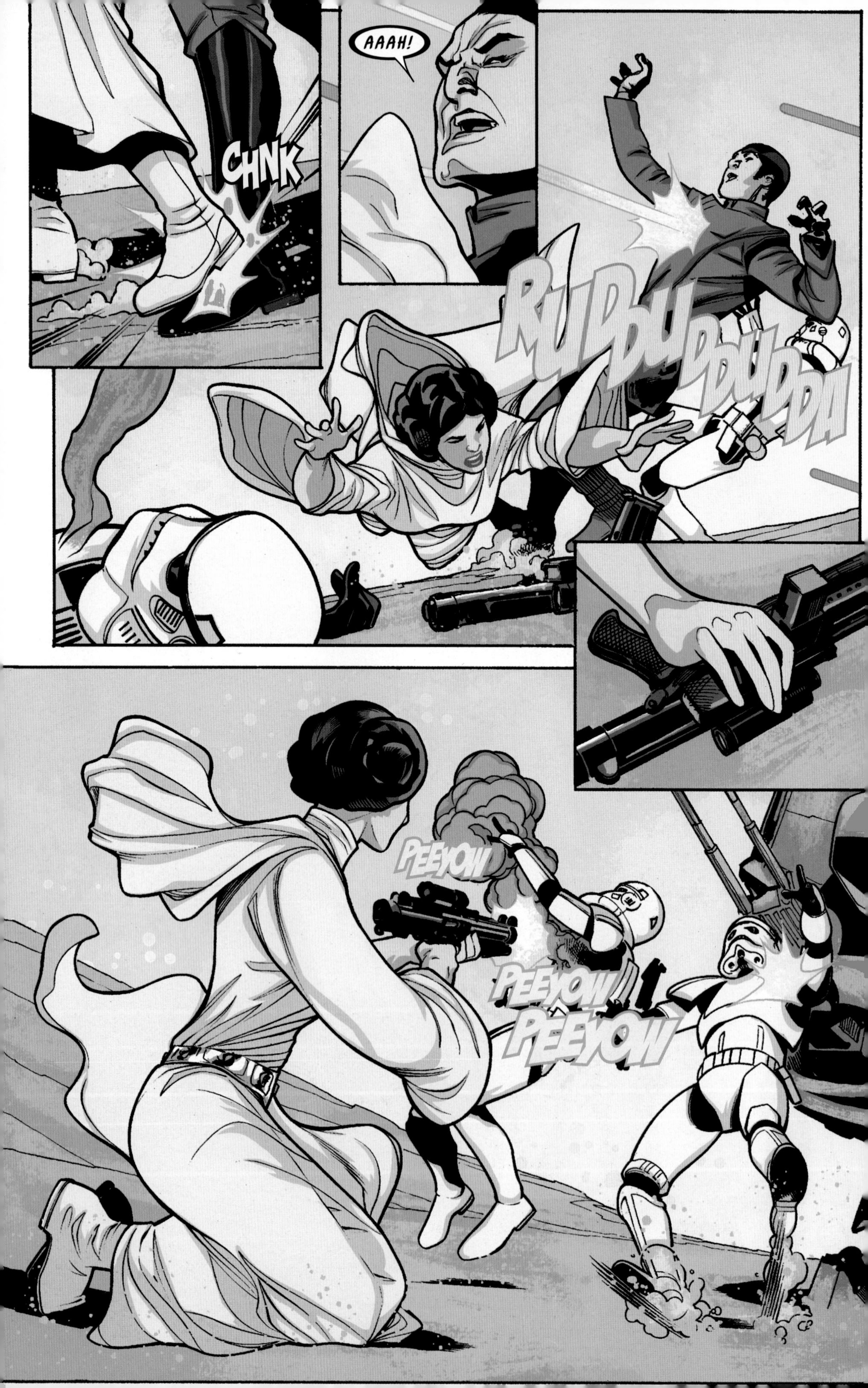
CHNK
AAAH!
RUDDUDDUDDA
PEEYOW
PEEYOW
PEEYOW

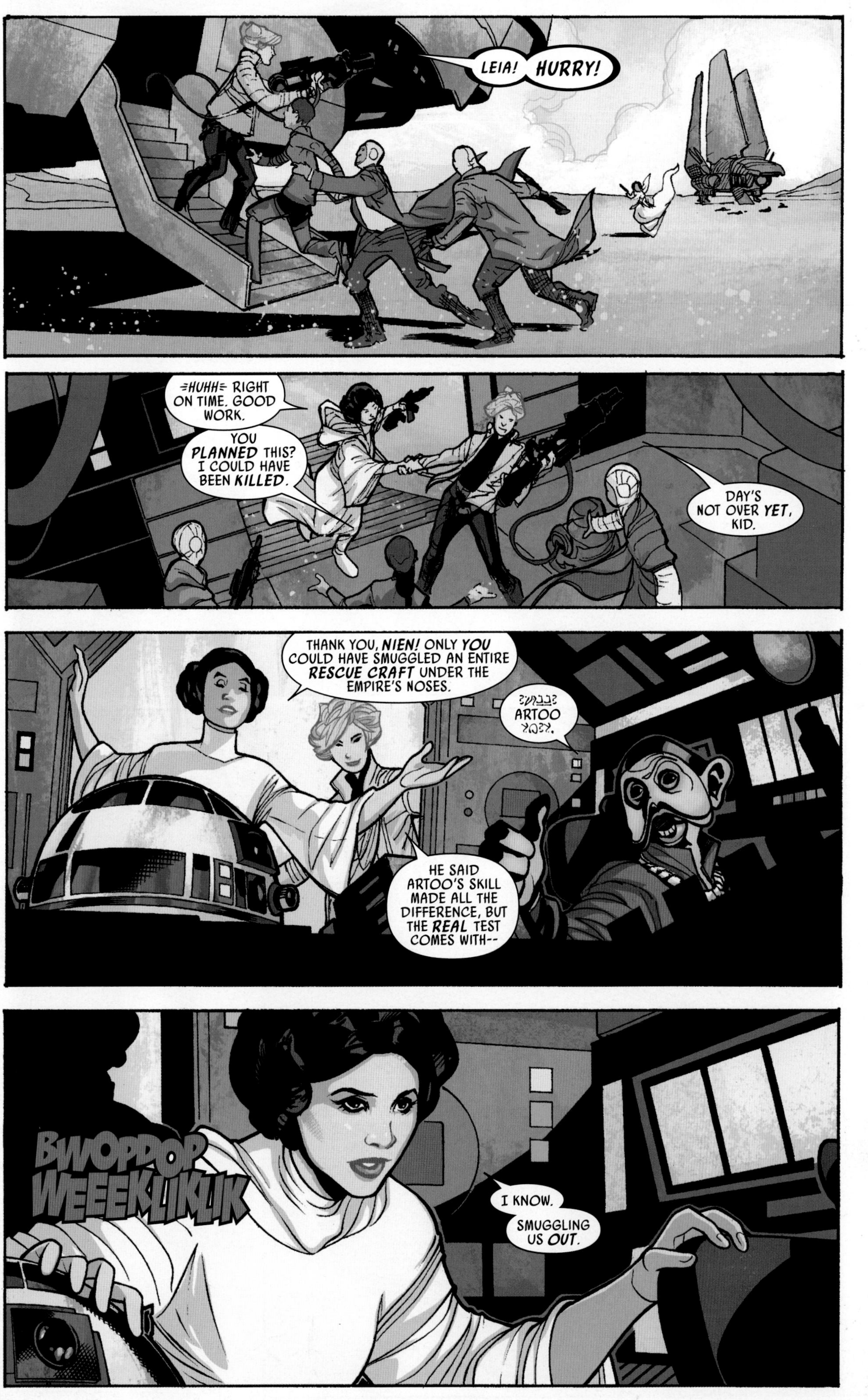
LEIA! HURRY!
=HUHH= RIGHT ON TIME. GOOD WORK.
YOU PLANNED THIS? I COULD HAVE BEEN KILLED.
DAY'S NOT OVER YET, KID.
THANK YOU, NIEN! ONLY YOU COULD HAVE SMUGGLED AN ENTIRE RESCUE CRAFT UNDER THE EMPIRE'S NOSES.
ARTOO
HE SAID ARTOO'S SKILL MADE ALL THE DIFFERENCE, BUT THE REAL TEST COMES WITH--
BWOPDOP WEEEKLIKLIK
I KNOW.
SMUGGLING US OUT.

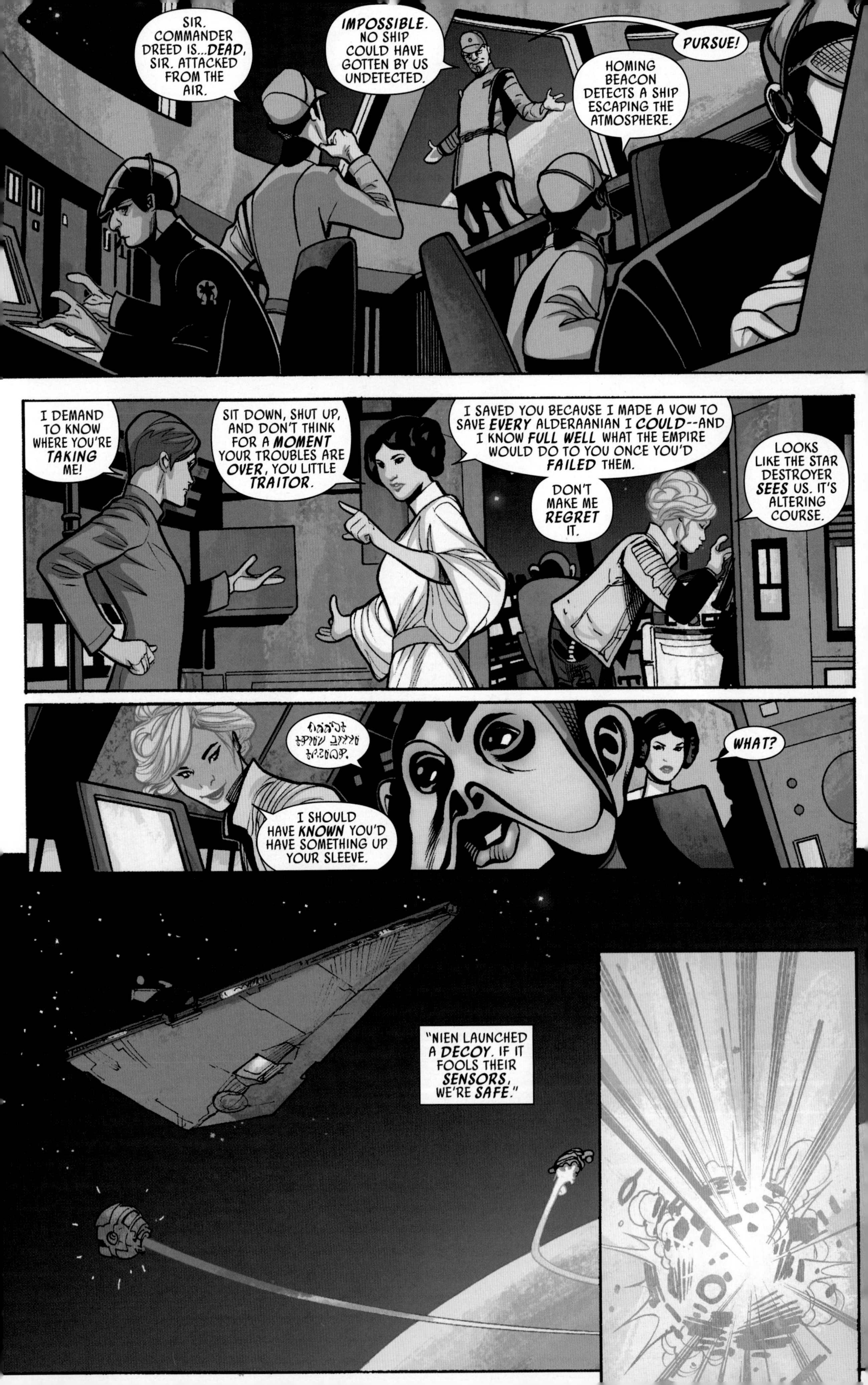

SIR. COMMANDER DREED IS...DEAD, SIR. ATTACKED FROM THE AIR.
IMPOSSIBLE. NO SHIP COULD HAVE GOTTEN BY US UNDETECTED.
HOMING BEACON DETECTS A SHIP ESCAPING THE ATMOSPHERE.
PURSUE!
I DEMAND TO KNOW WHERE YOU'RE TAKING ME!
SIT DOWN, SHUT UP, AND DON'T THINK FOR A MOMENT YOUR TROUBLES ARE OVER, YOU LITTLE TRAITOR.
I SAVED YOU BECAUSE I MADE A VOW TO SAVE EVERY ALDERAANIAN I COULD--AND I KNOW FULL WELL WHAT THE EMPIRE WOULD DO TO YOU ONCE YOU'D FAILED THEM.
DON'T MAKE ME REGRET IT.
LOOKS LIKE THE STAR DESTROYER SEES US. IT'S ALTERING COURSE.
WHAT?
I SHOULD HAVE KNOWN YOU'D HAVE SOMETHING UP YOUR SLEEVE.
"NIEN LAUNCHED A DECOY. IF IT FOOLS THEIR SENSORS, WE'RE SAFE."

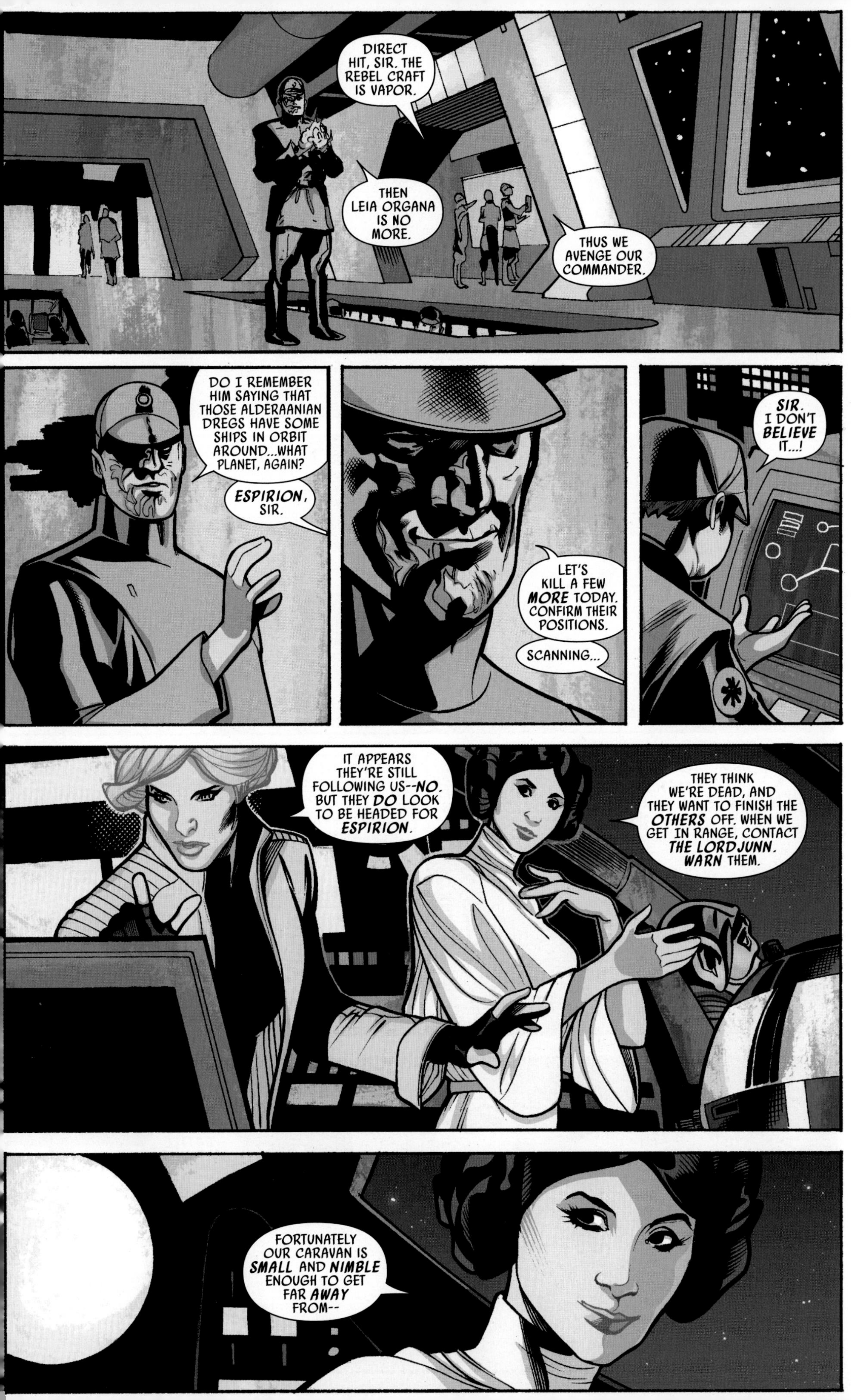
DIRECT HIT, SIR. THE REBEL CRAFT IS VAPOR.
THEN LEIA ORGANA IS NO MORE.
THUS WE AVENGE OUR COMMANDER.
DO I REMEMBER HIM SAYING THAT THOSE ALDERAANIAN DREGS HAVE SOME SHIPS IN ORBIT AROUND...WHAT PLANET, AGAIN?
ESPIRION, SIR.
LET'S KILL A FEW MORE TODAY. CONFIRM THEIR POSITIONS.
SCANNING...
SIR. I DON'T BELIEVE IT...!
IT APPEARS THEY'RE STILL FOLLOWING US--NO. BUT THEY DO LOOK TO BE HEADED FOR ESPIRION.
THEY THINK WE'RE DEAD, AND THEY WANT TO FINISH THE OTHERS OFF. WHEN WE GET IN RANGE, CONTACT THE LORD JUNN. WARN THEM.
FORTUNATELY OUR CARAVAN IS SMALL AND NIMBLE ENOUGH TO GET FAR AWAY FROM--

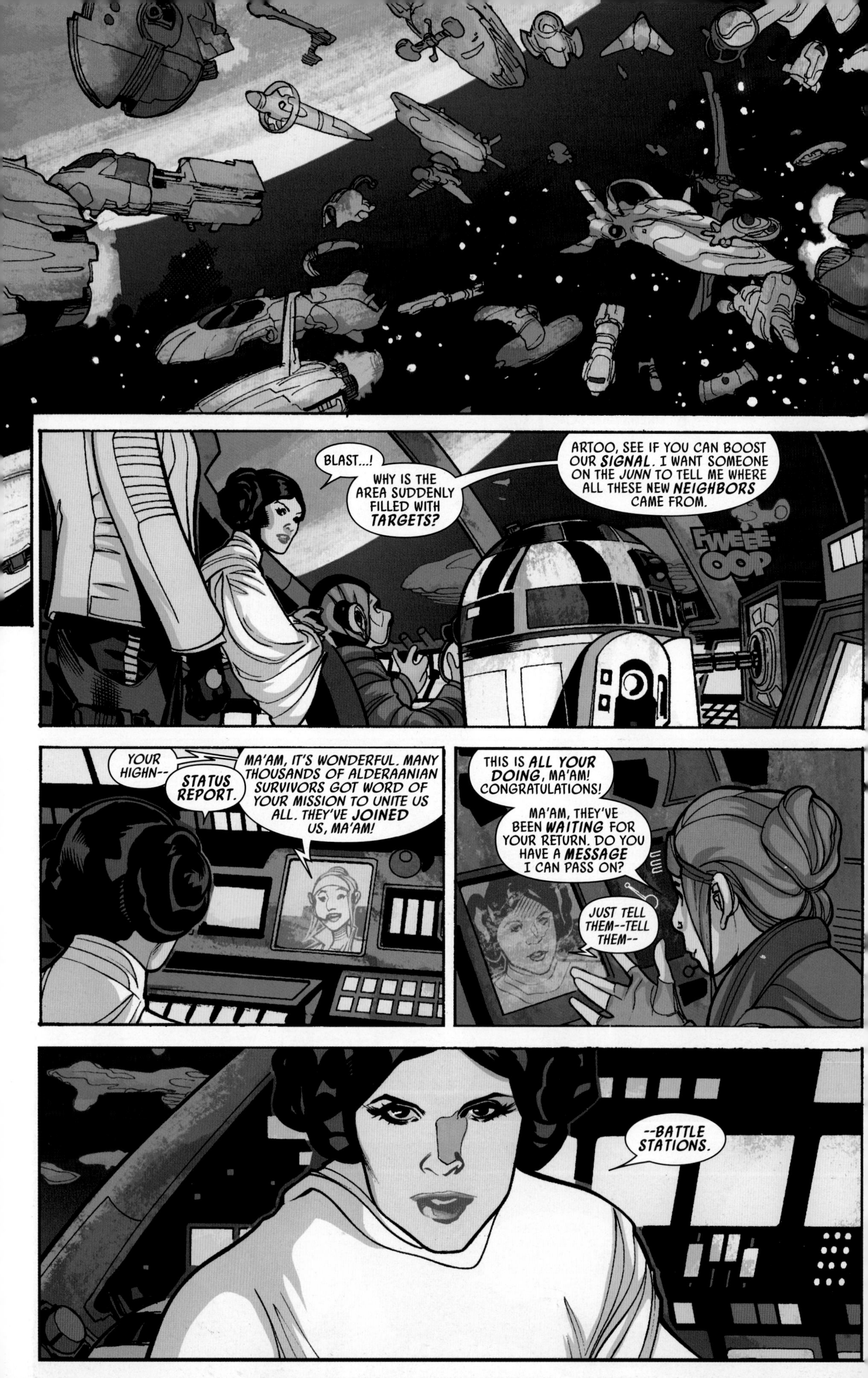

BLAST...!
WHY IS THE AREA SUDDENLY FILLED WITH TARGETS?
ARTOO, SEE IF YOU CAN BOOST OUR SIGNAL. I WANT SOMEONE ON THE JUNN TO TELL ME WHERE ALL THESE NEW NEIGHBORS CAME FROM.
FWEEE-OOP
YOUR HIGHN--
STATUS REPORT.
MA'AM, IT'S WONDERFUL. MANY THOUSANDS OF ALDERAANIAN SURVIVORS GOT WORD OF YOUR MISSION TO UNITE US ALL. THEY'VE JOINED US, MA'AM!
THIS IS ALL YOUR DOING, MA'AM! CONGRATULATIONS!
MA'AM, THEY'VE BEEN WAITING FOR YOUR RETURN. DO YOU HAVE A MESSAGE I CAN PASS ON?
JUST TELL THEM--TELL THEM--
--BATTLE STATIONS.

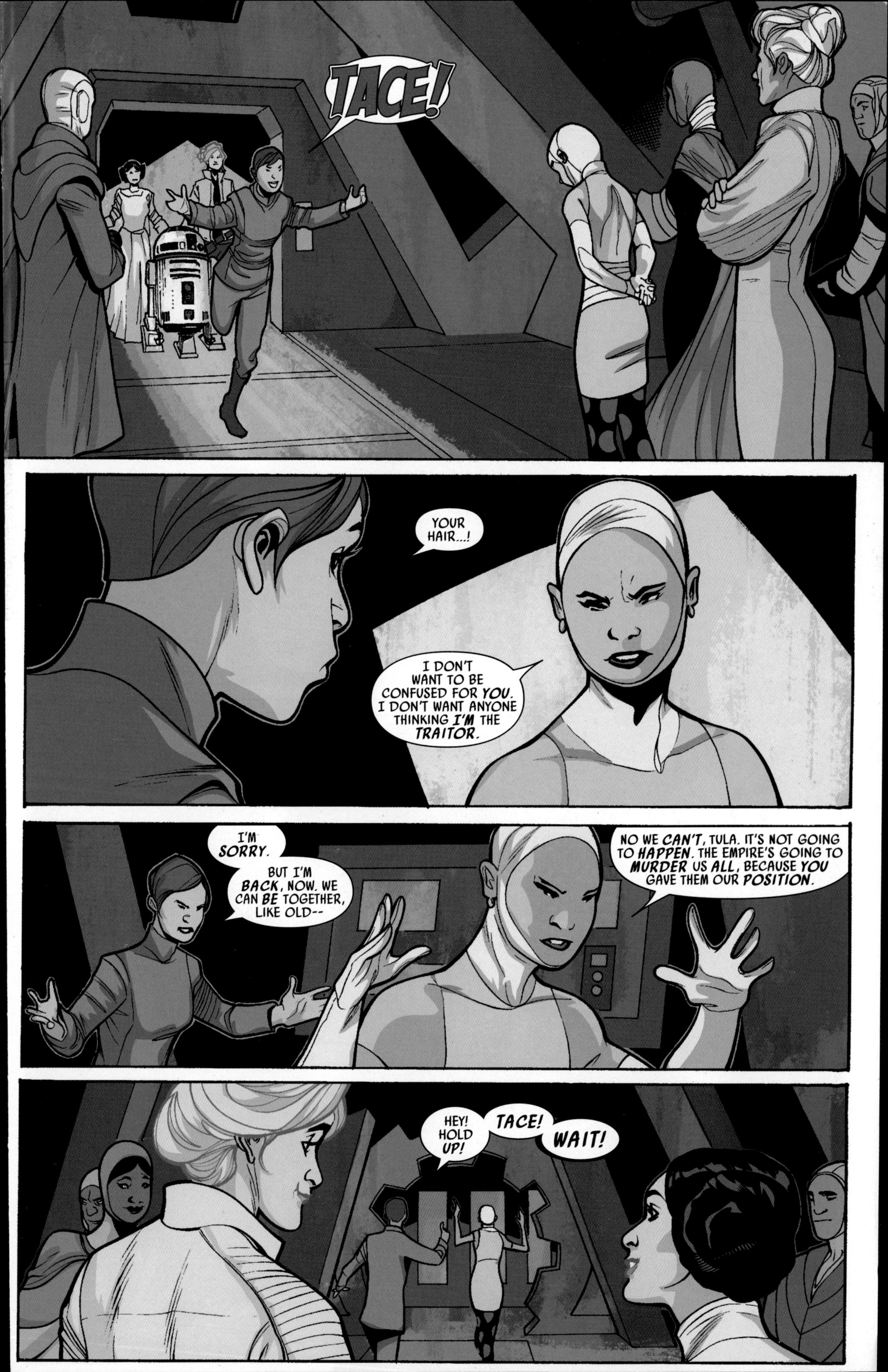
TACE!
YOUR HAIR...!
I DON'T WANT TO BE CONFUSED FOR YOU. I DON'T WANT ANYONE THINKING I'M THE TRAITOR.
I'M SORRY.
BUT I'M BACK, NOW. WE CAN BE TOGETHER, LIKE OLD--
NO WE CAN'T, TULA. IT'S NOT GOING TO HAPPEN. THE EMPIRE'S GOING TO MURDER US ALL, BECAUSE YOU GAVE THEM OUR POSITION.
HEY! HOLD UP!
TACE!
WAIT!

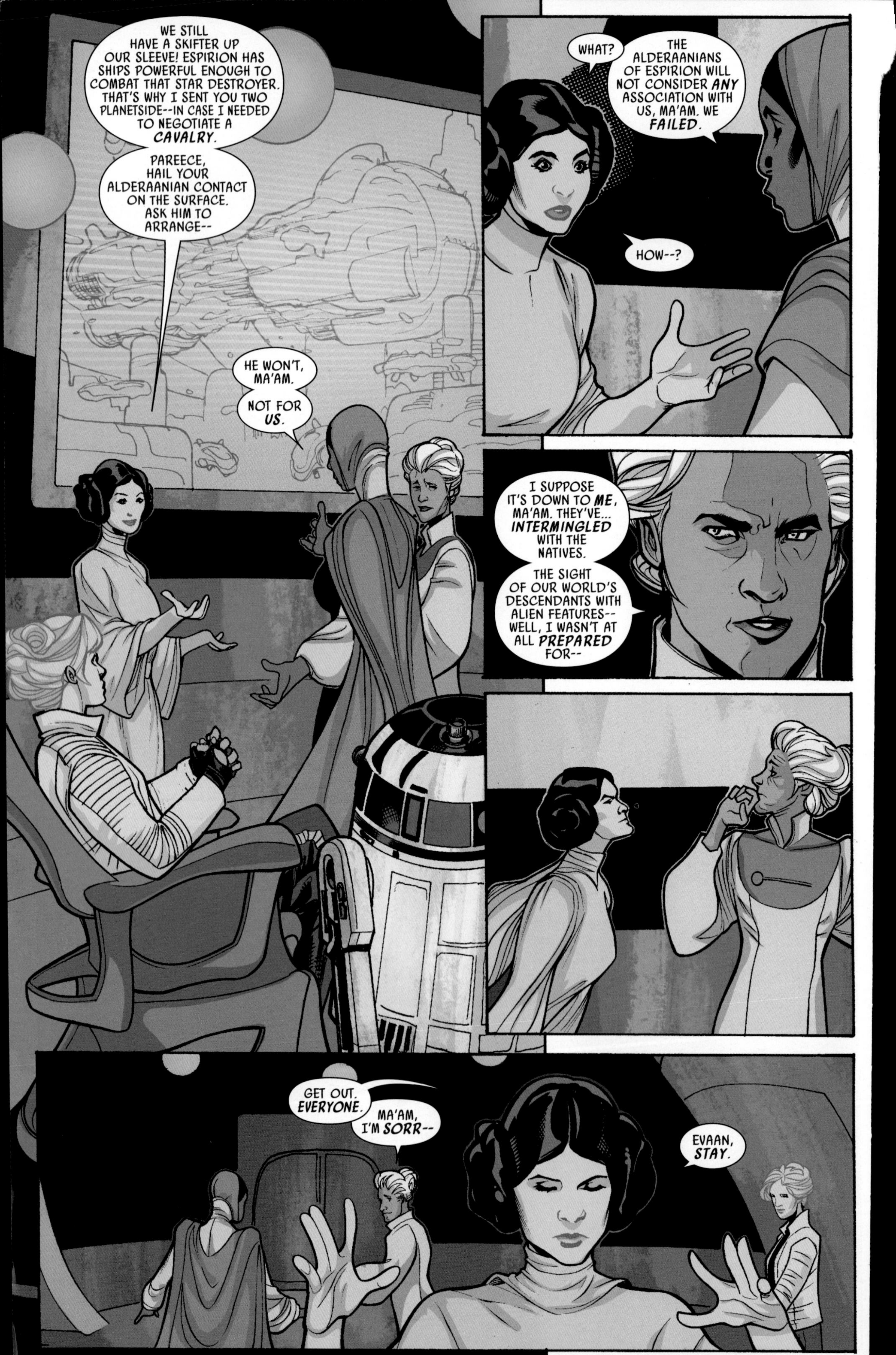
WE STILL HAVE A SKIFTER UP OUR SLEEVE! ESPIRION HAS SHIPS POWERFUL ENOUGH TO COMBAT THAT STAR DESTROYER. THAT'S WHY I SENT YOU TWO PLANETSIDE--IN CASE I NEEDED TO NEGOTIATE A CAVALRY.
PAREECE, HAIL YOUR ALDERAANIAN CONTACT ON THE SURFACE. ASK HIM TO ARRANGE--
HE WON'T, MA'AM.
NOT FOR US.
WHAT?
THE ALDERAANIANS OF ESPIRION WILL NOT CONSIDER ANY ASSOCIATION WITH US, MA'AM. WE FAILED.
HOW--?
I SUPPOSE IT'S DOWN TO ME, MA'AM. THEY'VE... INTERMINGLED WITH THE NATIVES.
THE SIGHT OF OUR WORLD'S DESCENDANTS WITH ALIEN FEATURES--WELL, I WASN'T AT ALL PREPARED FOR--
GET OUT. EVERYONE.
MA'AM, I'M SORR--
EVAAN, STAY.

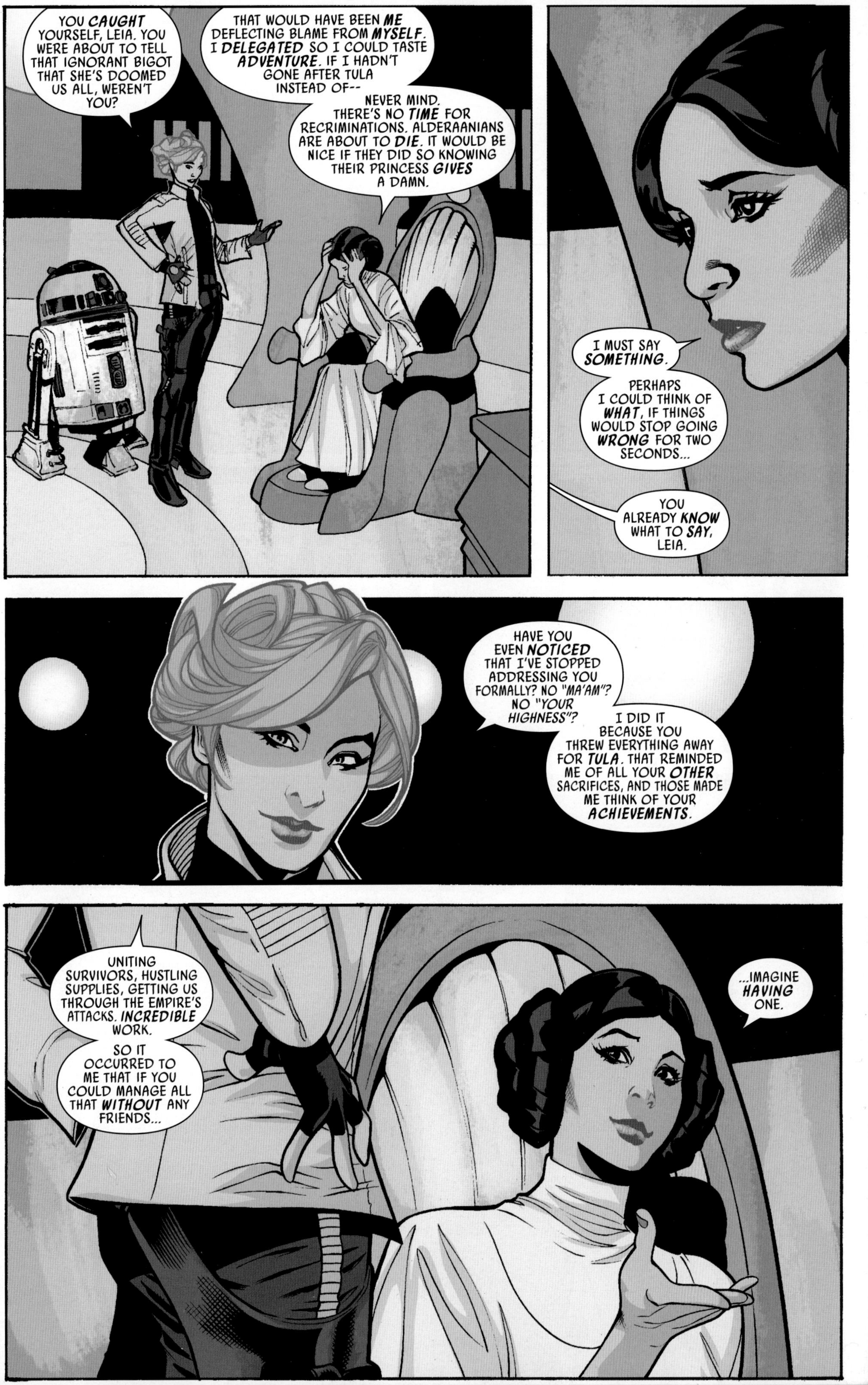

YOU CAUGHT YOURSELF, LEIA. YOU WERE ABOUT TO TELL THAT IGNORANT BIGOT THAT SHE'S DOOMED US ALL, WEREN'T YOU?
THAT WOULD HAVE BEEN ME DEFLECTING BLAME FROM MYSELF. I DELEGATED SO I COULD TASTE ADVENTURE. IF I HADN'T GONE AFTER TULA INSTEAD OF--
NEVER MIND. THERE'S NO TIME FOR RECRIMINATIONS. ALDERAANIANS ARE ABOUT TO DIE. IT WOULD BE NICE IF THEY DID SO KNOWING THEIR PRINCESS GIVES A DAMN.
I MUST SAY SOMETHING.
PERHAPS I COULD THINK OF WHAT, IF THINGS WOULD STOP GOING WRONG FOR TWO SECONDS...
YOU ALREADY KNOW WHAT TO SAY, LEIA.
HAVE YOU EVEN NOTICED THAT I'VE STOPPED ADDRESSING YOU FORMALLY? NO "MA'AM"? NO "YOUR HIGHNESS"?
I DID IT BECAUSE YOU THREW EVERYTHING AWAY FOR TULA. THAT REMINDED ME OF ALL YOUR OTHER SACRIFICES, AND THOSE MADE ME THINK OF YOUR ACHIEVEMENTS.
UNITING SURVIVORS, HUSTLING SUPPLIES, GETTING US THROUGH THE EMPIRE'S ATTACKS. INCREDIBLE WORK.
SO IT OCCURRED TO ME THAT IF YOU COULD MANAGE ALL THAT WITHOUT ANY FRIENDS...
...IMAGINE HAVING ONE.

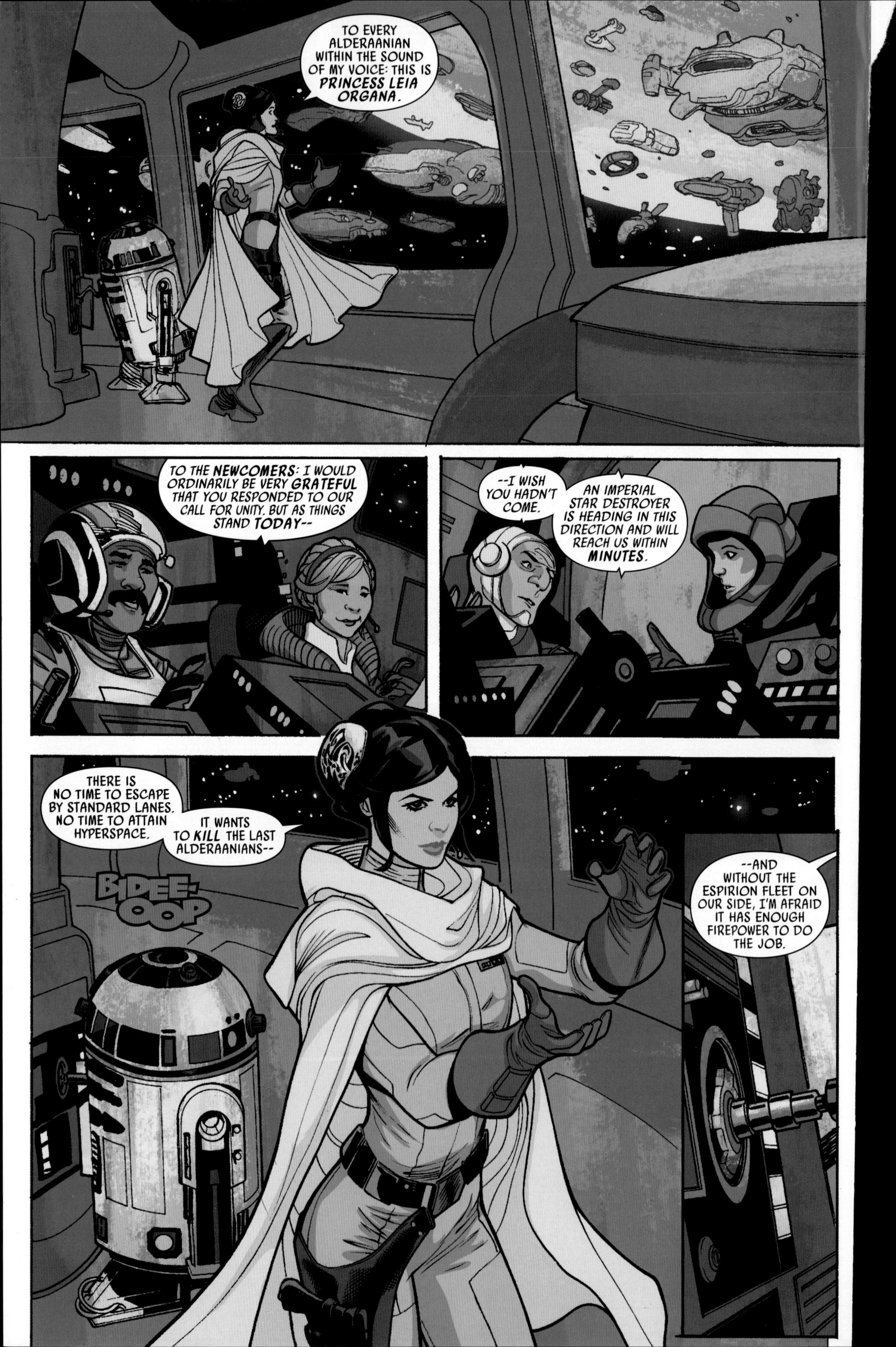
TO EVERY ALDERAANIAN WITHIN THE SOUND OF MY VOICE: THIS IS PRINCESS LEIA ORGANA.
TO THE NEWCOMERS: I WOULD ORDINARILY BE VERY GRATEFUL THAT YOU RESPONDED TO OUR CALL FOR UNITY. BUT AS THINGS STAND TODAY--
--I WISH YOU HADN'T COME.
AN IMPERIAL STAR DESTROYER IS HEADING IN THIS DIRECTION AND WILL REACH US WITHIN MINUTES.
THERE IS NO TIME TO ESCAPE BY STANDARD LANES. NO TIME TO ATTAIN HYPERSPACE.
IT WANTS TO KILL THE LAST ALDERAANIANS--
BIDEE-OOP
--AND WITHOUT THE ESPIRION FLEET ON OUR SIDE, I'M AFRAID IT HAS ENOUGH FIREPOWER TO DO THE JOB.

=SKREE=--AS ENOUGH FIREPOWER TO DO THE JOB.

BUT WE WILL **NOT** SURRENDER.

Espirion.

WE **WILL** DEFEND OURSELVES.

BUT WE WON'T LAND ONE MORE BLOW THAN NECESSARY.

WE ARE NOT OUR ENEMY.

WE ARE ALDERAAN.

WE ANSWER RAGE WITH WISDOM.

WE ANSWER FEAR WITH IMAGINATION.

WE ANSWER WAR WITH HOPE.

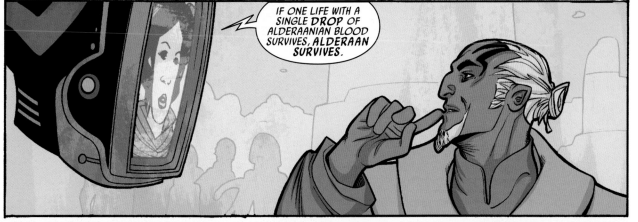

IF ONE LIFE WITH A SINGLE **DROP** OF ALDERAANIAN BLOOD SURVIVES, **ALDERAAN SURVIVES.**

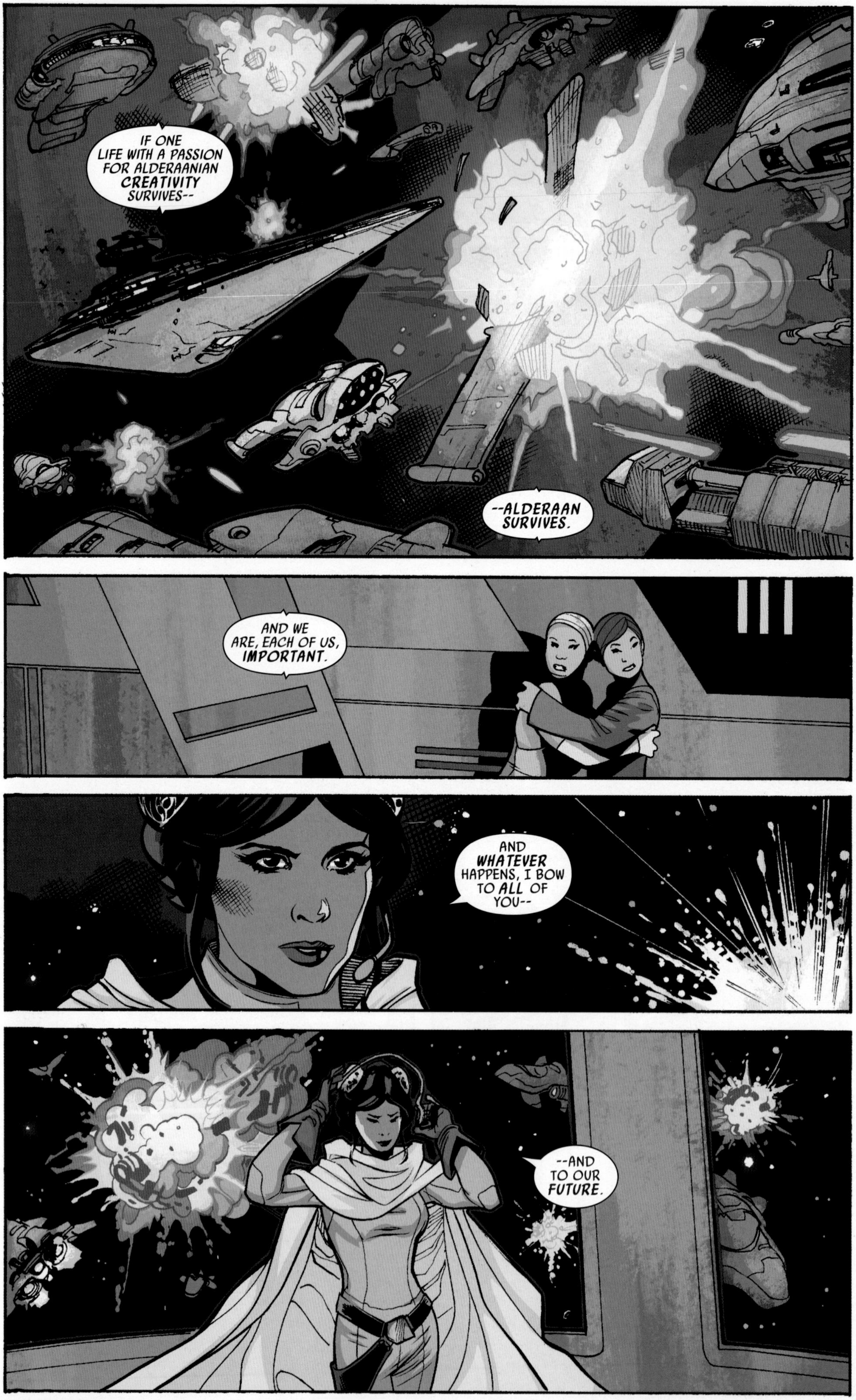
IF ONE LIFE WITH A PASSION FOR ALDERAANIAN CREATIVITY SURVIVES--
--ALDERAAN SURVIVES.
AND WE ARE, EACH OF US, IMPORTANT.
AND WHATEVER HAPPENS, I BOW TO ALL OF YOU--
--AND TO OUR FUTURE.

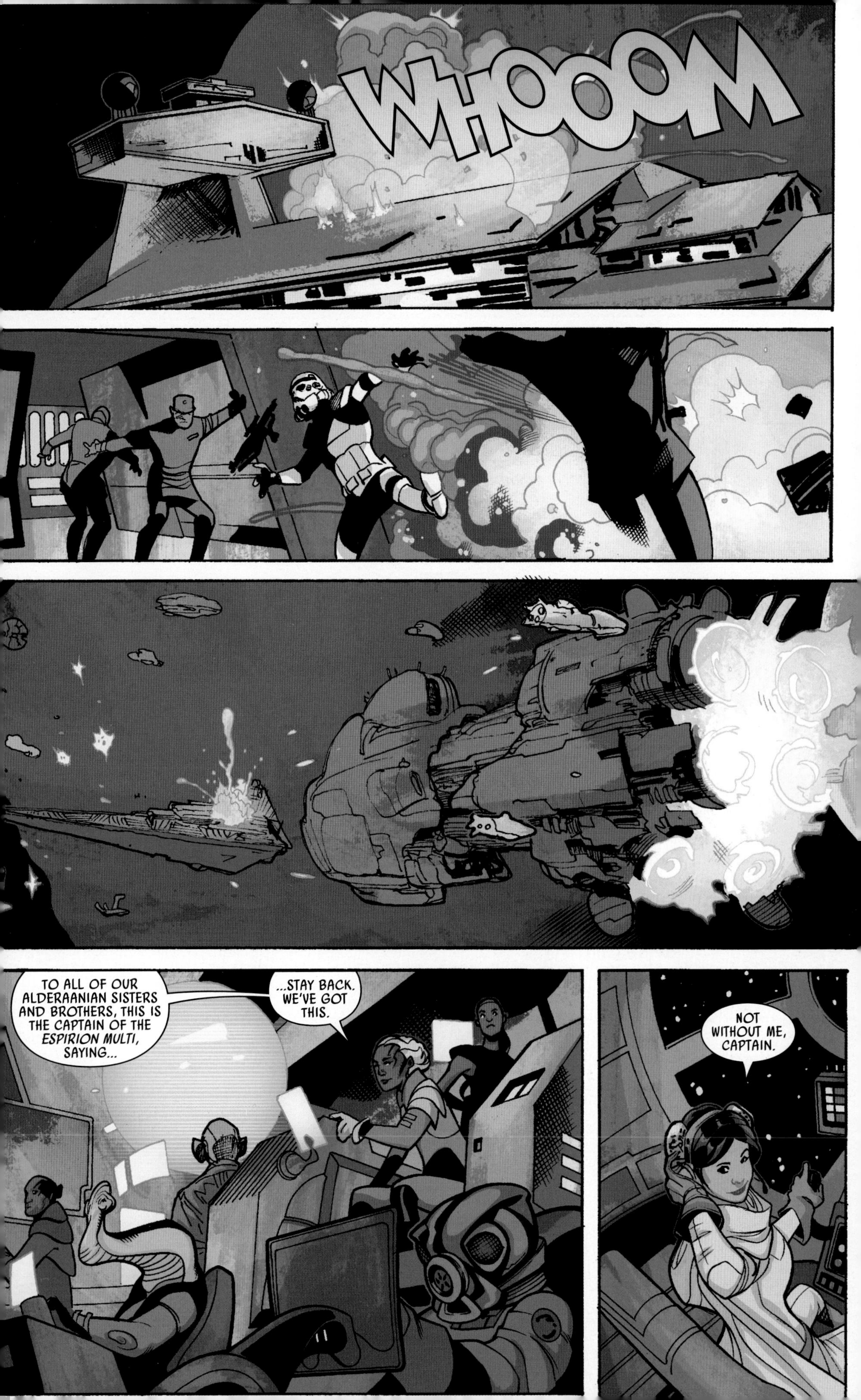
WHOOOM
TO ALL OF OUR ALDERAANIAN SISTERS AND BROTHERS, THIS IS THE CAPTAIN OF THE ESPIRION MULTI, SAYING...
...STAY BACK. WE'VE GOT THIS.
NOT WITHOUT ME, CAPTAIN.

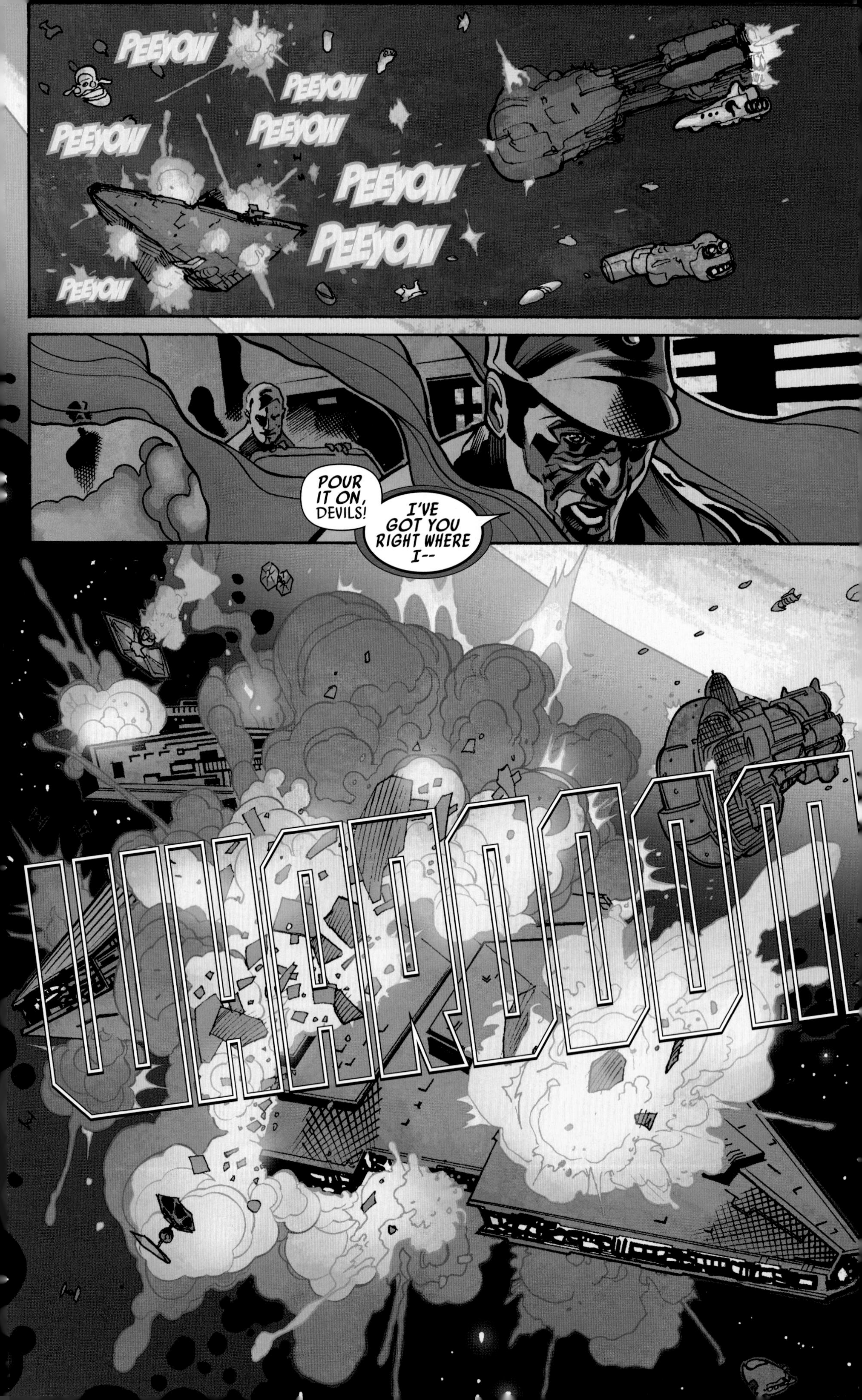
PEEYOW
PEEYOW
PEEYOW
PEEYOW
PEEYOW
PEEYOW
PEEYOW
POUR IT ON, DEVILS!
I'VE GOT YOU RIGHT WHERE I--
WHAROOOM

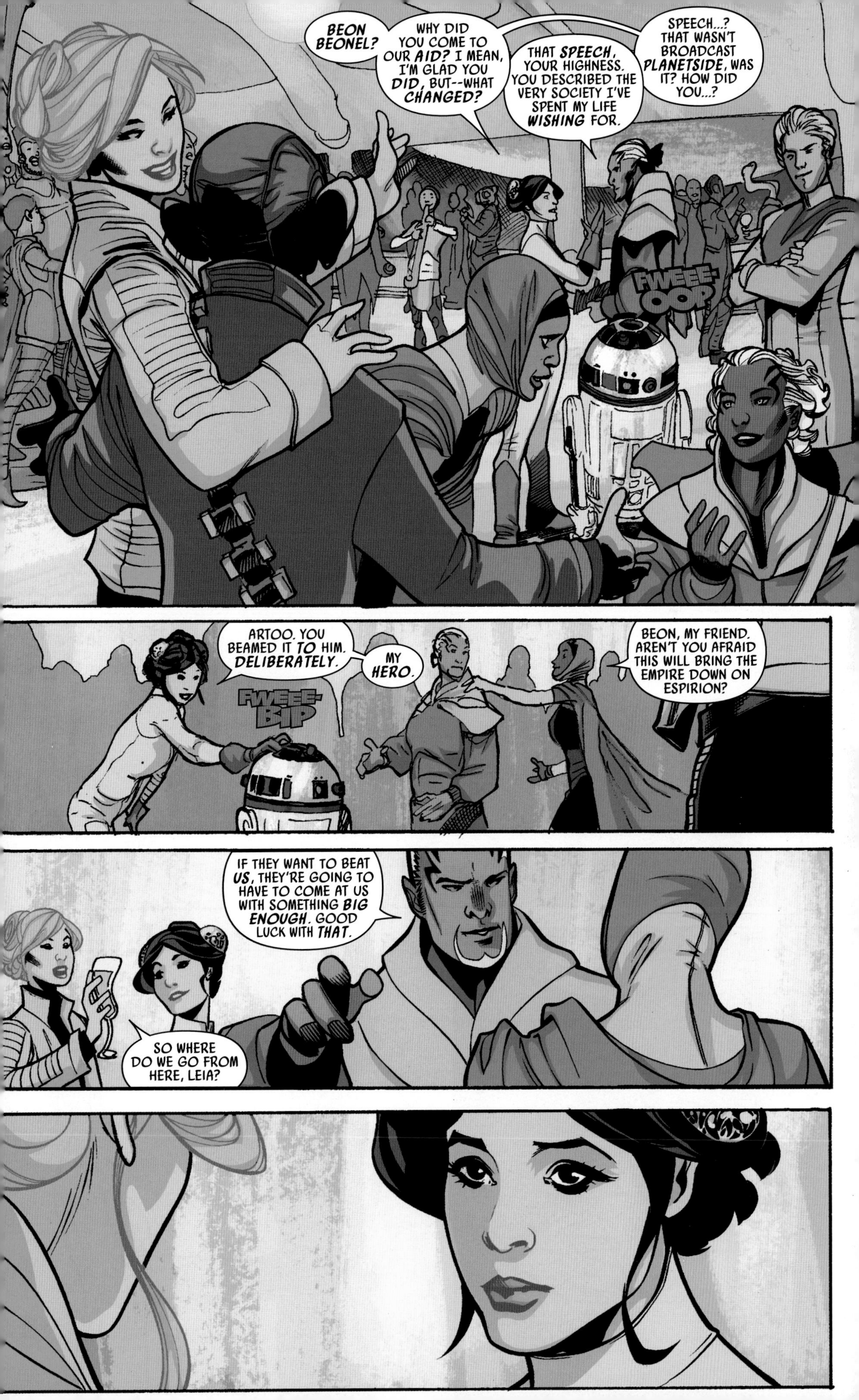
BEON BEONEL?
WHY DID YOU COME TO OUR AID? I MEAN, I'M GLAD YOU DID, BUT--WHAT CHANGED?
THAT SPEECH, YOUR HIGHNESS. YOU DESCRIBED THE VERY SOCIETY I'VE SPENT MY LIFE WISHING FOR.
SPEECH...? THAT WASN'T BROADCAST PLANETSIDE, WAS IT? HOW DID YOU...?
FWEEE-OOP
ARTOO. YOU BEAMED IT TO HIM. DELIBERATELY.
MY HERO.
FWEEE-BIP
BEON, MY FRIEND. AREN'T YOU AFRAID THIS WILL BRING THE EMPIRE DOWN ON ESPIRION?
IF THEY WANT TO BEAT US, THEY'RE GOING TO HAVE TO COME AT US WITH SOMETHING BIG ENOUGH. GOOD LUCK WITH THAT.
SO WHERE DO WE GO FROM HERE, LEIA?

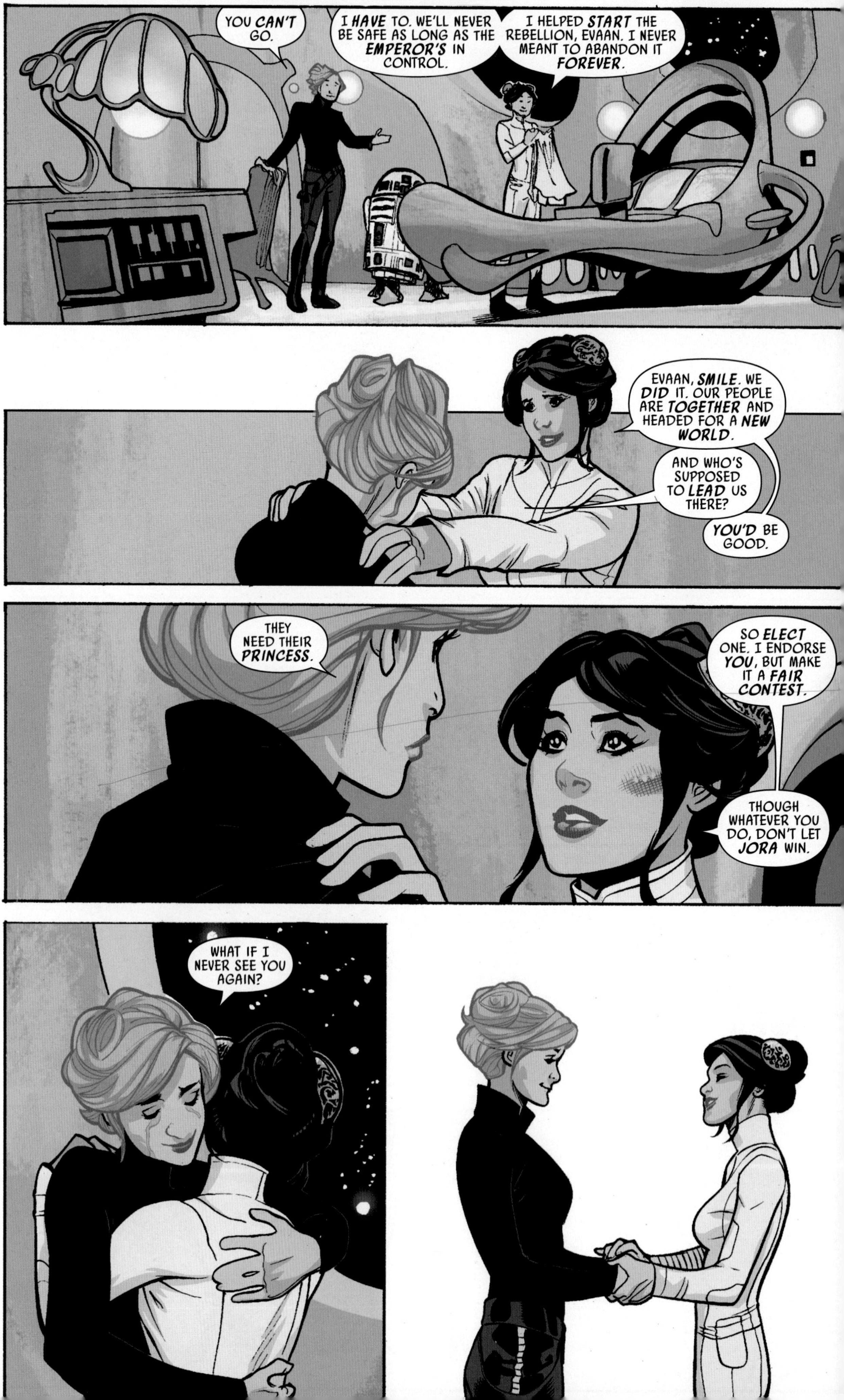
YOU CAN'T GO.
I HAVE TO. WE'LL NEVER BE SAFE AS LONG AS THE EMPEROR'S IN CONTROL.
I HELPED START THE REBELLION, EVAAN. I NEVER MEANT TO ABANDON IT FOREVER.
EVAAN, SMILE. WE DID IT. OUR PEOPLE ARE TOGETHER AND HEADED FOR A NEW WORLD.
AND WHO'S SUPPOSED TO LEAD US THERE?
YOU'D BE GOOD.
THEY NEED THEIR PRINCESS.
SO ELECT ONE. I ENDORSE YOU, BUT MAKE IT A FAIR CONTEST.
THOUGH WHATEVER YOU DO, DON'T LET JORA WIN.
WHAT IF I NEVER SEE YOU AGAIN?

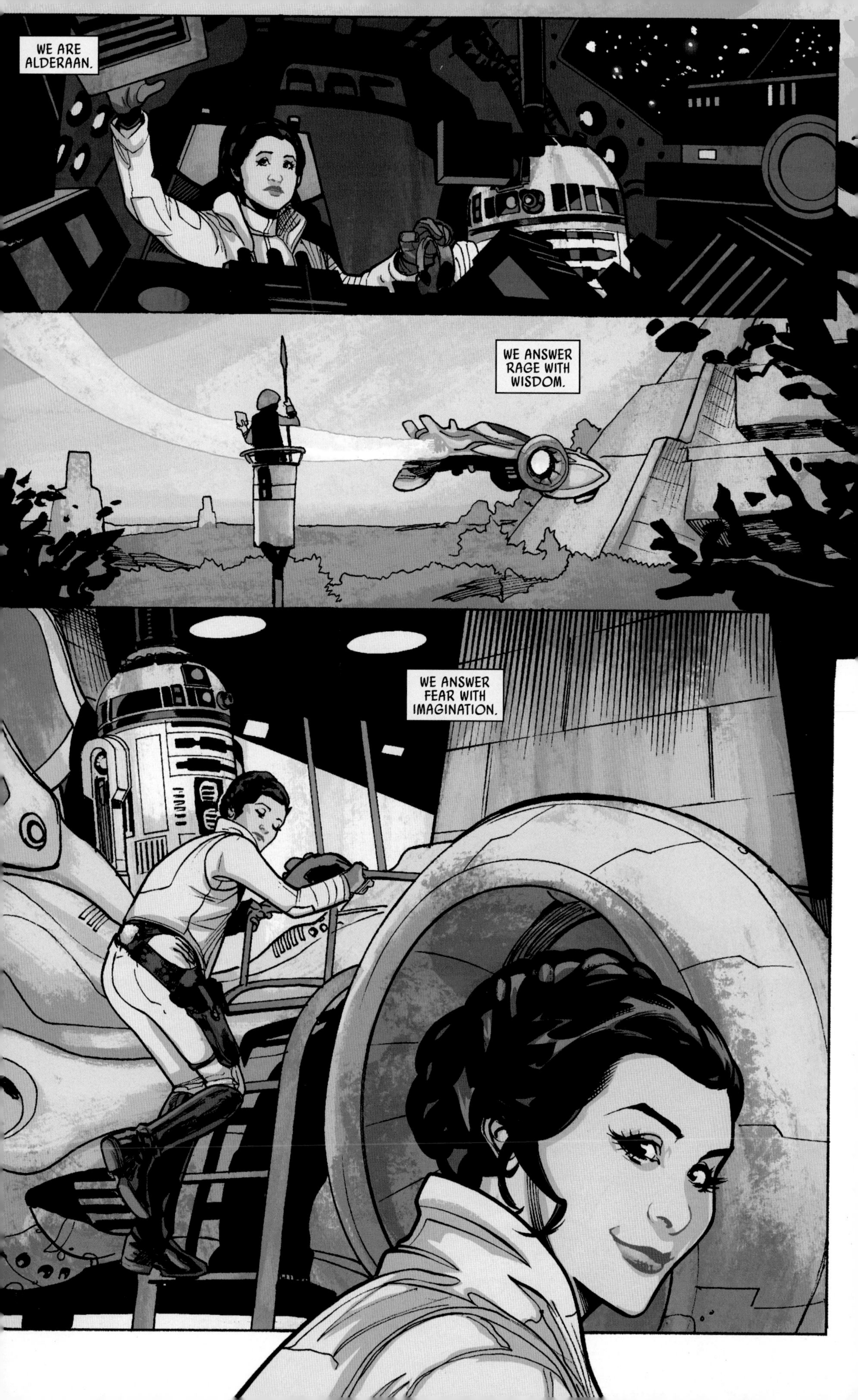
WE ARE ALDERAAN.
WE ANSWER RAGE WITH WISDOM.
WE ANSWER FEAR WITH IMAGINATION.

WE ANSWER *WAR* WITH HOPE.

WE ARE, EACH OF US, **IMPORTANT**.

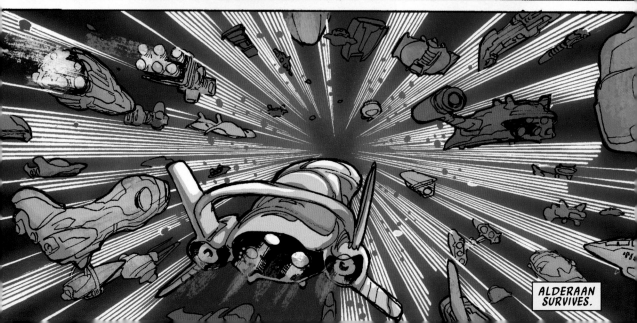

ALDERAAN SURVIVES.

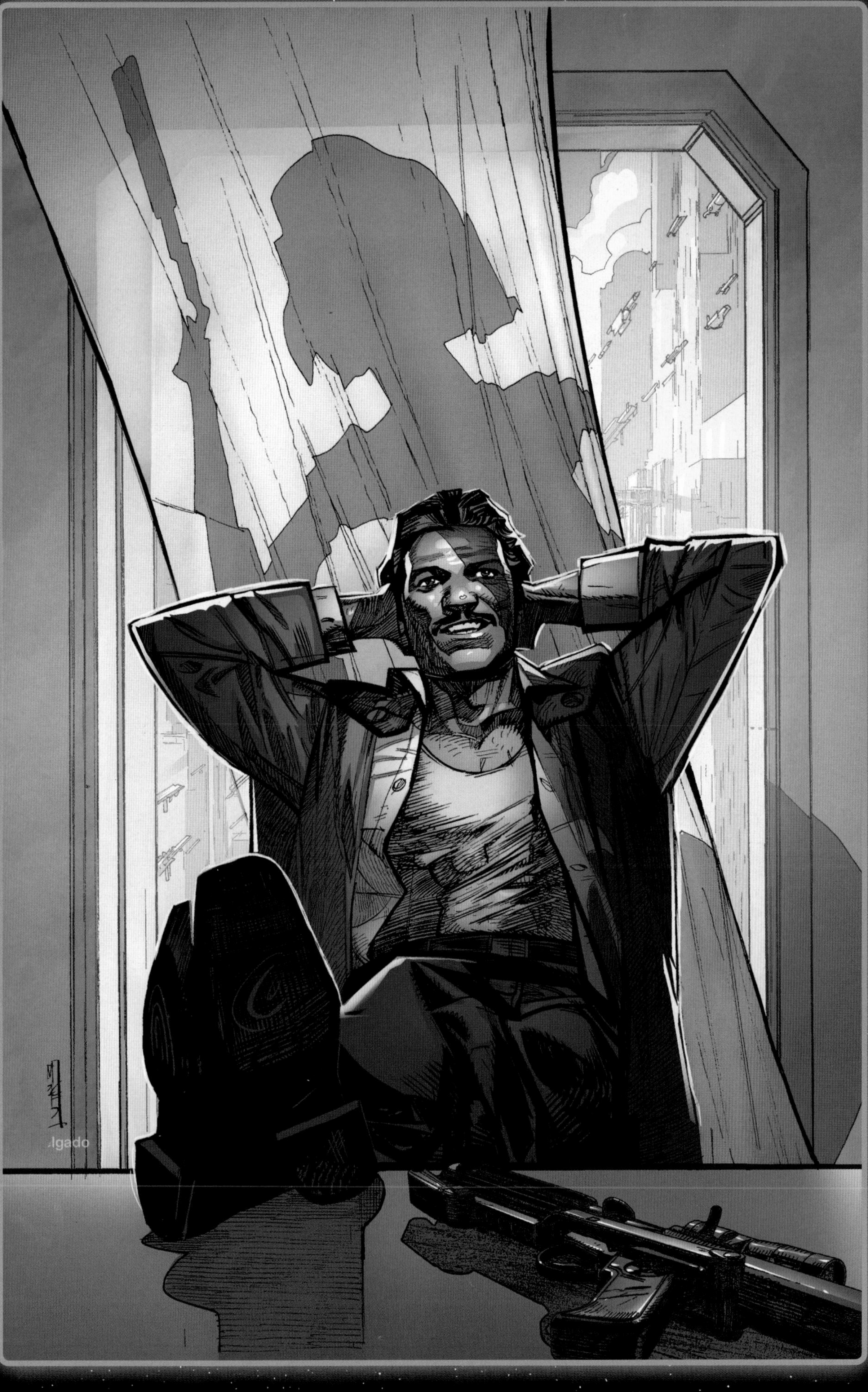

LANDO 1

LANDO

It is a period of scarce opportunity. In a galaxy overrun by an oppressive and evil Galactic Empire, there is little hope for a future free from the Emperor's iron rule.

But with the Imperials distracted by a growing alliance of rebels, smugglers and pirates travel the galaxy for fortunes found only by those daring enough to grasp them.

LANDO CALRISSIAN, a man trying to make his way through an uncaring universe, is willing to bet all he has for a single score – and it begins with the deal of a lifetime....

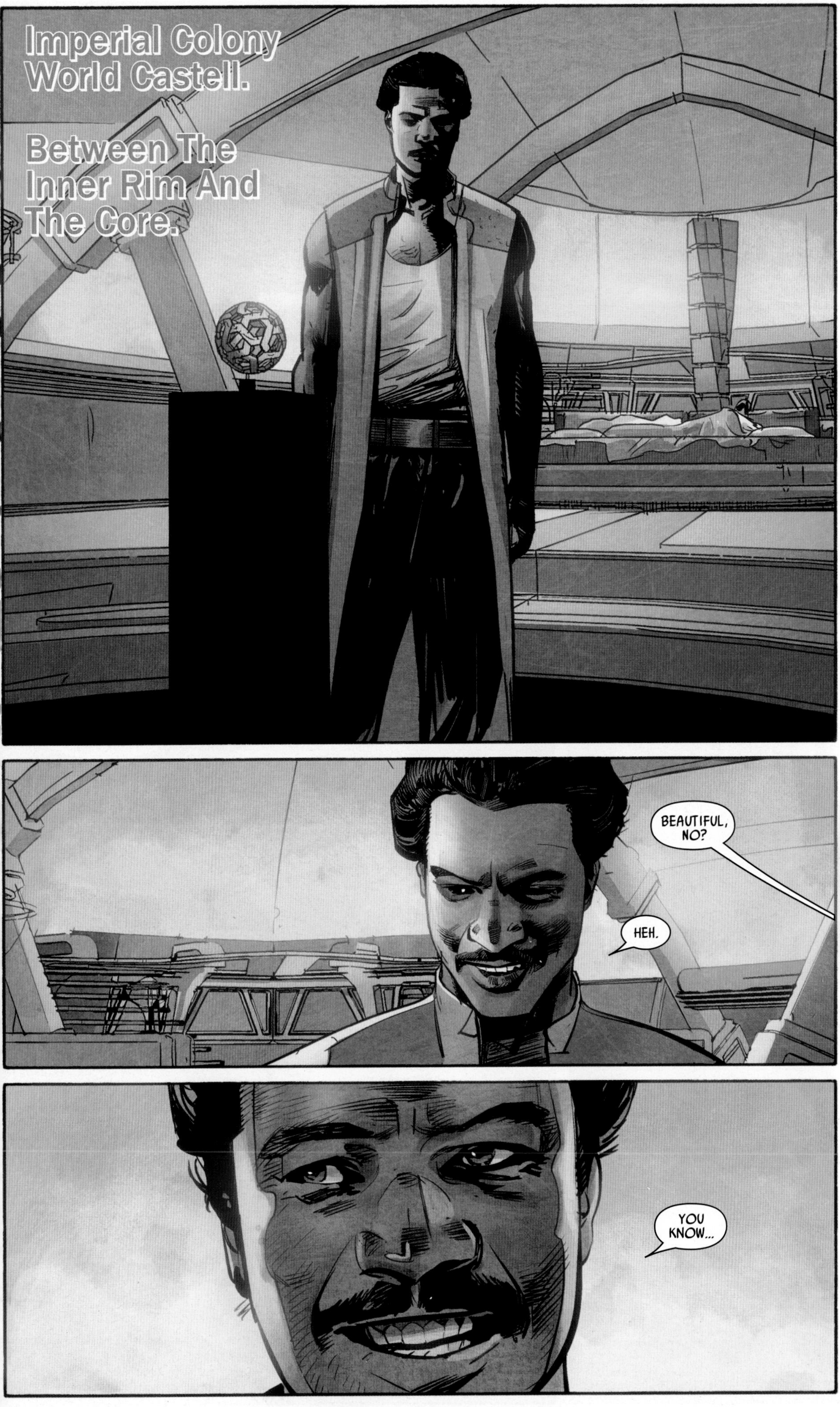
Imperial Colony World Castell.
Between The Inner Rim And The Core.
BEAUTIFUL, NO?
HEH.
YOU KNOW...

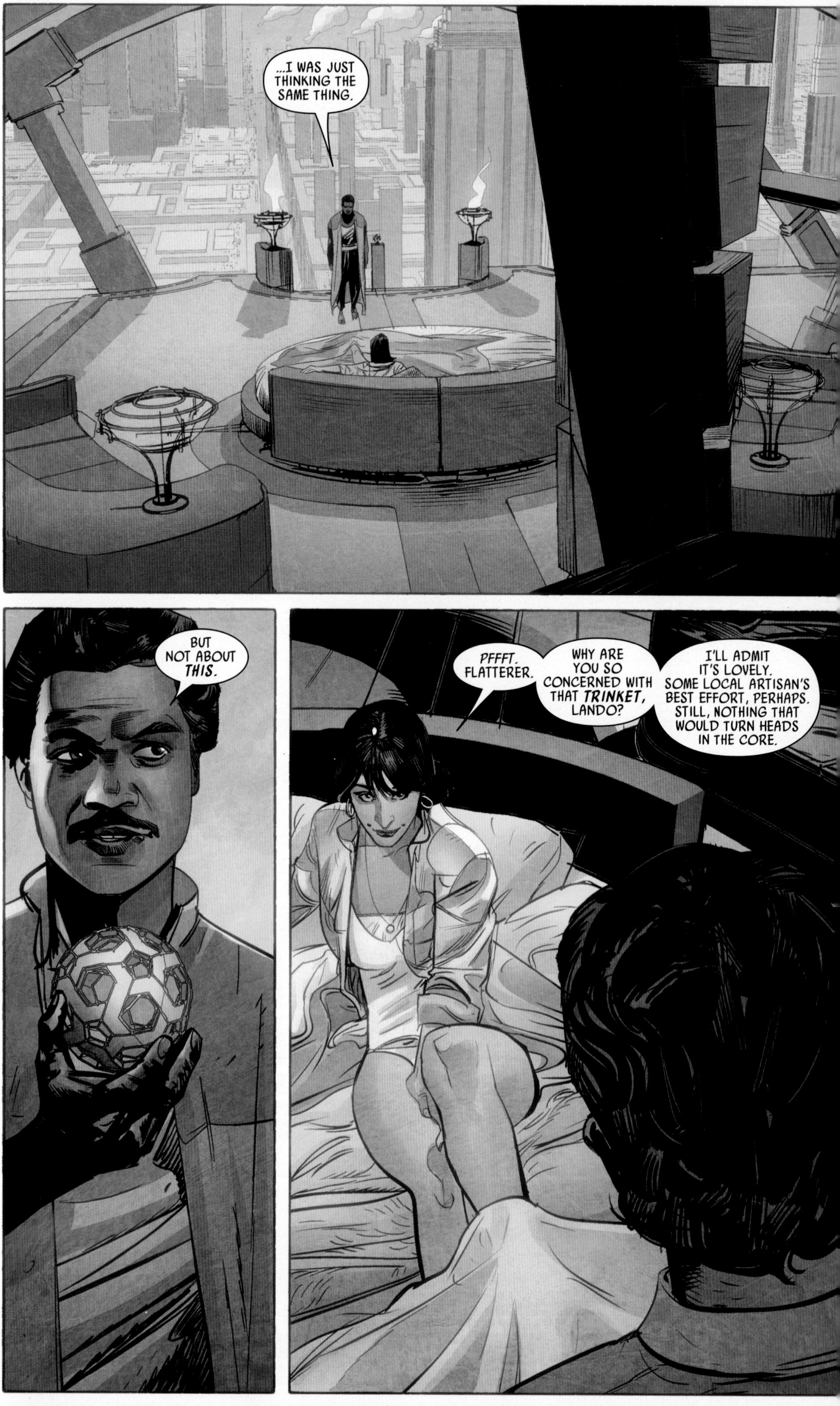
...I WAS JUST THINKING THE SAME THING.
BUT NOT ABOUT THIS.
PFFFT. FLATTERER.
WHY ARE YOU SO CONCERNED WITH THAT TRINKET, LANDO?
I'LL ADMIT IT'S LOVELY. SOME LOCAL ARTISAN'S BEST EFFORT, PERHAPS. STILL, NOTHING THAT WOULD TURN HEADS IN THE CORE.

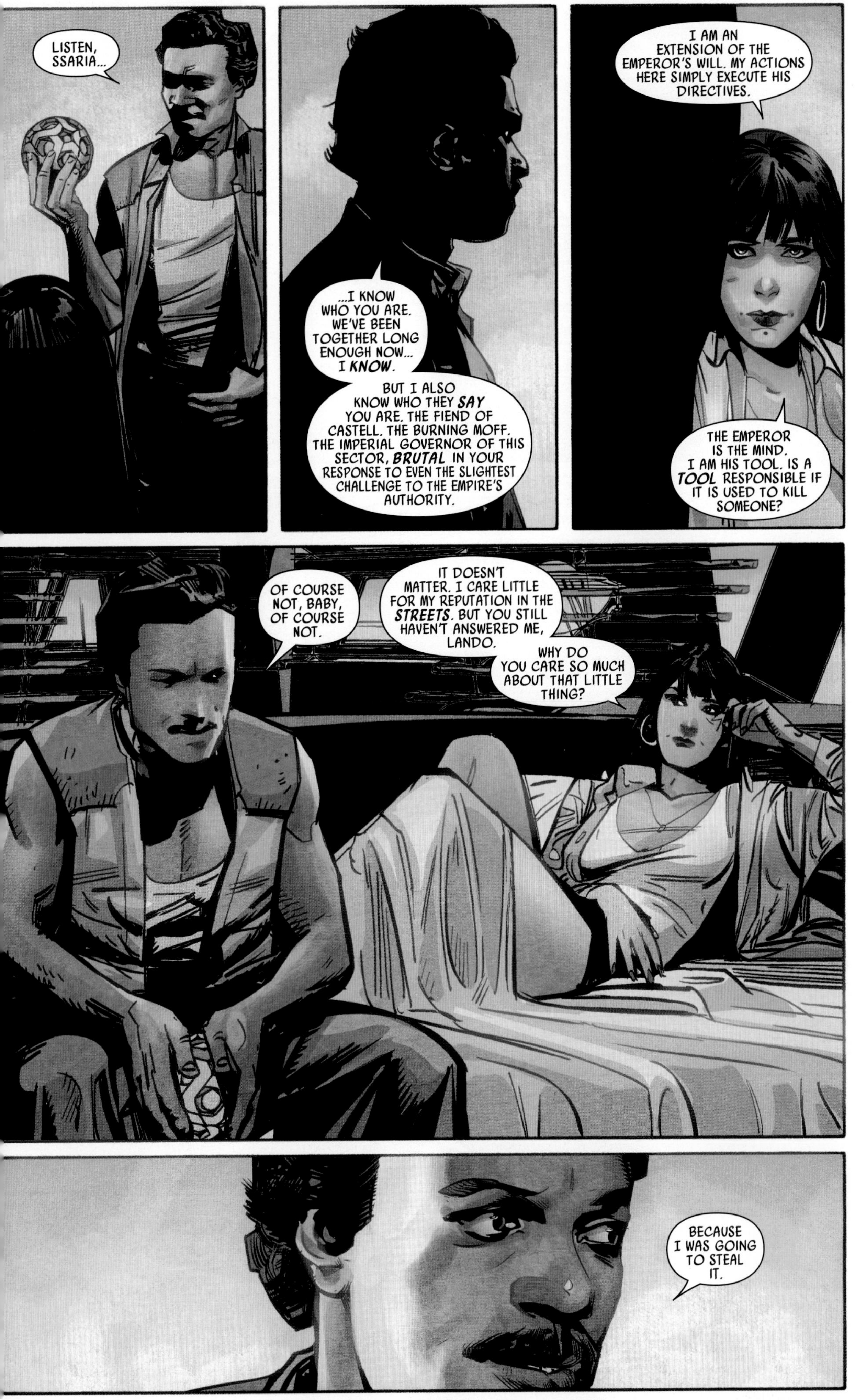
LISTEN, SSARIA...
...I KNOW WHO YOU ARE. WE'VE BEEN TOGETHER LONG ENOUGH NOW... I KNOW.
BUT I ALSO KNOW WHO THEY SAY YOU ARE. THE FIEND OF CASTELL. THE BURNING MOFF. THE IMPERIAL GOVERNOR OF THIS SECTOR, BRUTAL IN YOUR RESPONSE TO EVEN THE SLIGHTEST CHALLENGE TO THE EMPIRE'S AUTHORITY.
I AM AN EXTENSION OF THE EMPEROR'S WILL. MY ACTIONS HERE SIMPLY EXECUTE HIS DIRECTIVES.
THE EMPEROR IS THE MIND. I AM HIS TOOL. IS A TOOL RESPONSIBLE IF IT IS USED TO KILL SOMEONE?
OF COURSE NOT, BABY, OF COURSE NOT.
IT DOESN'T MATTER. I CARE LITTLE FOR MY REPUTATION IN THE STREETS. BUT YOU STILL HAVEN'T ANSWERED ME, LANDO.
WHY DO YOU CARE SO MUCH ABOUT THAT LITTLE THING?
BECAUSE I WAS GOING TO STEAL IT.

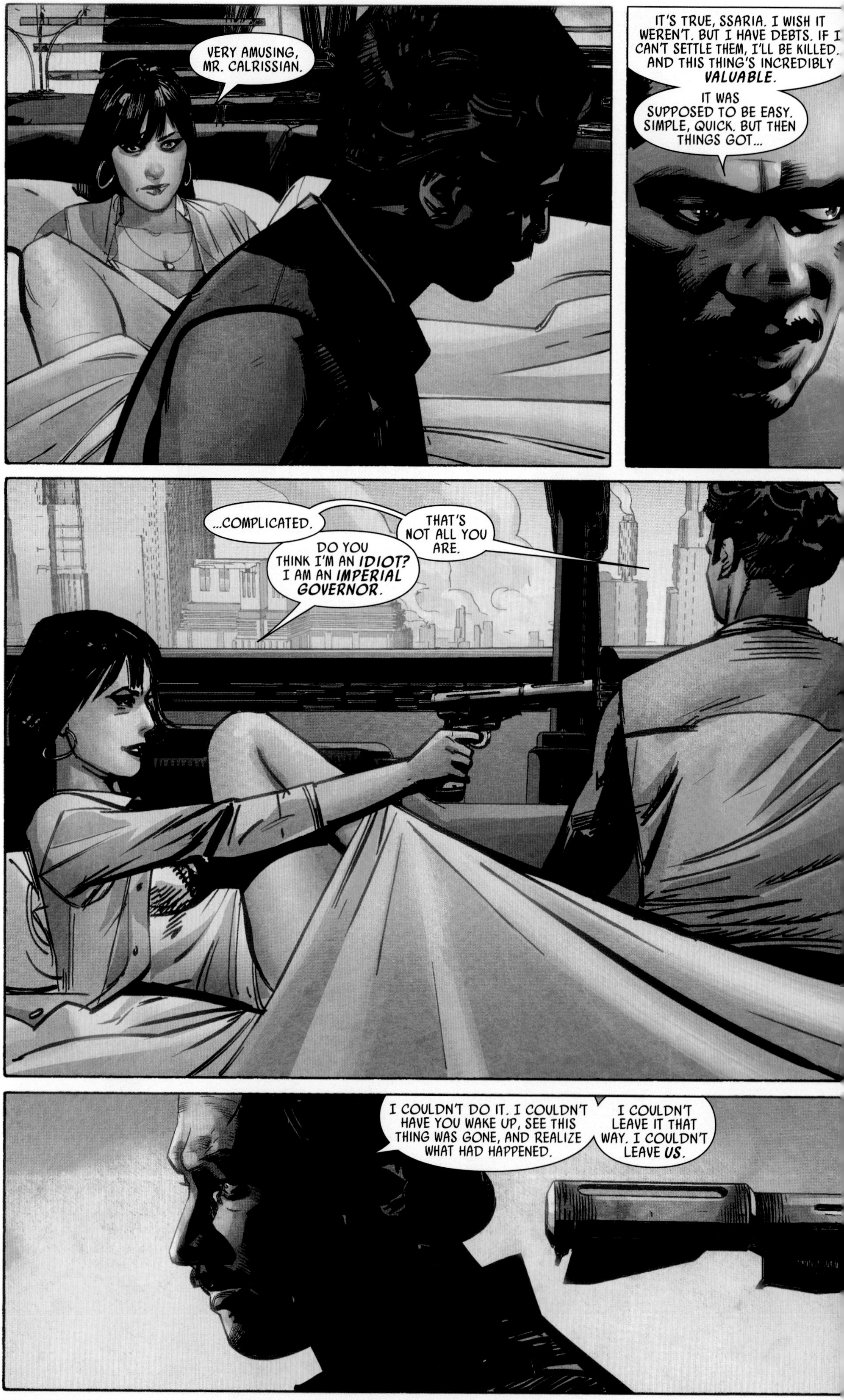
VERY AMUSING, MR. CALRISSIAN.
IT'S TRUE, SSARIA. I WISH IT WEREN'T. BUT I HAVE DEBTS. IF I CAN'T SETTLE THEM, I'LL BE KILLED. AND THIS THING'S INCREDIBLY VALUABLE.
IT WAS SUPPOSED TO BE EASY. SIMPLE, QUICK. BUT THEN THINGS GOT...
...COMPLICATED.
DO YOU THINK I'M AN IDIOT? I AM AN IMPERIAL GOVERNOR.
THAT'S NOT ALL YOU ARE.
I COULDN'T DO IT. I COULDN'T HAVE YOU WAKE UP, SEE THIS THING WAS GONE, AND REALIZE WHAT HAD HAPPENED.
I COULDN'T LEAVE IT THAT WAY. I COULDN'T LEAVE US.

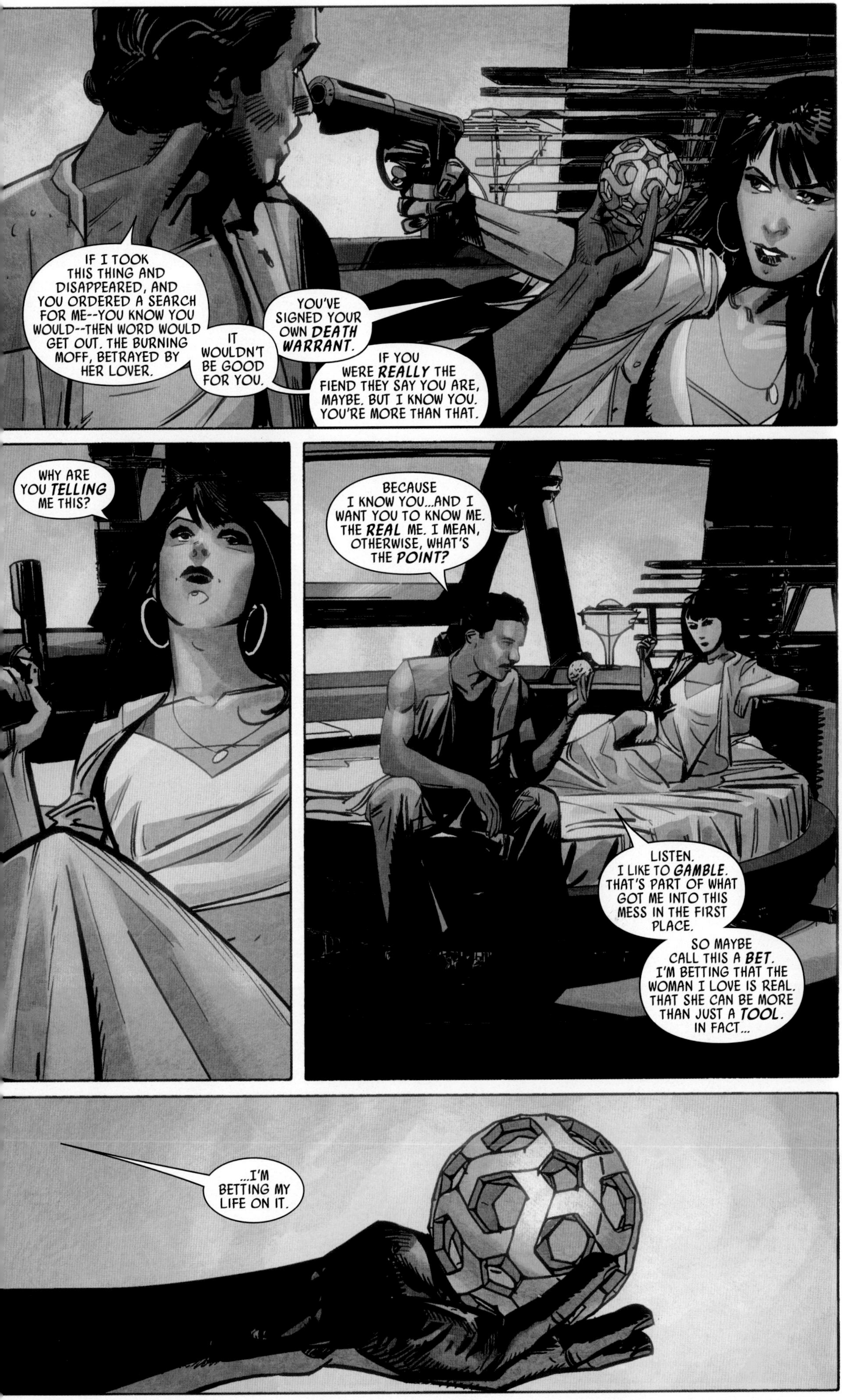
IF I TOOK THIS THING AND DISAPPEARED, AND YOU ORDERED A SEARCH FOR ME--YOU KNOW YOU WOULD--THEN WORD WOULD GET OUT. THE BURNING MOFF, BETRAYED BY HER LOVER.
IT WOULDN'T BE GOOD FOR YOU.
YOU'VE SIGNED YOUR OWN DEATH WARRANT.
IF YOU WERE REALLY THE FIEND THEY SAY YOU ARE, MAYBE. BUT I KNOW YOU. YOU'RE MORE THAN THAT.
WHY ARE YOU TELLING ME THIS?
BECAUSE I KNOW YOU...AND I WANT YOU TO KNOW ME. THE REAL ME. I MEAN, OTHERWISE, WHAT'S THE POINT?
LISTEN. I LIKE TO GAMBLE. THAT'S PART OF WHAT GOT ME INTO THIS MESS IN THE FIRST PLACE.
SO MAYBE CALL THIS A BET. I'M BETTING THAT THE WOMAN I LOVE IS REAL. THAT SHE CAN BE MORE THAN JUST A TOOL. IN FACT...
...I'M BETTING MY LIFE ON IT.

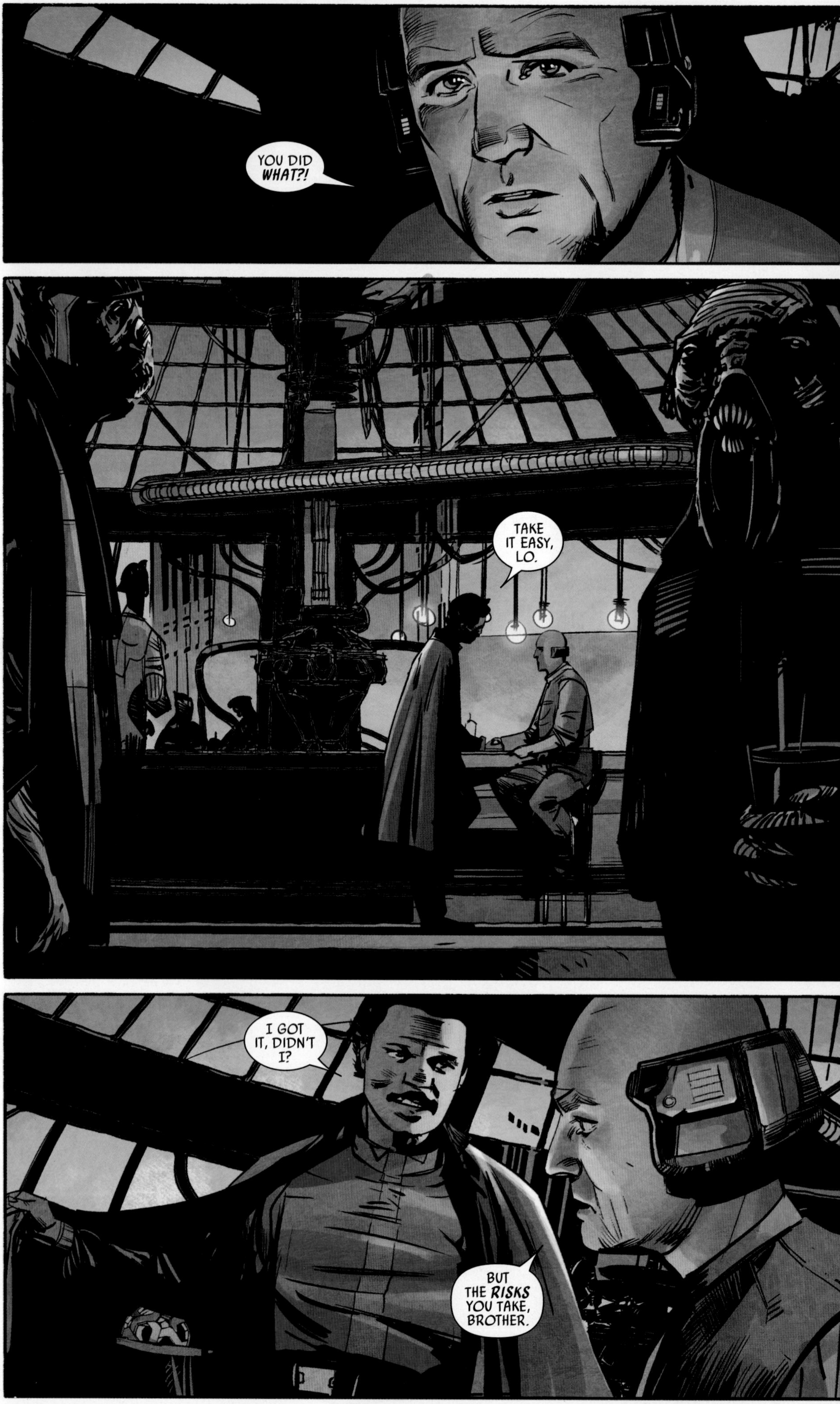
YOU DID WHAT?!
TAKE IT EASY, LO.
I GOT IT, DIDN'T I?
BUT THE RISKS YOU TAKE, BROTHER.

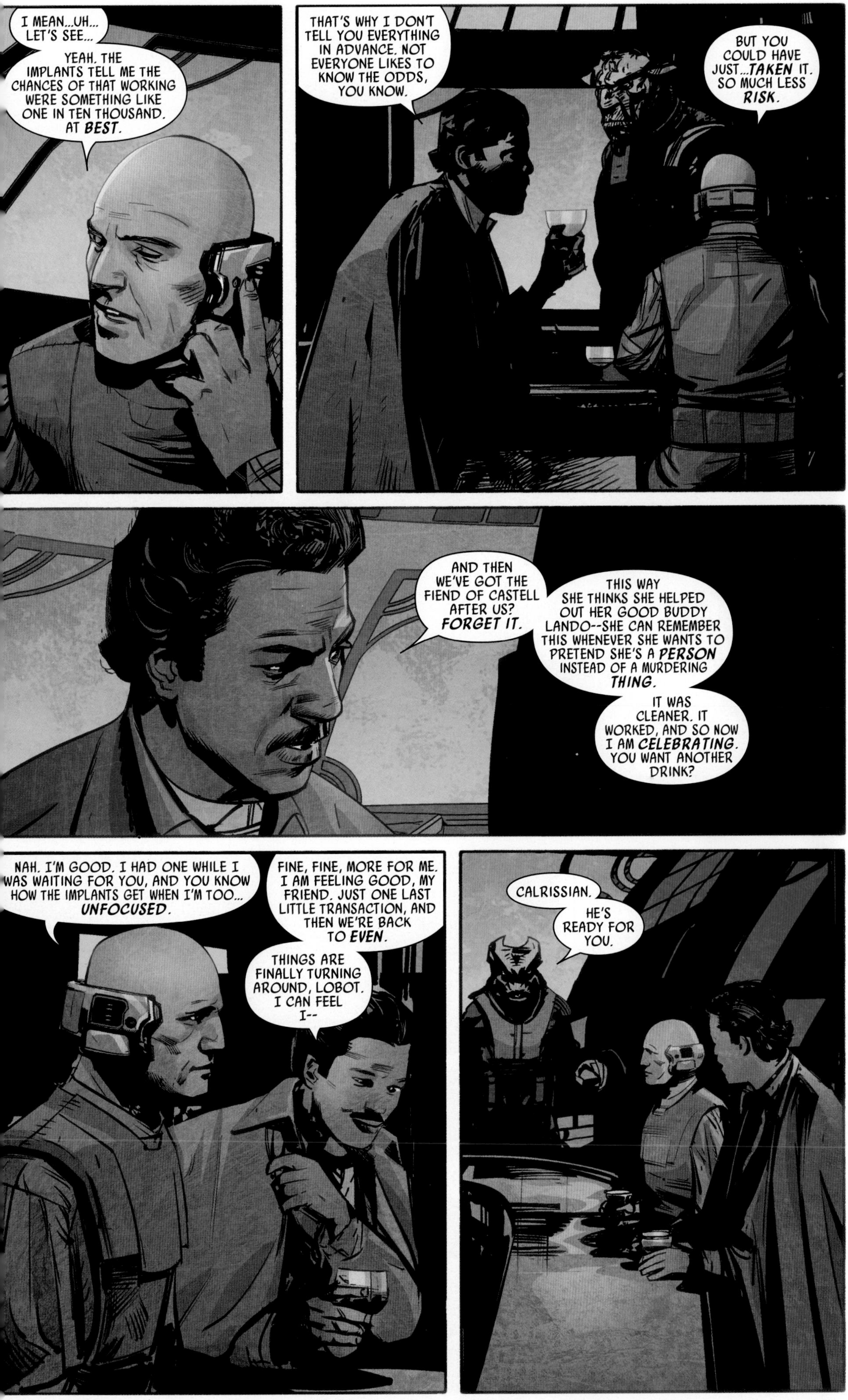
I MEAN...UH... LET'S SEE...
YEAH. THE IMPLANTS TELL ME THE CHANCES OF THAT WORKING WERE SOMETHING LIKE ONE IN TEN THOUSAND. AT *BEST*.
THAT'S WHY I DON'T TELL YOU EVERYTHING IN ADVANCE. NOT EVERYONE LIKES TO KNOW THE ODDS, YOU KNOW.
BUT YOU COULD HAVE JUST...*TAKEN* IT. SO MUCH LESS *RISK*.
AND THEN WE'VE GOT THE FIEND OF CASTELL AFTER US? *FORGET IT.*
THIS WAY SHE THINKS SHE HELPED OUT HER GOOD BUDDY LANDO--SHE CAN REMEMBER THIS WHENEVER SHE WANTS TO PRETEND SHE'S A *PERSON* INSTEAD OF A MURDERING *THING*.
IT WAS CLEANER. IT WORKED, AND SO NOW I AM *CELEBRATING*. YOU WANT ANOTHER DRINK?
NAH. I'M GOOD. I HAD ONE WHILE I WAS WAITING FOR YOU, AND YOU KNOW HOW THE IMPLANTS GET WHEN I'M TOO... *UNFOCUSED*.
FINE, FINE, MORE FOR ME. I AM FEELING GOOD, MY FRIEND. JUST ONE LAST LITTLE TRANSACTION, AND THEN WE'RE BACK TO *EVEN*.
THINGS ARE FINALLY TURNING AROUND, LOBOT. I CAN FEEL I--
CALRISSIAN.
HE'S READY FOR YOU.

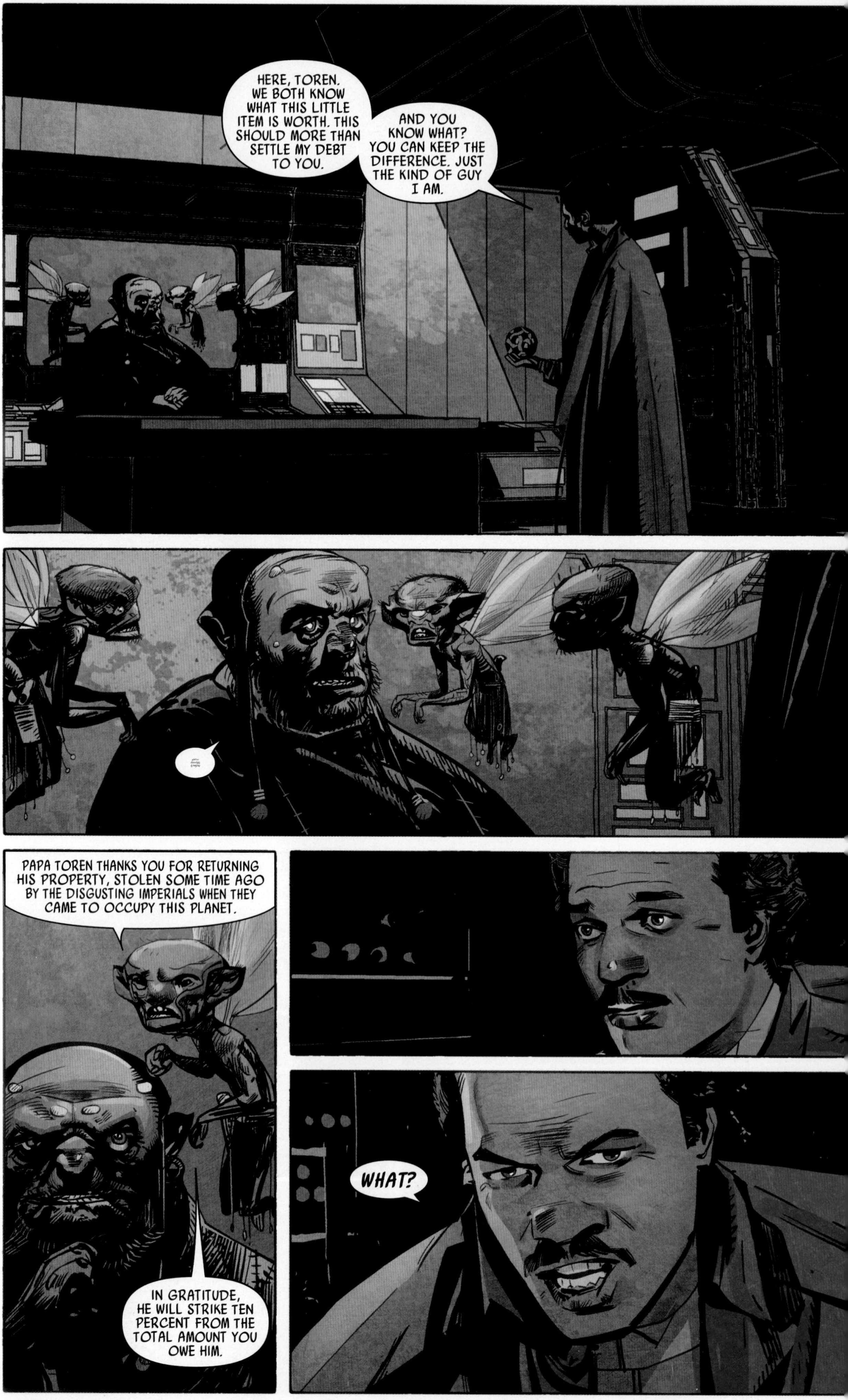
HERE, TOREN. WE BOTH KNOW WHAT THIS LITTLE ITEM IS WORTH. THIS SHOULD MORE THAN SETTLE MY DEBT TO YOU.
AND YOU KNOW WHAT? YOU CAN KEEP THE DIFFERENCE. JUST THE KIND OF GUY I AM.
PAPA TOREN THANKS YOU FOR RETURNING HIS PROPERTY, STOLEN SOME TIME AGO BY THE DISGUSTING IMPERIALS WHEN THEY CAME TO OCCUPY THIS PLANET.
IN GRATITUDE, HE WILL STRIKE TEN PERCENT FROM THE TOTAL AMOUNT YOU OWE HIM.
WHAT?

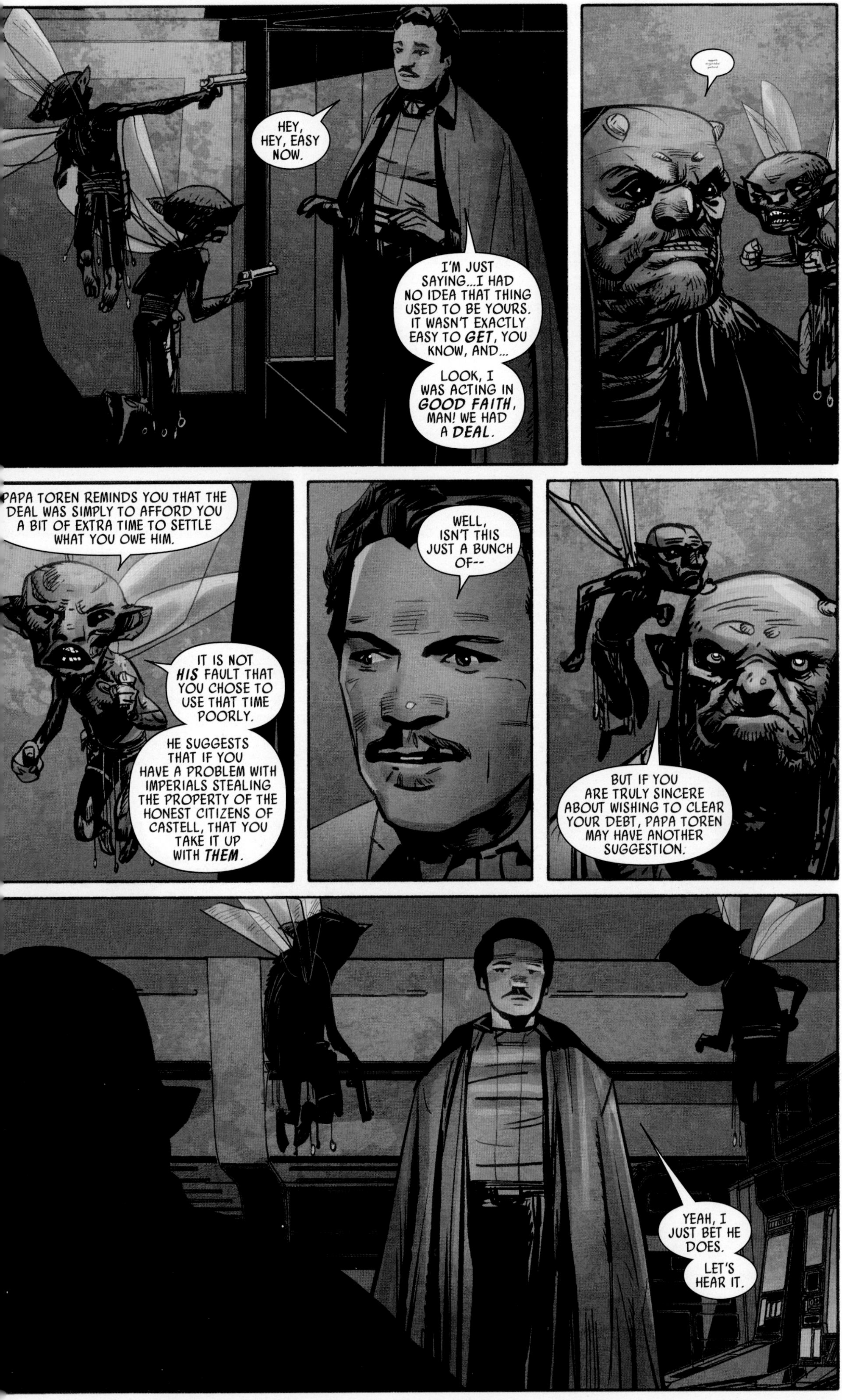
HEY, HEY, EASY NOW.
I'M JUST SAYING...I HAD NO IDEA THAT THING USED TO BE YOURS. IT WASN'T EXACTLY EASY TO GET, YOU KNOW, AND...
LOOK, I WAS ACTING IN GOOD FAITH, MAN! WE HAD A DEAL.
PAPA TOREN REMINDS YOU THAT THE DEAL WAS SIMPLY TO AFFORD YOU A BIT OF EXTRA TIME TO SETTLE WHAT YOU OWE HIM.
IT IS NOT HIS FAULT THAT YOU CHOSE TO USE THAT TIME POORLY.
HE SUGGESTS THAT IF YOU HAVE A PROBLEM WITH IMPERIALS STEALING THE PROPERTY OF THE HONEST CITIZENS OF CASTELL, THAT YOU TAKE IT UP WITH THEM.
WELL, ISN'T THIS JUST A BUNCH OF--
BUT IF YOU ARE TRULY SINCERE ABOUT WISHING TO CLEAR YOUR DEBT, PAPA TOREN MAY HAVE ANOTHER SUGGESTION.
YEAH, I JUST BET HE DOES.
LET'S HEAR IT.

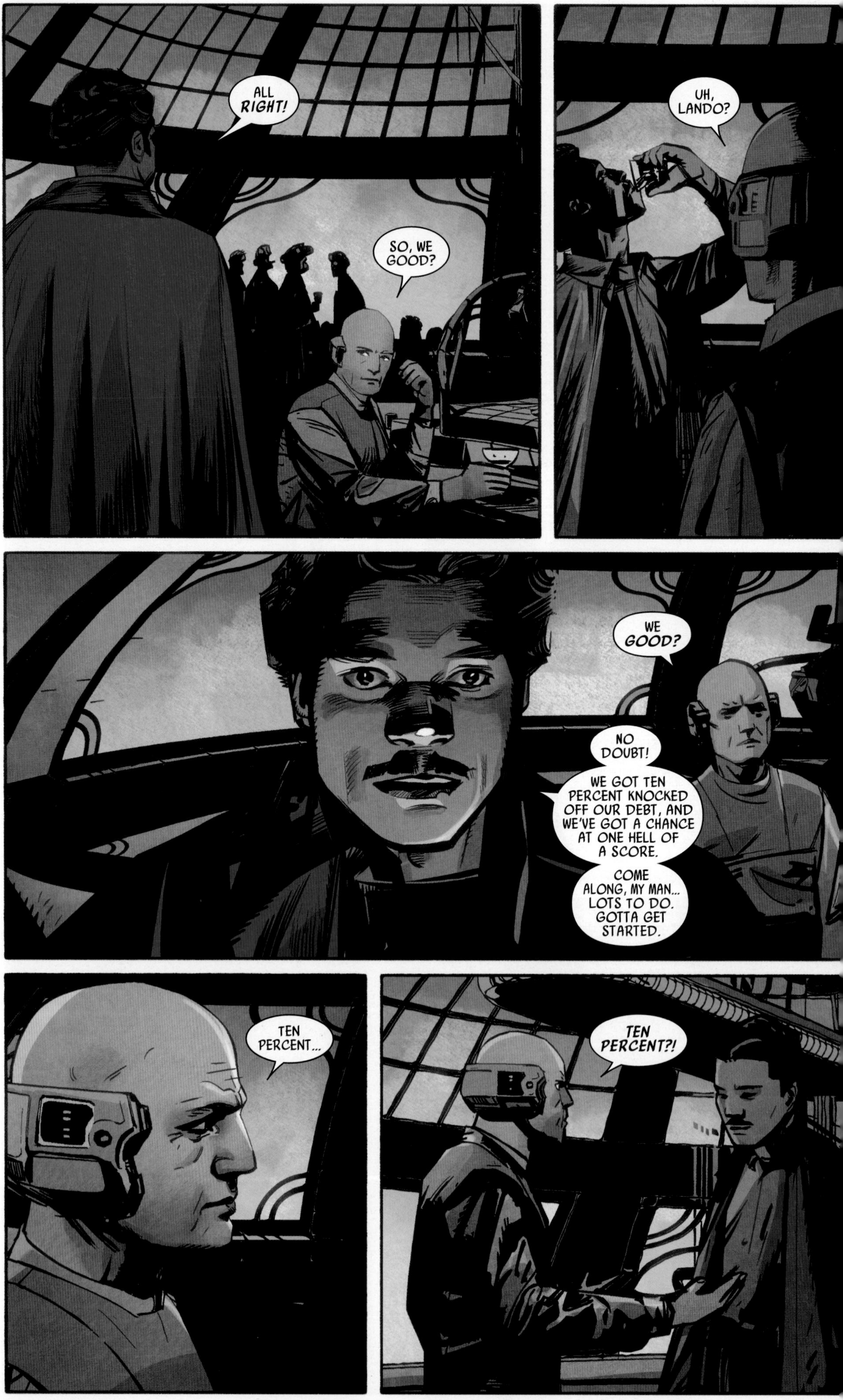
ALL RIGHT!
SO, WE GOOD?
UH, LANDO?
WE GOOD?
NO DOUBT!
WE GOT TEN PERCENT KNOCKED OFF OUR DEBT, AND WE'VE GOT A CHANCE AT ONE HELL OF A SCORE.
COME ALONG, MY MAN... LOTS TO DO. GOTTA GET STARTED.
TEN PERCENT...
TEN PERCENT?!

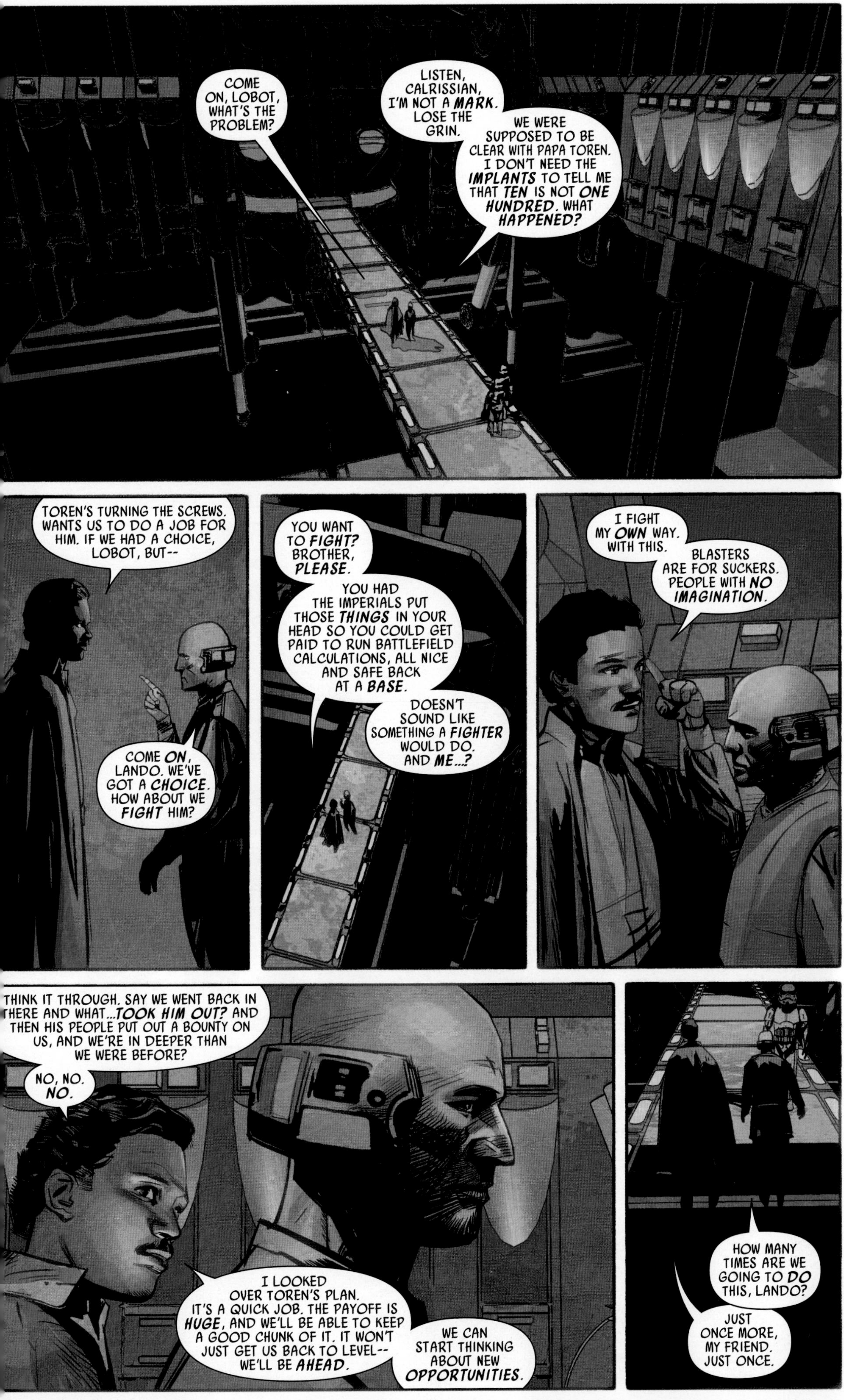
COME ON, LOBOT, WHAT'S THE PROBLEM?
LISTEN, CALRISSIAN, I'M NOT A MARK. LOSE THE GRIN.
WE WERE SUPPOSED TO BE CLEAR WITH PAPA TOREN. I DON'T NEED THE IMPLANTS TO TELL ME THAT TEN IS NOT ONE HUNDRED. WHAT HAPPENED?
TOREN'S TURNING THE SCREWS. WANTS US TO DO A JOB FOR HIM. IF WE HAD A CHOICE, LOBOT, BUT--
COME ON, LANDO. WE'VE GOT A CHOICE. HOW ABOUT WE FIGHT HIM?
YOU WANT TO FIGHT? BROTHER, PLEASE.
YOU HAD THE IMPERIALS PUT THOSE THINGS IN YOUR HEAD SO YOU COULD GET PAID TO RUN BATTLEFIELD CALCULATIONS, ALL NICE AND SAFE BACK AT A BASE.
DOESN'T SOUND LIKE SOMETHING A FIGHTER WOULD DO. AND ME...?
I FIGHT MY OWN WAY. WITH THIS.
BLASTERS ARE FOR SUCKERS. PEOPLE WITH NO IMAGINATION.
THINK IT THROUGH. SAY WE WENT BACK IN THERE AND WHAT...TOOK HIM OUT? AND THEN HIS PEOPLE PUT OUT A BOUNTY ON US, AND WE'RE IN DEEPER THAN WE WERE BEFORE?
NO, NO. NO.
I LOOKED OVER TOREN'S PLAN. IT'S A QUICK JOB. THE PAYOFF IS HUGE, AND WE'LL BE ABLE TO KEEP A GOOD CHUNK OF IT. IT WON'T JUST GET US BACK TO LEVEL-- WE'LL BE AHEAD.
WE CAN START THINKING ABOUT NEW OPPORTUNITIES.
HOW MANY TIMES ARE WE GOING TO DO THIS, LANDO?
JUST ONCE MORE, MY FRIEND. JUST ONCE.

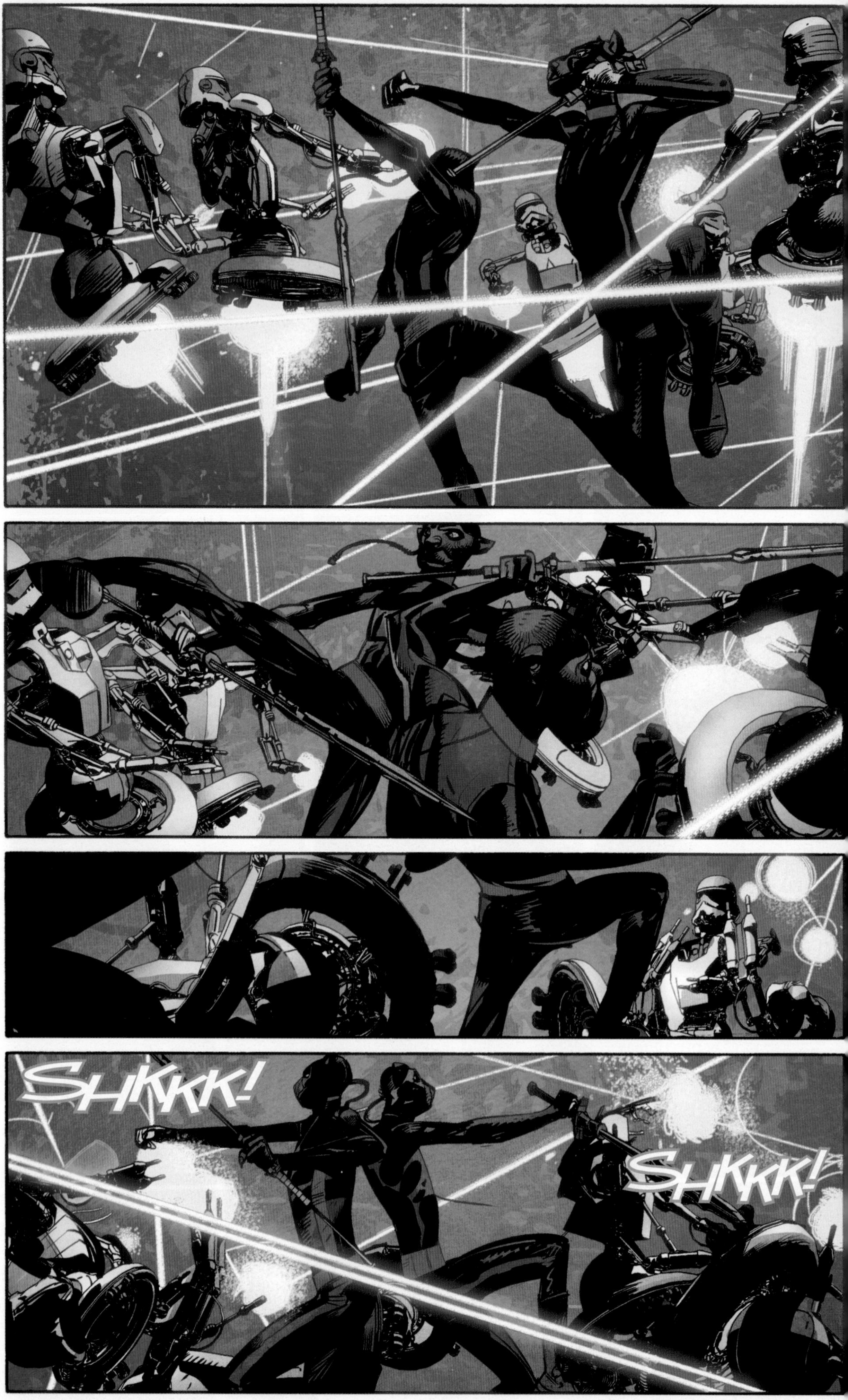
SHKKK!
SHKKK!

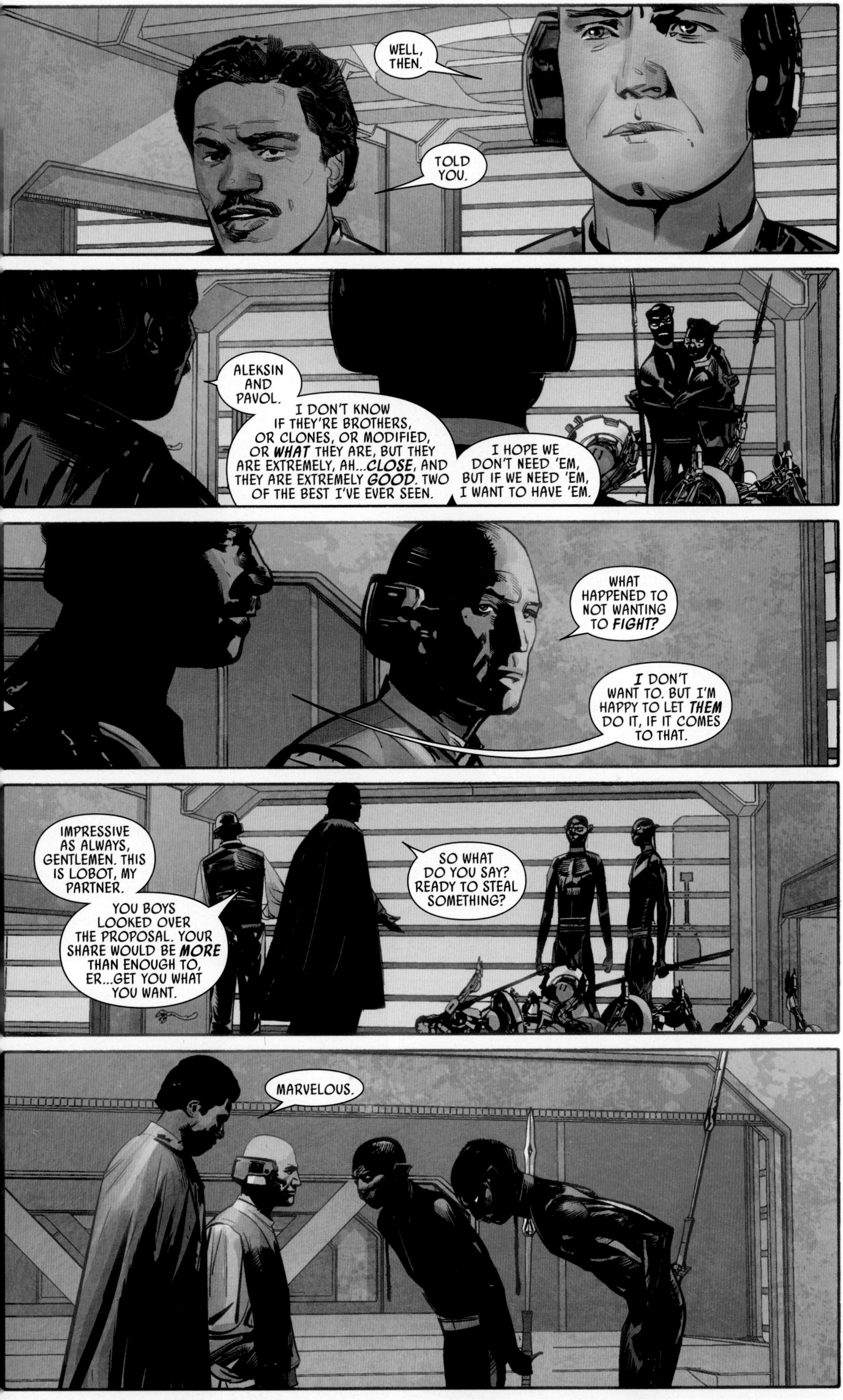
WELL, THEN.
TOLD YOU.
ALEKSIN AND PAVOL.
I DON'T KNOW IF THEY'RE BROTHERS, OR CLONES, OR MODIFIED, OR WHAT THEY ARE, BUT THEY ARE EXTREMELY, AH...CLOSE, AND THEY ARE EXTREMELY GOOD. TWO OF THE BEST I'VE EVER SEEN.
I HOPE WE DON'T NEED 'EM, BUT IF WE NEED 'EM, I WANT TO HAVE 'EM.
WHAT HAPPENED TO NOT WANTING TO FIGHT?
I DON'T WANT TO. BUT I'M HAPPY TO LET THEM DO IT, IF IT COMES TO THAT.
IMPRESSIVE AS ALWAYS, GENTLEMEN. THIS IS LOBOT, MY PARTNER.
YOU BOYS LOOKED OVER THE PROPOSAL. YOUR SHARE WOULD BE MORE THAN ENOUGH TO, ER...GET YOU WHAT YOU WANT.
SO WHAT DO YOU SAY? READY TO STEAL SOMETHING?
MARVELOUS.

YOU ARE OUT OF YOUR PORUK-FILLED MIND.

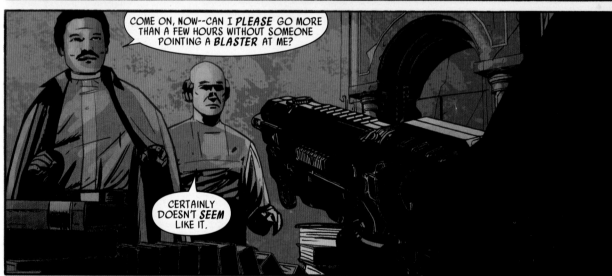

COME ON, NOW--CAN I *PLEASE* GO MORE THAN A FEW HOURS WITHOUT SOMEONE POINTING A *BLASTER* AT ME?

CERTAINLY DOESN'T *SEEM* LIKE IT.

KORIN, LISTEN--I KNOW WE HAVE A *HISTORY*, BUT THAT'S WHY I'M HERE.

HISTORY? *HISTORY?* I LOST AN *EYE*, CALRISSIAN, YOU *FLIT.*

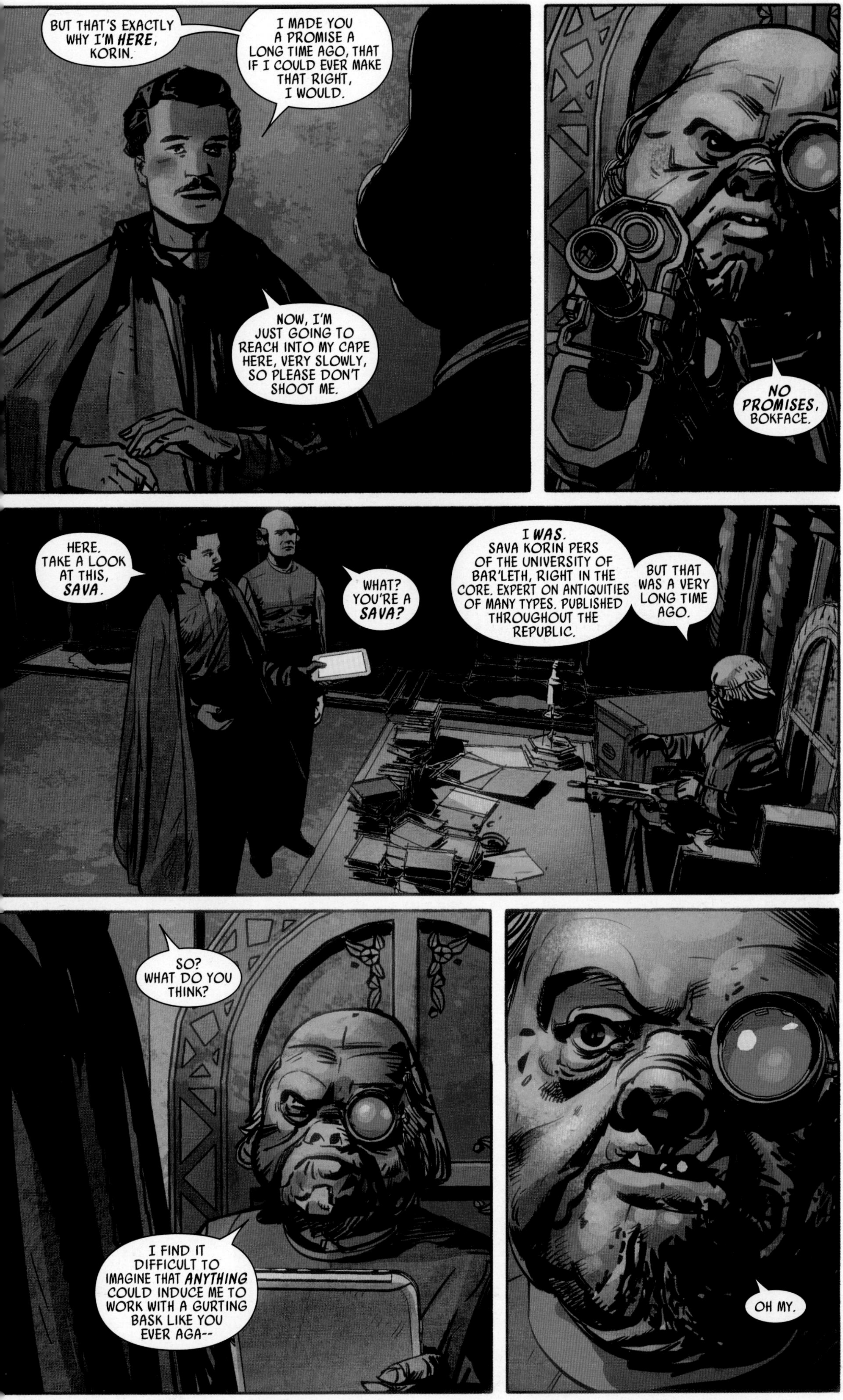
BUT THAT'S EXACTLY WHY I'M *HERE*, KORIN.
I MADE YOU A PROMISE A LONG TIME AGO, THAT IF I COULD EVER MAKE THAT RIGHT, I WOULD.
NOW, I'M JUST GOING TO REACH INTO MY CAPE HERE, VERY SLOWLY, SO PLEASE DON'T SHOOT ME.
NO PROMISES, BOKFACE.
HERE. TAKE A LOOK AT THIS, *SAVA*.
WHAT? YOU'RE A *SAVA?*
I *WAS*. SAVA KORIN PERS OF THE UNIVERSITY OF BAR'LETH, RIGHT IN THE CORE. EXPERT ON ANTIQUITIES OF MANY TYPES. PUBLISHED THROUGHOUT THE REPUBLIC.
BUT THAT WAS A VERY LONG TIME AGO.
SO? WHAT DO YOU THINK?
I FIND IT DIFFICULT TO IMAGINE THAT *ANYTHING* COULD INDUCE ME TO WORK WITH A GURTING BASK LIKE YOU EVER AGA--
OH MY.

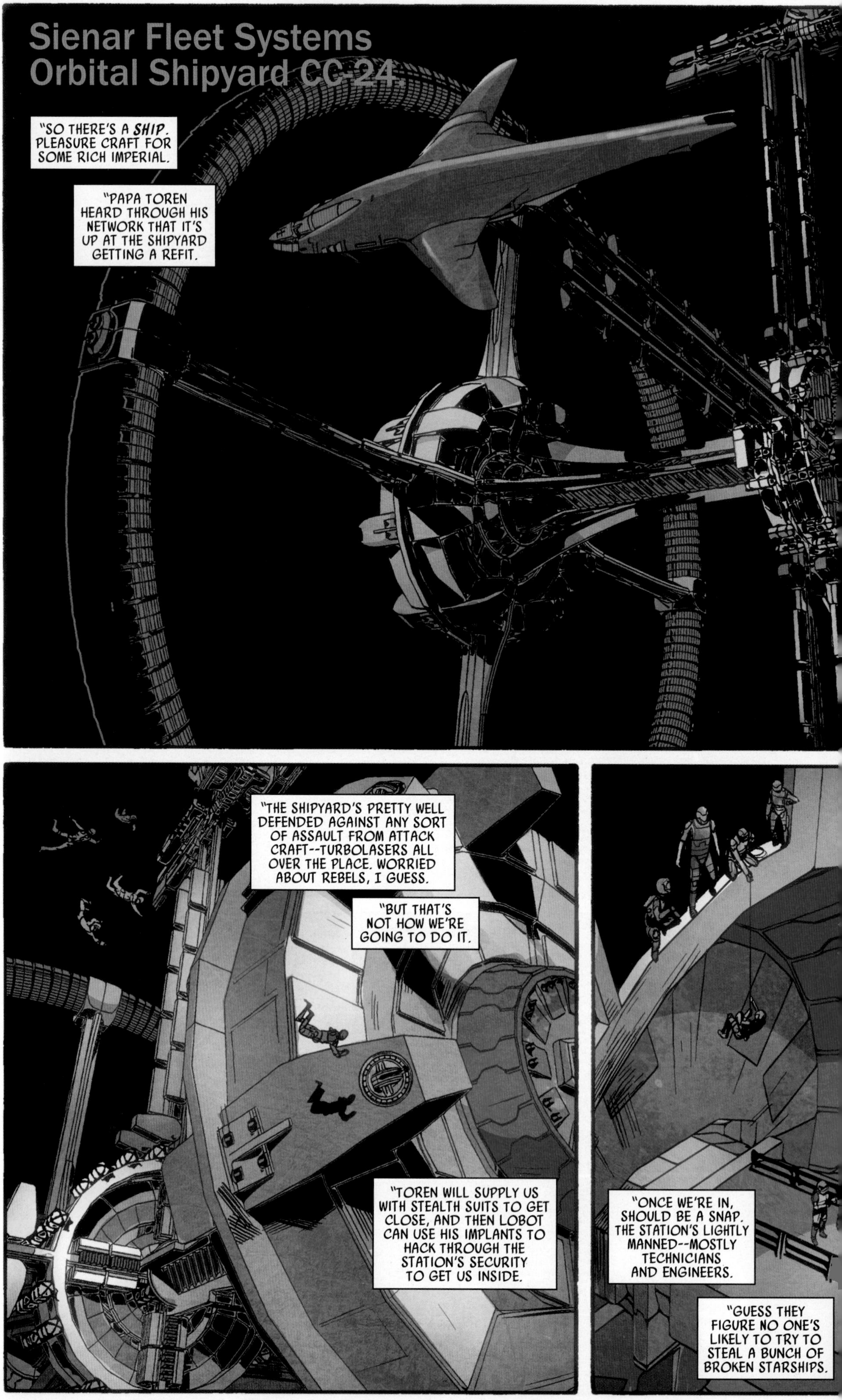
Sienar Fleet Systems
Orbital Shipyard CC-24.
"SO THERE'S A SHIP. PLEASURE CRAFT FOR SOME RICH IMPERIAL.
"PAPA TOREN HEARD THROUGH HIS NETWORK THAT IT'S UP AT THE SHIPYARD GETTING A REFIT.
"THE SHIPYARD'S PRETTY WELL DEFENDED AGAINST ANY SORT OF ASSAULT FROM ATTACK CRAFT--TURBOLASERS ALL OVER THE PLACE. WORRIED ABOUT REBELS, I GUESS.
"BUT THAT'S NOT HOW WE'RE GOING TO DO IT.
"TOREN WILL SUPPLY US WITH STEALTH SUITS TO GET CLOSE, AND THEN LOBOT CAN USE HIS IMPLANTS TO HACK THROUGH THE STATION'S SECURITY TO GET US INSIDE.
"ONCE WE'RE IN, SHOULD BE A SNAP. THE STATION'S LIGHTLY MANNED--MOSTLY TECHNICIANS AND ENGINEERS.
"GUESS THEY FIGURE NO ONE'S LIKELY TO TRY TO STEAL A BUNCH OF BROKEN STARSHIPS.

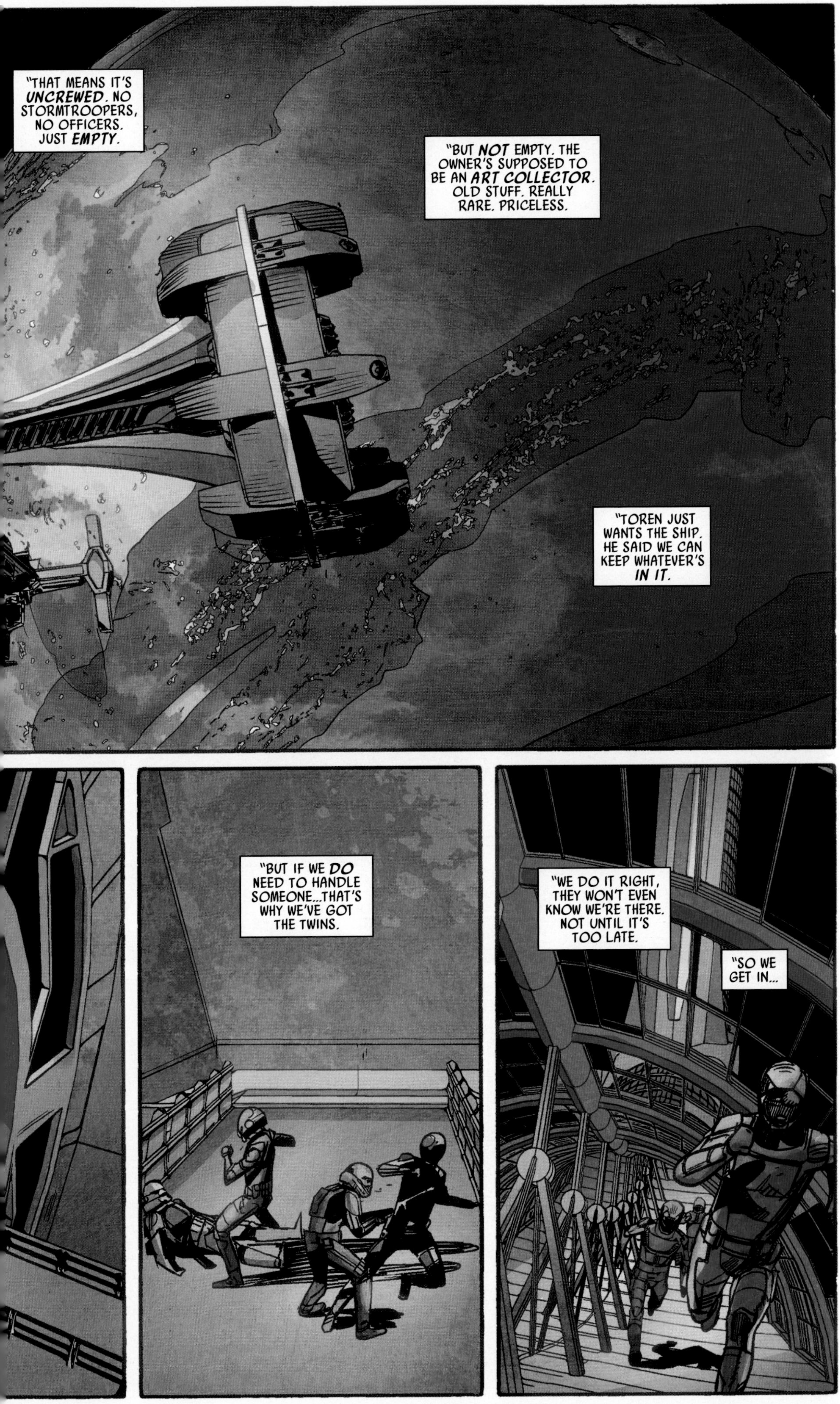
"THAT MEANS IT'S UNCREWED. NO STORMTROOPERS, NO OFFICERS. JUST EMPTY.
"BUT NOT EMPTY. THE OWNER'S SUPPOSED TO BE AN ART COLLECTOR. OLD STUFF. REALLY RARE. PRICELESS.
"TOREN JUST WANTS THE SHIP. HE SAID WE CAN KEEP WHATEVER'S IN IT.
"BUT IF WE DO NEED TO HANDLE SOMEONE...THAT'S WHY WE'VE GOT THE TWINS.
"SO WE GET IN...
"WE DO IT RIGHT, THEY WON'T EVEN KNOW WE'RE THERE. NOT UNTIL IT'S TOO LATE.

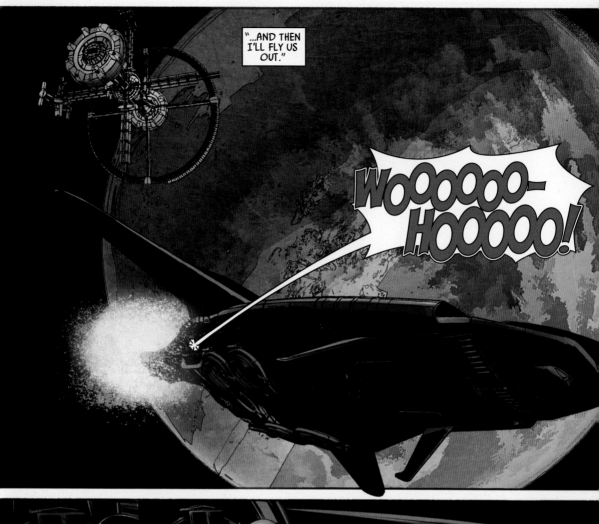

"...AND THEN I'LL FLY US OUT."

WOOOOOO-HOOOOO!

SEE? WHAT'D I TELL YA? EASY MONEY. EASY MONEY!

I'LL BELIEVE THAT WHEN I'M SPENDING IT.

COME ON, BROTHER. WE GOT AWAY CLEAN. HONESTLY...

"...I ALMOST FEEL BAD FOR WHOEVER'S IN CHARGE OF THAT SHIPYARD.

"YOU NEVER REALLY HEAR STORIES ABOUT THE IMPERIALS FORGIVING PEOPLE."

NO, NO, NO, NO, NO!

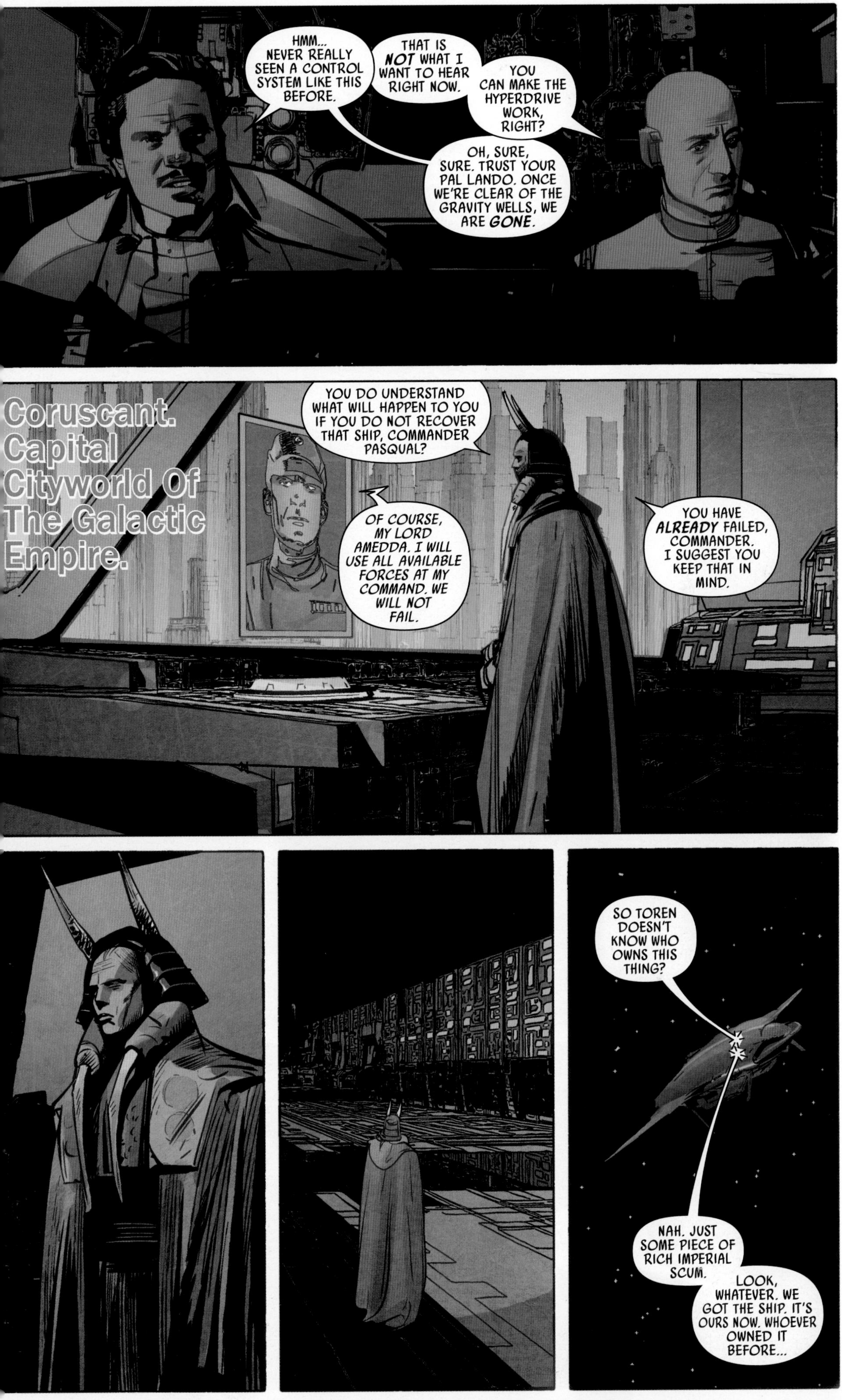
HMM... NEVER REALLY SEEN A CONTROL SYSTEM LIKE THIS BEFORE.
THAT IS NOT WHAT I WANT TO HEAR RIGHT NOW.
YOU CAN MAKE THE HYPERDRIVE WORK, RIGHT?
OH, SURE, SURE. TRUST YOUR PAL LANDO. ONCE WE'RE CLEAR OF THE GRAVITY WELLS, WE ARE GONE.
Coruscant. Capital Cityworld Of The Galactic Empire.
YOU DO UNDERSTAND WHAT WILL HAPPEN TO YOU IF YOU DO NOT RECOVER THAT SHIP, COMMANDER PASQUAL?
OF COURSE, MY LORD AMEDDA. I WILL USE ALL AVAILABLE FORCES AT MY COMMAND. WE WILL NOT FAIL.
YOU HAVE ALREADY FAILED, COMMANDER. I SUGGEST YOU KEEP THAT IN MIND.
SO TOREN DOESN'T KNOW WHO OWNS THIS THING?
NAH. JUST SOME PIECE OF RICH IMPERIAL SCUM.
LOOK, WHATEVER. WE GOT THE SHIP. IT'S OURS NOW. WHOEVER OWNED IT BEFORE...

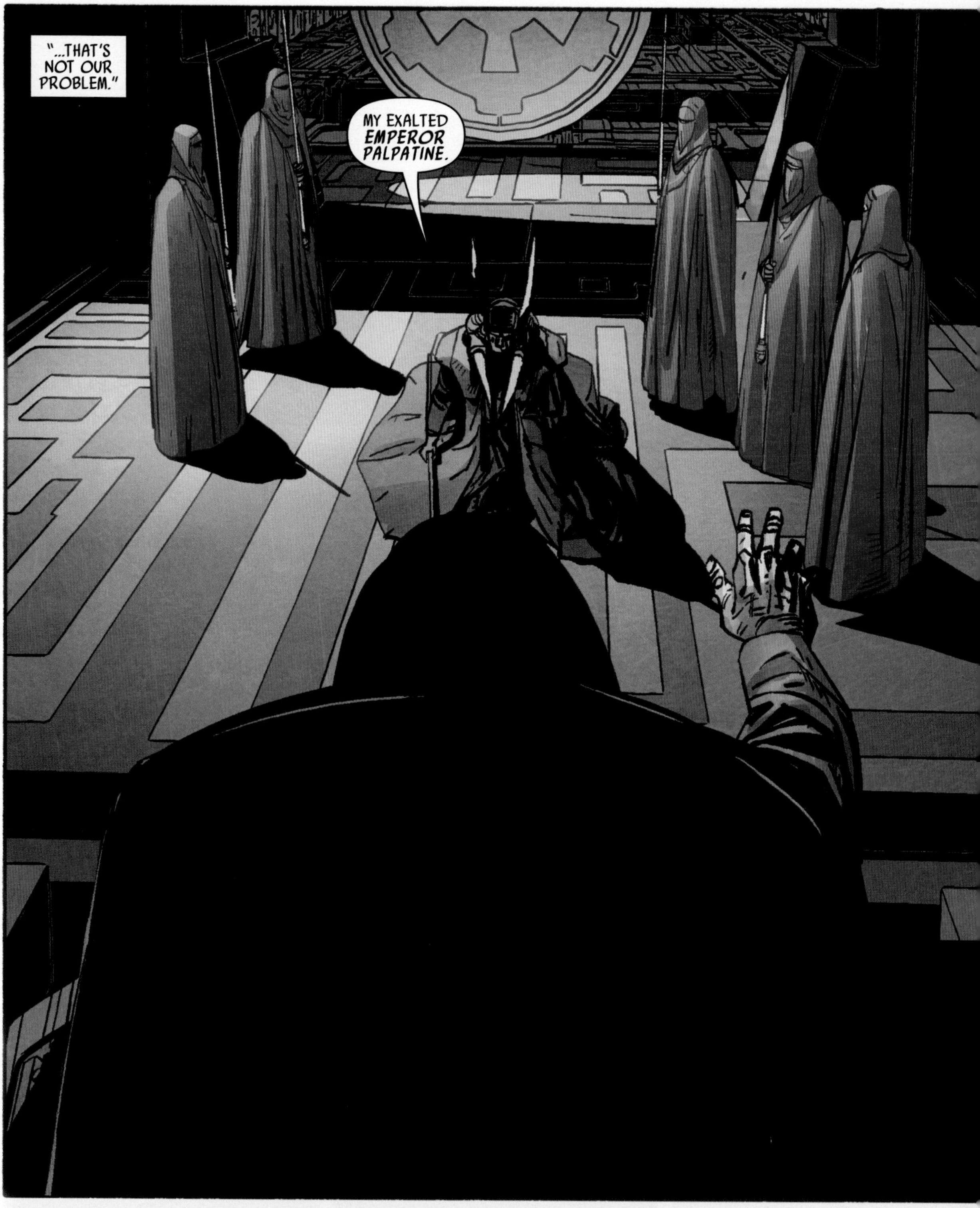
"...THAT'S NOT OUR PROBLEM."
MY EXALTED EMPEROR PALPATINE.

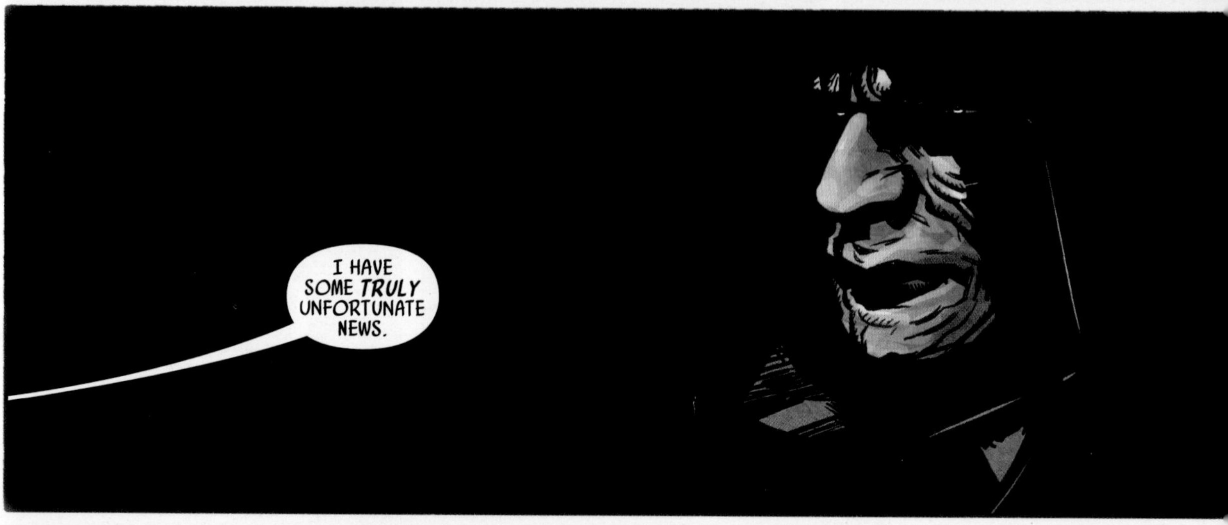
I HAVE SOME TRULY UNFORTUNATE NEWS.

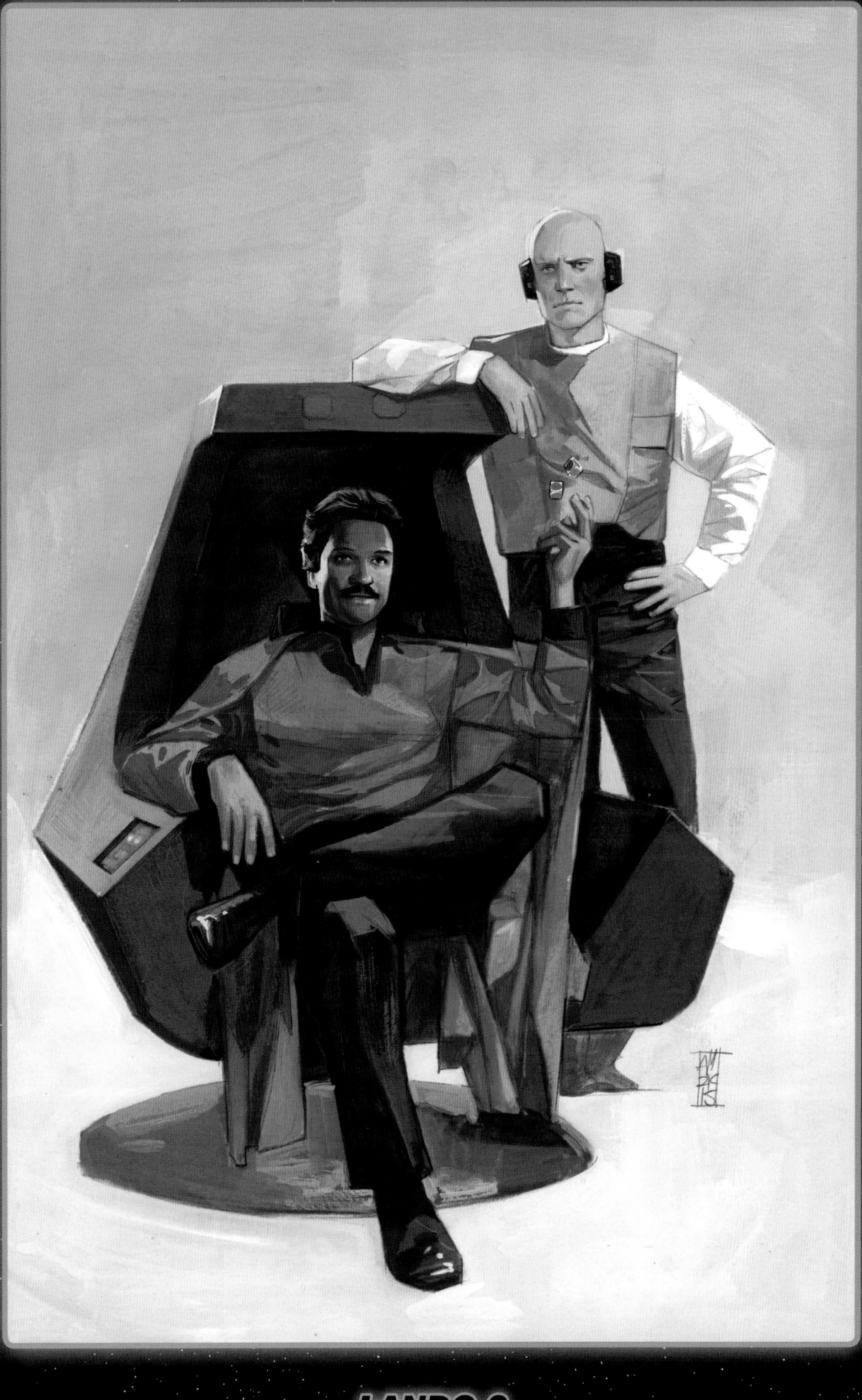

LANDO 2

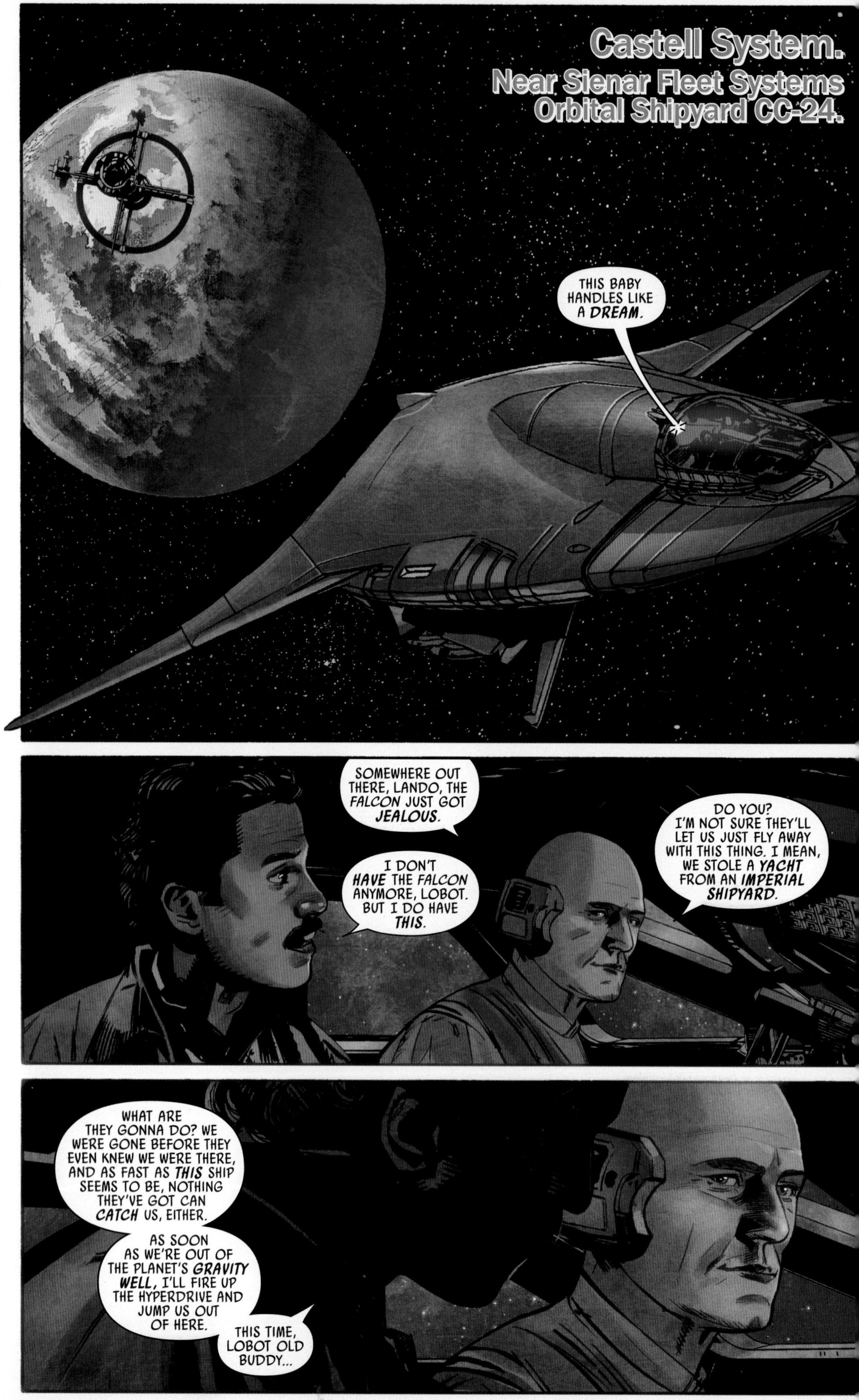

Castell System.
Near Sienar Fleet Systems Orbital Shipyard CC-24.
THIS BABY HANDLES LIKE A *DREAM*.
SOMEWHERE OUT THERE, LANDO, THE *FALCON* JUST GOT *JEALOUS*.
I DON'T *HAVE* THE *FALCON* ANYMORE, LOBOT. BUT I DO HAVE *THIS*.
DO YOU? I'M NOT SURE THEY'LL LET US JUST FLY AWAY WITH THIS THING. I MEAN, WE STOLE A *YACHT* FROM AN *IMPERIAL SHIPYARD*.
WHAT ARE THEY GONNA DO? WE WERE GONE BEFORE THEY EVEN KNEW WE WERE THERE, AND AS FAST AS *THIS* SHIP SEEMS TO BE, NOTHING THEY'VE GOT CAN *CATCH* US, EITHER.
AS SOON AS WE'RE OUT OF THE PLANET'S *GRAVITY WELL*, I'LL FIRE UP THE HYPERDRIVE AND JUMP US OUT OF HERE.
THIS TIME, LOBOT OLD BUDDY...

"...FINALLY...

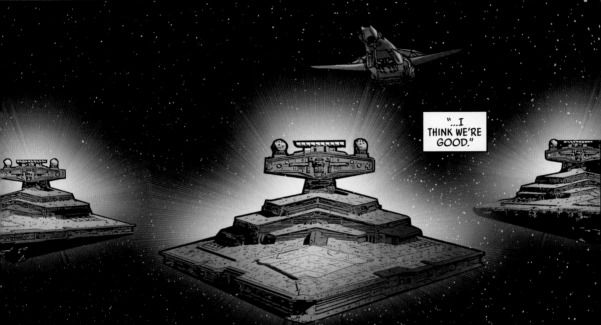

"...I THINK WE'RE GOOD."

YOU SURE ABOUT THAT?

THREE? THEY SENT THREE STAR DESTROYERS?

BAD NEWS.

NO, THIS IS GOOD.

CAN YOU IMAGINE HOW MUCH THIS THING MUST BE WORTH?

TO US? NOTHING, ONCE WE ARE DEAD.

CHEER UP, PAL. SUDDENLY...

...I FEEL VERY MUCH ALIVE.

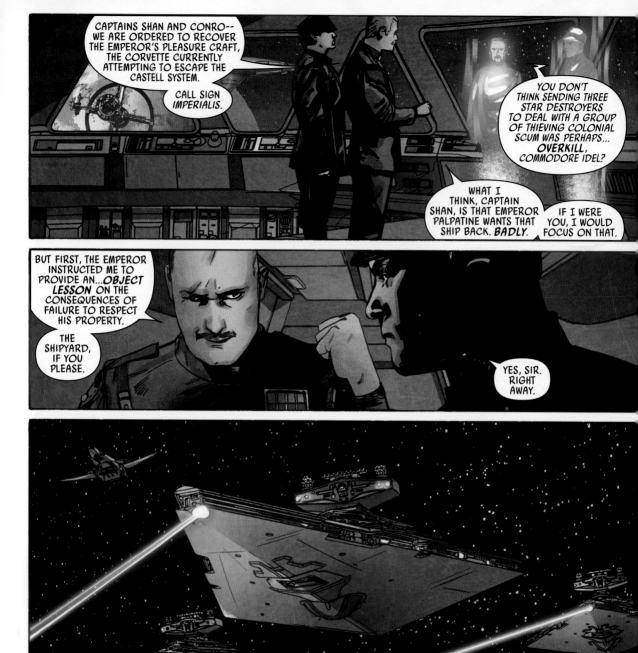

CAPTAINS SHAN AND CONRO-- WE ARE ORDERED TO RECOVER THE EMPEROR'S PLEASURE CRAFT, THE CORVETTE CURRENTLY ATTEMPTING TO ESCAPE THE CASTELL SYSTEM.

CALL SIGN IMPERIALIS.

YOU DON'T THINK SENDING THREE STAR DESTROYERS TO DEAL WITH A GROUP OF THIEVING COLONIAL SCUM WAS PERHAPS... *OVERKILL*, COMMODORE IDEL?

WHAT I THINK, CAPTAIN SHAN, IS THAT EMPEROR PALPATINE WANTS THAT SHIP BACK. *BADLY.*

IF I WERE YOU, I WOULD FOCUS ON THAT.

BUT FIRST, THE EMPEROR INSTRUCTED ME TO PROVIDE AN...*OBJECT LESSON* ON THE CONSEQUENCES OF FAILURE TO RESPECT HIS PROPERTY.

THE SHIPYARD, IF YOU PLEASE.

YES, SIR. RIGHT AWAY.

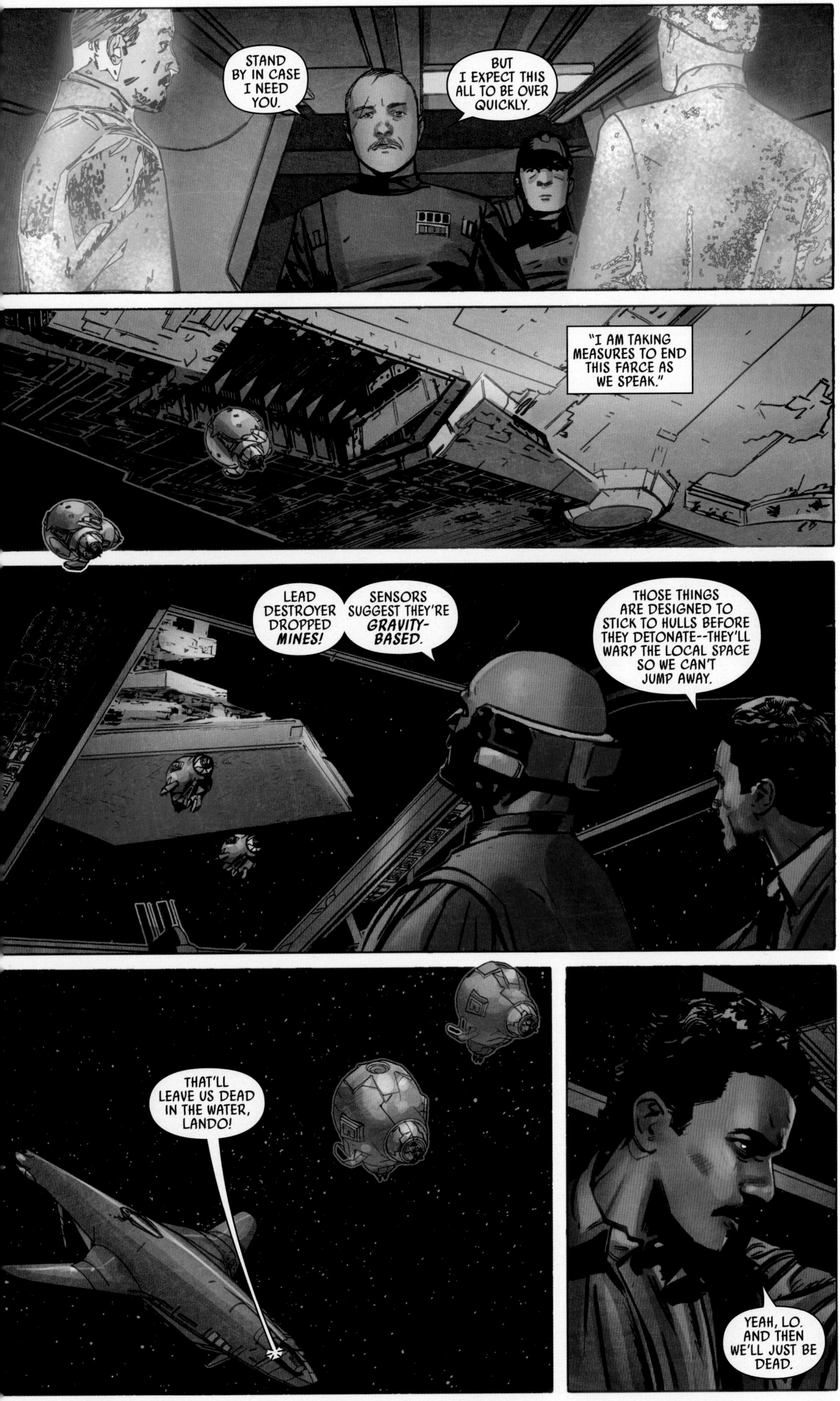
STAND BY IN CASE I NEED YOU.
BUT I EXPECT THIS ALL TO BE OVER QUICKLY.
"I AM TAKING MEASURES TO END THIS FARCE AS WE SPEAK."
LEAD DESTROYER DROPPED MINES!
SENSORS SUGGEST THEY'RE GRAVITY-BASED.
THOSE THINGS ARE DESIGNED TO STICK TO HULLS BEFORE THEY DETONATE--THEY'LL WARP THE LOCAL SPACE SO WE CAN'T JUMP AWAY.
THAT'LL LEAVE US DEAD IN THE WATER, LANDO!
YEAH, LO. AND THEN WE'LL JUST BE DEAD.

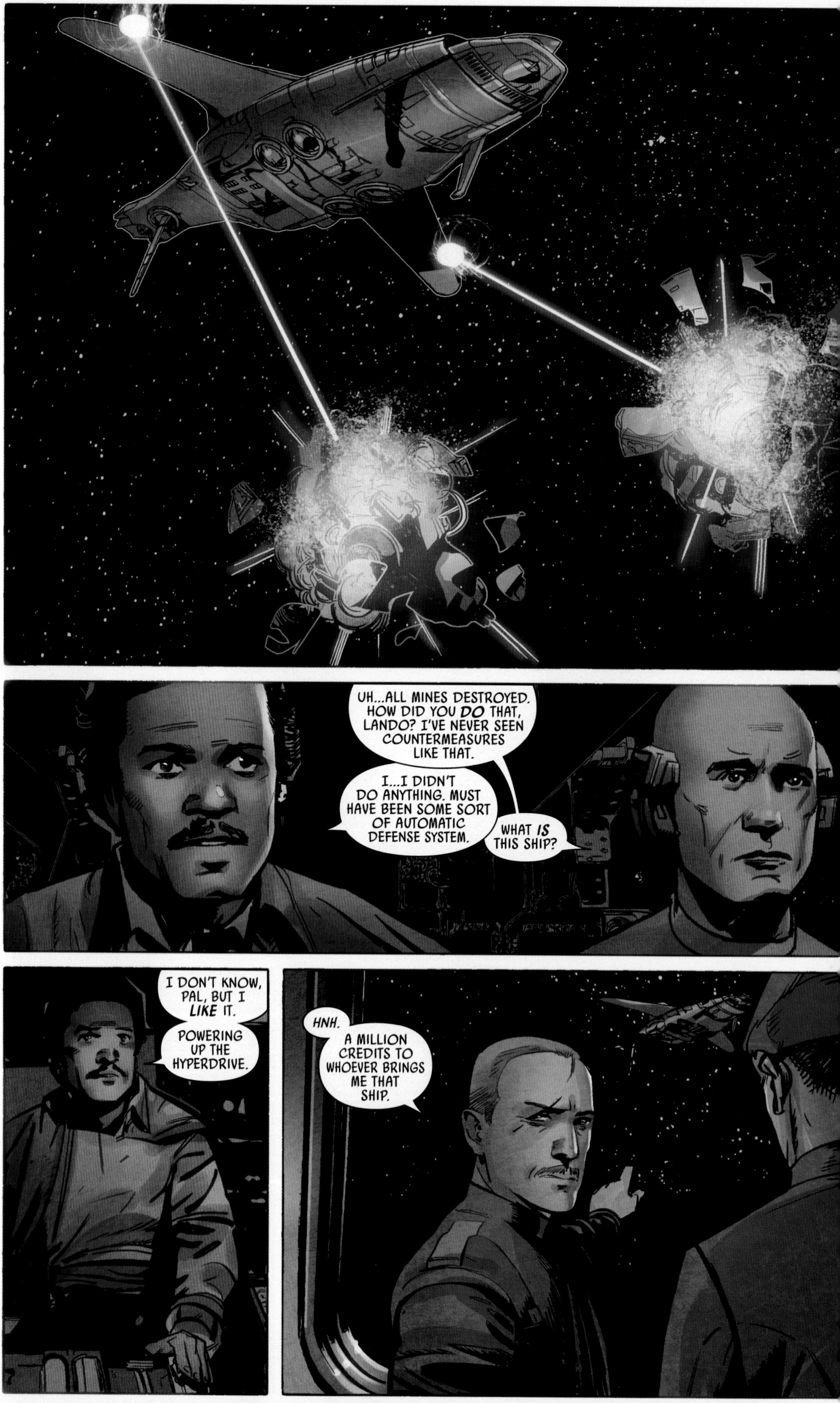
UH...ALL MINES DESTROYED. HOW DID YOU DO THAT, LANDO? I'VE NEVER SEEN COUNTERMEASURES LIKE THAT.
I...I DIDN'T DO ANYTHING. MUST HAVE BEEN SOME SORT OF AUTOMATIC DEFENSE SYSTEM.
WHAT IS THIS SHIP?
I DON'T KNOW, PAL, BUT I LIKE IT.
POWERING UP THE HYPERDRIVE.
HNH.
A MILLION CREDITS TO WHOEVER BRINGS ME THAT SHIP.

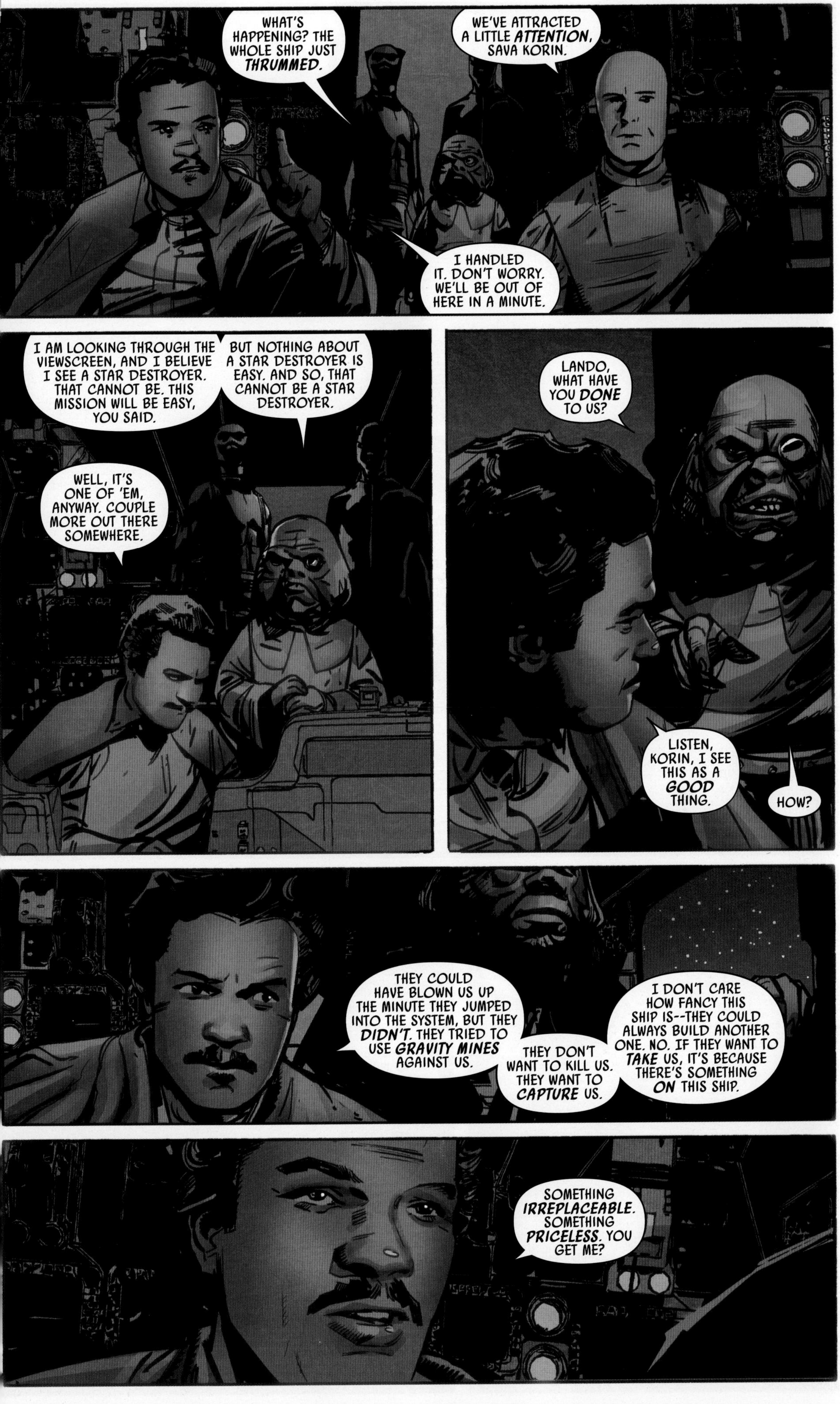
WHAT'S HAPPENING? THE WHOLE SHIP JUST THRUMMED.
WE'VE ATTRACTED A LITTLE ATTENTION, SAVA KORIN.
I HANDLED IT. DON'T WORRY. WE'LL BE OUT OF HERE IN A MINUTE.
I AM LOOKING THROUGH THE VIEWSCREEN, AND I BELIEVE I SEE A STAR DESTROYER. THAT CANNOT BE. THIS MISSION WILL BE EASY, YOU SAID.
BUT NOTHING ABOUT A STAR DESTROYER IS EASY. AND SO, THAT CANNOT BE A STAR DESTROYER.
WELL, IT'S ONE OF 'EM, ANYWAY. COUPLE MORE OUT THERE SOMEWHERE.
LANDO, WHAT HAVE YOU DONE TO US?
LISTEN, KORIN, I SEE THIS AS A GOOD THING.
HOW?
THEY COULD HAVE BLOWN US UP THE MINUTE THEY JUMPED INTO THE SYSTEM, BUT THEY DIDN'T. THEY TRIED TO USE GRAVITY MINES AGAINST US.
THEY DON'T WANT TO KILL US. THEY WANT TO CAPTURE US.
I DON'T CARE HOW FANCY THIS SHIP IS--THEY COULD ALWAYS BUILD ANOTHER ONE. NO. IF THEY WANT TO TAKE US, IT'S BECAUSE THERE'S SOMETHING ON THIS SHIP.
SOMETHING IRREPLACEABLE. SOMETHING PRICELESS. YOU GET ME?

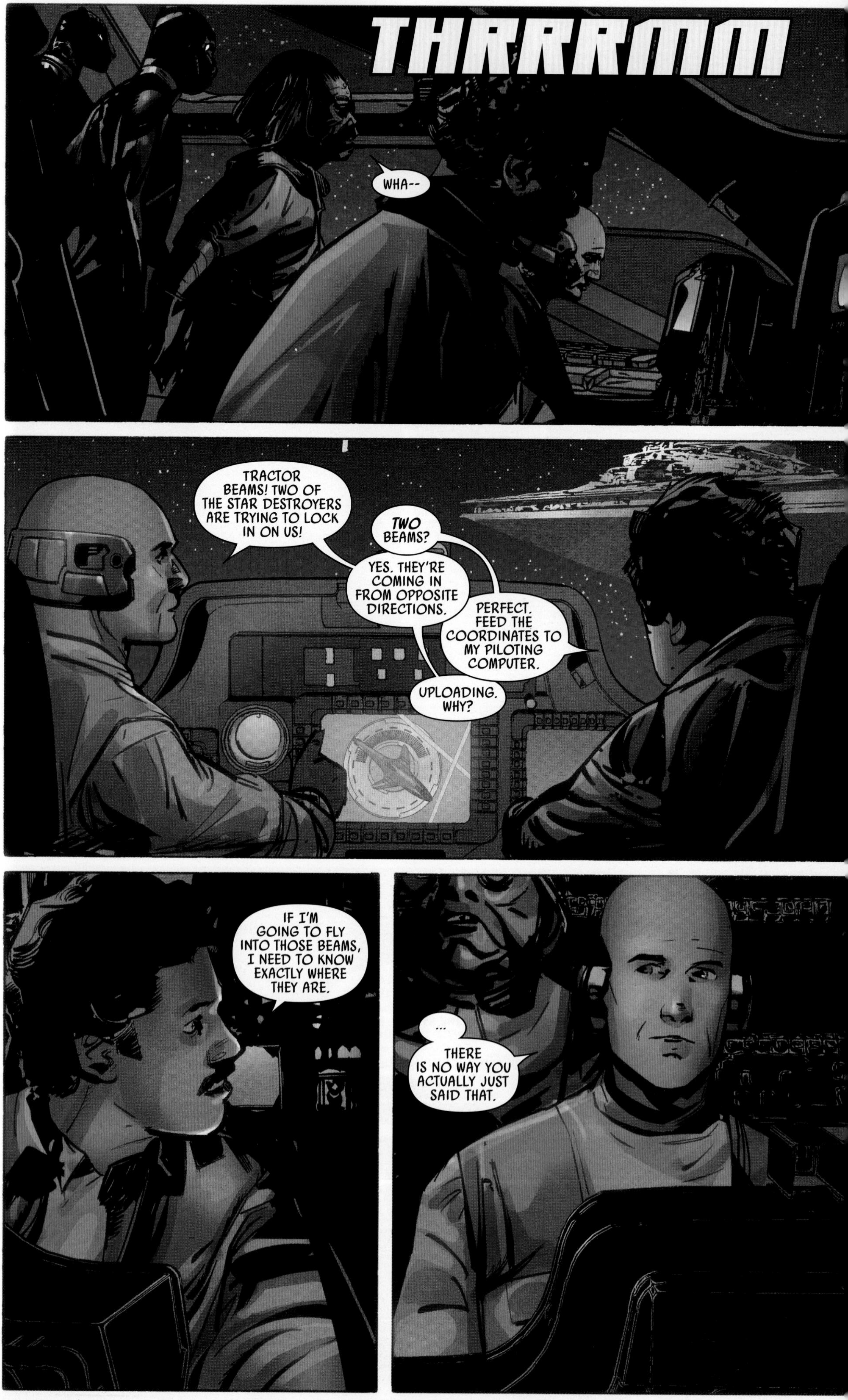
THRRRMM
WHA--
TRACTOR BEAMS! TWO OF THE STAR DESTROYERS ARE TRYING TO LOCK IN ON US!
TWO BEAMS?
YES. THEY'RE COMING IN FROM OPPOSITE DIRECTIONS.
PERFECT. FEED THE COORDINATES TO MY PILOTING COMPUTER.
UPLOADING. WHY?
IF I'M GOING TO FLY INTO THOSE BEAMS, I NEED TO KNOW EXACTLY WHERE THEY ARE.
...
THERE IS NO WAY YOU ACTUALLY JUST SAID THAT.

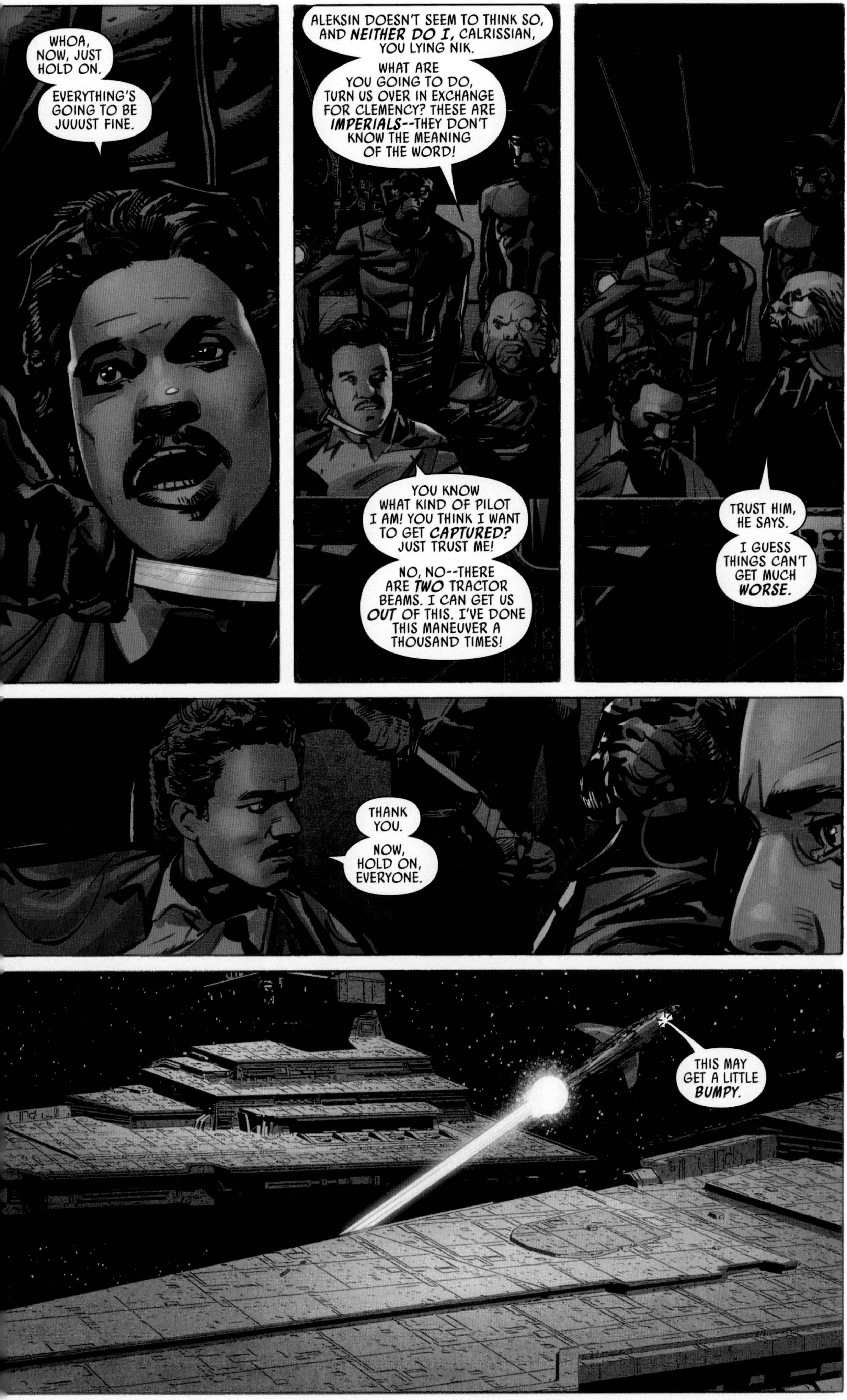

WHOA, NOW, JUST HOLD ON.
EVERYTHING'S GOING TO BE JUUUST FINE.
ALEKSIN DOESN'T SEEM TO THINK SO, AND NEITHER DO I, CALRISSIAN, YOU LYING NIK.
WHAT ARE YOU GOING TO DO, TURN US OVER IN EXCHANGE FOR CLEMENCY? THESE ARE IMPERIALS--THEY DON'T KNOW THE MEANING OF THE WORD!
YOU KNOW WHAT KIND OF PILOT I AM! YOU THINK I WANT TO GET CAPTURED? JUST TRUST ME!
NO, NO--THERE ARE TWO TRACTOR BEAMS. I CAN GET US OUT OF THIS. I'VE DONE THIS MANEUVER A THOUSAND TIMES!
TRUST HIM, HE SAYS.
I GUESS THINGS CAN'T GET MUCH WORSE.
THANK YOU.
NOW, HOLD ON, EVERYONE.
THIS MAY GET A LITTLE BUMPY.

TRACTOR BEAMS ORIENTING TOWARDS TARGET, CAPTAIN CONRO. THE IMPERIALIS IS MOVING FAST, BUT WE SHOULD HAVE HER IN A MATTER OF MOMENTS.

WHAT IS SHEN'S SHIP DOING?

SENSORS INDICATE THEY HAVE ALSO DEPLOYED THEIR TRACTOR BEAM. WE SHOULD GET THERE FIRST, THOUGH.

SEE THAT YOU DO, LIEUTENANT.

EASY, EASY...

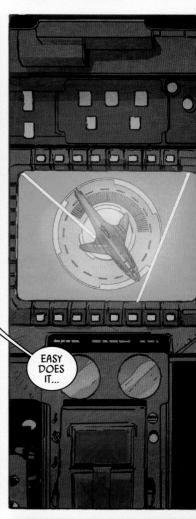

EASY DOES IT...

BEAM LOCKED, SIR. WE HAVE THE IMPERIALIS.

WELL DONE! BRING HER ABOARD, AND SEND CAPTAIN CONRO OUR VERY SINCERE CONDOLENCES.

WAIT...

HA!

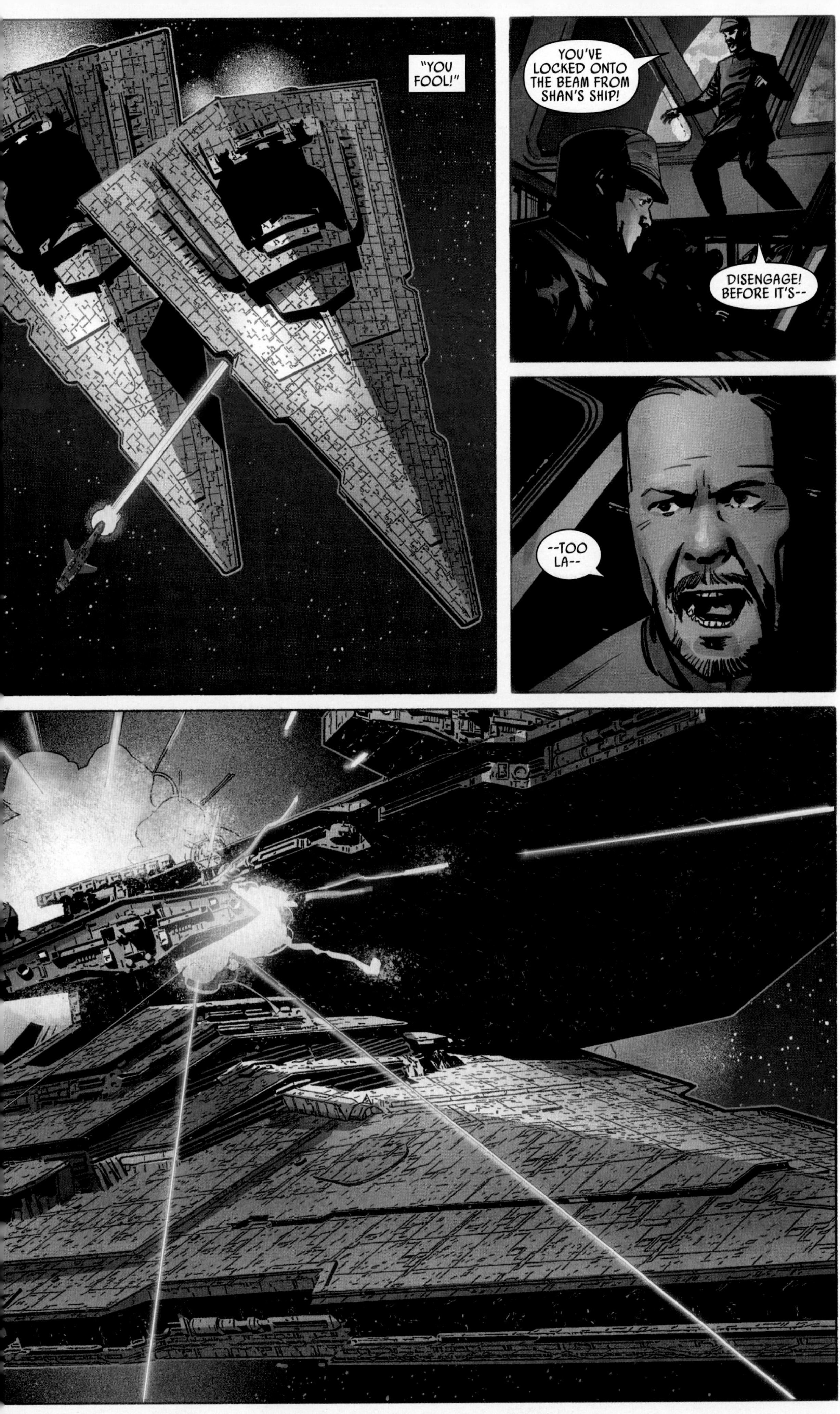
"YOU FOOL!"
YOU'VE LOCKED ONTO THE BEAM FROM SHAN'S SHIP!
DISENGAGE! BEFORE IT'S--
--TOO LA--

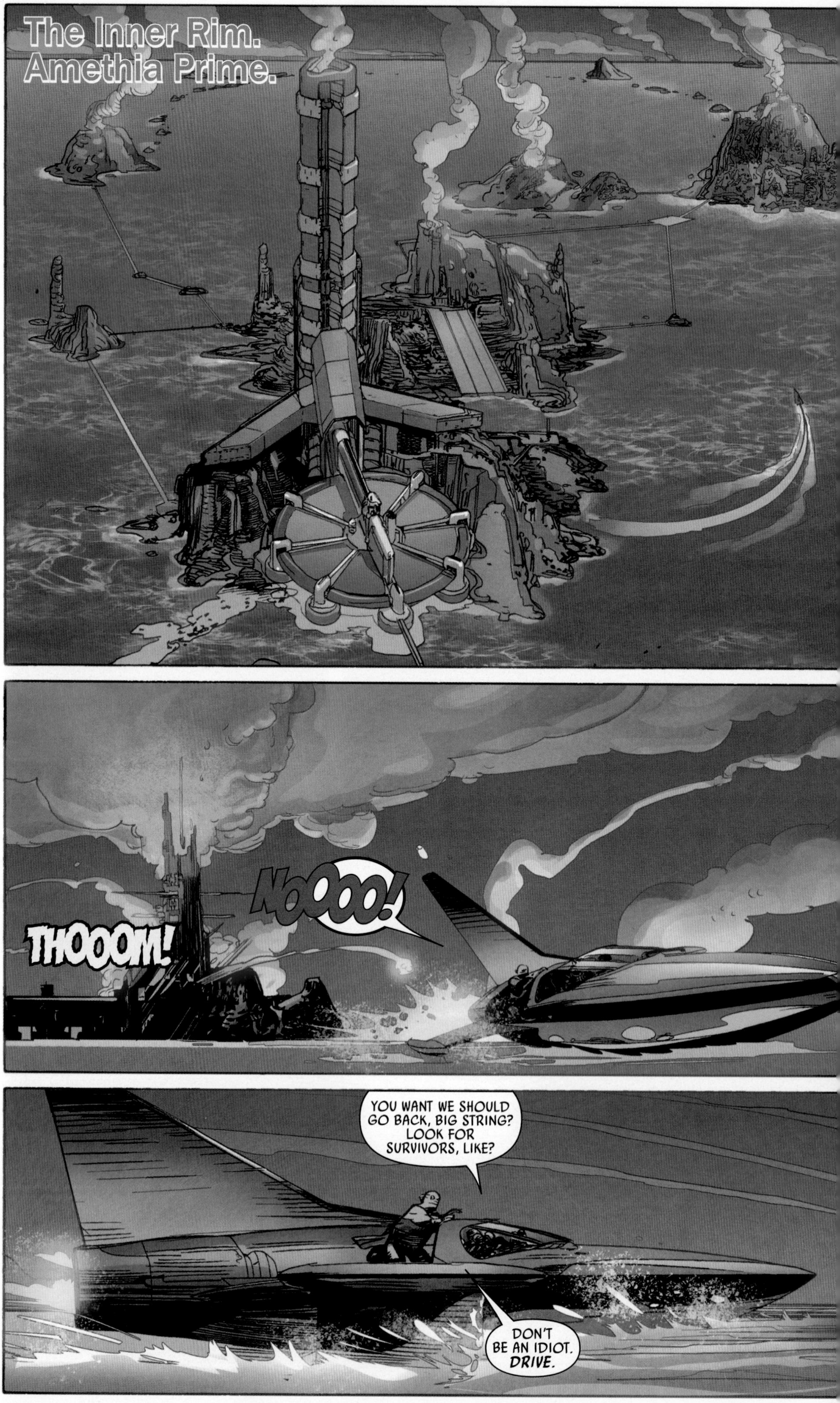
The Inner Rim.
Amethia Prime.
THOOOM!
NOOOO!
YOU WANT WE SHOULD GO BACK, BIG STRING? LOOK FOR SURVIVORS, LIKE?
DON'T BE AN IDIOT. DRIVE.

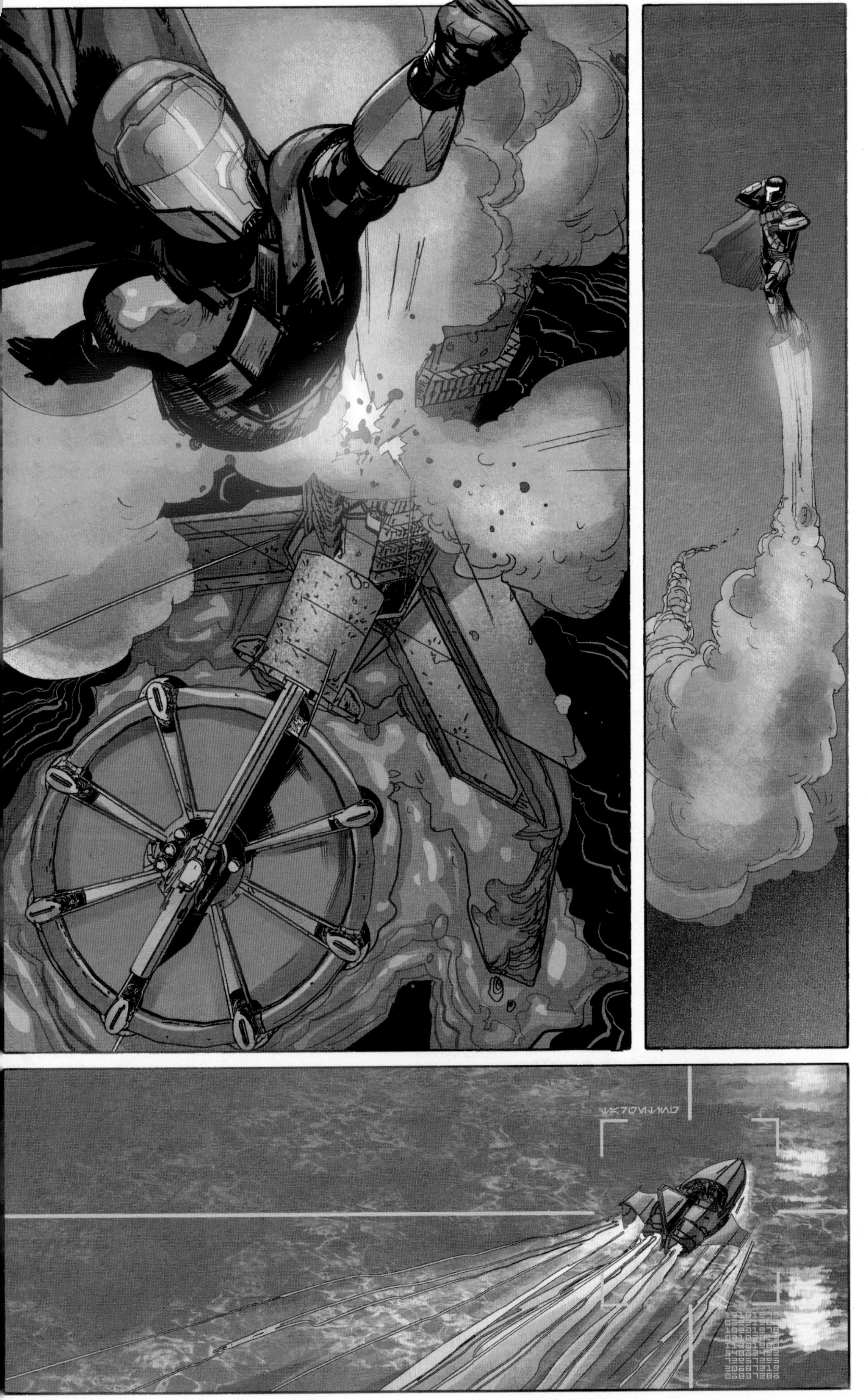

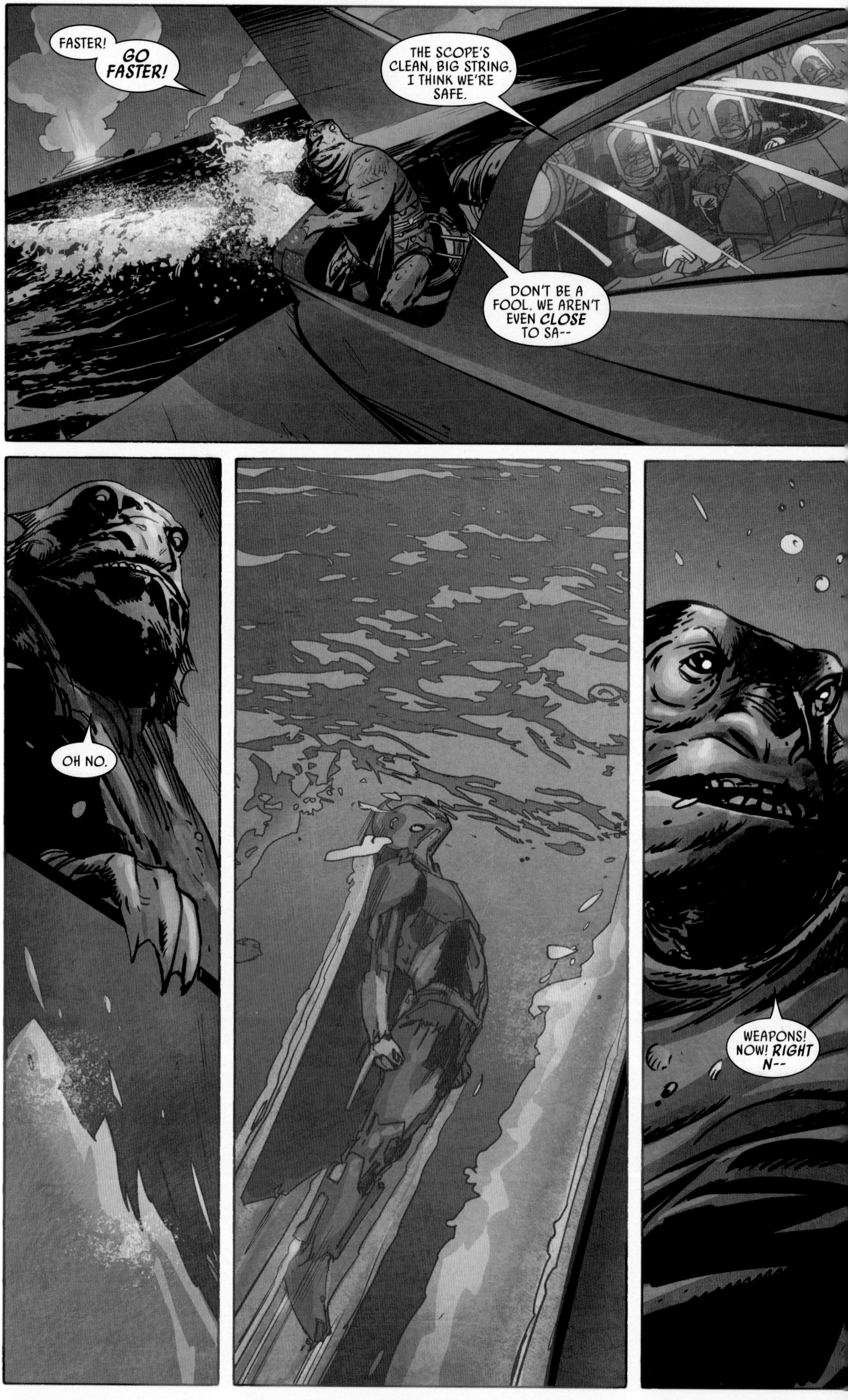
FASTER! GO FASTER!
THE SCOPE'S CLEAN, BIG STRING. I THINK WE'RE SAFE.
DON'T BE A FOOL. WE AREN'T EVEN CLOSE TO SA--
OH NO.
WEAPONS! NOW! RIGHT N--

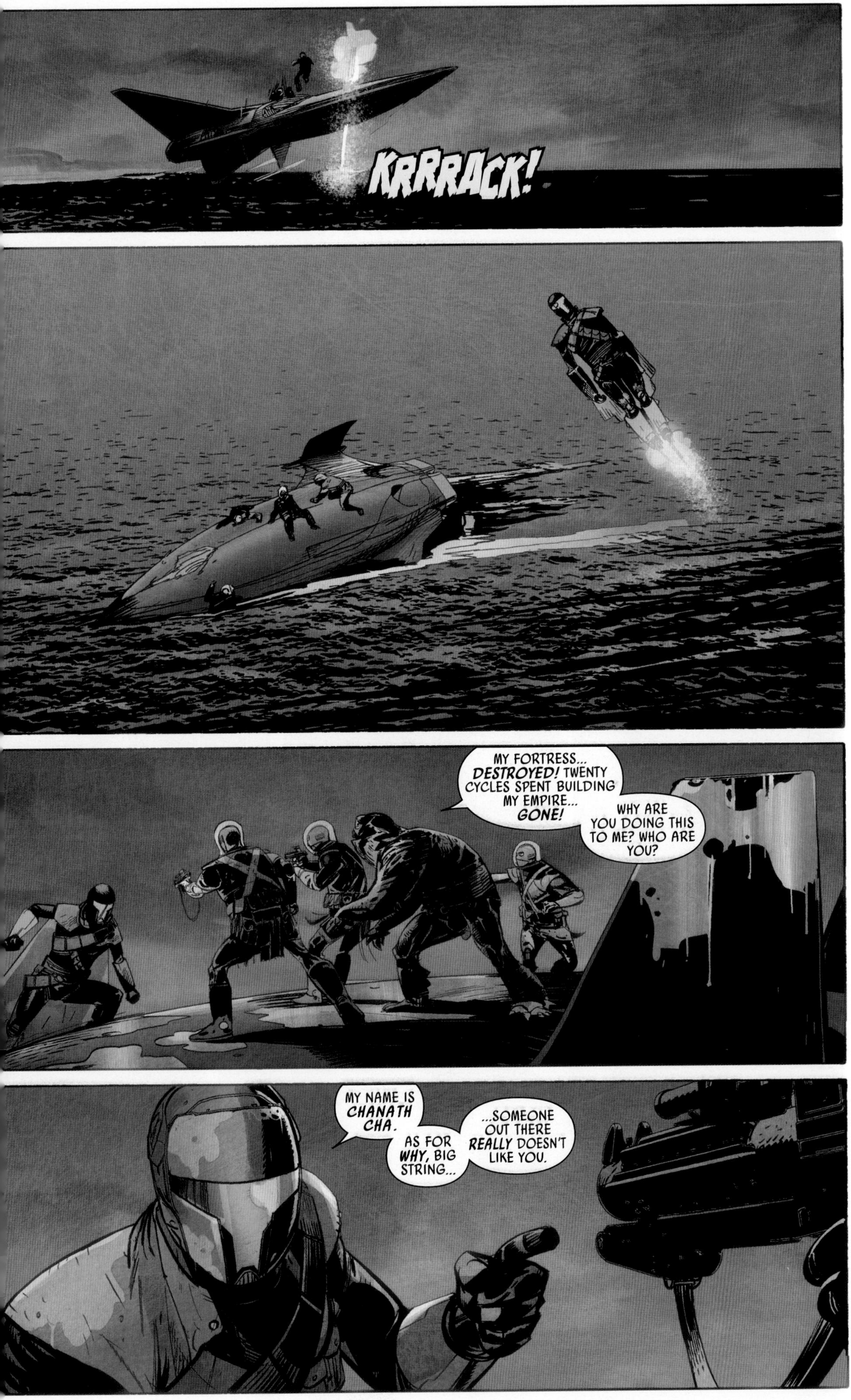
KRRRACK!
MY FORTRESS... DESTROYED! TWENTY CYCLES SPENT BUILDING MY EMPIRE... GONE!
WHY ARE YOU DOING THIS TO ME? WHO ARE YOU?
MY NAME IS CHANATH CHA.
AS FOR WHY, BIG STRING...
...SOMEONE OUT THERE REALLY DOESN'T LIKE YOU.

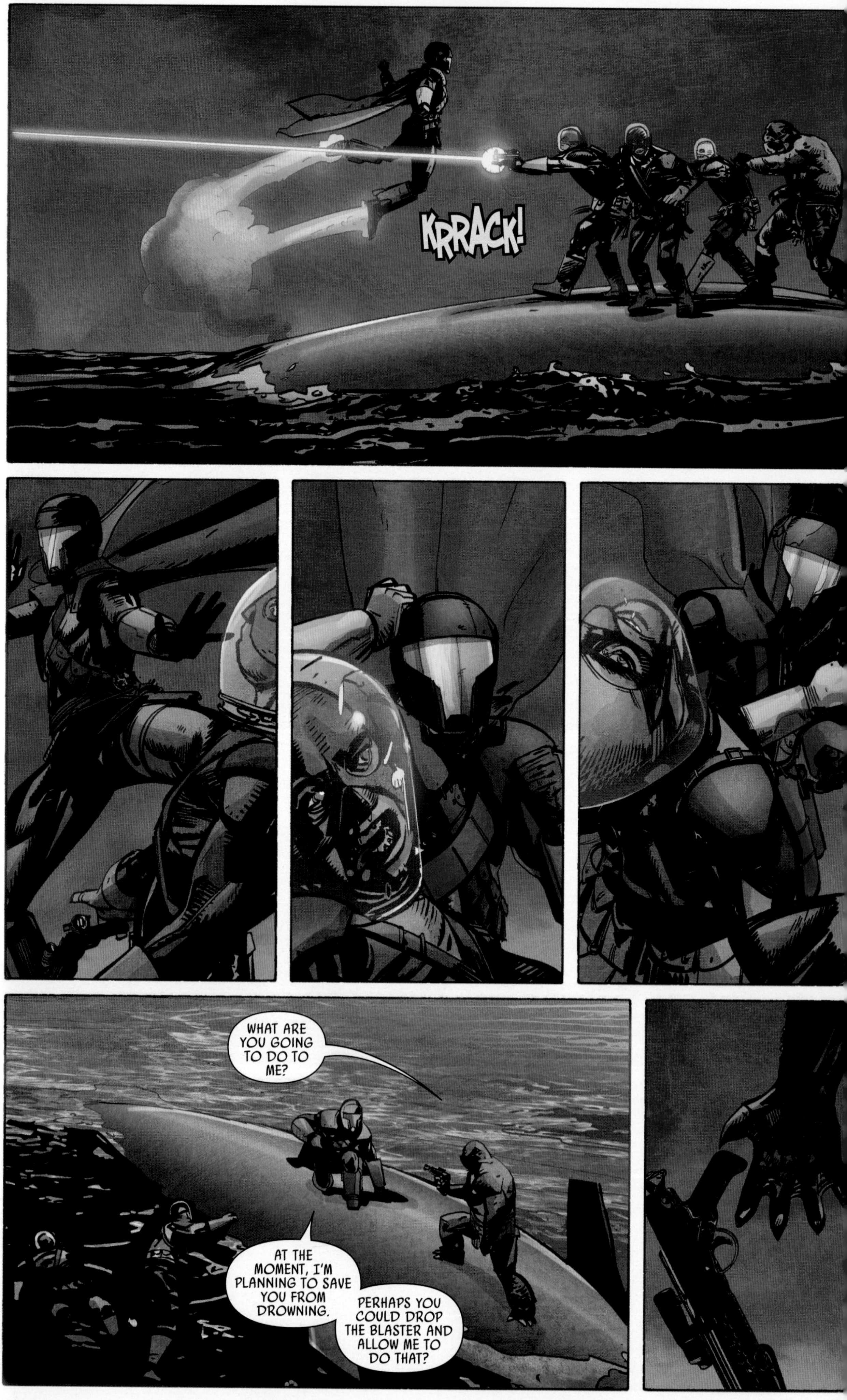
KRRACK!
WHAT ARE YOU GOING TO DO TO ME?
AT THE MOMENT, I'M PLANNING TO SAVE YOU FROM DROWNING.
PERHAPS YOU COULD DROP THE BLASTER AND ALLOW ME TO DO THAT?

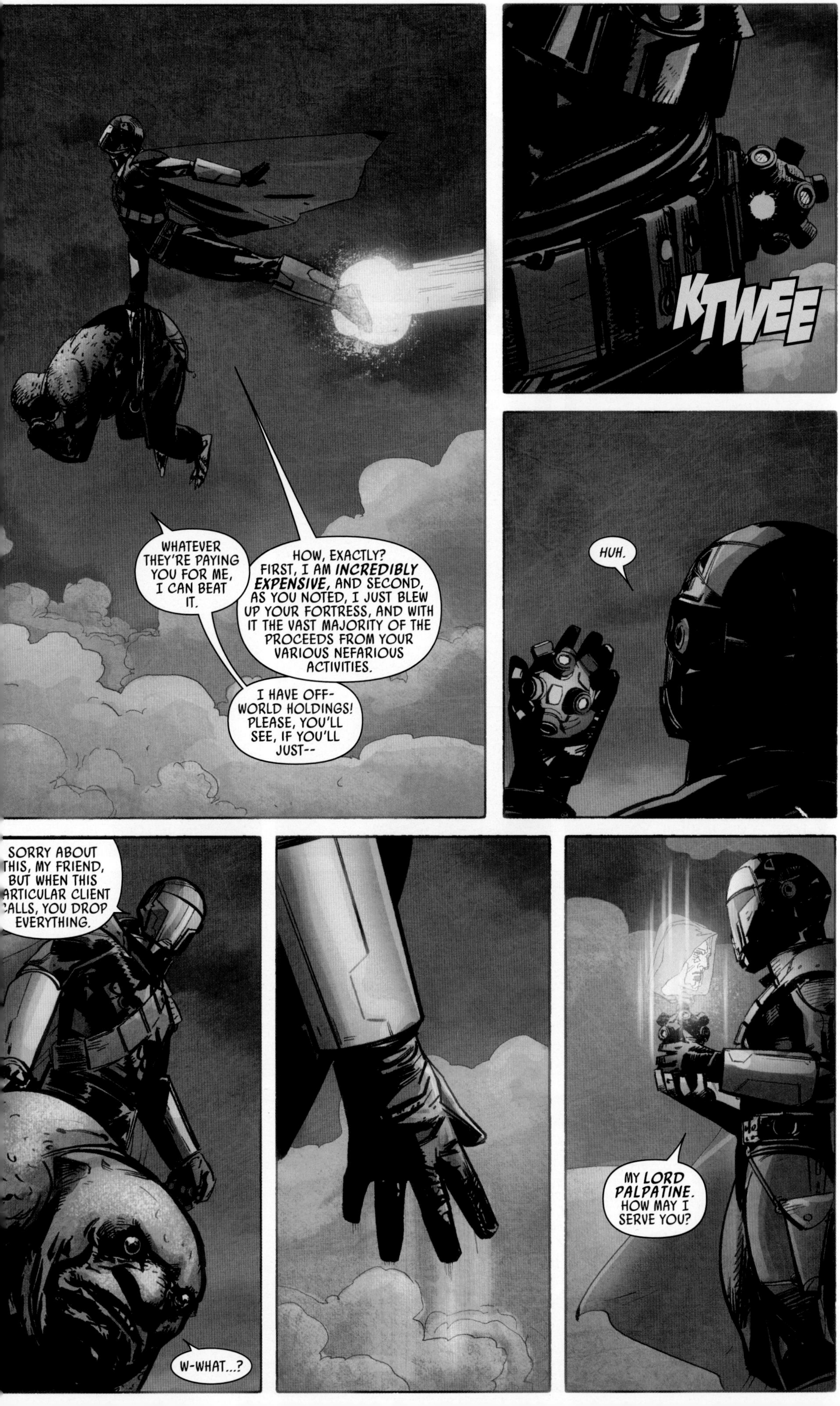
KTWEE
WHATEVER THEY'RE PAYING YOU FOR ME, I CAN BEAT IT.
HOW, EXACTLY? FIRST, I AM INCREDIBLY EXPENSIVE, AND SECOND, AS YOU NOTED, I JUST BLEW UP YOUR FORTRESS, AND WITH IT THE VAST MAJORITY OF THE PROCEEDS FROM YOUR VARIOUS NEFARIOUS ACTIVITIES.
I HAVE OFF-WORLD HOLDINGS! PLEASE, YOU'LL SEE, IF YOU'LL JUST--
HUH.
SORRY ABOUT THIS, MY FRIEND, BUT WHEN THIS ARTICULAR CLIENT CALLS, YOU DROP EVERYTHING.
W-WHAT...?
MY LORD PALPATINE. HOW MAY I SERVE YOU?

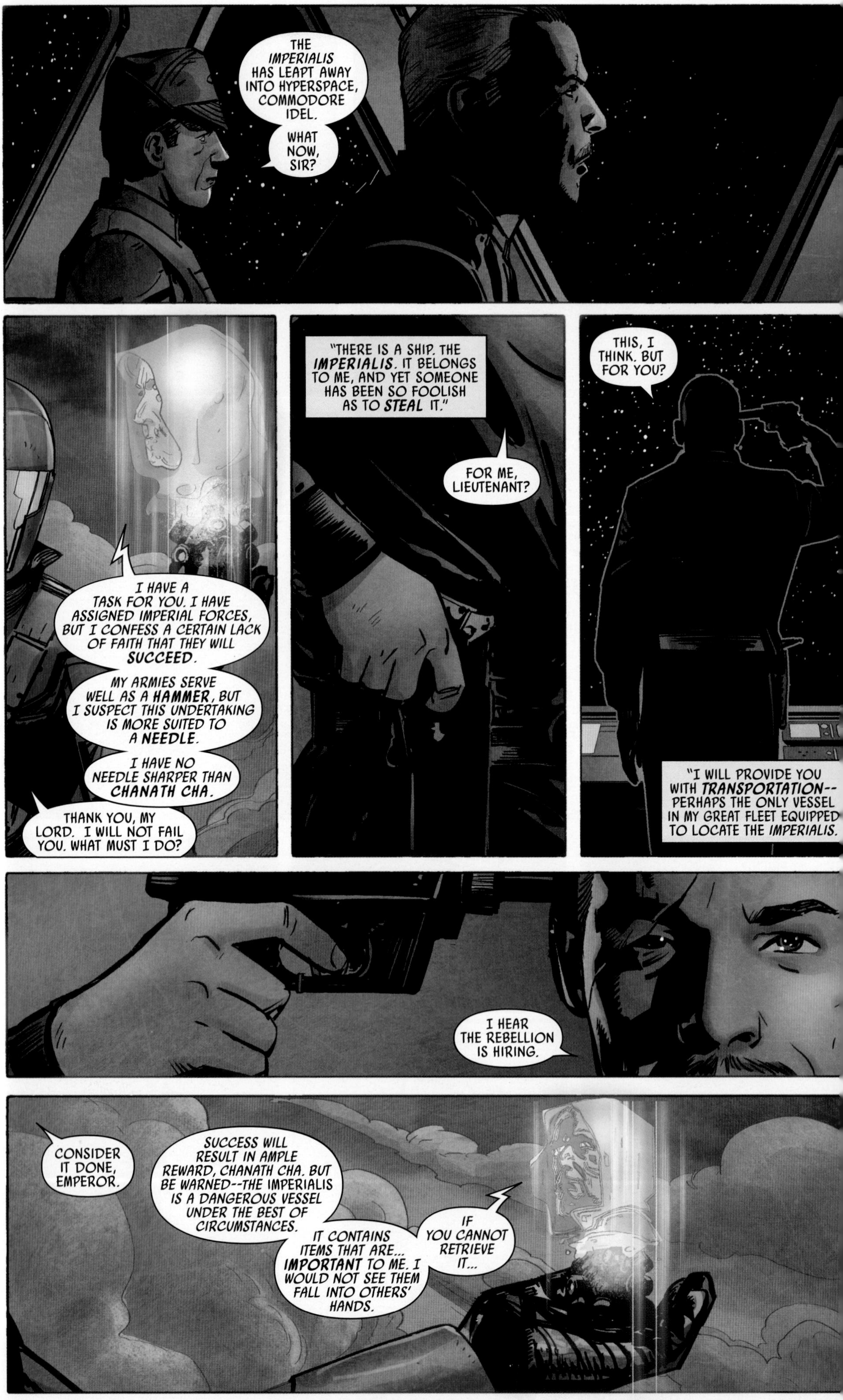

THE IMPERIALIS HAS LEAPT AWAY INTO HYPERSPACE, COMMODORE IDEL.
WHAT NOW, SIR?
I HAVE A TASK FOR YOU. I HAVE ASSIGNED IMPERIAL FORCES, BUT I CONFESS A CERTAIN LACK OF FAITH THAT THEY WILL SUCCEED.
MY ARMIES SERVE WELL AS A HAMMER, BUT I SUSPECT THIS UNDERTAKING IS MORE SUITED TO A NEEDLE.
I HAVE NO NEEDLE SHARPER THAN CHANATH CHA.
THANK YOU, MY LORD. I WILL NOT FAIL YOU. WHAT MUST I DO?
"THERE IS A SHIP. THE IMPERIALIS. IT BELONGS TO ME, AND YET SOMEONE HAS BEEN SO FOOLISH AS TO STEAL IT."
FOR ME, LIEUTENANT?
THIS, I THINK. BUT FOR YOU?
"I WILL PROVIDE YOU WITH TRANSPORTATION-- PERHAPS THE ONLY VESSEL IN MY GREAT FLEET EQUIPPED TO LOCATE THE IMPERIALIS.
I HEAR THE REBELLION IS HIRING.
CONSIDER IT DONE, EMPEROR.
SUCCESS WILL RESULT IN AMPLE REWARD, CHANATH CHA. BUT BE WARNED--THE IMPERIALIS IS A DANGEROUS VESSEL UNDER THE BEST OF CIRCUMSTANCES.
IT CONTAINS ITEMS THAT ARE... IMPORTANT TO ME. I WOULD NOT SEE THEM FALL INTO OTHERS' HANDS.
IF YOU CANNOT RETRIEVE IT...

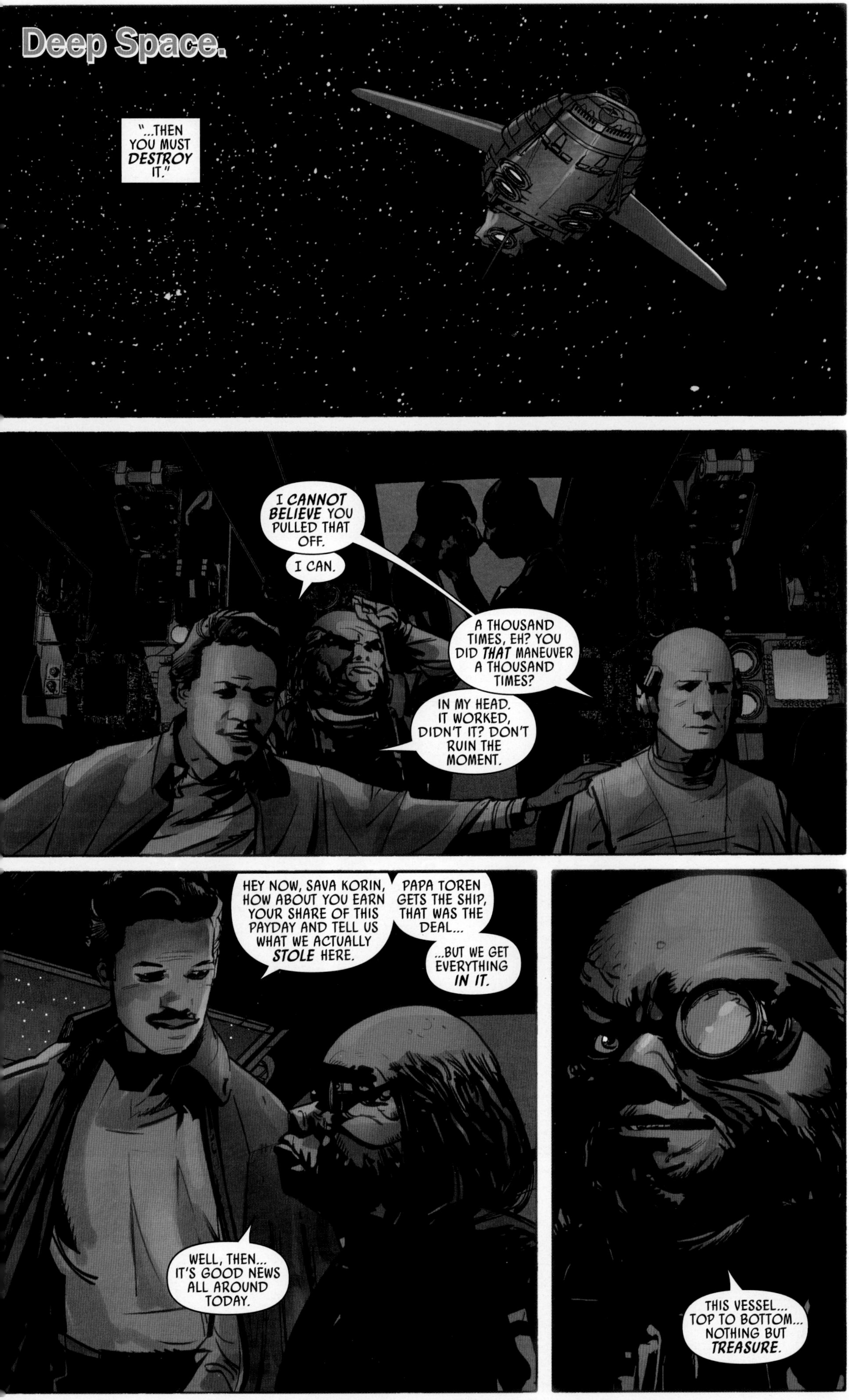
Deep Space.
"...THEN YOU MUST DESTROY IT."
I CANNOT BELIEVE YOU PULLED THAT OFF.
I CAN.
A THOUSAND TIMES, EH? YOU DID THAT MANEUVER A THOUSAND TIMES?
IN MY HEAD. IT WORKED, DIDN'T IT? DON'T RUIN THE MOMENT.
HEY NOW, SAVA KORIN, HOW ABOUT YOU EARN YOUR SHARE OF THIS PAYDAY AND TELL US WHAT WE ACTUALLY STOLE HERE.
PAPA TOREN GETS THE SHIP, THAT WAS THE DEAL...
...BUT WE GET EVERYTHING IN IT.
WELL, THEN... IT'S GOOD NEWS ALL AROUND TODAY.
THIS VESSEL... TOP TO BOTTOM... NOTHING BUT TREASURE.

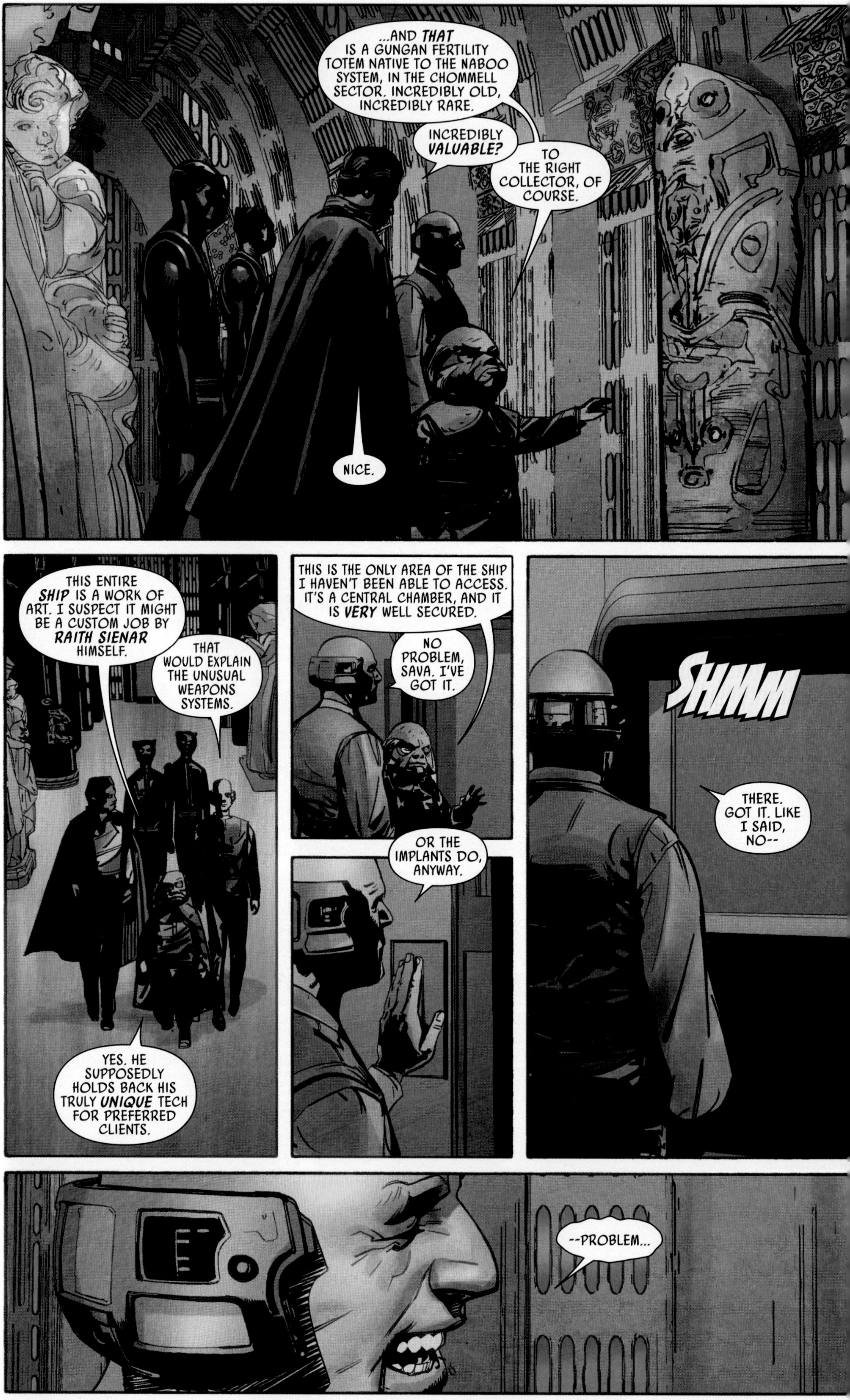
...AND THAT IS A GUNGAN FERTILITY TOTEM NATIVE TO THE NABOO SYSTEM, IN THE CHOMMELL SECTOR. INCREDIBLY OLD, INCREDIBLY RARE.
INCREDIBLY VALUABLE?
TO THE RIGHT COLLECTOR, OF COURSE.
NICE.
THIS ENTIRE SHIP IS A WORK OF ART. I SUSPECT IT MIGHT BE A CUSTOM JOB BY RAITH SIENAR HIMSELF.
THAT WOULD EXPLAIN THE UNUSUAL WEAPONS SYSTEMS.
YES. HE SUPPOSEDLY HOLDS BACK HIS TRULY UNIQUE TECH FOR PREFERRED CLIENTS.
THIS IS THE ONLY AREA OF THE SHIP I HAVEN'T BEEN ABLE TO ACCESS. IT'S A CENTRAL CHAMBER, AND IT IS VERY WELL SECURED.
NO PROBLEM, SAVA. I'VE GOT IT.
OR THE IMPLANTS DO, ANYWAY.
SHMM
THERE. GOT IT. LIKE I SAID, NO--
--PROBLEM...

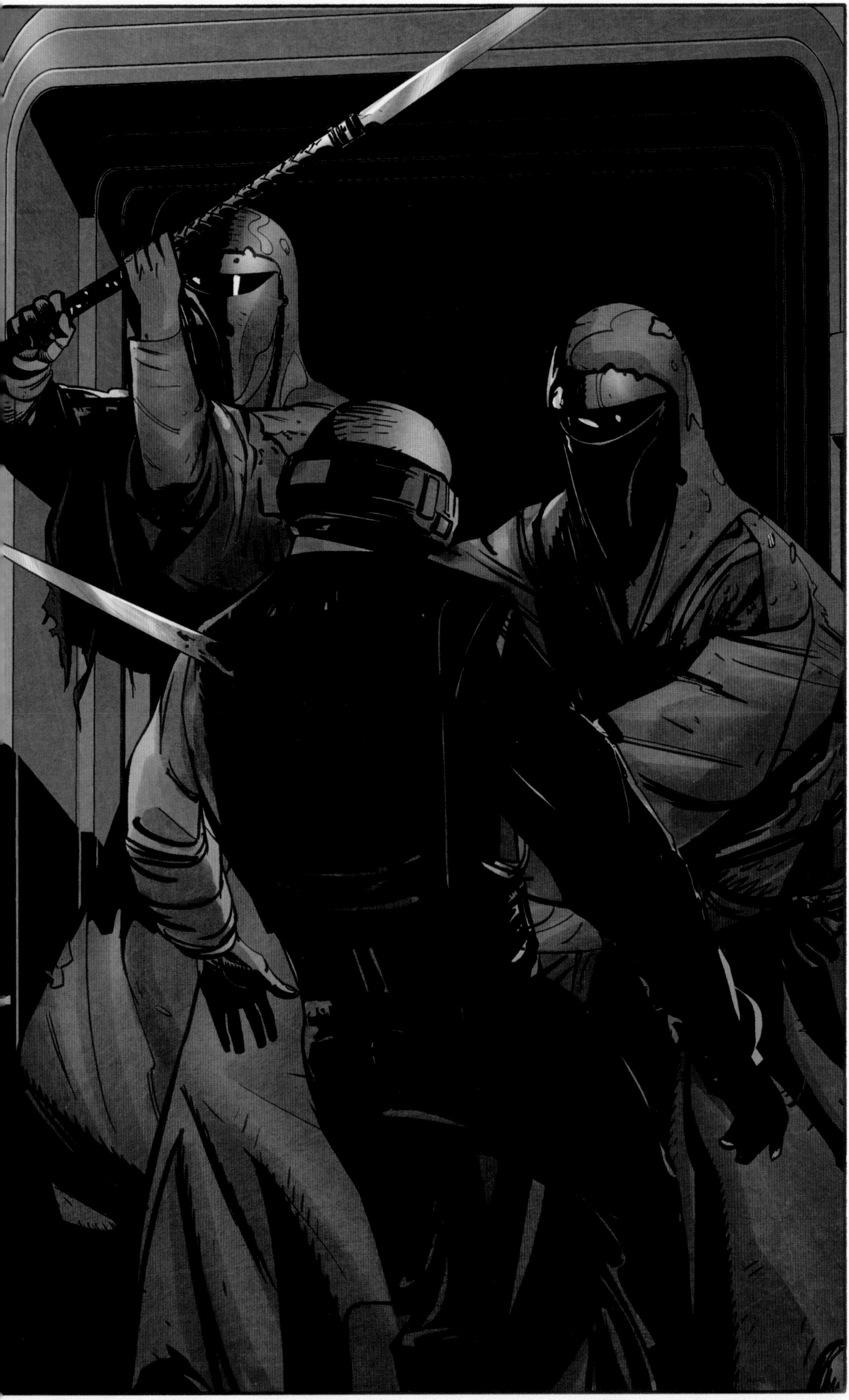

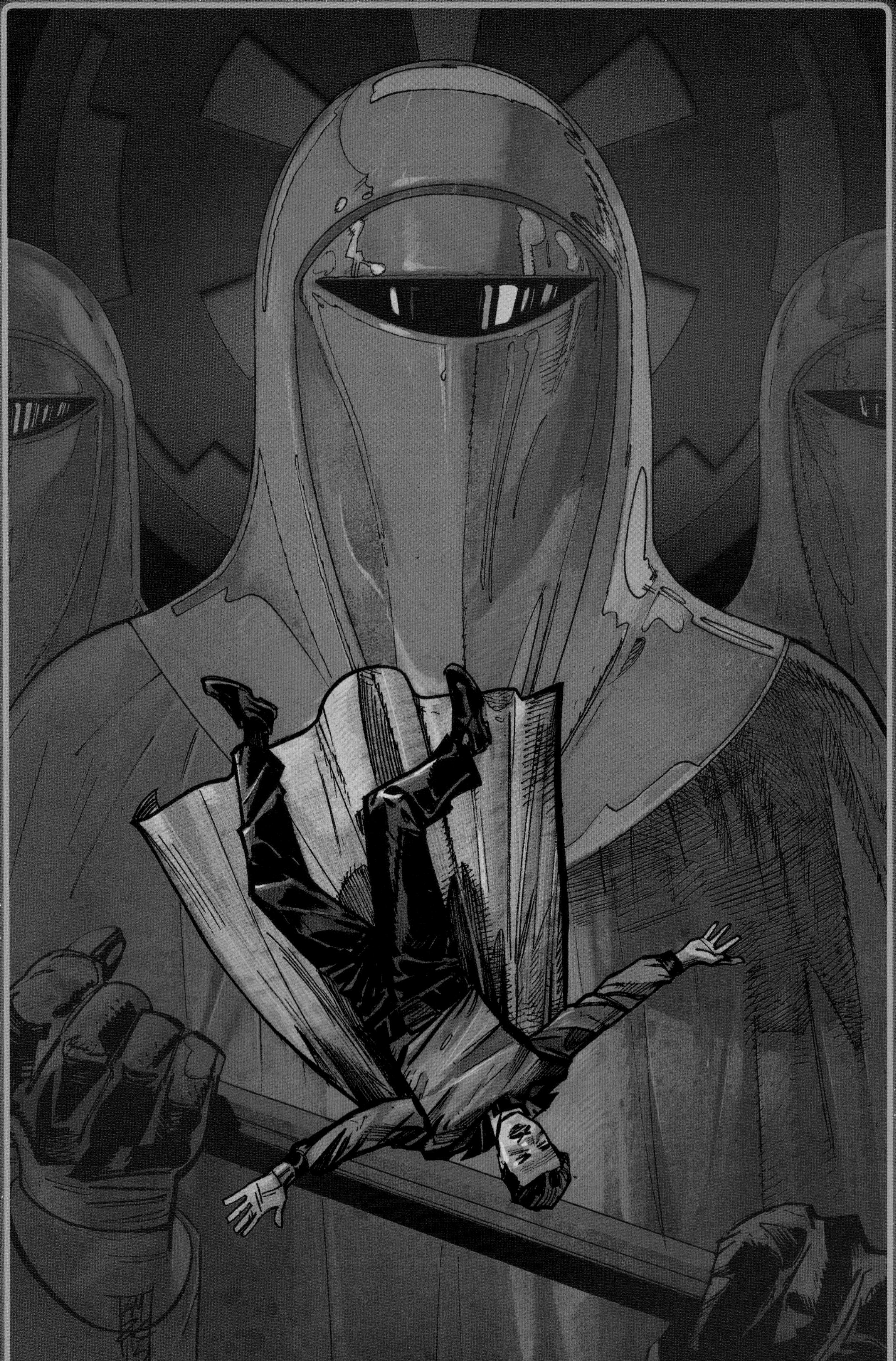

LANDO 3

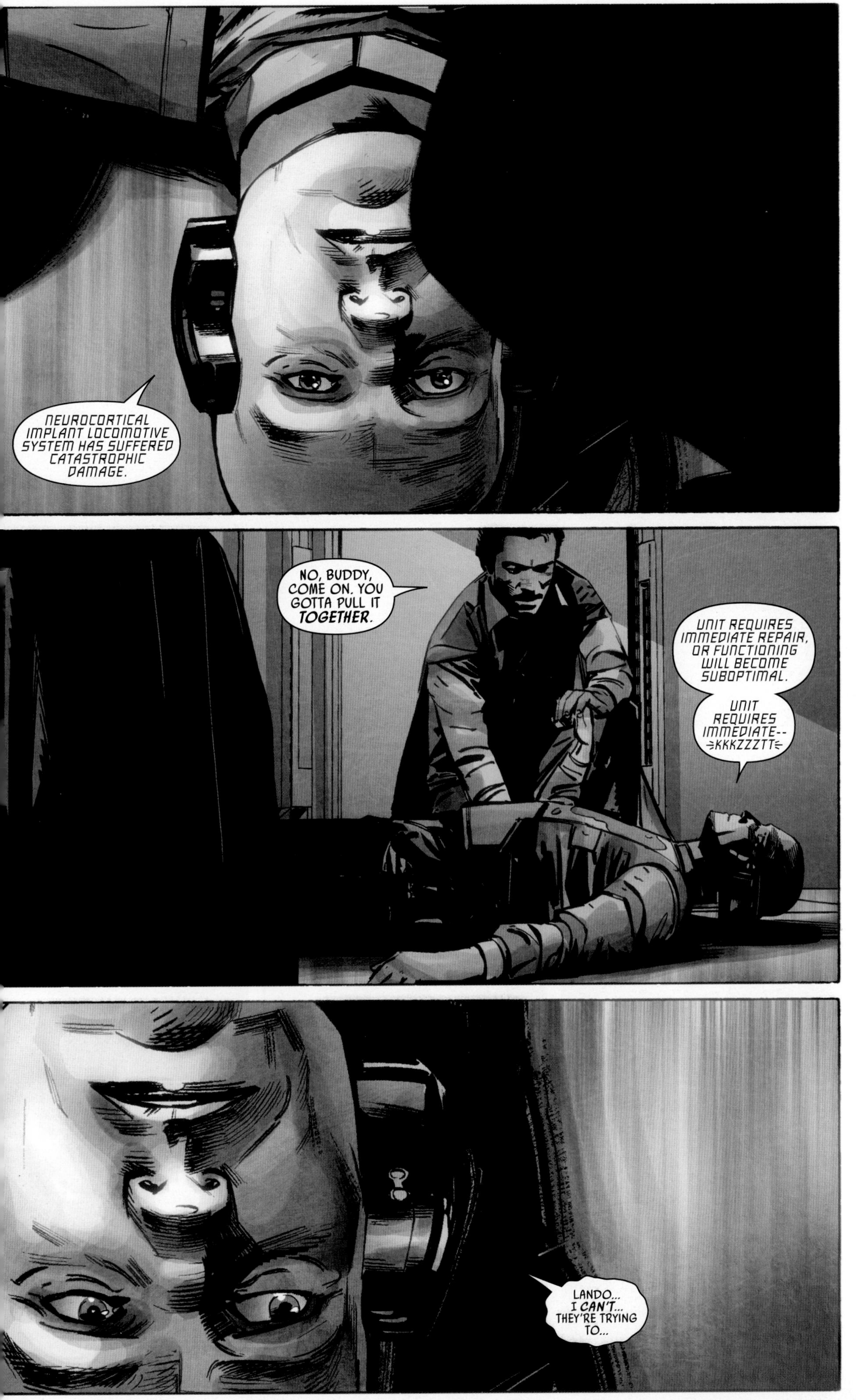
NEUROCORTICAL IMPLANT LOCOMOTIVE SYSTEM HAS SUFFERED CATASTROPHIC DAMAGE.
NO, BUDDY, COME ON. YOU GOTTA PULL IT *TOGETHER*.
UNIT REQUIRES IMMEDIATE REPAIR, OR FUNCTIONING WILL BECOME SUBOPTIMAL.
UNIT REQUIRES IMMEDIATE-- KKKZZZTT
LANDO... I *CAN'T*... THEY'RE TRYING TO...

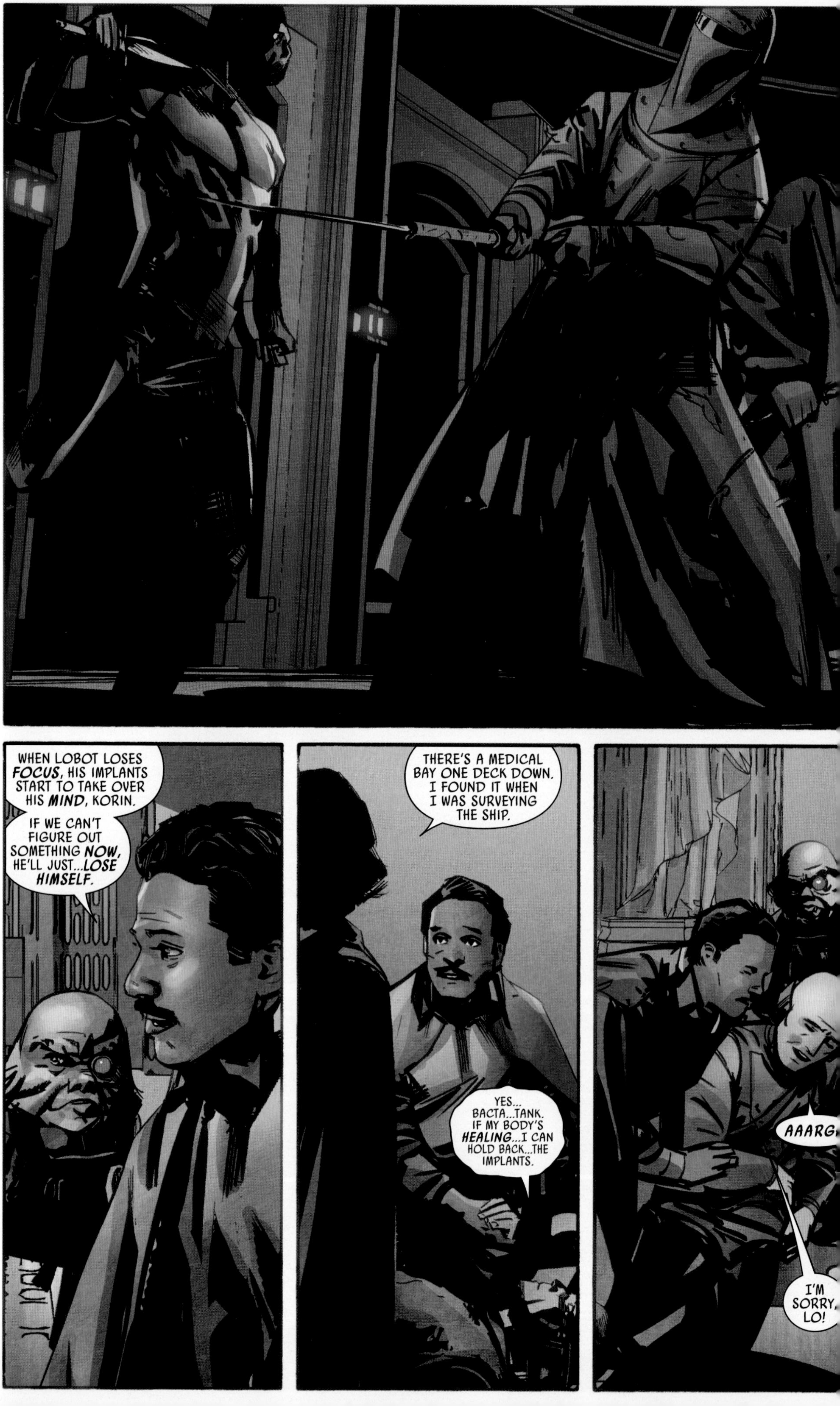
WHEN LOBOT LOSES FOCUS, HIS IMPLANTS START TO TAKE OVER HIS MIND, KORIN.
IF WE CAN'T FIGURE OUT SOMETHING NOW, HE'LL JUST...LOSE HIMSELF.
THERE'S A MEDICAL BAY ONE DECK DOWN. I FOUND IT WHEN I WAS SURVEYING THE SHIP.
YES... BACTA...TANK. IF MY BODY'S HEALING...I CAN HOLD BACK...THE IMPLANTS.
AAARG
I'M SORRY, LO!

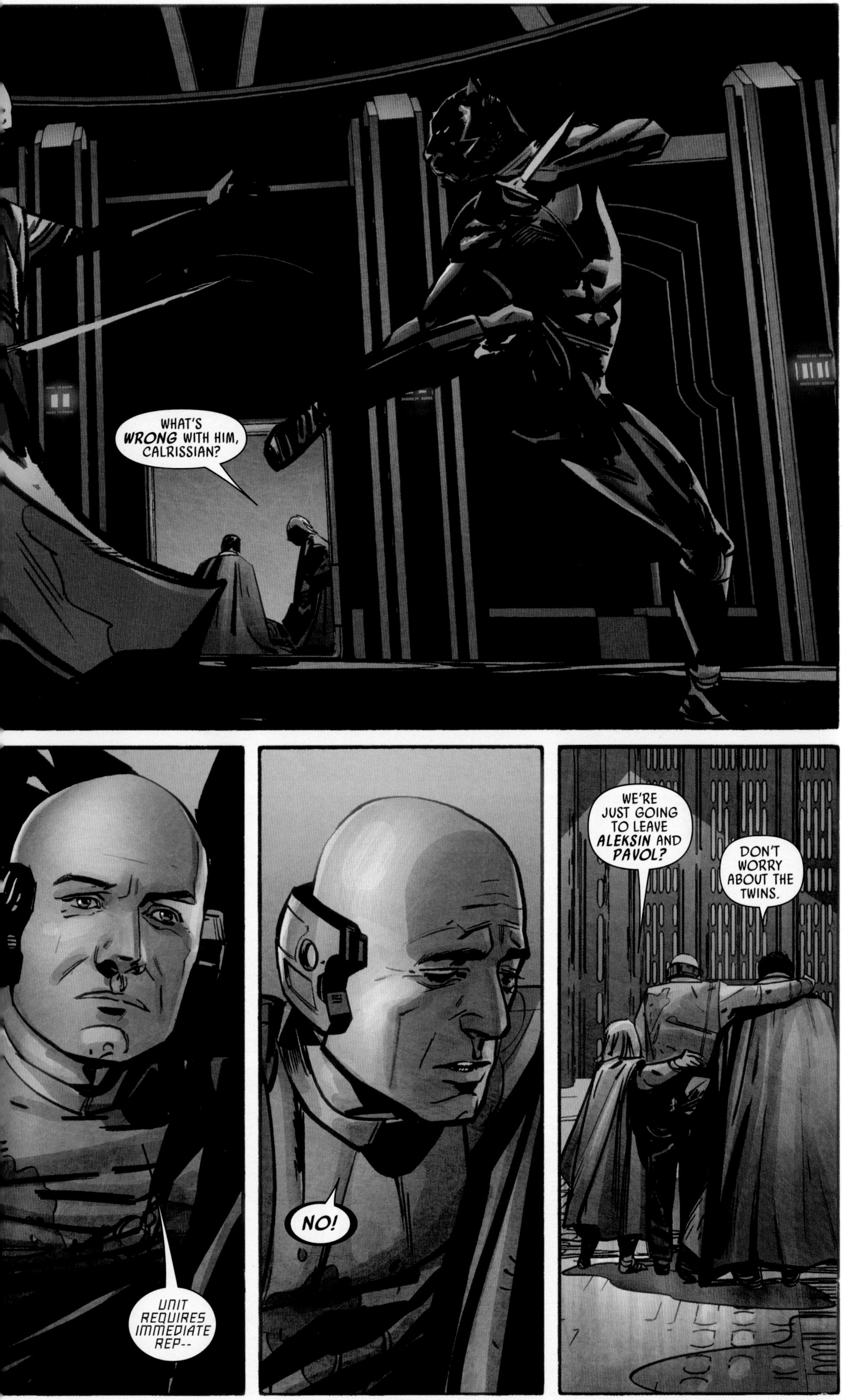
WHAT'S WRONG WITH HIM, CALRISSIAN?
UNIT REQUIRES IMMEDIATE REP--
NO!
WE'RE JUST GOING TO LEAVE ALEKSIN AND PAVOL?
DON'T WORRY ABOUT THE TWINS.

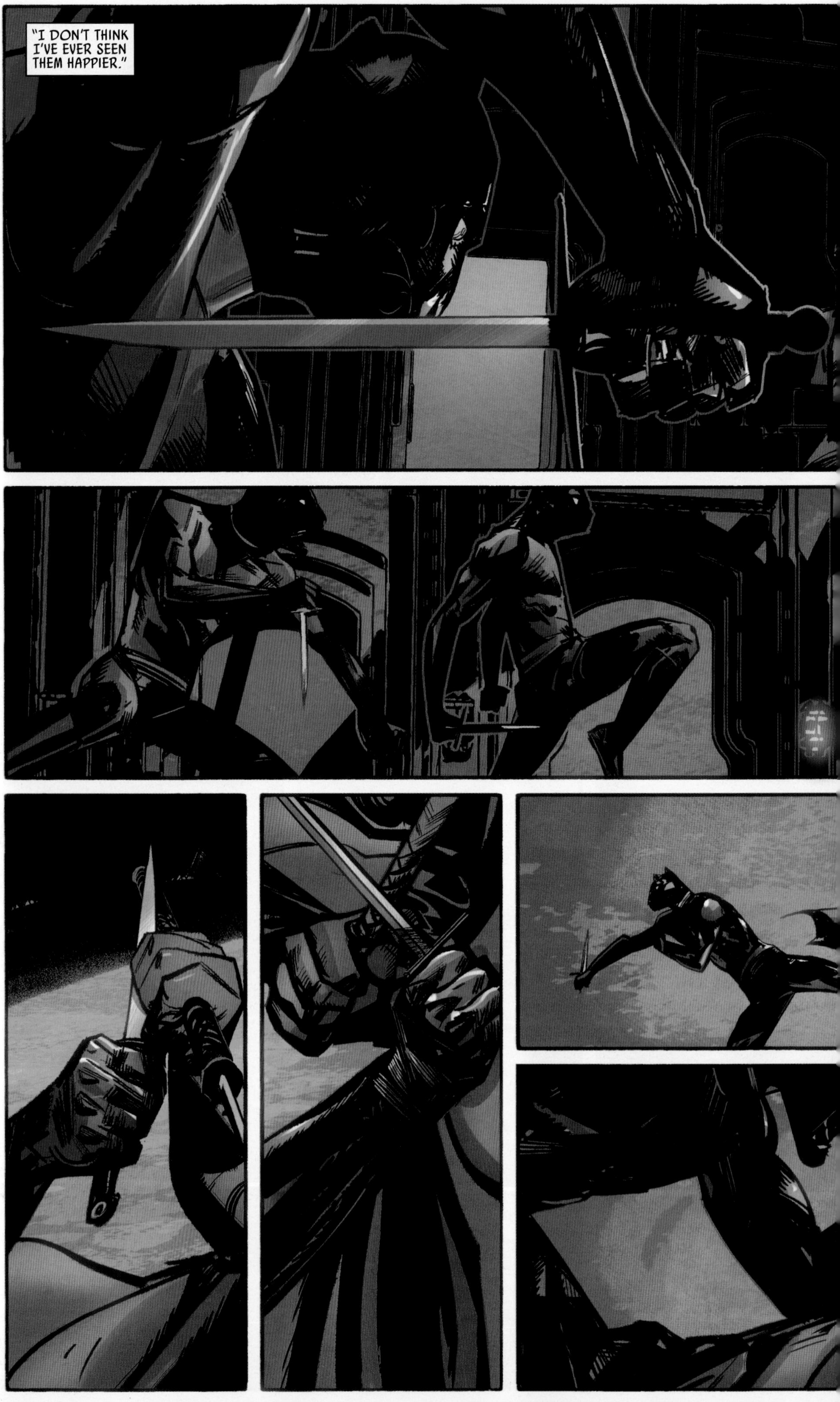
"I DON'T THINK I'VE EVER SEEN THEM HAPPIER."

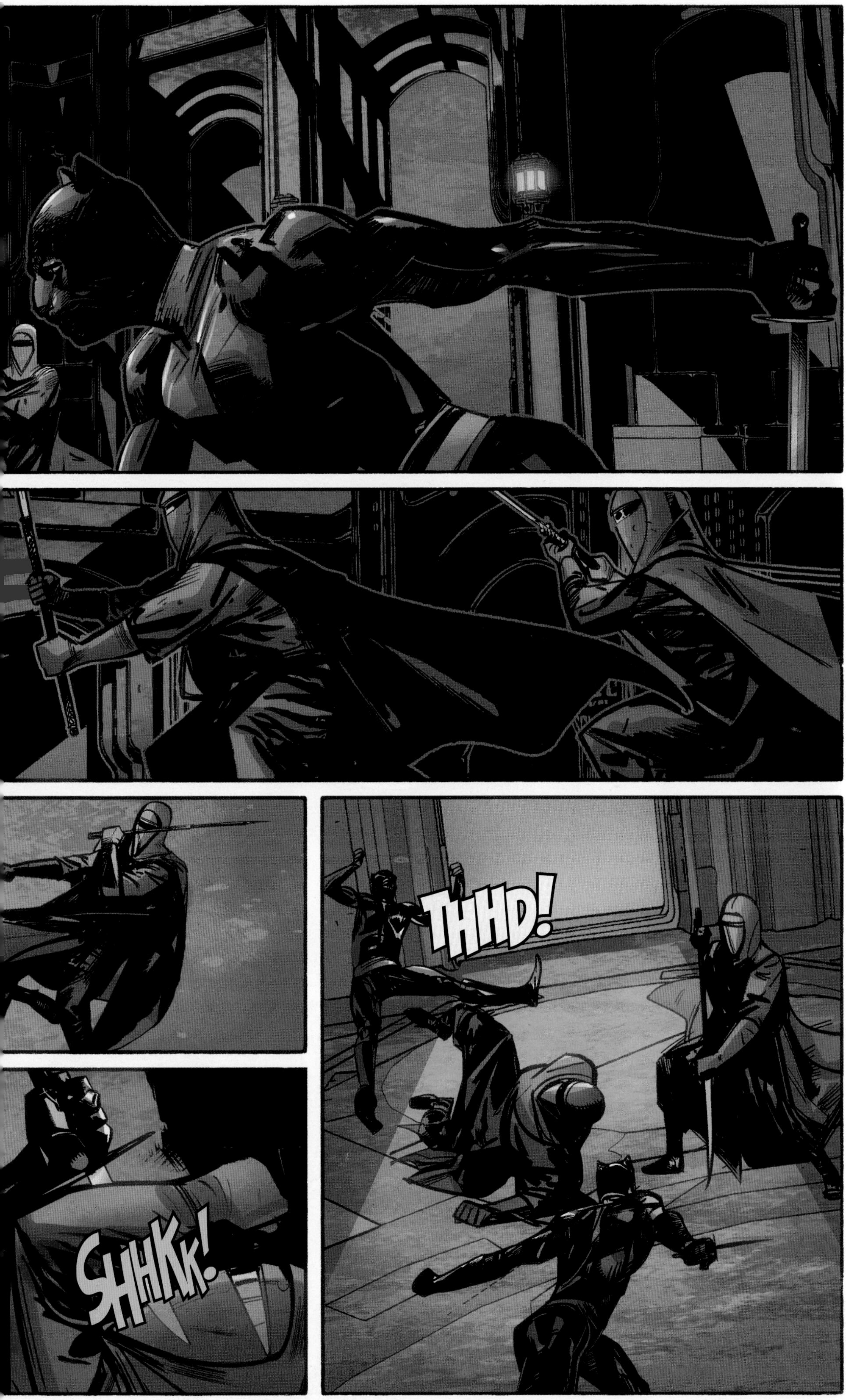
SHHKK!
THHD!

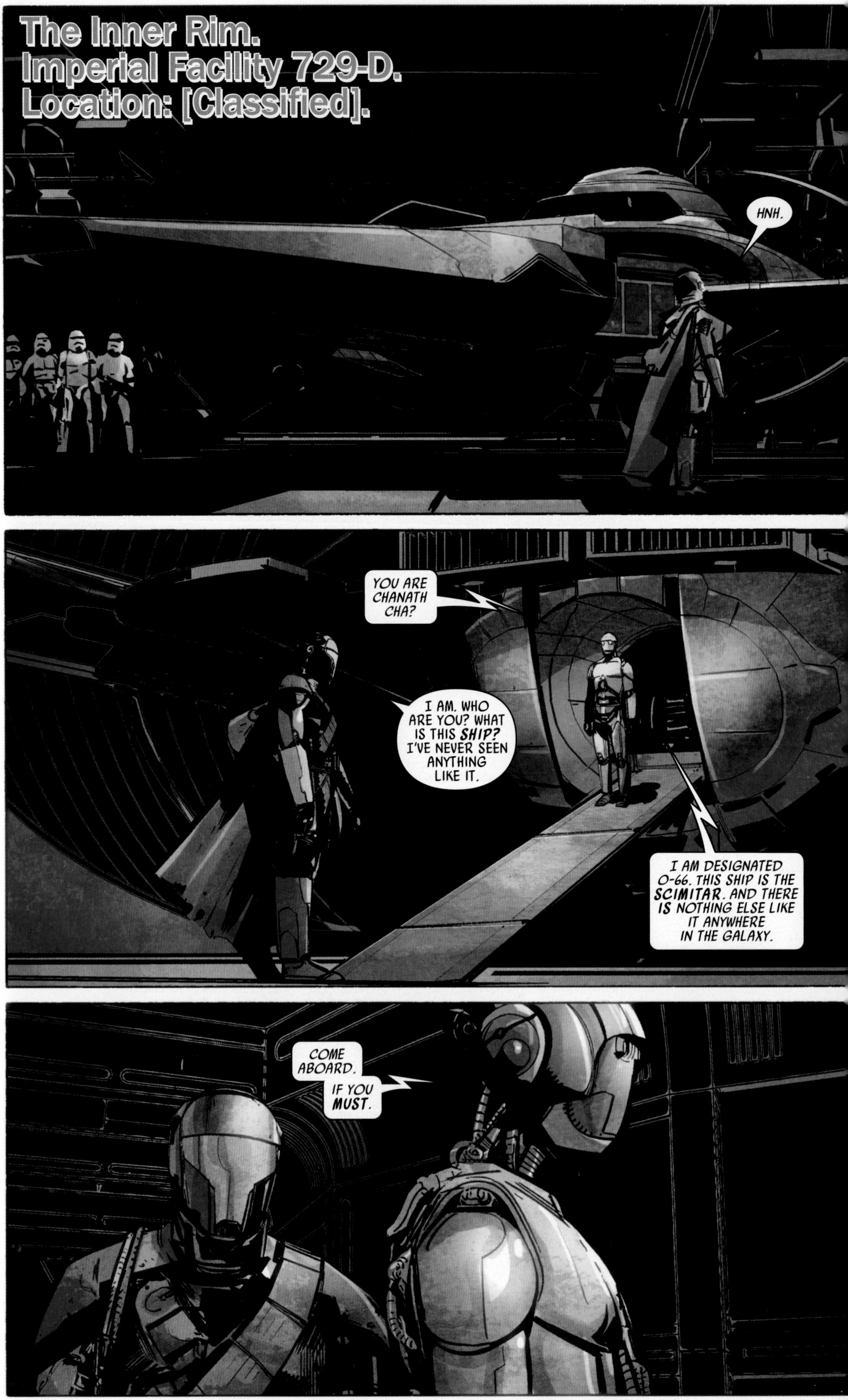
The Inner Rim.
Imperial Facility 729-D.
Location: [Classified].
HNH.
YOU ARE CHANATH CHA?
I AM. WHO ARE YOU? WHAT IS THIS SHIP? I'VE NEVER SEEN ANYTHING LIKE IT.
I AM DESIGNATED 0-66. THIS SHIP IS THE SCIMITAR. AND THERE IS NOTHING ELSE LIKE IT ANYWHERE IN THE GALAXY.
COME ABOARD.
IF YOU MUST.

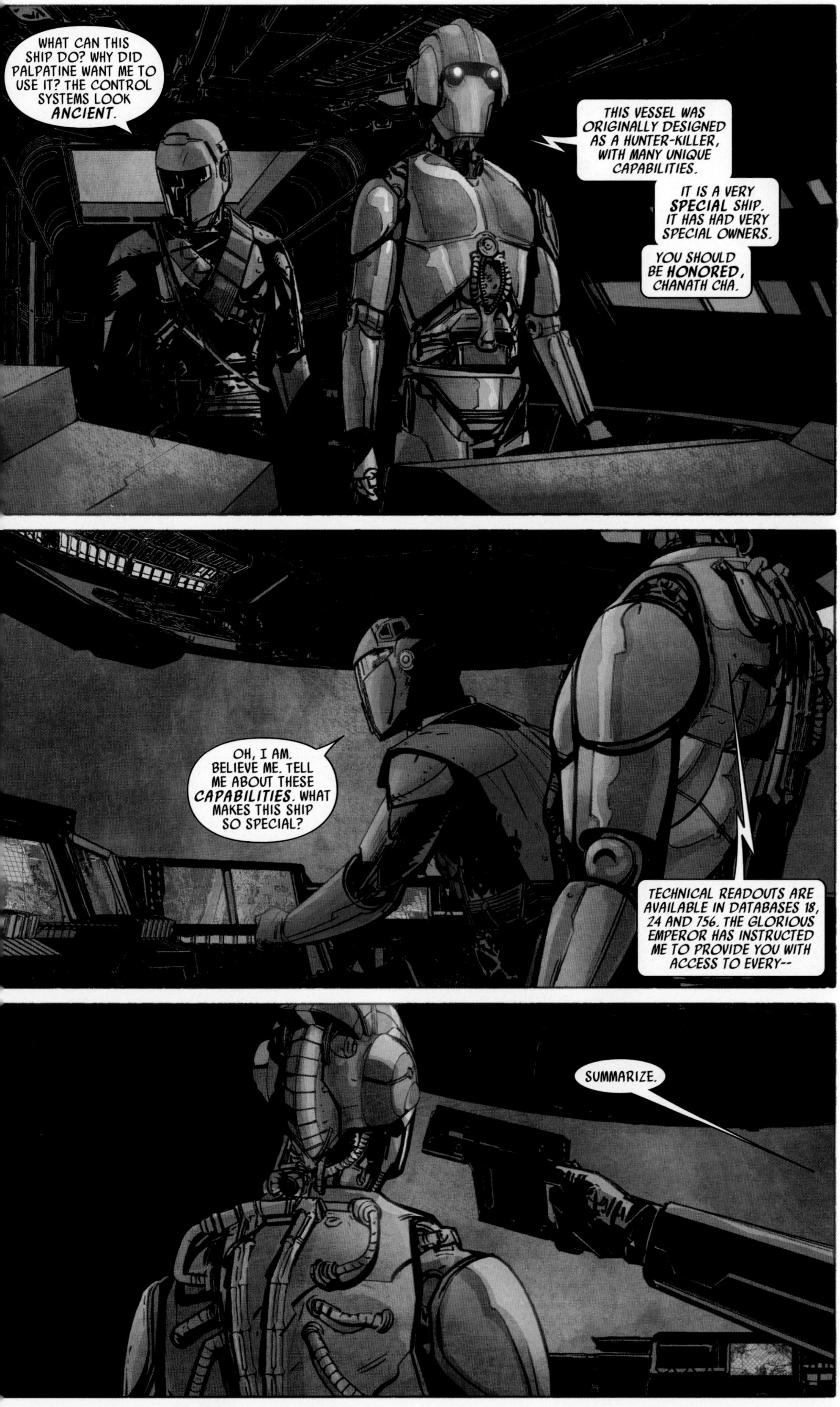
WHAT CAN THIS SHIP DO? WHY DID PALPATINE WANT ME TO USE IT? THE CONTROL SYSTEMS LOOK ANCIENT.
THIS VESSEL WAS ORIGINALLY DESIGNED AS A HUNTER-KILLER, WITH MANY UNIQUE CAPABILITIES.
IT IS A VERY SPECIAL SHIP. IT HAS HAD VERY SPECIAL OWNERS.
YOU SHOULD BE HONORED, CHANATH CHA.
OH, I AM. BELIEVE ME. TELL ME ABOUT THESE CAPABILITIES. WHAT MAKES THIS SHIP SO SPECIAL?
TECHNICAL READOUTS ARE AVAILABLE IN DATABASES 18, 24 AND 756. THE GLORIOUS EMPEROR HAS INSTRUCTED ME TO PROVIDE YOU WITH ACCESS TO EVERY--
SUMMARIZE.

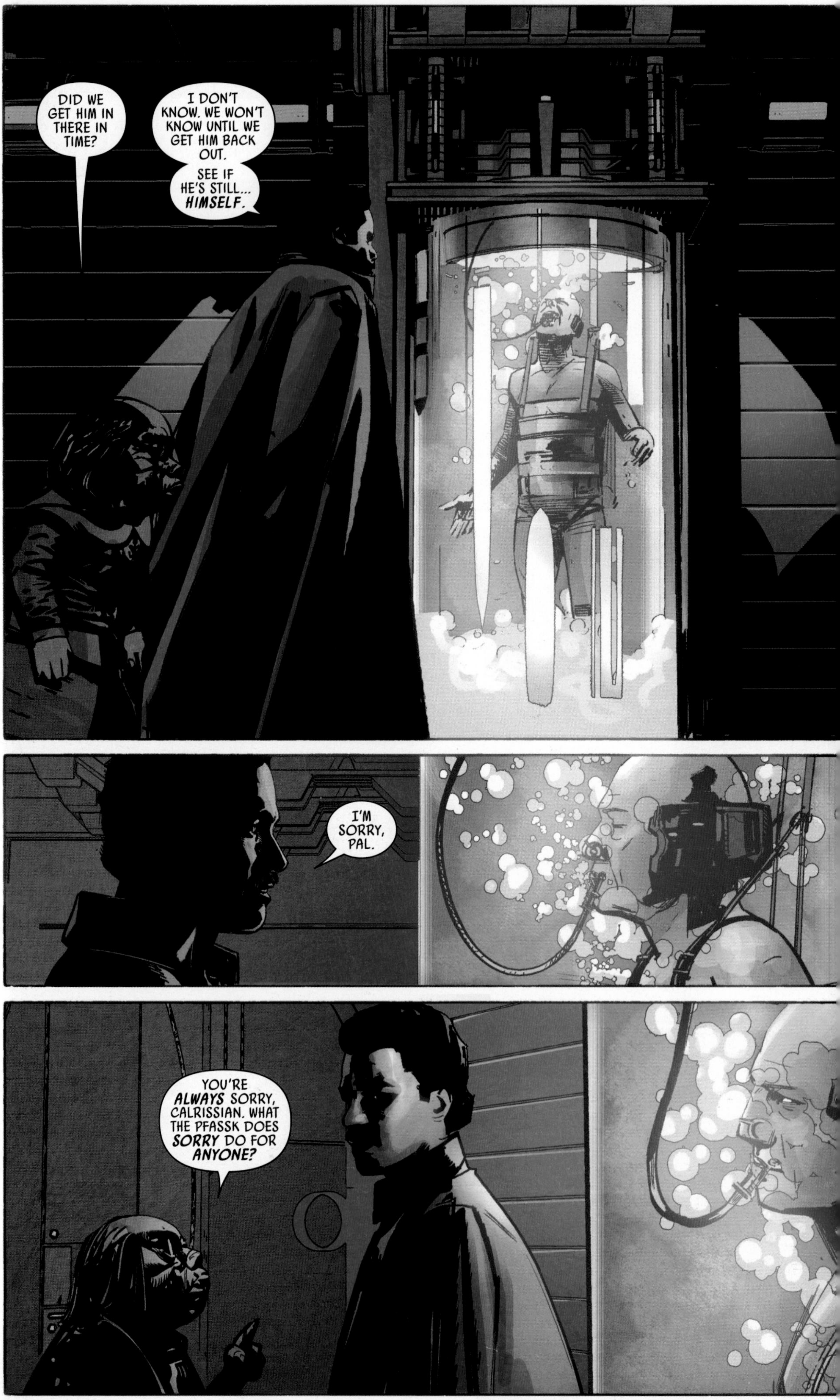
DID WE GET HIM IN THERE IN TIME?
I DON'T KNOW. WE WON'T KNOW UNTIL WE GET HIM BACK OUT.
SEE IF HE'S STILL... HIMSELF.
I'M SORRY, PAL.
YOU'RE ALWAYS SORRY, CALRISSIAN. WHAT THE PFASSK DOES SORRY DO FOR ANYONE?

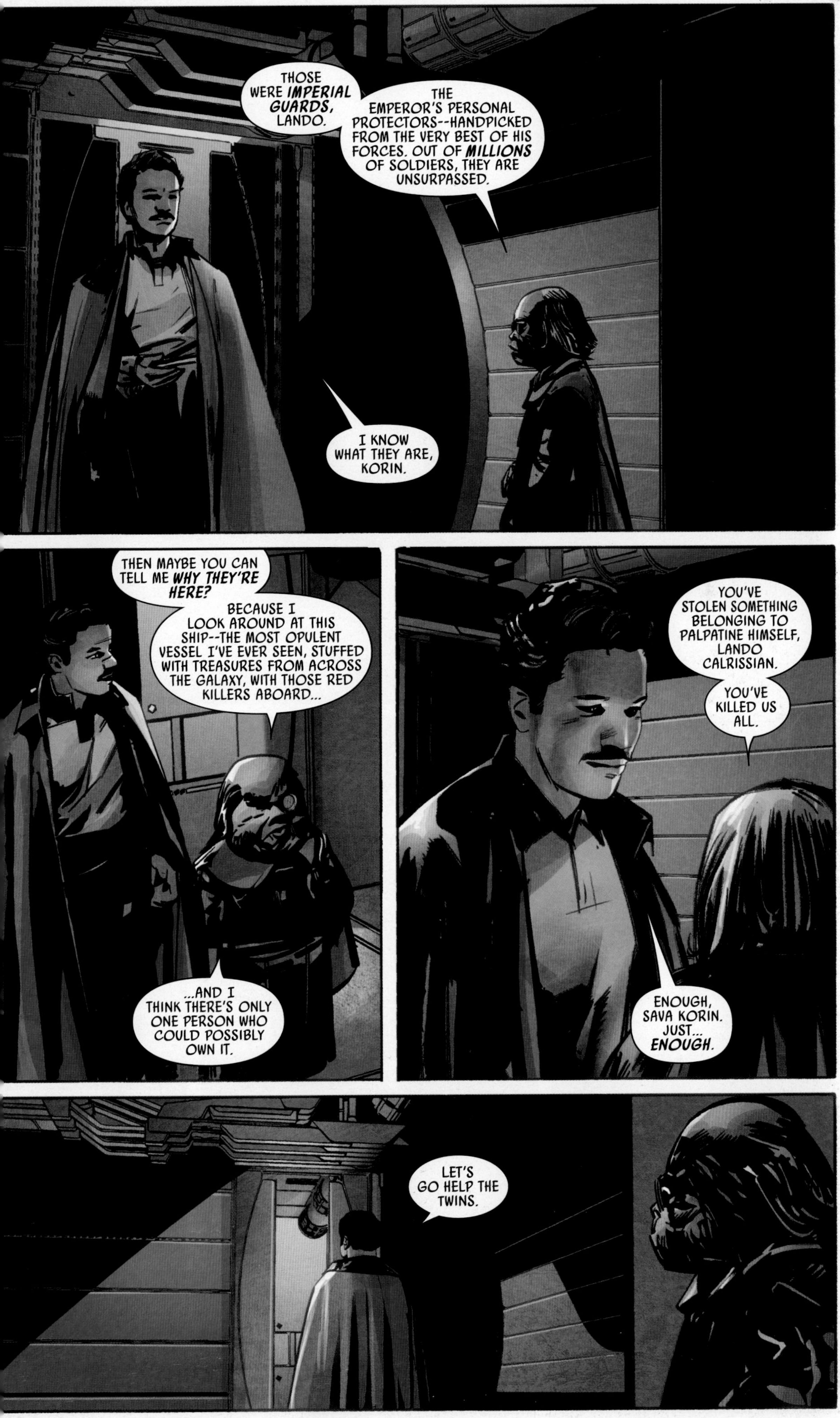
THOSE WERE IMPERIAL GUARDS, LANDO.
THE EMPEROR'S PERSONAL PROTECTORS--HANDPICKED FROM THE VERY BEST OF HIS FORCES. OUT OF MILLIONS OF SOLDIERS, THEY ARE UNSURPASSED.
I KNOW WHAT THEY ARE, KORIN.
THEN MAYBE YOU CAN TELL ME WHY THEY'RE HERE?
BECAUSE I LOOK AROUND AT THIS SHIP--THE MOST OPULENT VESSEL I'VE EVER SEEN, STUFFED WITH TREASURES FROM ACROSS THE GALAXY, WITH THOSE RED KILLERS ABOARD...
...AND I THINK THERE'S ONLY ONE PERSON WHO COULD POSSIBLY OWN IT.
YOU'VE STOLEN SOMETHING BELONGING TO PALPATINE HIMSELF, LANDO CALRISSIAN.
YOU'VE KILLED US ALL.
ENOUGH, SAVA KORIN. JUST... ENOUGH.
LET'S GO HELP THE TWINS.

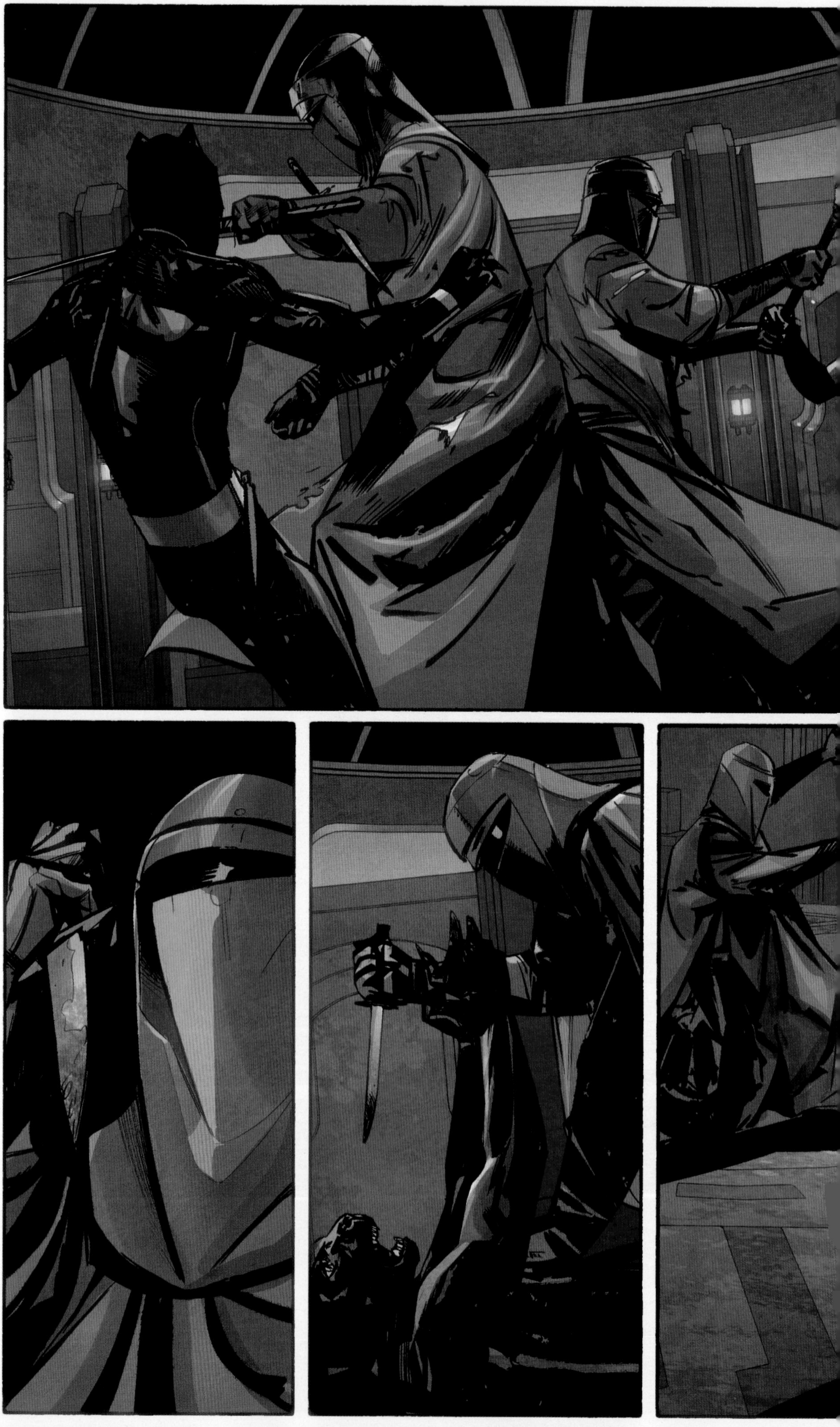

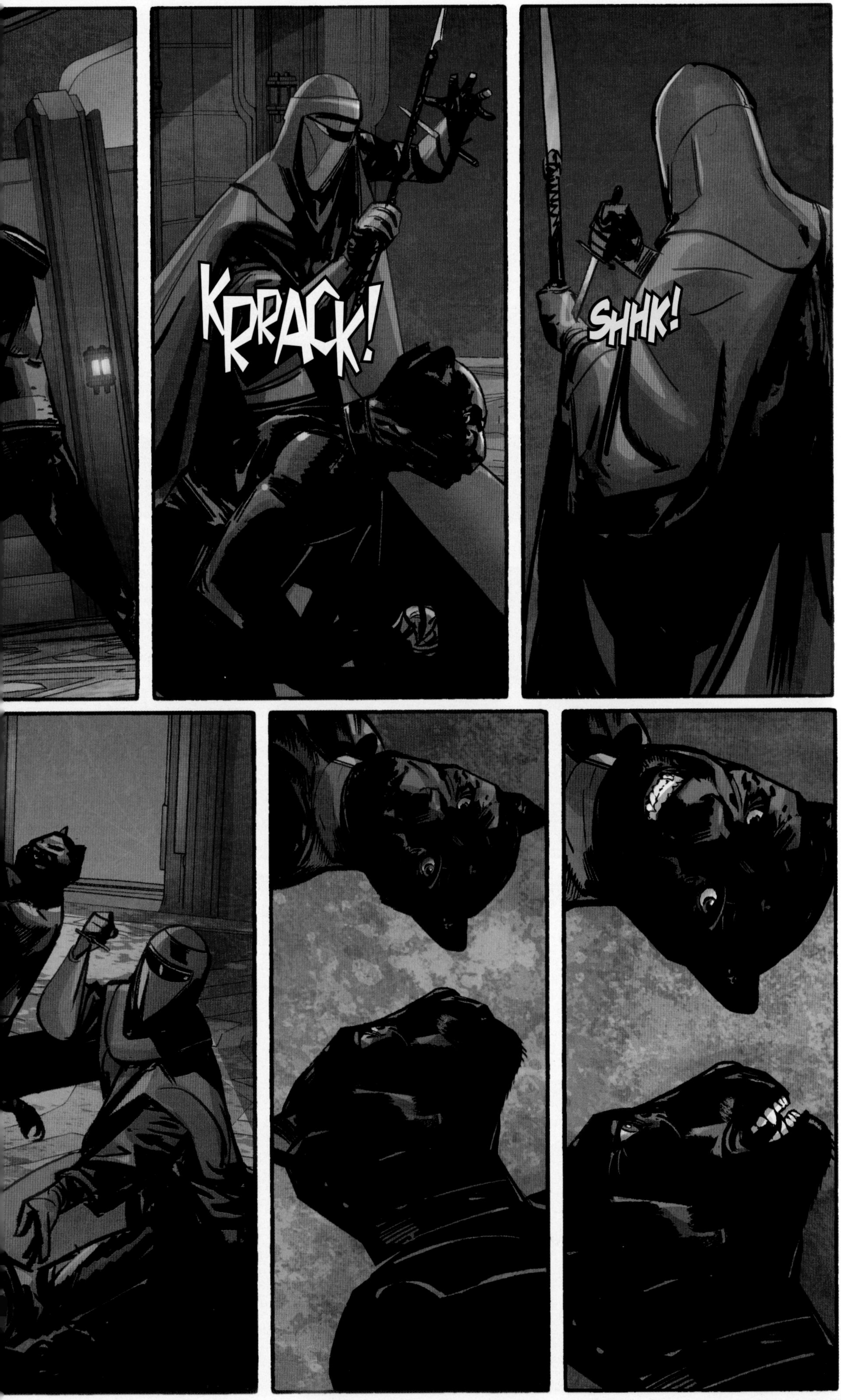
KRRACK!
SHHK!

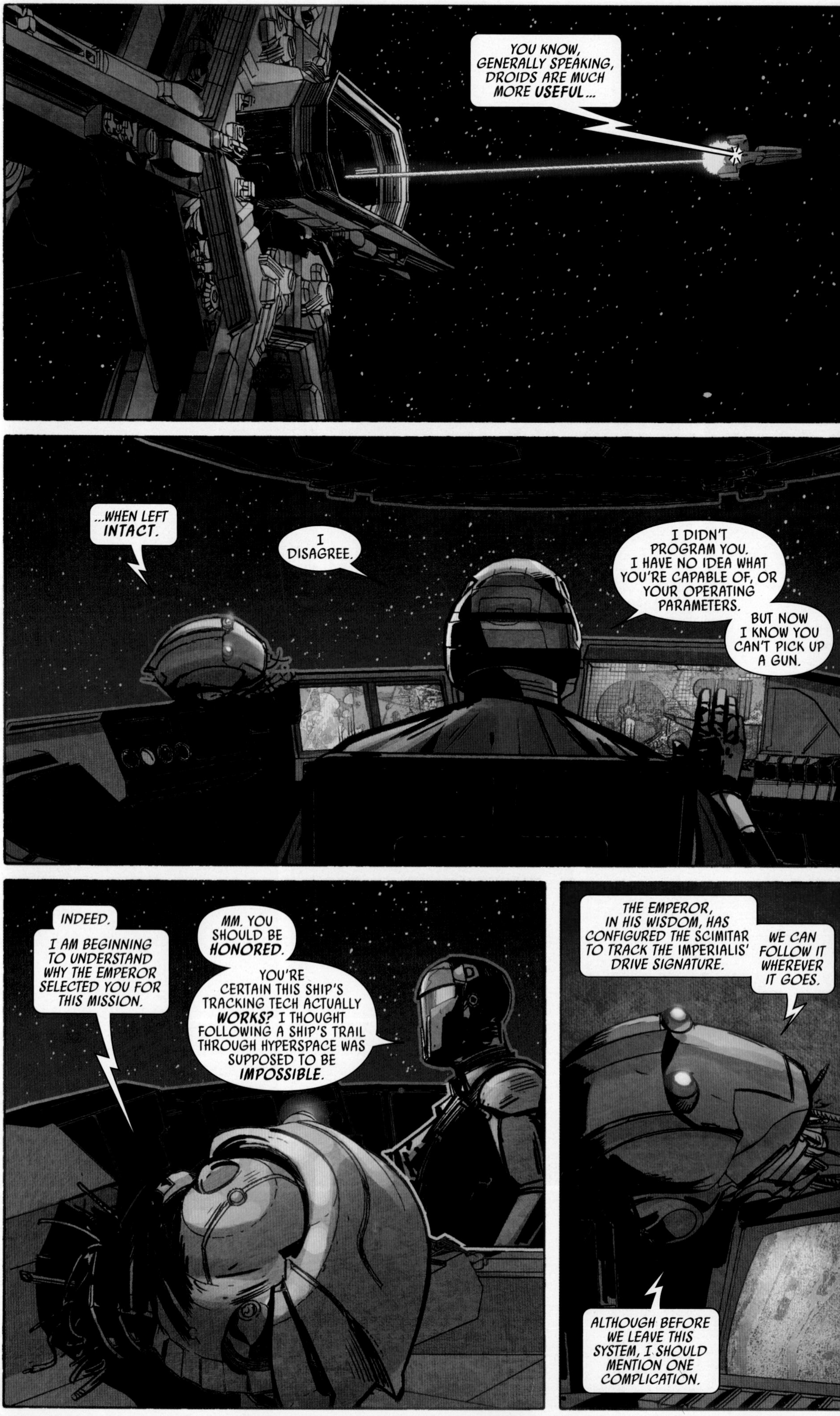
YOU KNOW, GENERALLY SPEAKING, DROIDS ARE MUCH MORE USEFUL...
...WHEN LEFT INTACT.
I DISAGREE.
I DIDN'T PROGRAM YOU. I HAVE NO IDEA WHAT YOU'RE CAPABLE OF, OR YOUR OPERATING PARAMETERS.
BUT NOW I KNOW YOU CAN'T PICK UP A GUN.
INDEED.
I AM BEGINNING TO UNDERSTAND WHY THE EMPEROR SELECTED YOU FOR THIS MISSION.
MM. YOU SHOULD BE HONORED.
YOU'RE CERTAIN THIS SHIP'S TRACKING TECH ACTUALLY WORKS? I THOUGHT FOLLOWING A SHIP'S TRAIL THROUGH HYPERSPACE WAS SUPPOSED TO BE IMPOSSIBLE.
THE EMPEROR, IN HIS WISDOM, HAS CONFIGURED THE SCIMITAR TO TRACK THE IMPERIALIS' DRIVE SIGNATURE.
WE CAN FOLLOW IT WHEREVER IT GOES.
ALTHOUGH BEFORE WE LEAVE THIS SYSTEM, I SHOULD MENTION ONE COMPLICATION.

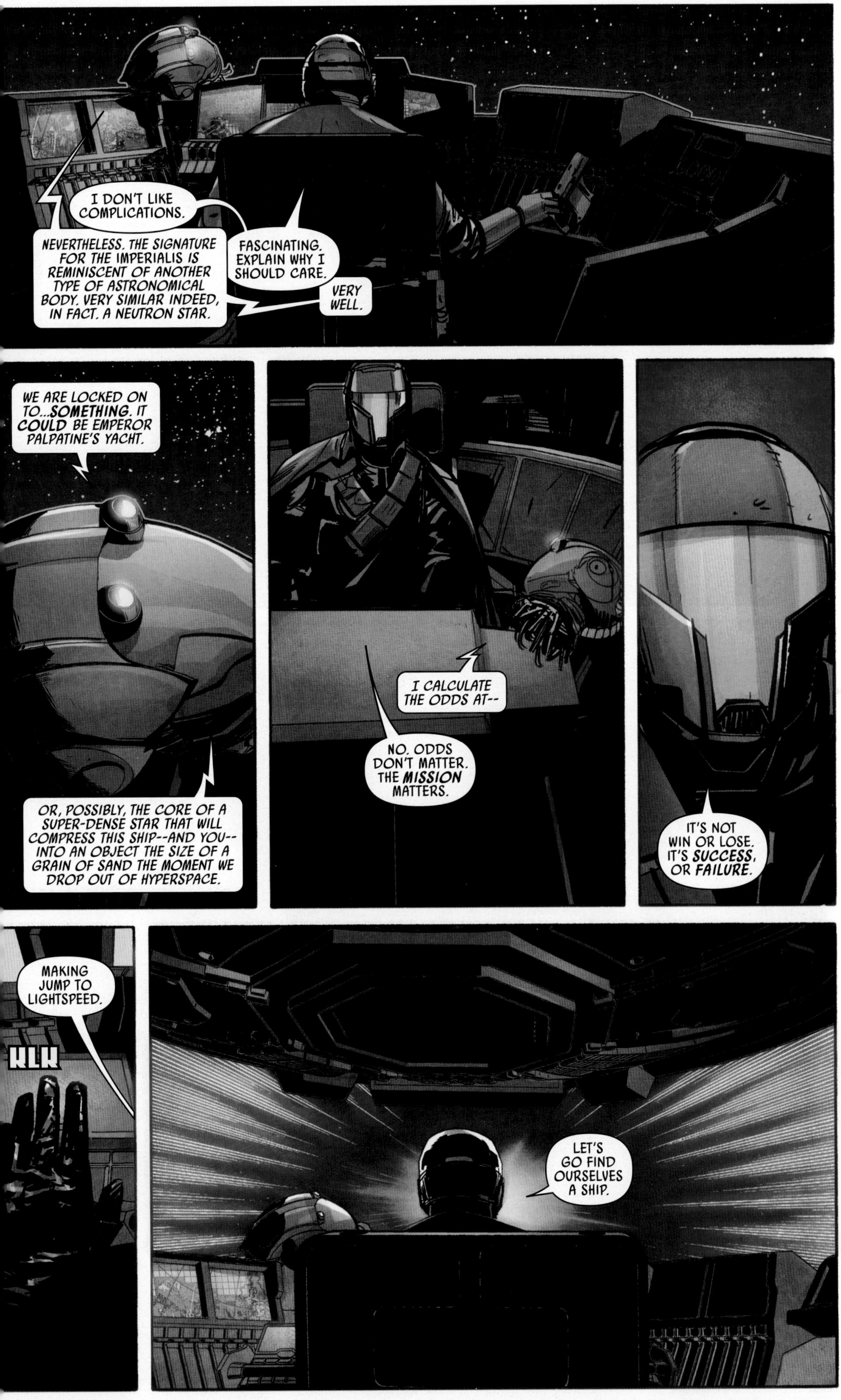
I DON'T LIKE COMPLICATIONS.
NEVERTHELESS. THE SIGNATURE FOR THE IMPERIALIS IS REMINISCENT OF ANOTHER TYPE OF ASTRONOMICAL BODY. VERY SIMILAR INDEED, IN FACT. A NEUTRON STAR.
FASCINATING. EXPLAIN WHY I SHOULD CARE.
VERY WELL.
WE ARE LOCKED ON TO...SOMETHING. IT COULD BE EMPEROR PALPATINE'S YACHT.
OR, POSSIBLY, THE CORE OF A SUPER-DENSE STAR THAT WILL COMPRESS THIS SHIP--AND YOU--INTO AN OBJECT THE SIZE OF A GRAIN OF SAND THE MOMENT WE DROP OUT OF HYPERSPACE.
I CALCULATE THE ODDS AT--
NO. ODDS DON'T MATTER. THE MISSION MATTERS.
IT'S NOT WIN OR LOSE. IT'S SUCCESS, OR FAILURE.
MAKING JUMP TO LIGHTSPEED.
KLK
LET'S GO FIND OURSELVES A SHIP.

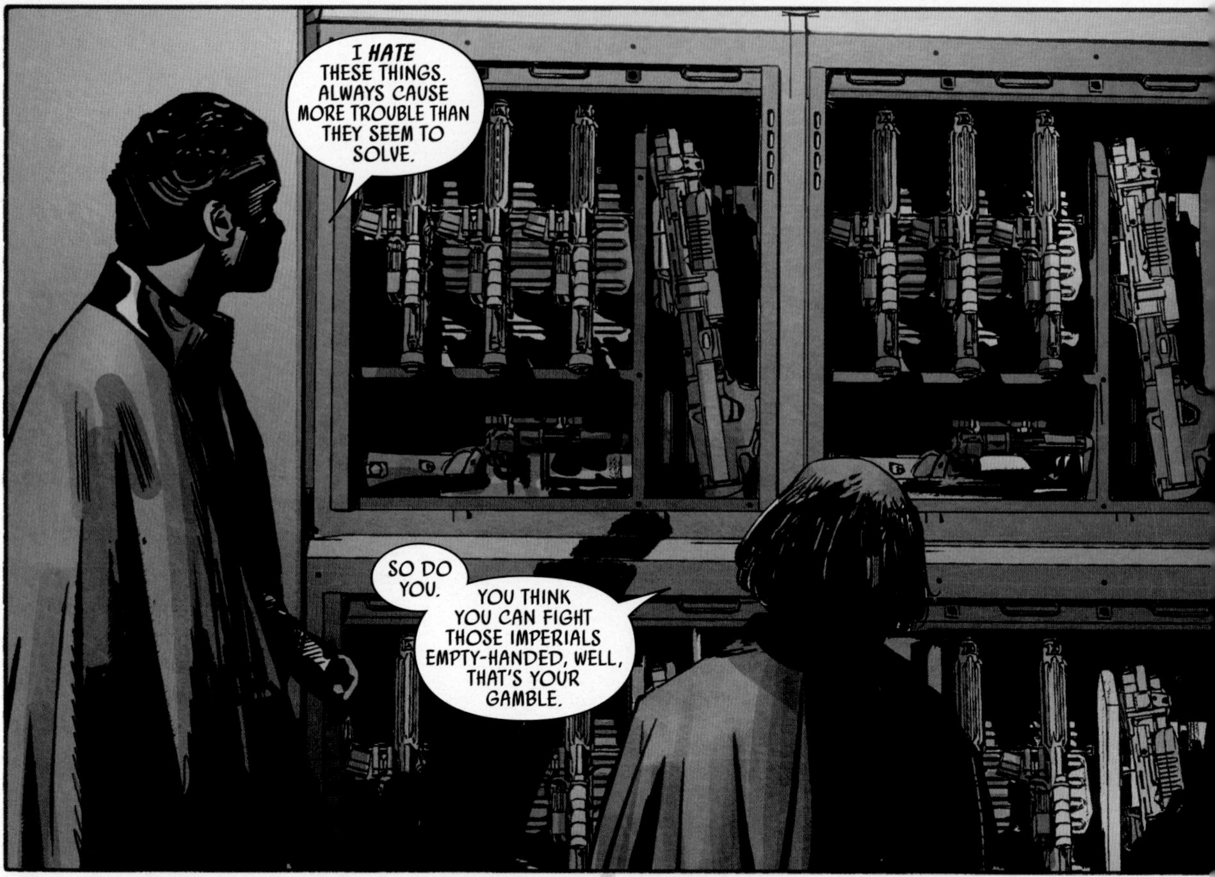
I HATE THESE THINGS. ALWAYS CAUSE MORE TROUBLE THAN THEY SEEM TO SOLVE.
SO DO YOU.
YOU THINK YOU CAN FIGHT THOSE IMPERIALS EMPTY-HANDED, WELL, THAT'S YOUR GAMBLE.

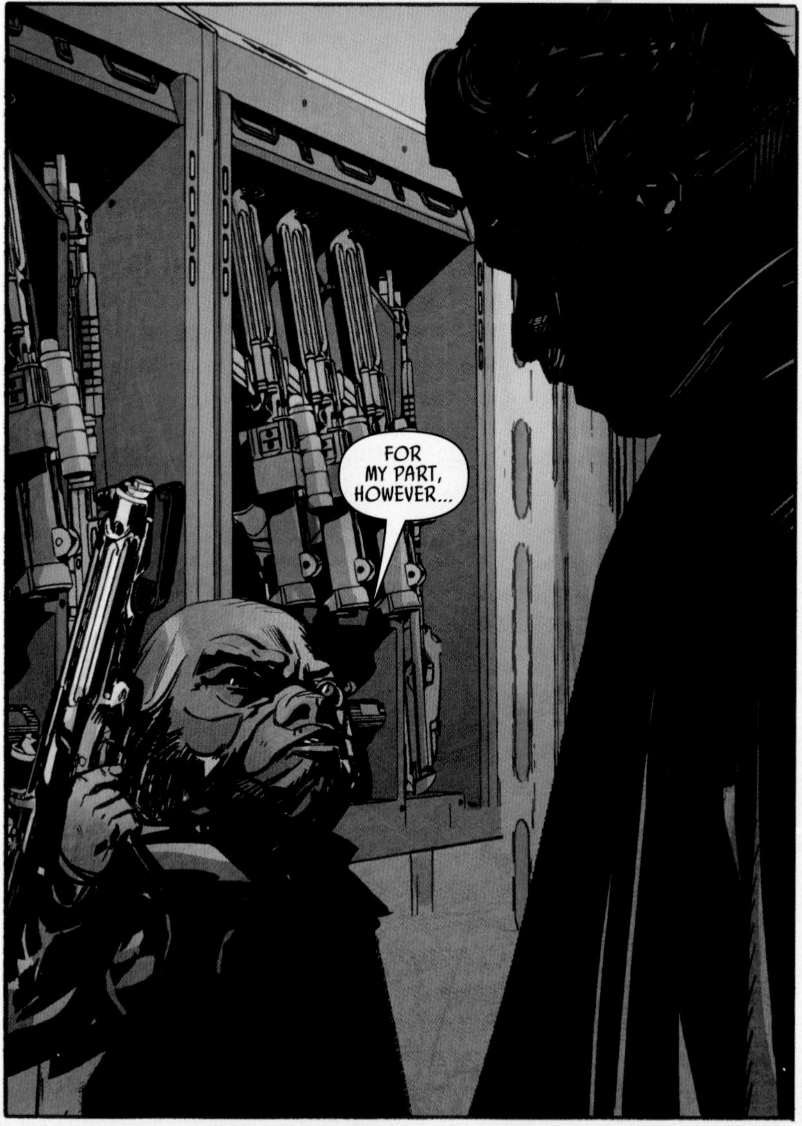
FOR MY PART, HOWEVER...

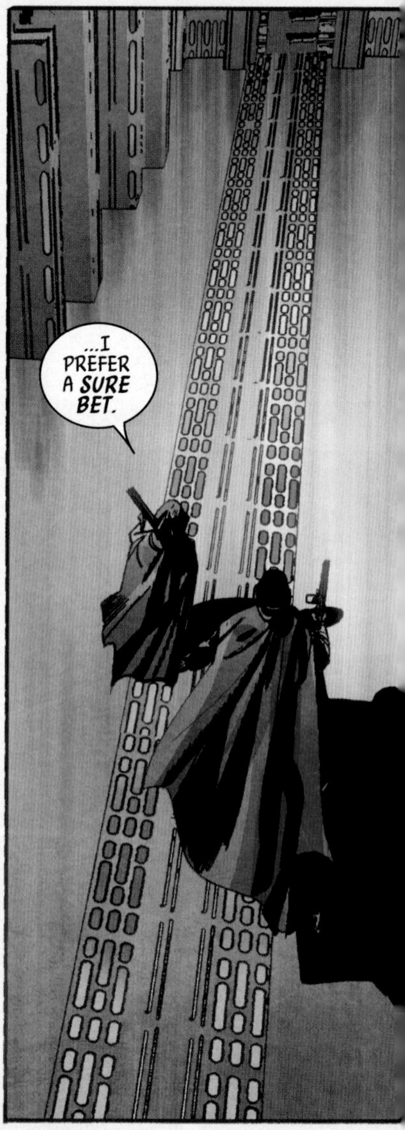
...I PREFER A SURE BET.

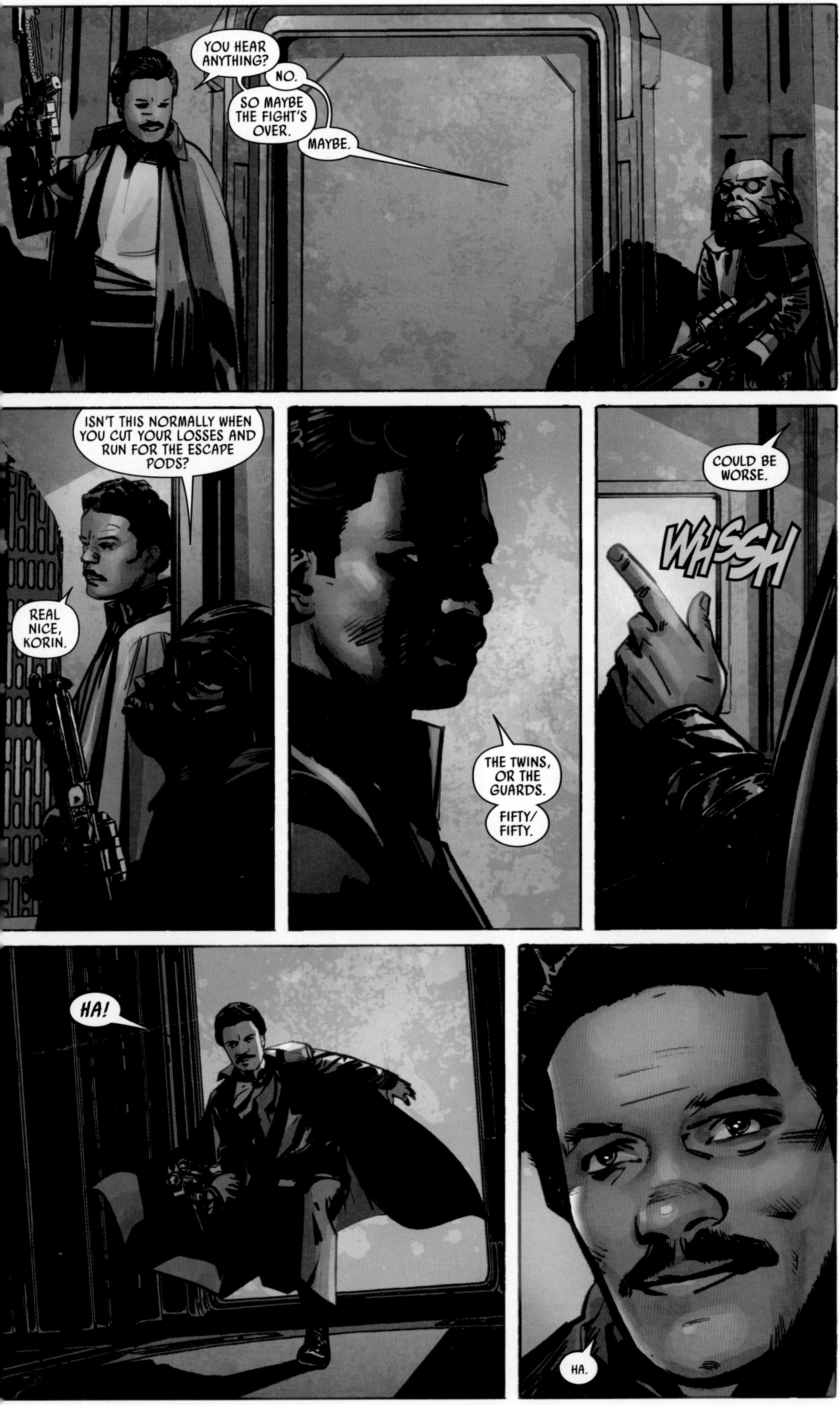
YOU HEAR ANYTHING?
NO.
SO MAYBE THE FIGHT'S OVER.
MAYBE.
ISN'T THIS NORMALLY WHEN YOU CUT YOUR LOSSES AND RUN FOR THE ESCAPE PODS?
REAL NICE, KORIN.
THE TWINS, OR THE GUARDS.
FIFTY/ FIFTY.
COULD BE WORSE.
WHSSH
HA!
HA.

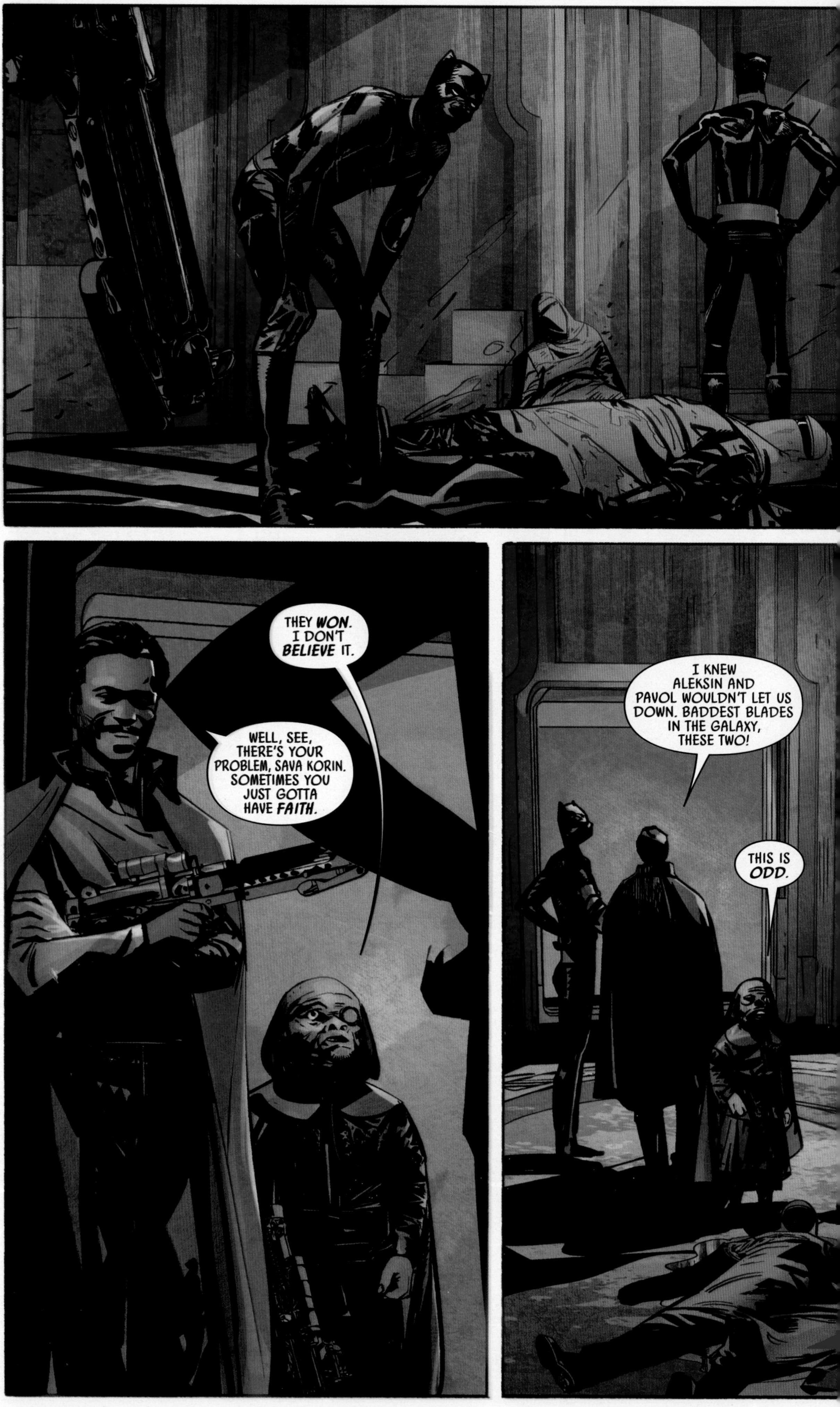
THEY **WON**. I DON'T **BELIEVE** IT.
WELL, SEE, THERE'S YOUR PROBLEM, SAVA KORIN. SOMETIMES YOU JUST GOTTA HAVE **FAITH**.
I KNEW ALEKSIN AND PAVOL WOULDN'T LET US DOWN. BADDEST BLADES IN THE GALAXY, THESE TWO!
THIS IS **ODD**.

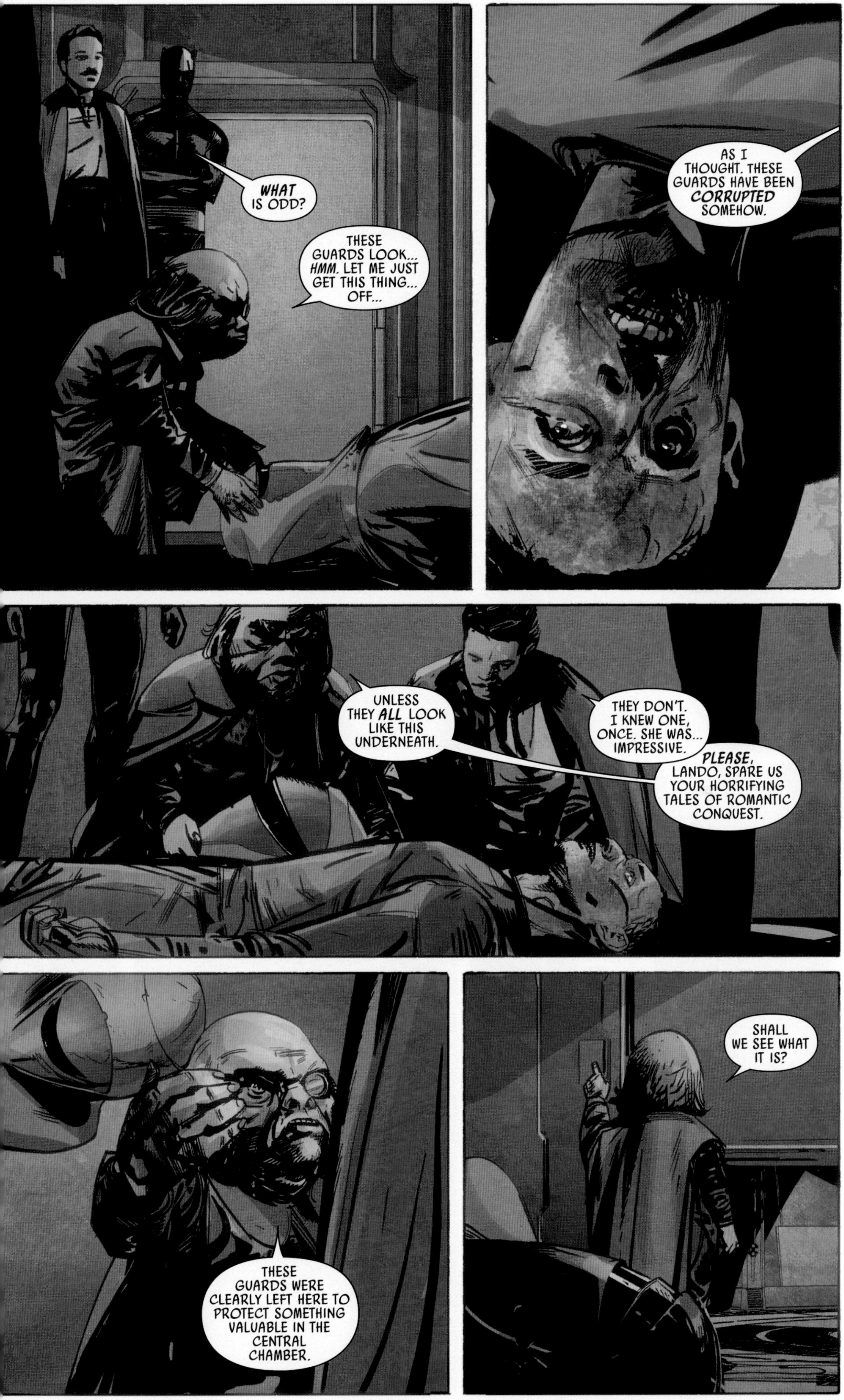
WHAT IS ODD?
THESE GUARDS LOOK... HMM. LET ME JUST GET THIS THING... OFF...
AS I THOUGHT. THESE GUARDS HAVE BEEN CORRUPTED SOMEHOW.
UNLESS THEY ALL LOOK LIKE THIS UNDERNEATH.
THEY DON'T. I KNEW ONE, ONCE. SHE WAS... IMPRESSIVE.
PLEASE, LANDO, SPARE US YOUR HORRIFYING TALES OF ROMANTIC CONQUEST.
THESE GUARDS WERE CLEARLY LEFT HERE TO PROTECT SOMETHING VALUABLE IN THE CENTRAL CHAMBER.
SHALL WE SEE WHAT IT IS?

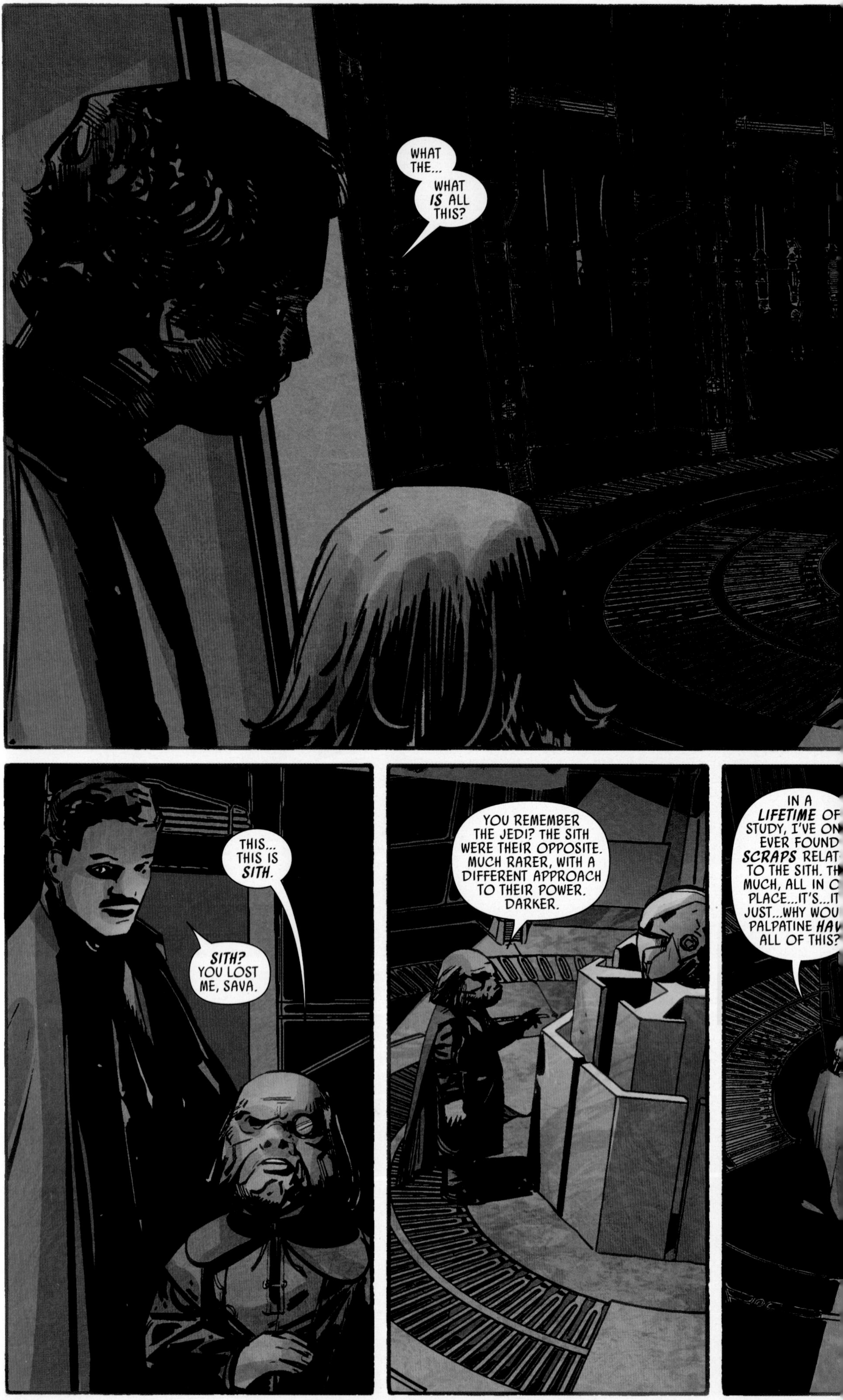
WHAT THE... WHAT IS ALL THIS?
THIS... THIS IS SITH.
SITH? YOU LOST ME, SAVA.
YOU REMEMBER THE JEDI? THE SITH WERE THEIR OPPOSITE. MUCH RARER, WITH A DIFFERENT APPROACH TO THEIR POWER. DARKER.
IN A LIFETIME OF STUDY, I'VE ON EVER FOUND SCRAPS RELAT TO THE SITH. TH MUCH, ALL IN C PLACE...IT'S...IT JUST...WHY WOU PALPATINE HAV ALL OF THIS?

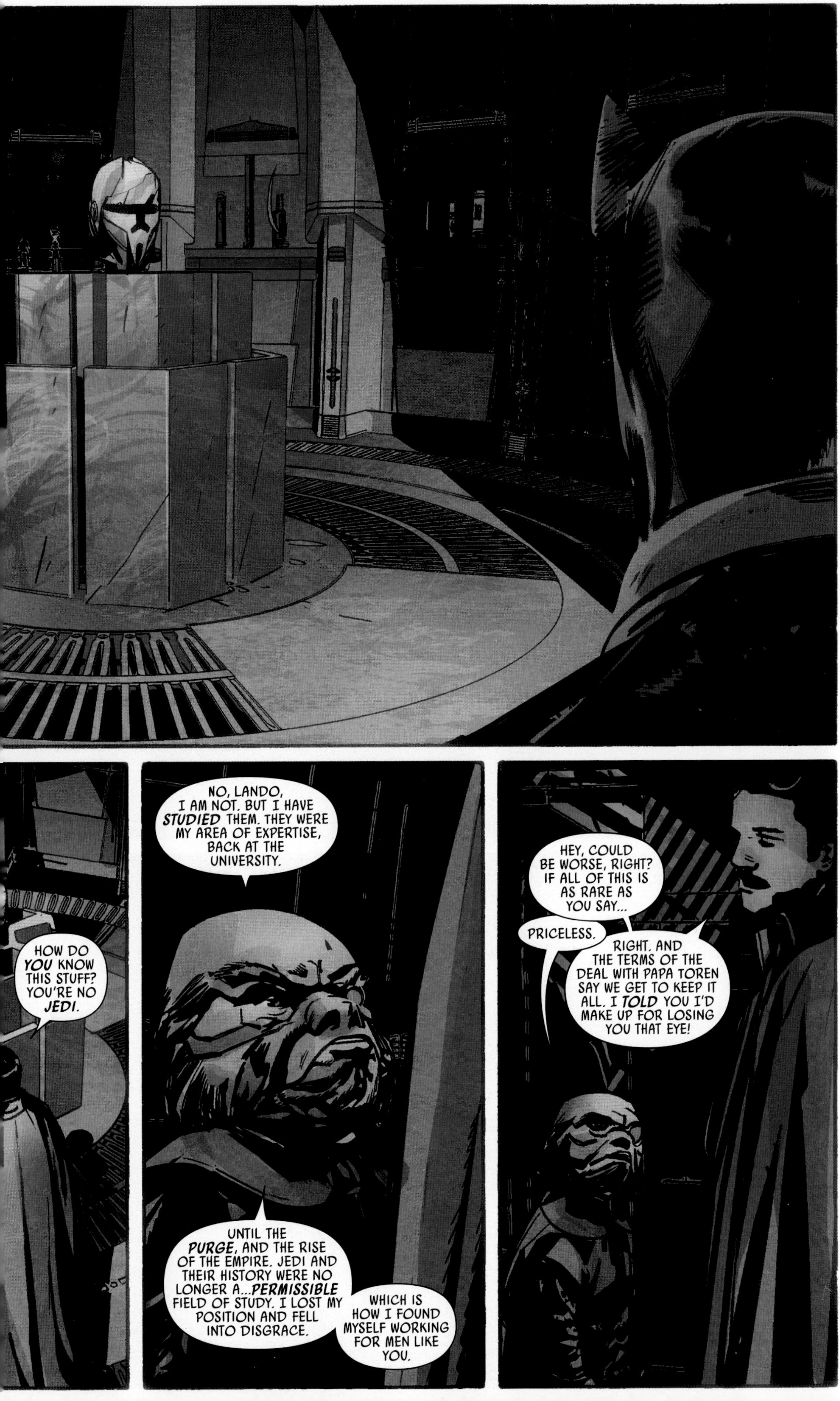
HOW DO *YOU* KNOW THIS STUFF? YOU'RE NO *JEDI*.
NO, LANDO, I AM NOT. BUT I HAVE *STUDIED* THEM. THEY WERE MY AREA OF EXPERTISE, BACK AT THE UNIVERSITY.
UNTIL THE *PURGE*, AND THE RISE OF THE EMPIRE. JEDI AND THEIR HISTORY WERE NO LONGER A...*PERMISSIBLE* FIELD OF STUDY. I LOST MY POSITION AND FELL INTO DISGRACE.
WHICH IS HOW I FOUND MYSELF WORKING FOR MEN LIKE YOU.
HEY, COULD BE WORSE, RIGHT? IF ALL OF THIS IS AS RARE AS YOU SAY...
PRICELESS.
RIGHT. AND THE TERMS OF THE DEAL WITH PAPA TOREN SAY WE GET TO KEEP IT ALL. I *TOLD* YOU I'D MAKE UP FOR LOSING YOU THAT EYE!

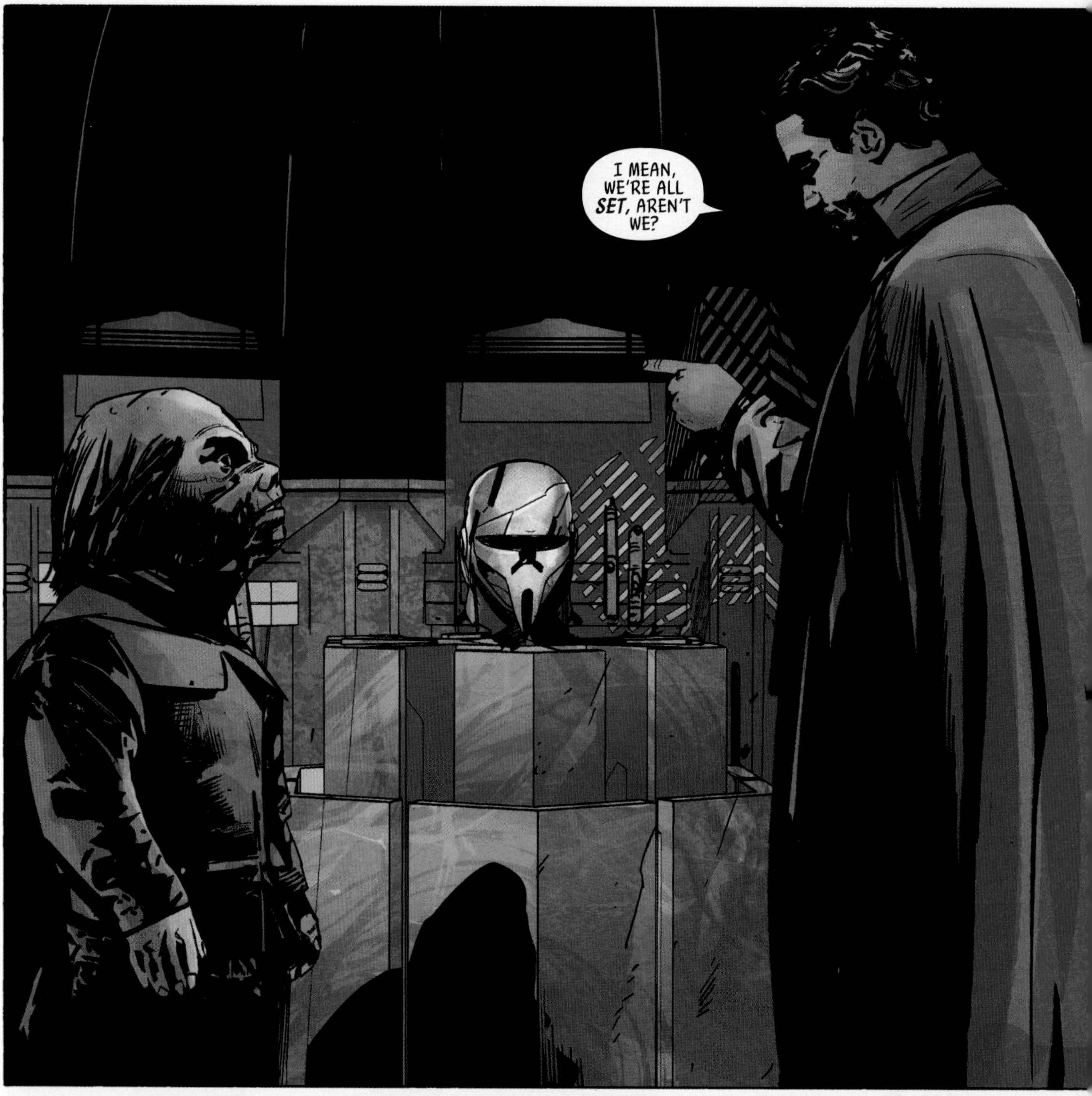
I MEAN, WE'RE ALL SET, AREN'T WE?
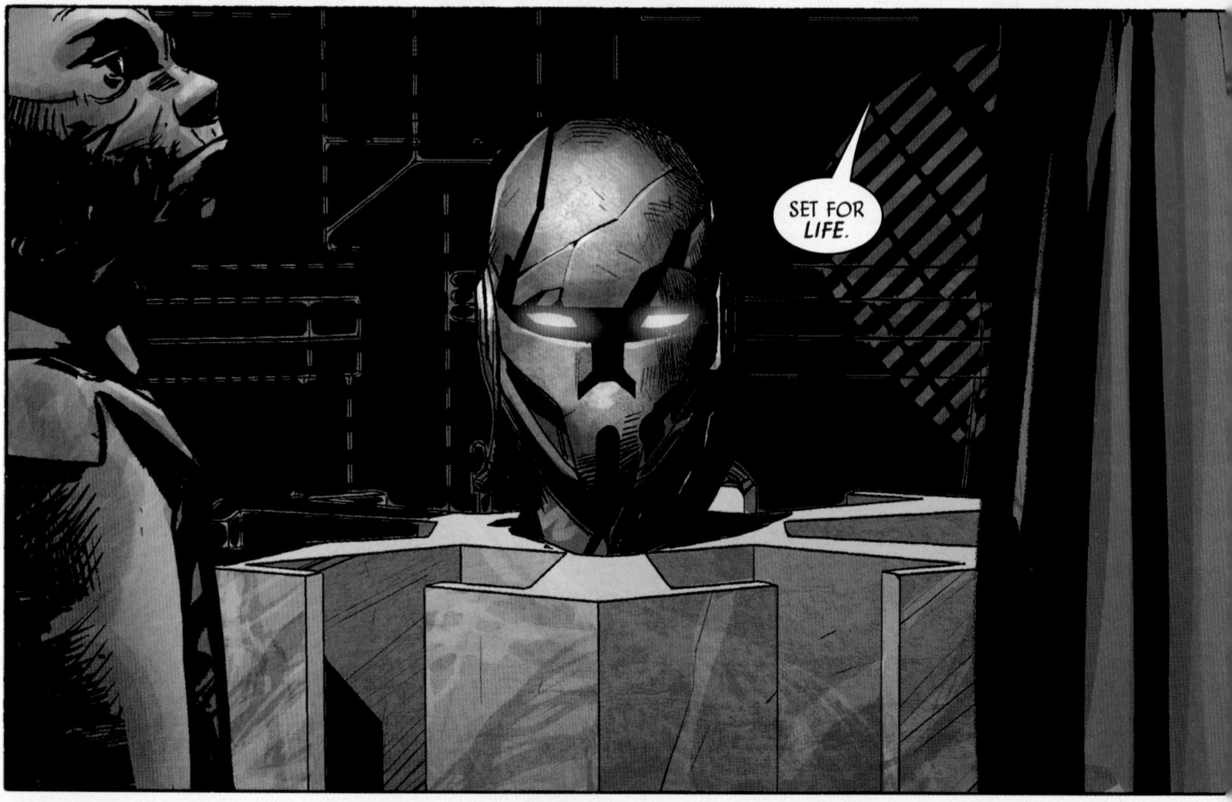
SET FOR LIFE.

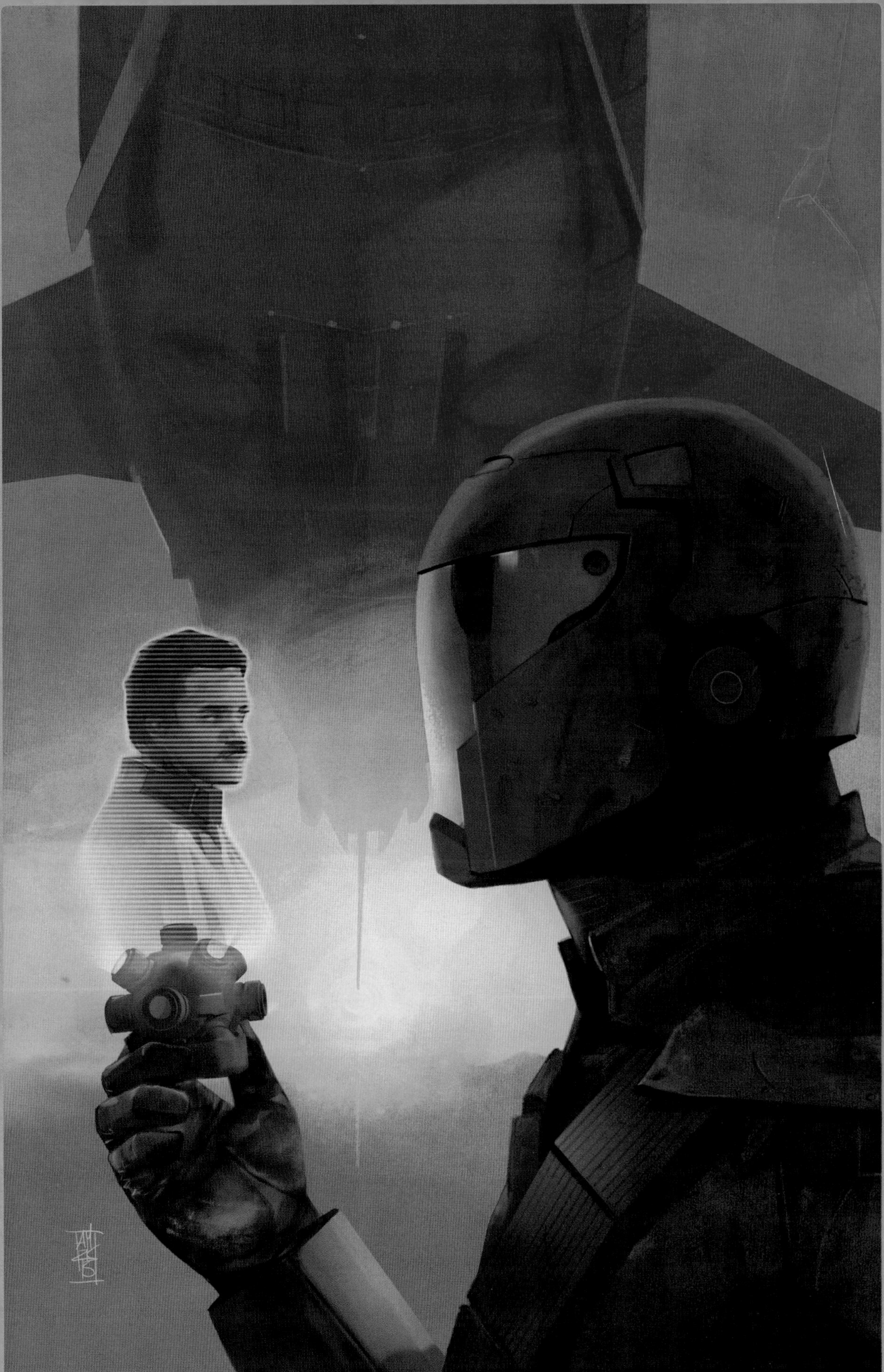

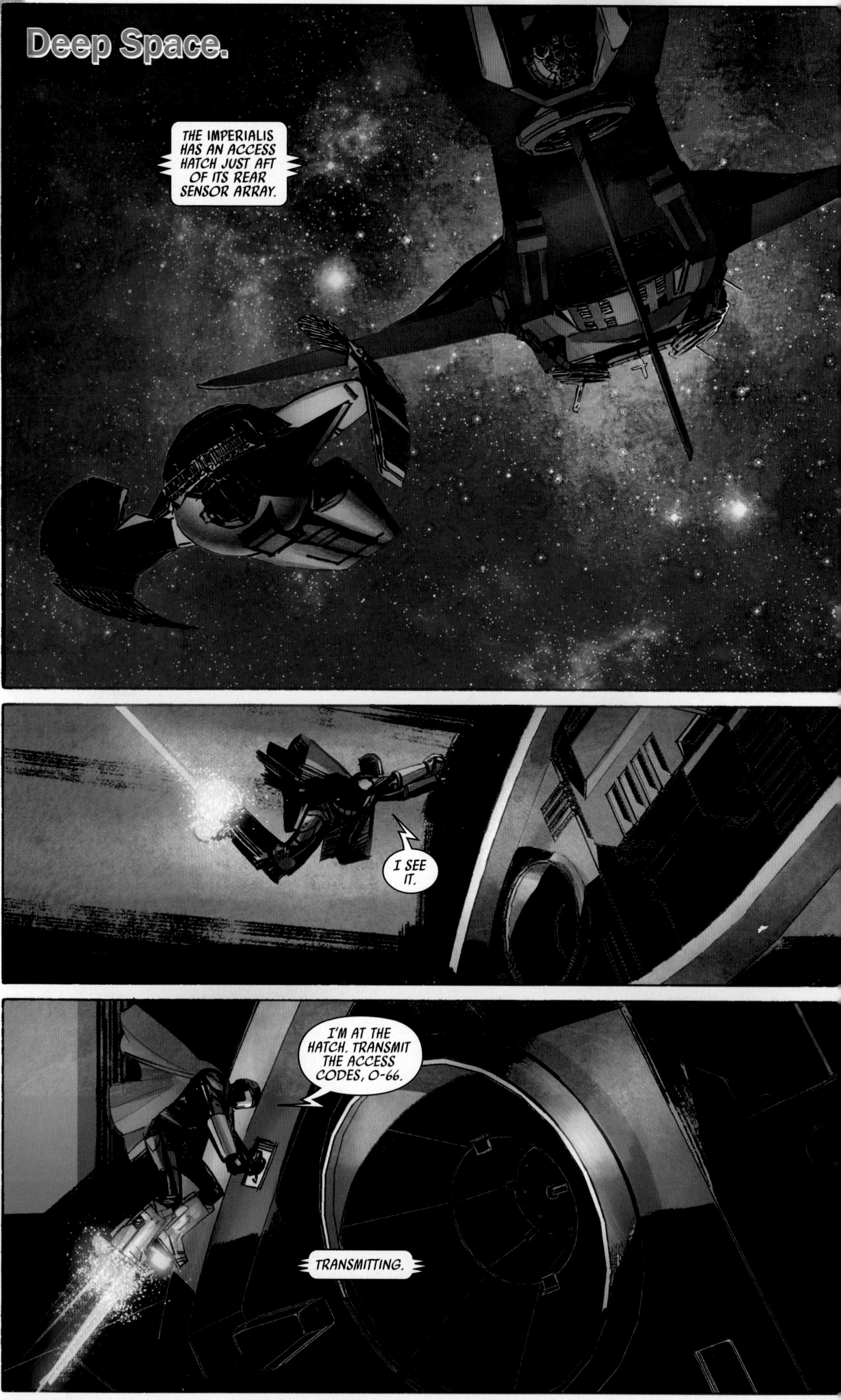
Deep Space.
THE IMPERIALIS HAS AN ACCESS HATCH JUST AFT OF ITS REAR SENSOR ARRAY.
I SEE IT.
I'M AT THE HATCH. TRANSMIT THE ACCESS CODES, 0-66.
TRANSMITTING.

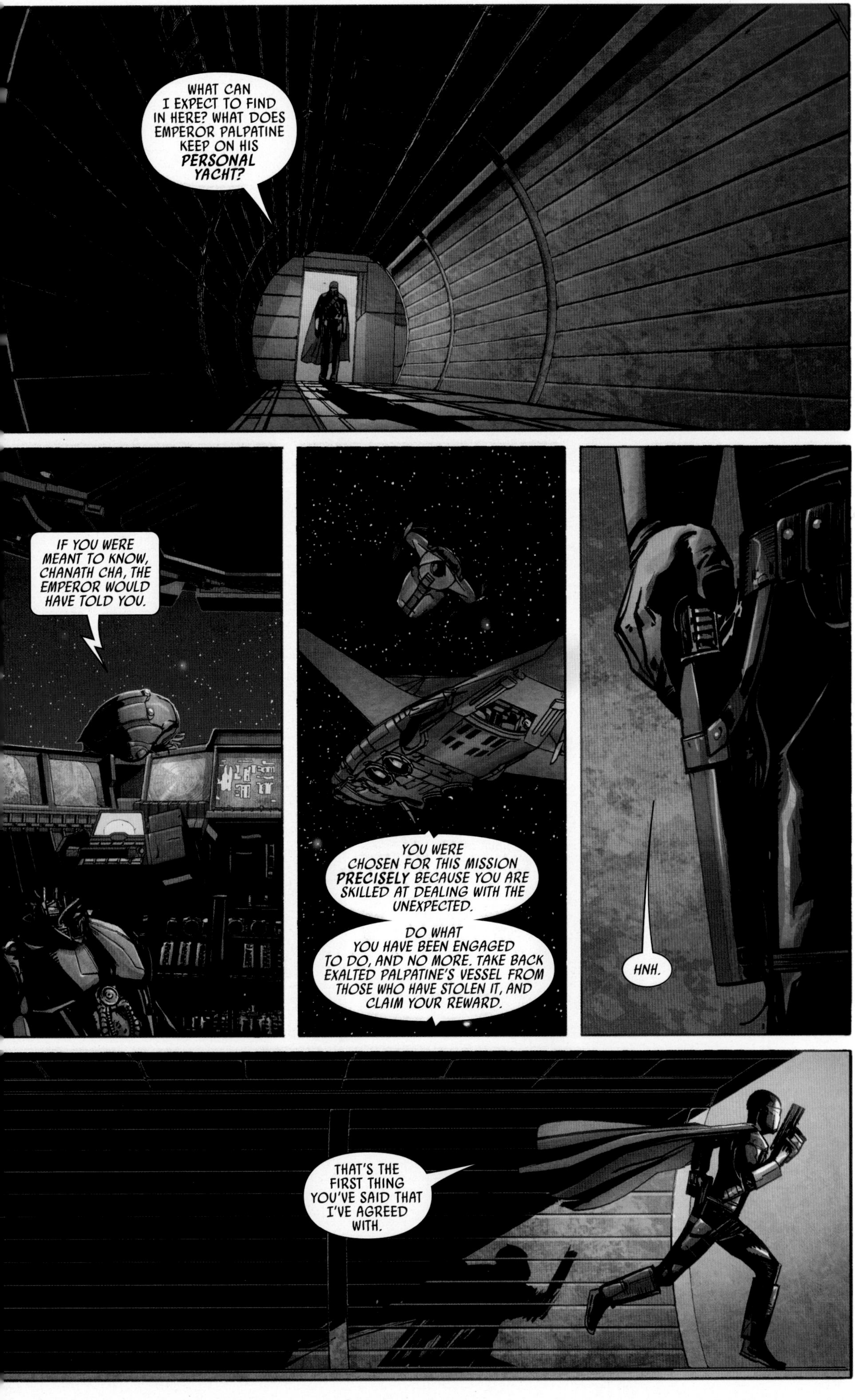
WHAT CAN I EXPECT TO FIND IN HERE? WHAT DOES EMPEROR PALPATINE KEEP ON HIS PERSONAL YACHT?
IF YOU WERE MEANT TO KNOW, CHANATH CHA, THE EMPEROR WOULD HAVE TOLD YOU.
YOU WERE CHOSEN FOR THIS MISSION PRECISELY BECAUSE YOU ARE SKILLED AT DEALING WITH THE UNEXPECTED.
DO WHAT YOU HAVE BEEN ENGAGED TO DO, AND NO MORE. TAKE BACK EXALTED PALPATINE'S VESSEL FROM THOSE WHO HAVE STOLEN IT, AND CLAIM YOUR REWARD.
HNH.
THAT'S THE FIRST THING YOU'VE SAID THAT I'VE AGREED WITH.

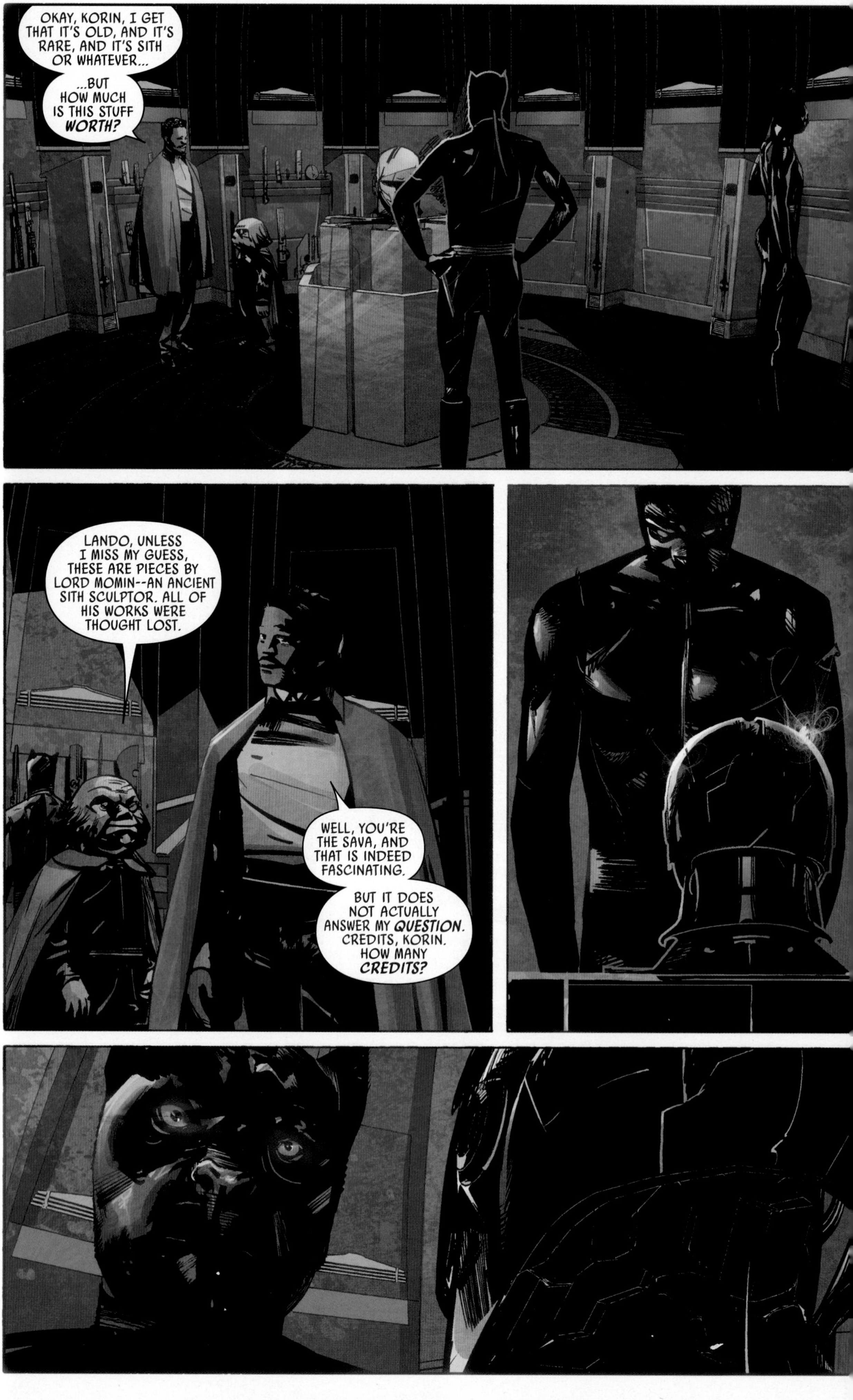
OKAY, KORIN, I GET THAT IT'S OLD, AND IT'S RARE, AND IT'S SITH OR WHATEVER...
...BUT HOW MUCH IS THIS STUFF *WORTH?*
LANDO, UNLESS I MISS MY GUESS, THESE ARE PIECES BY LORD MOMIN--AN ANCIENT SITH SCULPTOR. ALL OF HIS WORKS WERE THOUGHT LOST.
WELL, YOU'RE THE SAVA, AND THAT IS INDEED FASCINATING.
BUT IT DOES NOT ACTUALLY ANSWER MY *QUESTION*. CREDITS, KORIN. HOW MANY *CREDITS?*

THERE AREN'T MANY BUYERS FOR ANTIQUITIES OF THIS TYPE, BUT THE ONES OUT THERE ARE *VERY* WILLING TO SPEND IF AND WHEN NEW ITEMS APPEAR ON THE MARKET.

IF WE CAN FIND ONE OF *THOSE* INDIVIDUALS, THIS COLLECTION COULD GET US EACH ENOUGH CREDITS FOR...OH...

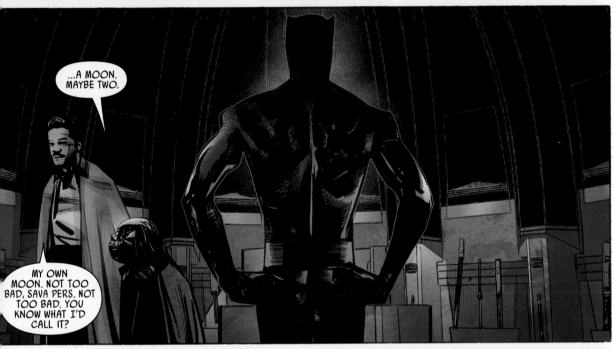

...A MOON. MAYBE TWO.

MY OWN MOON. NOT TOO BAD, SAVA PERS. NOT TOO BAD. YOU KNOW WHAT I'D CALL IT?

DO TELL.

I'D CALL IT LANDO LAND. GALAXY *NEEDS* A LANDO LAND.

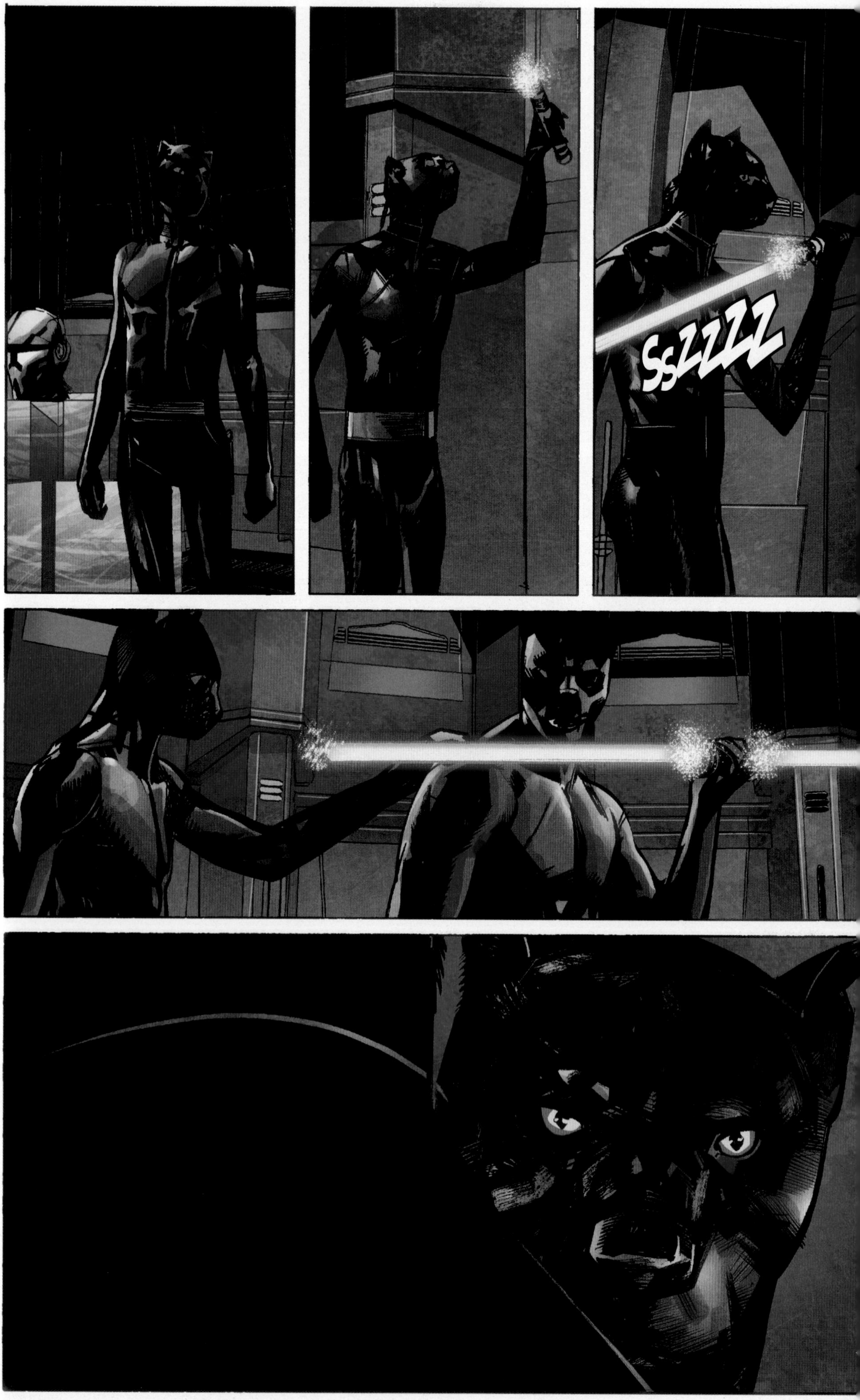
SsZZZZ

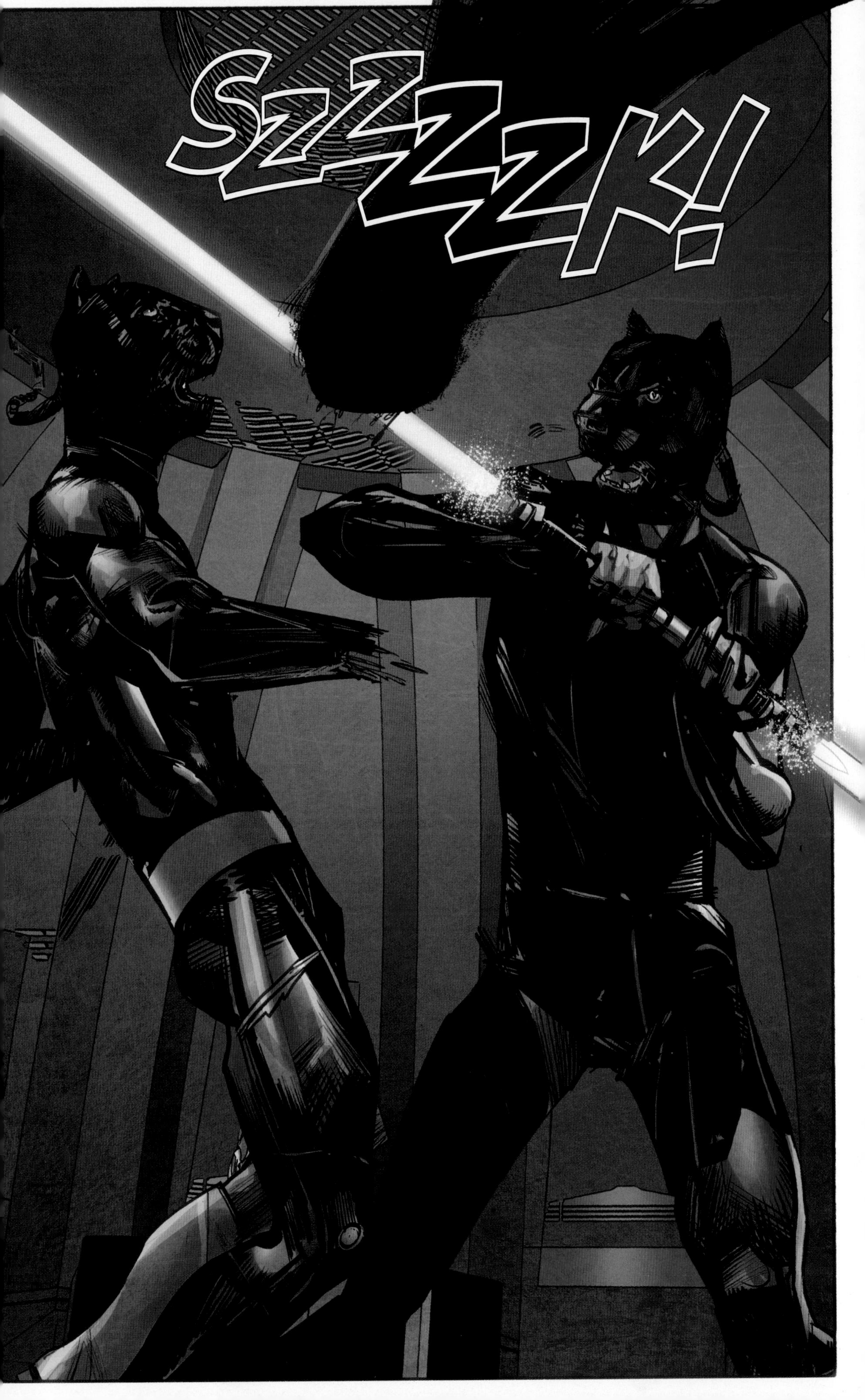
SZZZZK!

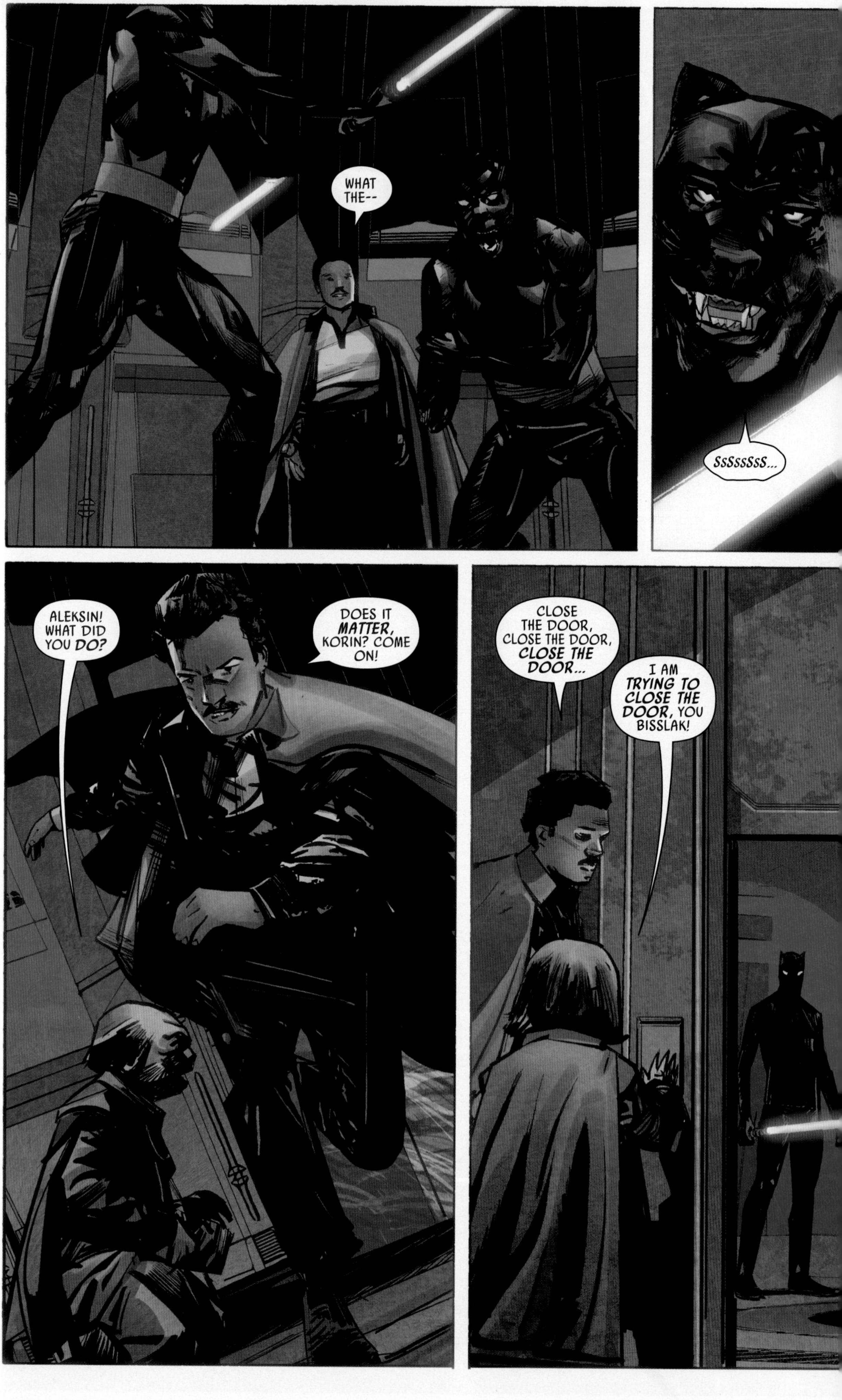
WHAT THE--
SSSSSSS...
ALEKSIN! WHAT DID YOU DO?
DOES IT MATTER, KORIN? COME ON!
CLOSE THE DOOR, CLOSE THE DOOR, CLOSE THE DOOR...
I AM TRYING TO CLOSE THE DOOR, YOU BISSLAK!

KTHHNK

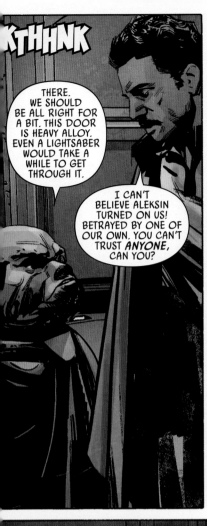

THERE. WE SHOULD BE ALL RIGHT FOR A BIT. THIS DOOR IS HEAVY ALLOY. EVEN A LIGHTSABER WOULD TAKE A WHILE TO GET THROUGH IT.

I CAN'T BELIEVE ALEKSIN TURNED ON US! BETRAYED BY ONE OF OUR OWN. YOU CAN'T TRUST *ANYONE*, CAN YOU?

... NOW DON'T YOU THROW THAT LOOK AT ME.

YOU CAN'T BLAME *ME* IF ALEKSIN DECIDED HE WANTED HIS OWN PAYDAY. IT'S NOT MY FAULT!

THIS TIME, MAYBE.

BUT I'M NOT SURE THIS IS JUST YOUR AVERAGE DOUBLE-CROSS.

IN MY RESEARCH BACK AT THE UNIVERSITY, I CAME ACROSS TALES WITH A COMMON THEME: THE IDEA THAT THE SITH WERE SOMEHOW *CORRUPTED*.

OR THAT THEY DID THE CORRUPTING... IT'S UNCLEAR.

THE JEDI DID AN EXCEPTIONALLY THOROUGH JOB SUPPRESSING KNOWLEDGE OF THE SITH. WHAT LITTLE I FOUND COULD EASILY HAVE BEEN ANTI-SITH PROPAGANDA FROM JEDI SOURCES.

BUT I *DO* KNOW THAT THIS TREASURE CHAMBER HOLDS MORE SITH ARTIFACTS THAN I BELIEVED STILL EXISTED.

PROXIMITY TO THESE ITEMS MAY HAVE *CHANGED* THESE ROYAL GUARDS IN SOME FASHION, AND POSSIBLY ALEKSIN AS WELL.

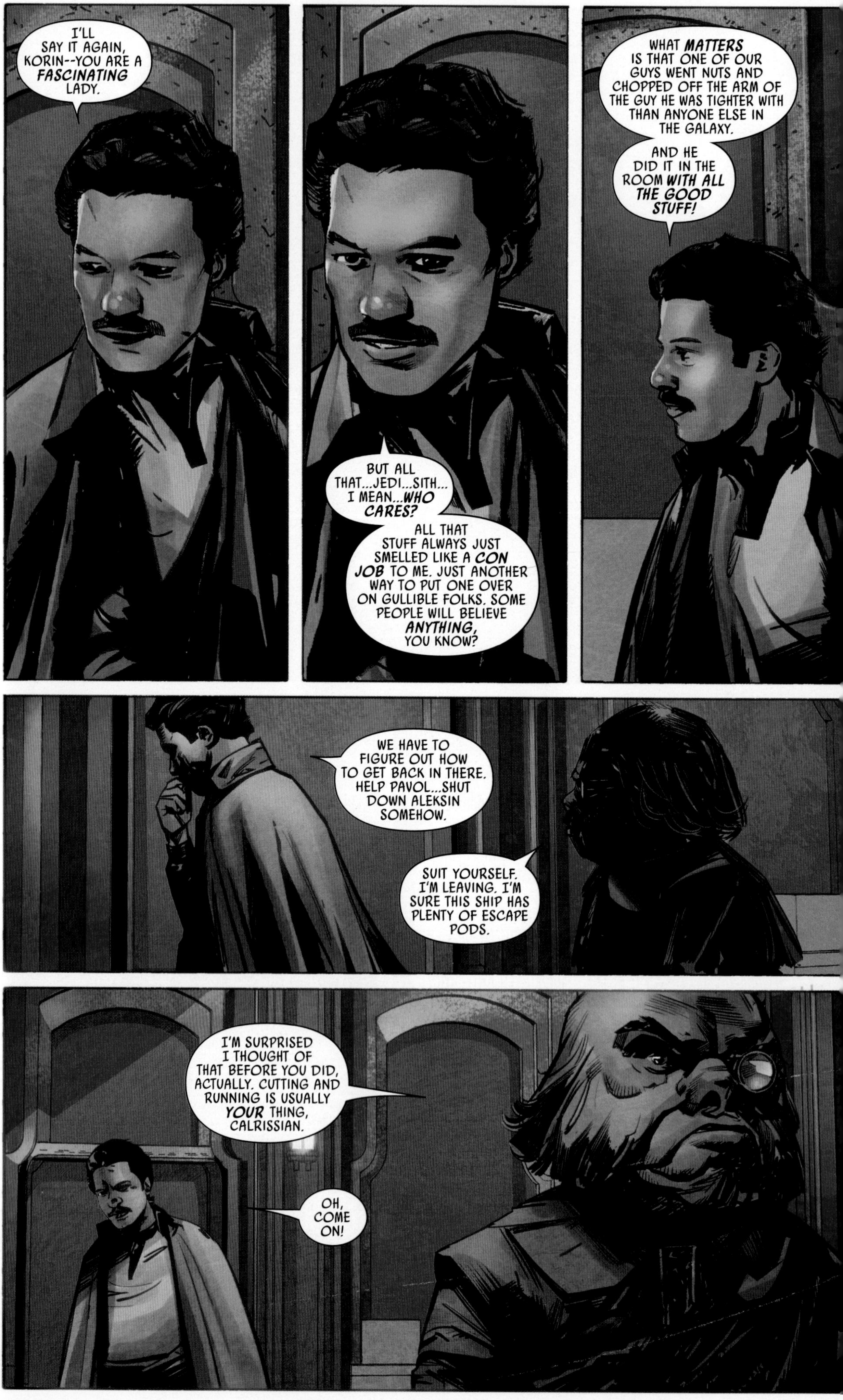
I'LL SAY IT AGAIN, KORIN--YOU ARE A FASCINATING LADY.
BUT ALL THAT...JEDI...SITH... I MEAN...WHO CARES?
ALL THAT STUFF ALWAYS JUST SMELLED LIKE A CON JOB TO ME. JUST ANOTHER WAY TO PUT ONE OVER ON GULLIBLE FOLKS. SOME PEOPLE WILL BELIEVE ANYTHING, YOU KNOW?
WHAT MATTERS IS THAT ONE OF OUR GUYS WENT NUTS AND CHOPPED OFF THE ARM OF THE GUY HE WAS TIGHTER WITH THAN ANYONE ELSE IN THE GALAXY.
AND HE DID IT IN THE ROOM WITH ALL THE GOOD STUFF!
WE HAVE TO FIGURE OUT HOW TO GET BACK IN THERE. HELP PAVOL...SHUT DOWN ALEKSIN SOMEHOW.
SUIT YOURSELF. I'M LEAVING. I'M SURE THIS SHIP HAS PLENTY OF ESCAPE PODS.
I'M SURPRISED I THOUGHT OF THAT BEFORE YOU DID, ACTUALLY. CUTTING AND RUNNING IS USUALLY YOUR THING, CALRISSIAN.
OH, COME ON!

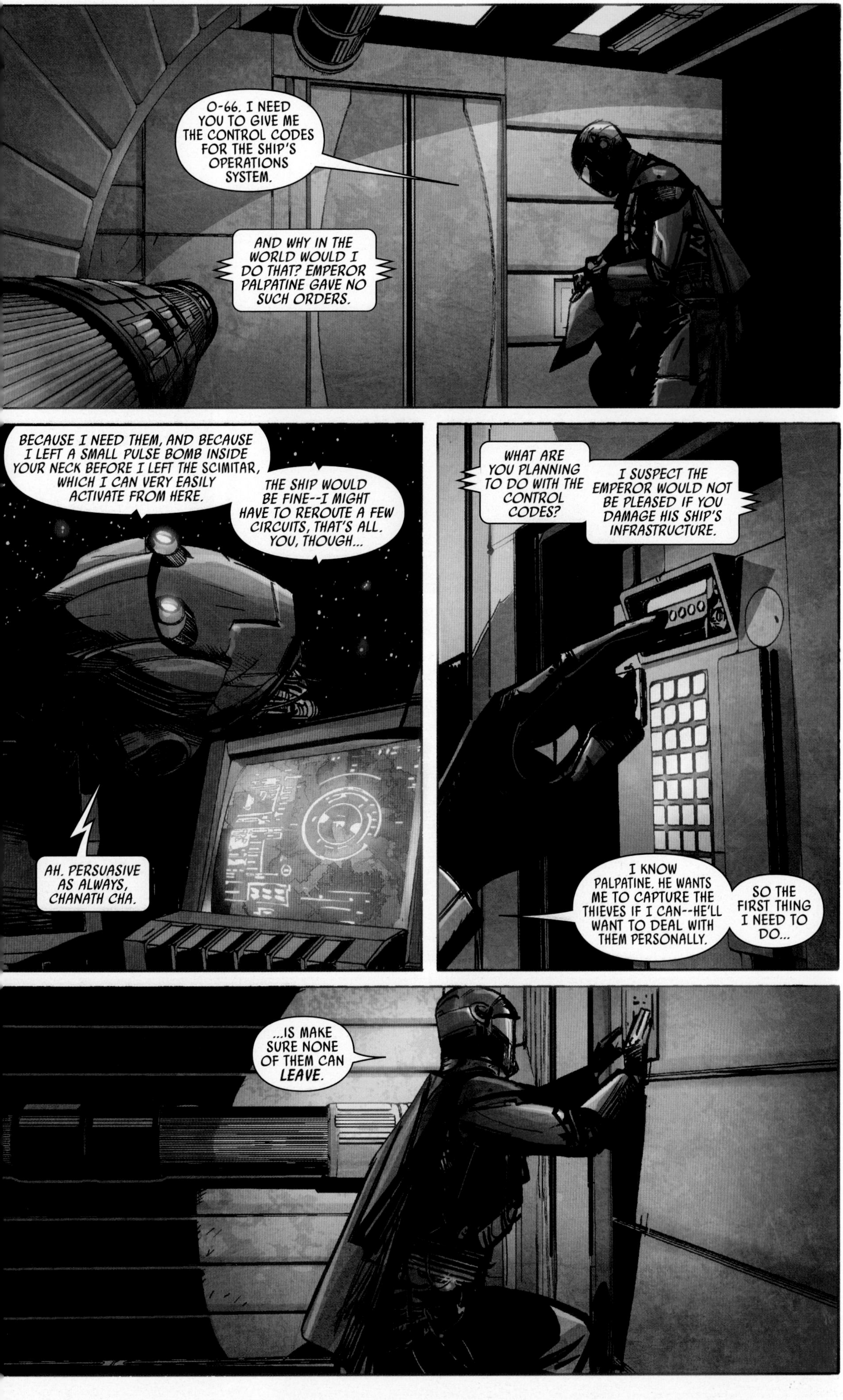
O-66. I NEED YOU TO GIVE ME THE CONTROL CODES FOR THE SHIP'S OPERATIONS SYSTEM.
AND WHY IN THE WORLD WOULD I DO THAT? EMPEROR PALPATINE GAVE NO SUCH ORDERS.
BECAUSE I NEED THEM, AND BECAUSE I LEFT A SMALL PULSE BOMB INSIDE YOUR NECK BEFORE I LEFT THE SCIMITAR, WHICH I CAN VERY EASILY ACTIVATE FROM HERE.
THE SHIP WOULD BE FINE--I MIGHT HAVE TO REROUTE A FEW CIRCUITS, THAT'S ALL. YOU, THOUGH...
AH. PERSUASIVE AS ALWAYS, CHANATH CHA.
WHAT ARE YOU PLANNING TO DO WITH THE CONTROL CODES?
I SUSPECT THE EMPEROR WOULD NOT BE PLEASED IF YOU DAMAGE HIS SHIP'S INFRASTRUCTURE.
I KNOW PALPATINE. HE WANTS ME TO CAPTURE THE THIEVES IF I CAN--HE'LL WANT TO DEAL WITH THEM PERSONALLY.
SO THE FIRST THING I NEED TO DO...
...IS MAKE SURE NONE OF THEM CAN LEAVE.

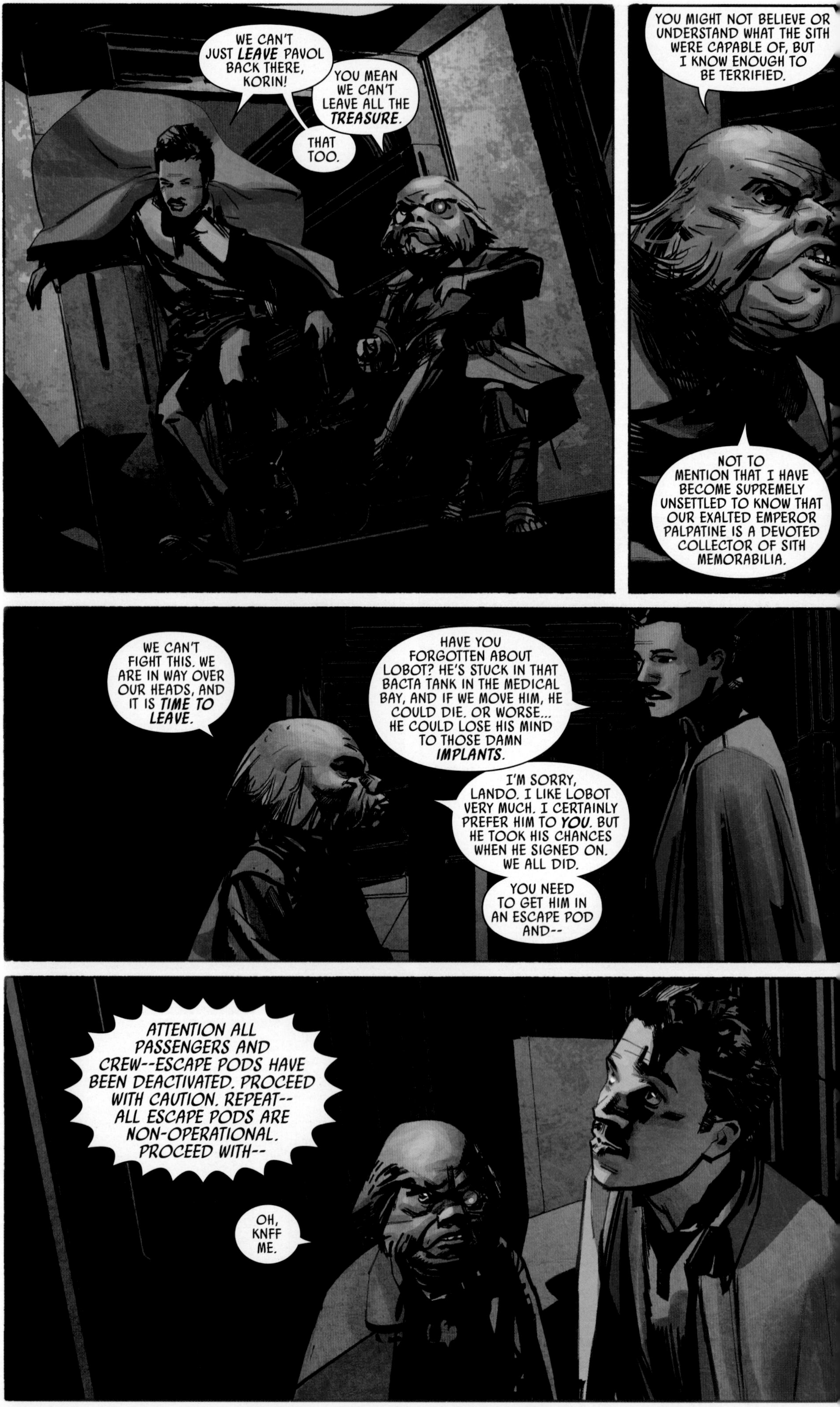
WE CAN'T JUST LEAVE PAVOL BACK THERE, KORIN!
YOU MEAN WE CAN'T LEAVE ALL THE TREASURE.
THAT TOO.
YOU MIGHT NOT BELIEVE OR UNDERSTAND WHAT THE SITH WERE CAPABLE OF, BUT I KNOW ENOUGH TO BE TERRIFIED.
NOT TO MENTION THAT I HAVE BECOME SUPREMELY UNSETTLED TO KNOW THAT OUR EXALTED EMPEROR PALPATINE IS A DEVOTED COLLECTOR OF SITH MEMORABILIA.
WE CAN'T FIGHT THIS. WE ARE IN WAY OVER OUR HEADS, AND IT IS TIME TO LEAVE.
HAVE YOU FORGOTTEN ABOUT LOBOT? HE'S STUCK IN THAT BACTA TANK IN THE MEDICAL BAY, AND IF WE MOVE HIM, HE COULD DIE. OR WORSE... HE COULD LOSE HIS MIND TO THOSE DAMN IMPLANTS.
I'M SORRY, LANDO. I LIKE LOBOT VERY MUCH. I CERTAINLY PREFER HIM TO YOU. BUT HE TOOK HIS CHANCES WHEN HE SIGNED ON. WE ALL DID.
YOU NEED TO GET HIM IN AN ESCAPE POD AND--
ATTENTION ALL PASSENGERS AND CREW--ESCAPE PODS HAVE BEEN DEACTIVATED. PROCEED WITH CAUTION. REPEAT-- ALL ESCAPE PODS ARE NON-OPERATIONAL. PROCEED WITH--
OH, KNFF ME.

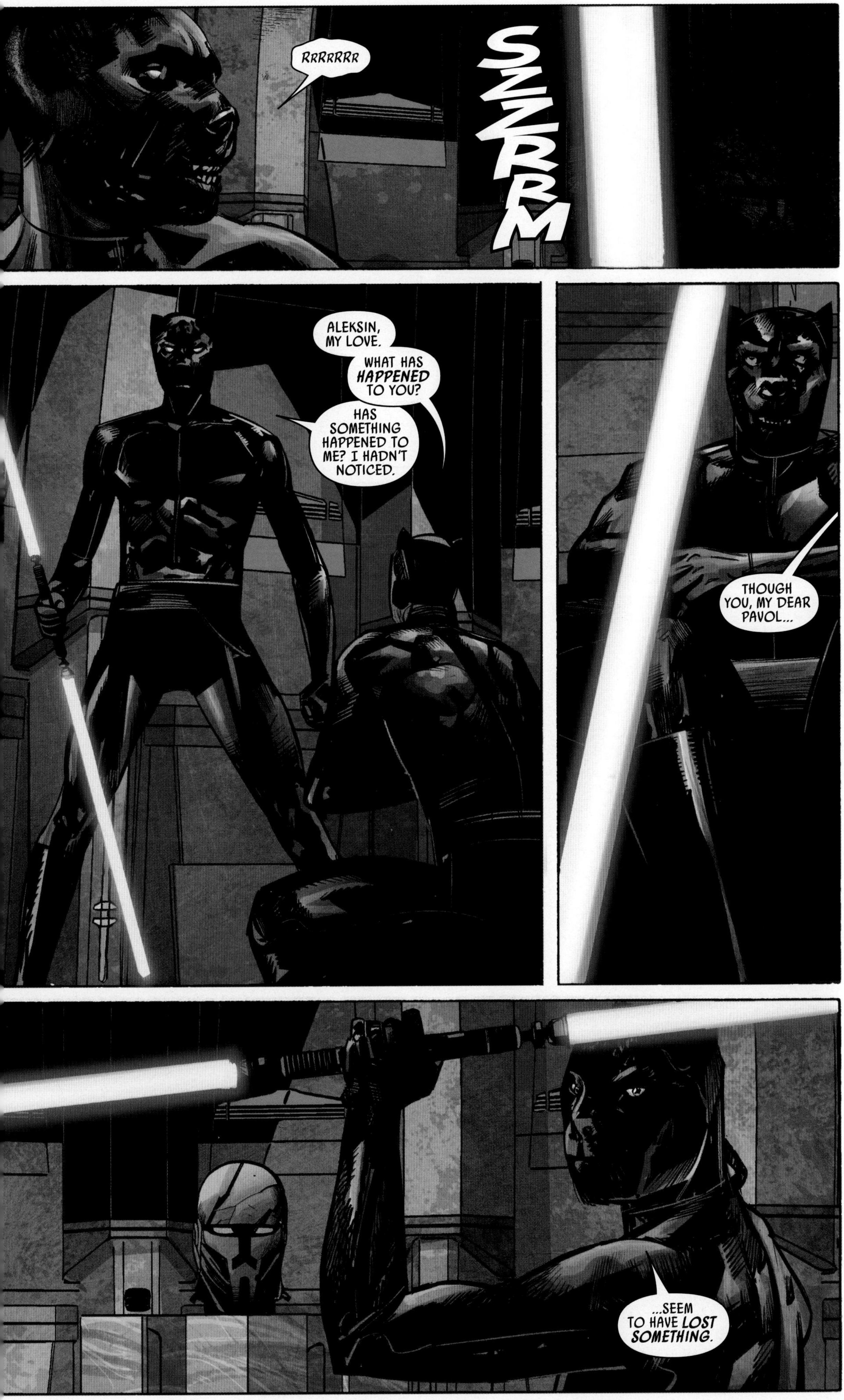
RRRRRRR
SZZRRM
ALEKSIN, MY LOVE.
WHAT HAS HAPPENED TO YOU?
HAS SOMETHING HAPPENED TO ME? I HADN'T NOTICED.
THOUGH YOU, MY DEAR PAVOL...
...SEEM TO HAVE LOST SOMETHING.

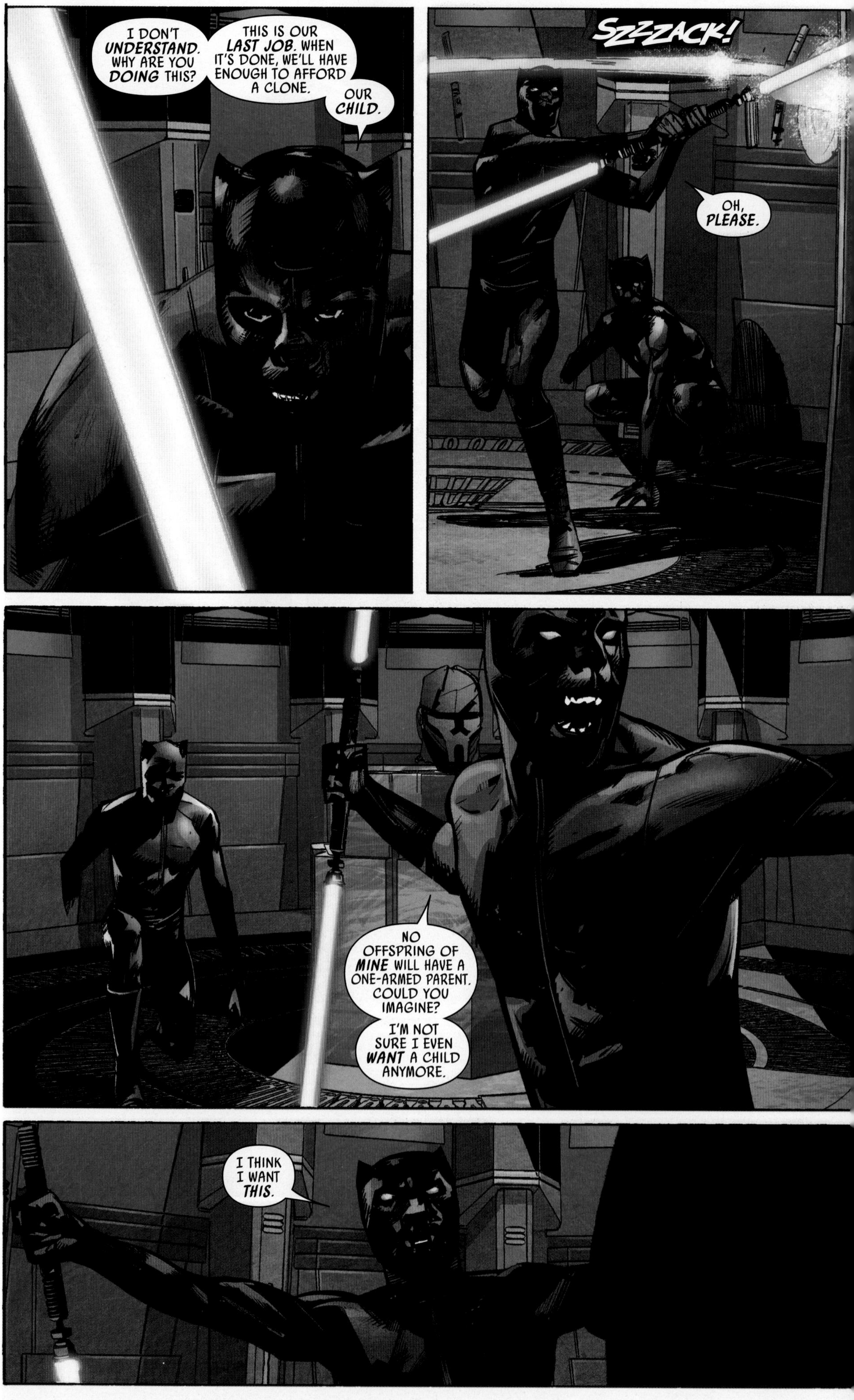
I DON'T UNDERSTAND. WHY ARE YOU DOING THIS?
THIS IS OUR LAST JOB. WHEN IT'S DONE, WE'LL HAVE ENOUGH TO AFFORD A CLONE.
OUR CHILD.
SZZZACK!
OH, PLEASE.
NO OFFSPRING OF MINE WILL HAVE A ONE-ARMED PARENT. COULD YOU IMAGINE?
I'M NOT SURE I EVEN WANT A CHILD ANYMORE.
I THINK I WANT THIS.

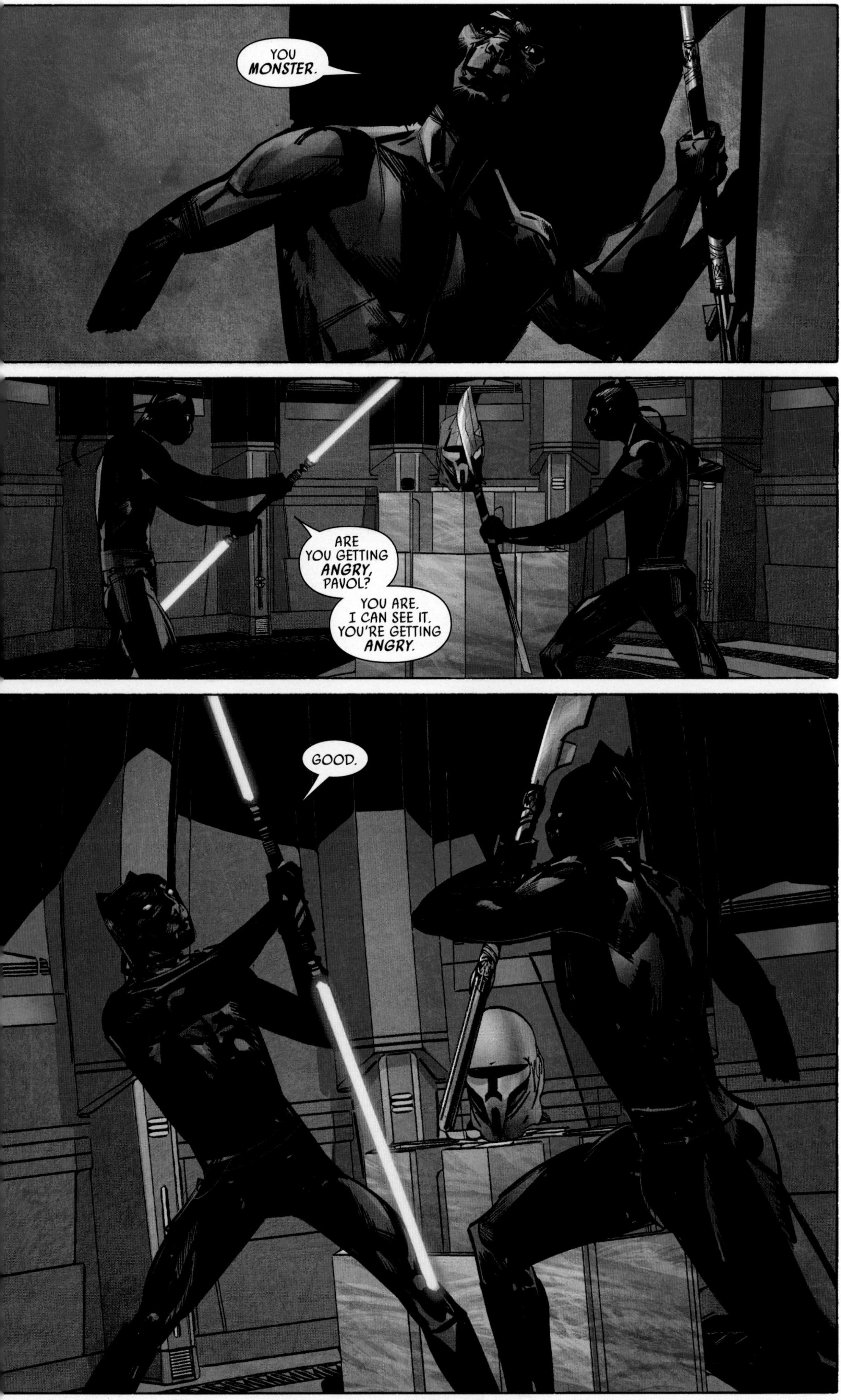
YOU MONSTER.
ARE YOU GETTING ANGRY, PAVOL?
YOU ARE. I CAN SEE IT. YOU'RE GETTING ANGRY.
GOOD.

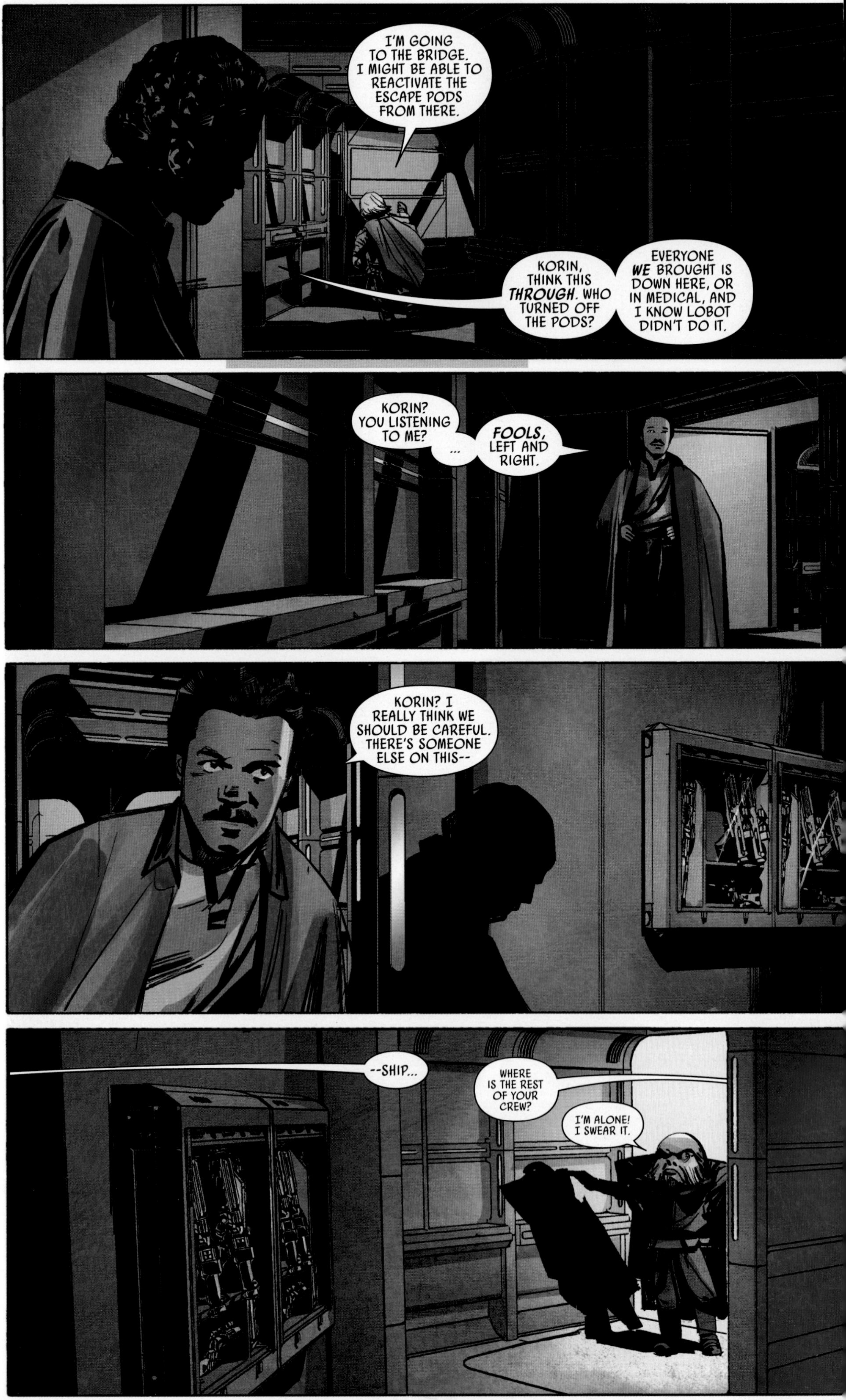
I'M GOING TO THE BRIDGE. I MIGHT BE ABLE TO REACTIVATE THE ESCAPE PODS FROM THERE.
KORIN, THINK THIS THROUGH. WHO TURNED OFF THE PODS?
EVERYONE WE BROUGHT IS DOWN HERE, OR IN MEDICAL, AND I KNOW LOBOT DIDN'T DO IT.
KORIN? YOU LISTENING TO ME?
...
FOOLS, LEFT AND RIGHT.
KORIN? I REALLY THINK WE SHOULD BE CAREFUL. THERE'S SOMEONE ELSE ON THIS--
--SHIP...
WHERE IS THE REST OF YOUR CREW?
I'M ALONE! I SWEAR IT.

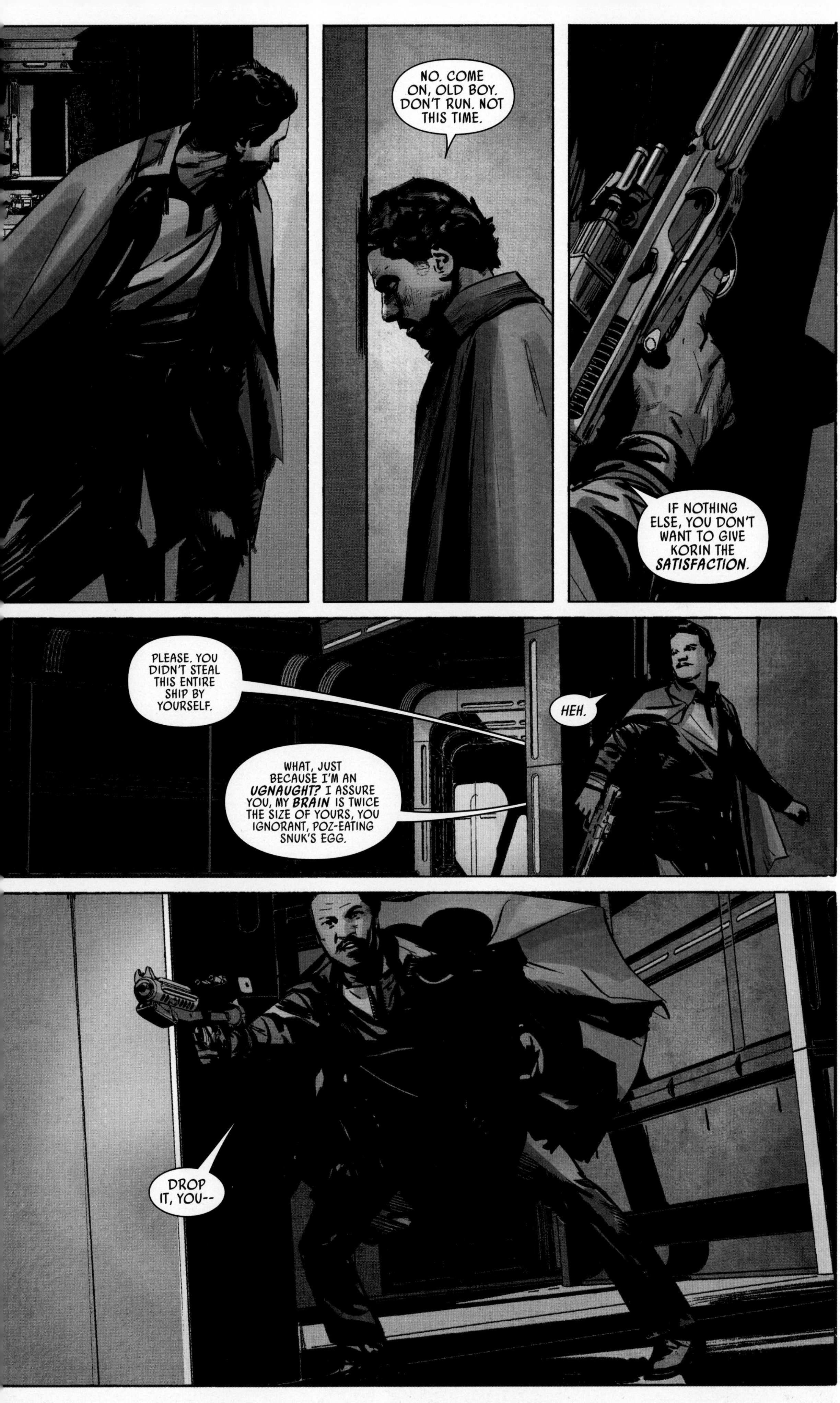
NO. COME ON, OLD BOY. DON'T RUN. NOT THIS TIME.
IF NOTHING ELSE, YOU DON'T WANT TO GIVE KORIN THE SATISFACTION.
PLEASE. YOU DIDN'T STEAL THIS ENTIRE SHIP BY YOURSELF.
HEH.
WHAT, JUST BECAUSE I'M AN UGNAUGHT? I ASSURE YOU, MY BRAIN IS TWICE THE SIZE OF YOURS, YOU IGNORANT, POZ-EATING SNUK'S EGG.
DROP IT, YOU--

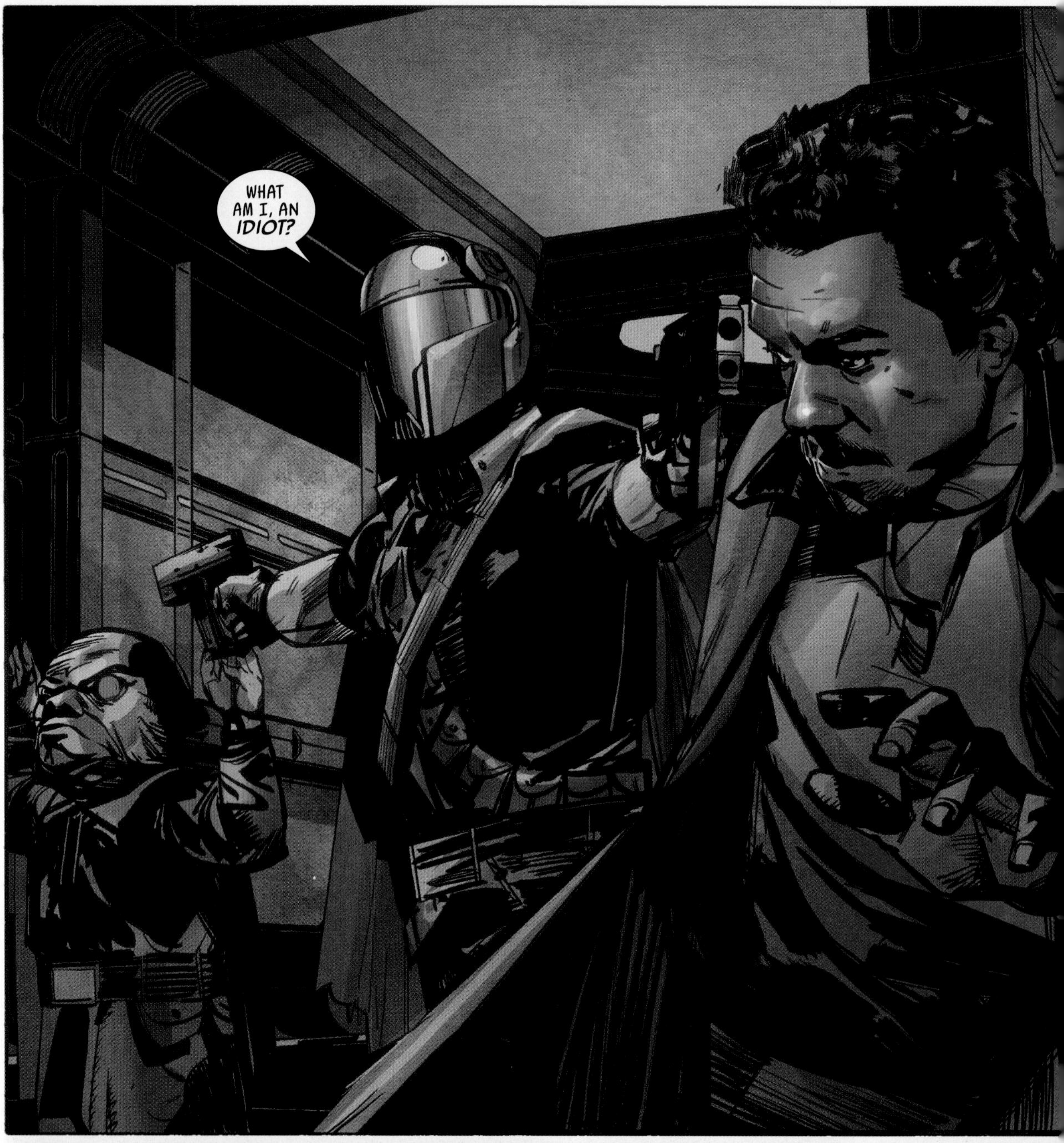
WHAT AM I, AN IDIOT?

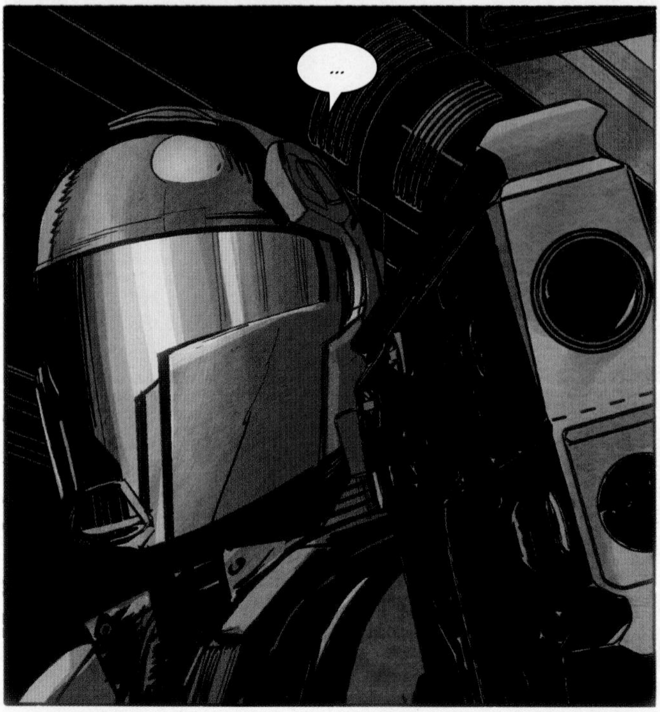
...

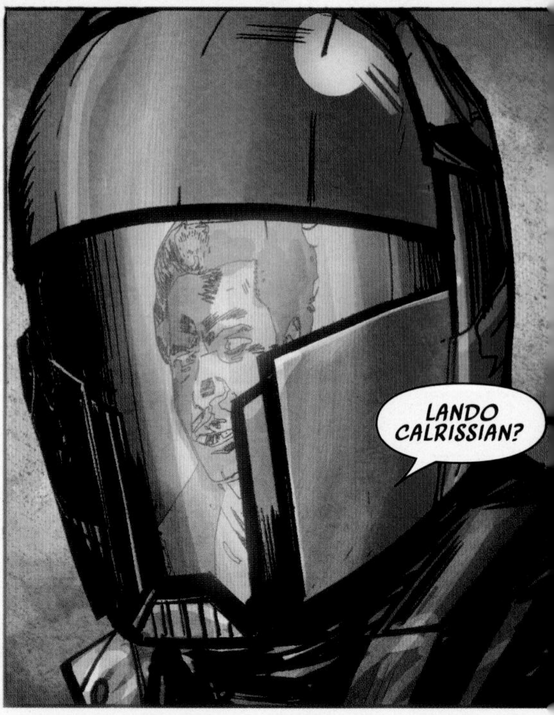
LANDO CALRISSIAN?

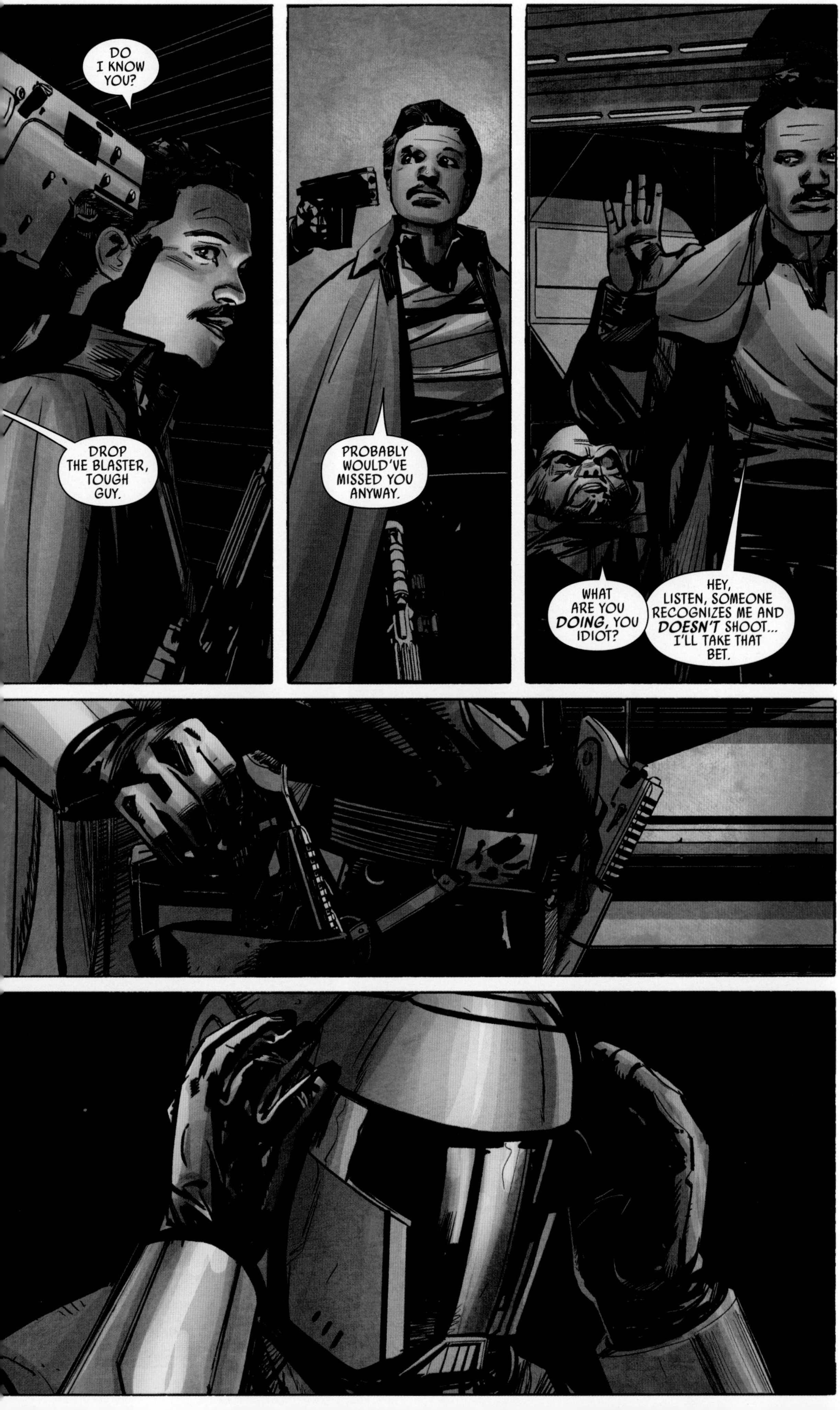
DO I KNOW YOU?
DROP THE BLASTER, TOUGH GUY.
PROBABLY WOULD'VE MISSED YOU ANYWAY.
WHAT ARE YOU DOING, YOU IDIOT?
HEY, LISTEN, SOMEONE RECOGNIZES ME AND DOESN'T SHOOT... I'LL TAKE THAT BET.

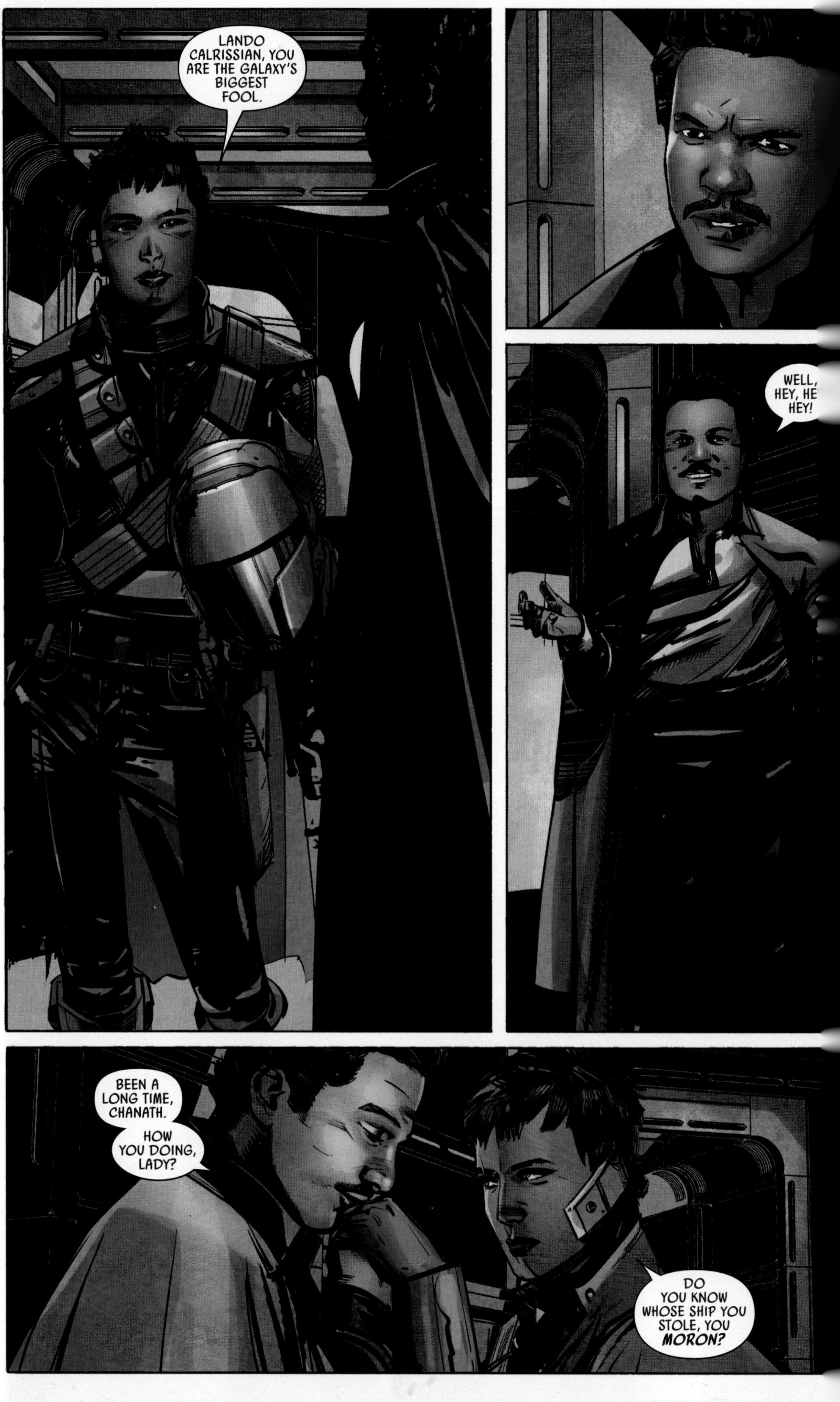
LANDO CALRISSIAN, YOU ARE THE GALAXY'S BIGGEST FOOL.
WELL, HEY, HEY HEY!
BEEN A LONG TIME, CHANATH.
HOW YOU DOING, LADY?
DO YOU KNOW WHOSE SHIP YOU STOLE, YOU *MORON?*

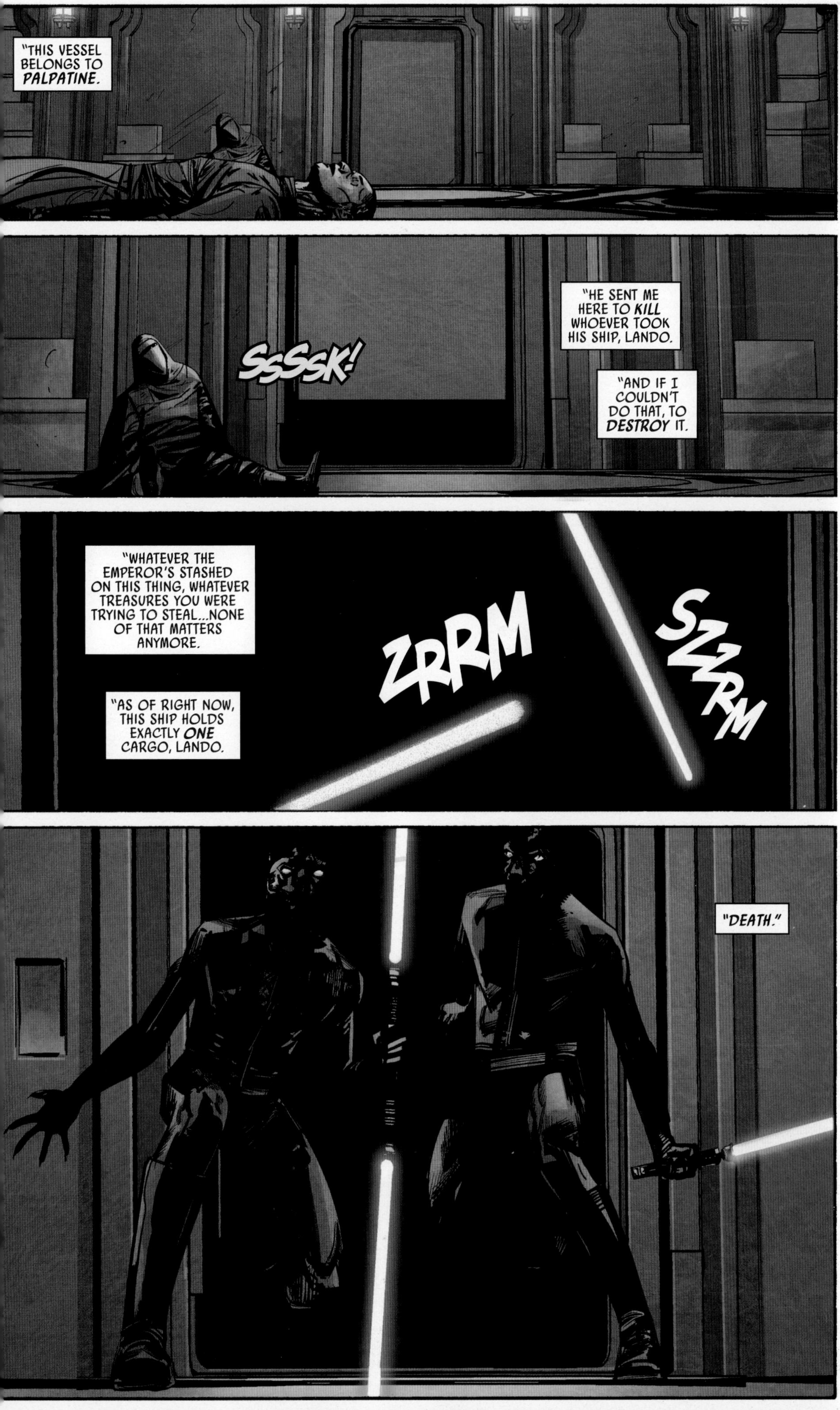
"THIS VESSEL BELONGS TO PALPATINE.
"HE SENT ME HERE TO KILL WHOEVER TOOK HIS SHIP, LANDO.
"AND IF I COULDN'T DO THAT, TO DESTROY IT.
SSSSK!
"WHATEVER THE EMPEROR'S STASHED ON THIS THING, WHATEVER TREASURES YOU WERE TRYING TO STEAL...NONE OF THAT MATTERS ANYMORE.
"AS OF RIGHT NOW, THIS SHIP HOLDS EXACTLY ONE CARGO, LANDO.
ZRRM
SZZRM
"DEATH."

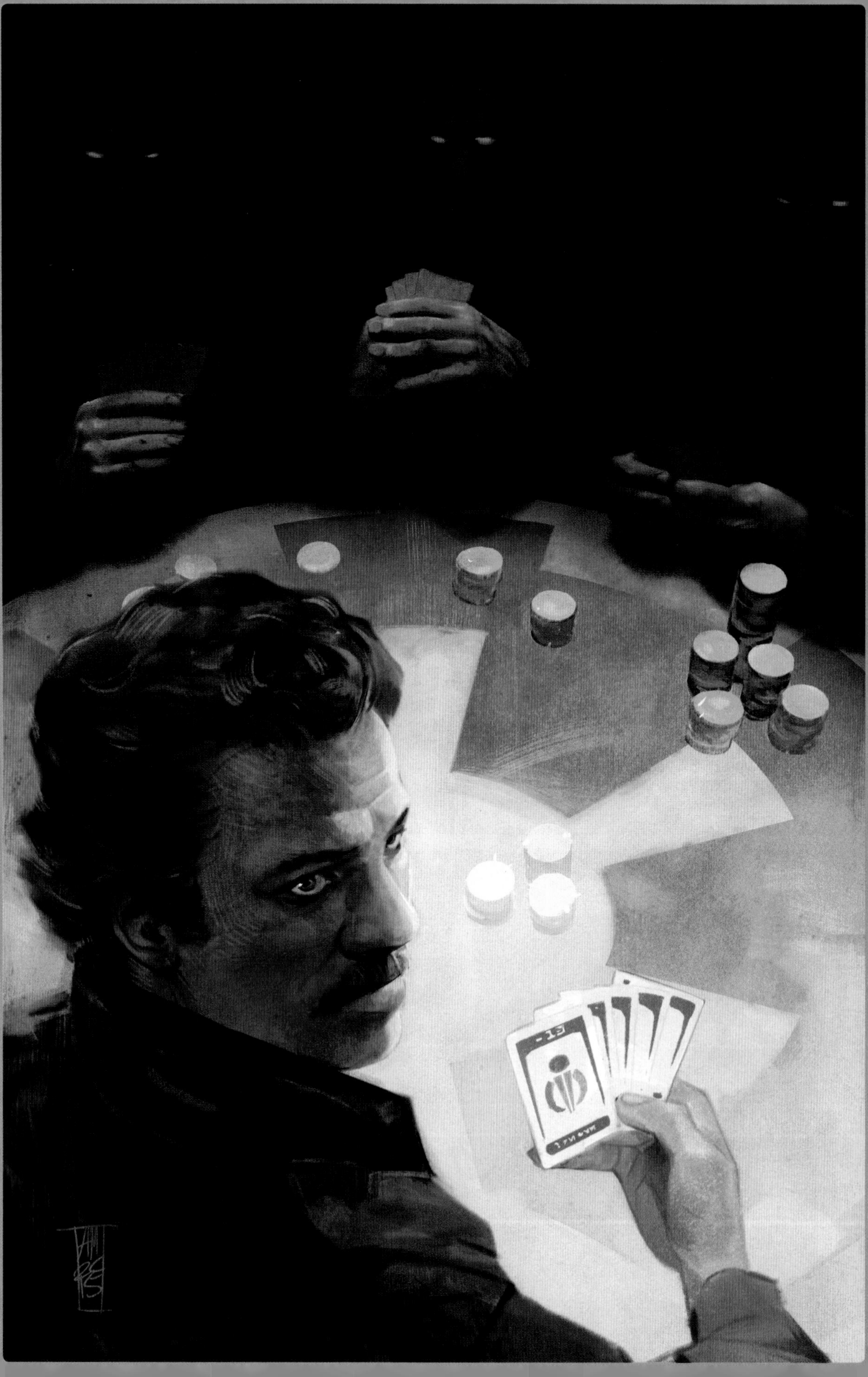

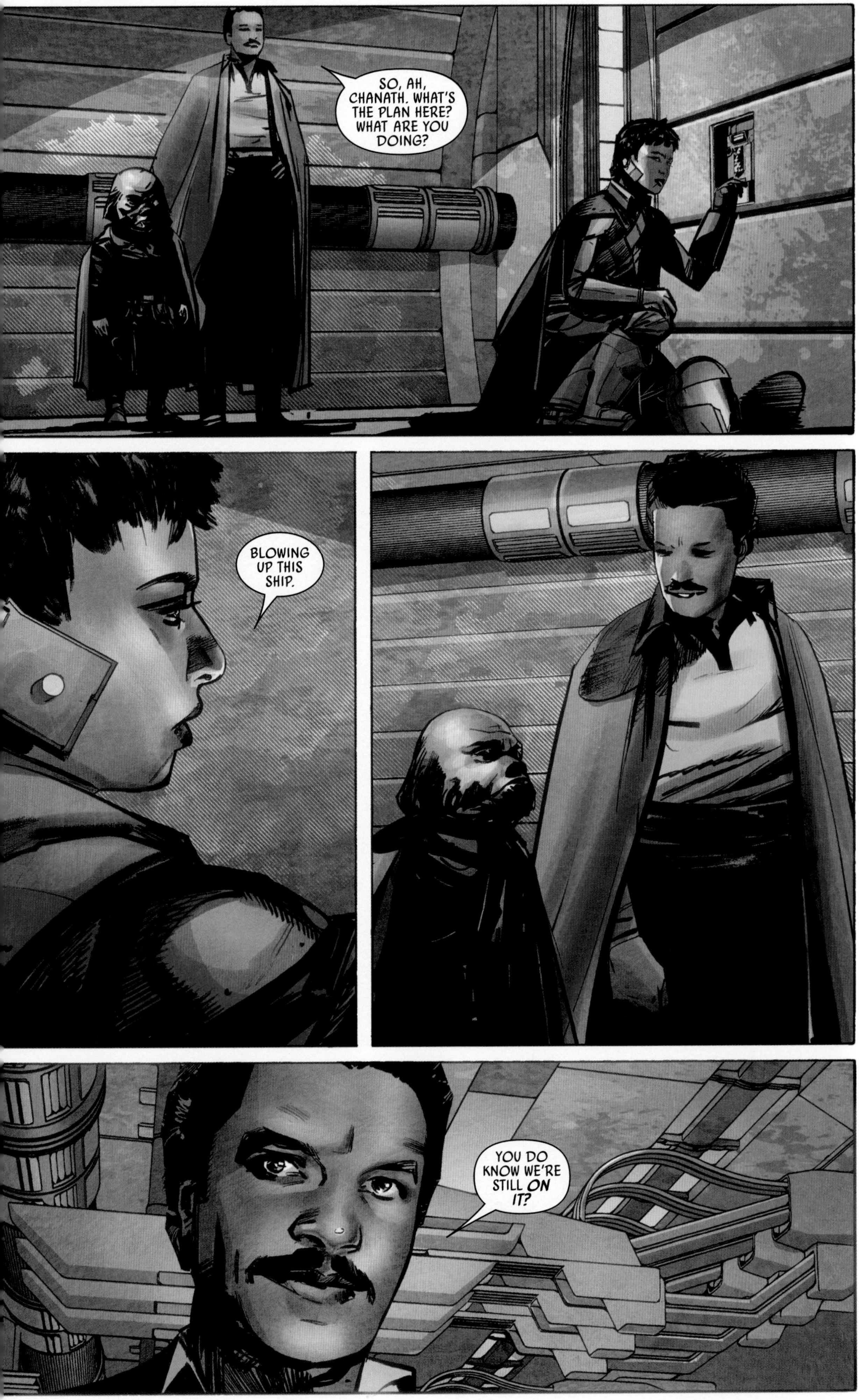
SO, AH, CHANATH. WHAT'S THE PLAN HERE? WHAT ARE YOU DOING?
BLOWING UP THIS SHIP.
YOU DO KNOW WE'RE STILL *ON* IT?

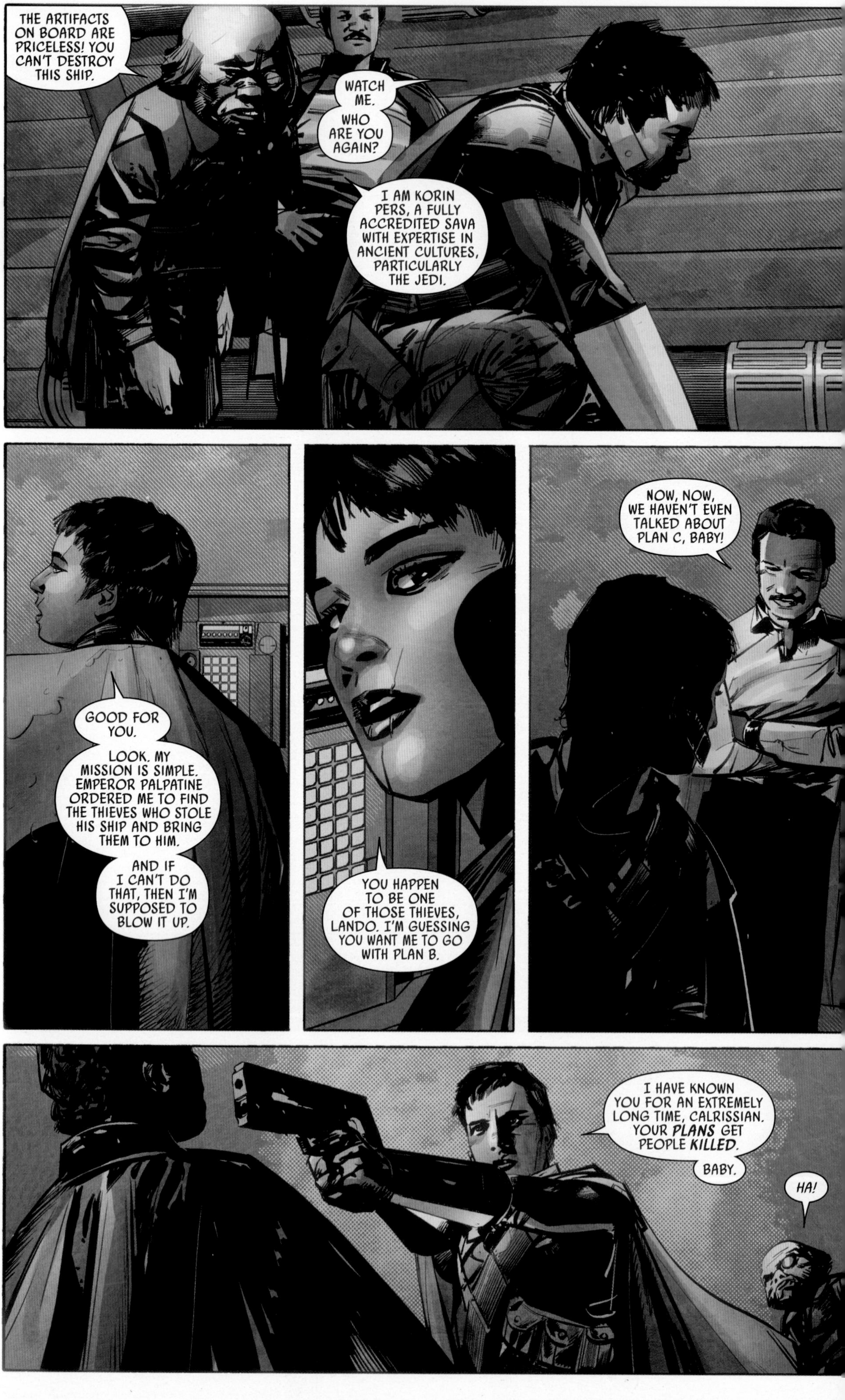
THE ARTIFACTS ON BOARD ARE PRICELESS! YOU CAN'T DESTROY THIS SHIP.
WATCH ME.
WHO ARE YOU AGAIN?
I AM KORIN PERS, A FULLY ACCREDITED SAVA WITH EXPERTISE IN ANCIENT CULTURES, PARTICULARLY THE JEDI.
GOOD FOR YOU.
LOOK. MY MISSION IS SIMPLE. EMPEROR PALPATINE ORDERED ME TO FIND THE THIEVES WHO STOLE HIS SHIP AND BRING THEM TO HIM.
AND IF I CAN'T DO THAT, THEN I'M SUPPOSED TO BLOW IT UP.
YOU HAPPEN TO BE ONE OF THOSE THIEVES, LANDO. I'M GUESSING YOU WANT ME TO GO WITH PLAN B.
NOW, NOW, WE HAVEN'T EVEN TALKED ABOUT PLAN C, BABY!
I HAVE KNOWN YOU FOR AN EXTREMELY LONG TIME, CALRISSIAN. YOUR *PLANS* GET PEOPLE *KILLED*.
BABY.
HA!

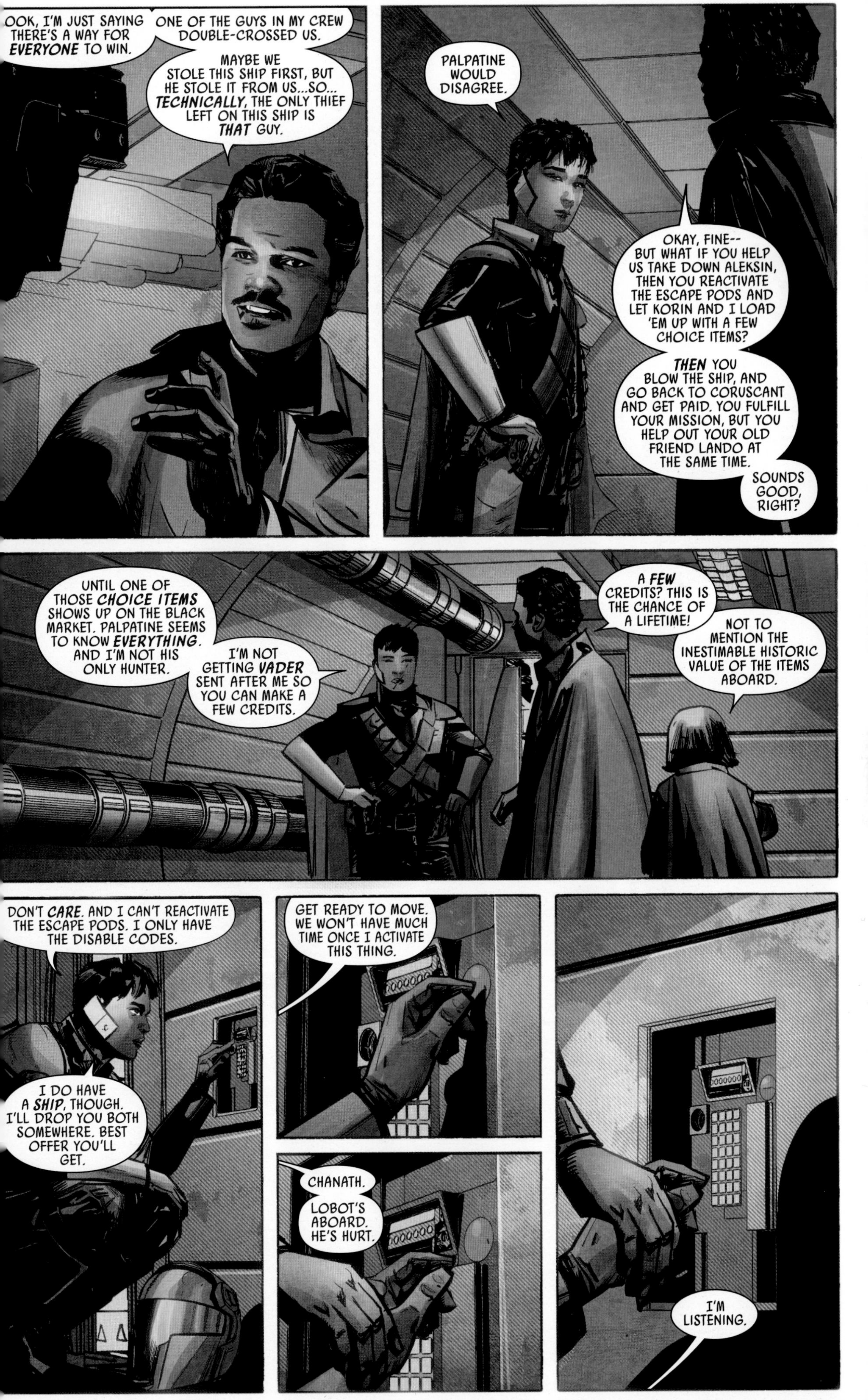
OOK, I'M JUST SAYING THERE'S A WAY FOR EVERYONE TO WIN.
ONE OF THE GUYS IN MY CREW DOUBLE-CROSSED US.
MAYBE WE STOLE THIS SHIP FIRST, BUT HE STOLE IT FROM US...SO... TECHNICALLY, THE ONLY THIEF LEFT ON THIS SHIP IS THAT GUY.
PALPATINE WOULD DISAGREE.
OKAY, FINE-- BUT WHAT IF YOU HELP US TAKE DOWN ALEKSIN, THEN YOU REACTIVATE THE ESCAPE PODS AND LET KORIN AND I LOAD 'EM UP WITH A FEW CHOICE ITEMS?
THEN YOU BLOW THE SHIP, AND GO BACK TO CORUSCANT AND GET PAID. YOU FULFILL YOUR MISSION, BUT YOU HELP OUT YOUR OLD FRIEND LANDO AT THE SAME TIME.
SOUNDS GOOD, RIGHT?
UNTIL ONE OF THOSE CHOICE ITEMS SHOWS UP ON THE BLACK MARKET. PALPATINE SEEMS TO KNOW EVERYTHING. AND I'M NOT HIS ONLY HUNTER.
I'M NOT GETTING VADER SENT AFTER ME SO YOU CAN MAKE A FEW CREDITS.
A FEW CREDITS? THIS IS THE CHANCE OF A LIFETIME!
NOT TO MENTION THE INESTIMABLE HISTORIC VALUE OF THE ITEMS ABOARD.
DON'T CARE. AND I CAN'T REACTIVATE THE ESCAPE PODS. I ONLY HAVE THE DISABLE CODES.
I DO HAVE A SHIP, THOUGH. I'LL DROP YOU BOTH SOMEWHERE. BEST OFFER YOU'LL GET.
GET READY TO MOVE. WE WON'T HAVE MUCH TIME ONCE I ACTIVATE THIS THING.
CHANATH.
LOBOT'S ABOARD. HE'S HURT.
I'M LISTENING.

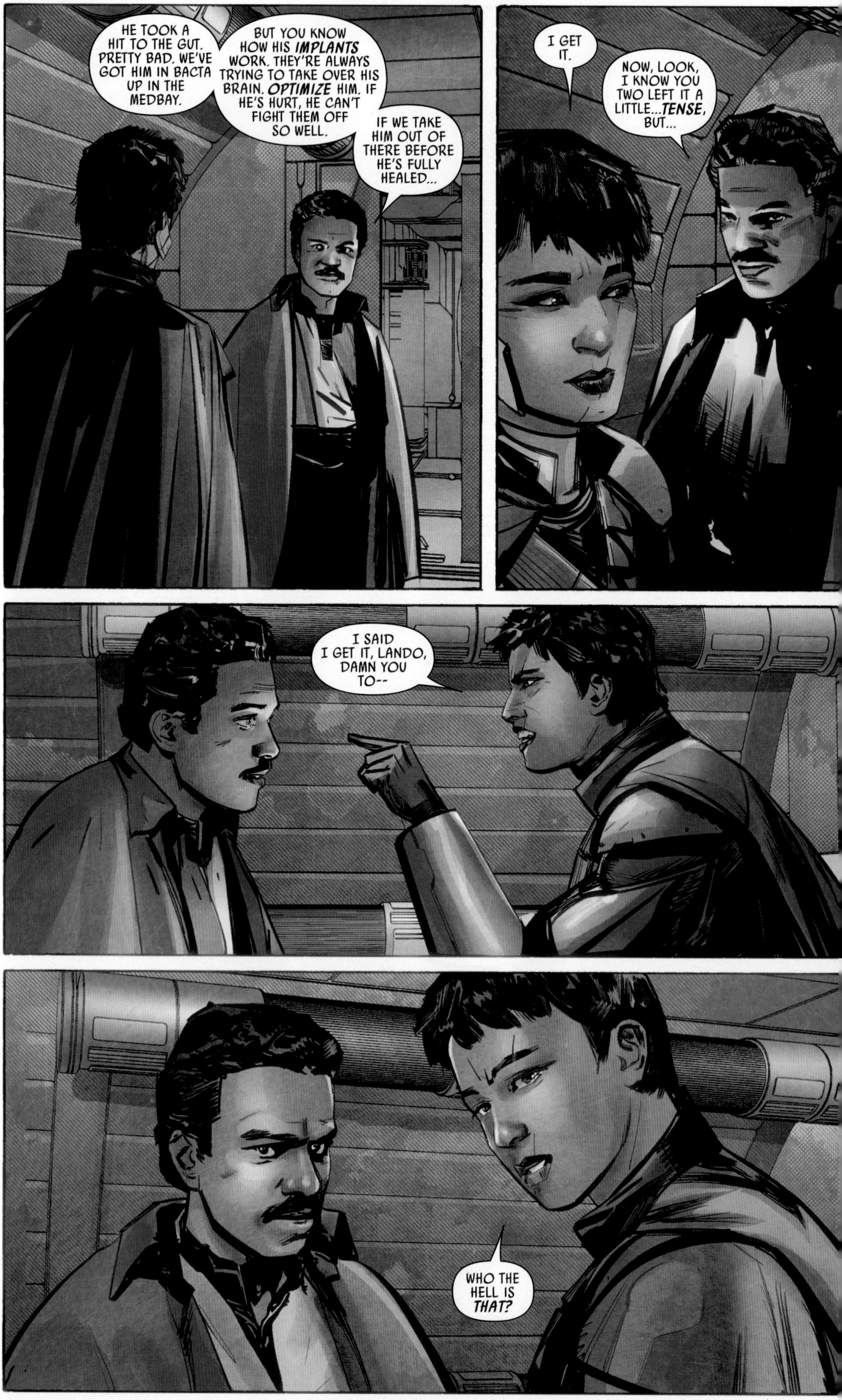
HE TOOK A HIT TO THE GUT. PRETTY BAD. WE'VE GOT HIM IN BACTA UP IN THE MEDBAY.
BUT YOU KNOW HOW HIS IMPLANTS WORK. THEY'RE ALWAYS TRYING TO TAKE OVER HIS BRAIN. OPTIMIZE HIM. IF HE'S HURT, HE CAN'T FIGHT THEM OFF SO WELL.
IF WE TAKE HIM OUT OF THERE BEFORE HE'S FULLY HEALED...
I GET IT.
NOW, LOOK, I KNOW YOU TWO LEFT IT A LITTLE...TENSE, BUT...
I SAID I GET IT, LANDO, DAMN YOU TO--
WHO THE HELL IS THAT?

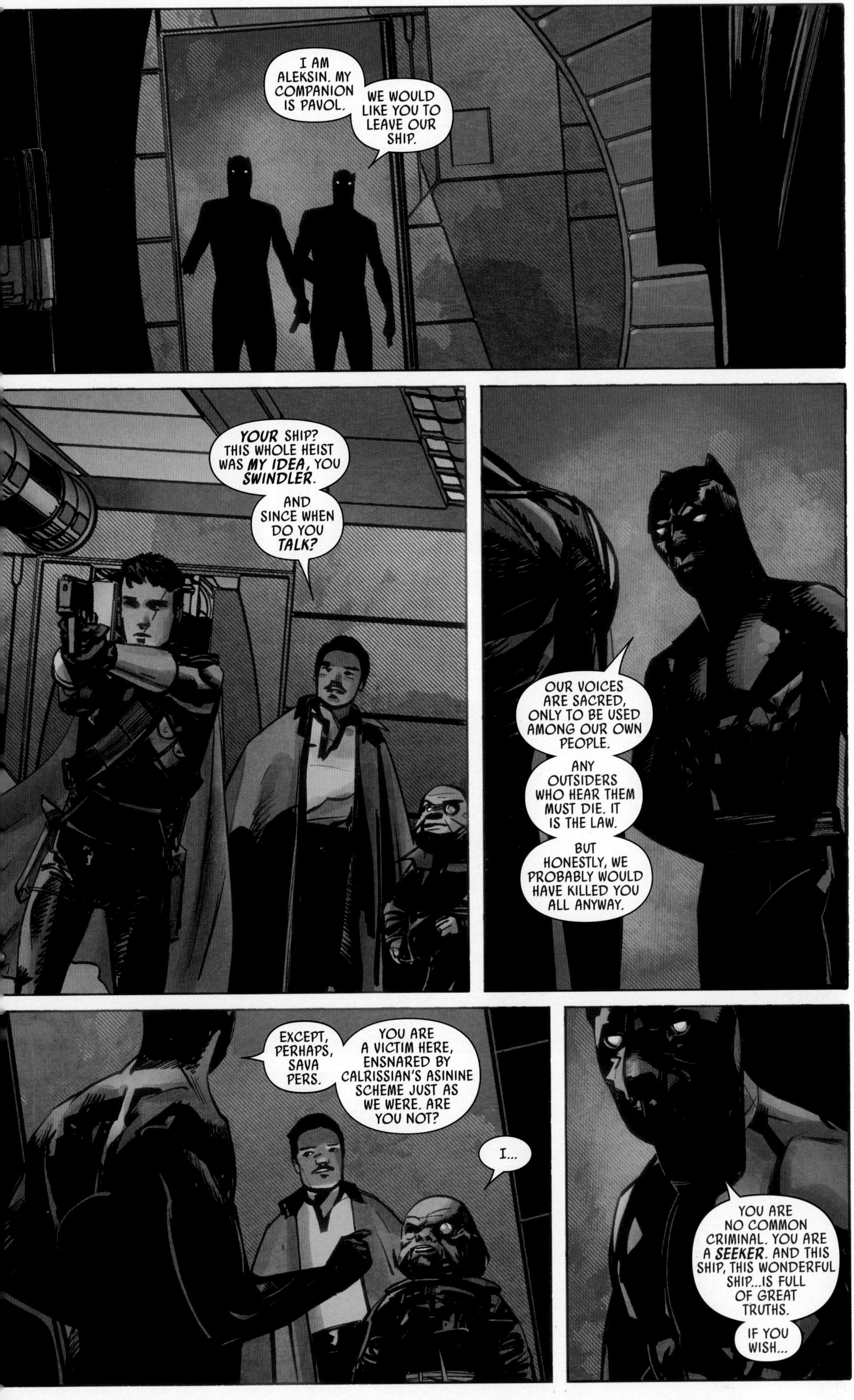
I AM ALEKSIN. MY COMPANION IS PAVOL.
WE WOULD LIKE YOU TO LEAVE OUR SHIP.
YOUR SHIP? THIS WHOLE HEIST WAS MY IDEA, YOU SWINDLER.
AND SINCE WHEN DO YOU TALK?
OUR VOICES ARE SACRED, ONLY TO BE USED AMONG OUR OWN PEOPLE.
ANY OUTSIDERS WHO HEAR THEM MUST DIE. IT IS THE LAW.
BUT HONESTLY, WE PROBABLY WOULD HAVE KILLED YOU ALL ANYWAY.
EXCEPT, PERHAPS, SAVA PERS.
YOU ARE A VICTIM HERE, ENSNARED BY CALRISSIAN'S ASININE SCHEME JUST AS WE WERE. ARE YOU NOT?
I...
YOU ARE NO COMMON CRIMINAL. YOU ARE A SEEKER. AND THIS SHIP, THIS WONDERFUL SHIP...IS FULL OF GREAT TRUTHS.
IF YOU WISH...

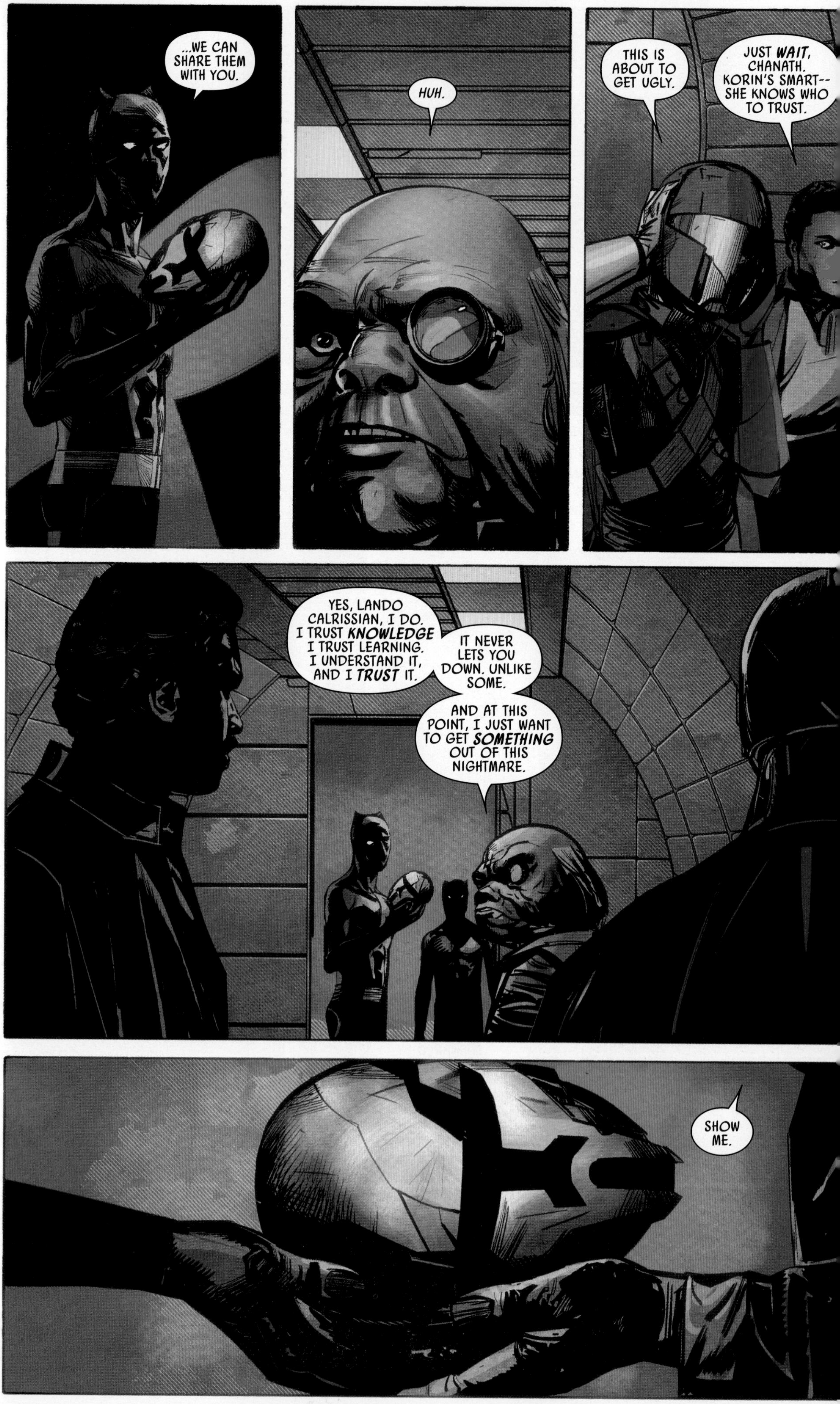
...WE CAN SHARE THEM WITH YOU.
HUH.
THIS IS ABOUT TO GET UGLY.
JUST WAIT, CHANATH. KORIN'S SMART-- SHE KNOWS WHO TO TRUST.
YES, LANDO CALRISSIAN, I DO. I TRUST KNOWLEDGE I TRUST LEARNING. I UNDERSTAND IT, AND I TRUST IT.
IT NEVER LETS YOU DOWN. UNLIKE SOME.
AND AT THIS POINT, I JUST WANT TO GET SOMETHING OUT OF THIS NIGHTMARE.
SHOW ME.

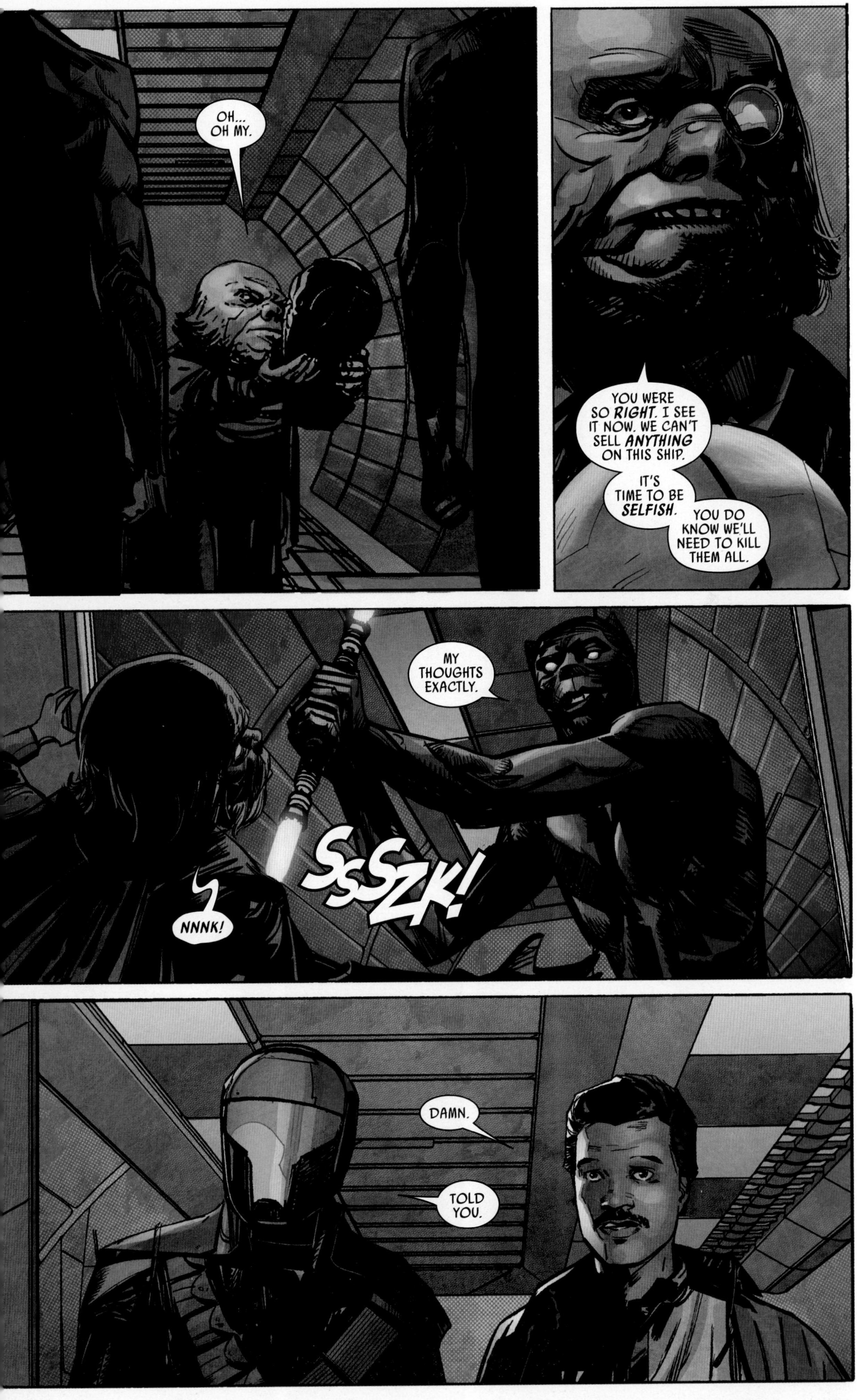
OH... OH MY.
YOU WERE SO RIGHT. I SEE IT NOW. WE CAN'T SELL ANYTHING ON THIS SHIP.
IT'S TIME TO BE SELFISH.
YOU DO KNOW WE'LL NEED TO KILL THEM ALL.
MY THOUGHTS EXACTLY.
NNNK!
SSSZK!
DAMN.
TOLD YOU.

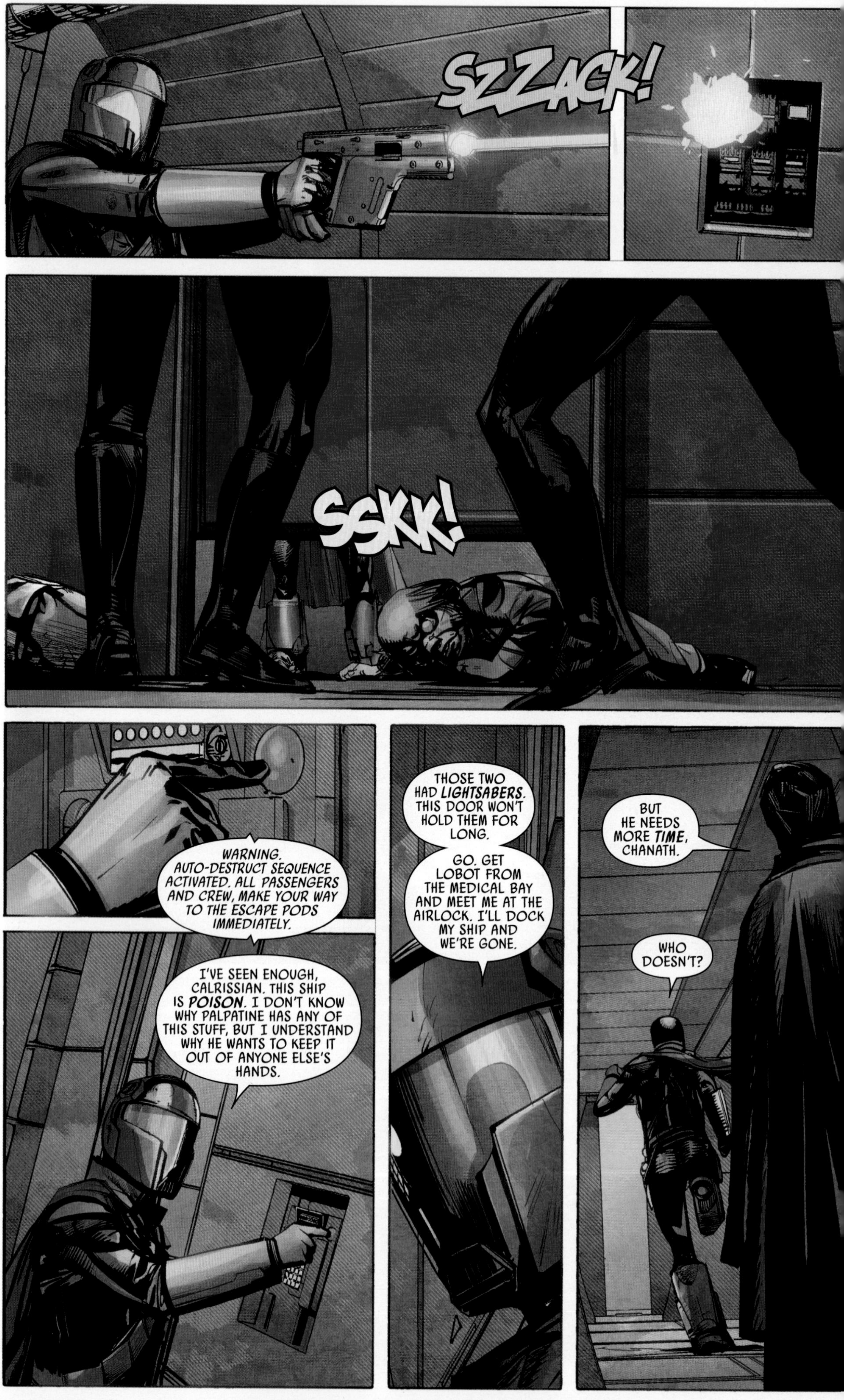
SZZACK!
SSKK!
WARNING. AUTO-DESTRUCT SEQUENCE ACTIVATED. ALL PASSENGERS AND CREW, MAKE YOUR WAY TO THE ESCAPE PODS IMMEDIATELY.
I'VE SEEN ENOUGH, CALRISSIAN. THIS SHIP IS POISON. I DON'T KNOW WHY PALPATINE HAS ANY OF THIS STUFF, BUT I UNDERSTAND WHY HE WANTS TO KEEP IT OUT OF ANYONE ELSE'S HANDS.
THOSE TWO HAD LIGHTSABERS. THIS DOOR WON'T HOLD THEM FOR LONG.
GO. GET LOBOT FROM THE MEDICAL BAY AND MEET ME AT THE AIRLOCK. I'LL DOCK MY SHIP AND WE'RE GONE.
BUT HE NEEDS MORE TIME, CHANATH.
WHO DOESN'T?

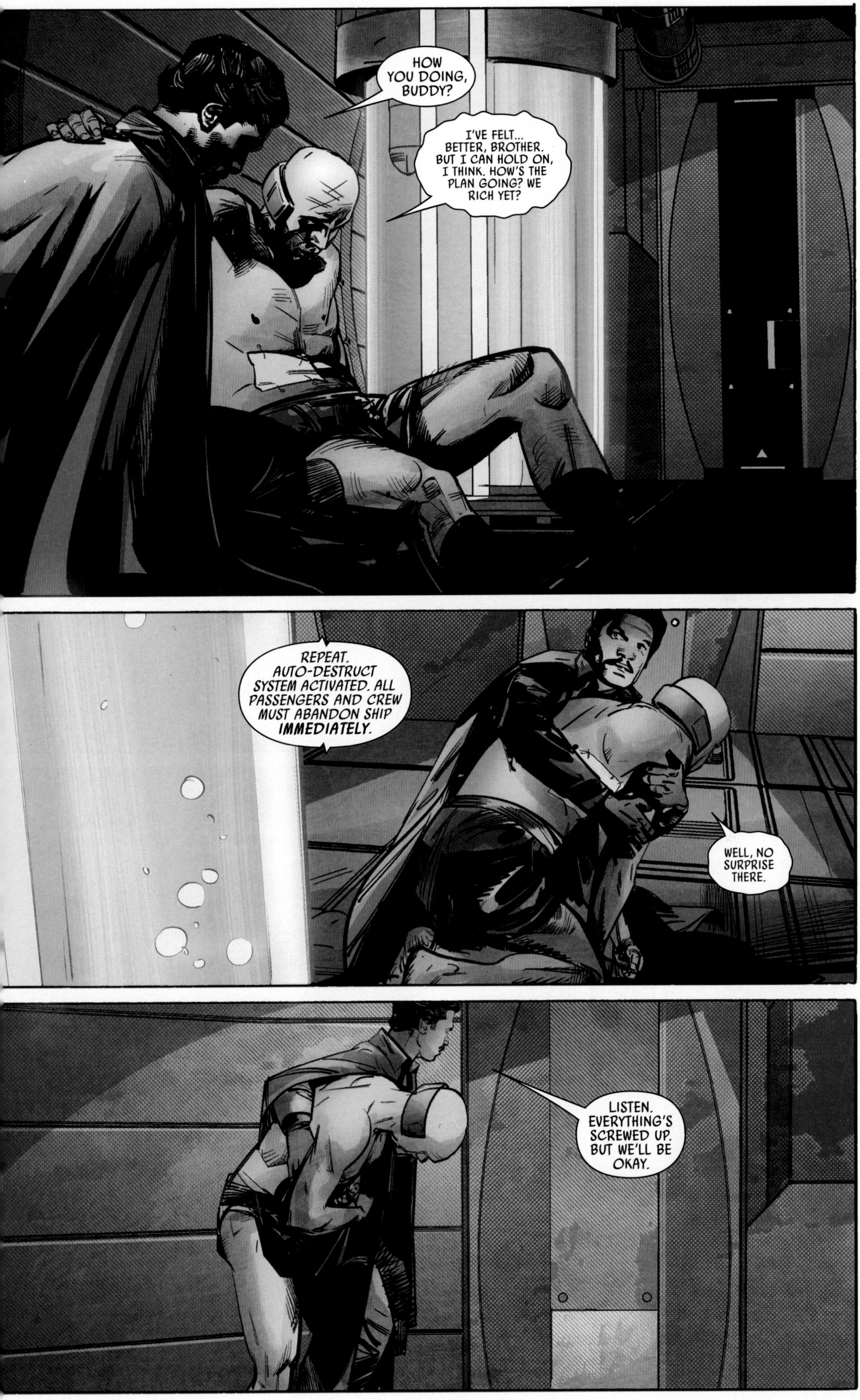
HOW YOU DOING, BUDDY?
I'VE FELT... BETTER, BROTHER. BUT I CAN HOLD ON, I THINK. HOW'S THE PLAN GOING? WE RICH YET?
REPEAT. AUTO-DESTRUCT SYSTEM ACTIVATED. ALL PASSENGERS AND CREW MUST ABANDON SHIP IMMEDIATELY.
WELL, NO SURPRISE THERE.
LISTEN. EVERYTHING'S SCREWED UP. BUT WE'LL BE OKAY.

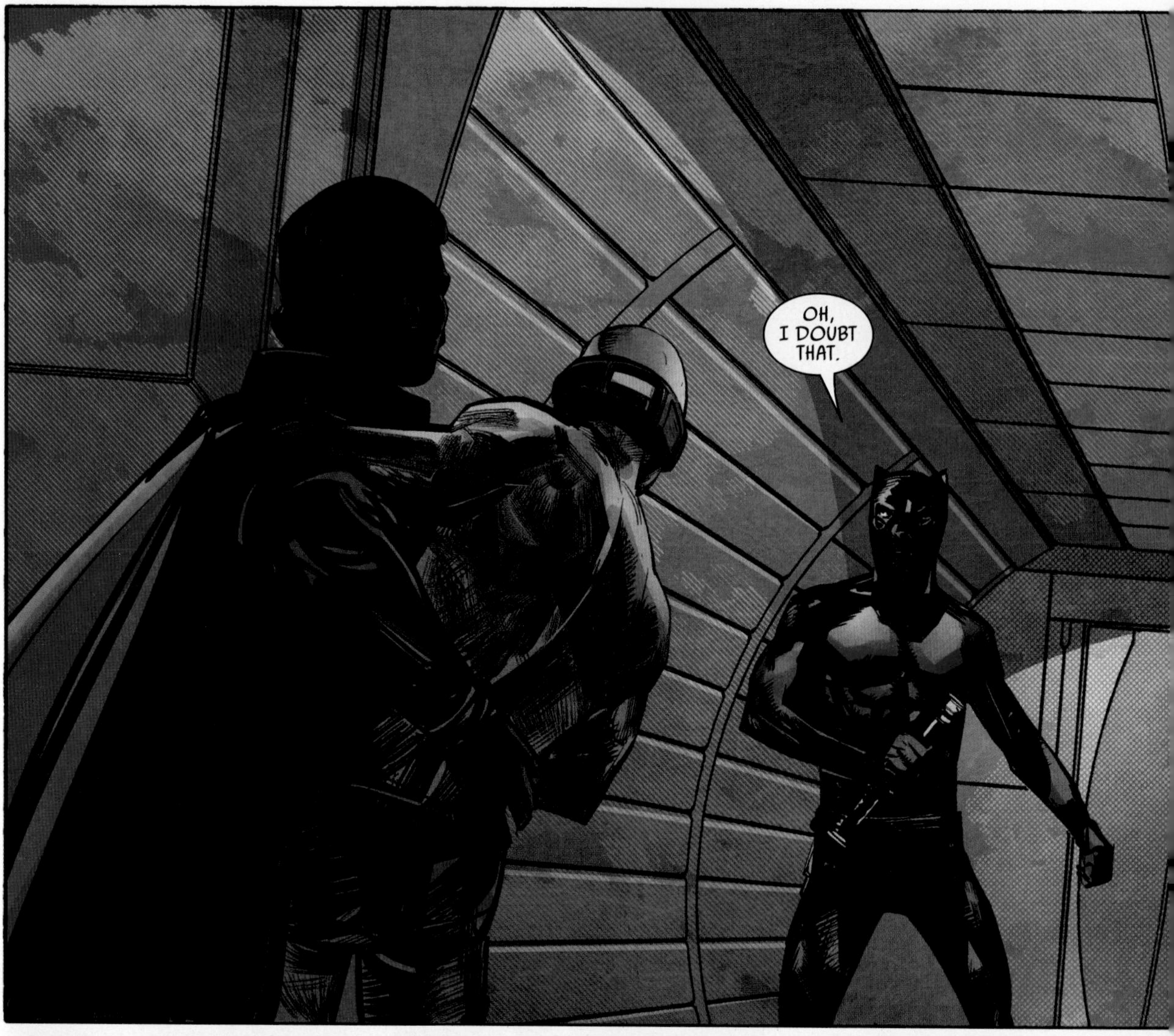
OH, I DOUBT THAT.

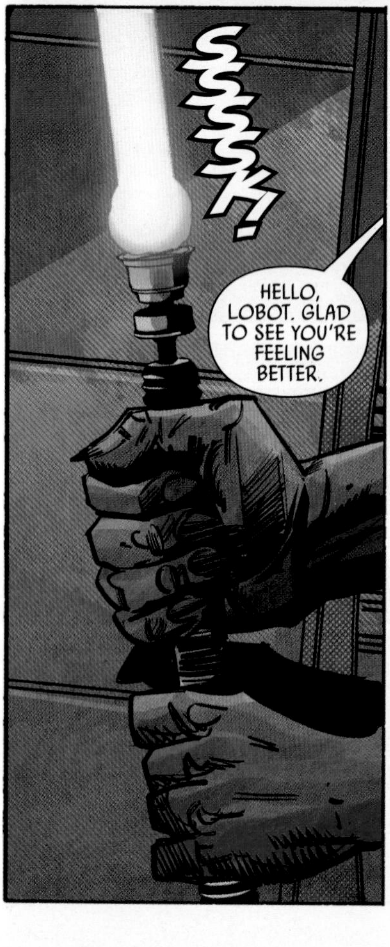
SSSSK!
HELLO, LOBOT. GLAD TO SEE YOU'RE FEELING BETTER.

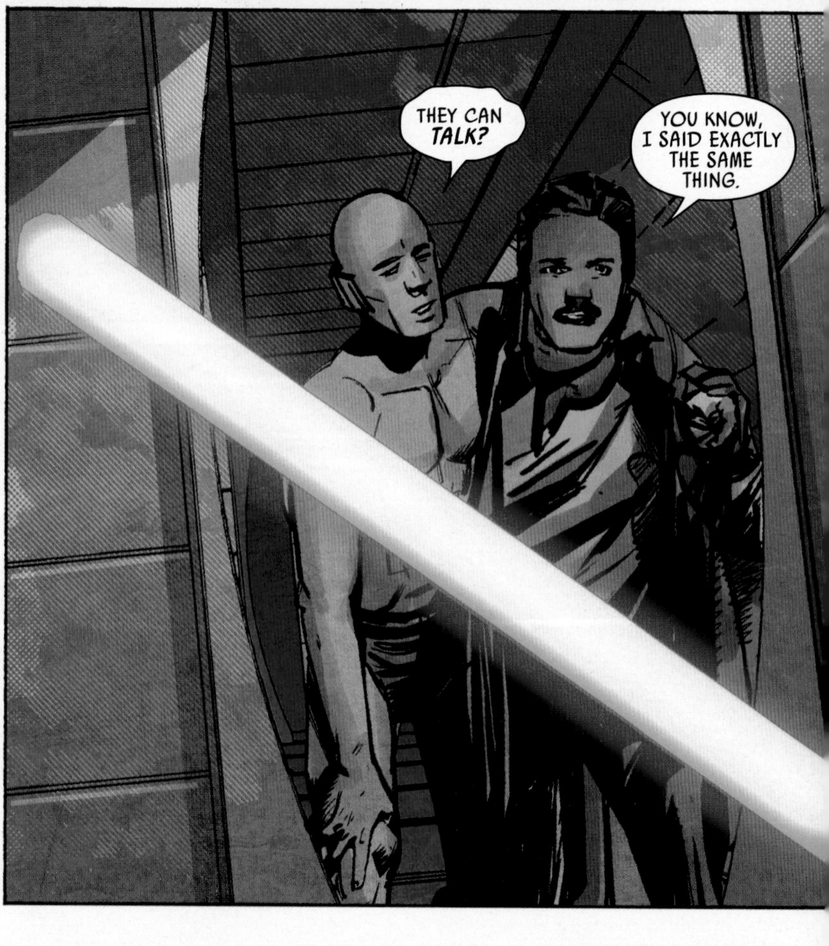
THEY CAN *TALK?*
YOU KNOW, I SAID EXACTLY THE SAME THING.

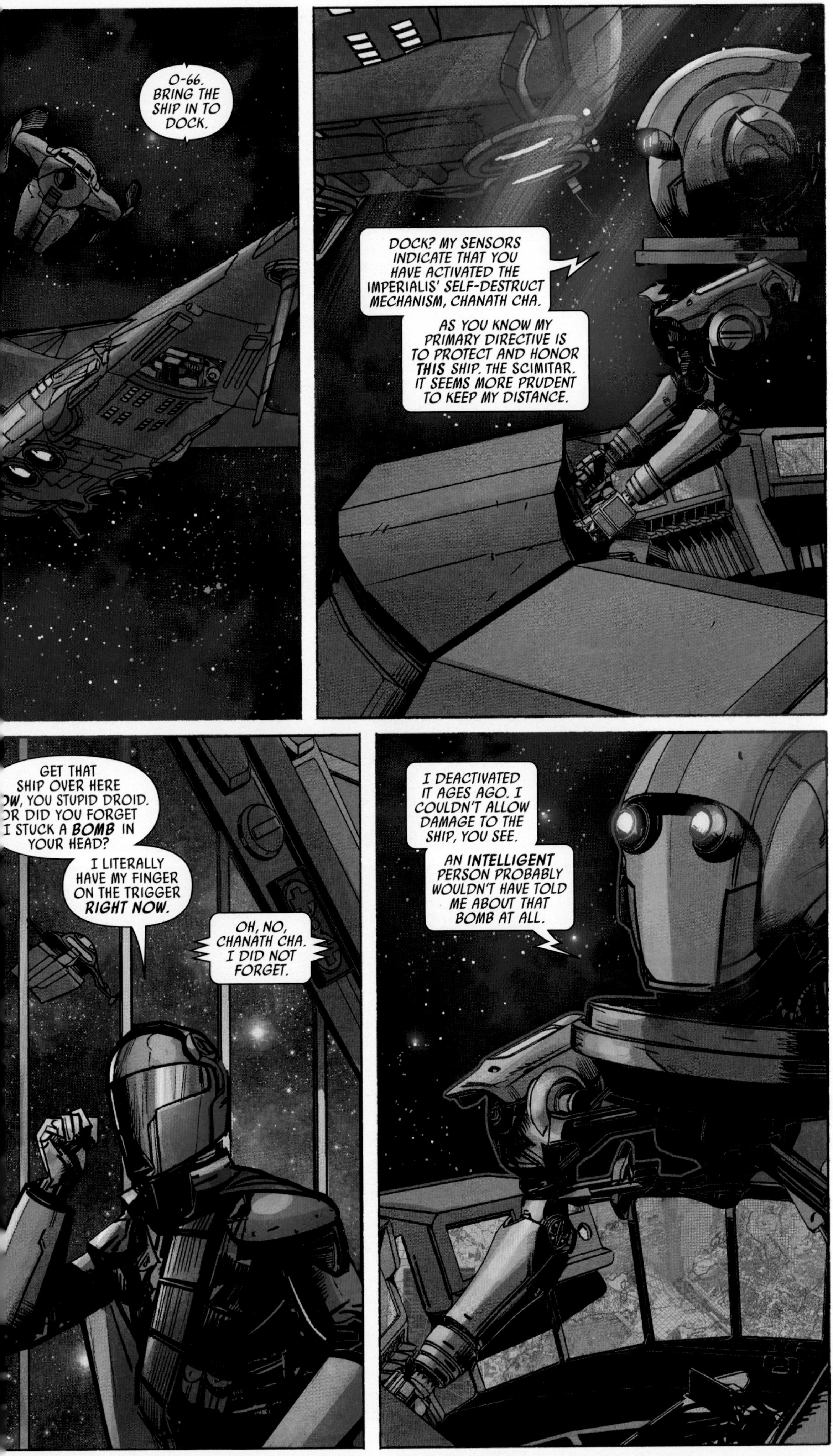
O-66. BRING THE SHIP IN TO DOCK.
DOCK? MY SENSORS INDICATE THAT YOU HAVE ACTIVATED THE IMPERIALIS' SELF-DESTRUCT MECHANISM, CHANATH CHA.
AS YOU KNOW MY PRIMARY DIRECTIVE IS TO PROTECT AND HONOR **THIS** SHIP. THE SCIMITAR. IT SEEMS MORE PRUDENT TO KEEP MY DISTANCE.
GET THAT SHIP OVER HERE OW, YOU STUPID DROID. OR DID YOU FORGET I STUCK A **BOMB** IN YOUR HEAD?
I LITERALLY HAVE MY FINGER ON THE TRIGGER **RIGHT NOW.**
OH, NO, CHANATH CHA. I DID NOT FORGET.
I DEACTIVATED IT AGES AGO. I COULDN'T ALLOW DAMAGE TO THE SHIP, YOU SEE.
AN **INTELLIGENT** PERSON PROBABLY WOULDN'T HAVE TOLD ME ABOUT THAT BOMB AT ALL.

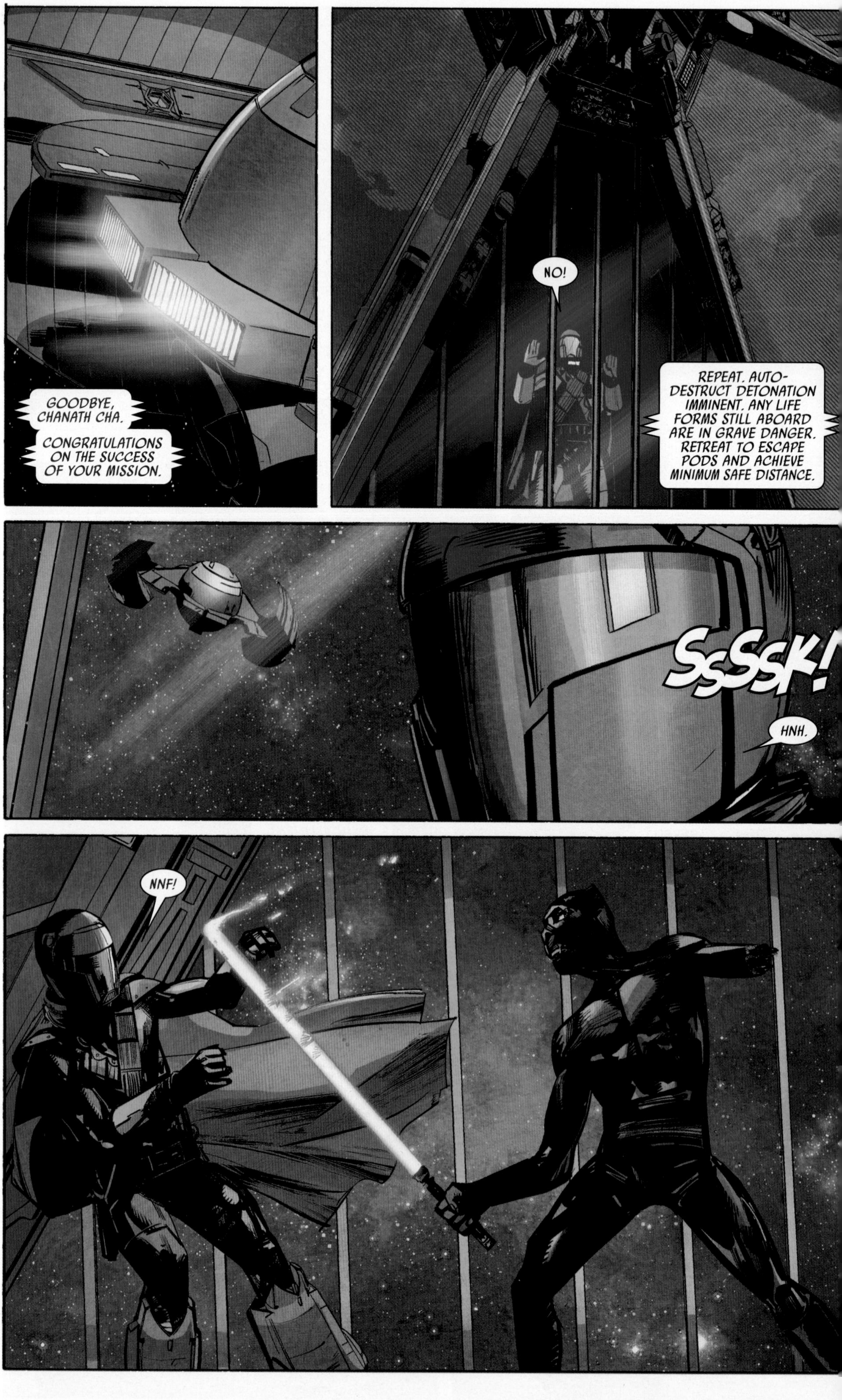
GOODBYE, CHANATH CHA.
CONGRATULATIONS ON THE SUCCESS OF YOUR MISSION.
NO!
REPEAT. AUTO-DESTRUCT DETONATION IMMINENT. ANY LIFE FORMS STILL ABOARD ARE IN GRAVE DANGER. RETREAT TO ESCAPE PODS AND ACHIEVE MINIMUM SAFE DISTANCE.
SsSSK!
HNH.
NNF!

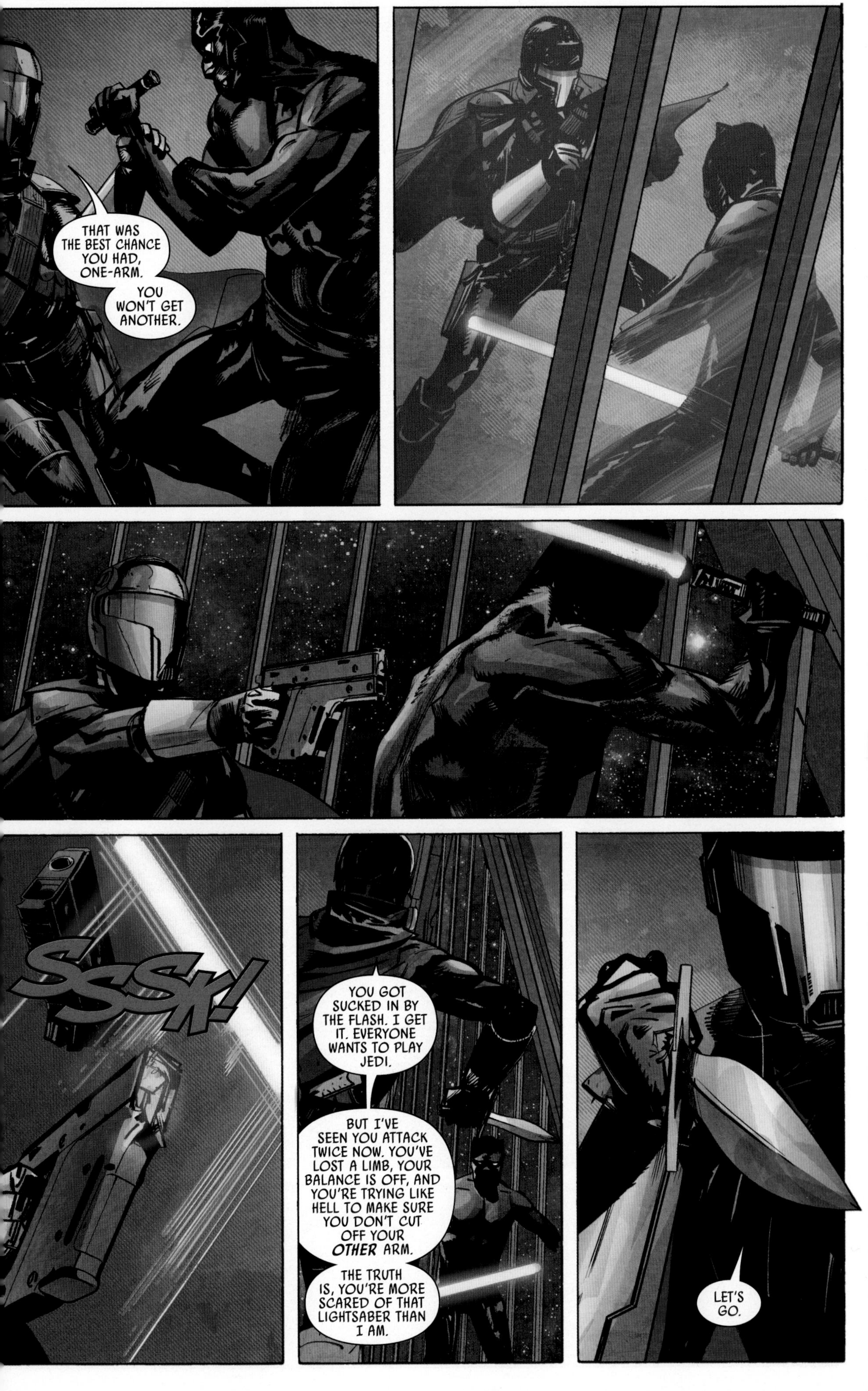
THAT WAS THE BEST CHANCE YOU HAD, ONE-ARM.
YOU WON'T GET ANOTHER.
SSSK!
YOU GOT SUCKED IN BY THE FLASH. I GET IT. EVERYONE WANTS TO PLAY JEDI.
BUT I'VE SEEN YOU ATTACK TWICE NOW. YOU'VE LOST A LIMB, YOUR BALANCE IS OFF, AND YOU'RE TRYING LIKE HELL TO MAKE SURE YOU DON'T CUT OFF YOUR OTHER ARM.
THE TRUTH IS, YOU'RE MORE SCARED OF THAT LIGHTSABER THAN I AM.
LET'S GO.

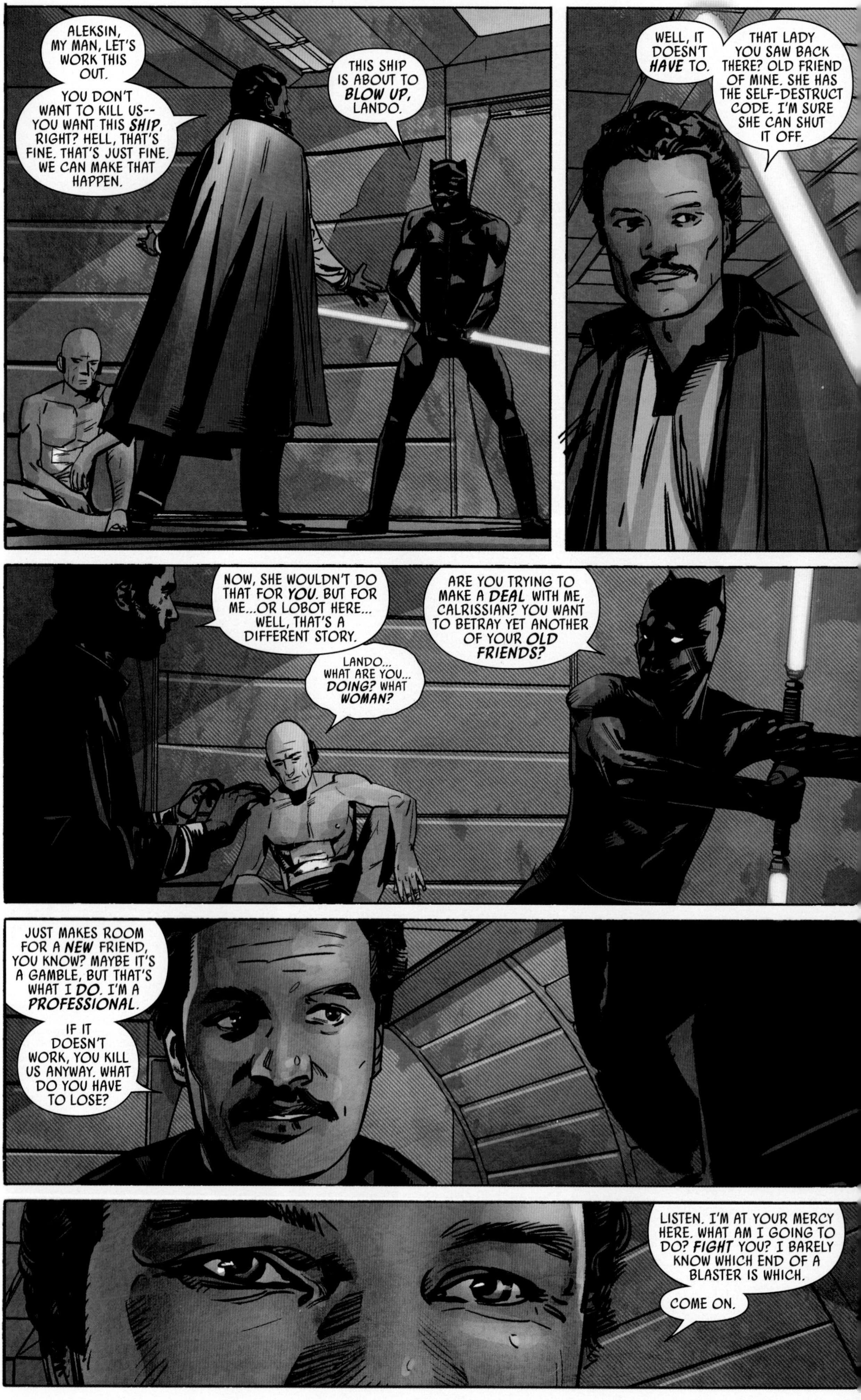
ALEKSIN, MY MAN, LET'S WORK THIS OUT.
YOU DON'T WANT TO KILL US-- YOU WANT THIS SHIP, RIGHT? HELL, THAT'S FINE. THAT'S JUST FINE. WE CAN MAKE THAT HAPPEN.
THIS SHIP IS ABOUT TO BLOW UP, LANDO.
WELL, IT DOESN'T HAVE TO.
THAT LADY YOU SAW BACK THERE? OLD FRIEND OF MINE. SHE HAS THE SELF-DESTRUCT CODE. I'M SURE SHE CAN SHUT IT OFF.
NOW, SHE WOULDN'T DO THAT FOR YOU. BUT FOR ME...OR LOBOT HERE... WELL, THAT'S A DIFFERENT STORY.
ARE YOU TRYING TO MAKE A DEAL WITH ME, CALRISSIAN? YOU WANT TO BETRAY YET ANOTHER OF YOUR OLD FRIENDS?
LANDO... WHAT ARE YOU... DOING? WHAT WOMAN?
JUST MAKES ROOM FOR A NEW FRIEND, YOU KNOW? MAYBE IT'S A GAMBLE, BUT THAT'S WHAT I DO. I'M A PROFESSIONAL.
IF IT DOESN'T WORK, YOU KILL US ANYWAY. WHAT DO YOU HAVE TO LOSE?
LISTEN. I'M AT YOUR MERCY HERE. WHAT AM I GOING TO DO? FIGHT YOU? I BARELY KNOW WHICH END OF A BLASTER IS WHICH.
COME ON.

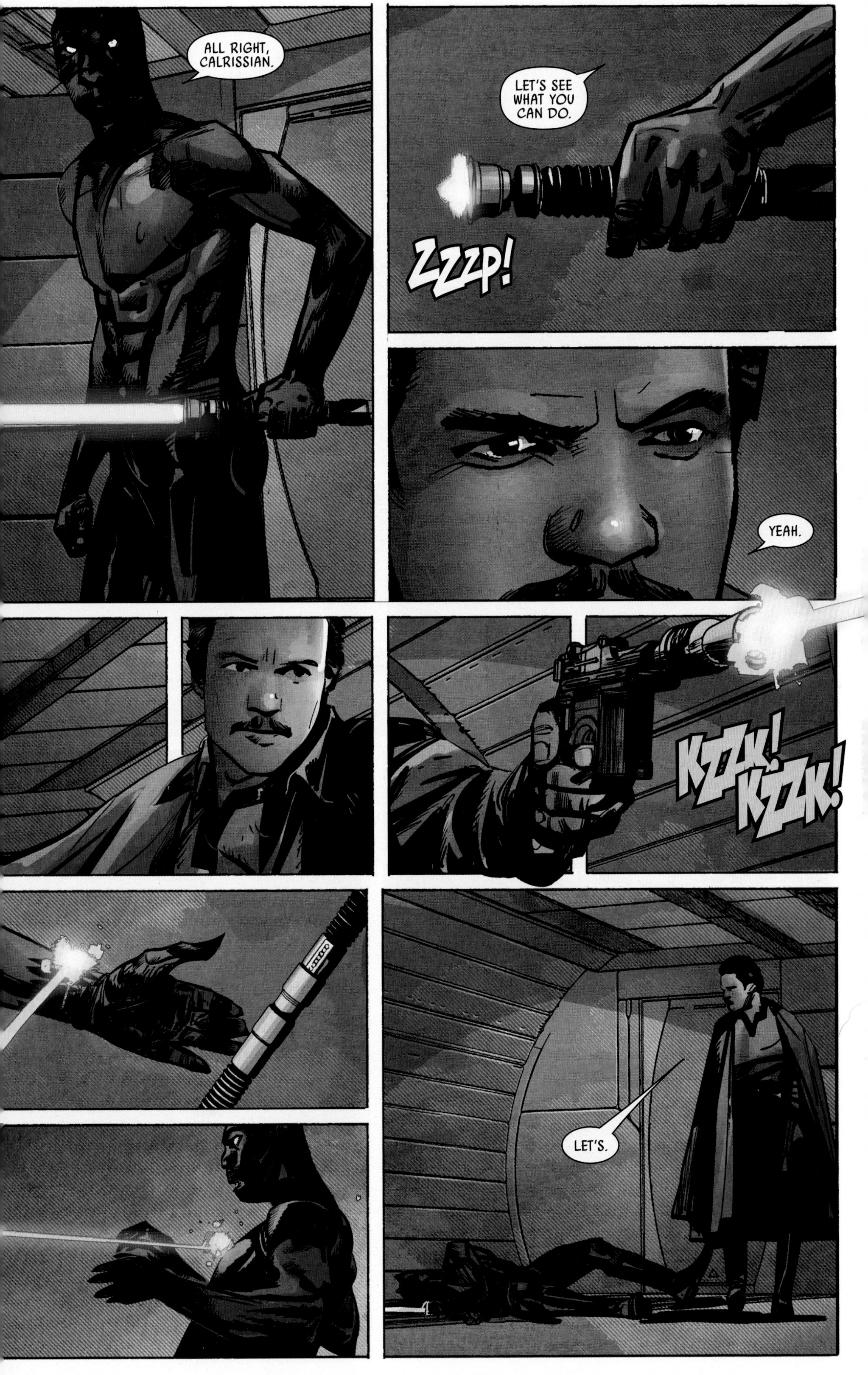
ALL RIGHT, CALRISSIAN.
LET'S SEE WHAT YOU CAN DO.
ZZZP!
YEAH.
KZZK! KZZK!
LET'S.

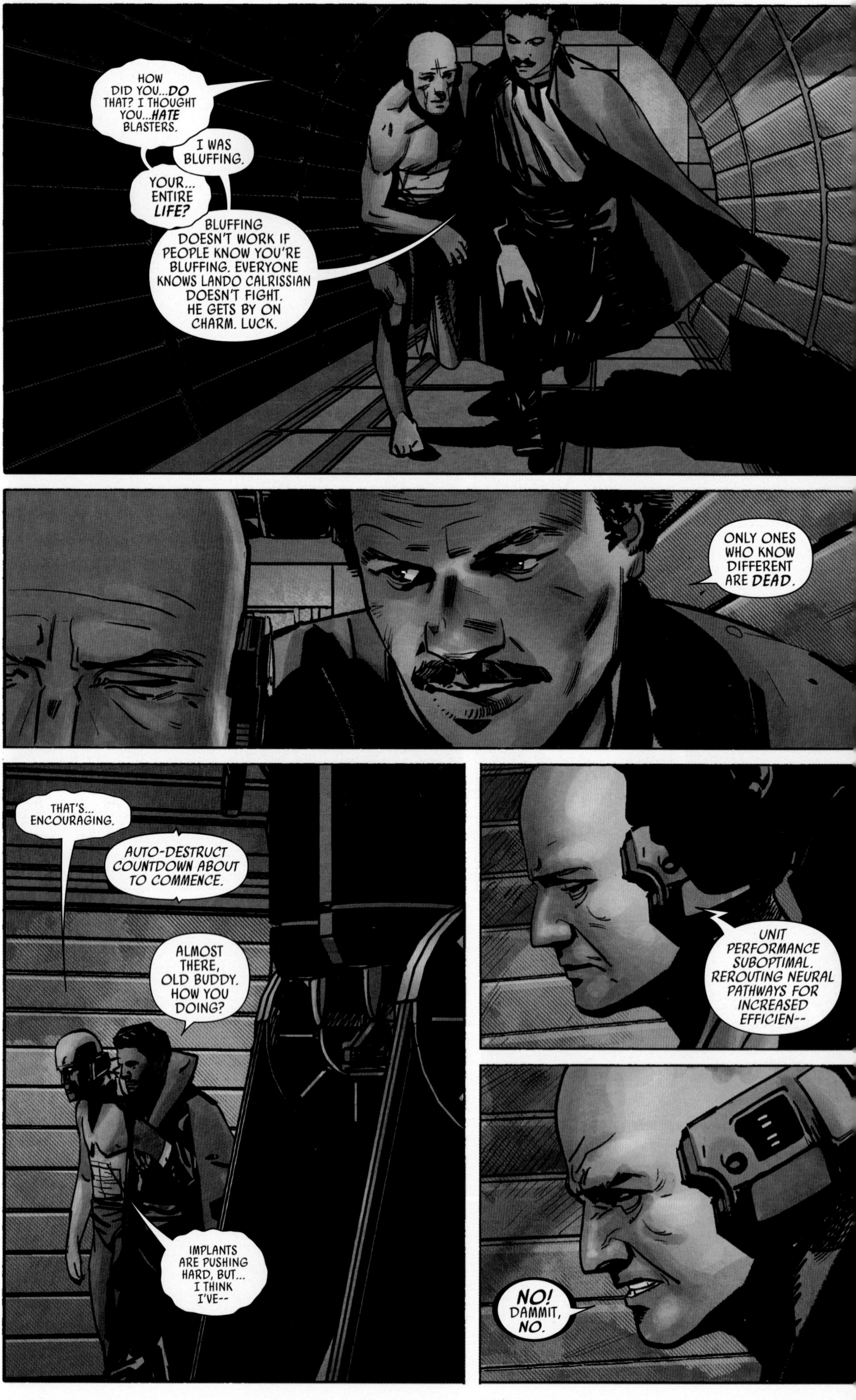
HOW DID YOU...DO THAT? I THOUGHT YOU...HATE BLASTERS.
I WAS BLUFFING.
YOUR... ENTIRE LIFE?
BLUFFING DOESN'T WORK IF PEOPLE KNOW YOU'RE BLUFFING. EVERYONE KNOWS LANDO CALRISSIAN DOESN'T FIGHT. HE GETS BY ON CHARM. LUCK.
ONLY ONES WHO KNOW DIFFERENT ARE DEAD.
THAT'S... ENCOURAGING.
AUTO-DESTRUCT COUNTDOWN ABOUT TO COMMENCE.
ALMOST THERE, OLD BUDDY. HOW YOU DOING?
IMPLANTS ARE PUSHING HARD, BUT... I THINK I'VE--
UNIT PERFORMANCE SUBOPTIMAL. REROUTING NEURAL PATHWAYS FOR INCREASED EFFICIEN--
NO! DAMMIT, NO.

CHANATH? *YOU'RE...THE WOMAN?*

LAST TIME I CHECKED. HOW ARE YOU, LOBOT?

BEEN... BETTER. GOOD TO SEE YOU... THOUGH. MISSED YOU.

YOU TWO CAN CATCH UP LATER--THIS WHOLE DAMN THING'S ABOUT TO BLOW. WHERE'S OUR RIDE, CHANATH?

GONE. I'M SORRY, BOYS. LOOKS LIKE THIS IS IT.

ESCAPE... PODS?

NO GOOD. CHANATH SHUT THOSE DOWN-- AND SHE DOESN'T HAVE THE CODE TO TURN THEM BACK ON.

GET ME TO AN INTERFACE.

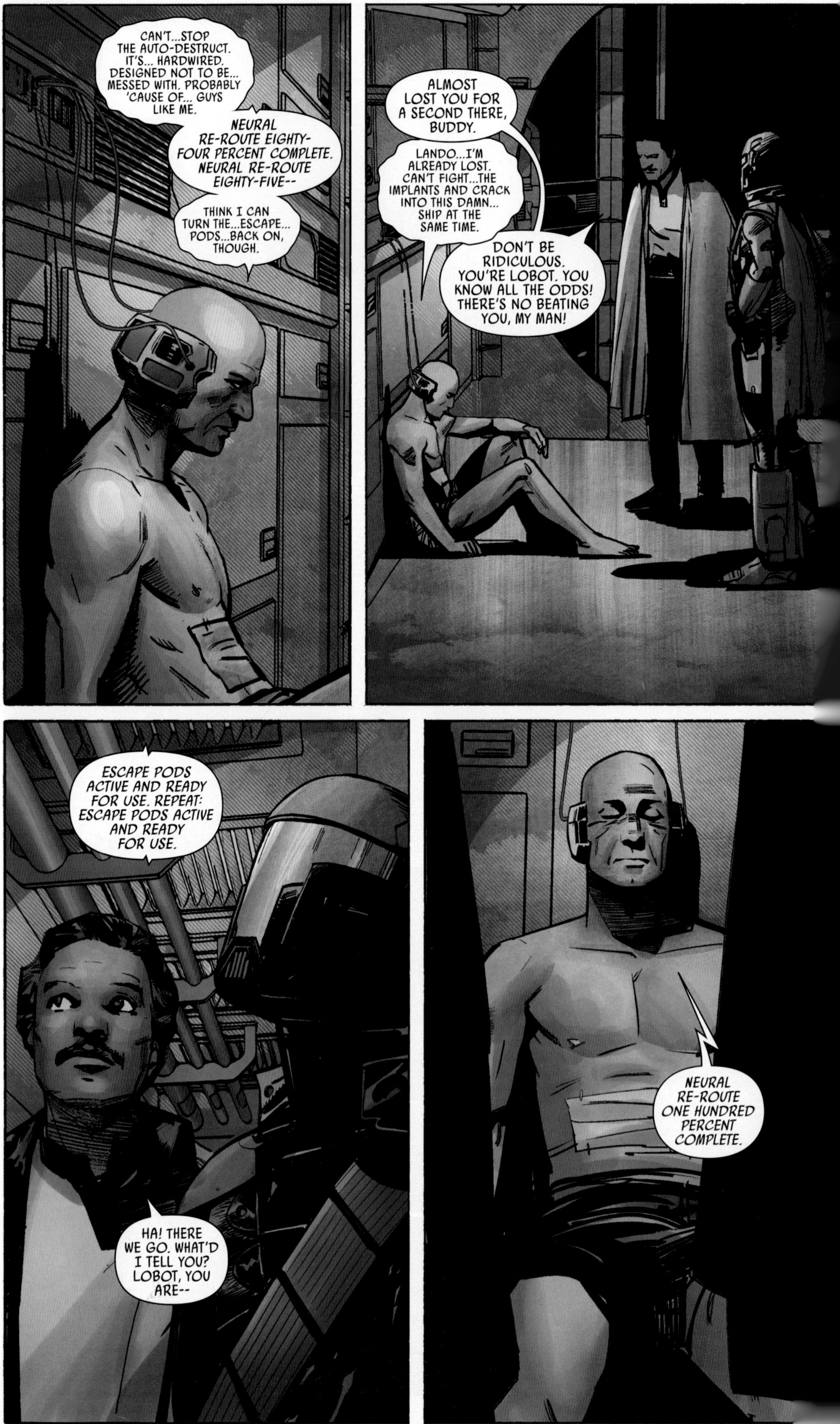
CAN'T...STOP THE AUTO-DESTRUCT. IT'S... HARDWIRED. DESIGNED NOT TO BE... MESSED WITH. PROBABLY 'CAUSE OF... GUYS LIKE ME.
NEURAL RE-ROUTE EIGHTY-FOUR PERCENT COMPLETE. NEURAL RE-ROUTE EIGHTY-FIVE--
THINK I CAN TURN THE...ESCAPE... PODS...BACK ON, THOUGH.
ALMOST LOST YOU FOR A SECOND THERE, BUDDY.
LANDO...I'M ALREADY LOST. CAN'T FIGHT...THE IMPLANTS AND CRACK INTO THIS DAMN... SHIP AT THE SAME TIME.
DON'T BE RIDICULOUS. YOU'RE LOBOT. YOU KNOW ALL THE ODDS! THERE'S NO BEATING YOU, MY MAN!
ESCAPE PODS ACTIVE AND READY FOR USE. REPEAT: ESCAPE PODS ACTIVE AND READY FOR USE.
HA! THERE WE GO. WHAT'D I TELL YOU? LOBOT, YOU ARE--
NEURAL RE-ROUTE ONE HUNDRED PERCENT COMPLETE.

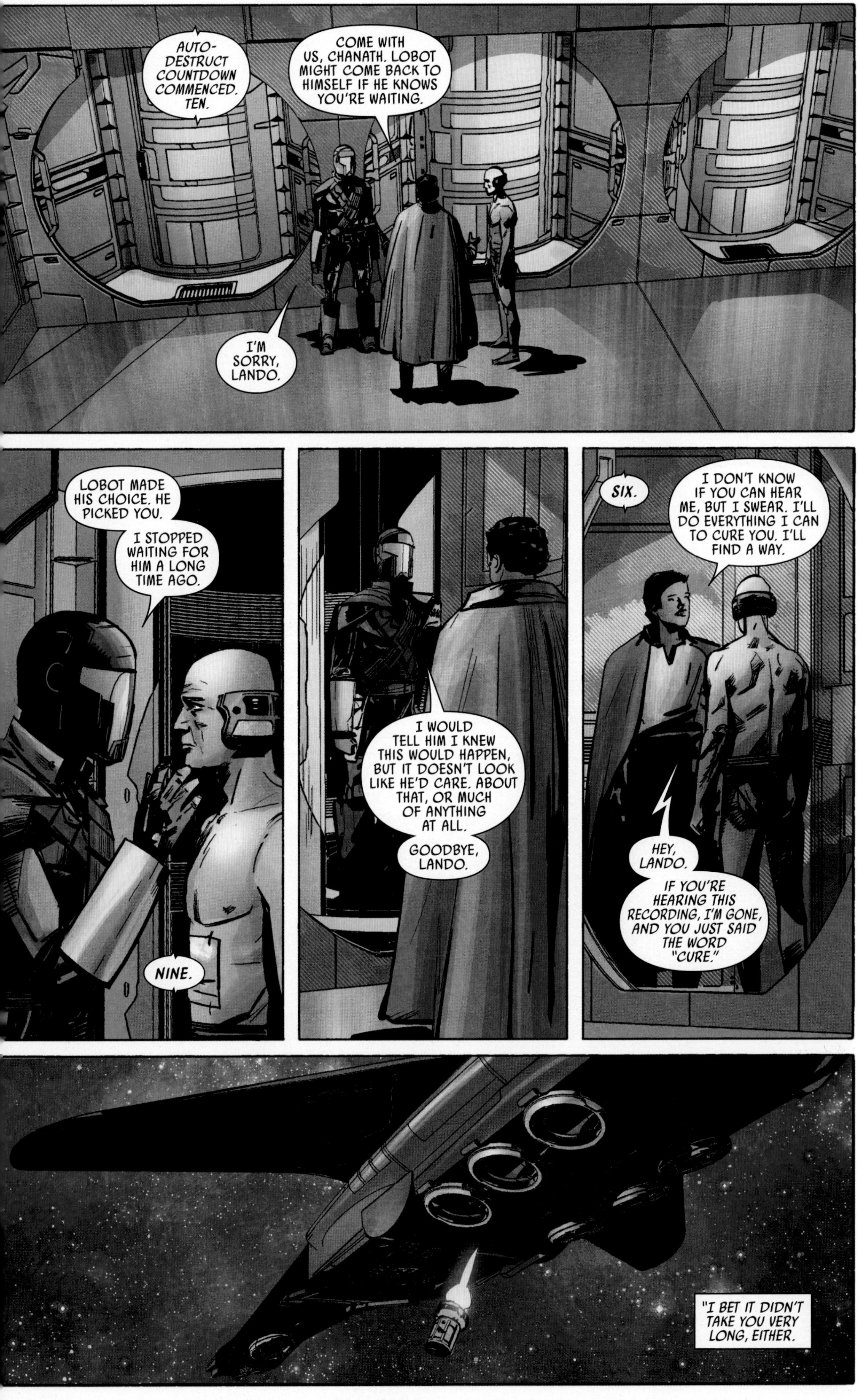
AUTO-DESTRUCT COUNTDOWN COMMENCED. TEN.
COME WITH US, CHANATH. LOBOT MIGHT COME BACK TO HIMSELF IF HE KNOWS YOU'RE WAITING.
I'M SORRY, LANDO.
LOBOT MADE HIS CHOICE. HE PICKED YOU.
I STOPPED WAITING FOR HIM A LONG TIME AGO.
NINE.
I WOULD TELL HIM I KNEW THIS WOULD HAPPEN, BUT IT DOESN'T LOOK LIKE HE'D CARE. ABOUT THAT, OR MUCH OF ANYTHING AT ALL.
GOODBYE, LANDO.
SIX.
I DON'T KNOW IF YOU CAN HEAR ME, BUT I SWEAR. I'LL DO EVERYTHING I CAN TO CURE YOU. I'LL FIND A WAY.
HEY, LANDO.
IF YOU'RE HEARING THIS RECORDING, I'M GONE, AND YOU JUST SAID THE WORD "CURE."
"I BET IT DIDN'T TAKE YOU VERY LONG, EITHER.

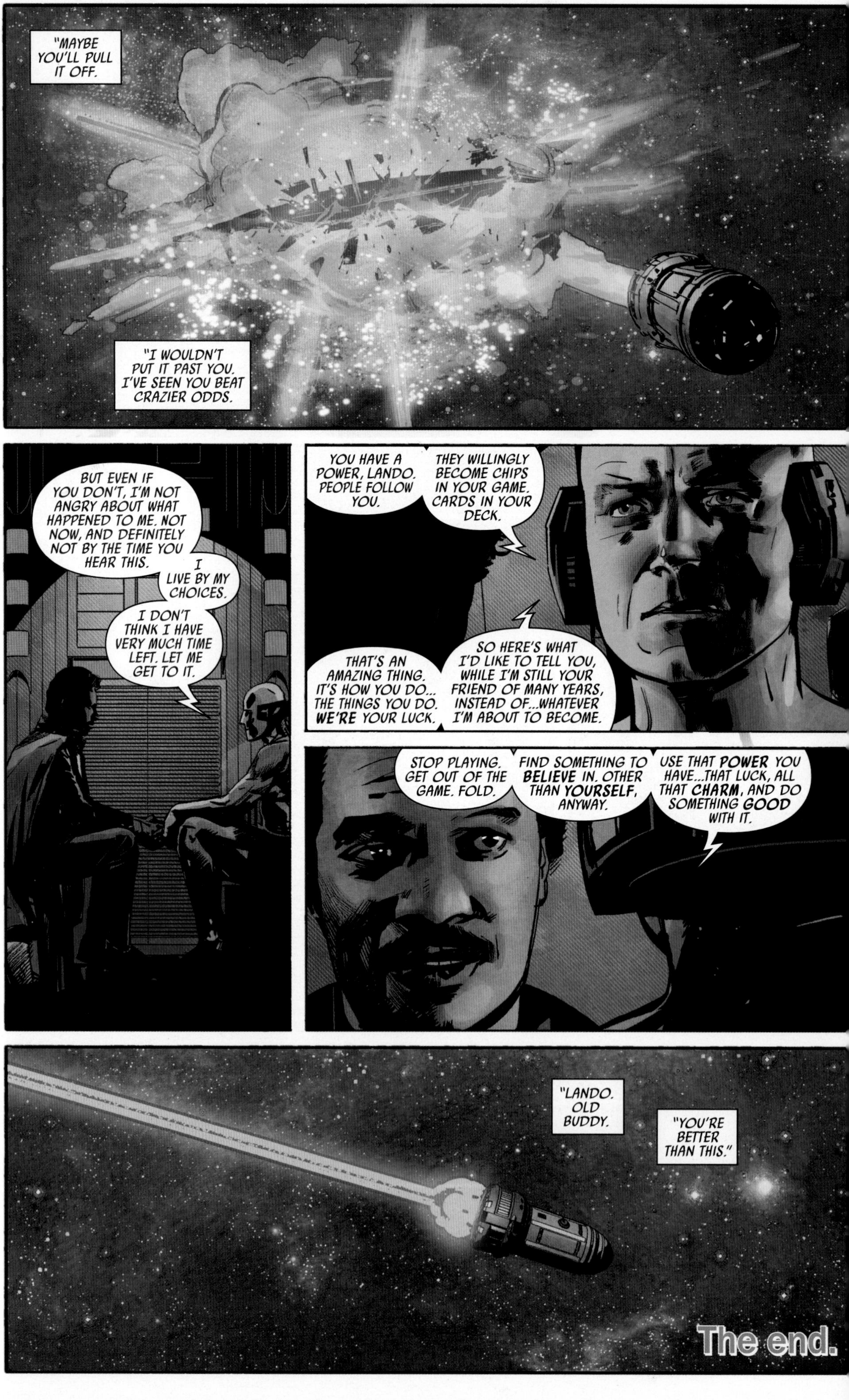
"MAYBE YOU'LL PULL IT OFF.
"I WOULDN'T PUT IT PAST YOU. I'VE SEEN YOU BEAT CRAZIER ODDS.
BUT EVEN IF YOU DON'T, I'M NOT ANGRY ABOUT WHAT HAPPENED TO ME. NOT NOW, AND DEFINITELY NOT BY THE TIME YOU HEAR THIS.
I LIVE BY MY CHOICES.
I DON'T THINK I HAVE VERY MUCH TIME LEFT. LET ME GET TO IT.
YOU HAVE A POWER, LANDO. PEOPLE FOLLOW YOU.
THEY WILLINGLY BECOME CHIPS IN YOUR GAME. CARDS IN YOUR DECK.
THAT'S AN AMAZING THING. IT'S HOW YOU DO... THE THINGS YOU DO. WE'RE YOUR LUCK.
SO HERE'S WHAT I'D LIKE TO TELL YOU, WHILE I'M STILL YOUR FRIEND OF MANY YEARS, INSTEAD OF...WHATEVER I'M ABOUT TO BECOME.
STOP PLAYING. GET OUT OF THE GAME. FOLD.
FIND SOMETHING TO BELIEVE IN. OTHER THAN YOURSELF, ANYWAY.
USE THAT POWER YOU HAVE...THAT LUCK, ALL THAT CHARM, AND DO SOMETHING GOOD WITH IT.
"LANDO. OLD BUDDY.
"YOU'RE BETTER THAN THIS."
The end.

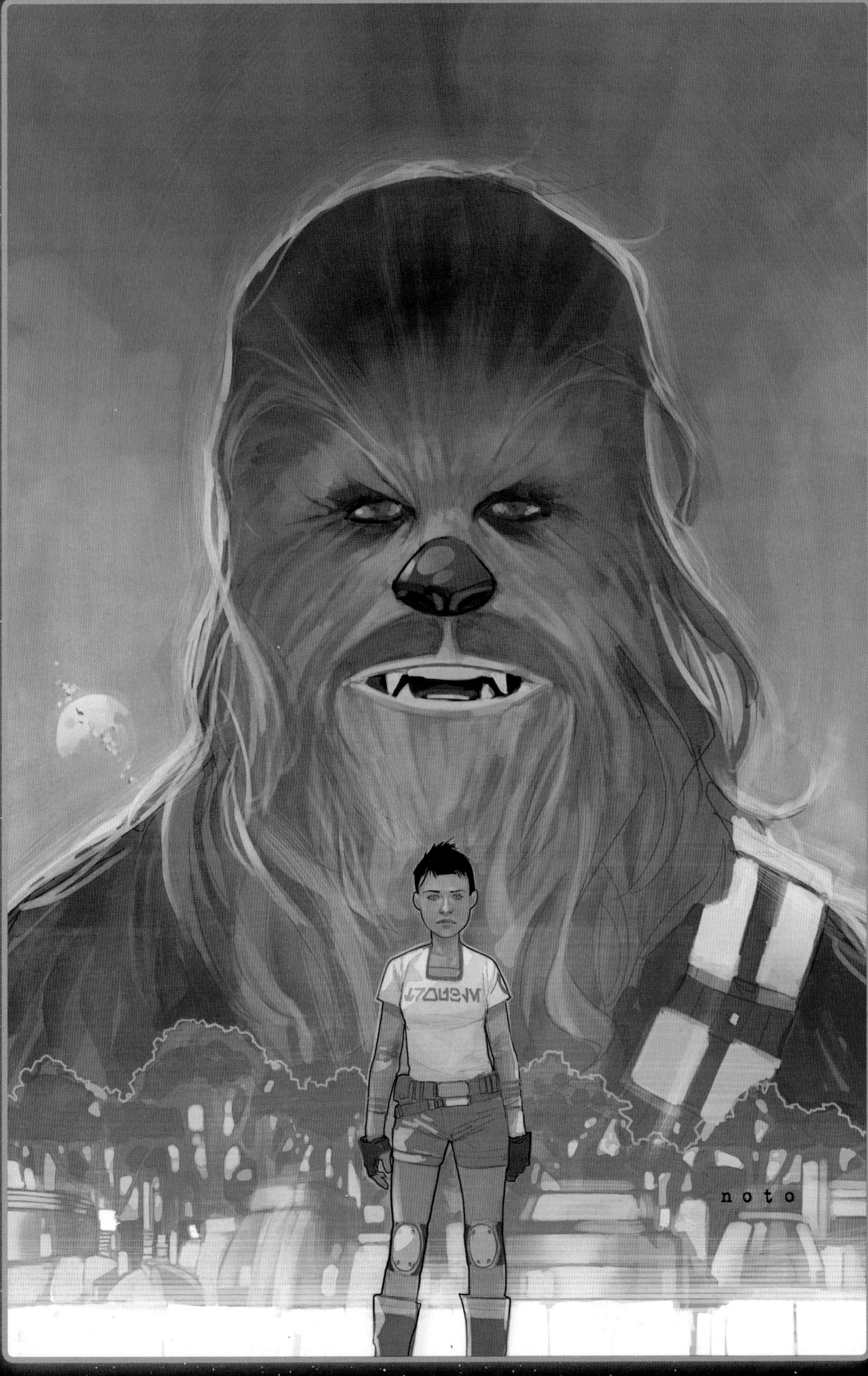
noto

CHEWBACCA 1

CHEWBACCA

It is a period of renewed hope for the rebellion.

The evil galactic Empire's greatest weapon, the Death Star, has been destroyed by CHEWBACCA, warrior son of the planet KASHYYYK...with some help from his trusty sidekick Han and his friends Luke and Leia. But Chewie is not one to grandstand. There is still much to accomplish.

The Battle of Yavin reverberates through the galaxy as our WOOKIEE hero embarks on a very important and personal secret mission. Unfortunately for Chewbacca, his loaner spacecraft proves to be what they refer to in the Outer Rim as a "hunk of junk"....

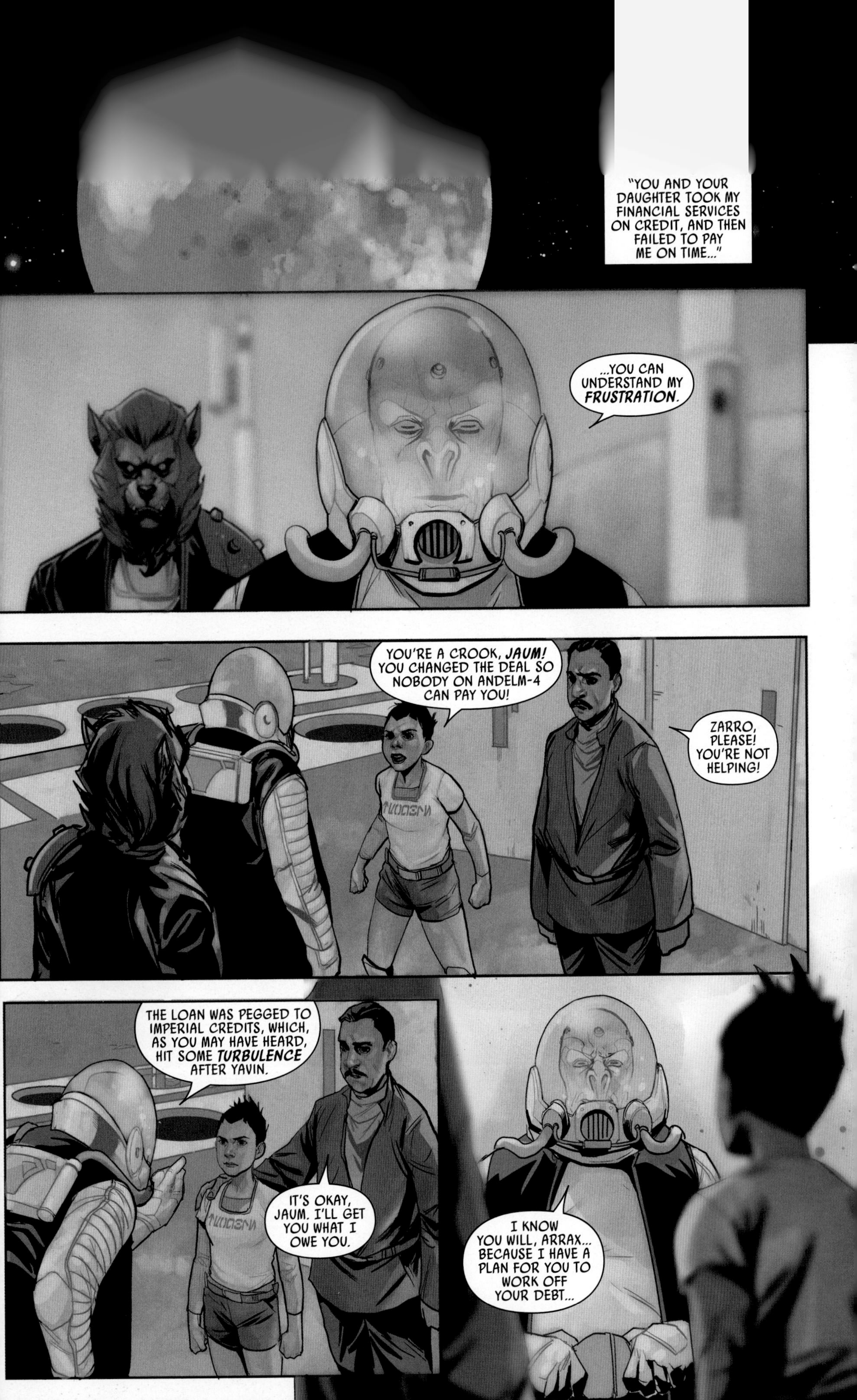
"YOU AND YOUR DAUGHTER TOOK MY FINANCIAL SERVICES ON CREDIT, AND THEN FAILED TO PAY ME ON TIME..."
...YOU CAN UNDERSTAND MY *FRUSTRATION*.
YOU'RE A CROOK, *JAUM!* YOU CHANGED THE DEAL SO NOBODY ON ANDELM-4 CAN PAY YOU!
ZARRO, PLEASE! YOU'RE NOT HELPING!
THE LOAN WAS PEGGED TO IMPERIAL CREDITS, WHICH, AS YOU MAY HAVE HEARD, HIT SOME *TURBULENCE* AFTER YAVIN.
IT'S OKAY, JAUM. I'LL GET YOU WHAT I OWE YOU.
I KNOW YOU WILL, ARRAX... BECAUSE I HAVE A PLAN FOR YOU TO WORK OFF YOUR DEBT...

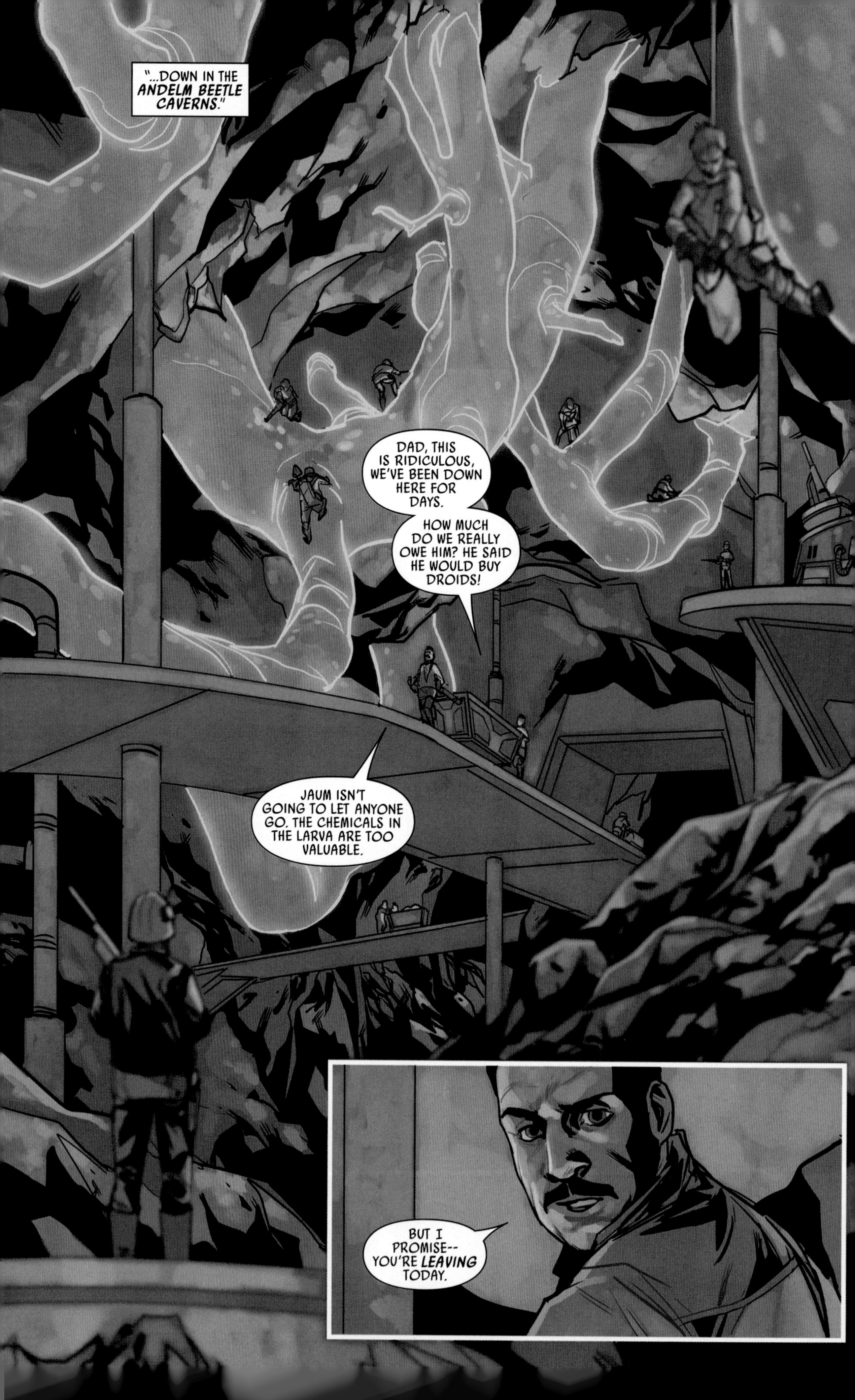
"...DOWN IN THE ANDELM BEETLE CAVERNS."
DAD, THIS IS RIDICULOUS, WE'VE BEEN DOWN HERE FOR DAYS.
HOW MUCH DO WE REALLY OWE HIM? HE SAID HE WOULD BUY DROIDS!
JAUM ISN'T GOING TO LET ANYONE GO. THE CHEMICALS IN THE LARVA ARE TOO VALUABLE.
BUT I PROMISE-- YOU'RE LEAVING TODAY.

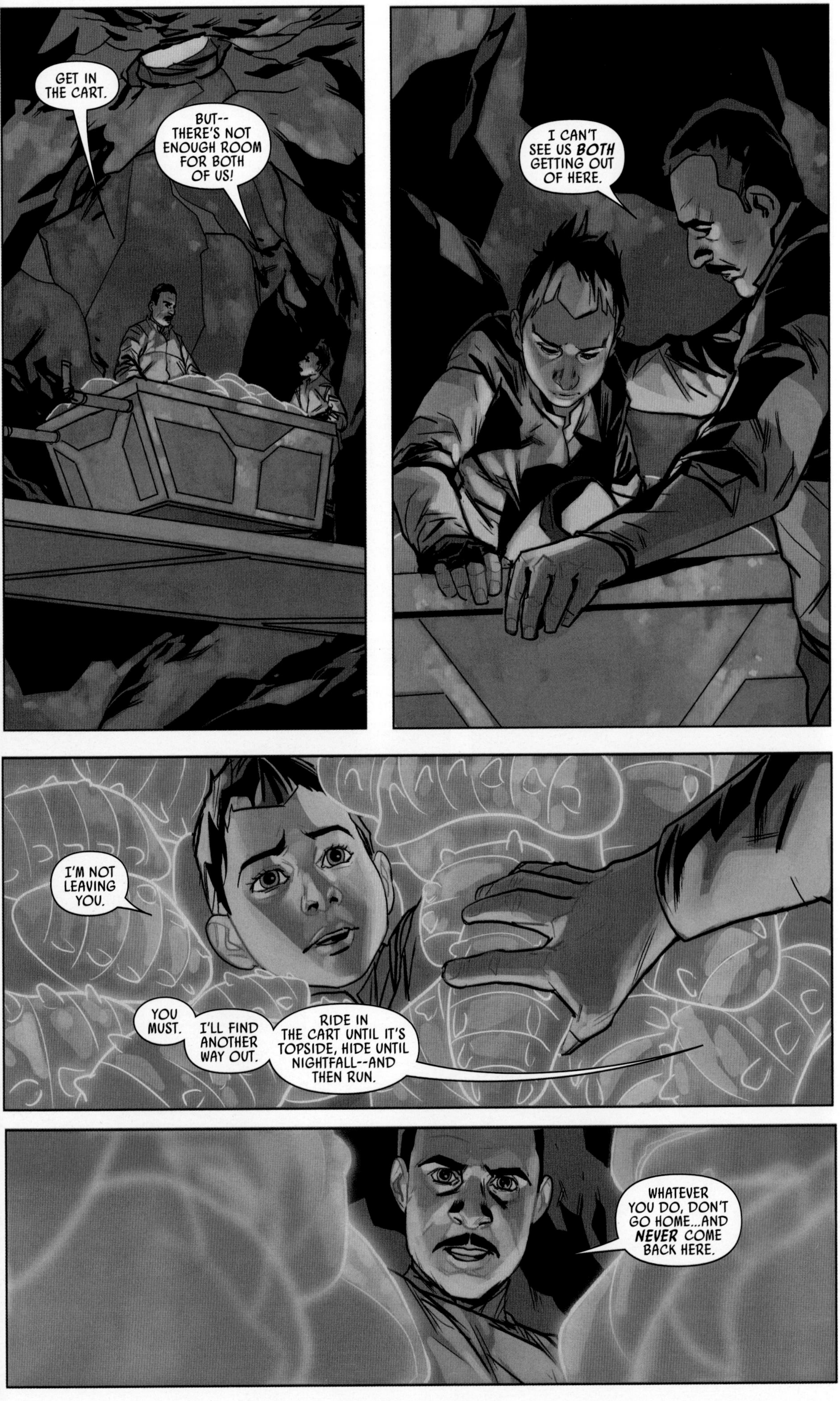
GET IN THE CART.
BUT-- THERE'S NOT ENOUGH ROOM FOR BOTH OF US!
I CAN'T SEE US **BOTH** GETTING OUT OF HERE.
I'M NOT LEAVING YOU.
YOU MUST.
I'LL FIND ANOTHER WAY OUT.
RIDE IN THE CART UNTIL IT'S TOPSIDE, HIDE UNTIL NIGHTFALL--AND THEN RUN.
WHATEVER YOU DO, DON'T GO HOME...AND **NEVER** COME BACK HERE.

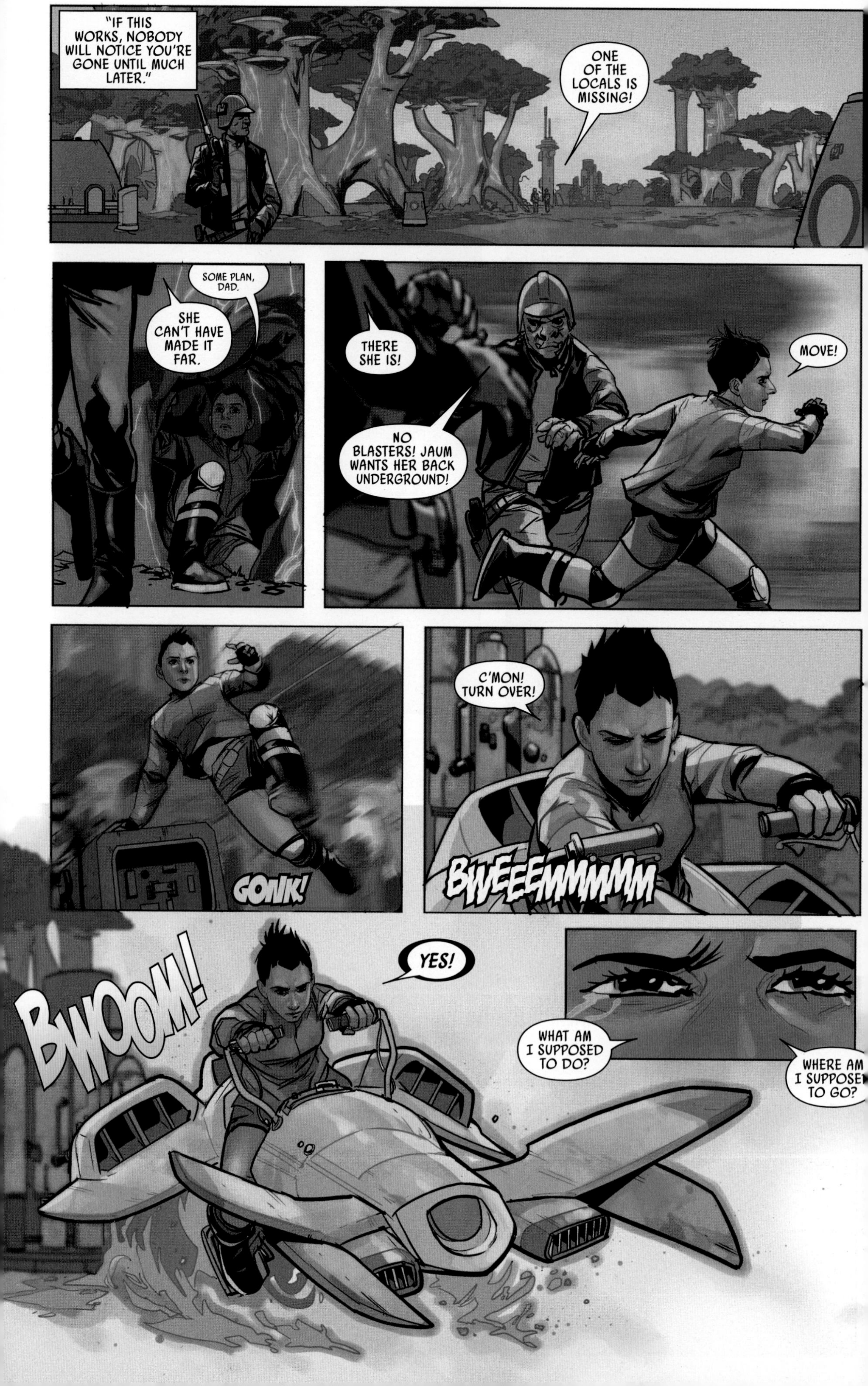
"IF THIS WORKS, NOBODY WILL NOTICE YOU'RE GONE UNTIL MUCH LATER."
ONE OF THE LOCALS IS MISSING!
SHE CAN'T HAVE MADE IT FAR.
SOME PLAN, DAD.
THERE SHE IS!
NO BLASTERS! JAUM WANTS HER BACK UNDERGROUND!
MOVE!
GONK!
C'MON! TURN OVER!
BWEEEMMMMM
BWOOM!
YES!
WHAT AM I SUPPOSED TO DO?
WHERE AM I SUPPOSE TO GO?

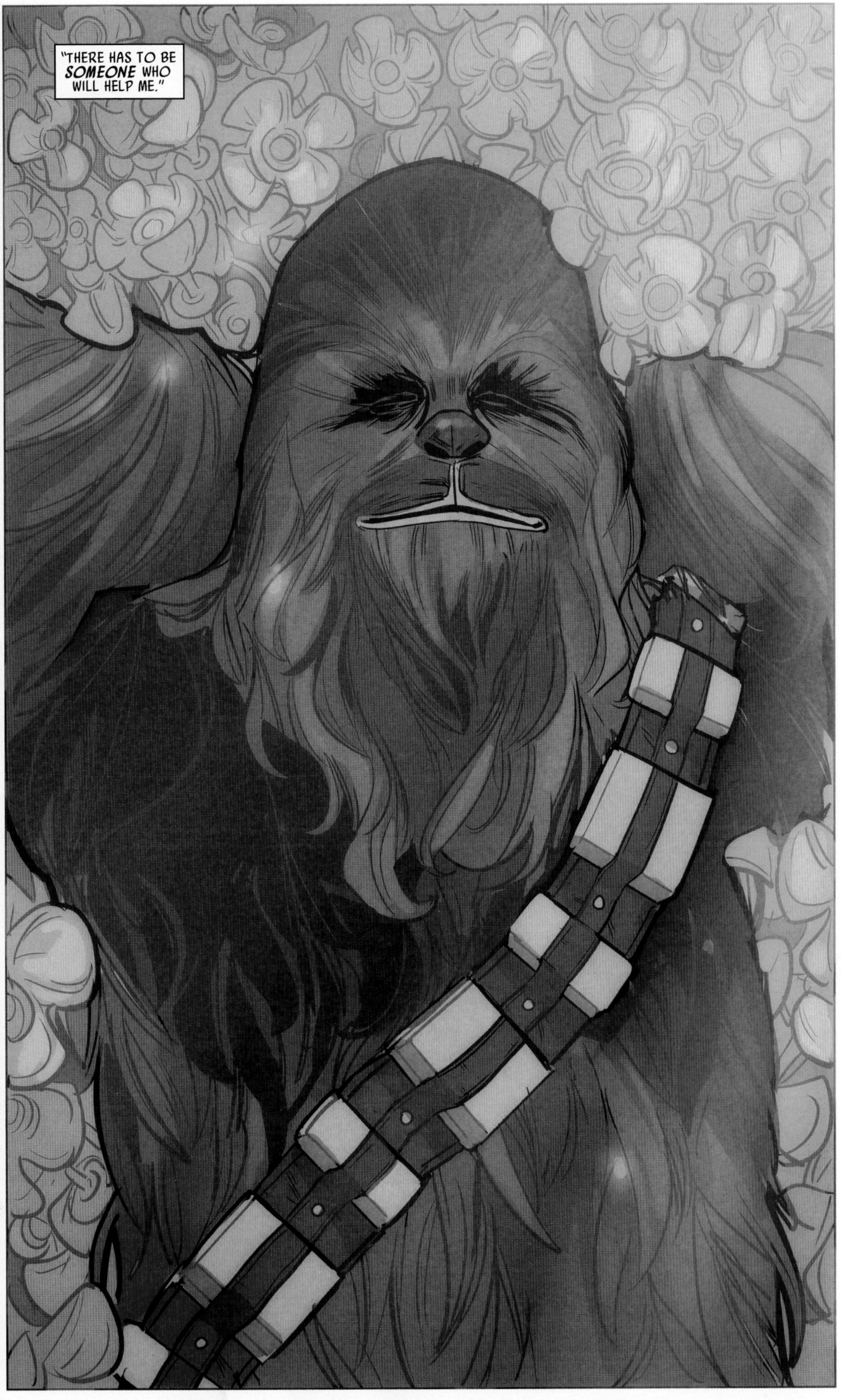
"THERE HAS TO BE SOMEONE WHO WILL HELP ME."

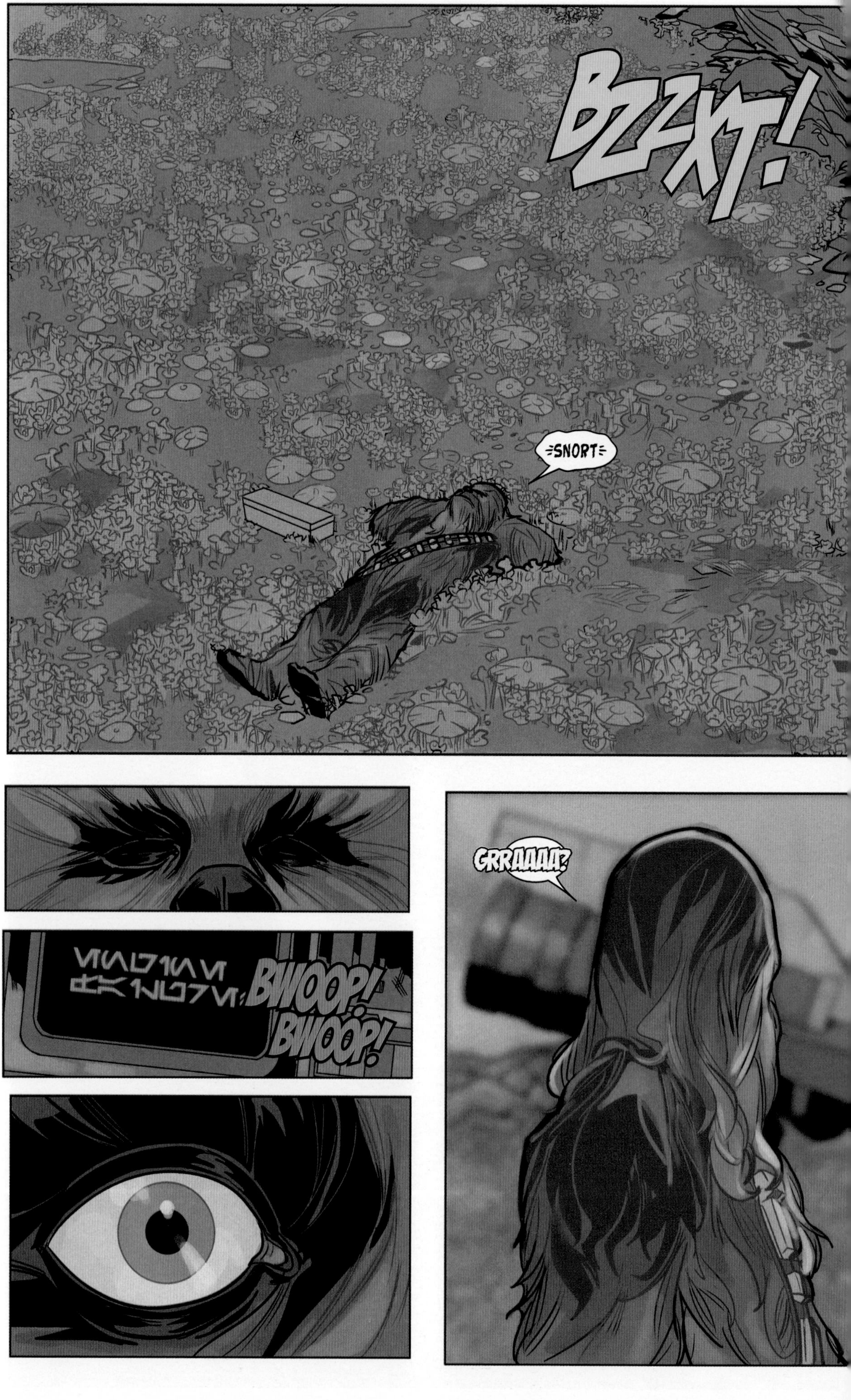
BZZXT!
SNORT
BWOOP!
BWOOP!
GRRAAAA?

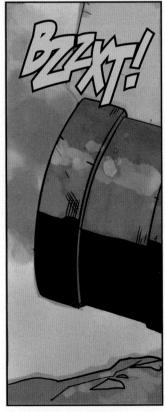

BZZXT!

HRRAAAA!
HRRUUNNGH!

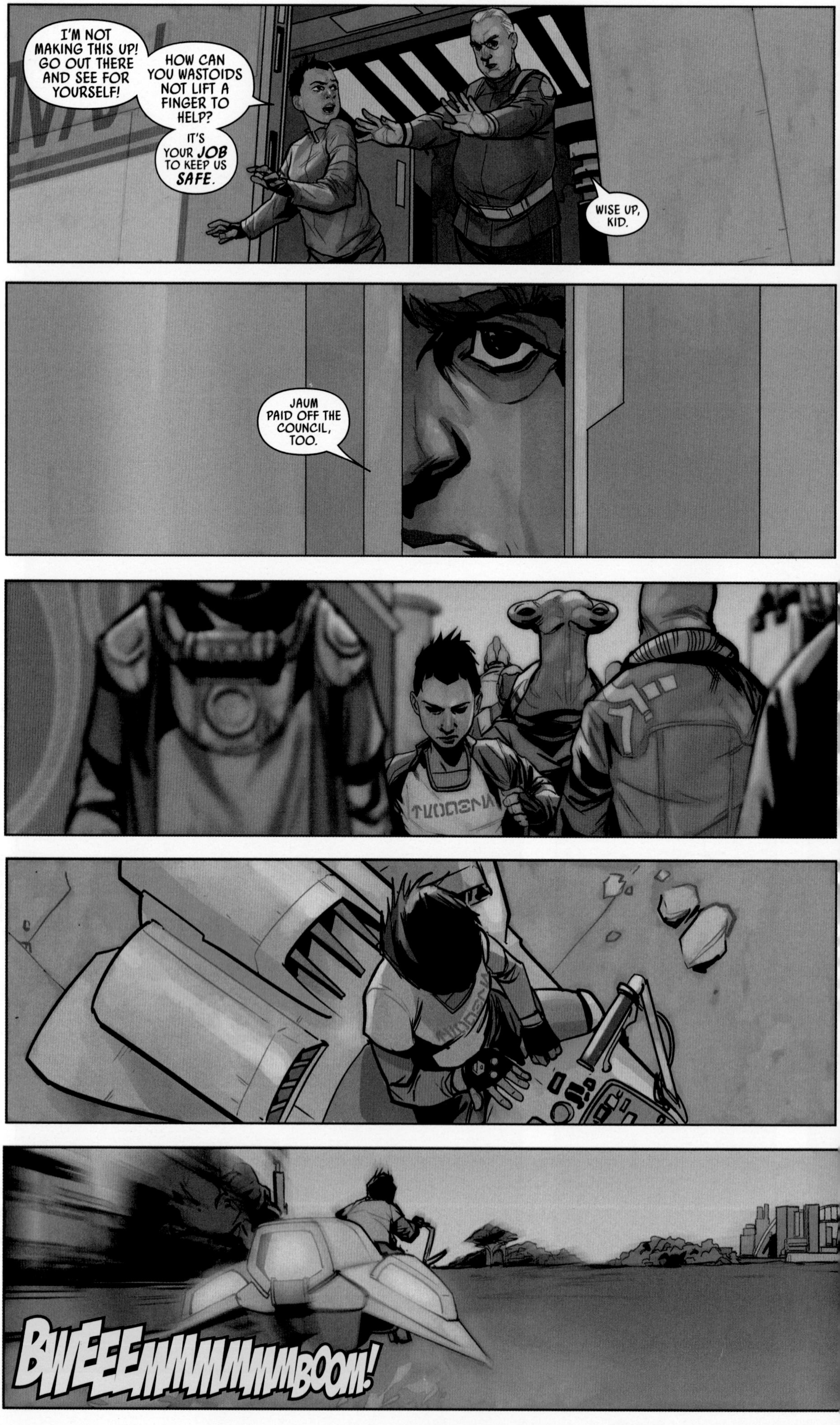
I'M NOT MAKING THIS UP! GO OUT THERE AND SEE FOR YOURSELF!
HOW CAN YOU WASTOIDS NOT LIFT A FINGER TO HELP?
IT'S YOUR JOB TO KEEP US SAFE.
WISE UP, KID.
JAUM PAID OFF THE COUNCIL, TOO.
BWEEEMMMMMMMMBOOM!

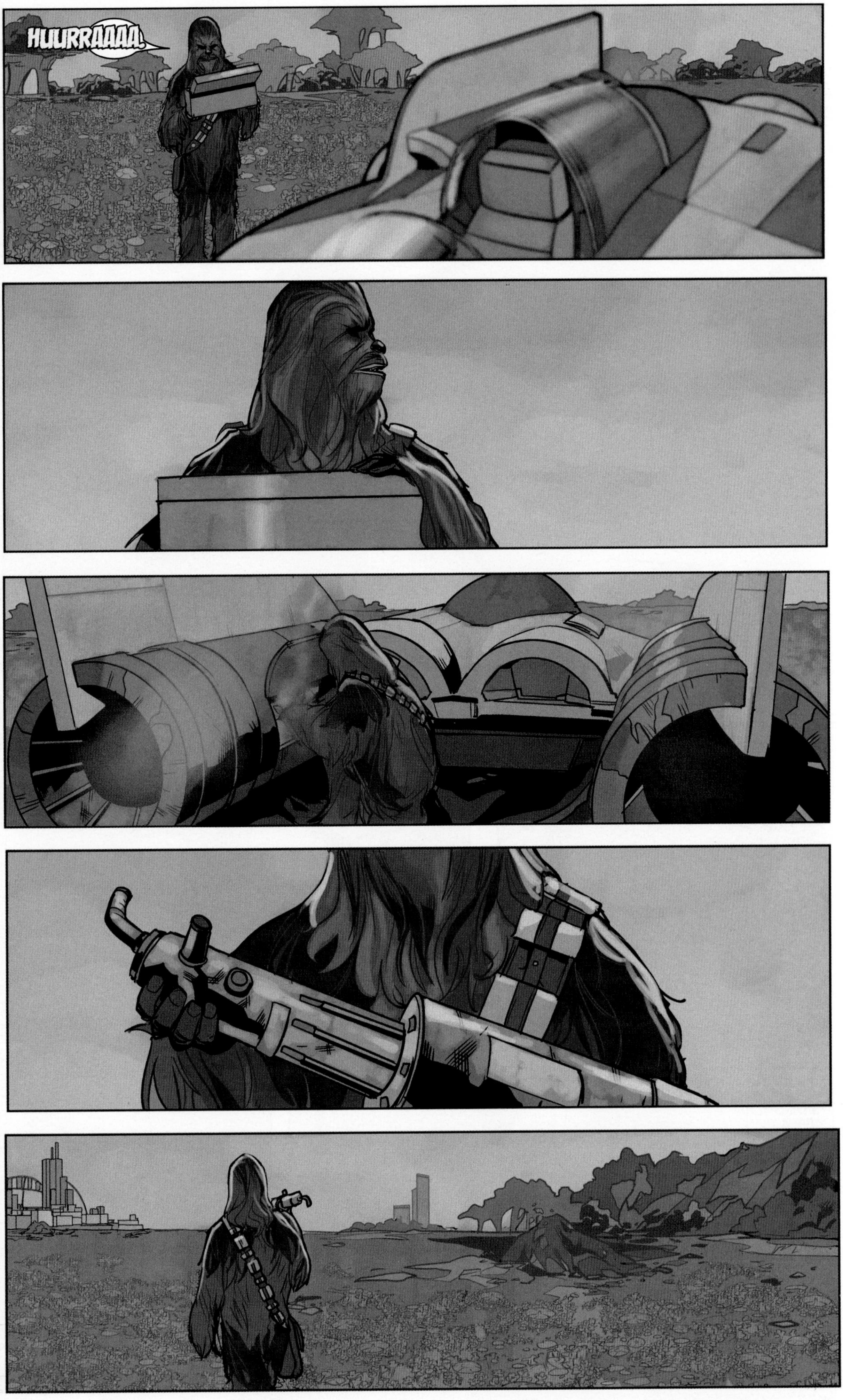
HUURRAAAA!

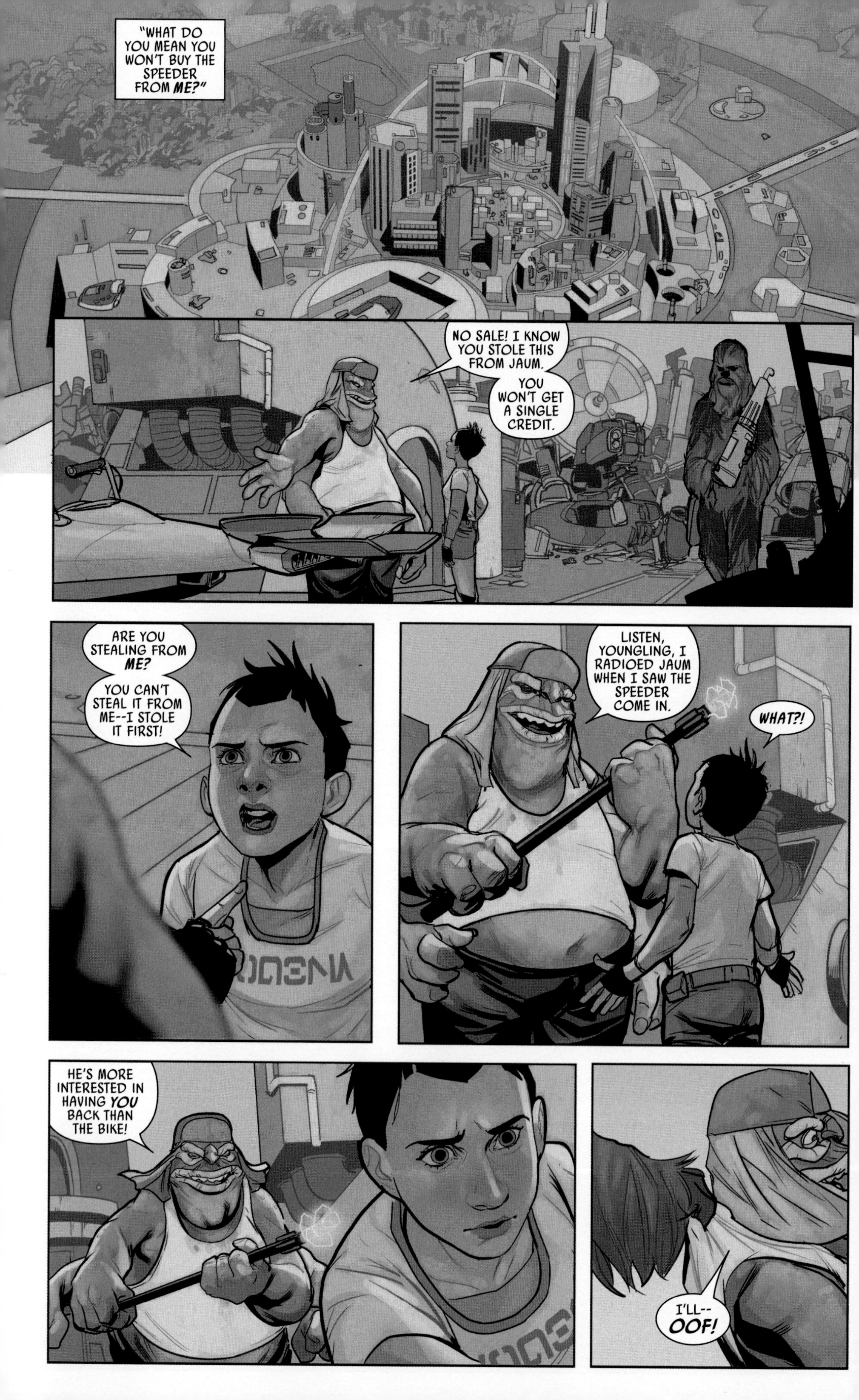
"WHAT DO YOU MEAN YOU WON'T BUY THE SPEEDER FROM *ME?*"
NO SALE! I KNOW YOU STOLE THIS FROM JAUM.
YOU WON'T GET A SINGLE CREDIT.
ARE YOU STEALING FROM *ME?*
YOU CAN'T STEAL IT FROM ME--I STOLE IT FIRST!
LISTEN, YOUNGLING, I RADIOED JAUM WHEN I SAW THE SPEEDER COME IN.
WHAT?!
HE'S MORE INTERESTED IN HAVING *YOU* BACK THAN THE BIKE!
I'LL--
OOF!

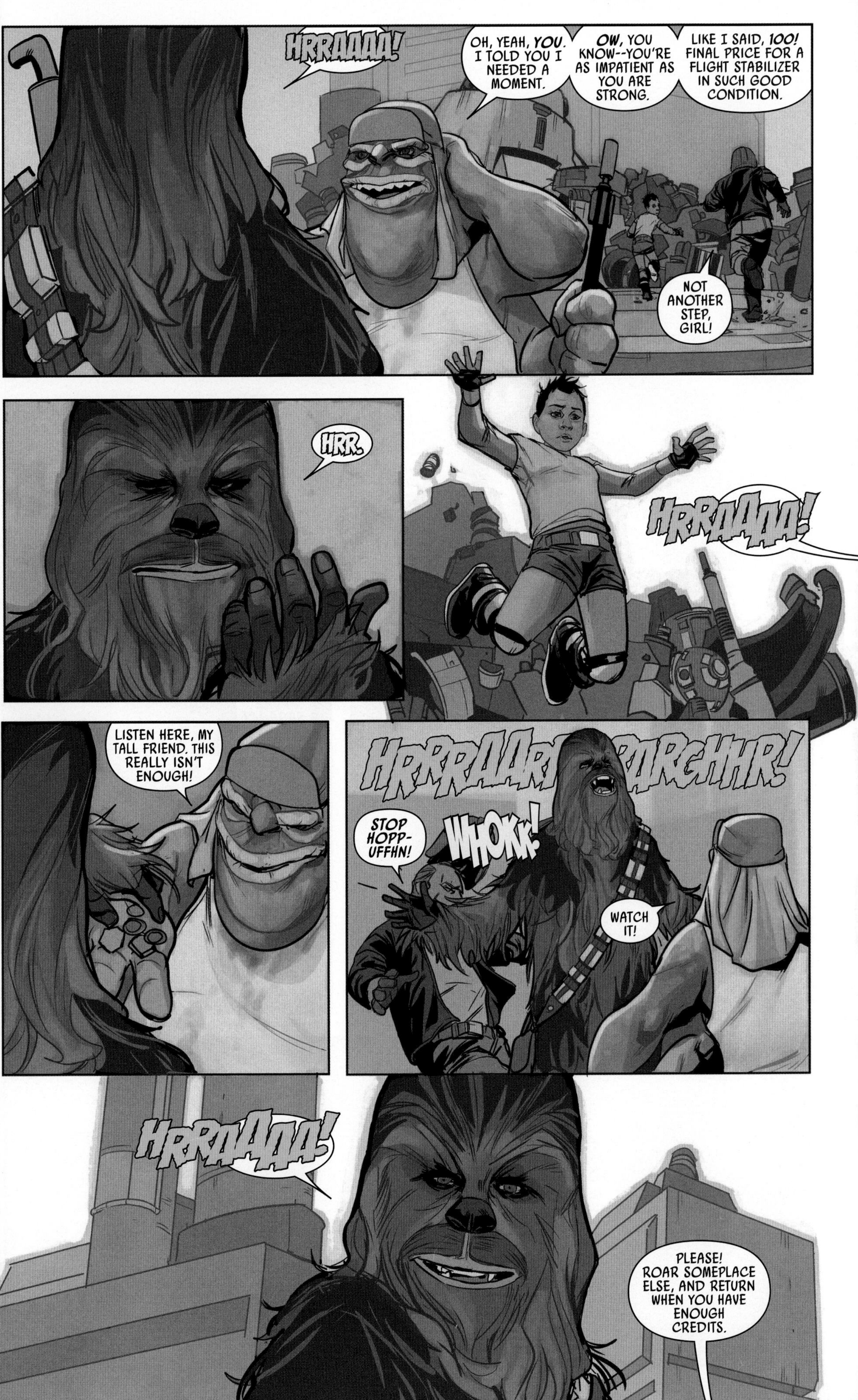
HRRAAAA!
OH, YEAH, YOU. I TOLD YOU I NEEDED A MOMENT.
OW, YOU KNOW--YOU'RE AS IMPATIENT AS YOU ARE STRONG.
LIKE I SAID, 100! FINAL PRICE FOR A FLIGHT STABILIZER IN SUCH GOOD CONDITION.
NOT ANOTHER STEP, GIRL!
HRR.
HRRAAAA!
LISTEN HERE, MY TALL FRIEND. THIS REALLY ISN'T ENOUGH!
STOP HOPP-UFFHN!
WHOKK!
WATCH IT!
HRRAAAA!
PLEASE! ROAR SOMEPLACE ELSE, AND RETURN WHEN YOU HAVE ENOUGH CREDITS.

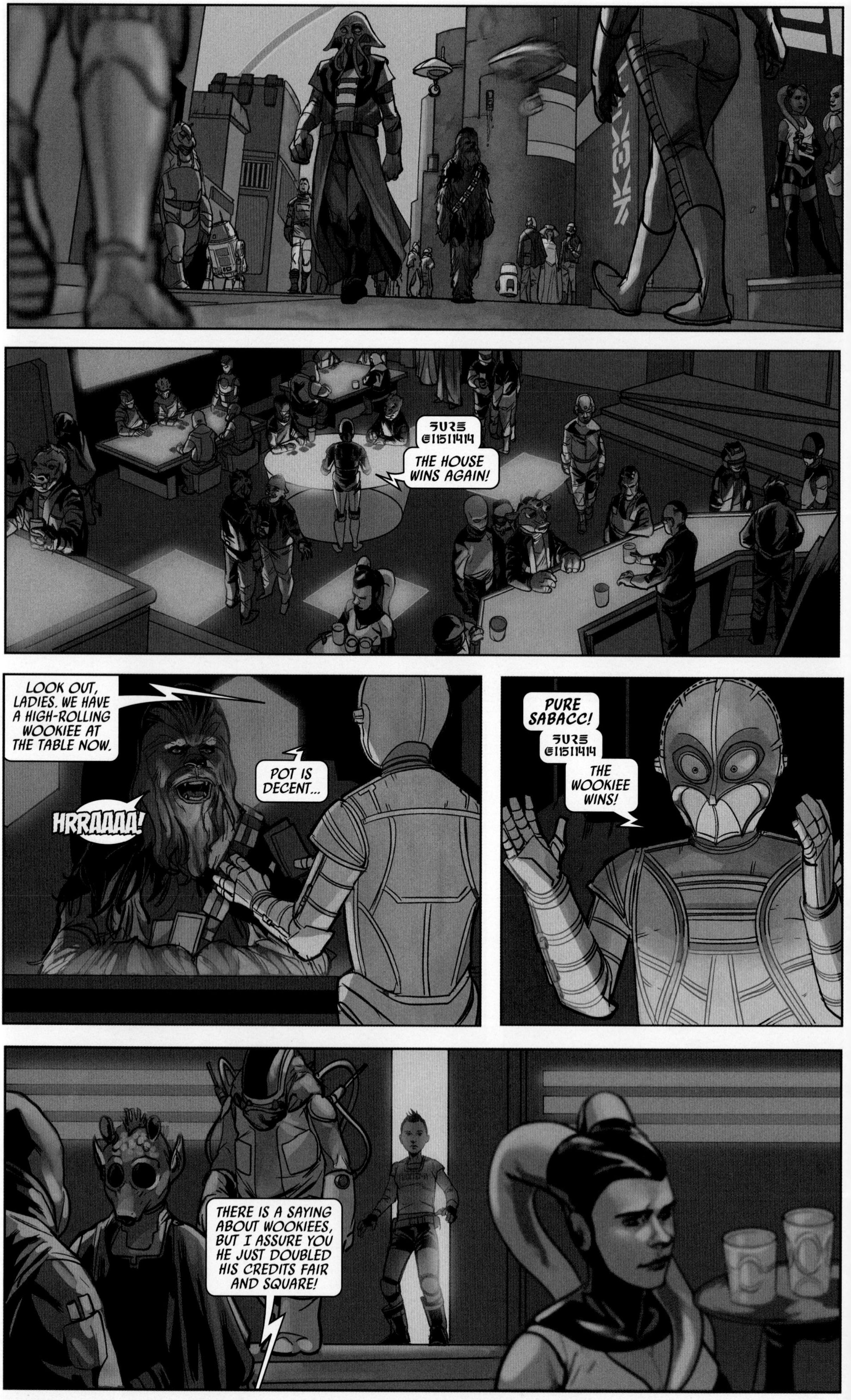
THE HOUSE WINS AGAIN!
LOOK OUT, LADIES. WE HAVE A HIGH-ROLLING WOOKIEE AT THE TABLE NOW.
HRRAAAA!
POT IS DECENT...
PURE SABACC!
THE WOOKIEE WINS!
THERE IS A SAYING ABOUT WOOKIEES, BUT I ASSURE YOU HE JUST DOUBLED HIS CREDITS FAIR AND SQUARE!

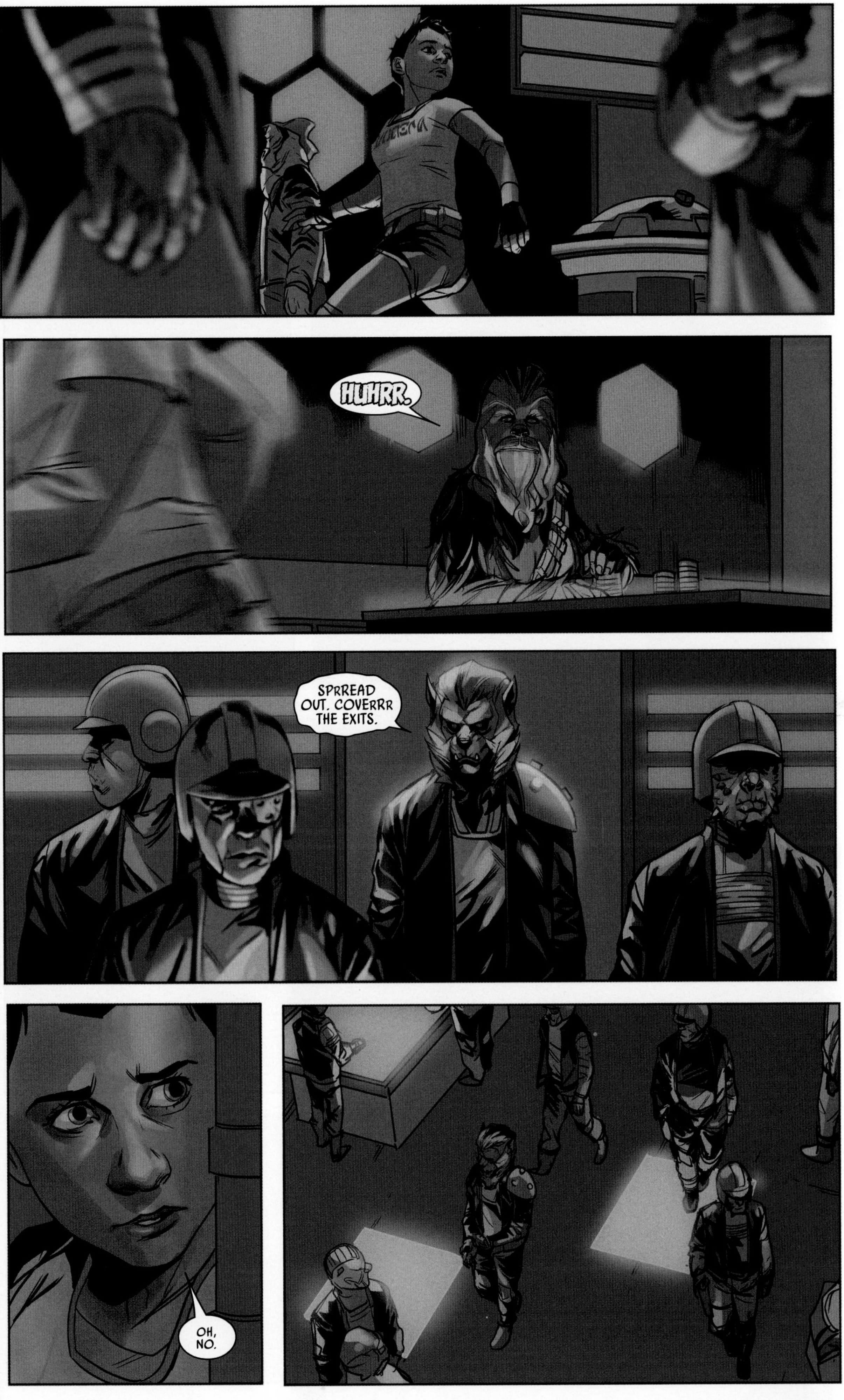
HUHRR.
SPRREAD OUT. COVERRR THE EXITS.
OH, NO.

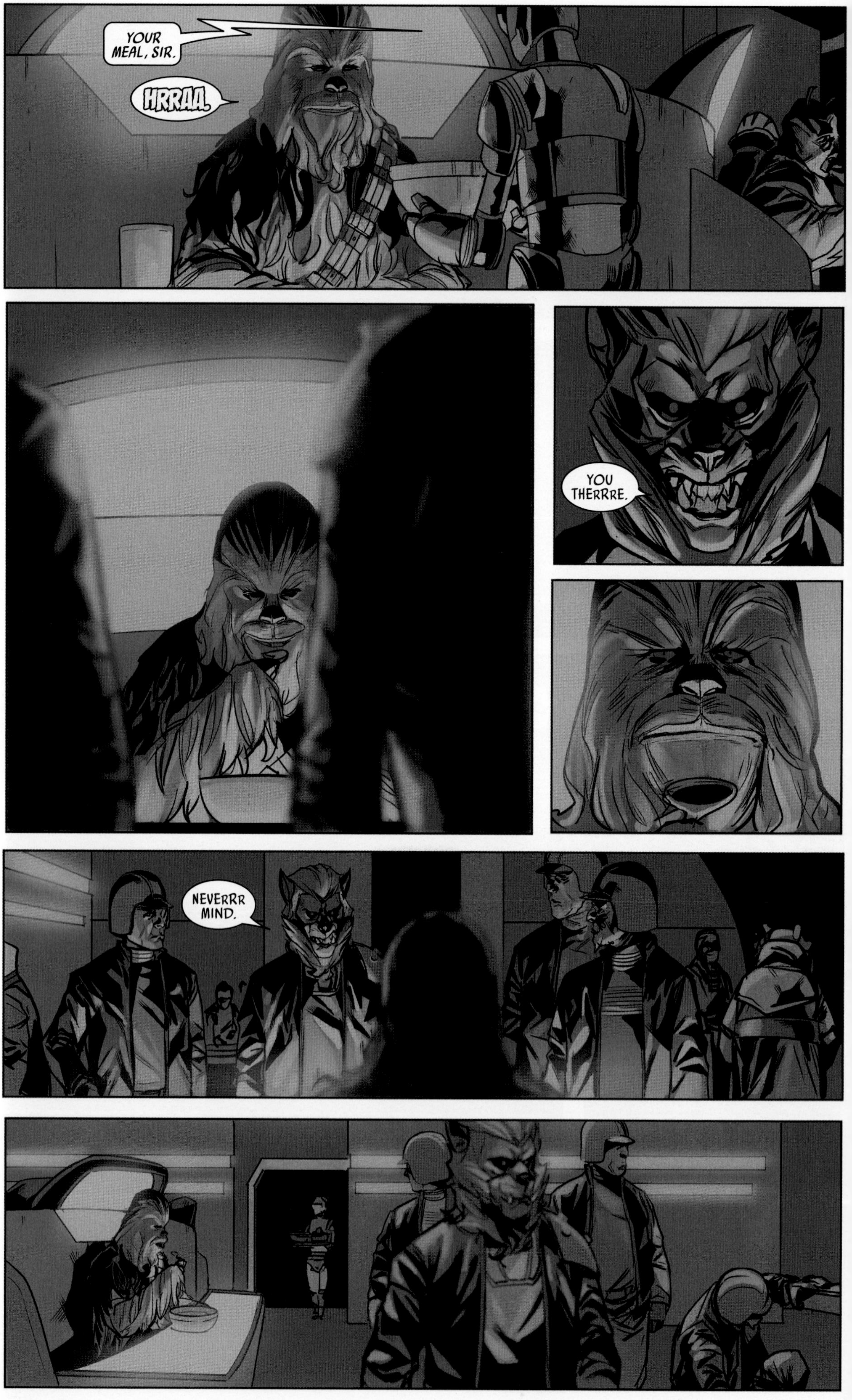
YOUR MEAL, SIR.
HRRAA.
YOU THERRRE.
NEVERRR MIND.

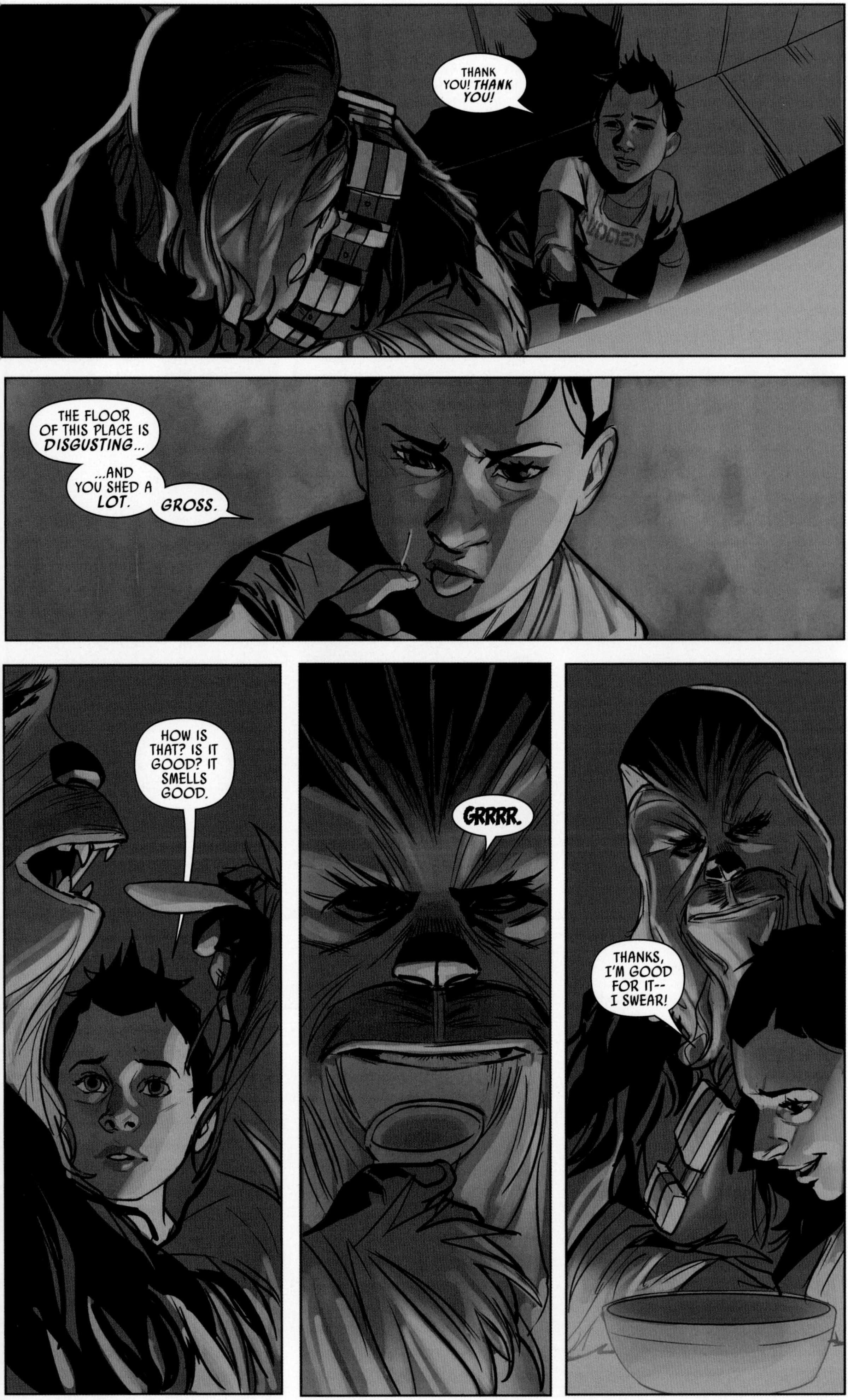
THANK YOU! THANK YOU!
THE FLOOR OF THIS PLACE IS DISGUSTING...
...AND YOU SHED A LOT.
GROSS.
HOW IS THAT? IS IT GOOD? IT SMELLS GOOD.
GRRRR.
THANKS, I'M GOOD FOR IT-- I SWEAR!

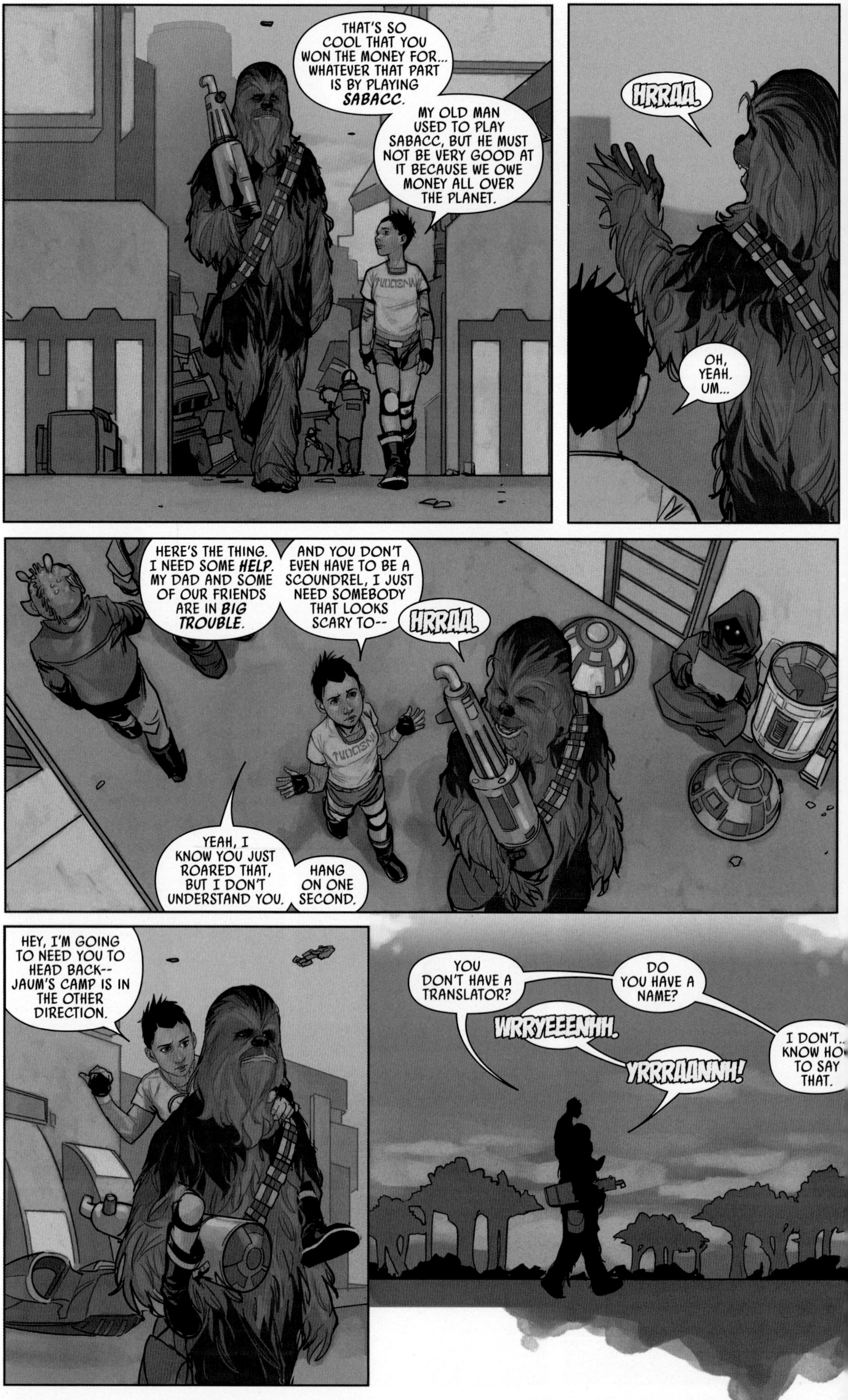
THAT'S SO COOL THAT YOU WON THE MONEY FOR... WHATEVER THAT PART IS BY PLAYING *SABACC*.
MY OLD MAN USED TO PLAY SABACC, BUT HE MUST NOT BE VERY GOOD AT IT BECAUSE WE OWE MONEY ALL OVER THE PLANET.
HRRAA.
OH, YEAH. UM...
HERE'S THE THING. I NEED SOME *HELP*. MY DAD AND SOME OF OUR FRIENDS ARE IN *BIG TROUBLE*.
AND YOU DON'T EVEN HAVE TO BE A SCOUNDREL, I JUST NEED SOMEBODY THAT LOOKS SCARY TO--
HRRAA.
YEAH, I KNOW YOU JUST ROARED THAT, BUT I DON'T UNDERSTAND YOU.
HANG ON ONE SECOND.
HEY, I'M GOING TO NEED YOU TO HEAD BACK-- JAUM'S CAMP IS IN THE OTHER DIRECTION.
YOU DON'T HAVE A TRANSLATOR?
WRRYEEENHH.
DO YOU HAVE A NAME?
YRRRAANNH!
I DON'T... KNOW HO TO SAY THAT.

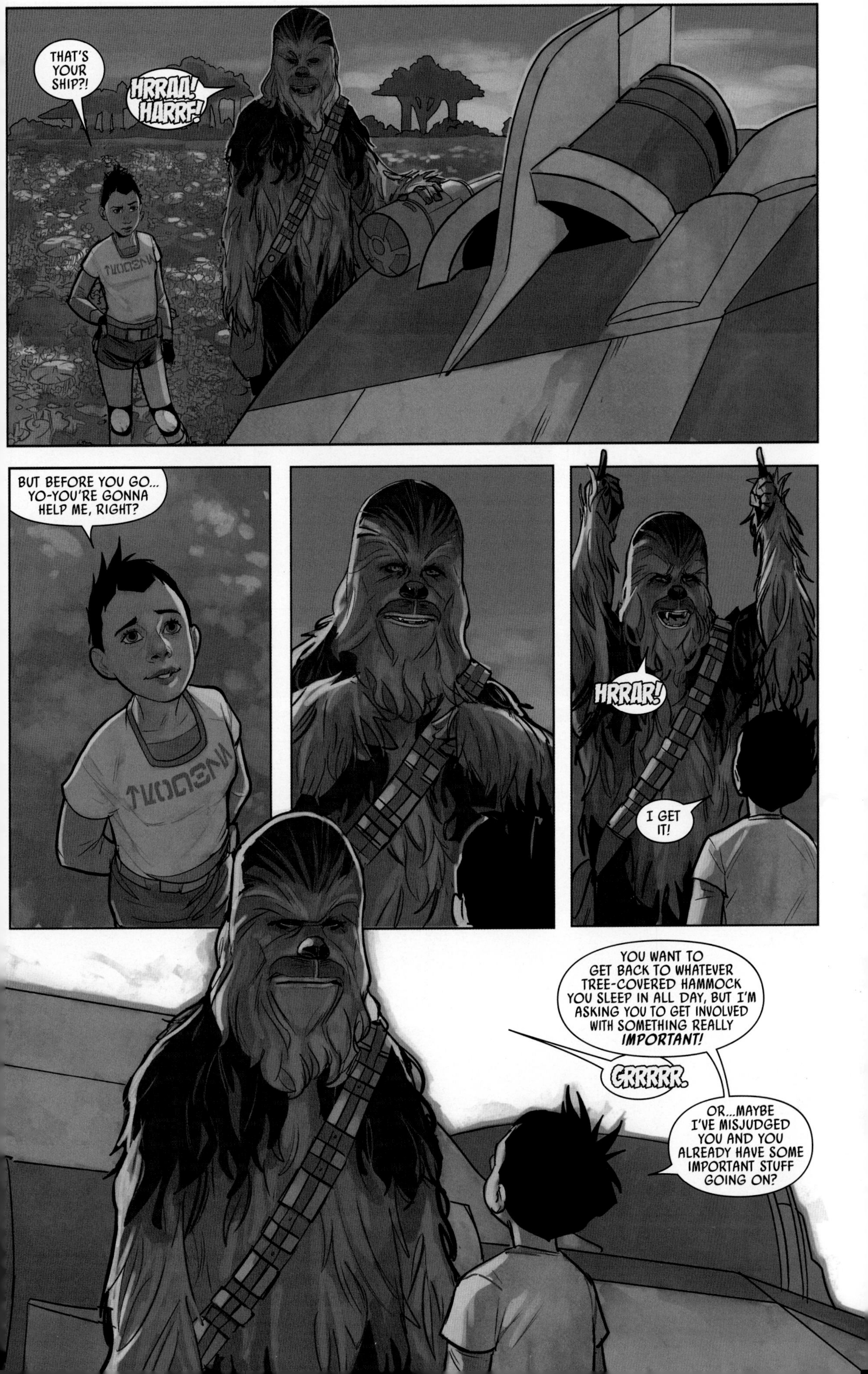
THAT'S YOUR SHIP?!
HRRAA! HARRF!
BUT BEFORE YOU GO... YO-YOU'RE GONNA HELP ME, RIGHT?
HRRAR!
I GET IT!
YOU WANT TO GET BACK TO WHATEVER TREE-COVERED HAMMOCK YOU SLEEP IN ALL DAY, BUT I'M ASKING YOU TO GET INVOLVED WITH SOMETHING REALLY IMPORTANT!
GRRRRR.
OR...MAYBE I'VE MISJUDGED YOU AND YOU ALREADY HAVE SOME IMPORTANT STUFF GOING ON?

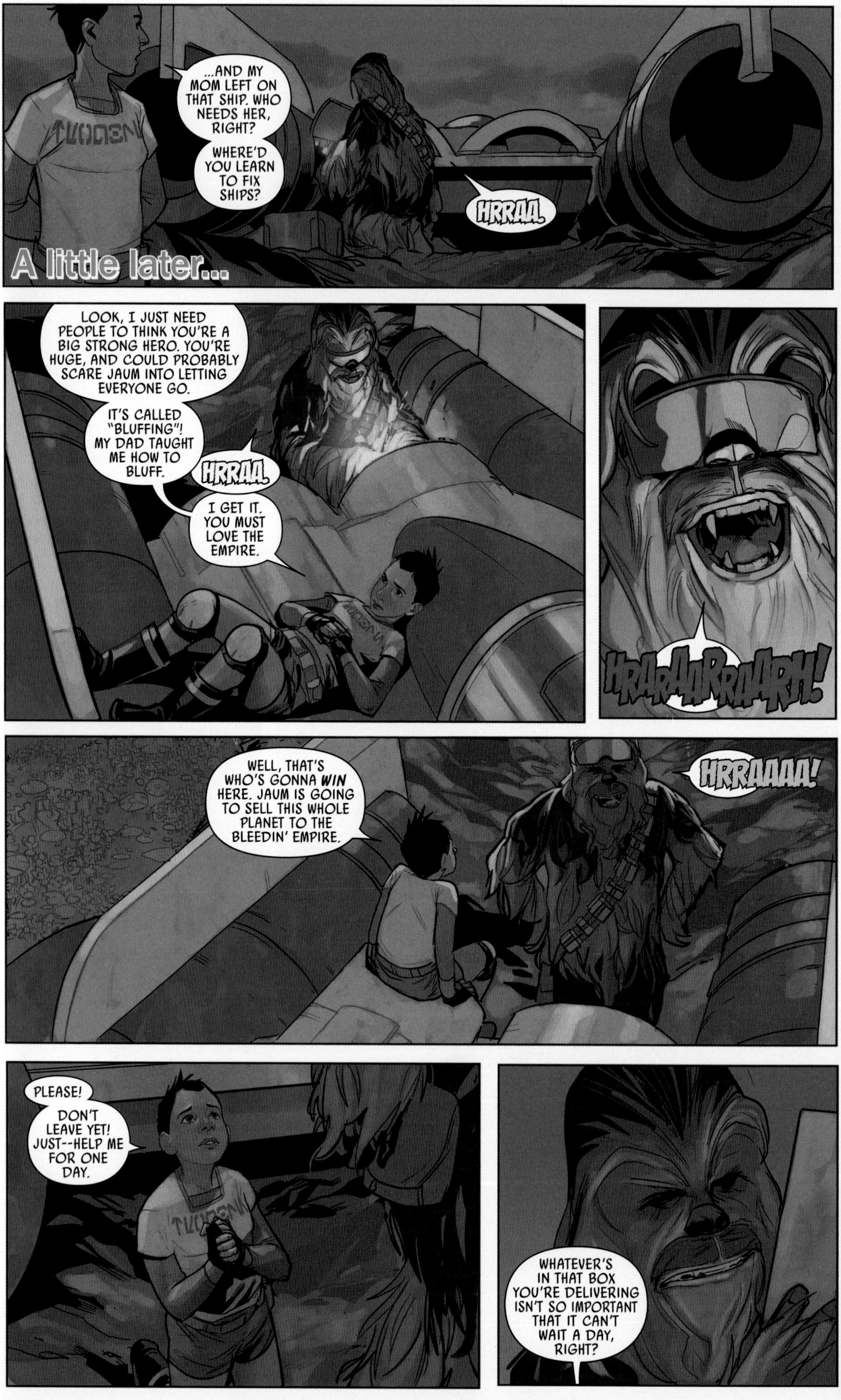
...AND MY MOM LEFT ON THAT SHIP. WHO NEEDS HER, RIGHT?
WHERE'D YOU LEARN TO FIX SHIPS?
HRRAAL
A little later...
LOOK, I JUST NEED PEOPLE TO THINK YOU'RE A BIG STRONG HERO. YOU'RE HUGE, AND COULD PROBABLY SCARE JAUM INTO LETTING EVERYONE GO.
IT'S CALLED "BLUFFING"! MY DAD TAUGHT ME HOW TO BLUFF.
HRRAAL
I GET IT. YOU MUST LOVE THE EMPIRE.
HRARAARRAARH!
WELL, THAT'S WHO'S GONNA WIN HERE. JAUM IS GOING TO SELL THIS WHOLE PLANET TO THE BLEEDIN' EMPIRE.
HRRAAAA!
PLEASE!
DON'T LEAVE YET! JUST--HELP ME FOR ONE DAY.
WHATEVER'S IN THAT BOX YOU'RE DELIVERING ISN'T SO IMPORTANT THAT IT CAN'T WAIT A DAY, RIGHT?

I DON'T KNOW WHAT TO DO--NOBODY WILL HELP ME!

MY DAD IS TRAPPED DOWN IN JAUM'S MINE!

HRRAAAA!

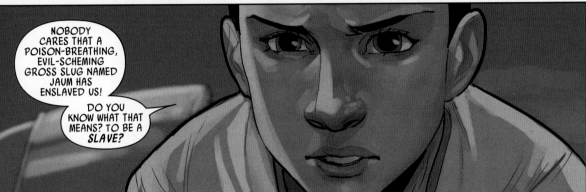

NOBODY CARES THAT A POISON-BREATHING, EVIL-SCHEMING GROSS SLUG NAMED JAUM HAS ENSLAVED US!

DO YOU KNOW WHAT THAT MEANS? TO BE A SLAVE?

HRRAAAA!
HRRAAAA!
HRRAAAA!

OKAY, DON'T RAGE OUT. I GOT THE MESSAGE. YOU'RE LEAVING. SAFE TRAVELS.

YERRRH...

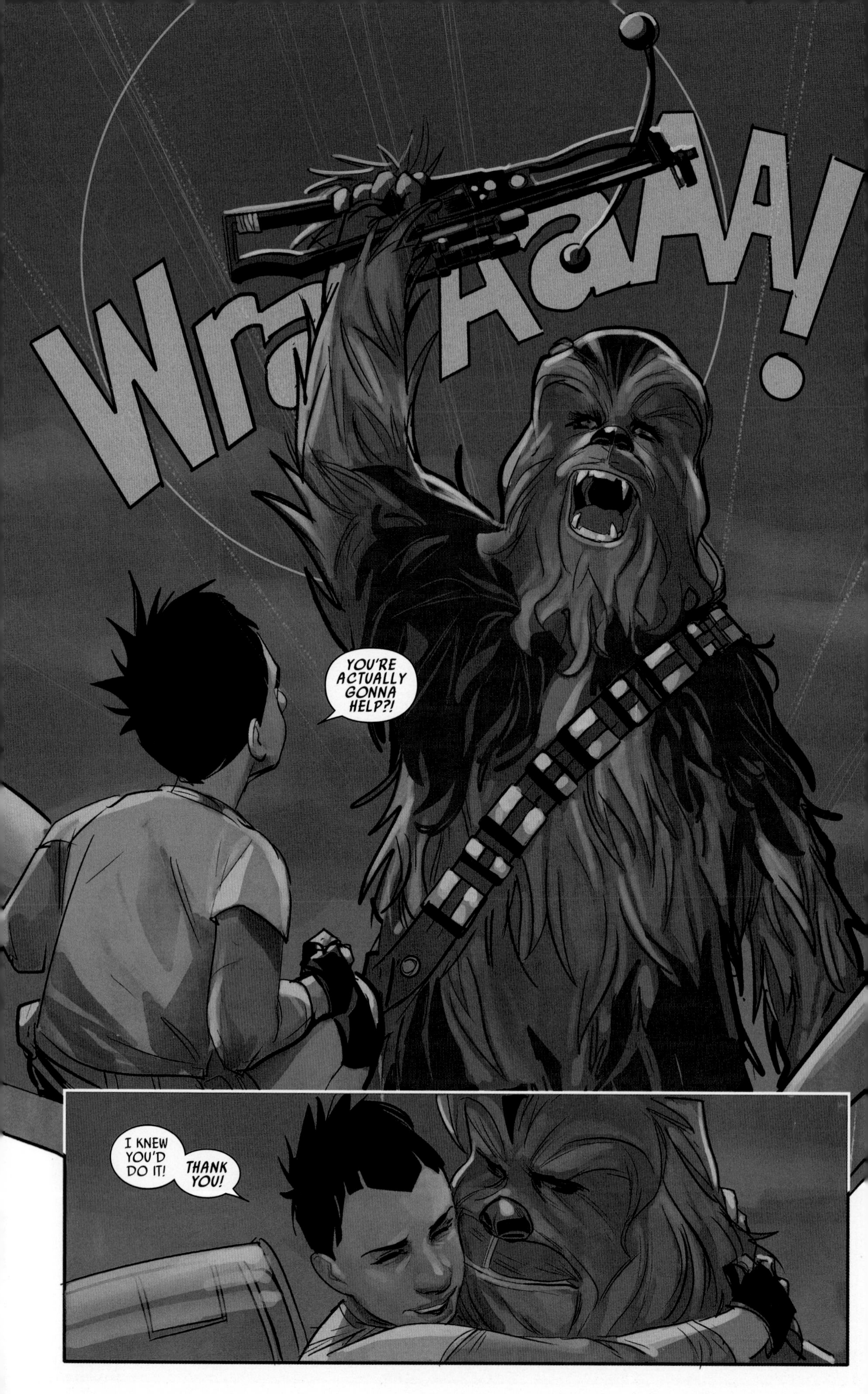
WRAAAAAA!
YOU'RE ACTUALLY GONNA HELP?!
I KNEW YOU'D DO IT!
THANK YOU!

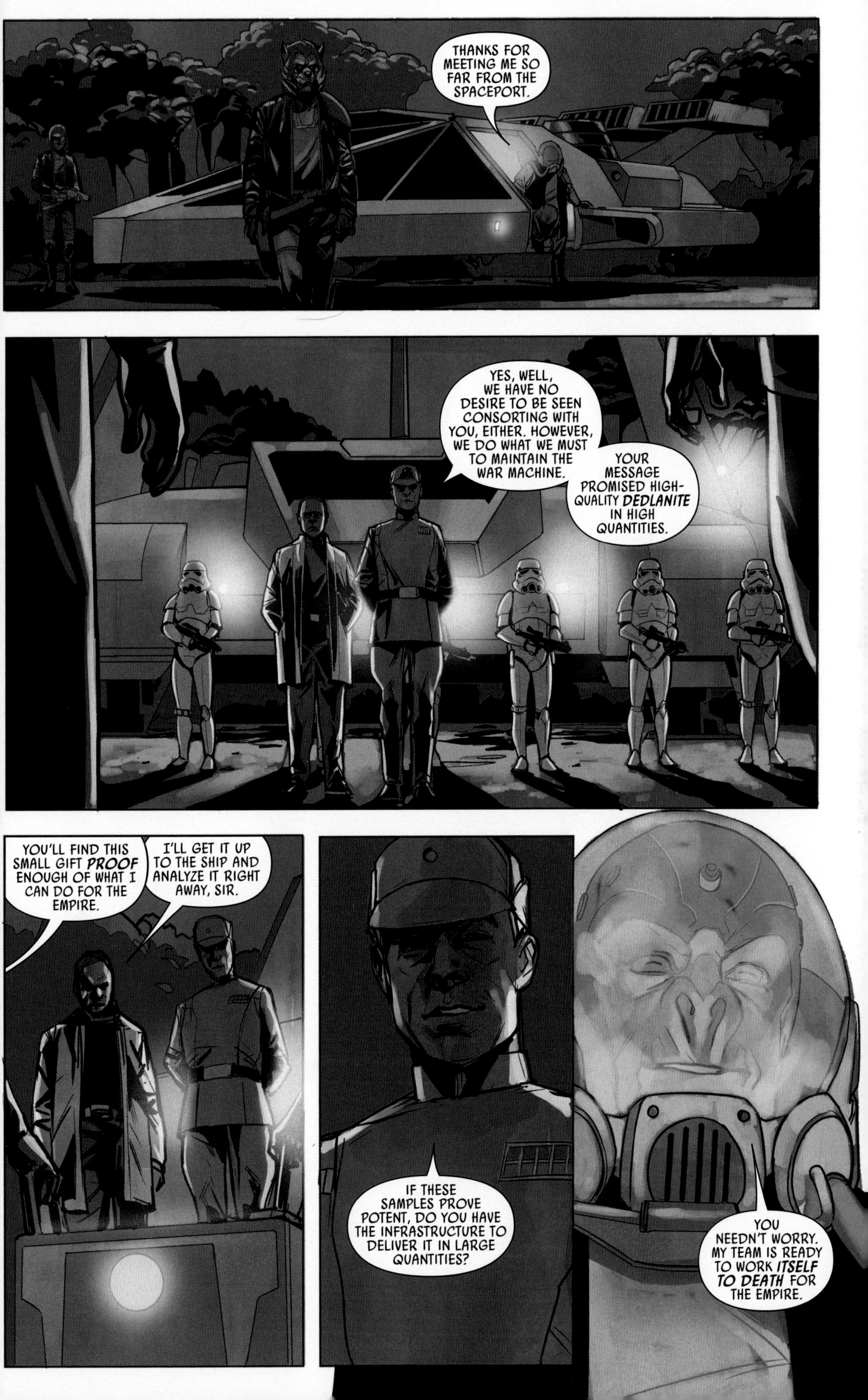
THANKS FOR MEETING ME SO FAR FROM THE SPACEPORT.
YES, WELL, WE HAVE NO DESIRE TO BE SEEN CONSORTING WITH YOU, EITHER. HOWEVER, WE DO WHAT WE MUST TO MAINTAIN THE WAR MACHINE.
YOUR MESSAGE PROMISED HIGH-QUALITY DEDLANITE IN HIGH QUANTITIES.
YOU'LL FIND THIS SMALL GIFT PROOF ENOUGH OF WHAT I CAN DO FOR THE EMPIRE.
I'LL GET IT UP TO THE SHIP AND ANALYZE IT RIGHT AWAY, SIR.
IF THESE SAMPLES PROVE POTENT, DO YOU HAVE THE INFRASTRUCTURE TO DELIVER IT IN LARGE QUANTITIES?
YOU NEEDN'T WORRY. MY TEAM IS READY TO WORK ITSELF TO DEATH FOR THE EMPIRE.

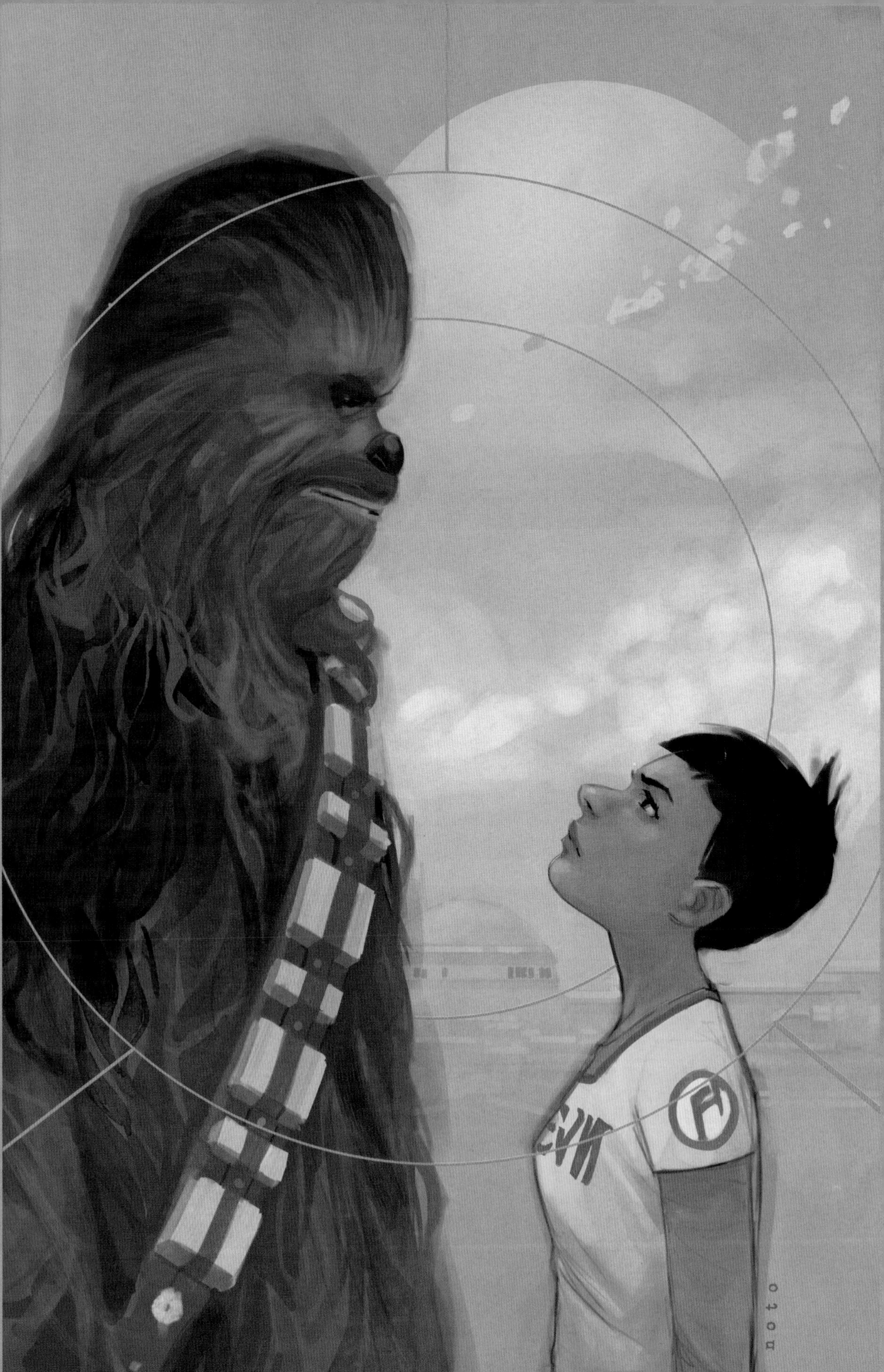
noto

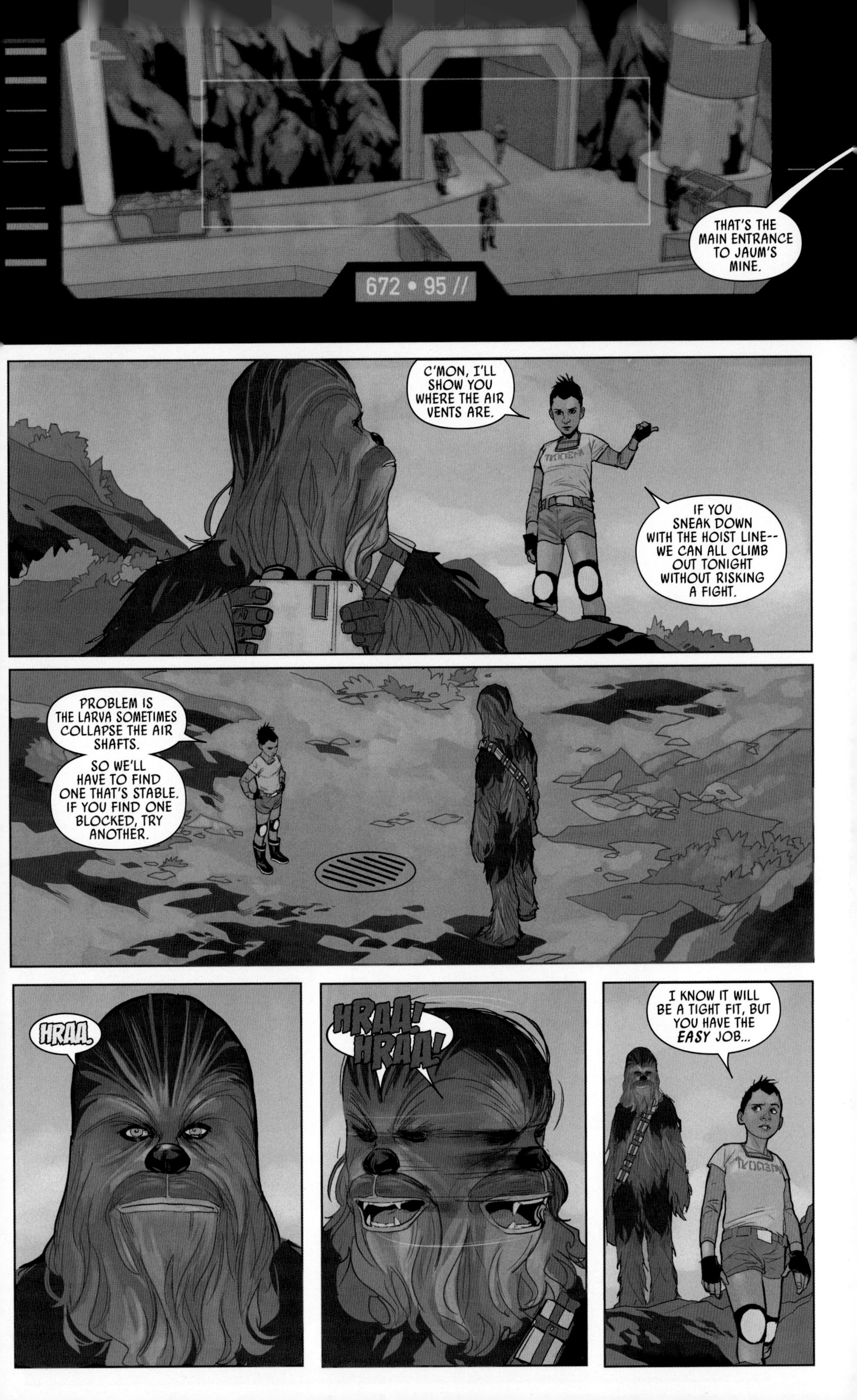
672 • 95 //
THAT'S THE MAIN ENTRANCE TO JAUM'S MINE.
C'MON, I'LL SHOW YOU WHERE THE AIR VENTS ARE.
IF YOU SNEAK DOWN WITH THE HOIST LINE-- WE CAN ALL CLIMB OUT TONIGHT WITHOUT RISKING A FIGHT.
PROBLEM IS THE LARVA SOMETIMES COLLAPSE THE AIR SHAFTS.
SO WE'LL HAVE TO FIND ONE THAT'S STABLE. IF YOU FIND ONE BLOCKED, TRY ANOTHER.
HRAA
HRAA! HRAA!
I KNOW IT WILL BE A TIGHT FIT, BUT YOU HAVE THE *EASY* JOB...

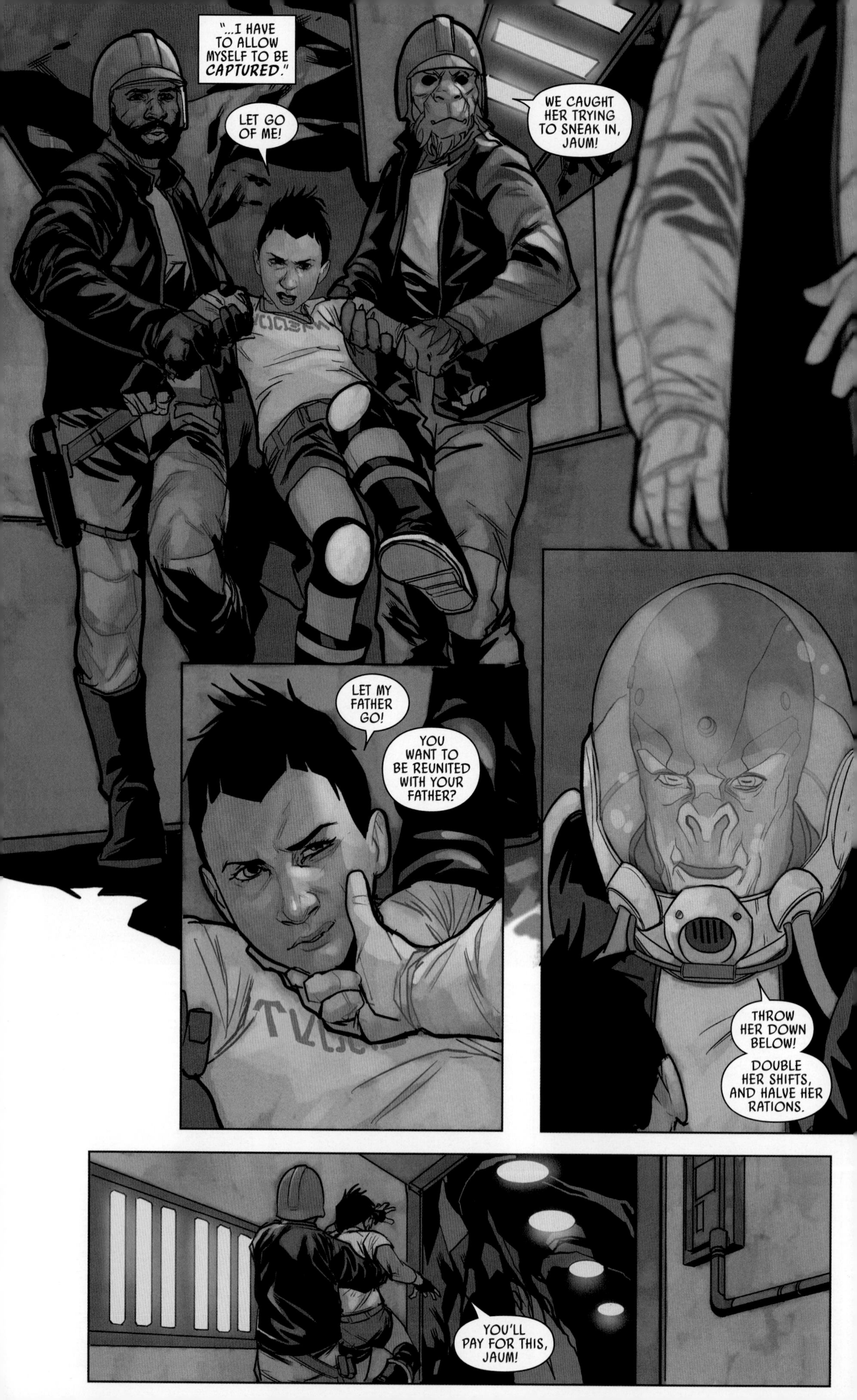
"...I HAVE TO ALLOW MYSELF TO BE CAPTURED."
LET GO OF ME!
WE CAUGHT HER TRYING TO SNEAK IN, JAUM!
LET MY FATHER GO!
YOU WANT TO BE REUNITED WITH YOUR FATHER?
THROW HER DOWN BELOW!
DOUBLE HER SHIFTS, AND HALVE HER RATIONS.
YOU'LL PAY FOR THIS, JAUM!

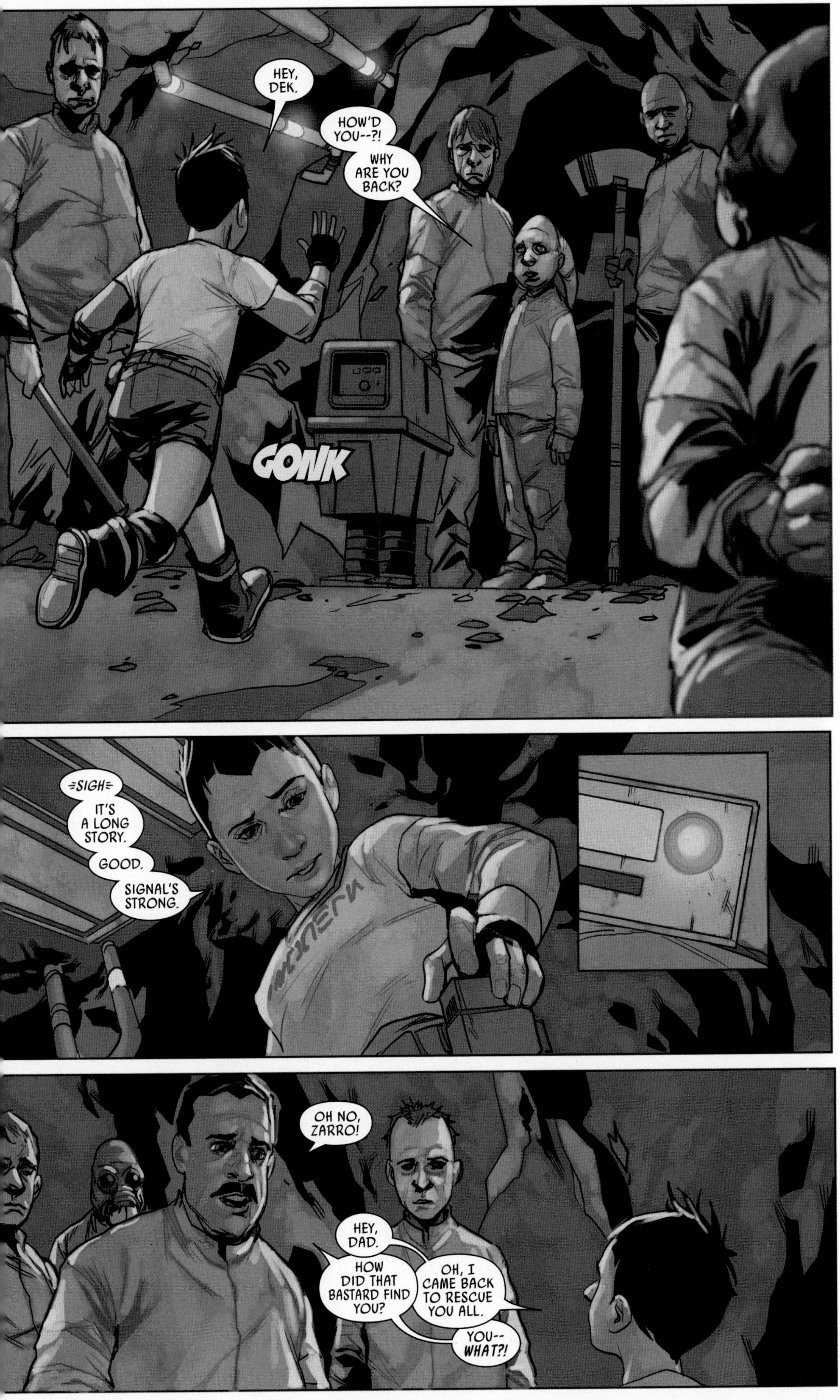
HEY, DEK.
HOW'D YOU--?!
WHY ARE YOU BACK?
GONK
=SIGH=
IT'S A LONG STORY.
GOOD.
SIGNAL'S STRONG.
OH NO, ZARRO!
HEY, DAD.
HOW DID THAT BASTARD FIND YOU?
OH, I CAME BACK TO RESCUE YOU ALL.
YOU-- WHAT?!

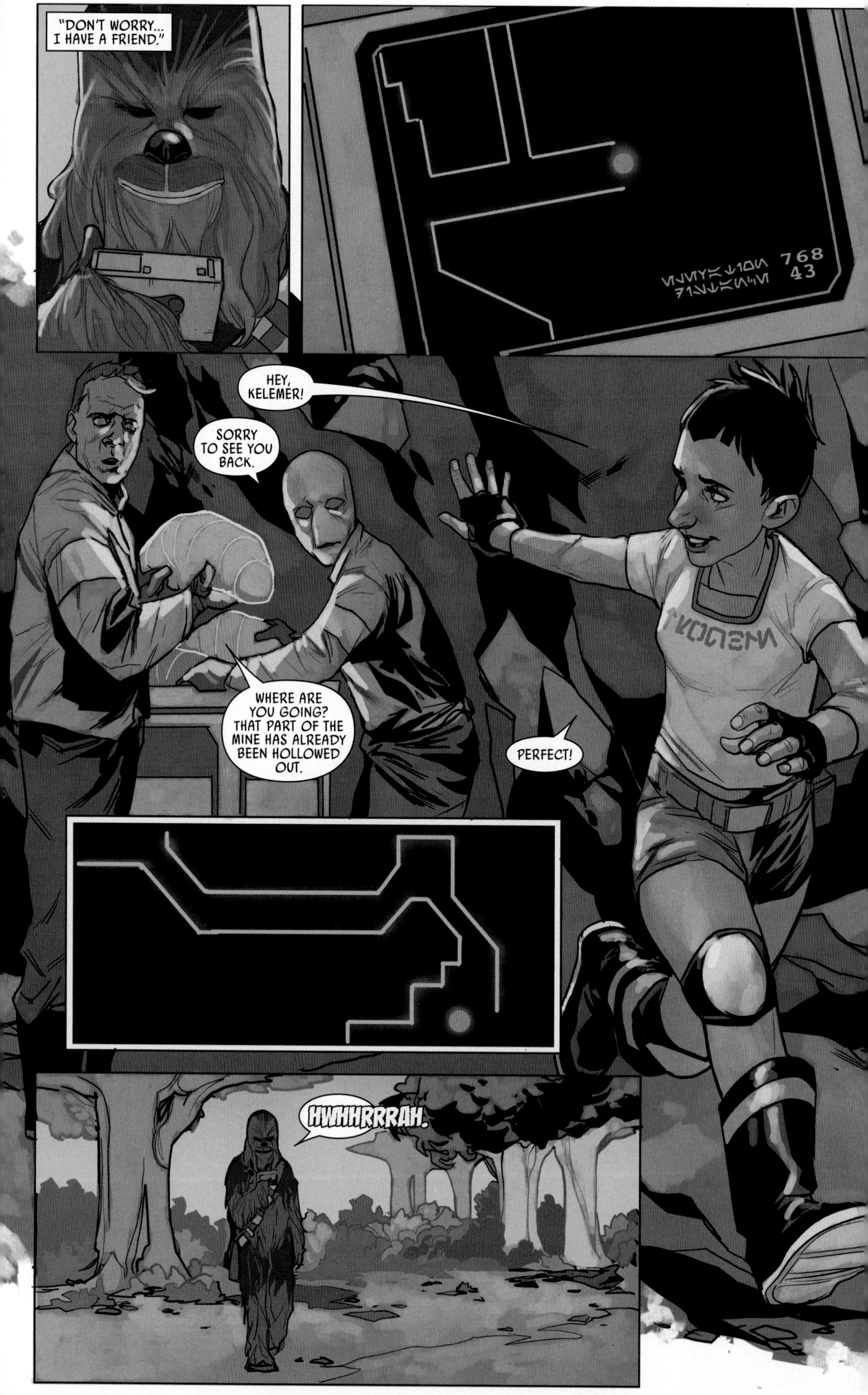
"DON'T WORRY... I HAVE A FRIEND."
768
43
HEY, KELEMER!
SORRY TO SEE YOU BACK.
WHERE ARE YOU GOING? THAT PART OF THE MINE HAS ALREADY BEEN HOLLOWED OUT.
PERFECT!
HWHHRRRAH.

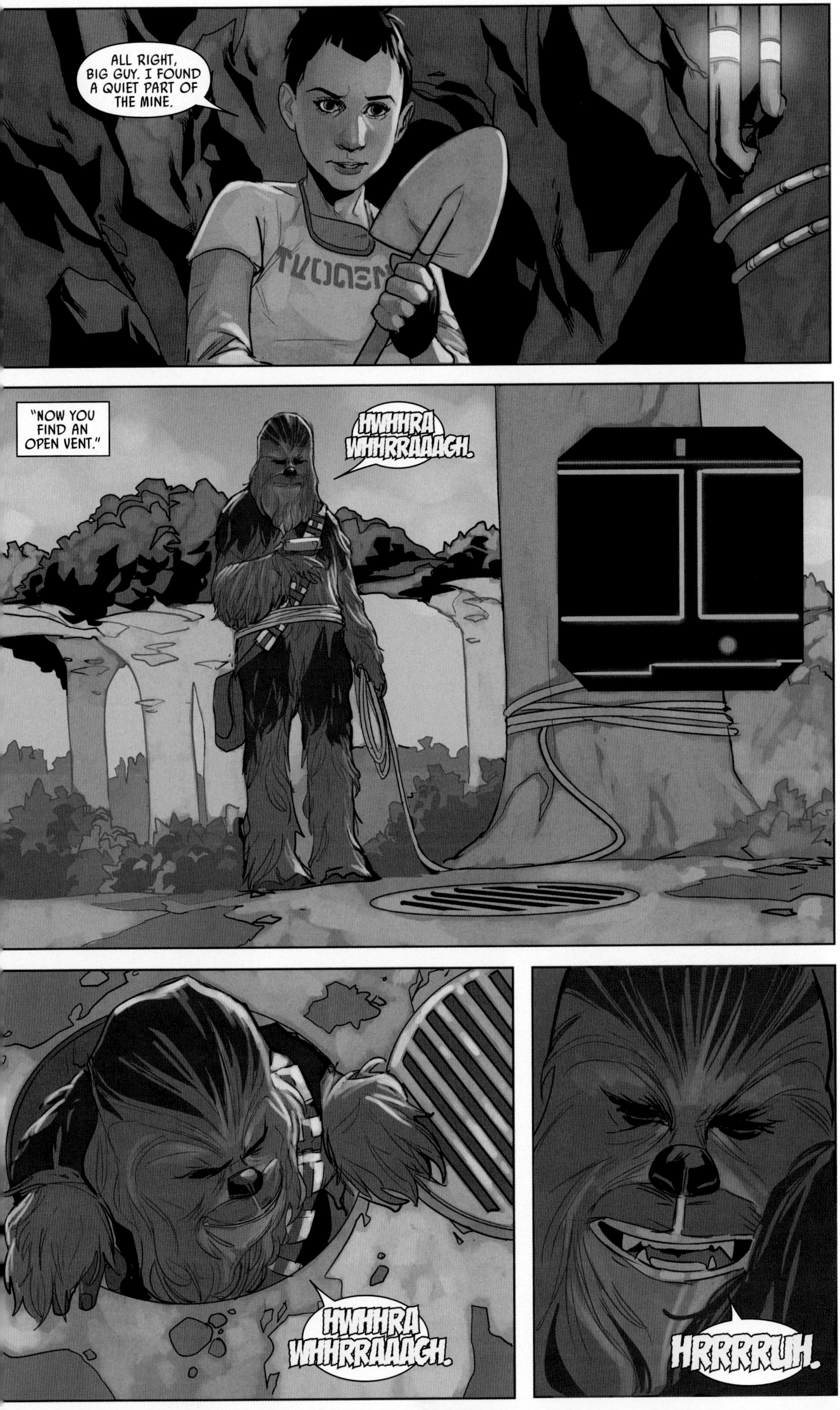
ALL RIGHT, BIG GUY. I FOUND A QUIET PART OF THE MINE.
"NOW YOU FIND AN OPEN VENT."
HWHHRA WHHRRAAAGH.
HWHHRA WHHRRAAAGH.
HRRRRUH.

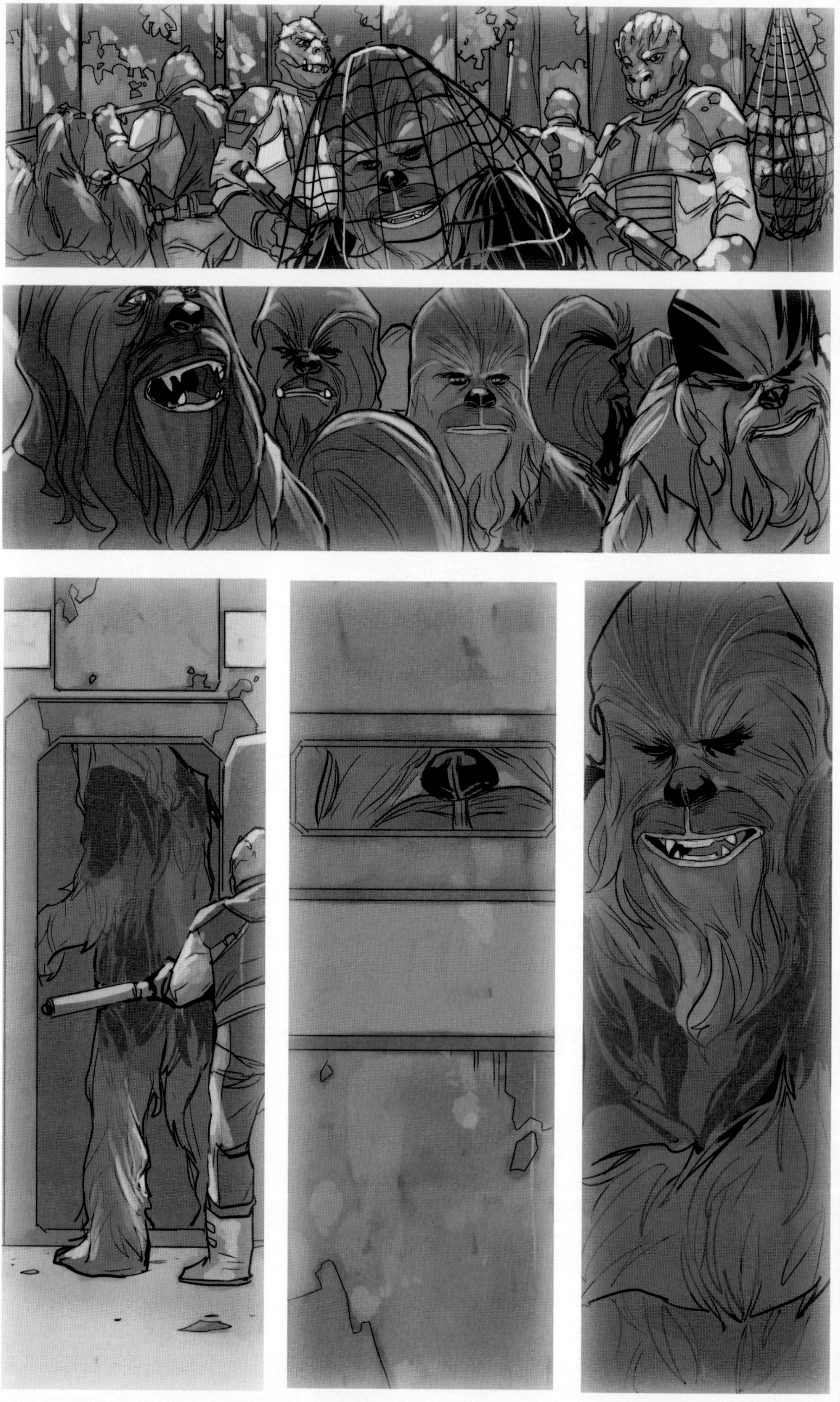

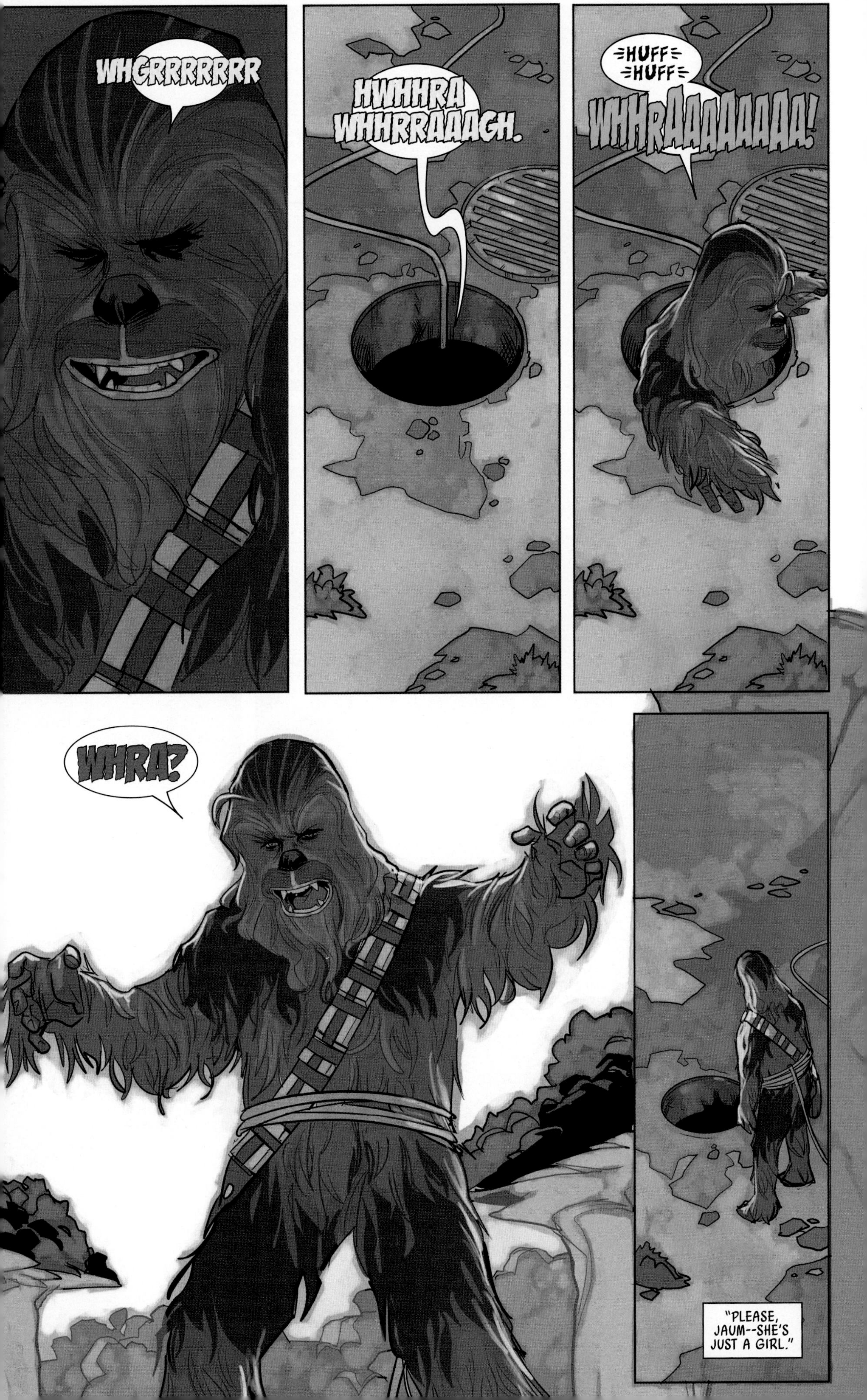
WHGRRRRRRR
HWHHRA WHHRRAAAGH.
HUFF HUFF
WHHRAAAAAAAA!
WHRA?
"PLEASE, JAUM--SHE'S JUST A GIRL."

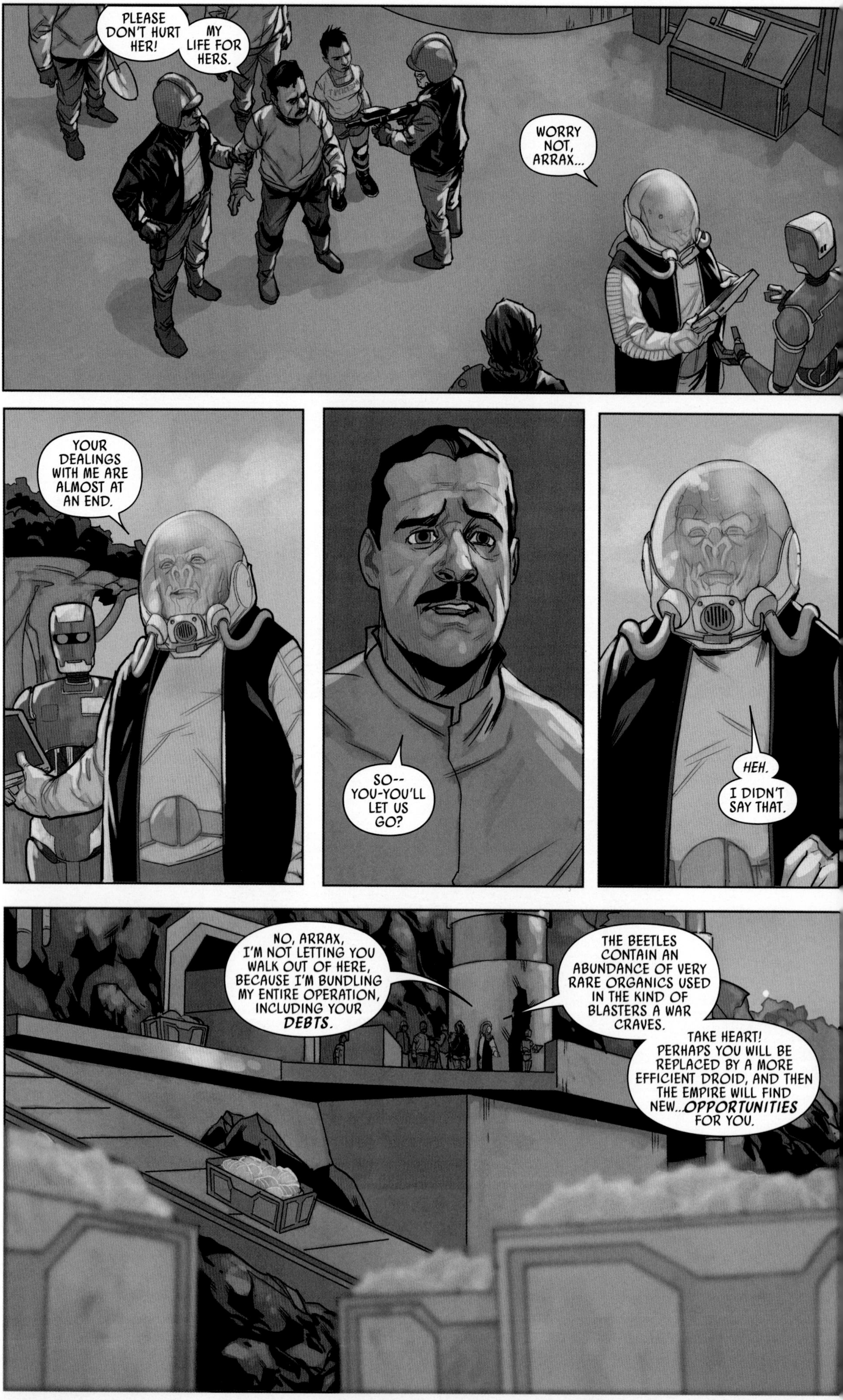
PLEASE DON'T HURT HER!
MY LIFE FOR HERS.
WORRY NOT, ARRAX...
YOUR DEALINGS WITH ME ARE ALMOST AT AN END.
SO-- YOU-YOU'LL LET US GO?
HEH.
I DIDN'T SAY THAT.
NO, ARRAX, I'M NOT LETTING YOU WALK OUT OF HERE, BECAUSE I'M BUNDLING MY ENTIRE OPERATION, INCLUDING YOUR DEBTS.
THE BEETLES CONTAIN AN ABUNDANCE OF VERY RARE ORGANICS USED IN THE KIND OF BLASTERS A WAR CRAVES.
TAKE HEART! PERHAPS YOU WILL BE REPLACED BY A MORE EFFICIENT DROID, AND THEN THE EMPIRE WILL FIND NEW...OPPORTUNITIES FOR YOU.

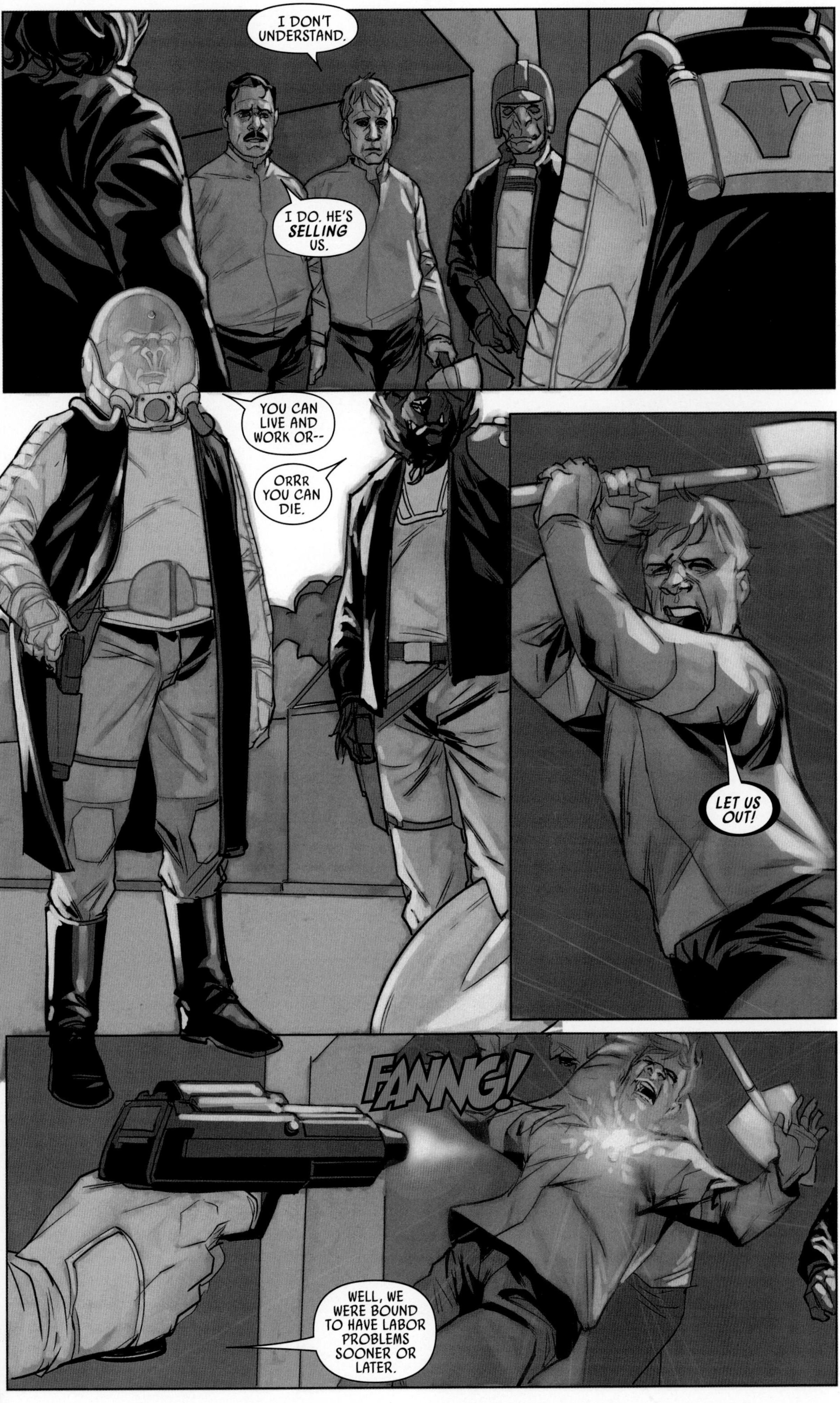
I DON'T UNDERSTAND.
I DO. HE'S SELLING US.
YOU CAN LIVE AND WORK OR--
ORRR YOU CAN DIE.
LET US OUT!
FANNG!
WELL, WE WERE BOUND TO HAVE LABOR PROBLEMS SOONER OR LATER.

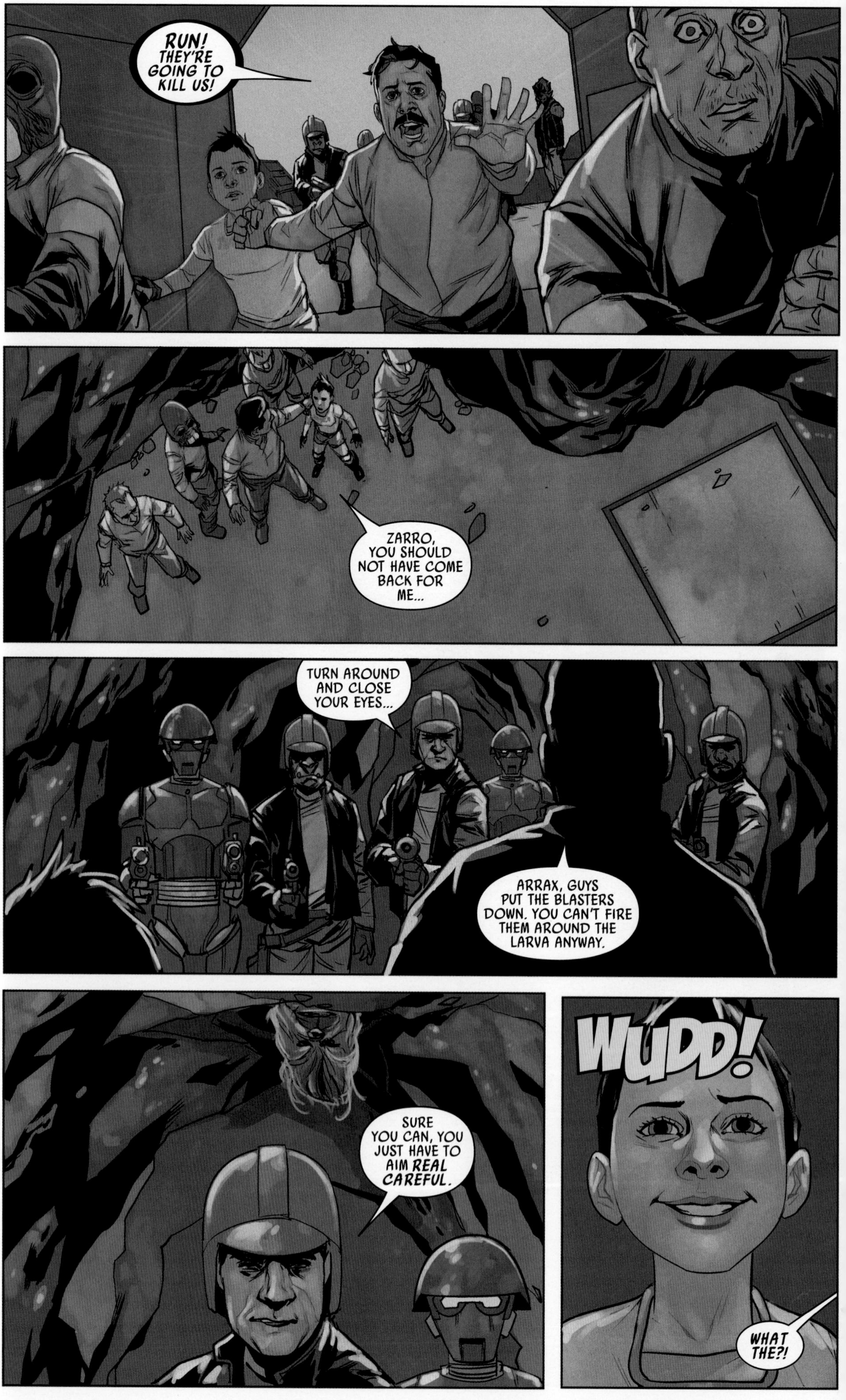
RUN! THEY'RE GOING TO KILL US!
ZARRO, YOU SHOULD NOT HAVE COME BACK FOR ME...
TURN AROUND AND CLOSE YOUR EYES...
ARRAX, GUYS PUT THE BLASTERS DOWN. YOU CAN'T FIRE THEM AROUND THE LARVA ANYWAY.
SURE YOU CAN, YOU JUST HAVE TO AIM REAL CAREFUL.
WUDD!
WHAT THE?!

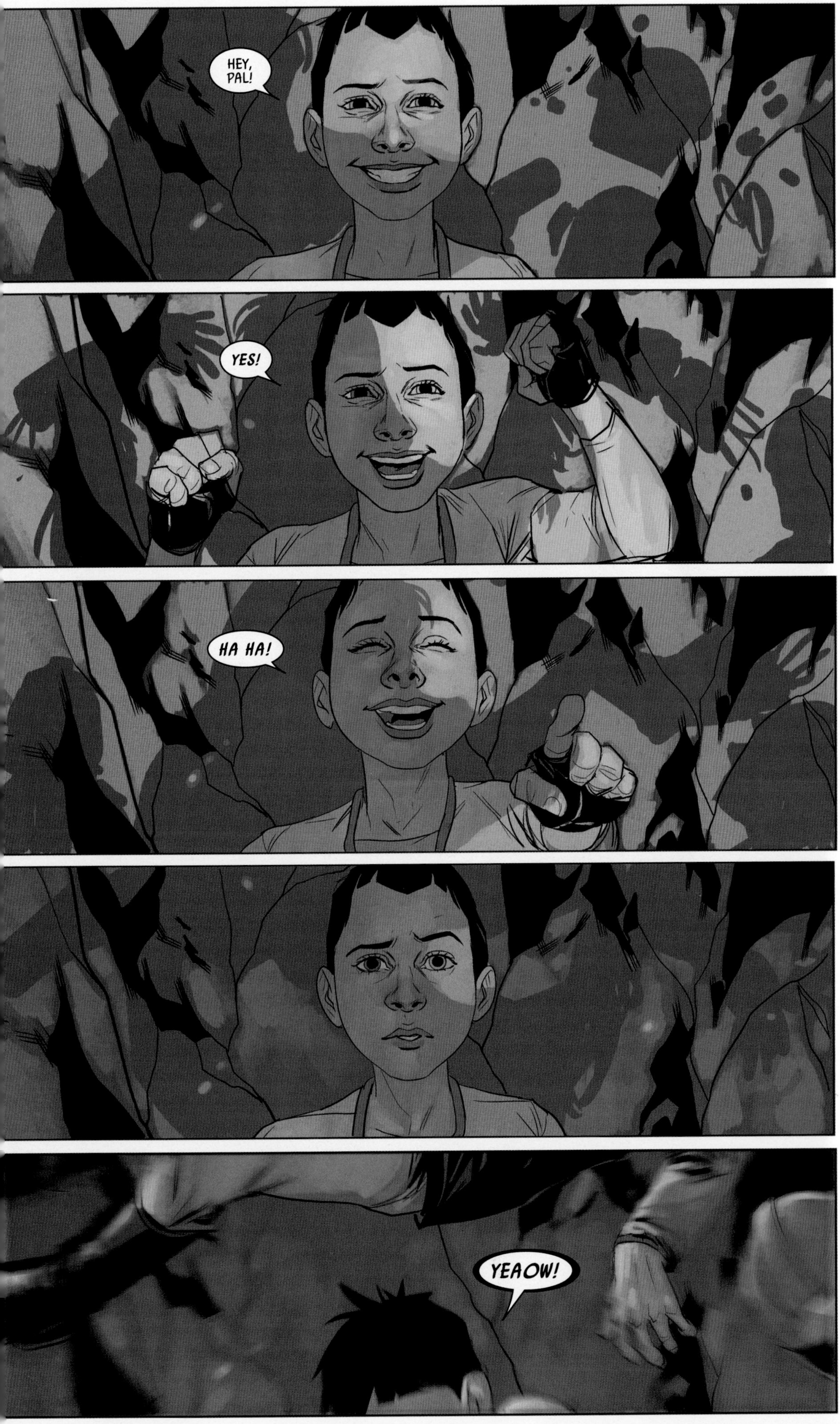
HEY, PAL!
YES!
HA HA!
YEAOW!

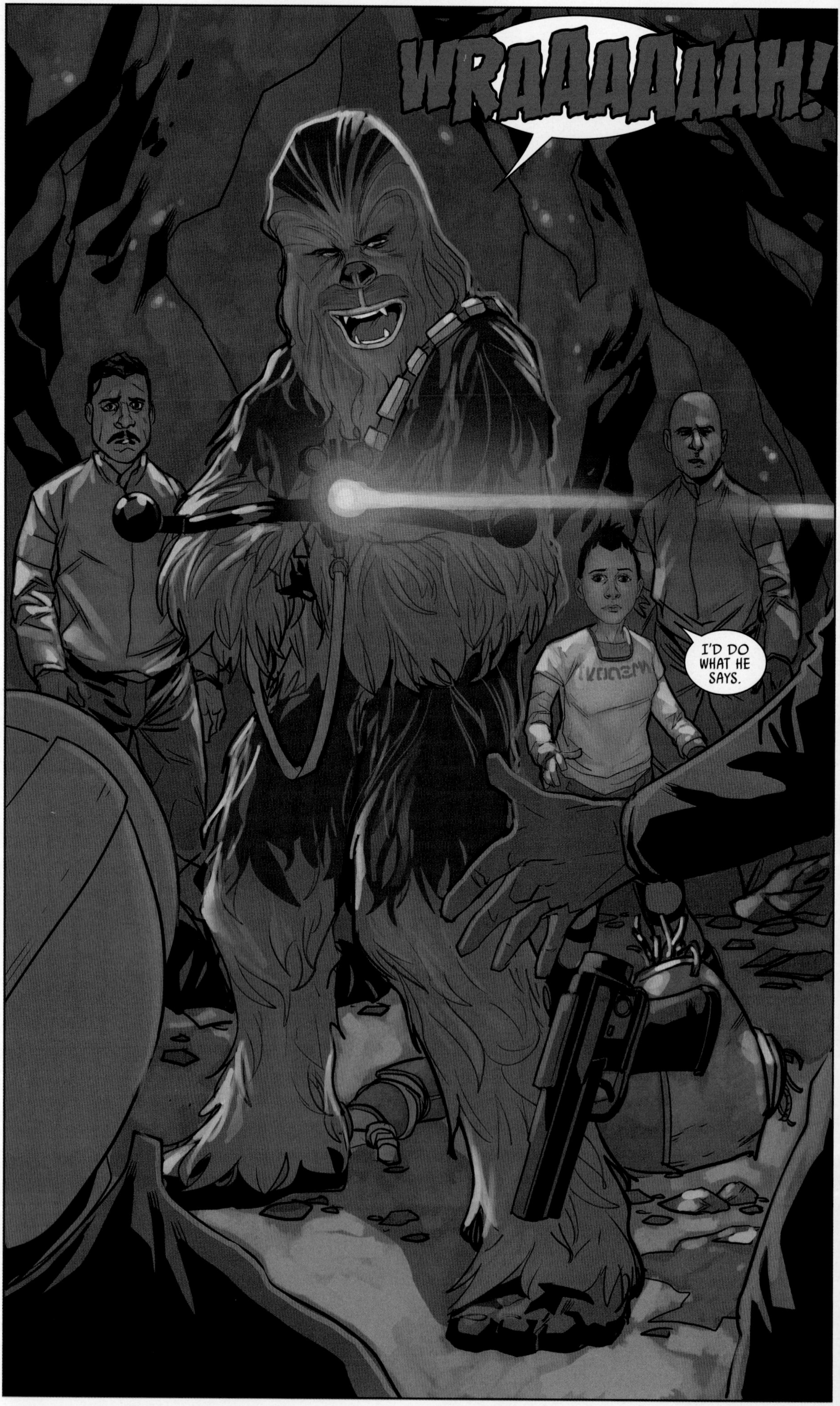
WRAAAAAAH!
I'D DO WHAT HE SAYS.

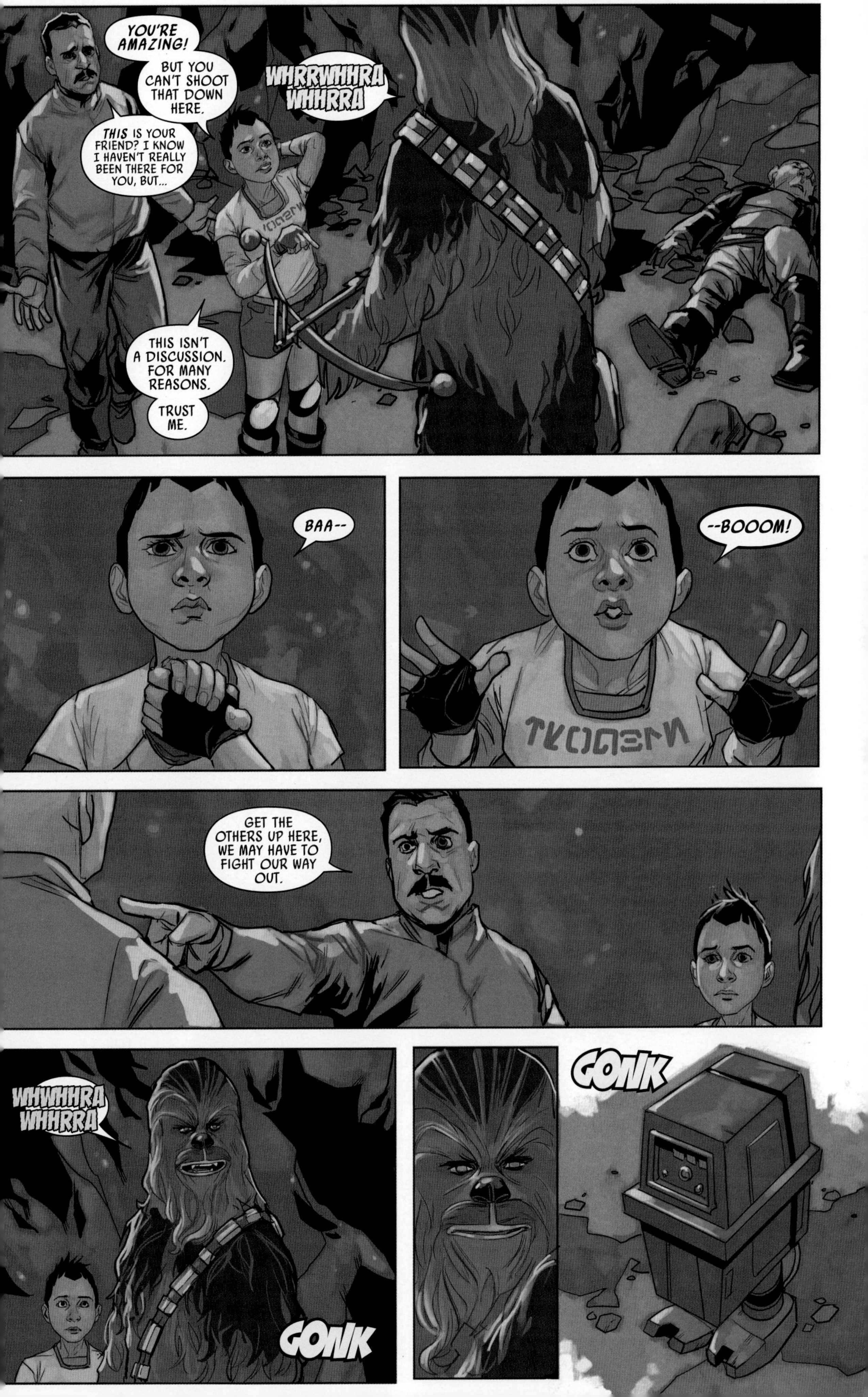
YOU'RE AMAZING!
BUT YOU CAN'T SHOOT THAT DOWN HERE.
WHRRWHHRA WHHRRA
THIS IS YOUR FRIEND? I KNOW I HAVEN'T REALLY BEEN THERE FOR YOU, BUT...
THIS ISN'T A DISCUSSION. FOR MANY REASONS.
TRUST ME.
BAA--
--BOOOM!
GET THE OTHERS UP HERE, WE MAY HAVE TO FIGHT OUR WAY OUT.
WHWHHRA WHHRRA
GONK
GONK

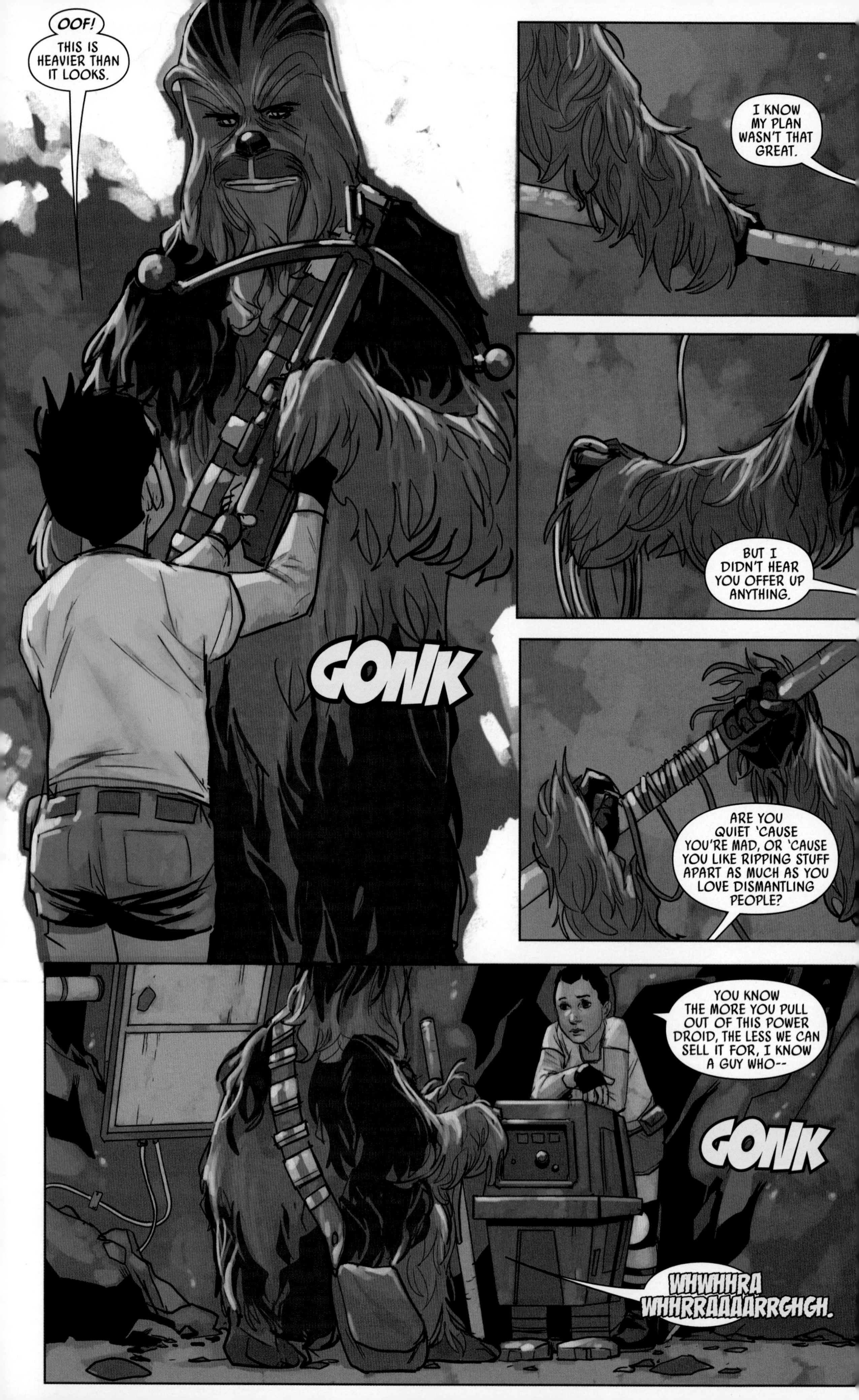
OOF! THIS IS HEAVIER THAN IT LOOKS.
GONK
I KNOW MY PLAN WASN'T THAT GREAT.
BUT I DIDN'T HEAR YOU OFFER UP ANYTHING.
ARE YOU QUIET 'CAUSE YOU'RE MAD, OR 'CAUSE YOU LIKE RIPPING STUFF APART AS MUCH AS YOU LOVE DISMANTLING PEOPLE?
YOU KNOW THE MORE YOU PULL OUT OF THIS POWER DROID, THE LESS WE CAN SELL IT FOR, I KNOW A GUY WHO--
GONK
WHWHHRA WHHRRAAAARRGHGH.

THIS IS AN UNAPPROVED WORK STOPPAGE. RETURN TO WORK!
RETURURBZZZZT
WHRRRRAANNH!
BZZACKK!
GONK
REBZZT WORK--
CATASTROPHIC DAMAGE...THANK THE MAKER.
WHAAAANNGH!
I THINK HE WANTS US TO FOLLOW HIM.
FINALLY I LIKE ONE OF YOUR FRIENDS!
BZZACKK!
GONK

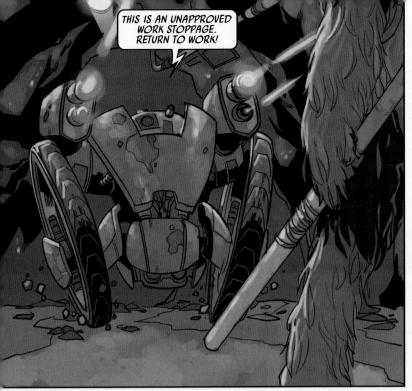

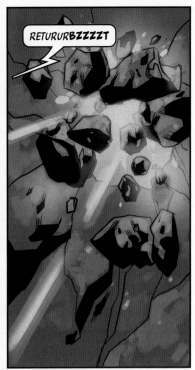

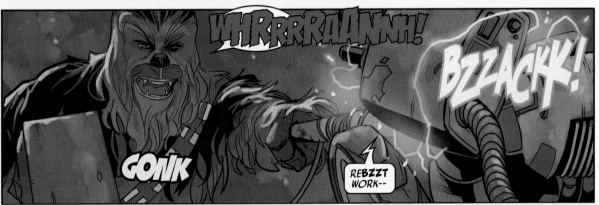

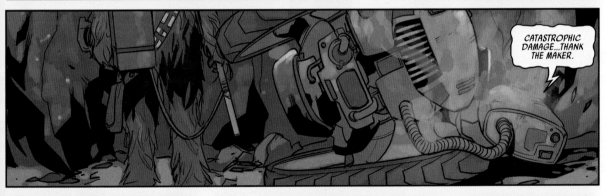

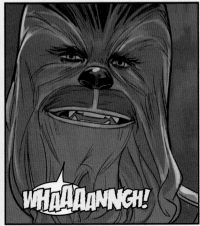

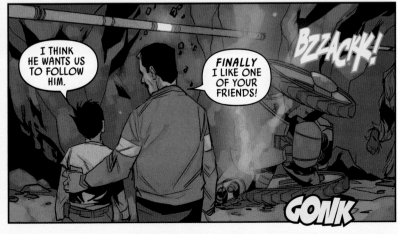

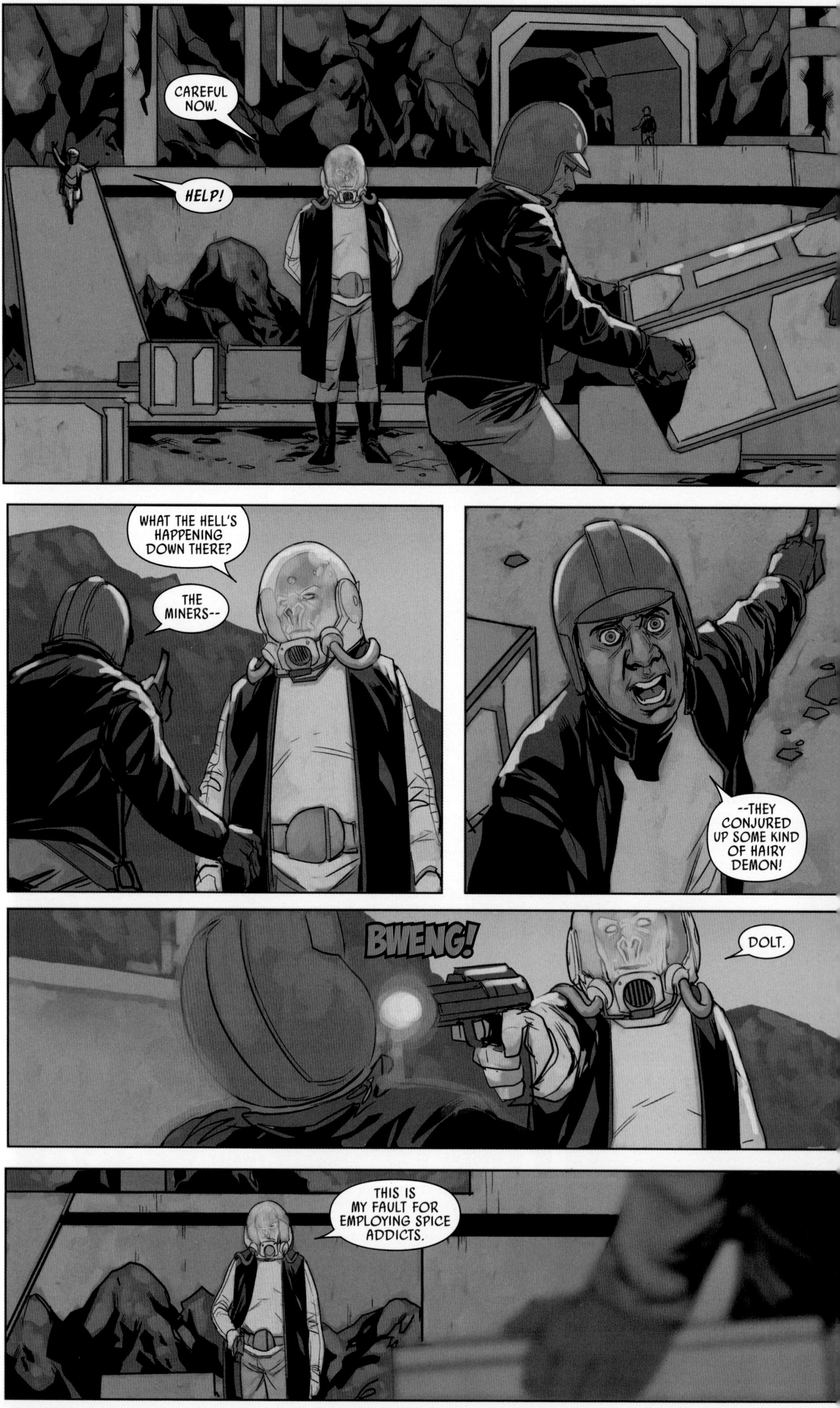
CAREFUL NOW.
HELP!
WHAT THE HELL'S HAPPENING DOWN THERE?
THE MINERS--
--THEY CONJURED UP SOME KIND OF HAIRY DEMON!
BWENG!
DOLT.
THIS IS MY FAULT FOR EMPLOYING SPICE ADDICTS.

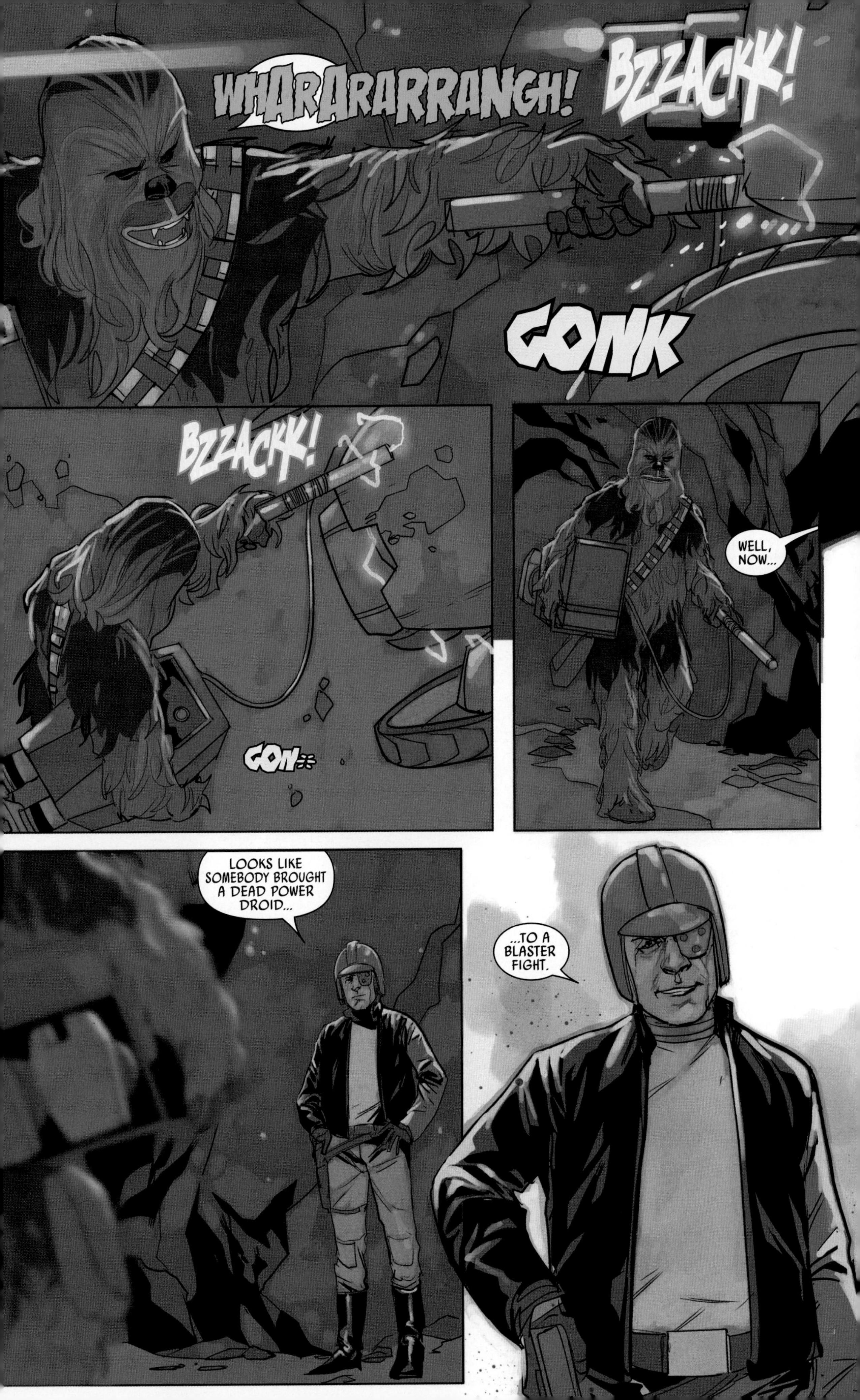
WHARARARRANGH!
BZZACKK!
GONK
BZZACKK!
GON--
WELL, NOW...
LOOKS LIKE SOMEBODY BROUGHT A DEAD POWER DROID...
...TO A BLASTER FIGHT.

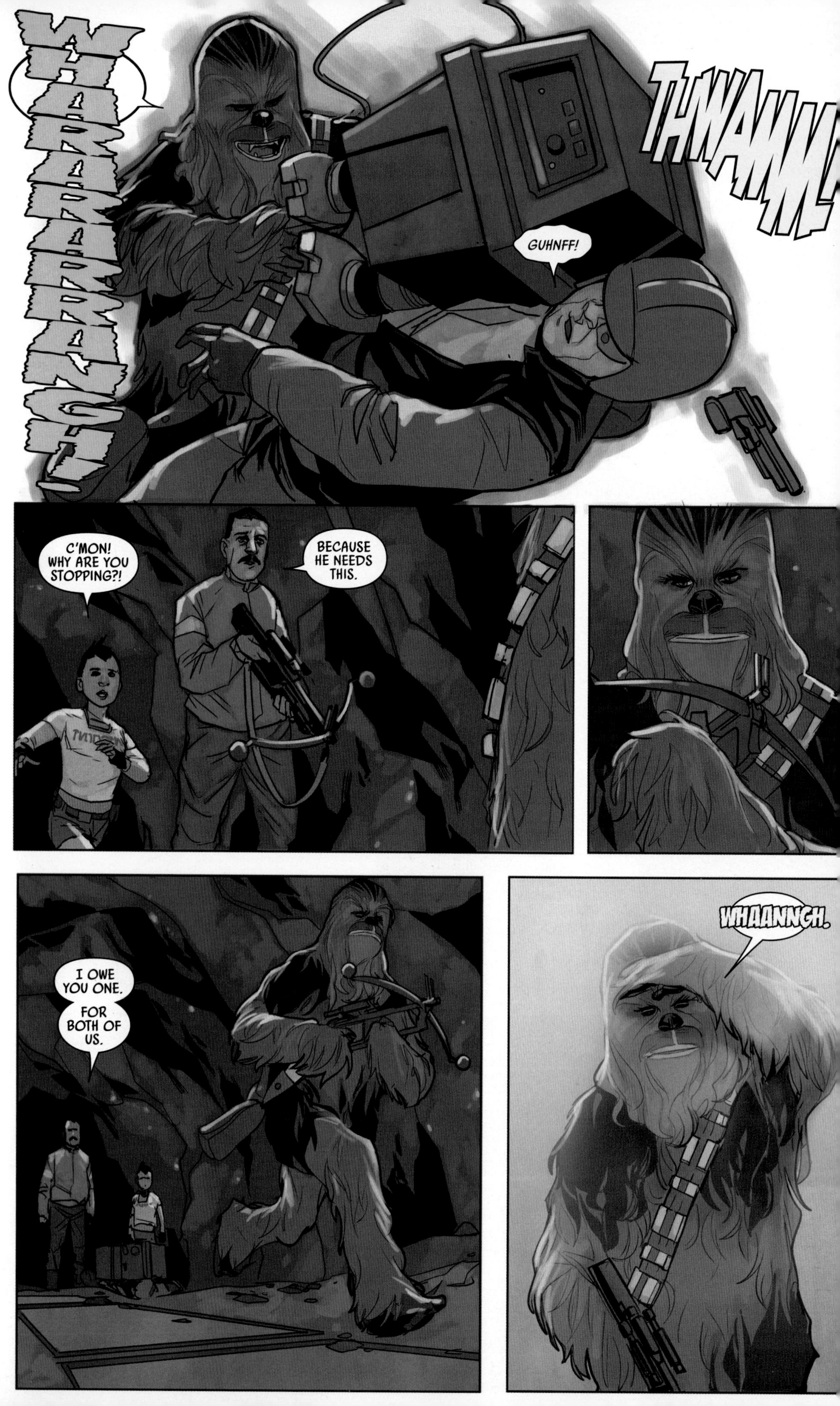
WHARARARRARGH!
THWAMM!
GUHNFF!
C'MON! WHY ARE YOU STOPPING?!
BECAUSE HE NEEDS THIS.
I OWE YOU ONE. FOR BOTH OF US.
WHAANNGH.

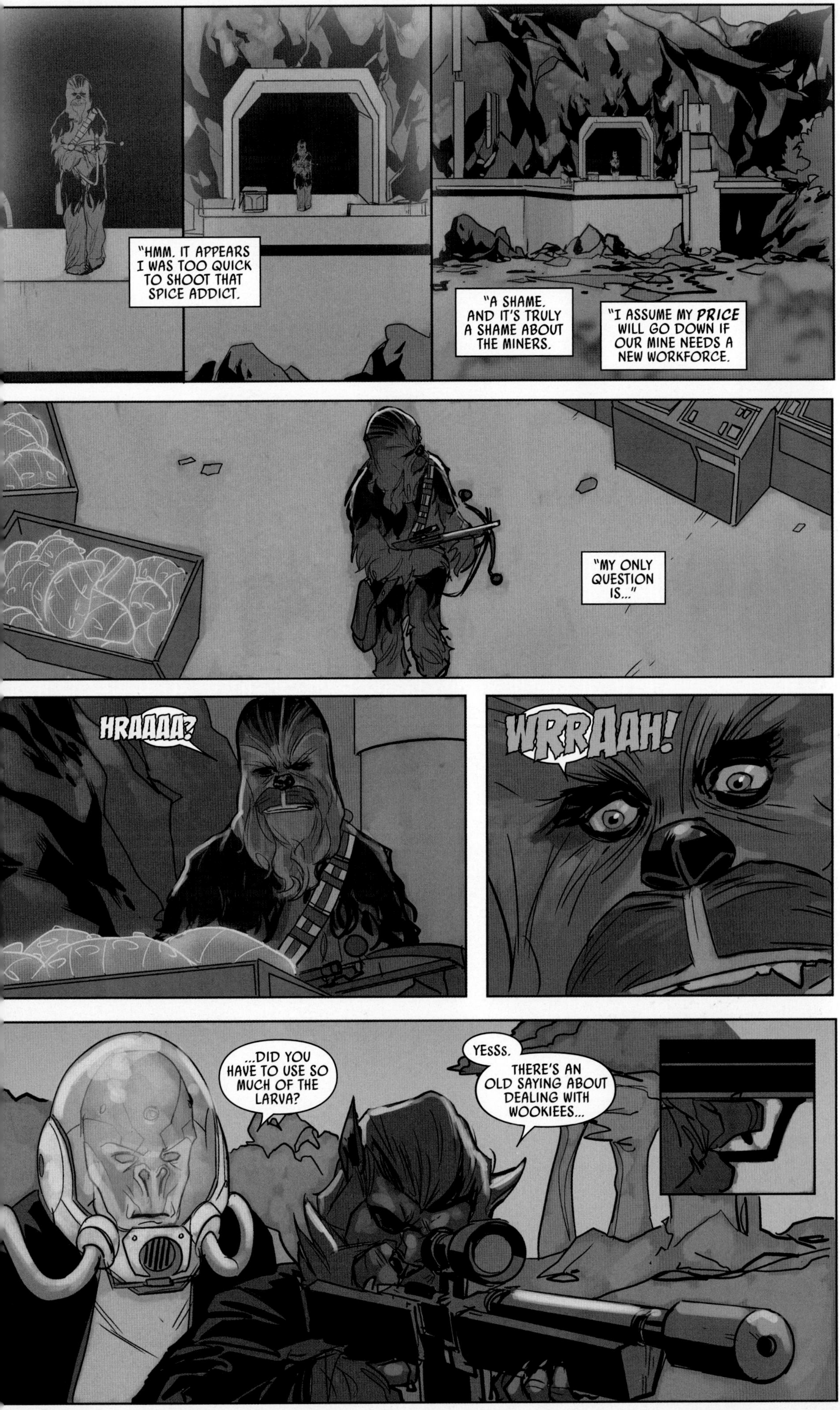
"HMM. IT APPEARS I WAS TOO QUICK TO SHOOT THAT SPICE ADDICT.
"A SHAME. AND IT'S TRULY A SHAME ABOUT THE MINERS.
"I ASSUME MY PRICE WILL GO DOWN IF OUR MINE NEEDS A NEW WORKFORCE.
"MY ONLY QUESTION IS..."
HRAAAA?
WRRAAH!
...DID YOU HAVE TO USE SO MUCH OF THE LARVA?
YESSS.
THERE'S AN OLD SAYING ABOUT DEALING WITH WOOKIEES...

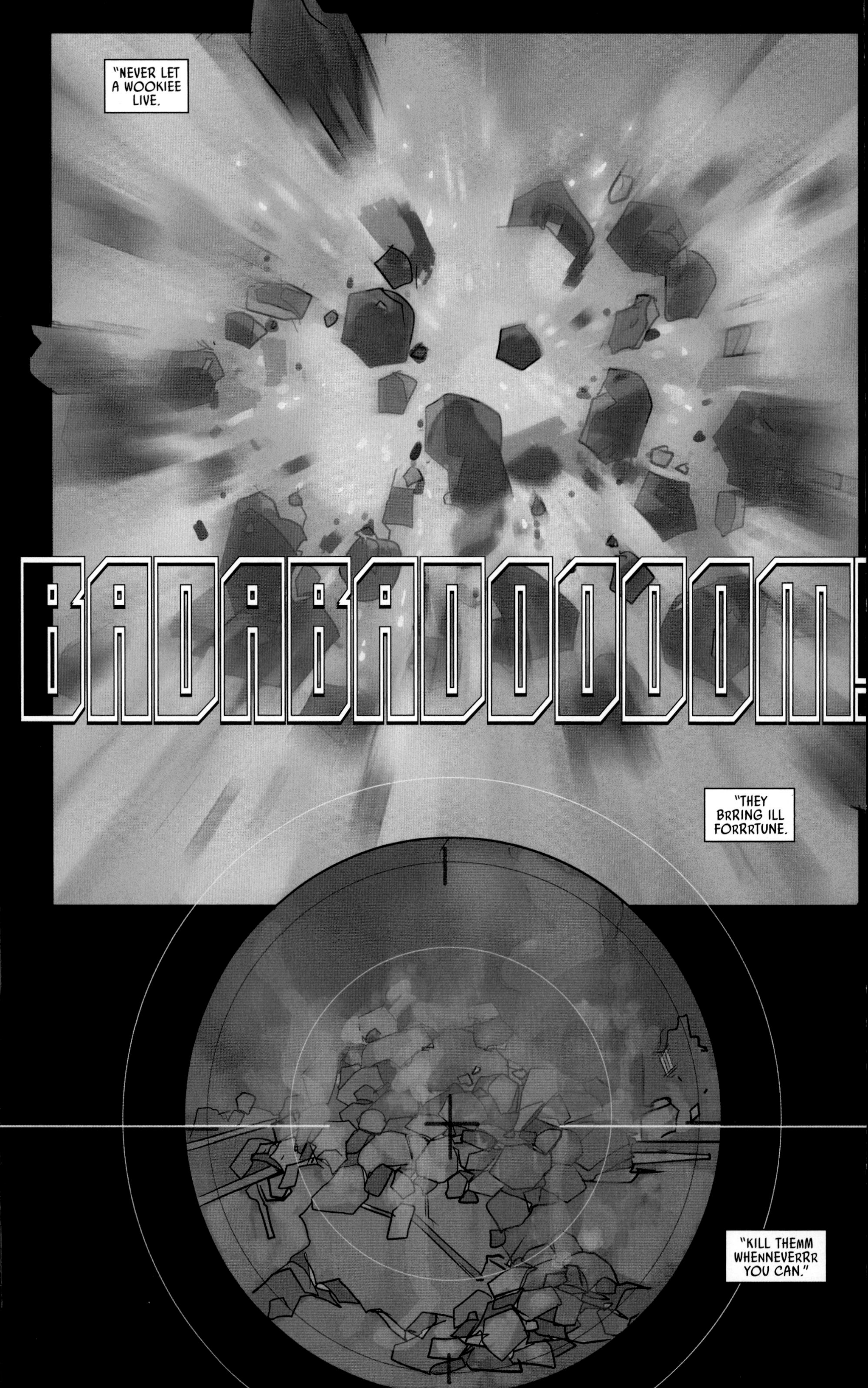
"NEVER LET A WOOKIEE LIVE.
BADABADOOOOOM!
"THEY BRRING ILL FORRRTUNE.
"KILL THEMM WHENNEVERRR YOU CAN."

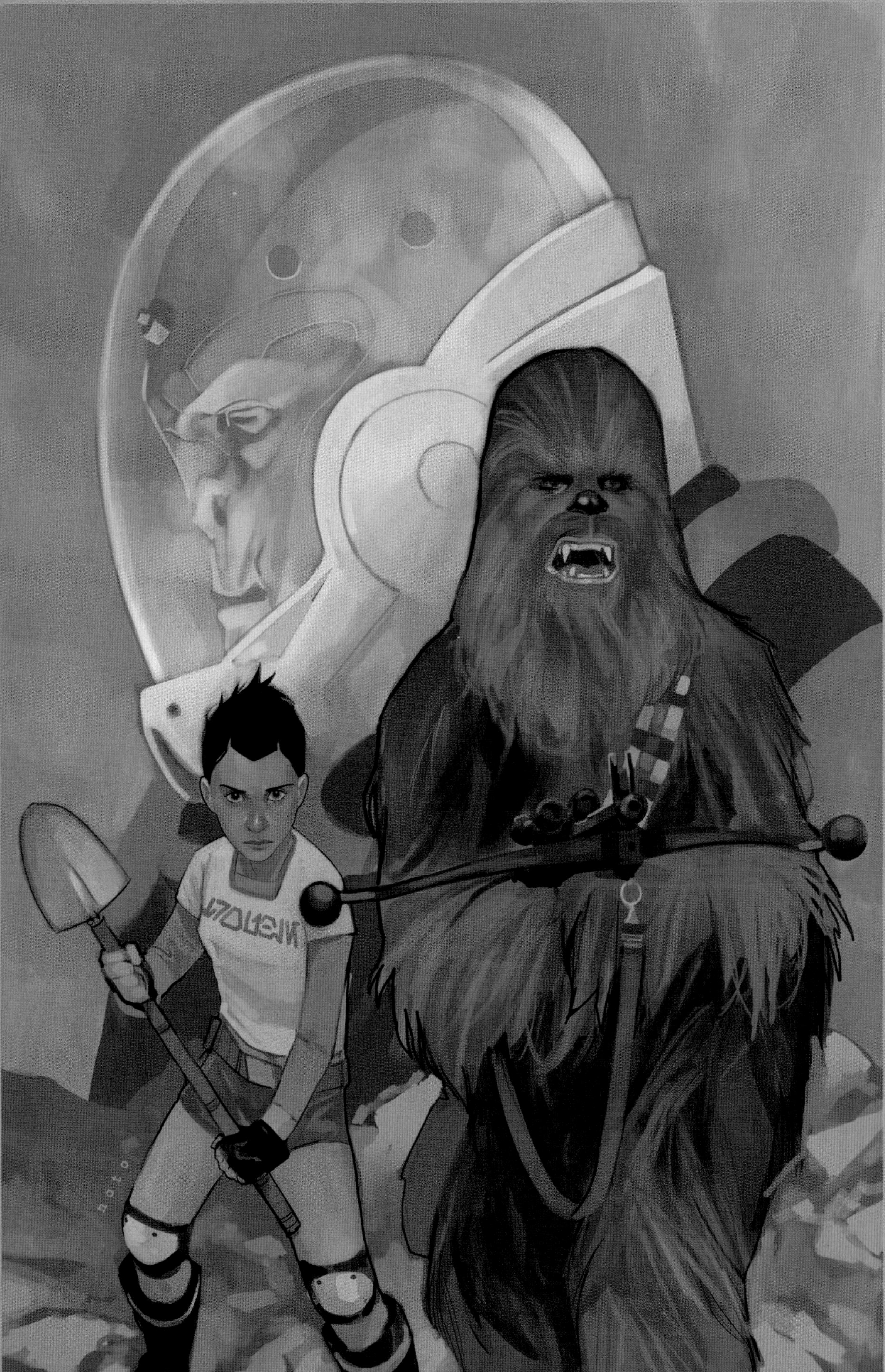

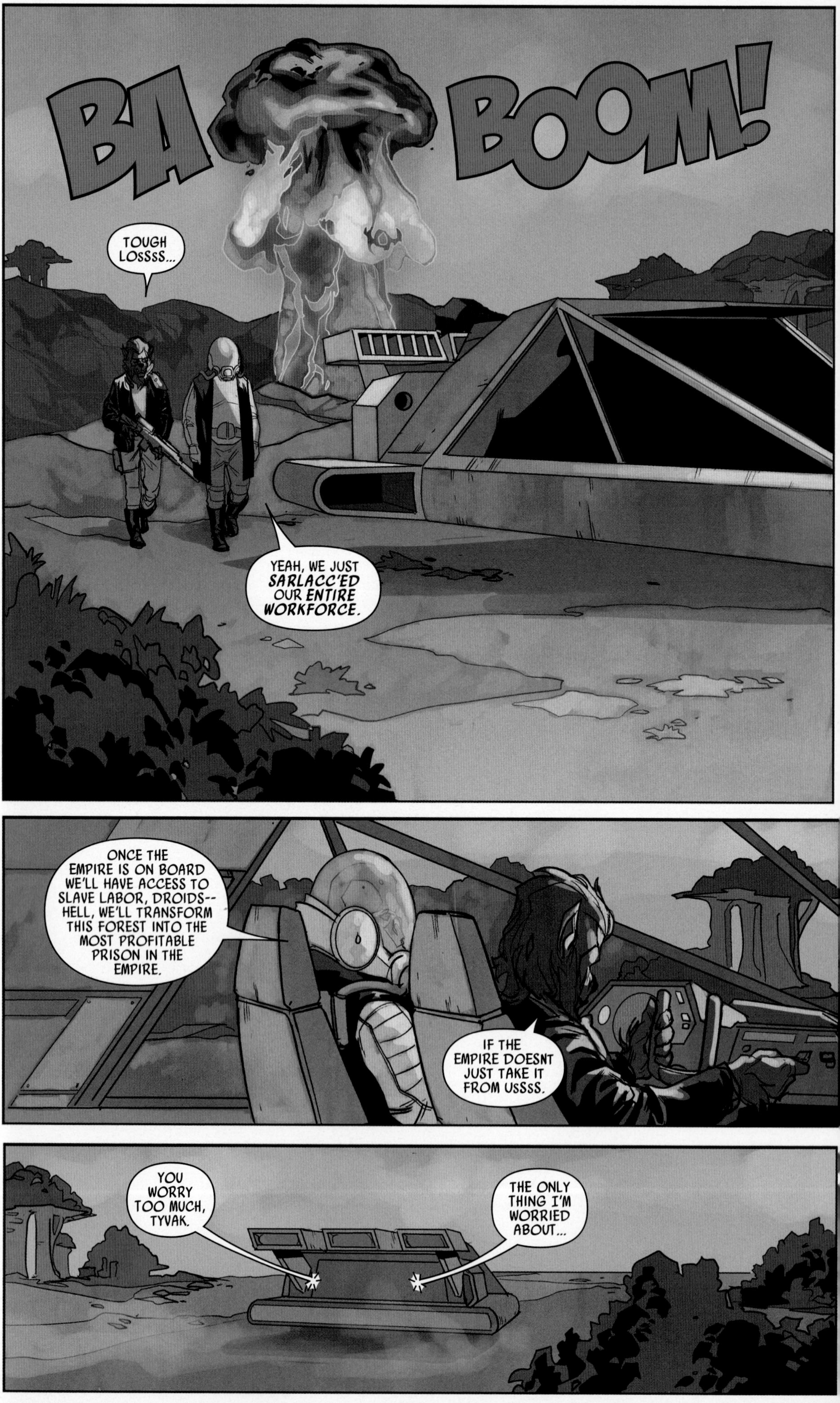
BA BOOM!
TOUGH LOSSSS...
YEAH, WE JUST SARLACC'ED OUR ENTIRE WORKFORCE.
ONCE THE EMPIRE IS ON BOARD WE'LL HAVE ACCESS TO SLAVE LABOR, DROIDS-- HELL, WE'LL TRANSFORM THIS FOREST INTO THE MOST PROFITABLE PRISON IN THE EMPIRE.
IF THE EMPIRE DOESNT JUST TAKE IT FROM USSSS.
YOU WORRY TOO MUCH, TYVAK.
THE ONLY THING I'M WORRIED ABOUT...

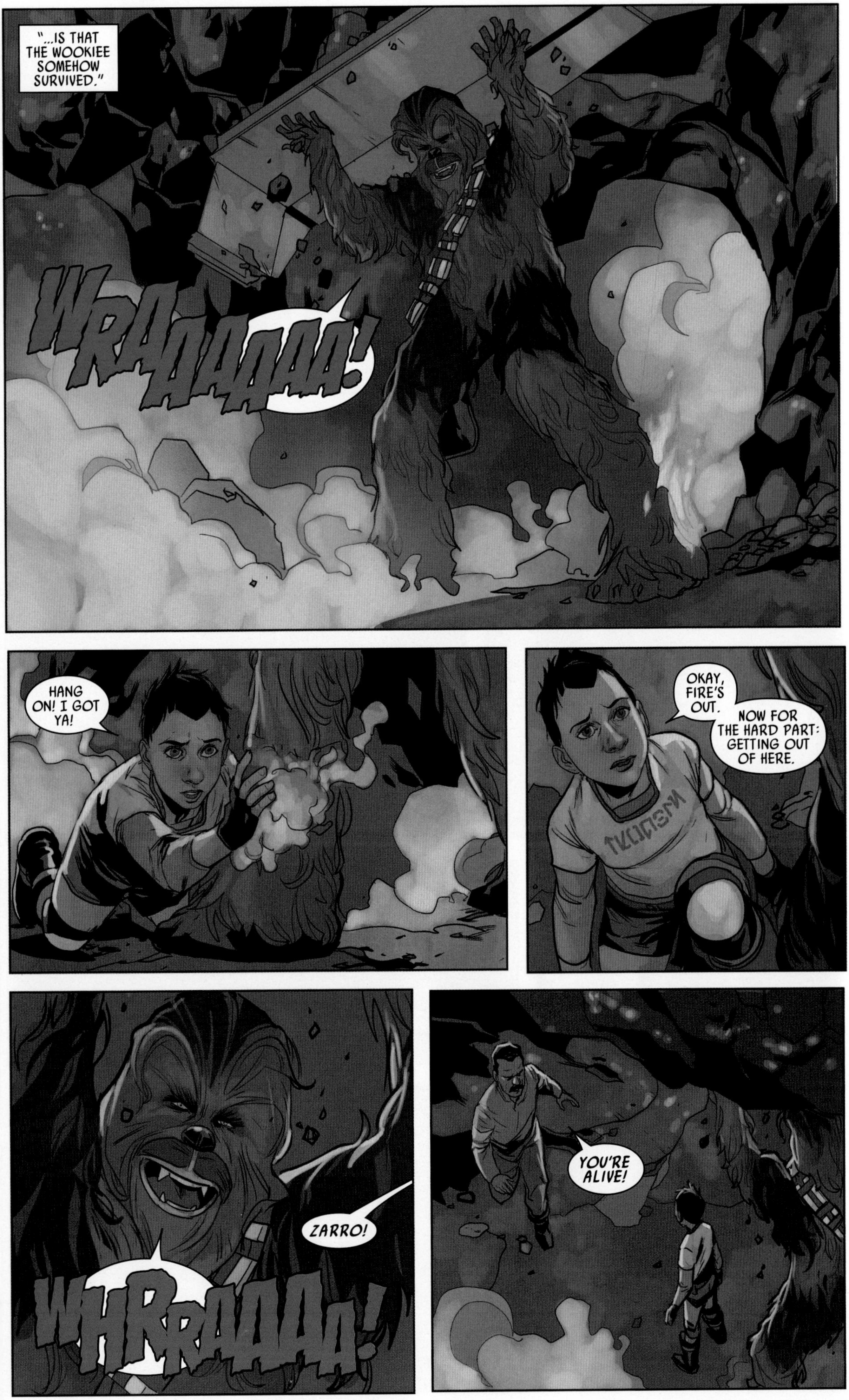
"...IS THAT THE WOOKIEE SOMEHOW SURVIVED."
WRAAAAAAA!
HANG ON! I GOT YA!
OKAY, FIRE'S OUT.
NOW FOR THE HARD PART: GETTING OUT OF HERE.
ZARRO!
WHRRAAAAA!
YOU'RE ALIVE!

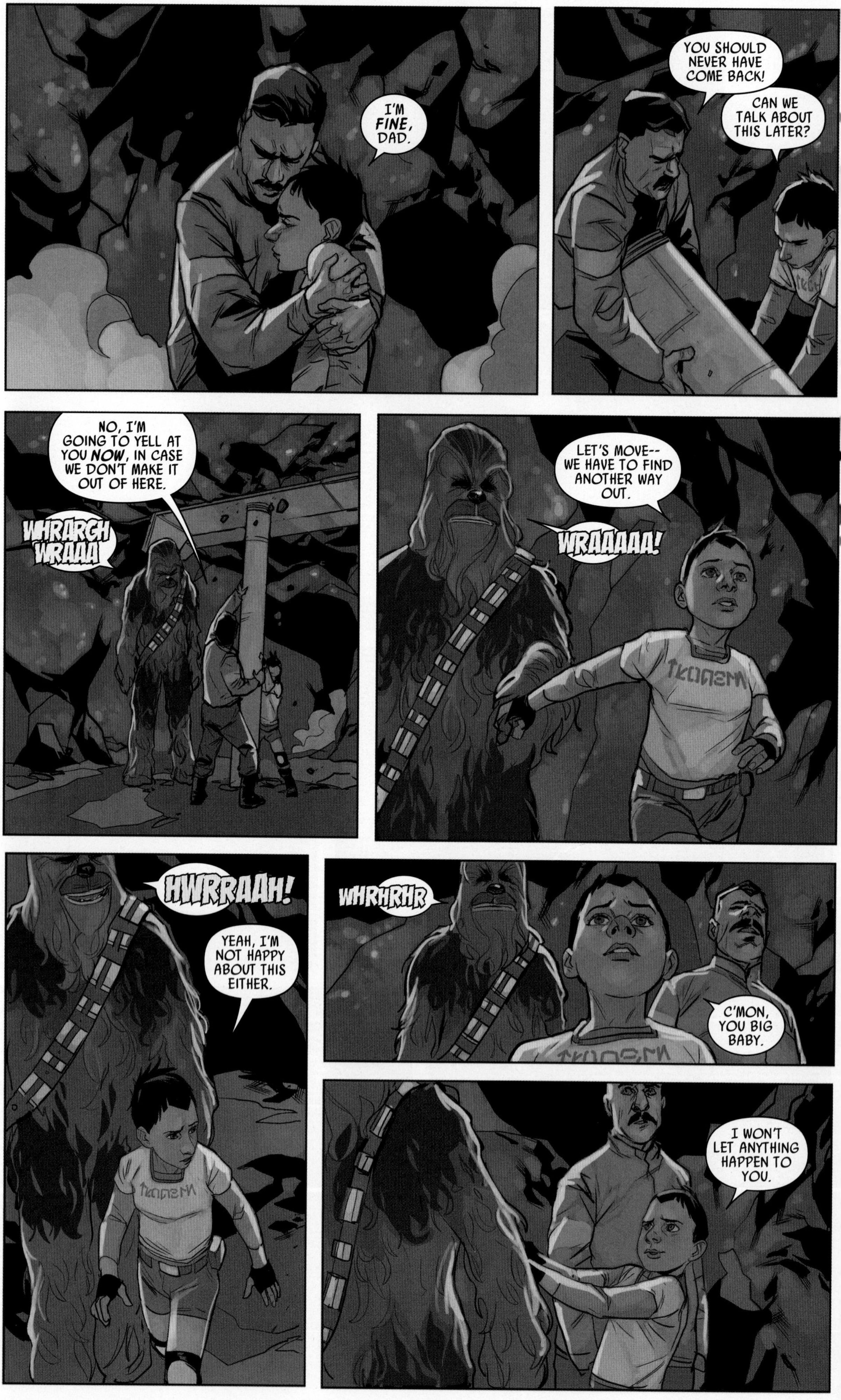
I'M FINE, DAD.
YOU SHOULD NEVER HAVE COME BACK!
CAN WE TALK ABOUT THIS LATER?
NO, I'M GOING TO YELL AT YOU NOW, IN CASE WE DON'T MAKE IT OUT OF HERE.
WHRARGH WRAAA
LET'S MOVE-- WE HAVE TO FIND ANOTHER WAY OUT.
WRAAAAA!
HWRRAAH!
YEAH, I'M NOT HAPPY ABOUT THIS EITHER.
WHRHRHR
C'MON, YOU BIG BABY.
I WON'T LET ANYTHING HAPPEN TO YOU.

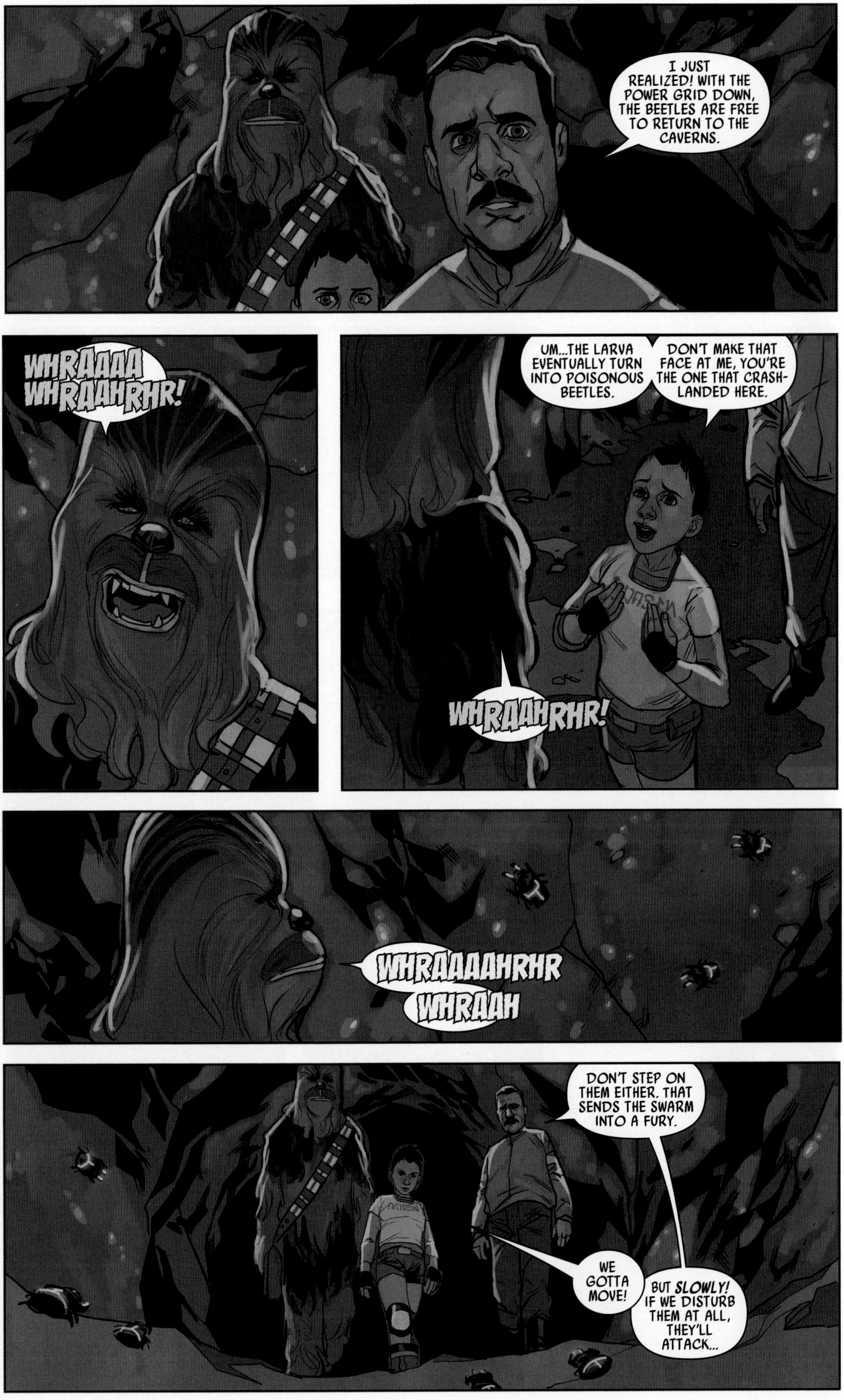

I JUST REALIZED! WITH THE POWER GRID DOWN, THE BEETLES ARE FREE TO RETURN TO THE CAVERNS.
WHRAAAA WHRAAHRHR!
UM...THE LARVA EVENTUALLY TURN INTO POISONOUS BEETLES.
DON'T MAKE THAT FACE AT ME, YOU'RE THE ONE THAT CRASH-LANDED HERE.
WHRAAHRHR!
WHRAAAAHRHR
WHRAAH
DON'T STEP ON THEM EITHER. THAT SENDS THE SWARM INTO A FURY.
WE GOTTA MOVE!
BUT *SLOWLY!* IF WE DISTURB THEM AT ALL, THEY'LL ATTACK...

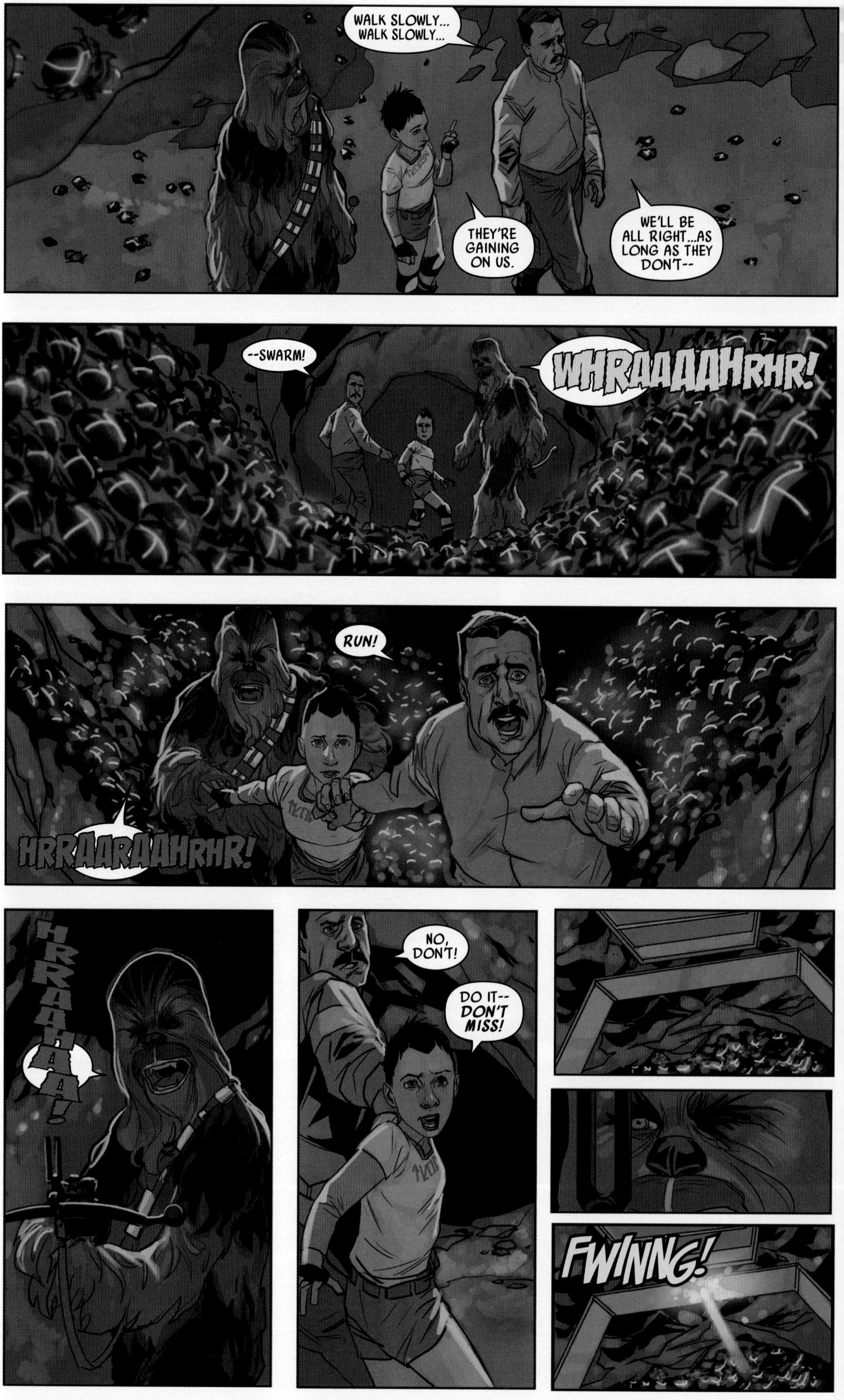

WALK SLOWLY... WALK SLOWLY...
THEY'RE GAINING ON US.
WE'LL BE ALL RIGHT...AS LONG AS THEY DON'T--
--SWARM!
WHRAAAAHRHR!
RUN!
HRRAARAAHRHR!
HRRAAHAA!
NO, DON'T!
DO IT-- DON'T MISS!
FWINNG!

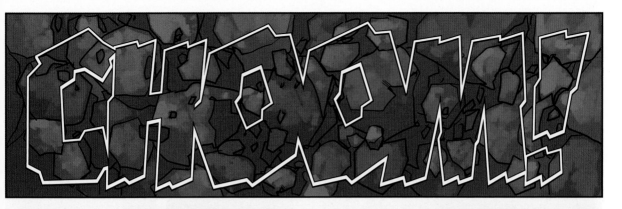

CHROOM!

GREAT SHOT!

THAT WAS OUR ONLY WAY OUT!

NOT ANYMORE IT'S NOT.

HHRAAAAAGH!

WHA' HAPPENED?

THE LAST THING I REMEMBER IS A GIANT, ANGRY--

...WOOKIEE?

WHOMP!

OOF!

IS THAT WHAT YOU ARE? A "WOOKIEE"?

LET'S CATCH OUR BREATH...

WHRHRAAAAAGH!

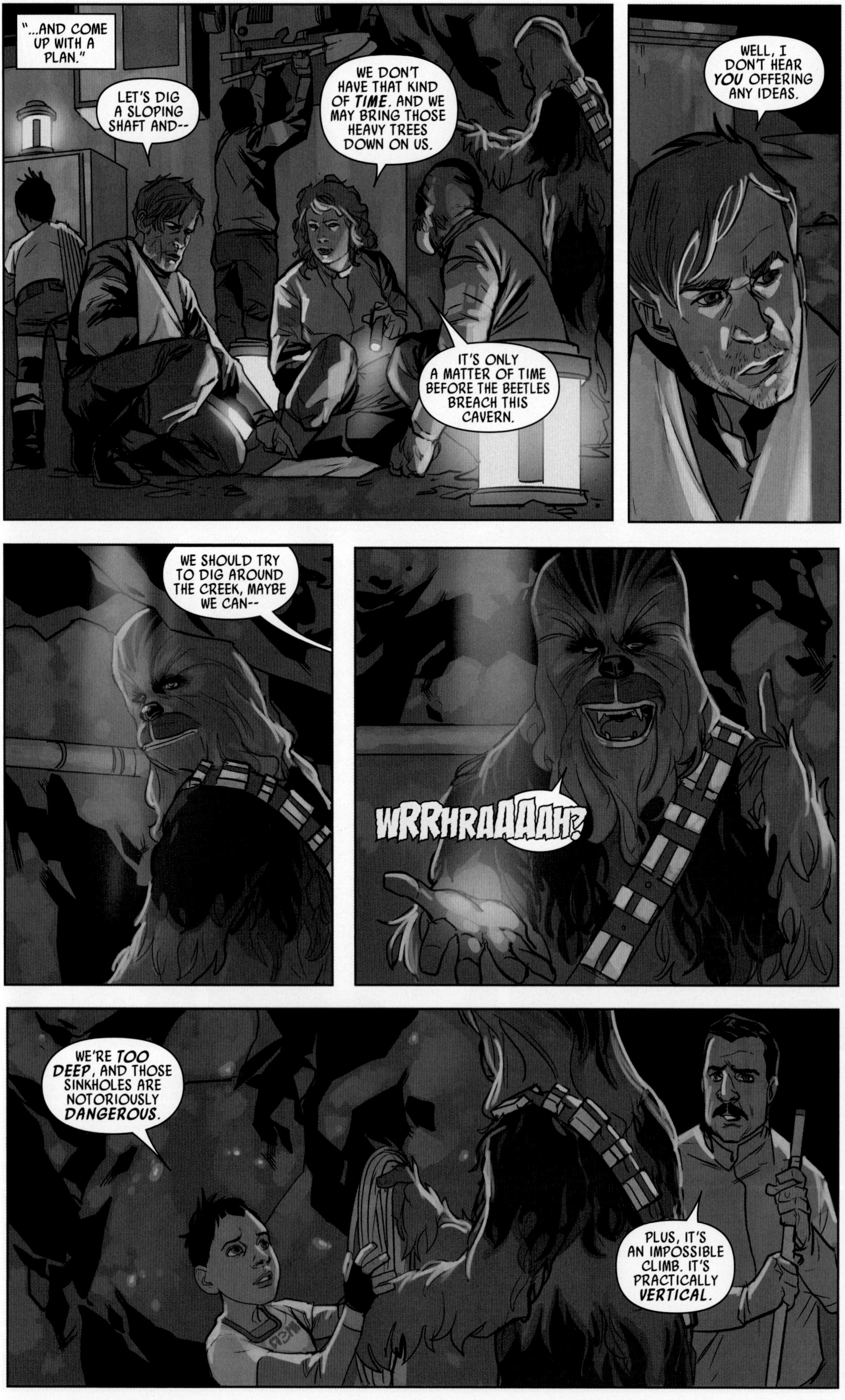

"...AND COME UP WITH A PLAN."
LET'S DIG A SLOPING SHAFT AND--
WE DON'T HAVE THAT KIND OF *TIME*. AND WE MAY BRING THOSE HEAVY TREES DOWN ON US.
IT'S ONLY A MATTER OF TIME BEFORE THE BEETLES BREACH THIS CAVERN.
WELL, I DON'T HEAR *YOU* OFFERING ANY IDEAS.
WE SHOULD TRY TO DIG AROUND THE CREEK, MAYBE WE CAN--
WRRHRAAAAH?
WE'RE *TOO DEEP*, AND THOSE SINKHOLES ARE NOTORIOUSLY *DANGEROUS*.
PLUS, IT'S AN IMPOSSIBLE CLIMB. IT'S PRACTICALLY *VERTICAL*.

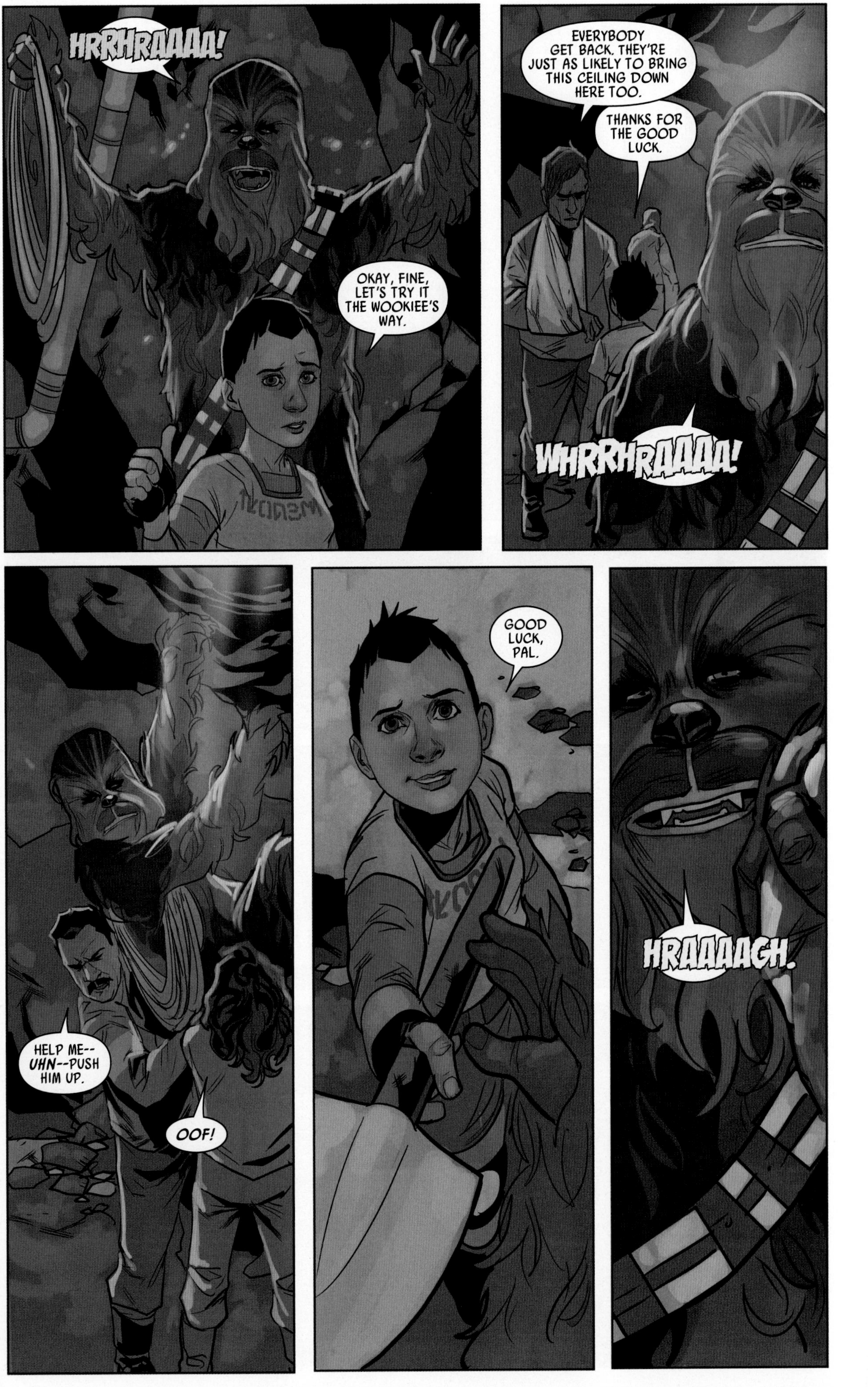
HRRHRAAAA!
OKAY, FINE, LET'S TRY IT THE WOOKIEE'S WAY.
EVERYBODY GET BACK. THEY'RE JUST AS LIKELY TO BRING THIS CEILING DOWN HERE TOO.
THANKS FOR THE GOOD LUCK.
WHRRHRAAAA!
HELP ME-- *UHN*--PUSH HIM UP.
OOF!
GOOD LUCK, PAL.
HRAAAAGH.

WHRAAAAGH!

HRA

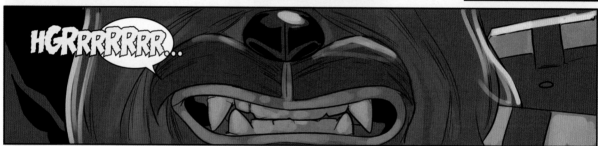

HGRRRRRRR...

WHRAAAARRR!

SKRAKK!

HRAAAGRAAA!

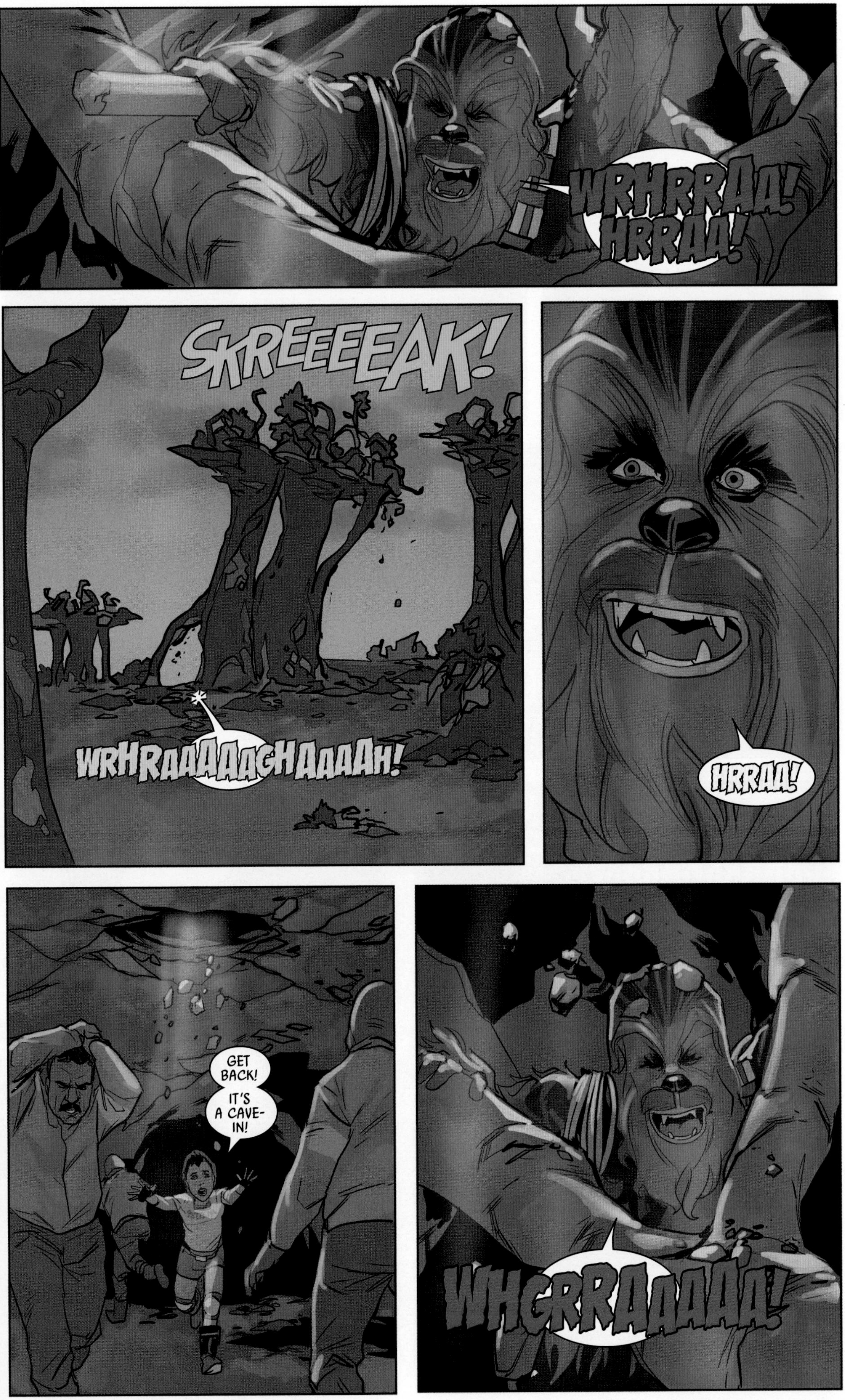

WRHRRAA! HRRAA!
SKREEEEEAK!
WRHRAAAAAGHAAAAH!
HRRAA!
GET BACK! IT'S A CAVE-IN!
WHGRRAAAAA!

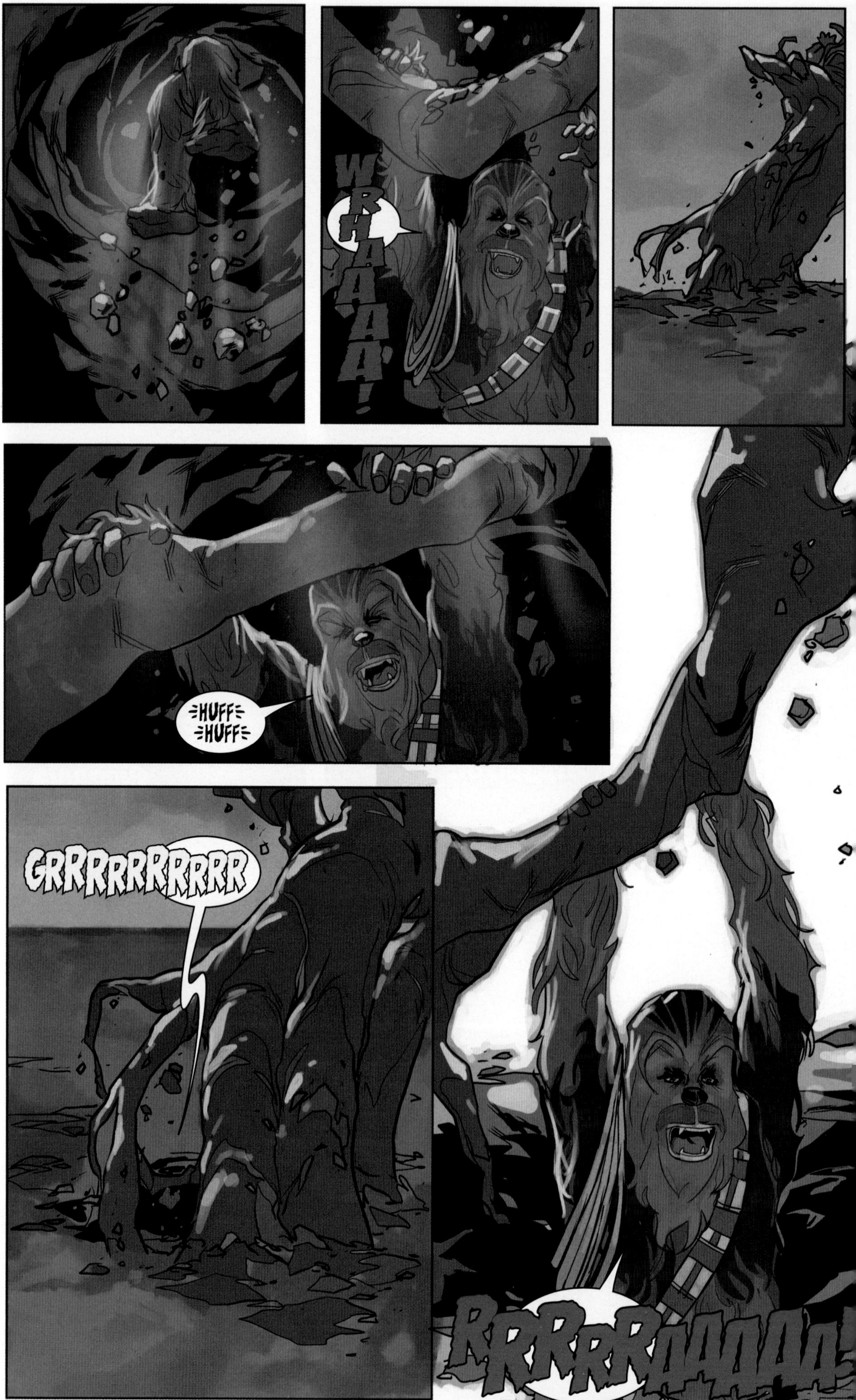
WRHAAAAA!
HUFF HUFF
GRRRRRRRRRR
RRRRRAAAAA

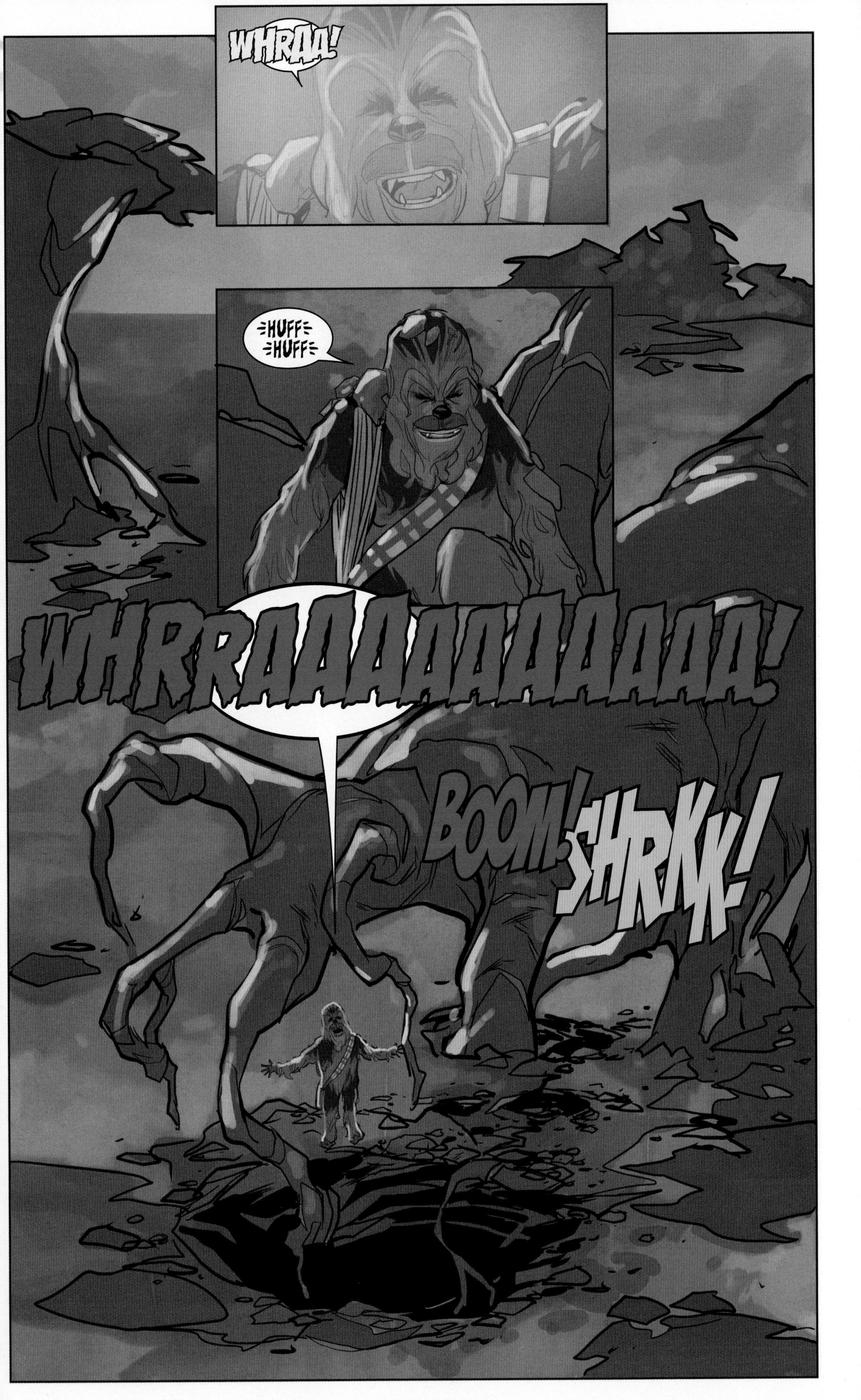
WHRAA!
HUFF HUFF
WHRRAAAAAAAAAAA!
BOOM!
SHRKK!

WHRAA RAAAH WRAHIAAAHG

YOU OKAY? ARE YOU HURT?

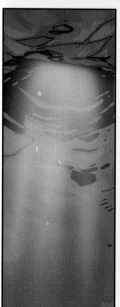

WOOKIEE?

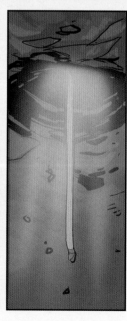

YES!

HE DID IT!

WE'RE SAVED!

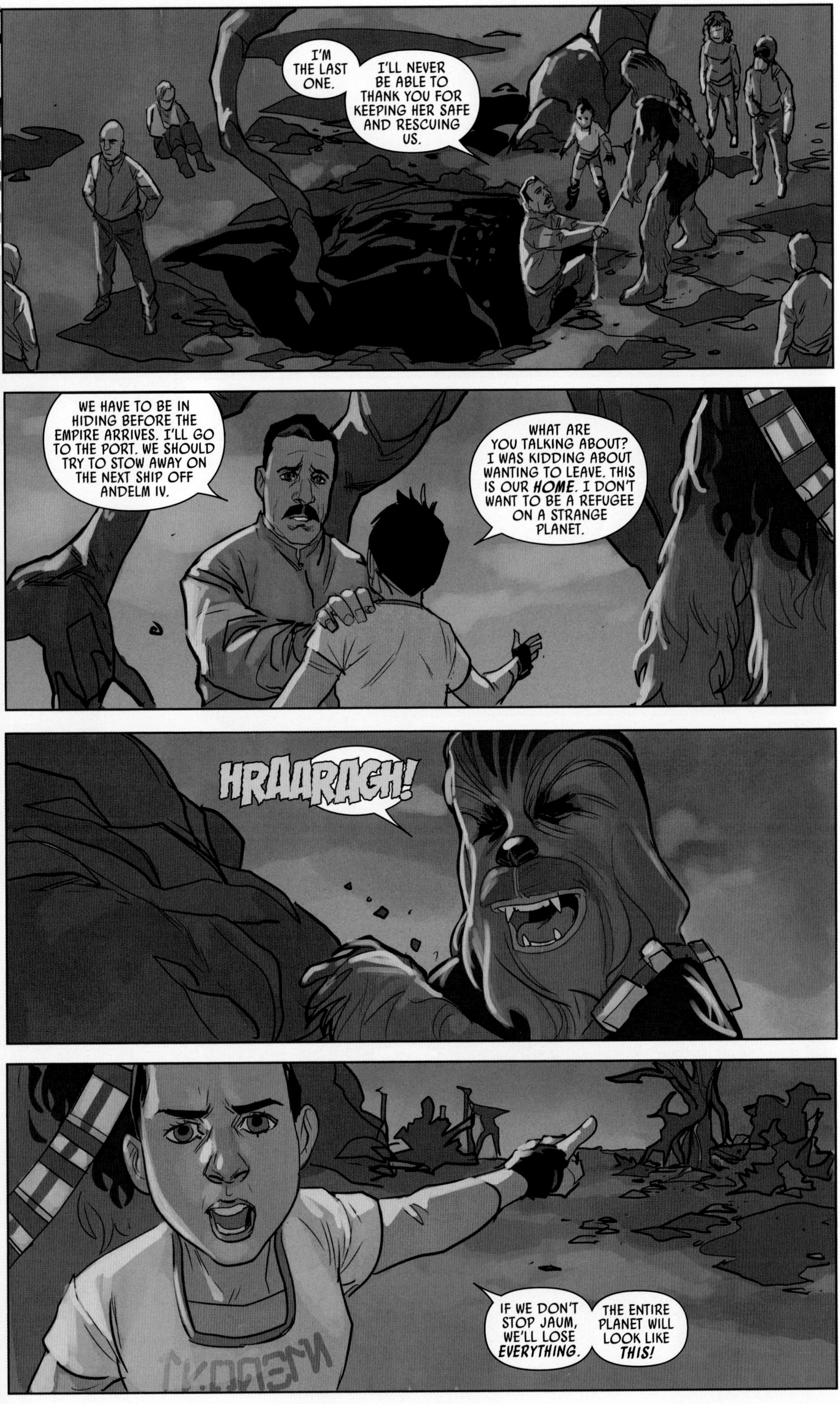
I'M THE LAST ONE.
I'LL NEVER BE ABLE TO THANK YOU FOR KEEPING HER SAFE AND RESCUING US.
WE HAVE TO BE IN HIDING BEFORE THE EMPIRE ARRIVES. I'LL GO TO THE PORT. WE SHOULD TRY TO STOW AWAY ON THE NEXT SHIP OFF ANDELM IV.
WHAT ARE YOU TALKING ABOUT? I WAS KIDDING ABOUT WANTING TO LEAVE. THIS IS OUR HOME. I DON'T WANT TO BE A REFUGEE ON A STRANGE PLANET.
HRAARAGH!
IF WE DON'T STOP JAUM, WE'LL LOSE EVERYTHING.
THE ENTIRE PLANET WILL LOOK LIKE THIS!

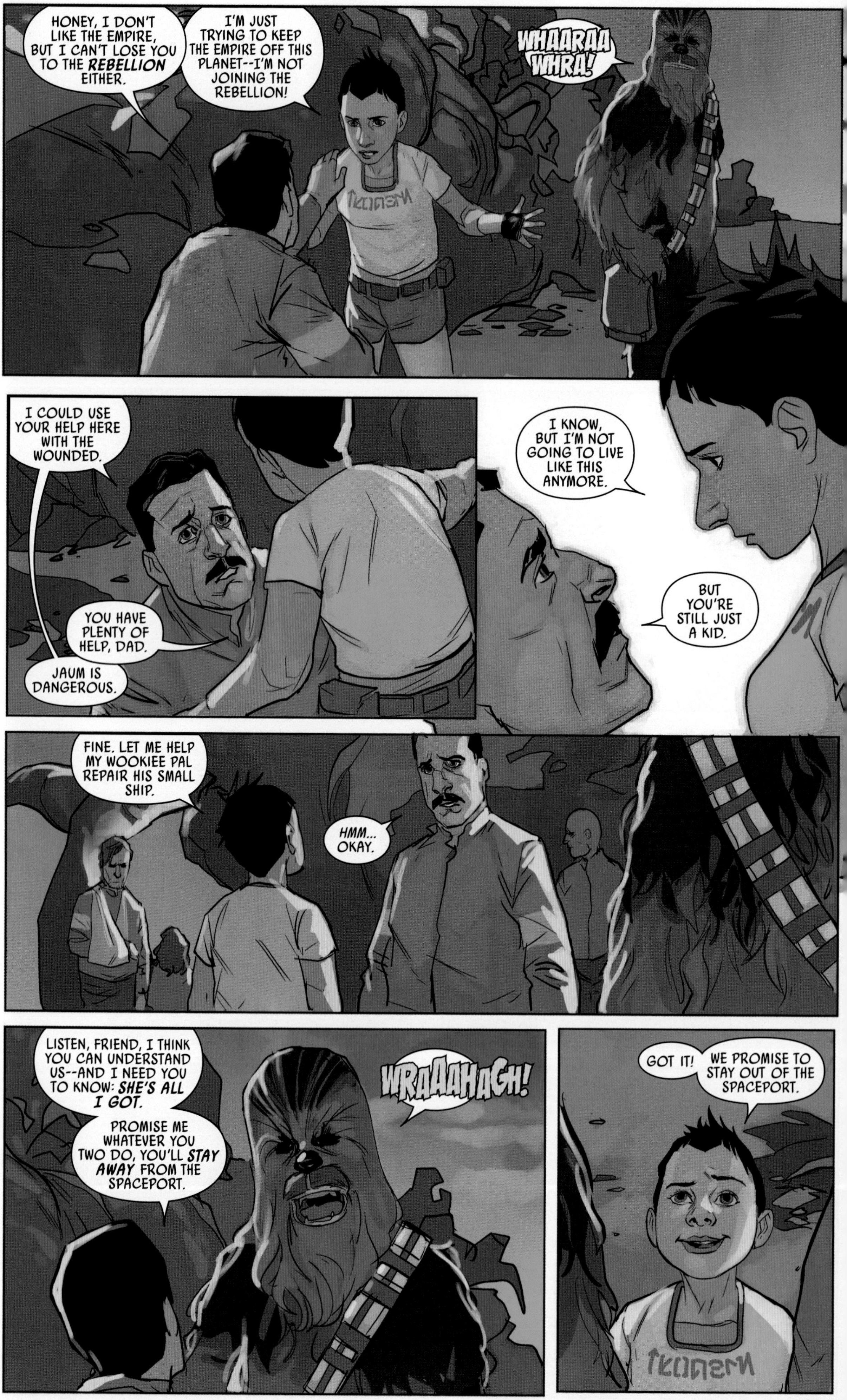
HONEY, I DON'T LIKE THE EMPIRE, BUT I CAN'T LOSE YOU TO THE *REBELLION* EITHER.
I'M JUST TRYING TO KEEP THE EMPIRE OFF THIS PLANET--I'M NOT JOINING THE REBELLION!
WHAARAA WHRA!
I COULD USE YOUR HELP HERE WITH THE WOUNDED.
YOU HAVE PLENTY OF HELP, DAD.
JAUM IS DANGEROUS.
I KNOW, BUT I'M NOT GOING TO LIVE LIKE THIS ANYMORE.
BUT YOU'RE STILL JUST A KID.
FINE. LET ME HELP MY WOOKIEE PAL REPAIR HIS SMALL SHIP.
HMM... OKAY.
LISTEN, FRIEND, I THINK YOU CAN UNDERSTAND US--AND I NEED YOU TO KNOW: *SHE'S ALL I GOT.*
PROMISE ME WHATEVER YOU TWO DO, YOU'LL *STAY AWAY* FROM THE SPACEPORT.
WRAAAHAGH!
GOT IT!
WE PROMISE TO STAY OUT OF THE SPACEPORT.

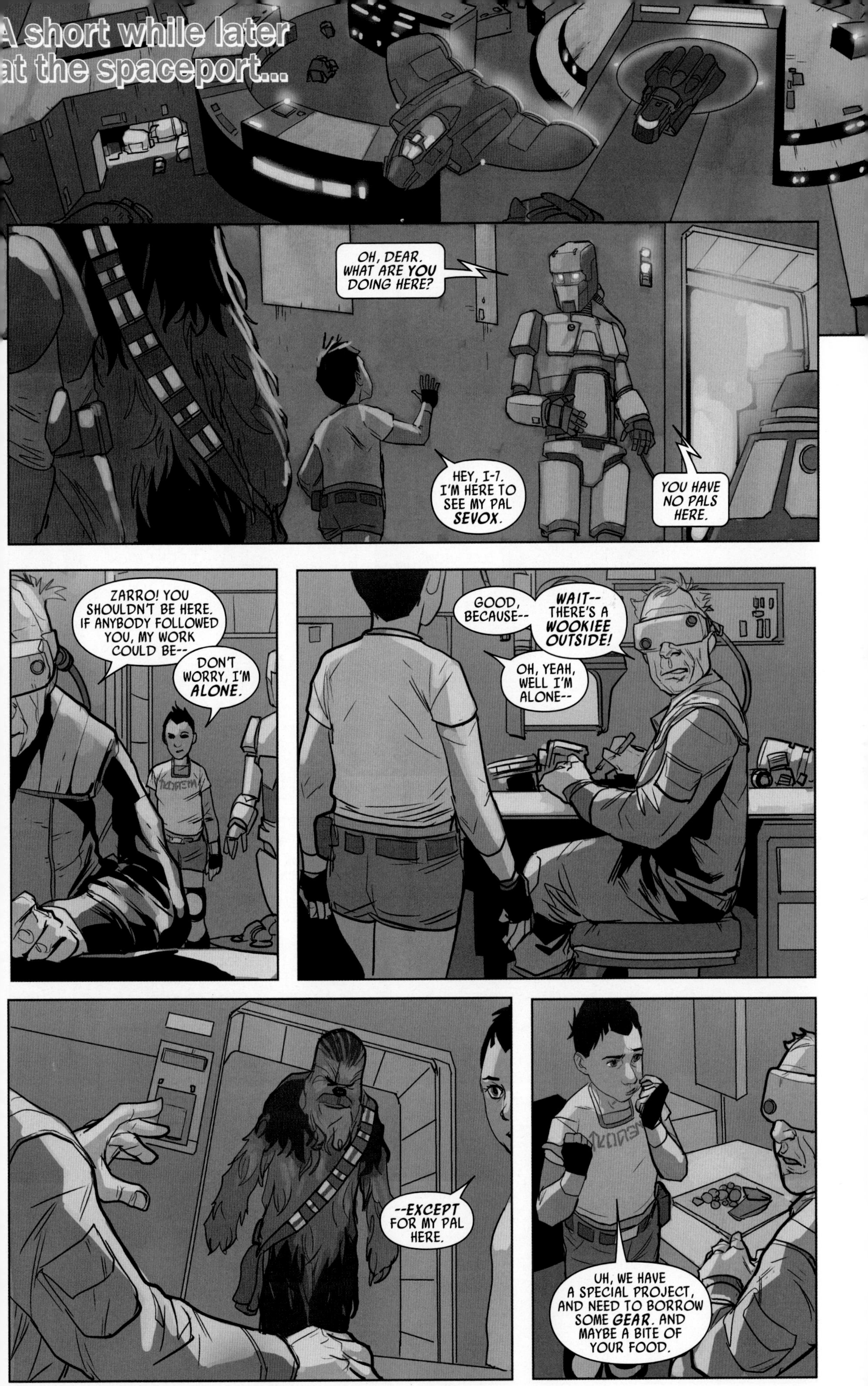
A short while later at the spaceport...
OH, DEAR. WHAT ARE YOU DOING HERE?
HEY, I-7. I'M HERE TO SEE MY PAL SEVOX.
YOU HAVE NO PALS HERE.
ZARRO! YOU SHOULDN'T BE HERE. IF ANYBODY FOLLOWED YOU, MY WORK COULD BE--
DON'T WORRY, I'M ALONE.
GOOD, BECAUSE--
WAIT-- THERE'S A WOOKIEE OUTSIDE!
OH, YEAH, WELL I'M ALONE--
--EXCEPT FOR MY PAL HERE.
UH, WE HAVE A SPECIAL PROJECT, AND NEED TO BORROW SOME GEAR. AND MAYBE A BITE OF YOUR FOOD.

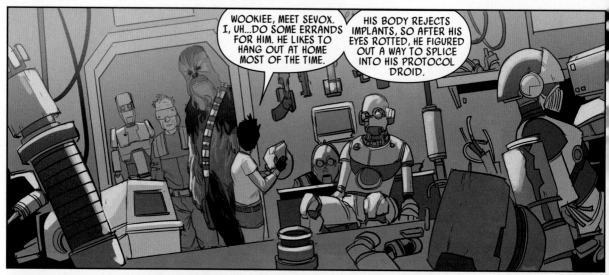

WOOKIEE, MEET SEVOX. I, UH...DO SOME ERRANDS FOR HIM. HE LIKES TO HANG OUT AT HOME MOST OF THE TIME.

HIS BODY REJECTS IMPLANTS, SO AFTER HIS EYES ROTTED, HE FIGURED OUT A WAY TO SPLICE INTO HIS PROTOCOL DROID.

WHRAAAARAGH!

HOW COULD YOU BRING A STRANGER HERE? WHO ELSE KNOWS ABOUT MY BUNKER?

I'M RUINED!

SEVOX WILL CALM DOWN IN A MINUTE, WOOKIEE. I HOPE HE HAS WHAT YOU WERE ROARING ABOUT, OTHERWISE I DON'T KNOW WHERE TO TAKE YOU.

GHRAAARACH! HAAGH!

SEVOX'S PREPARED FOR THE EMPIRE COMING HERE. OR THE REBELLION. WHOEVER IS COMING, HE'S PREPARED.

THIS IS A VIOLATION OF TRUST!

HRAARH HRAARGH

I DON'T KNOW WHAT YOU'RE PLANNING, SO THERE'S NO WAY THAT JAUM WILL SEE US COMING!

"LOOKS LIKE WE GOT TROUBLE, JAUM."

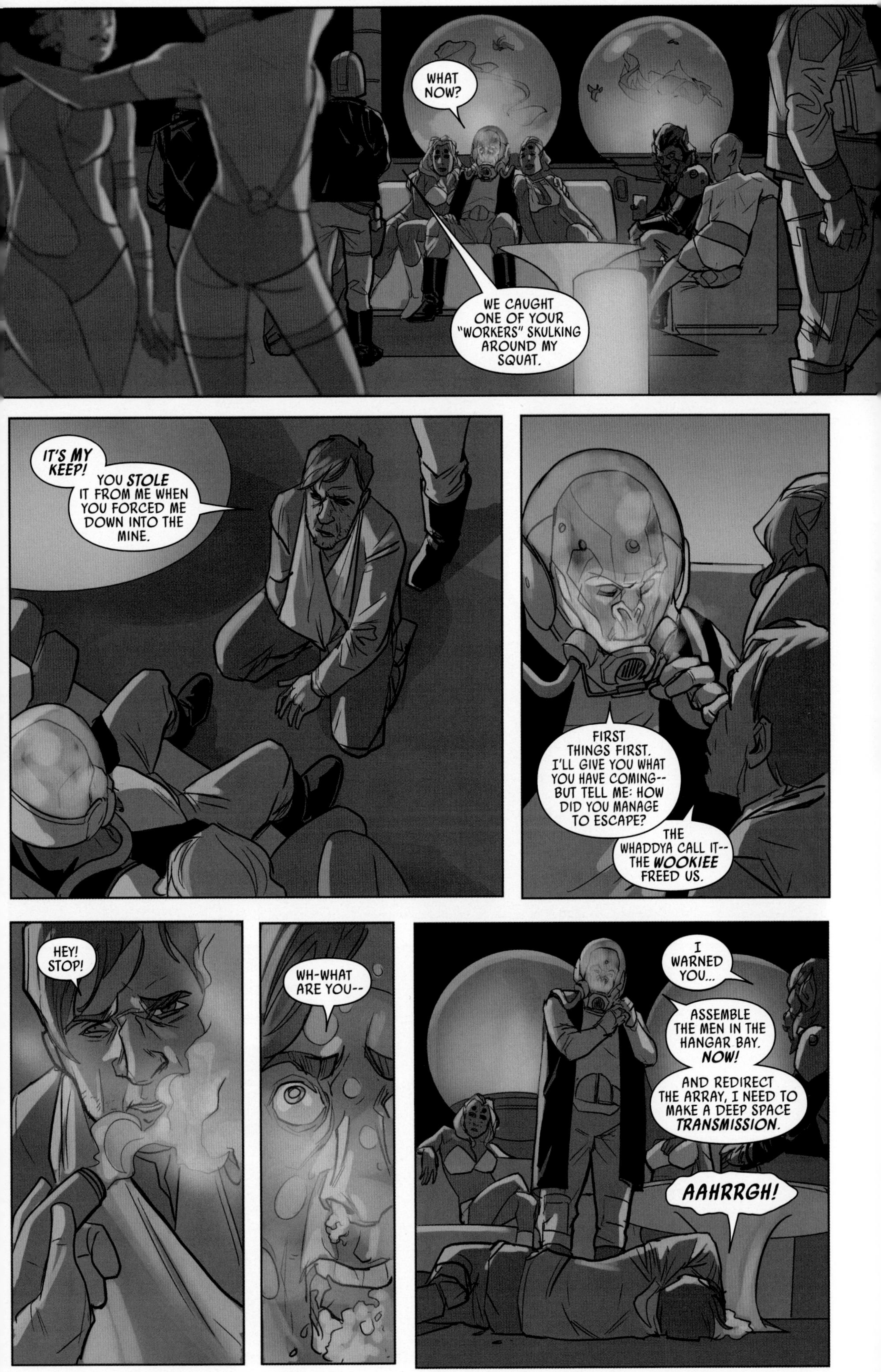
WHAT NOW?
WE CAUGHT ONE OF YOUR "WORKERS" SKULKING AROUND MY SQUAT.
IT'S MY KEEP!
YOU STOLE IT FROM ME WHEN YOU FORCED ME DOWN INTO THE MINE.
FIRST THINGS FIRST. I'LL GIVE YOU WHAT YOU HAVE COMING-- BUT TELL ME: HOW DID YOU MANAGE TO ESCAPE?
THE WHADDYA CALL IT-- THE WOOKIEE FREED US.
HEY! STOP!
WH-WHAT ARE YOU--
I WARNED YOU...
ASSEMBLE THE MEN IN THE HANGAR BAY. NOW!
AND REDIRECT THE ARRAY, I NEED TO MAKE A DEEP SPACE TRANSMISSION.
AAHRRGH!

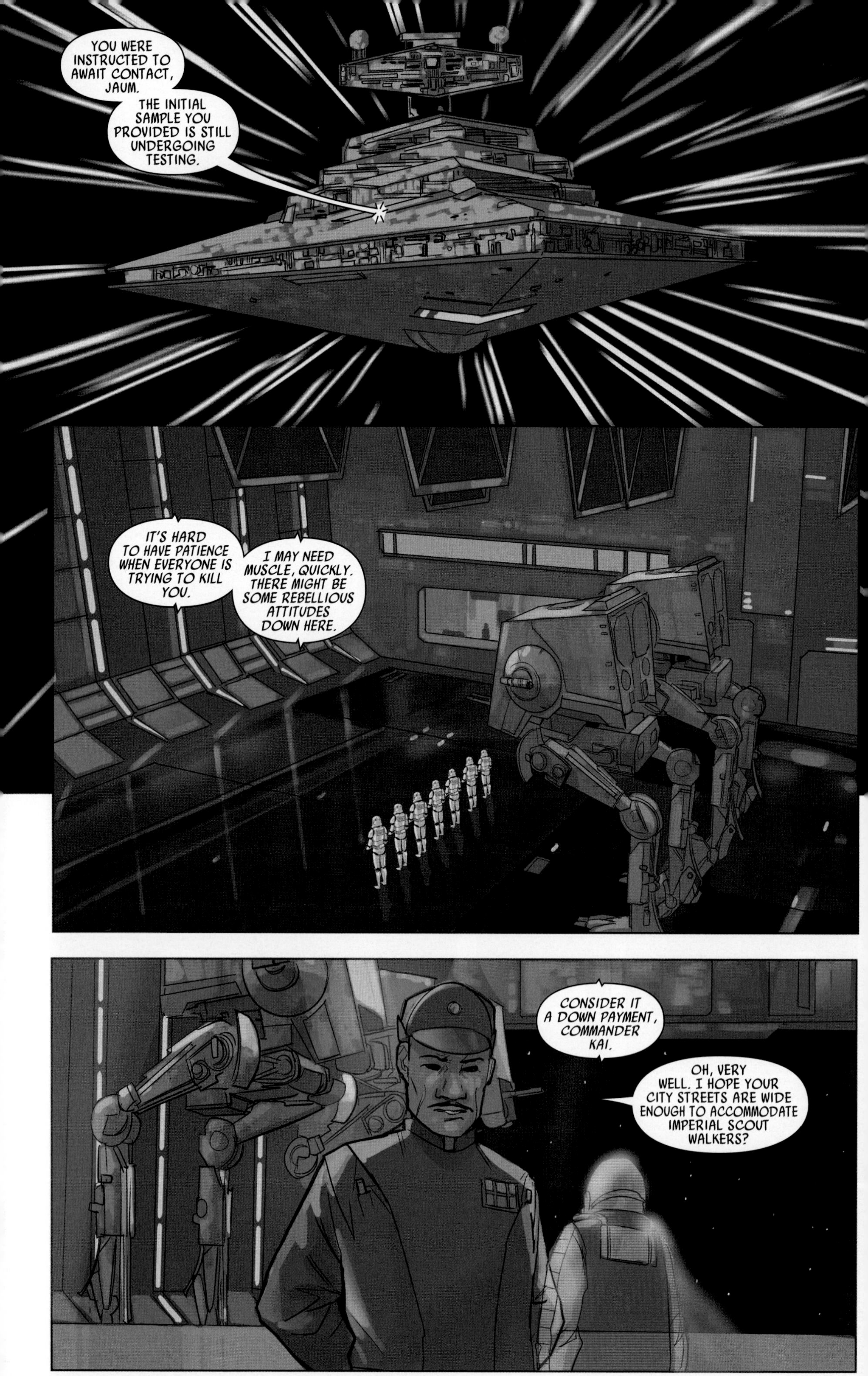
YOU WERE INSTRUCTED TO AWAIT CONTACT, JAUM.
THE INITIAL SAMPLE YOU PROVIDED IS STILL UNDERGOING TESTING.
IT'S HARD TO HAVE PATIENCE WHEN EVERYONE IS TRYING TO KILL YOU.
I MAY NEED MUSCLE, QUICKLY. THERE MIGHT BE SOME REBELLIOUS ATTITUDES DOWN HERE.
CONSIDER IT A DOWN PAYMENT, COMMANDER KAI.
OH, VERY WELL. I HOPE YOUR CITY STREETS ARE WIDE ENOUGH TO ACCOMMODATE IMPERIAL SCOUT WALKERS?

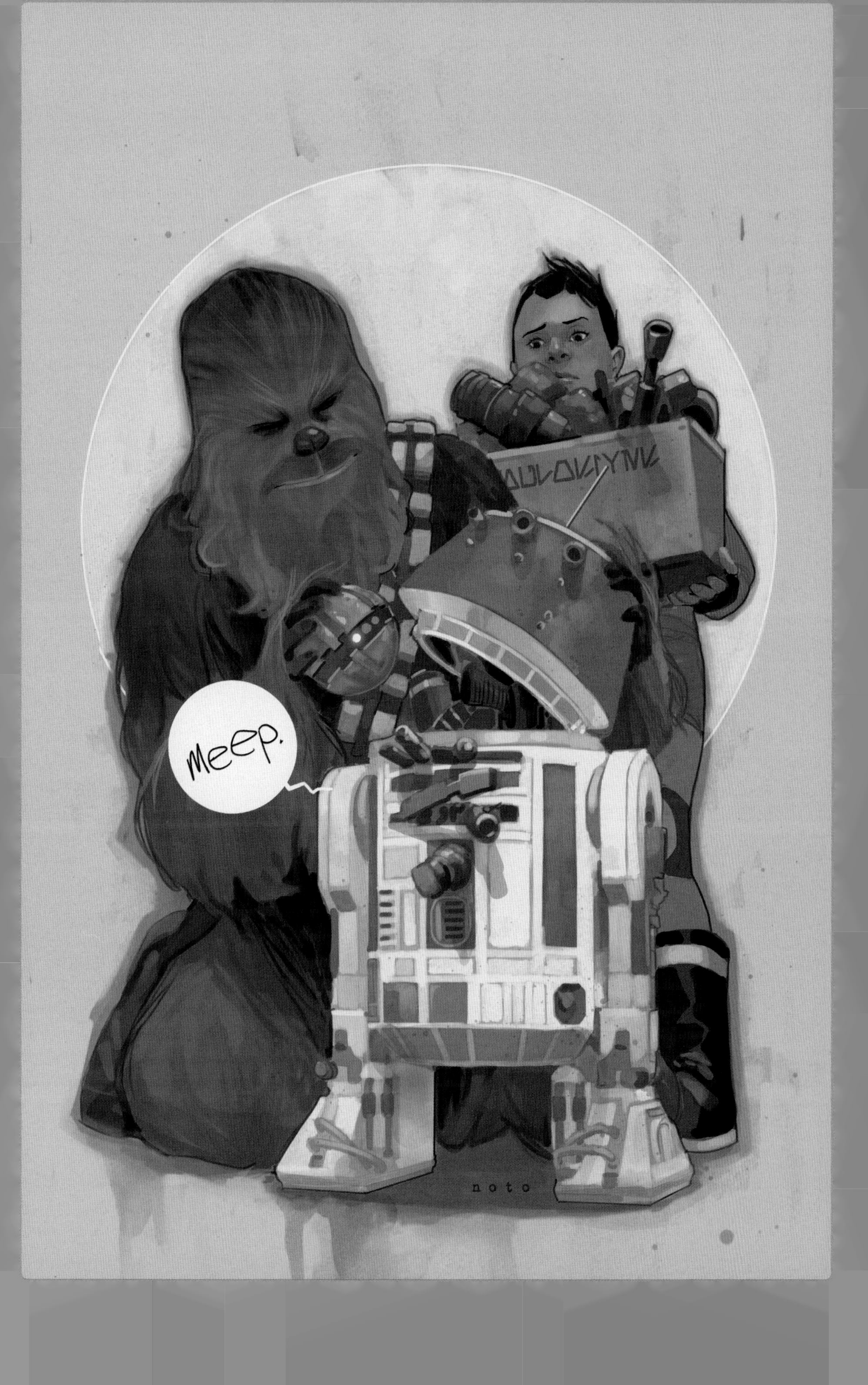
Meep.
noto

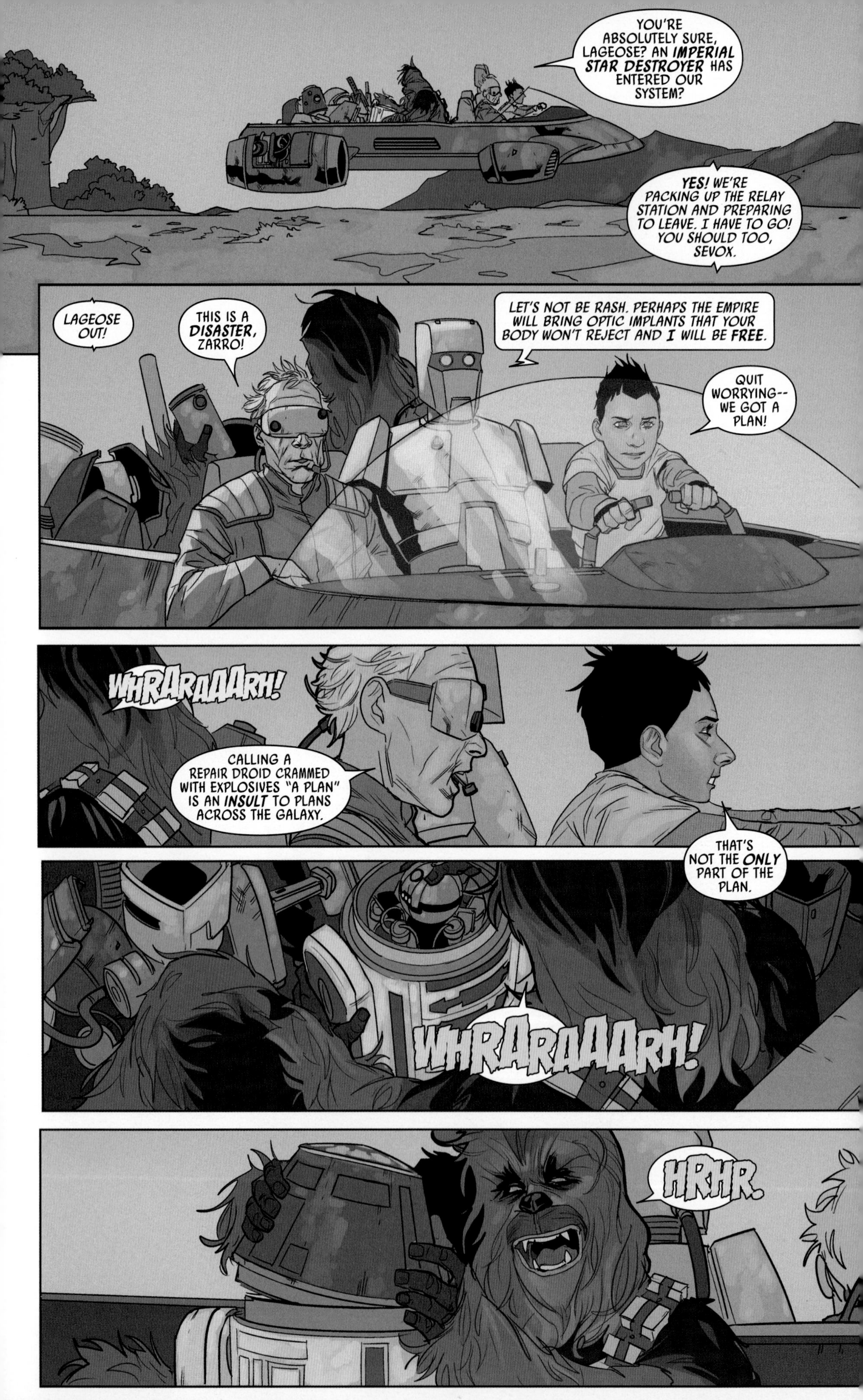
YOU'RE ABSOLUTELY SURE, LAGEOSE? AN IMPERIAL STAR DESTROYER HAS ENTERED OUR SYSTEM?
YES! WE'RE PACKING UP THE RELAY STATION AND PREPARING TO LEAVE. I HAVE TO GO! YOU SHOULD TOO, SEVOX.
LAGEOSE OUT!
THIS IS A DISASTER, ZARRO!
LET'S NOT BE RASH. PERHAPS THE EMPIRE WILL BRING OPTIC IMPLANTS THAT YOUR BODY WON'T REJECT AND I WILL BE FREE.
QUIT WORRYING-- WE GOT A PLAN!
WHRARAAARH!
CALLING A REPAIR DROID CRAMMED WITH EXPLOSIVES "A PLAN" IS AN INSULT TO PLANS ACROSS THE GALAXY.
THAT'S NOT THE ONLY PART OF THE PLAN.
WHRARAAARH!
HRHR.

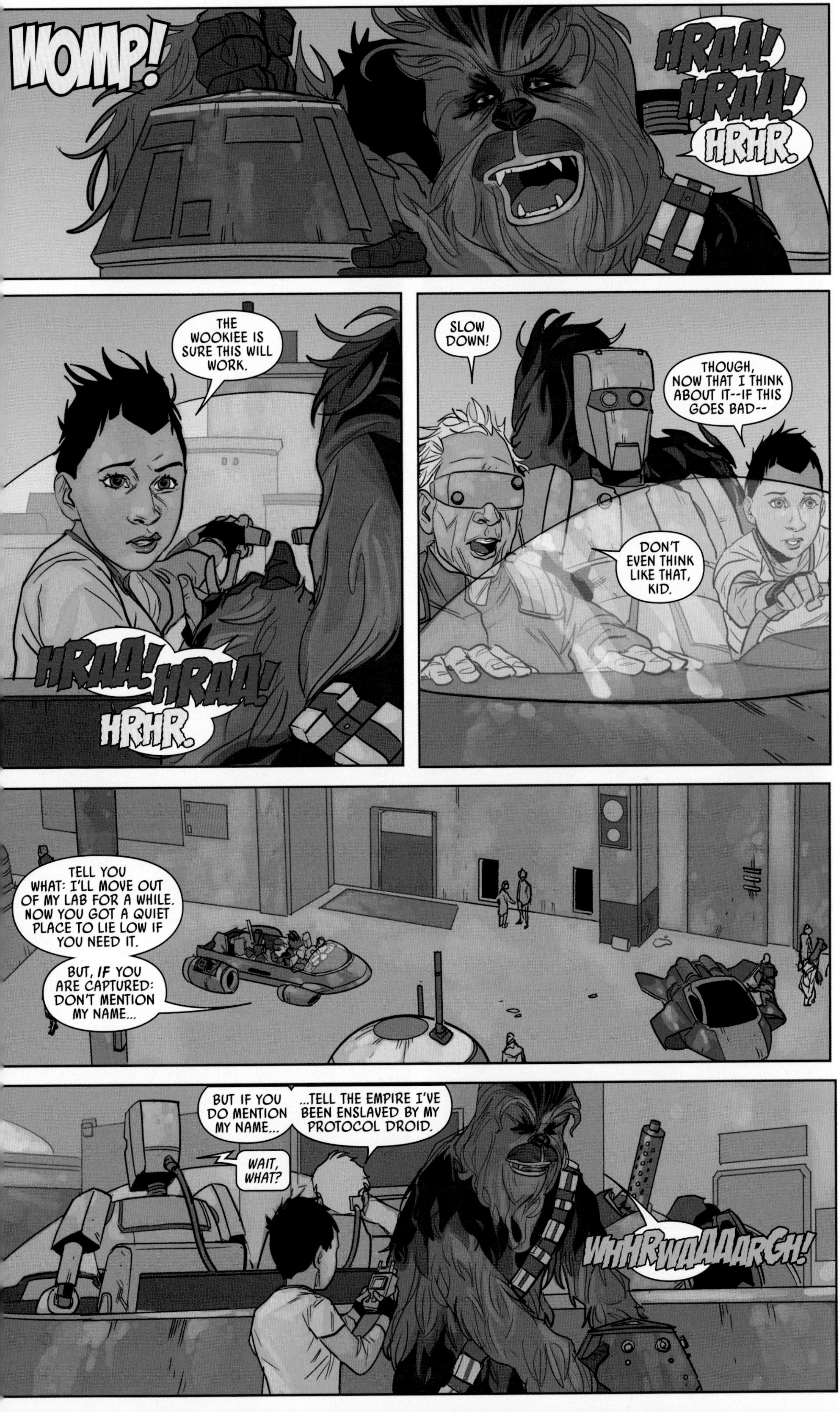
WOMP!
HRAA! HRAA! HRHR.
THE WOOKIEE IS SURE THIS WILL WORK.
HRAA! HRAA! HRHR.
SLOW DOWN!
THOUGH, NOW THAT I THINK ABOUT IT--IF THIS GOES BAD--
DON'T EVEN THINK LIKE THAT, KID.
TELL YOU WHAT: I'LL MOVE OUT OF MY LAB FOR A WHILE. NOW YOU GOT A QUIET PLACE TO LIE LOW IF YOU NEED IT.
BUT, *IF* YOU ARE CAPTURED: DON'T MENTION MY NAME...
BUT IF YOU DO MENTION MY NAME...
...TELL THE EMPIRE I'VE BEEN ENSLAVED BY MY PROTOCOL DROID.
WAIT, WHAT?
WHHRWAAAARGH!

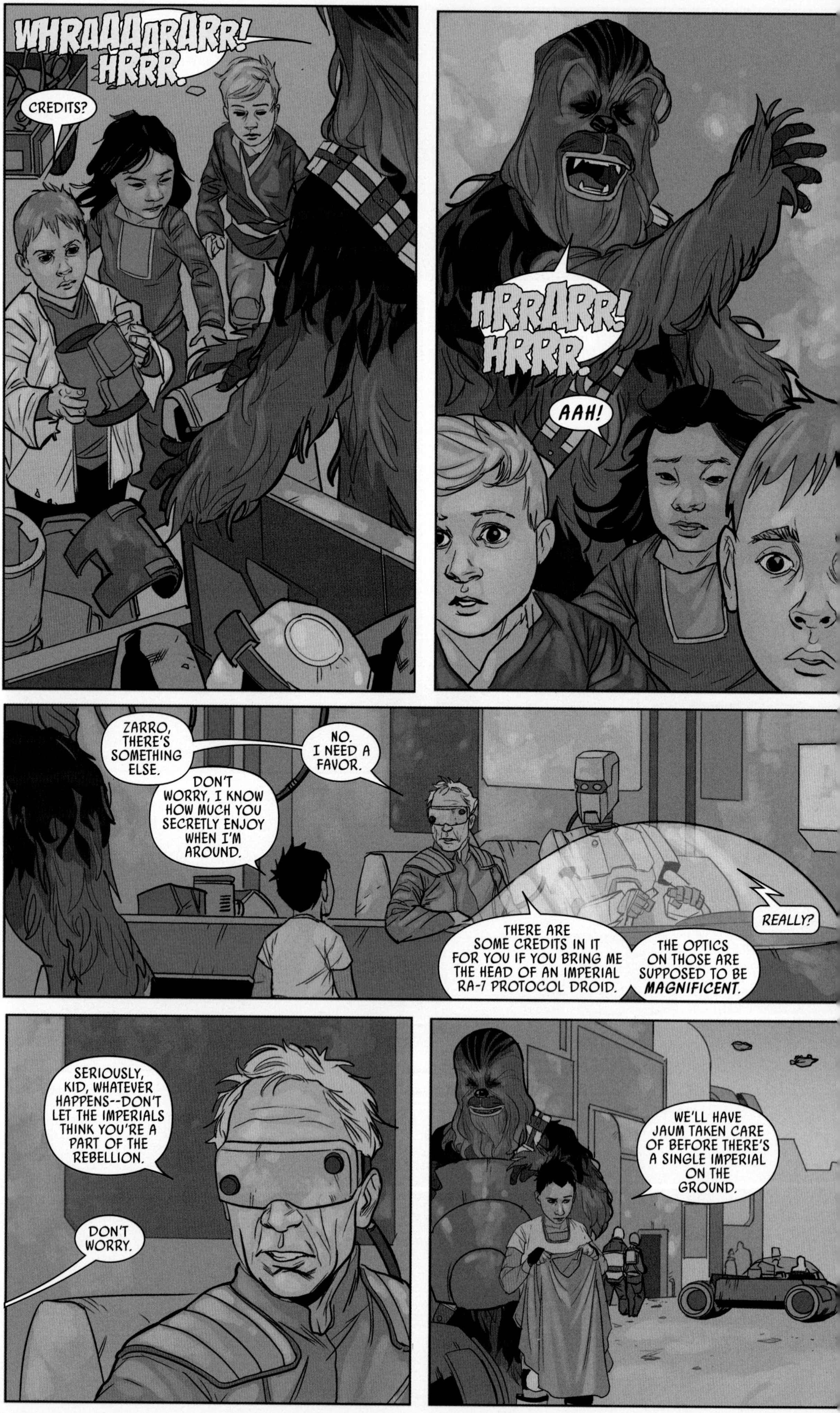
WHRAAAARARR! HRRR.
CREDITS?
HRRARR! HRRR.
AAH!
ZARRO, THERE'S SOMETHING ELSE.
NO. I NEED A FAVOR.
DON'T WORRY, I KNOW HOW MUCH YOU SECRETLY ENJOY WHEN I'M AROUND.
THERE ARE SOME CREDITS IN IT FOR YOU IF YOU BRING ME THE HEAD OF AN IMPERIAL RA-7 PROTOCOL DROID.
THE OPTICS ON THOSE ARE SUPPOSED TO BE MAGNIFICENT.
REALLY?
SERIOUSLY, KID, WHATEVER HAPPENS--DON'T LET THE IMPERIALS THINK YOU'RE A PART OF THE REBELLION.
DON'T WORRY.
WE'LL HAVE JAUM TAKEN CARE OF BEFORE THERE'S A SINGLE IMPERIAL ON THE GROUND.

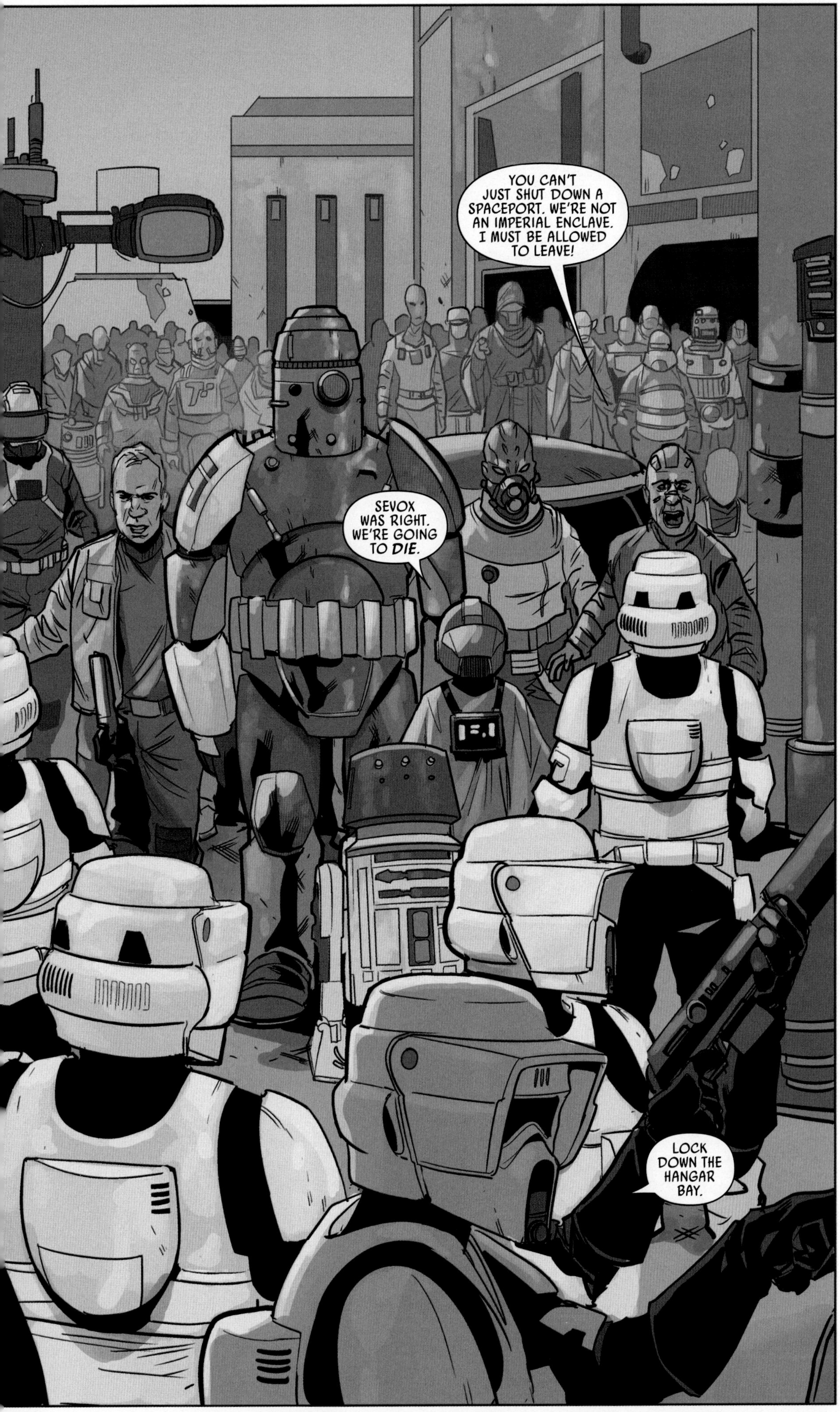
YOU CAN'T JUST SHUT DOWN A SPACEPORT. WE'RE NOT AN IMPERIAL ENCLAVE. I MUST BE ALLOWED TO LEAVE!
SEVOX WAS RIGHT. WE'RE GOING TO *DIE*.
LOCK DOWN THE HANGAR BAY.

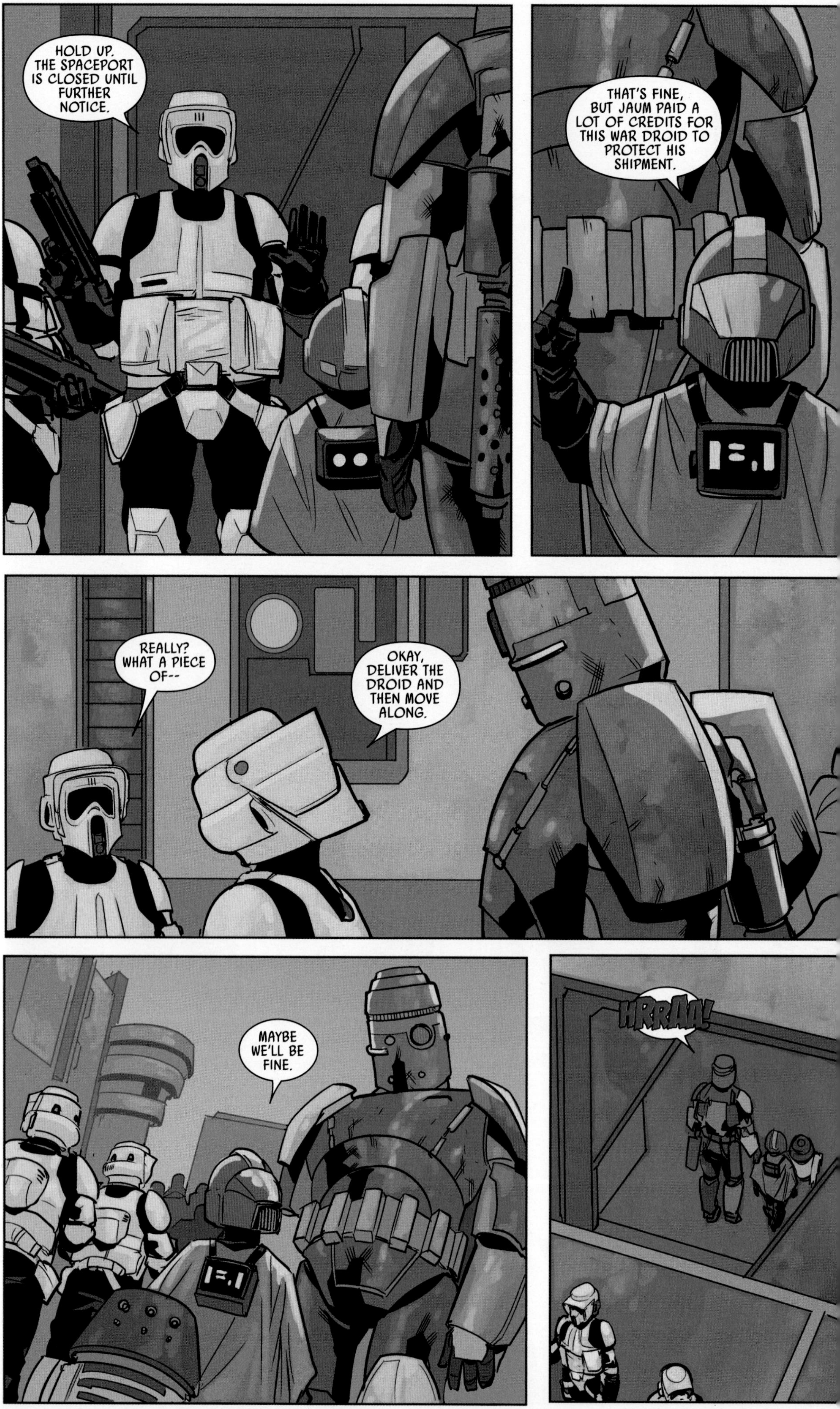

HOLD UP. THE SPACEPORT IS CLOSED UNTIL FURTHER NOTICE.
THAT'S FINE, BUT JAUM PAID A LOT OF CREDITS FOR THIS WAR DROID TO PROTECT HIS SHIPMENT.
REALLY? WHAT A PIECE OF--
OKAY, DELIVER THE DROID AND THEN MOVE ALONG.
MAYBE WE'LL BE FINE.
HRRAA!

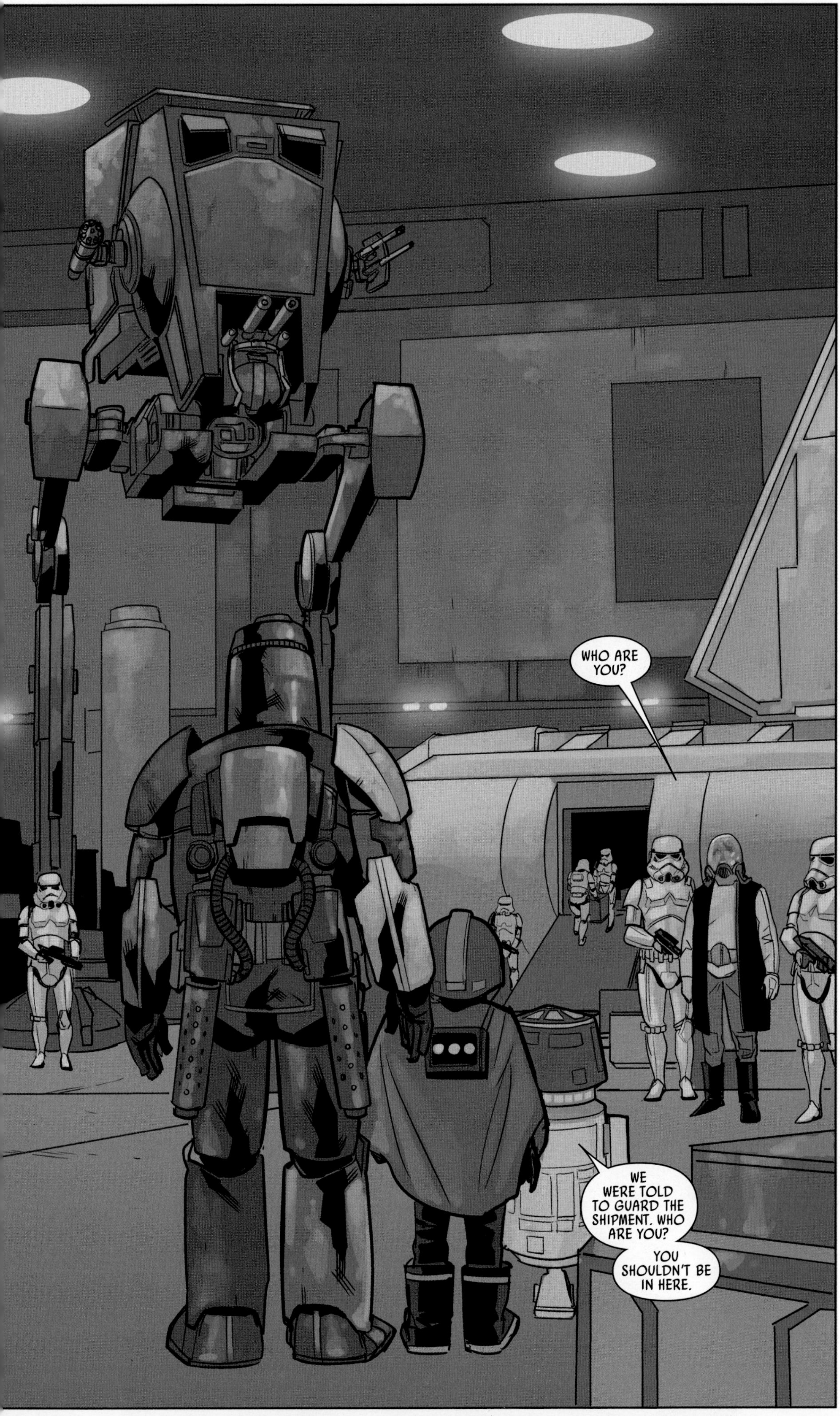
WHO ARE YOU?
WE WERE TOLD TO GUARD THE SHIPMENT. WHO ARE YOU?
YOU SHOULDN'T BE IN HERE.

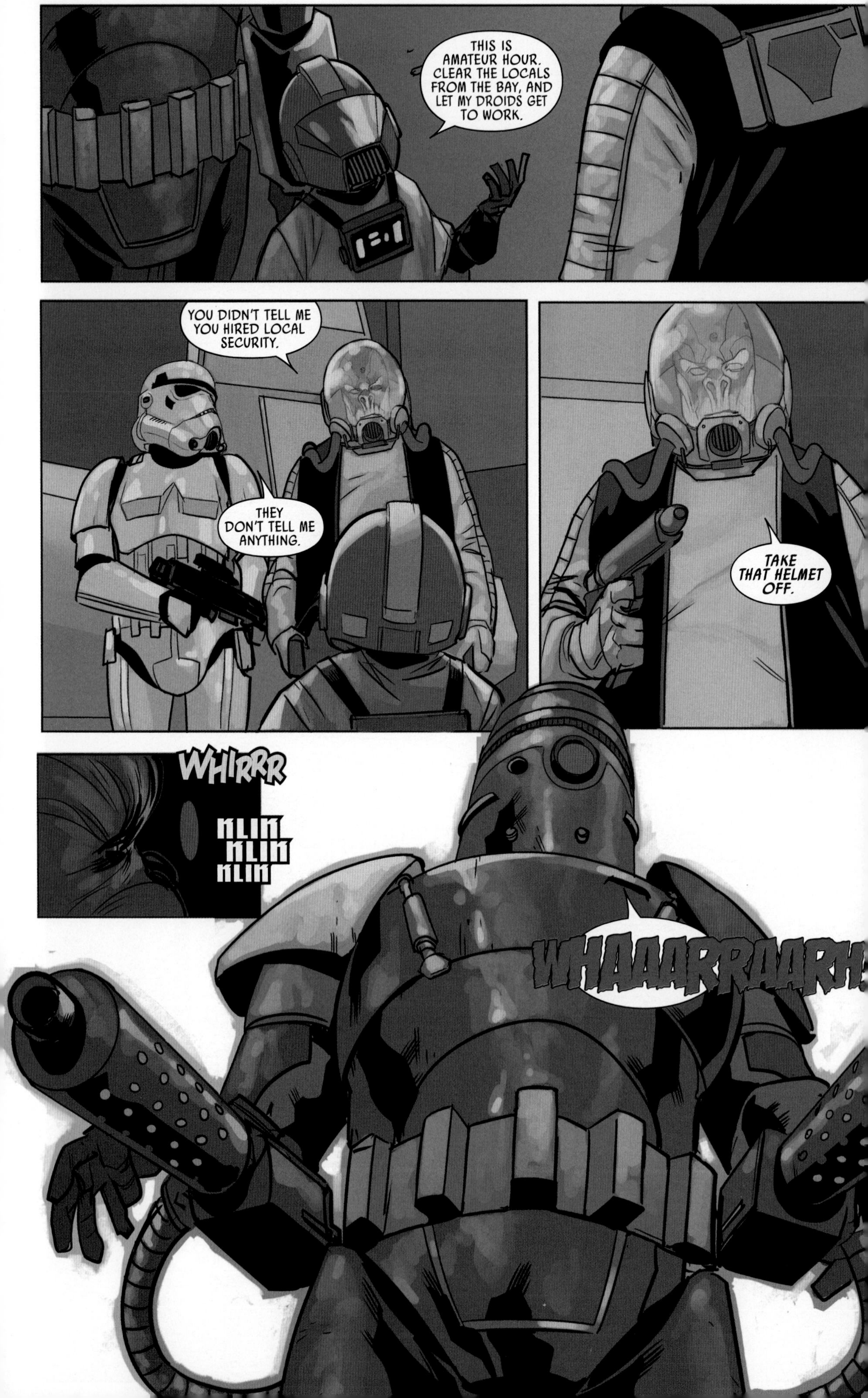
THIS IS AMATEUR HOUR. CLEAR THE LOCALS FROM THE BAY, AND LET MY DROIDS GET TO WORK.
YOU DIDN'T TELL ME YOU HIRED LOCAL SECURITY.
THEY DON'T TELL ME ANYTHING.
TAKE THAT HELMET OFF.
WHIRRR
KLIK KLIK KLIK
WHAAARRAARH!

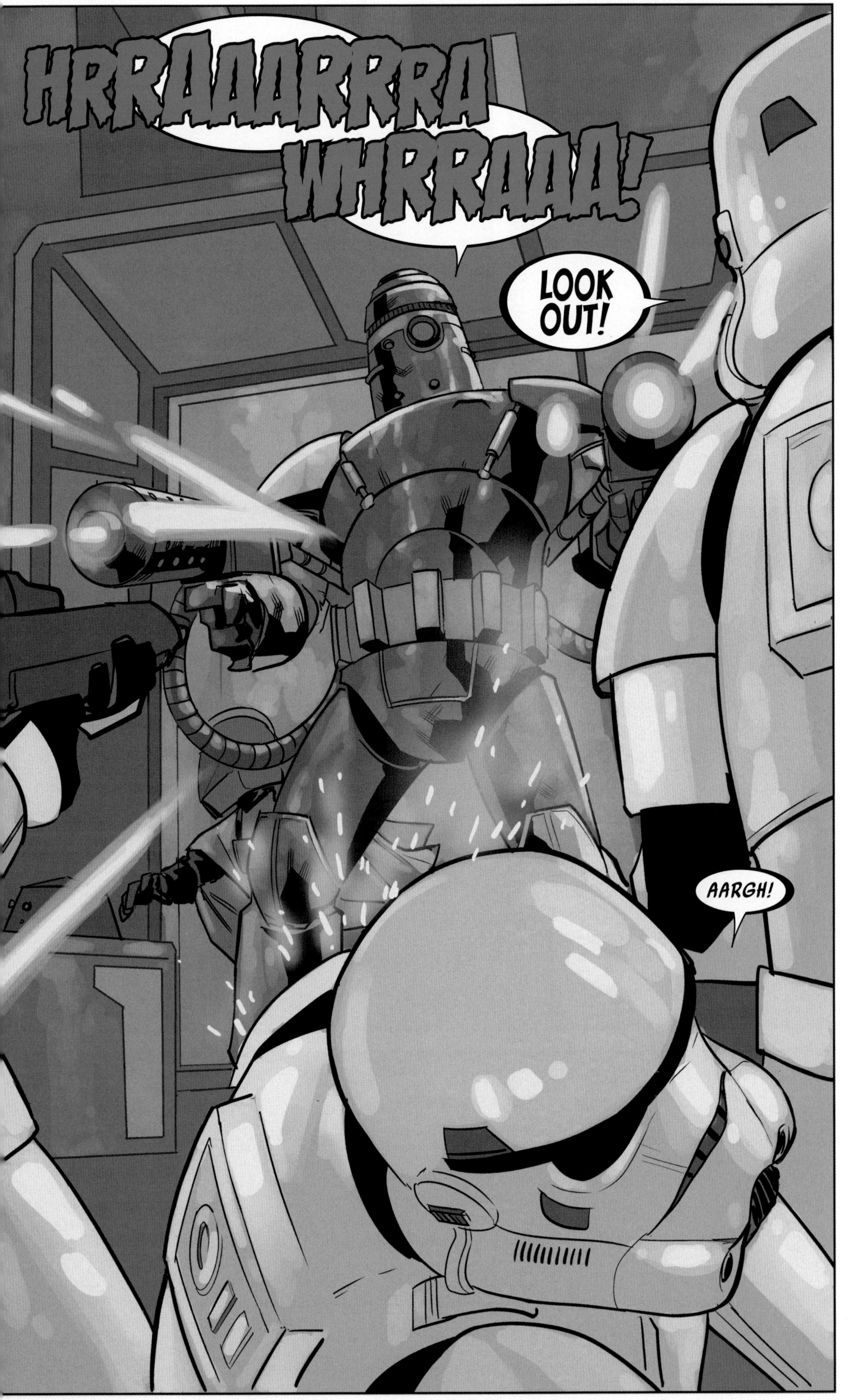
HRRAAARRRA WHRRAAA!
LOOK OUT!
AARGH!

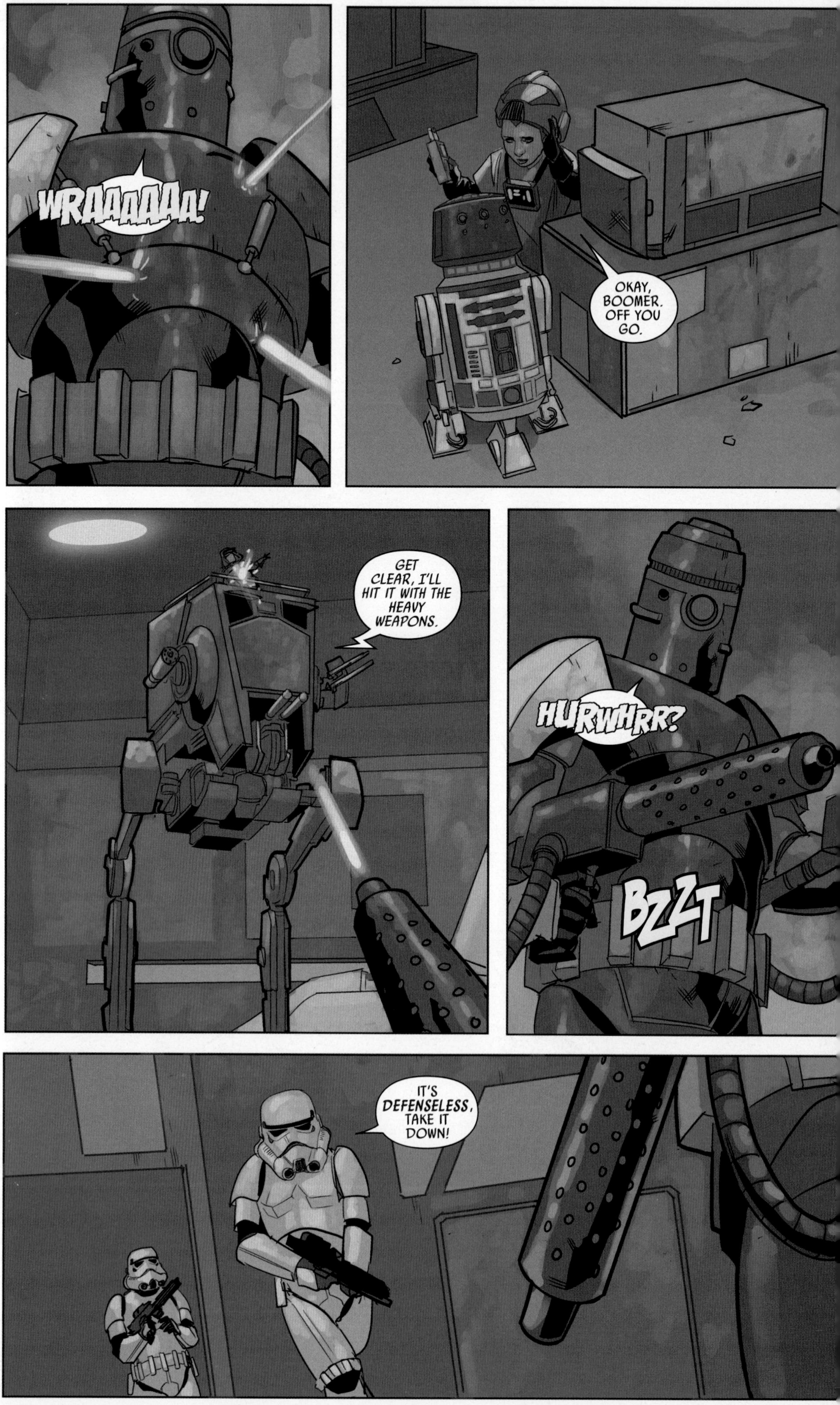
WRAAAAAA!
OKAY, BOOMER. OFF YOU GO.
GET CLEAR, I'LL HIT IT WITH THE HEAVY WEAPONS.
HURWHRR?
BZZT
IT'S DEFENSELESS, TAKE IT DOWN!

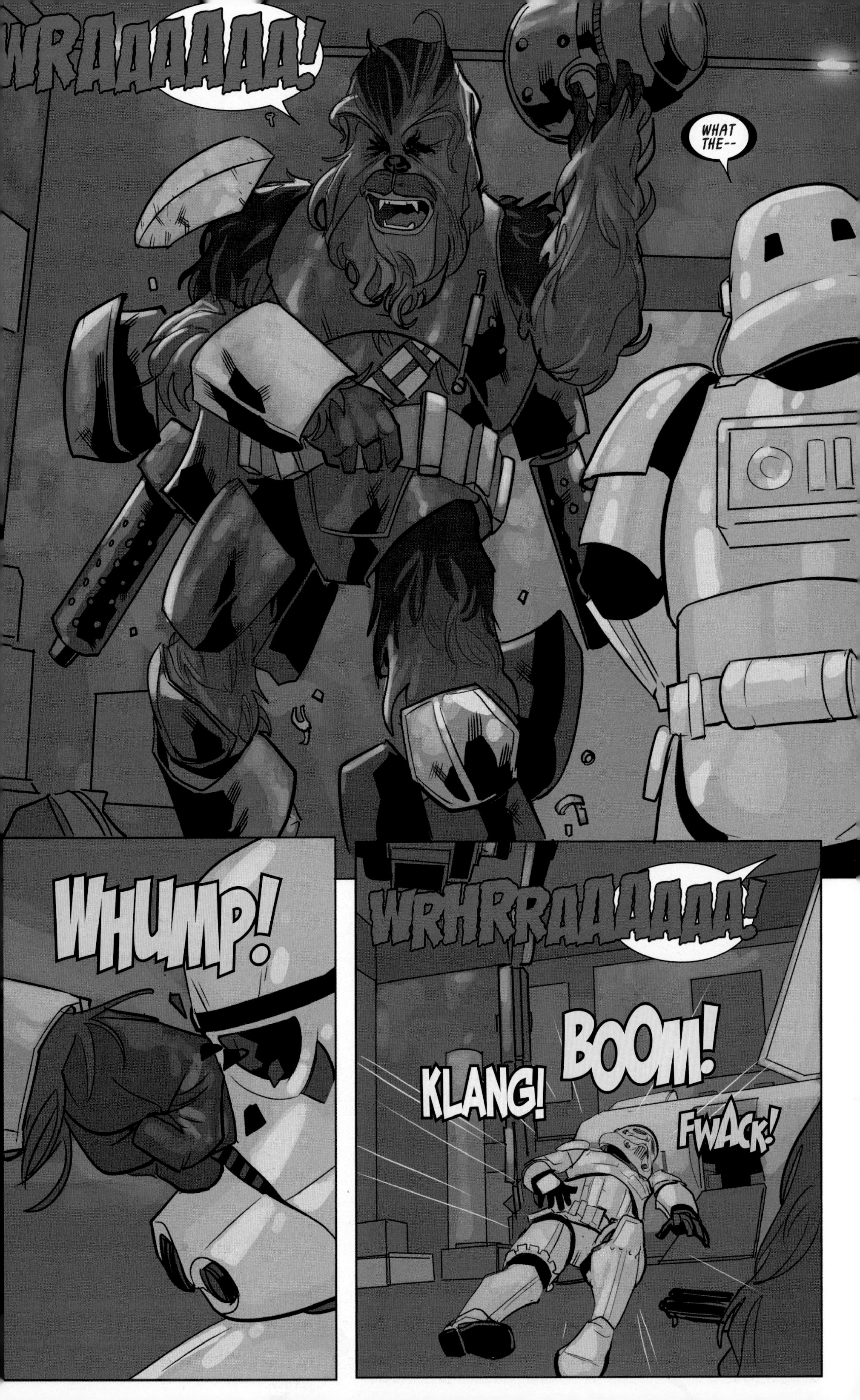
WRAAAAAA!
WHAT THE--
WHUMP!
WRHRRAAAAAAA!
BOOM!
KLANG!
FWACK!

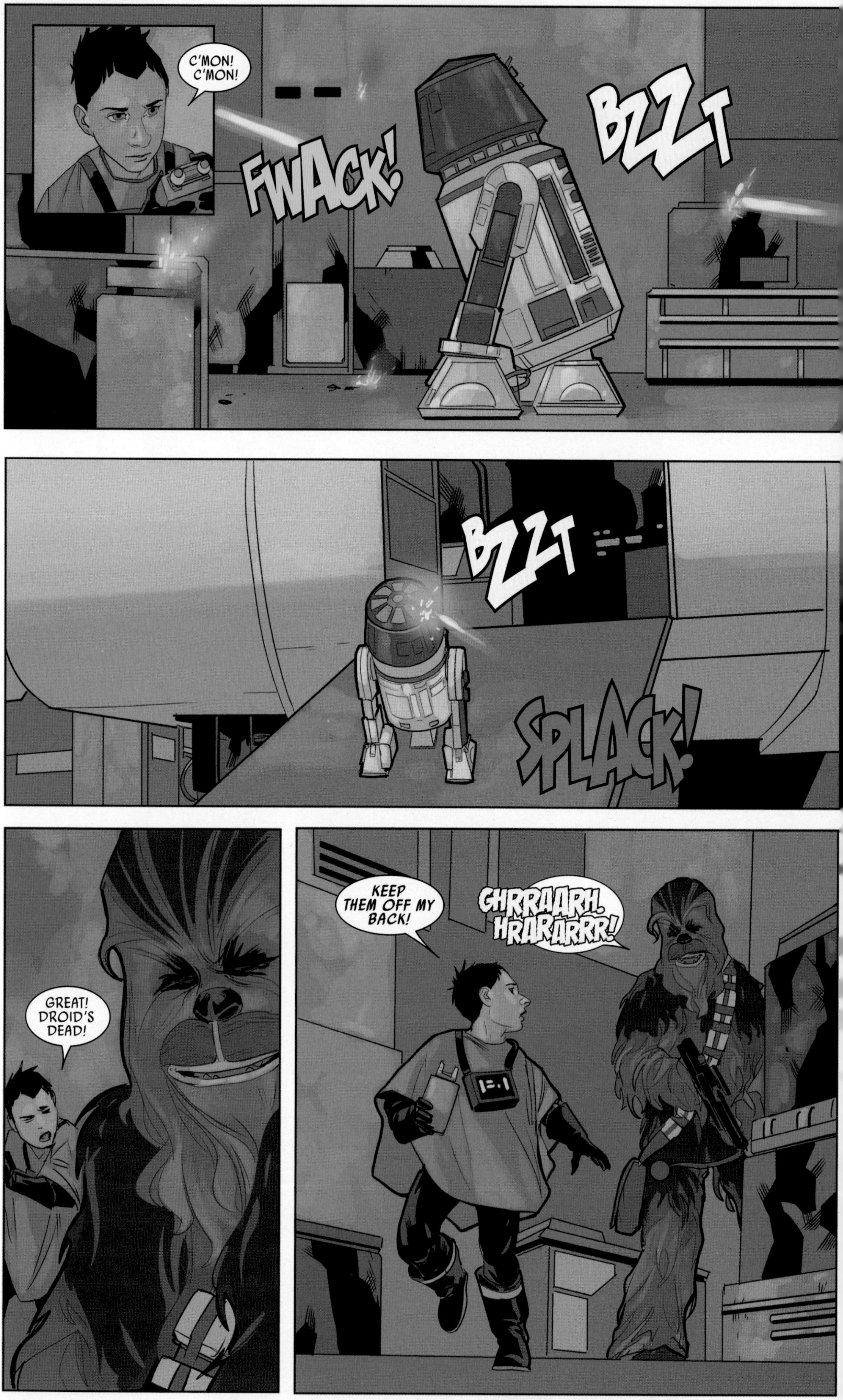
C'MON! C'MON!
FWACK!
BZZT
BZZT
SPLACK!
GREAT! DROID'S DEAD!
KEEP THEM OFF MY BACK!
GHRRAARH. HRARARRR!

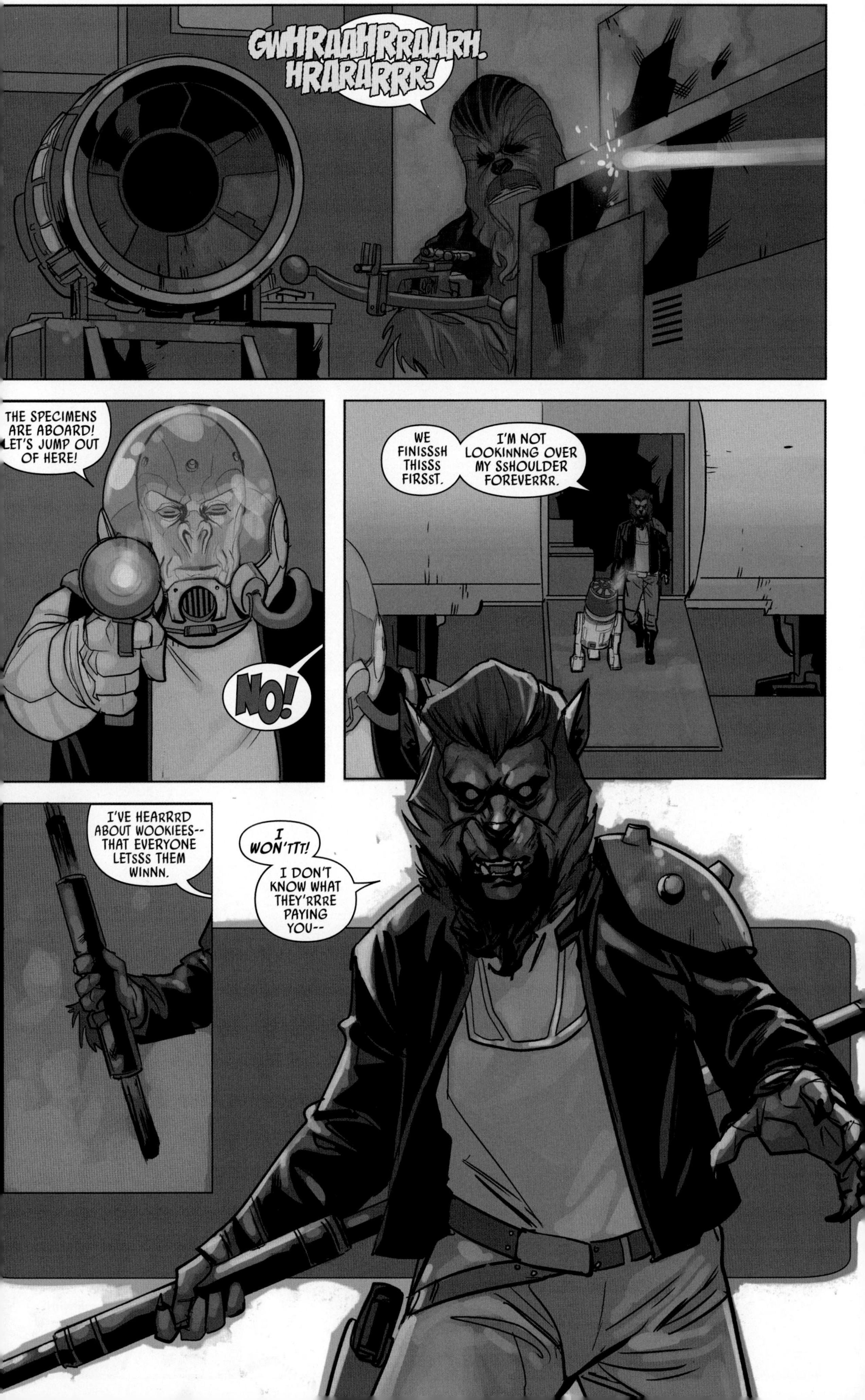
GWHRAAHRRAARH. HRARARRR!
THE SPECIMENS ARE ABOARD! LET'S JUMP OUT OF HERE!
NO!
WE FINISSSH THISSS FIRSST.
I'M NOT LOOKINNNG OVER MY SSHOULDER FOREVERRR.
I'VE HEARRRD ABOUT WOOKIEES-- THAT EVERYONE LETSSS THEM WINNN.
I WON'TTT!
I DON'T KNOW WHAT THEY'RRRE PAYING YOU--

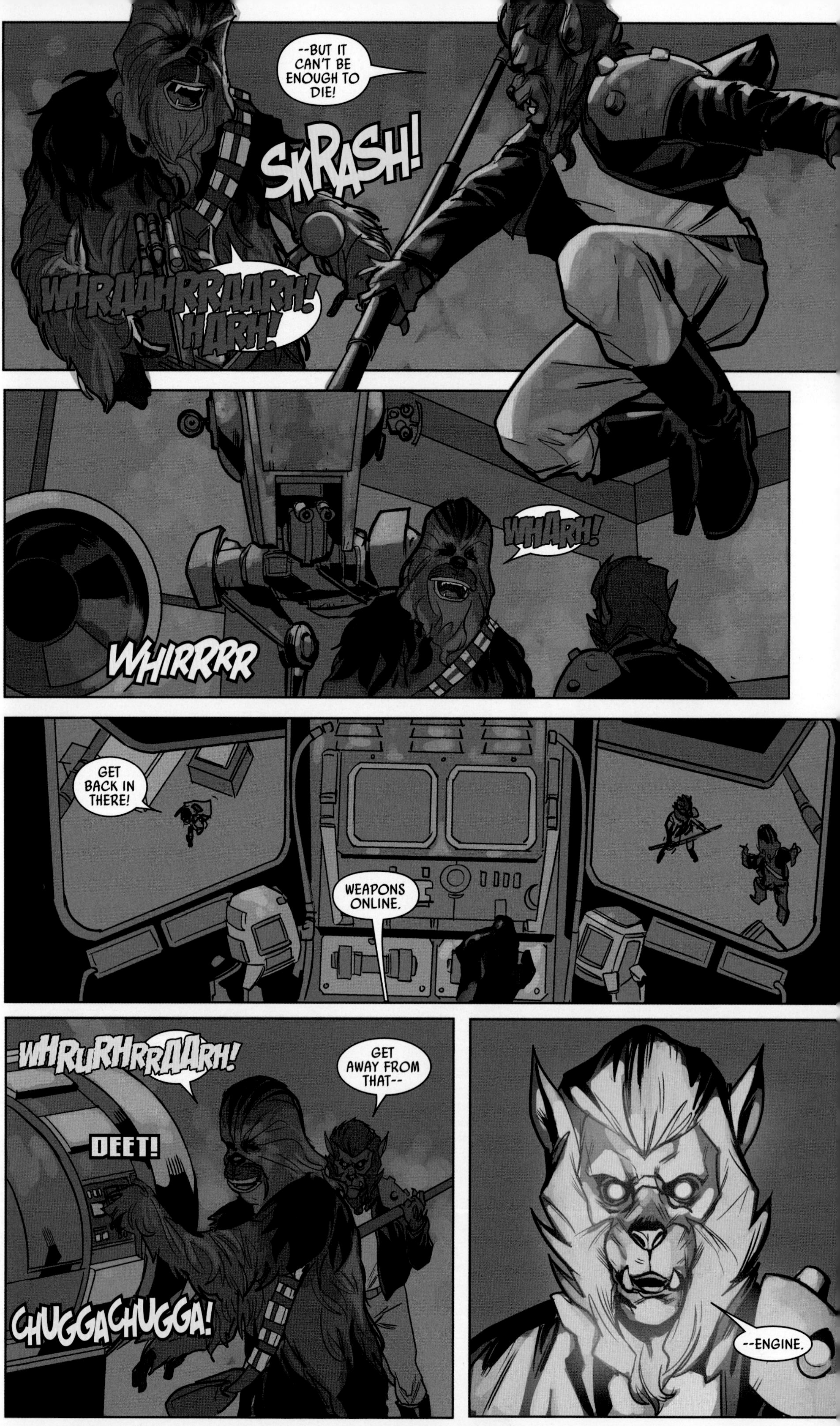
--BUT IT CAN'T BE ENOUGH TO DIE!
SKRASH!
WHRAAHRRAARH! HARH!
WHARH!
WHIRRRR
GET BACK IN THERE!
WEAPONS ONLINE.
WHRURHRRAARH!
GET AWAY FROM THAT--
DEET!
CHUGGACHUGGA!
--ENGINE.

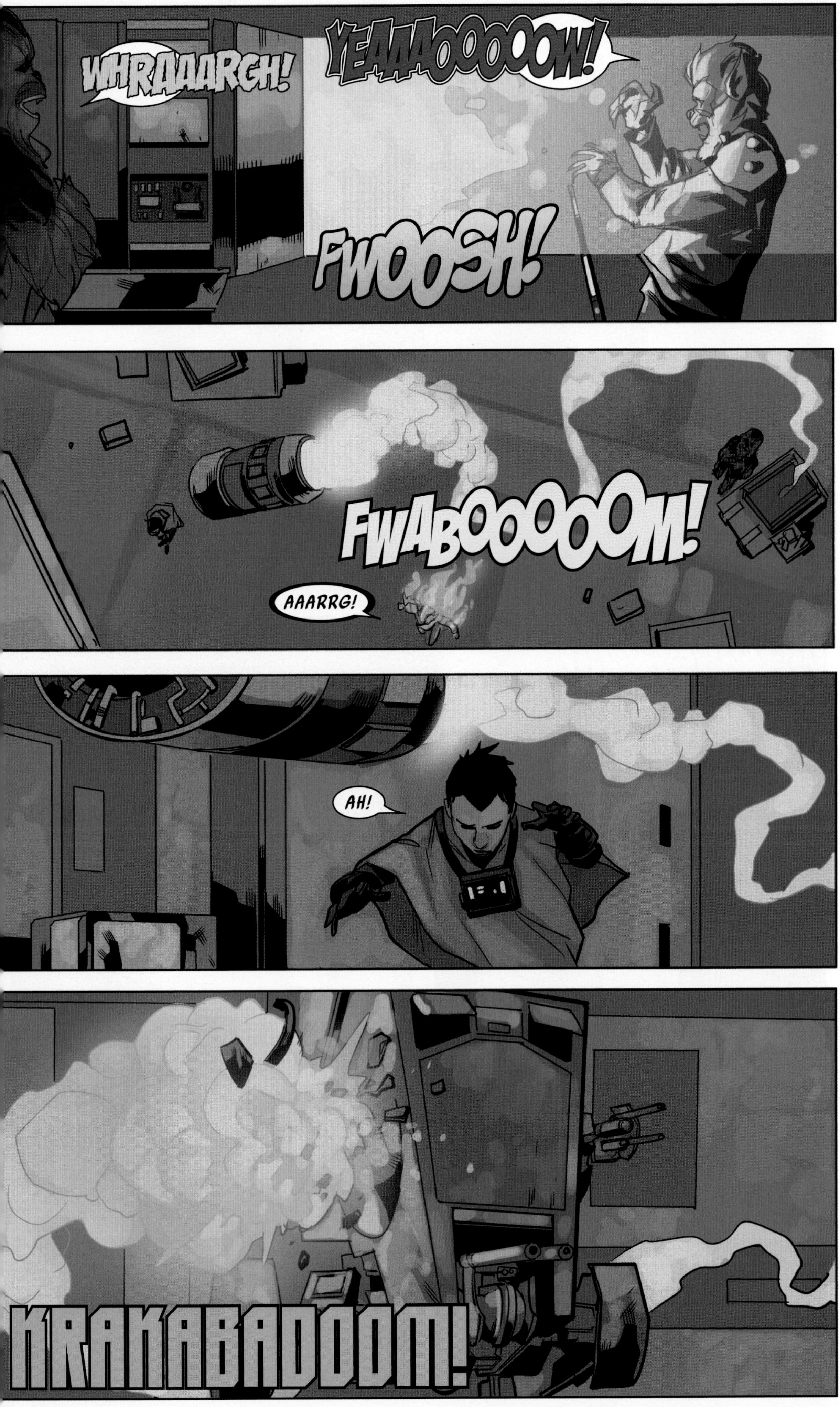
WHRAAARGH!
YEAAAOOOOOW!
FWOOSH!
FWABOOOOOOM!
AAARRG!
AH!
KRAKABADOOM!

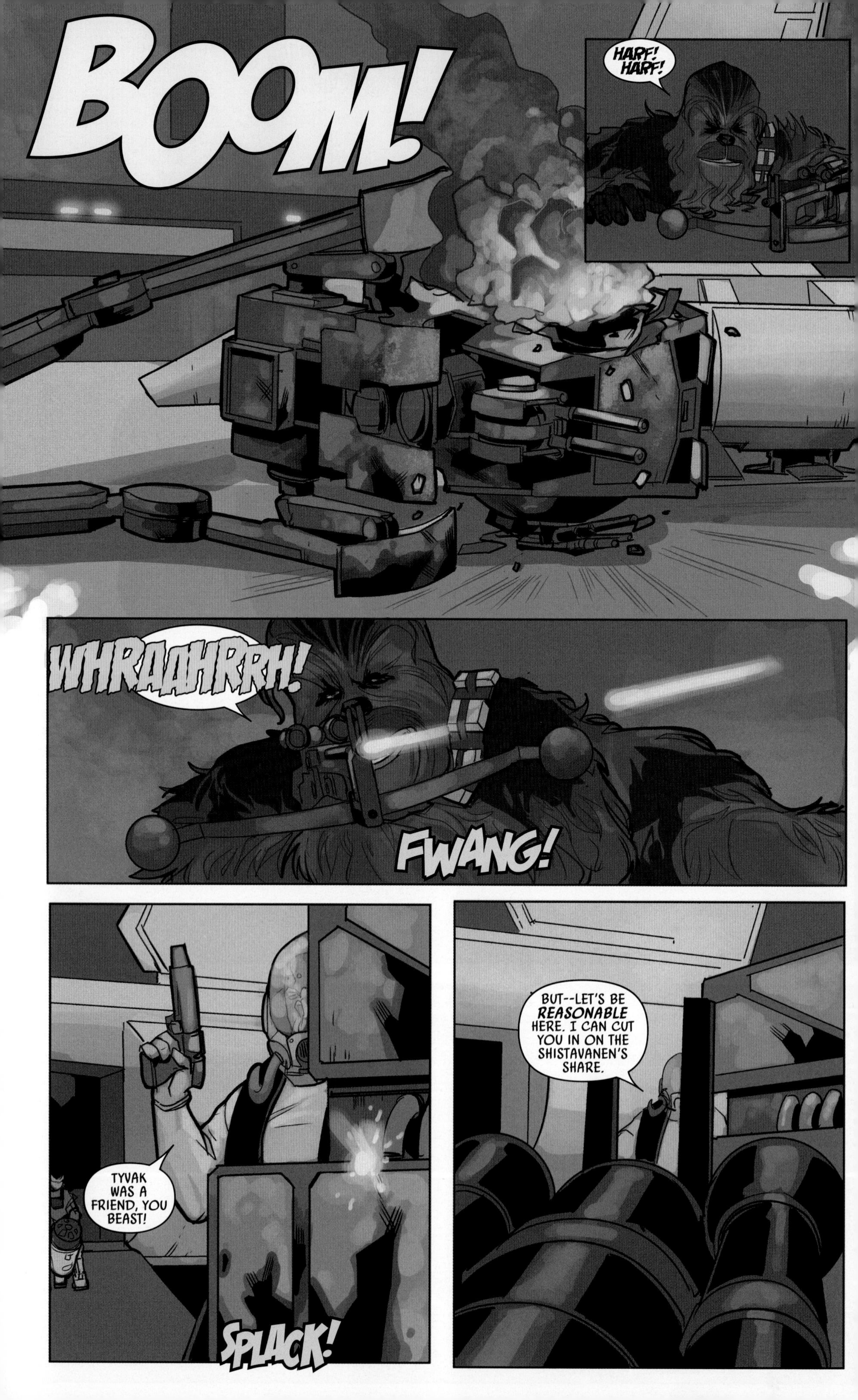
BOOM!
HARF! HARF!
WHRAAHRRH!
FWANG!
TYVAK WAS A FRIEND, YOU BEAST!
SPLACK!
BUT--LET'S BE REASONABLE HERE. I CAN CUT YOU IN ON THE SHISTAVANEN'S SHARE.

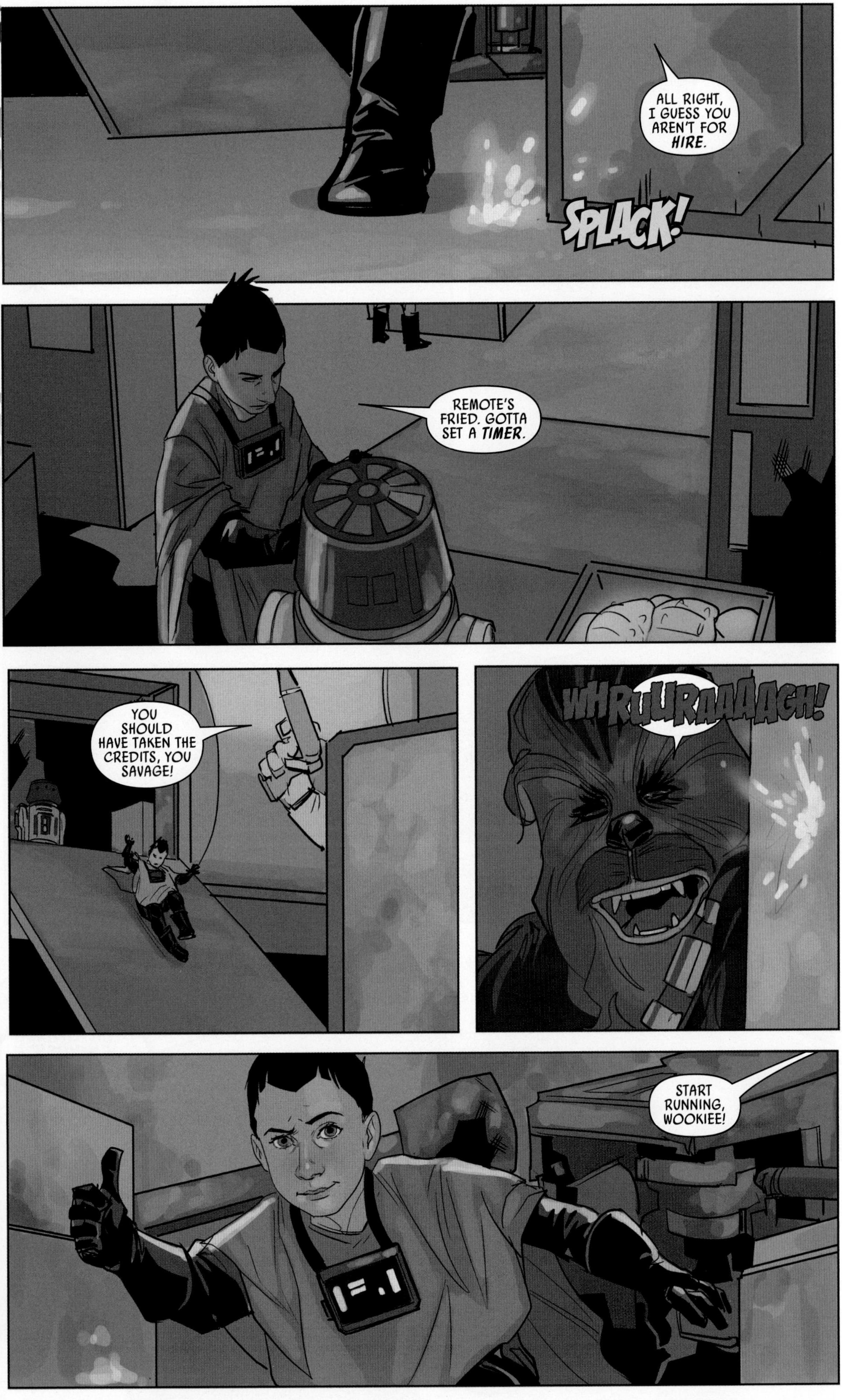
ALL RIGHT, I GUESS YOU AREN'T FOR *HIRE*.
SPLACK!
REMOTE'S FRIED. GOTTA SET A *TIMER*.
YOU SHOULD HAVE TAKEN THE CREDITS, YOU SAVAGE!
WHRUURAAAAGH!
START RUNNING, WOOKIEE!

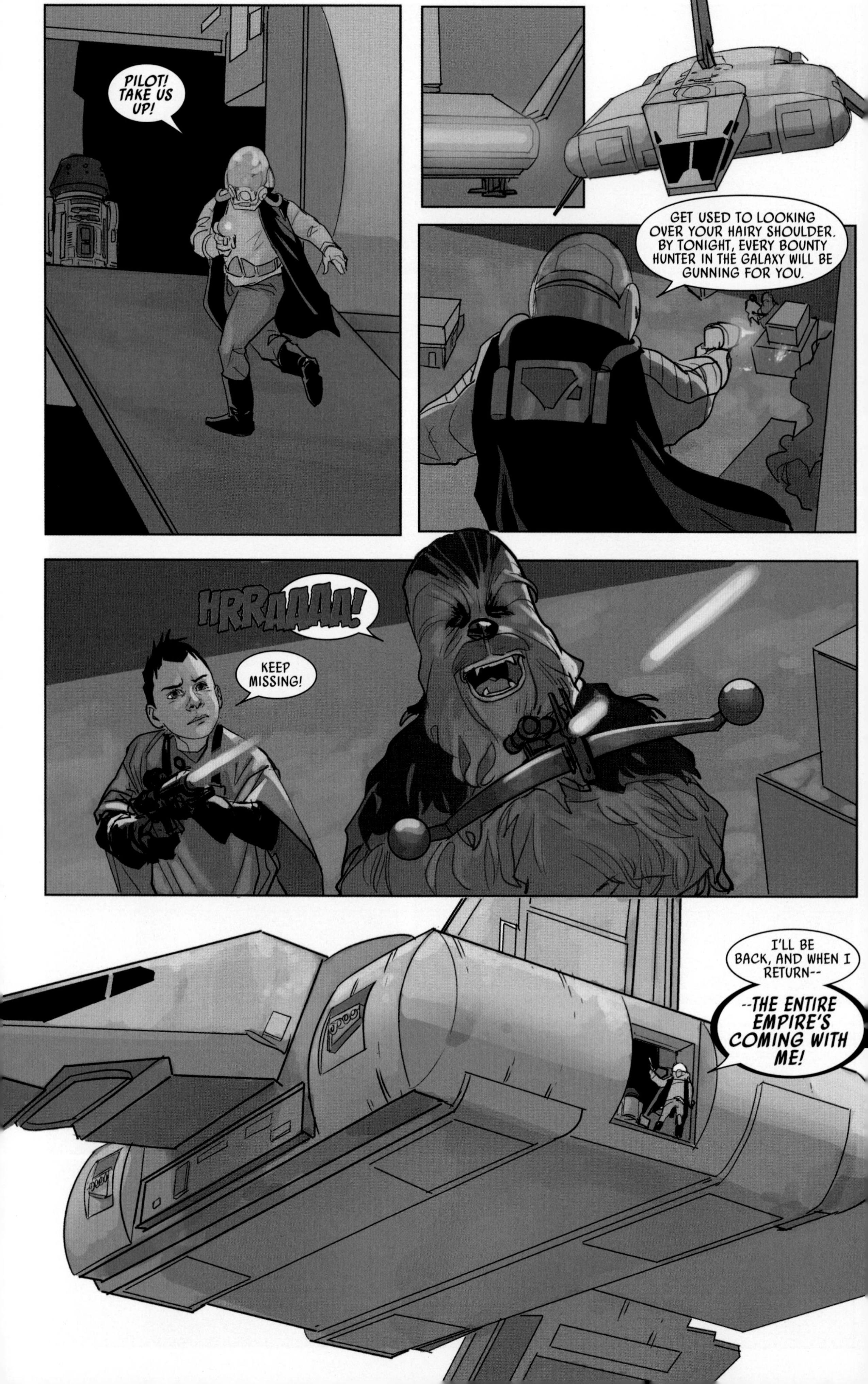
PILOT! TAKE US UP!
GET USED TO LOOKING OVER YOUR HAIRY SHOULDER. BY TONIGHT, EVERY BOUNTY HUNTER IN THE GALAXY WILL BE GUNNING FOR YOU.
HRRAAAA!
KEEP MISSING!
I'LL BE BACK, AND WHEN I RETURN--
--THE ENTIRE EMPIRE'S COMING WITH ME!

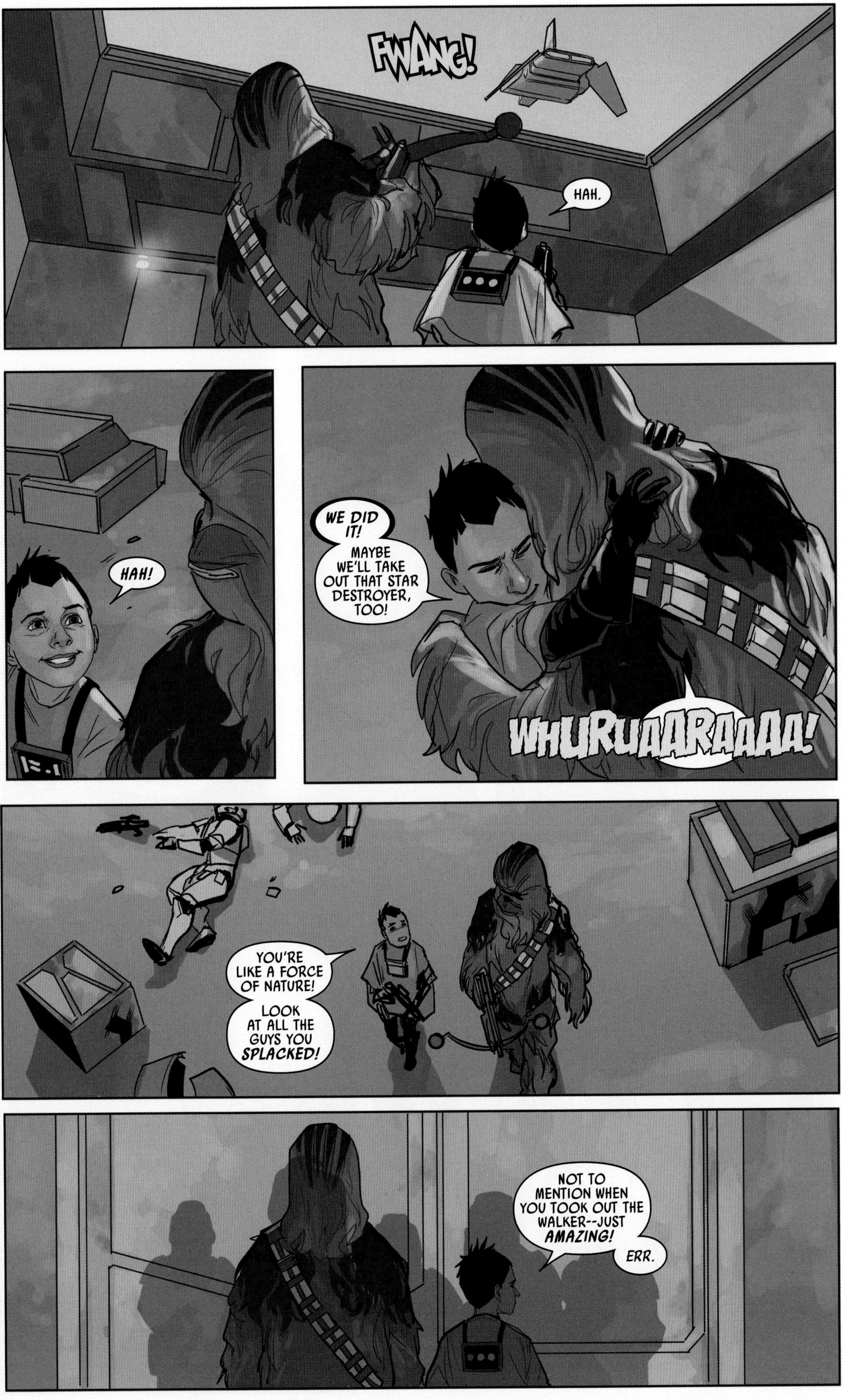
FWANG!
HAH.
HAH!
WE DID IT!
MAYBE WE'LL TAKE OUT THAT STAR DESTROYER, TOO!
WHURUAARAAAA!
YOU'RE LIKE A FORCE OF NATURE!
LOOK AT ALL THE GUYS YOU SPLACKED!
NOT TO MENTION WHEN YOU TOOK OUT THE WALKER--JUST AMAZING!
ERR.

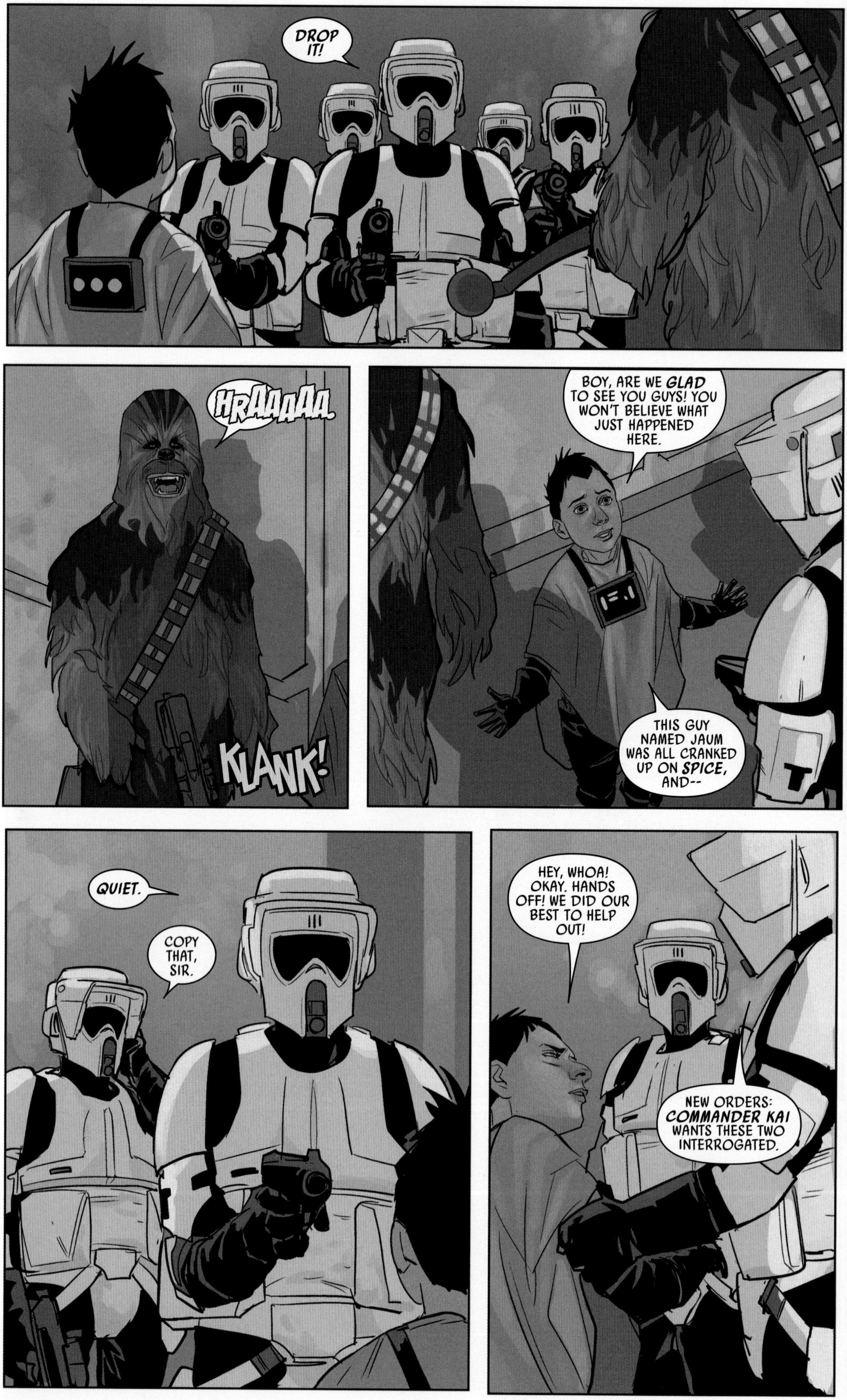
DROP IT!
HRAAAAA
KLANK!
BOY, ARE WE GLAD TO SEE YOU GUYS! YOU WON'T BELIEVE WHAT JUST HAPPENED HERE.
THIS GUY NAMED JAUM WAS ALL CRANKED UP ON SPICE, AND--
QUIET.
COPY THAT, SIR.
HEY, WHOA! OKAY. HANDS OFF! WE DID OUR BEST TO HELP OUT!
NEW ORDERS: COMMANDER KAI WANTS THESE TWO INTERROGATED.

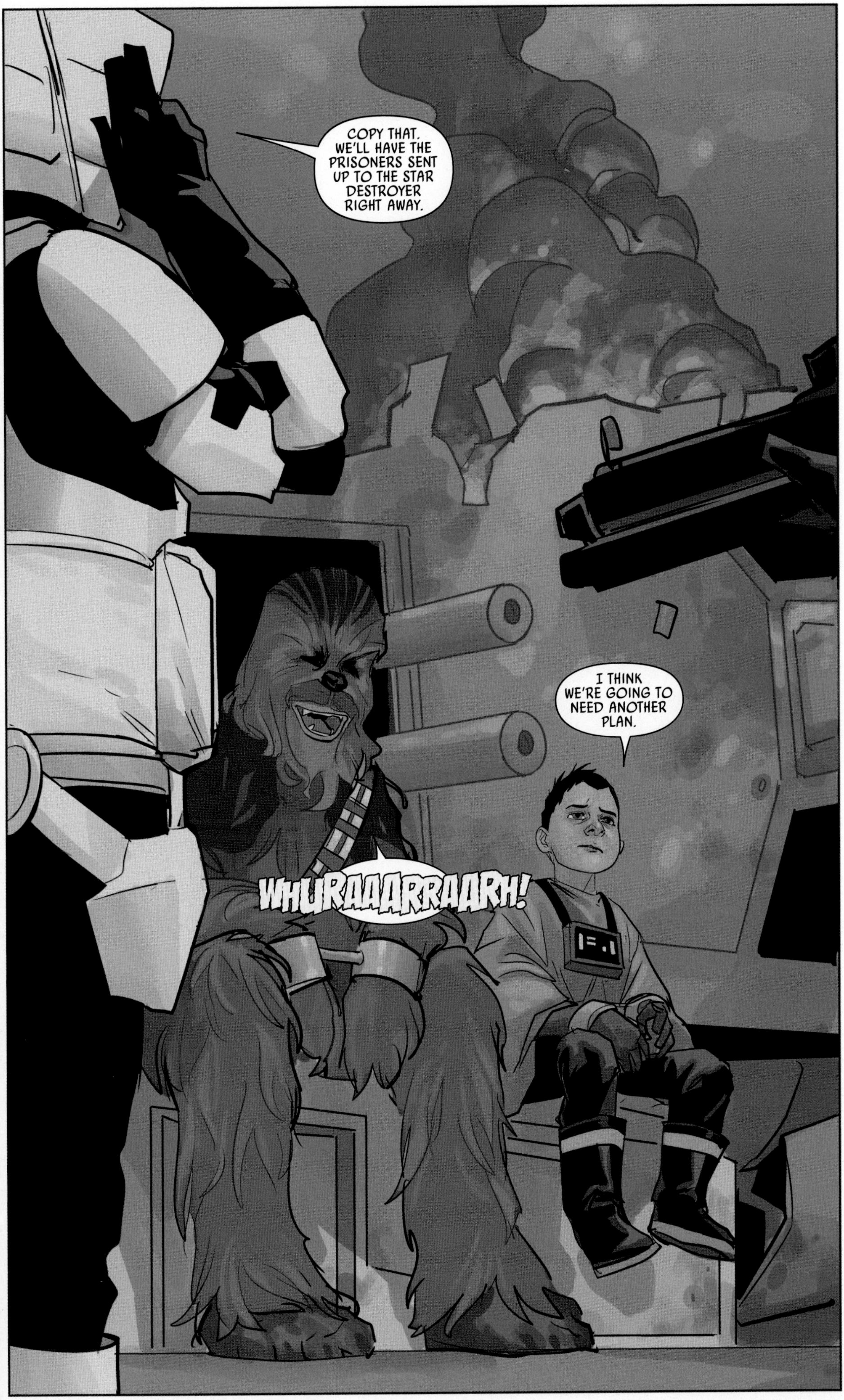
COPY THAT. WE'LL HAVE THE PRISONERS SENT UP TO THE STAR DESTROYER RIGHT AWAY.
I THINK WE'RE GOING TO NEED ANOTHER PLAN.
WHURAAARRAARH!

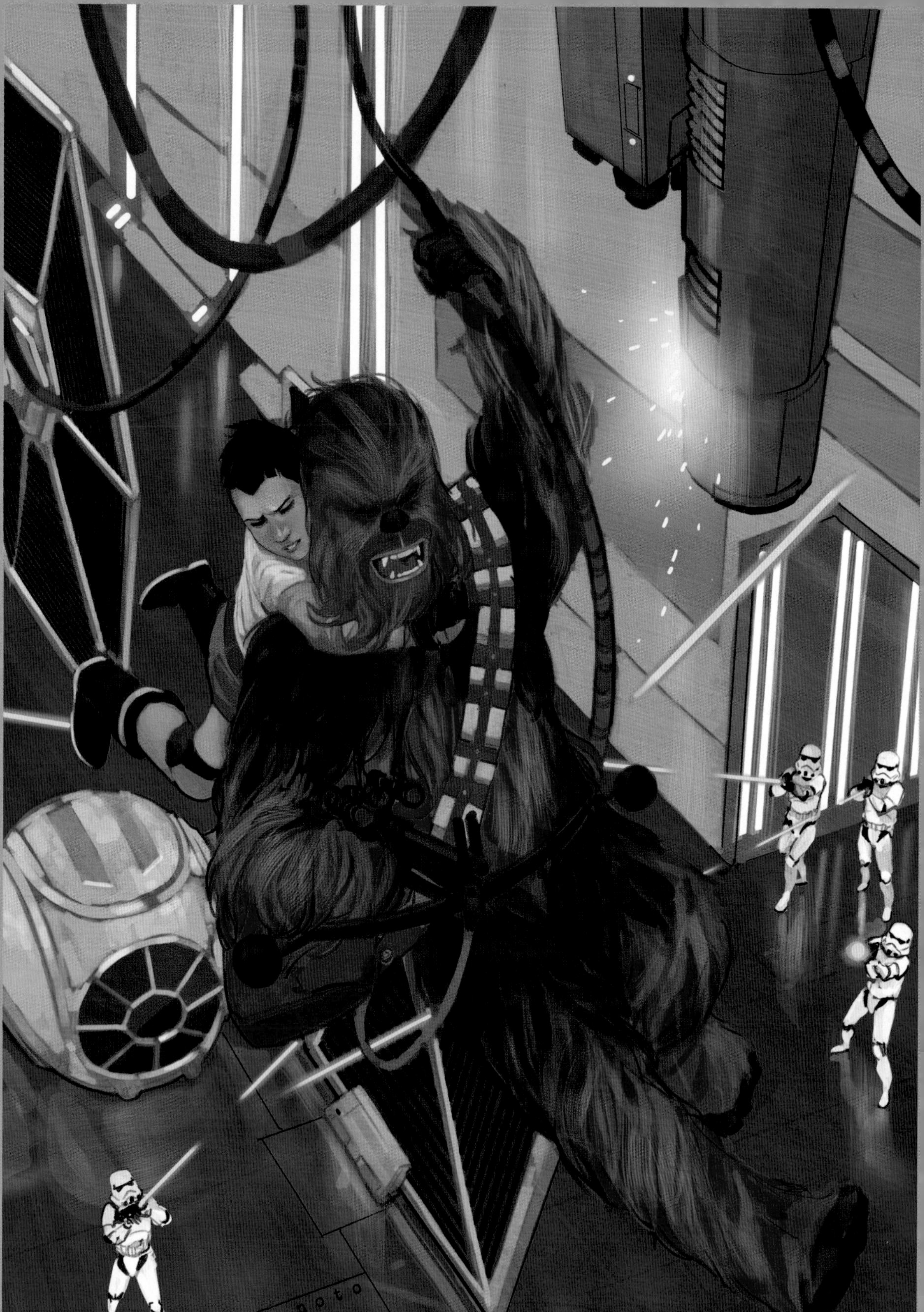
noto

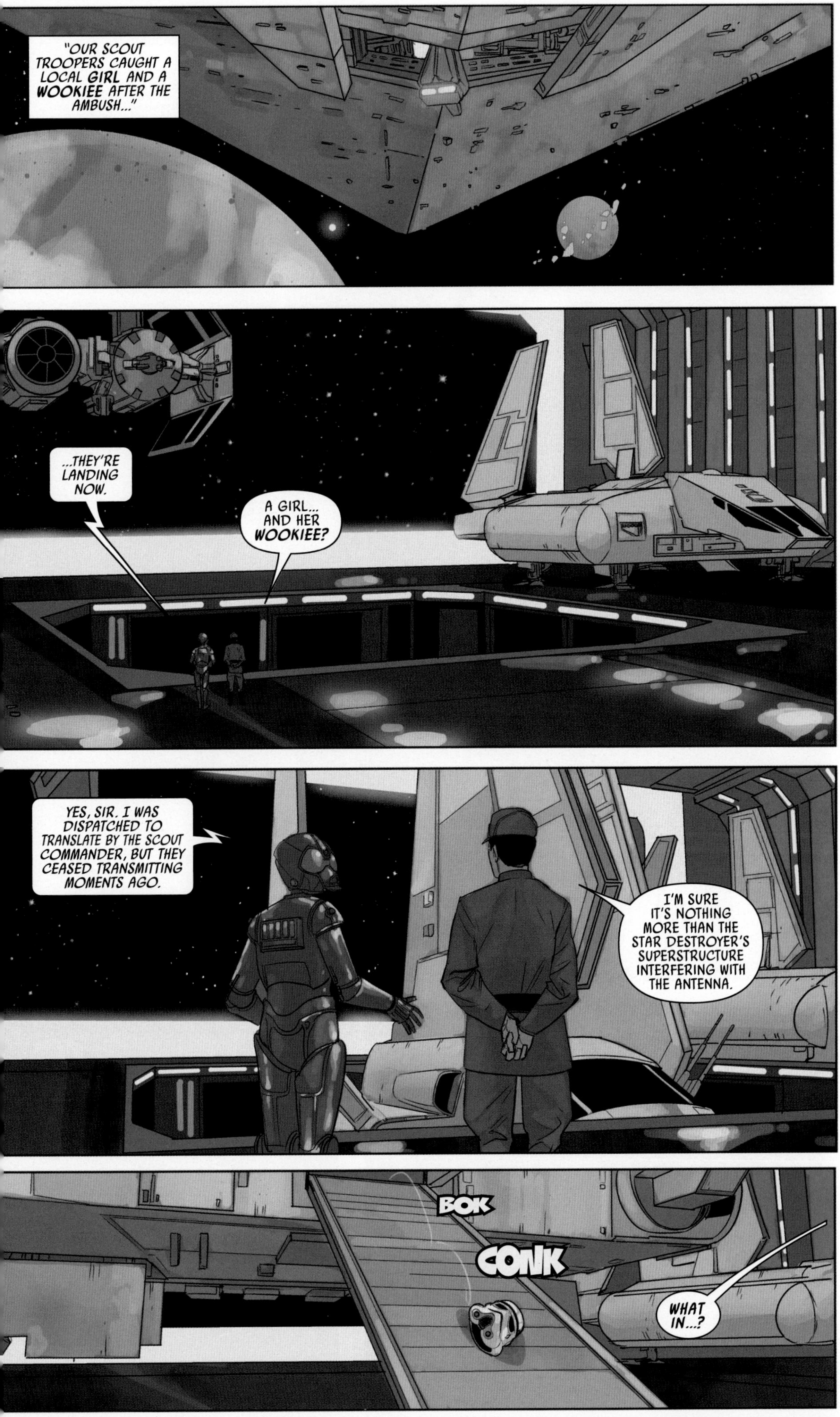
"OUR SCOUT TROOPERS CAUGHT A LOCAL GIRL AND A WOOKIEE AFTER THE AMBUSH..."
...THEY'RE LANDING NOW.
A GIRL... AND HER WOOKIEE?
YES, SIR. I WAS DISPATCHED TO TRANSLATE BY THE SCOUT COMMANDER, BUT THEY CEASED TRANSMITTING MOMENTS AGO.
I'M SURE IT'S NOTHING MORE THAN THE STAR DESTROYER'S SUPERSTRUCTURE INTERFERING WITH THE ANTENNA.
BOK
CONK
WHAT IN...?

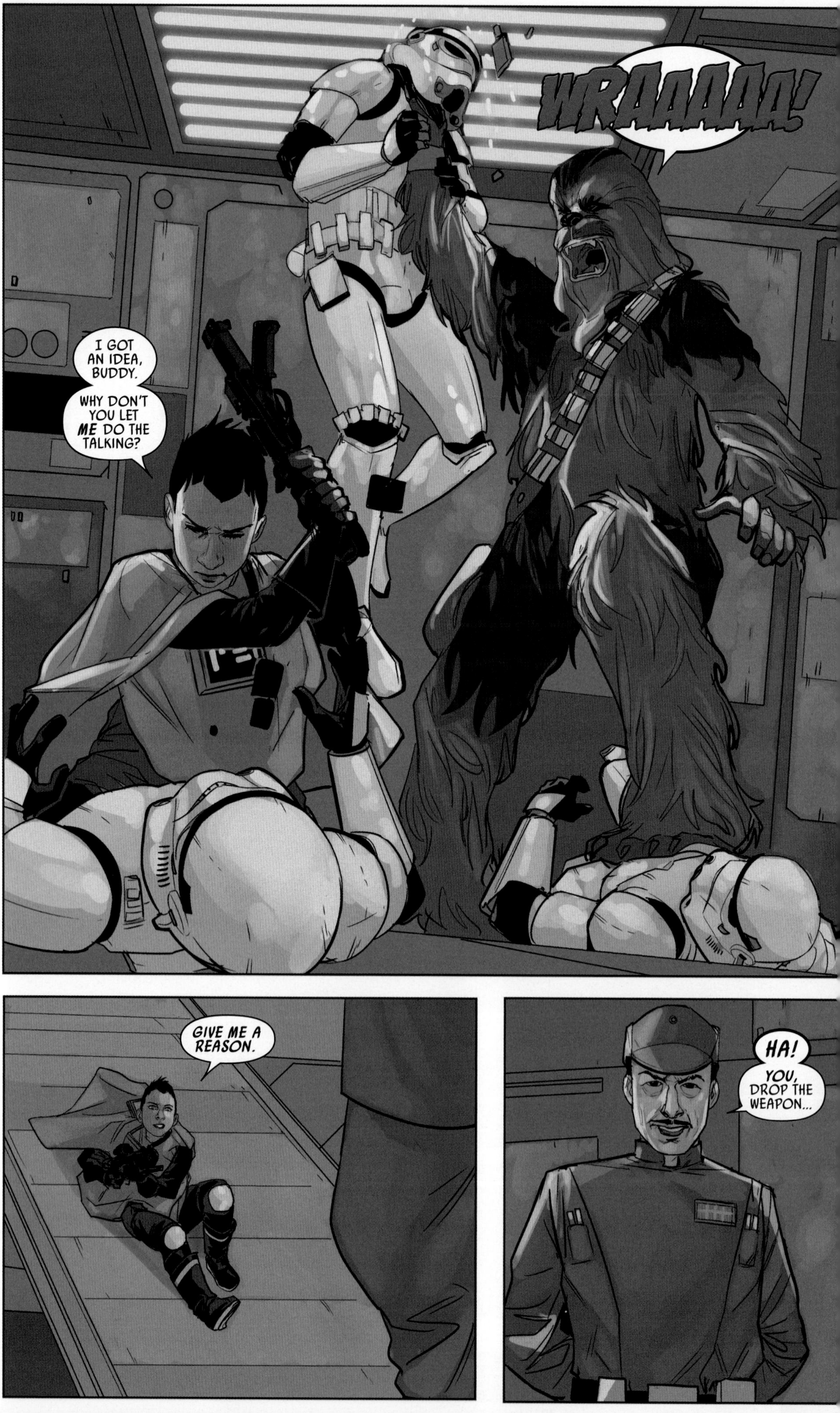
WRAAAAA!
I GOT AN IDEA, BUDDY.
WHY DON'T YOU LET ME DO THE TALKING?
GIVE ME A REASON.
HA!
YOU, DROP THE WEAPON...

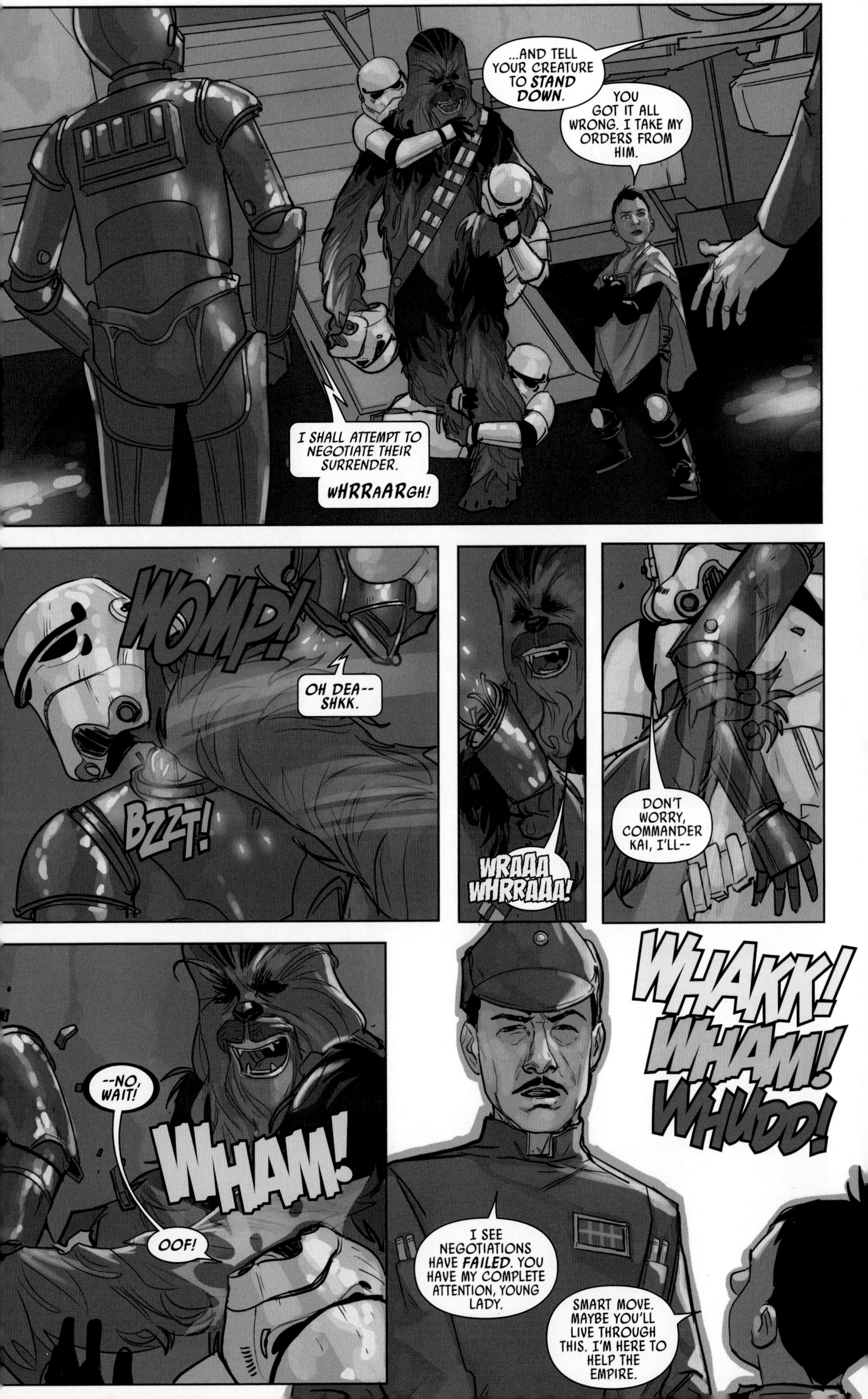
...AND TELL YOUR CREATURE TO STAND DOWN.
YOU GOT IT ALL WRONG. I TAKE MY ORDERS FROM HIM.
I SHALL ATTEMPT TO NEGOTIATE THEIR SURRENDER.
WHRRAARGH!
WOMP!
OH DEA-- SHKK.
BZZT!
WRAAA WHRRAAA!
DON'T WORRY, COMMANDER KAI, I'LL--
--NO, WAIT!
WHAM!
OOF!
WHAKK! WHAM! WHUDD!
I SEE NEGOTIATIONS HAVE FAILED. YOU HAVE MY COMPLETE ATTENTION, YOUNG LADY.
SMART MOVE. MAYBE YOU'LL LIVE THROUGH THIS. I'M HERE TO HELP THE EMPIRE.

JAUM IS HERE TO SELL YOU SOME *LIES*, SWIPE YOUR *CREDITS*--HE SAYS HE'S A GANGSTER, BUT HE'S NOT. HE'S A *REBEL SPY*.

IF YOU INSPECT THE SURFACE, HE DOESN'T EVEN HAVE A MINING OPERATION AT ALL.

BUT--WE'VE INSPECTED HIS SAMPLES.

THOSE ARE ALL IMPORTS FROM WHO KNOWS WHERE.

DID YOU SCAN HIS DROID CAREFULLY? I SAW HIM CRAMMING IT WITH *EXPLOSIVES*.

ARE YOU SAYING--

THAT DROID'S A BOMB!

WE'VE BEEN DECEIVED!

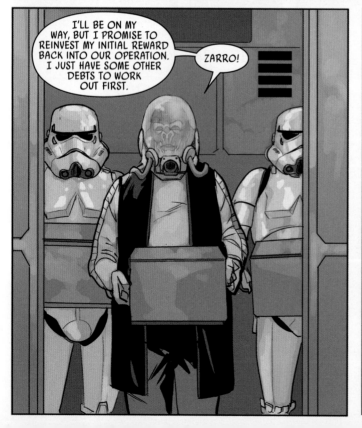

I'LL BE ON MY WAY, BUT I PROMISE TO REINVEST MY INITIAL REWARD BACK INTO OUR OPERATION. I JUST HAVE SOME OTHER DEBTS TO WORK OUT FIRST.

ZARRO!

WHAT ARE THESE TWO DOING HERE?

WRAAAAA!

IT'S OVER, JAUM--I'VE TOLD THEM THE TRUTH ABOUT YOU.

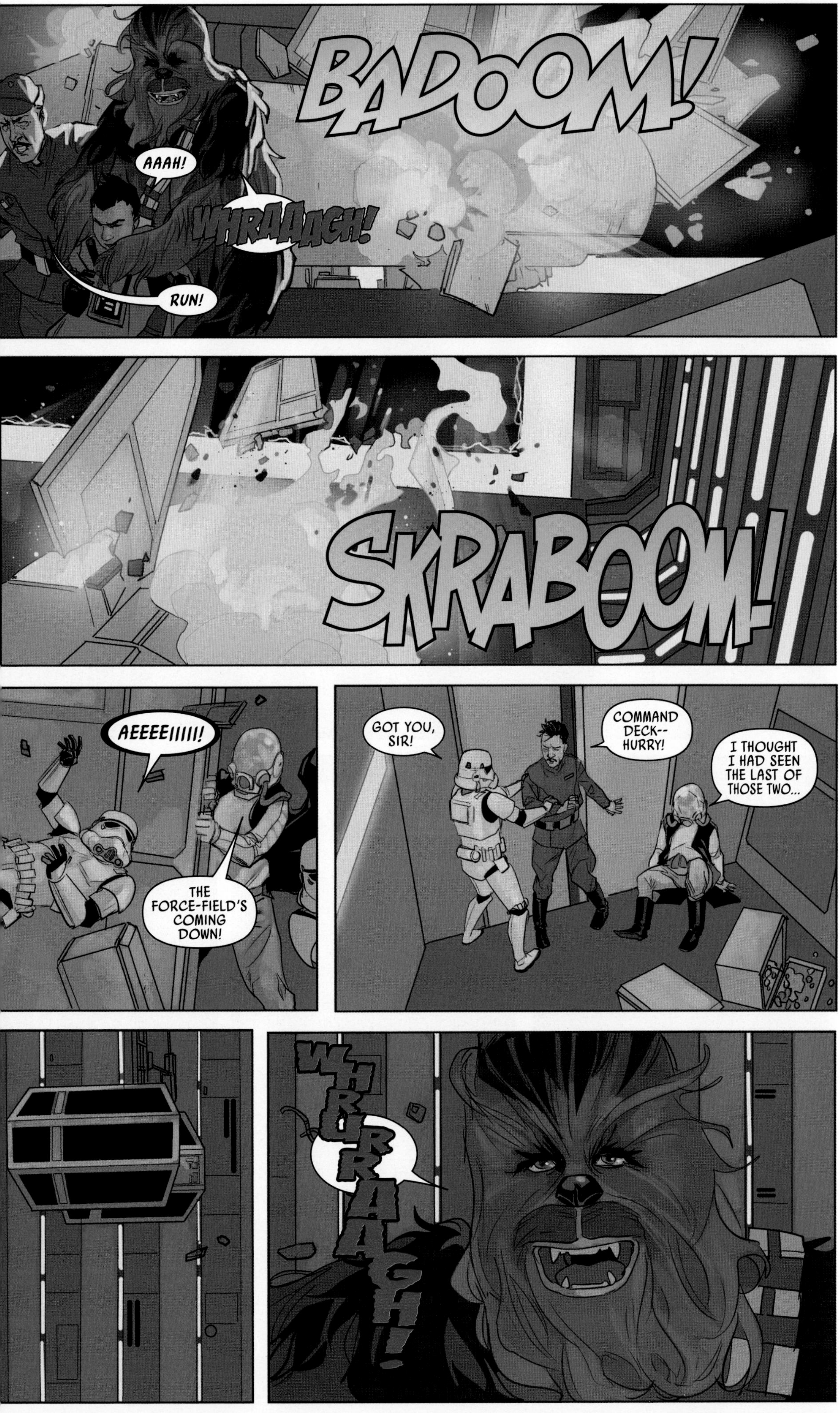
BADOOM!
AAAH!
WHRAAAAGH!
RUN!
SKRABOOM!
AEEEEIIIII!
THE FORCE-FIELD'S COMING DOWN!
GOT YOU, SIR!
COMMAND DECK--HURRY!
I THOUGHT I HAD SEEN THE LAST OF THOSE TWO...
WHRRRAAAGH!

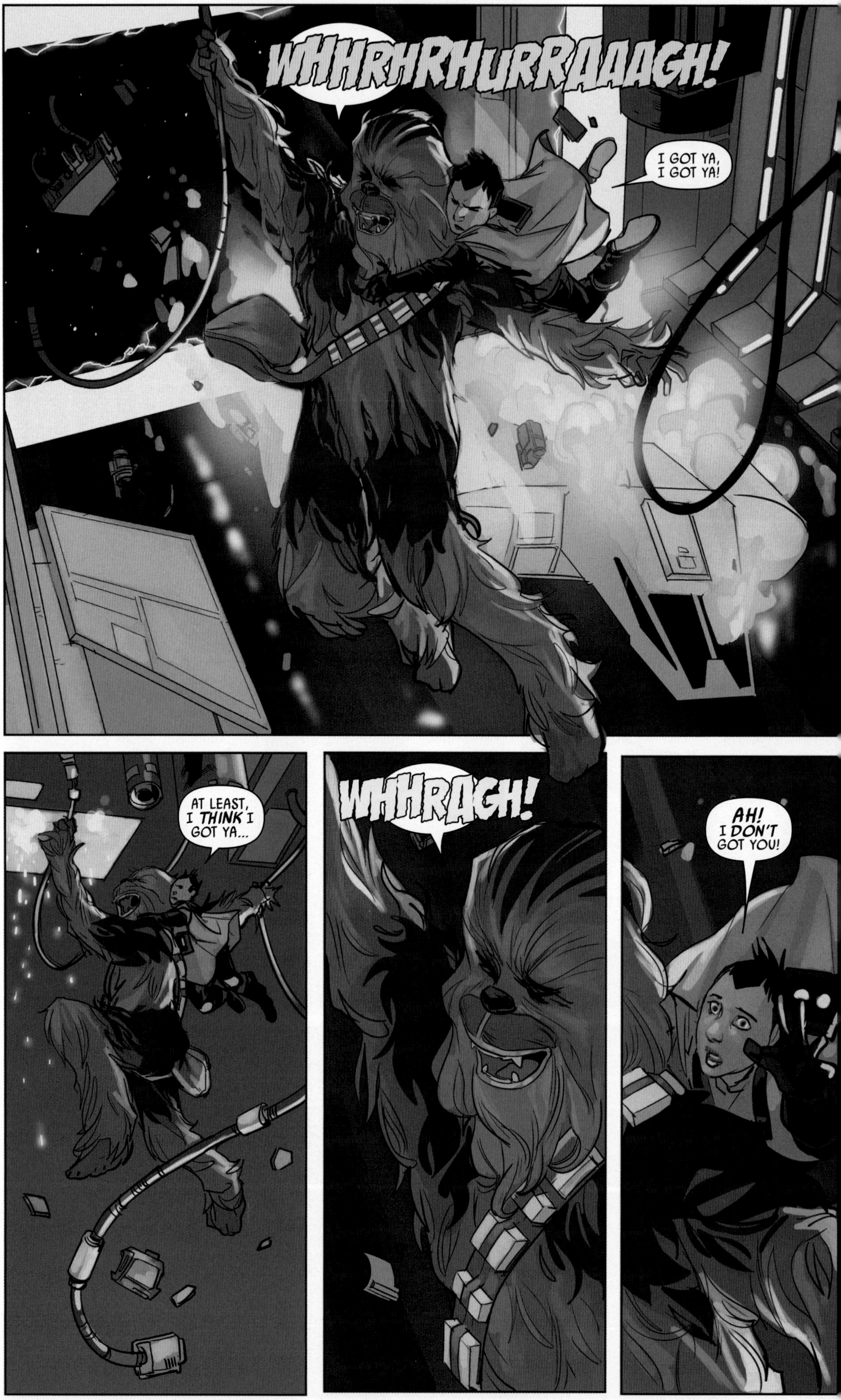
WHHRHRHURRAAAGH!
I GOT YA, I GOT YA!
AT LEAST, I THINK I GOT YA...
WHHRAGH!
AH! I DON'T GOT YOU!

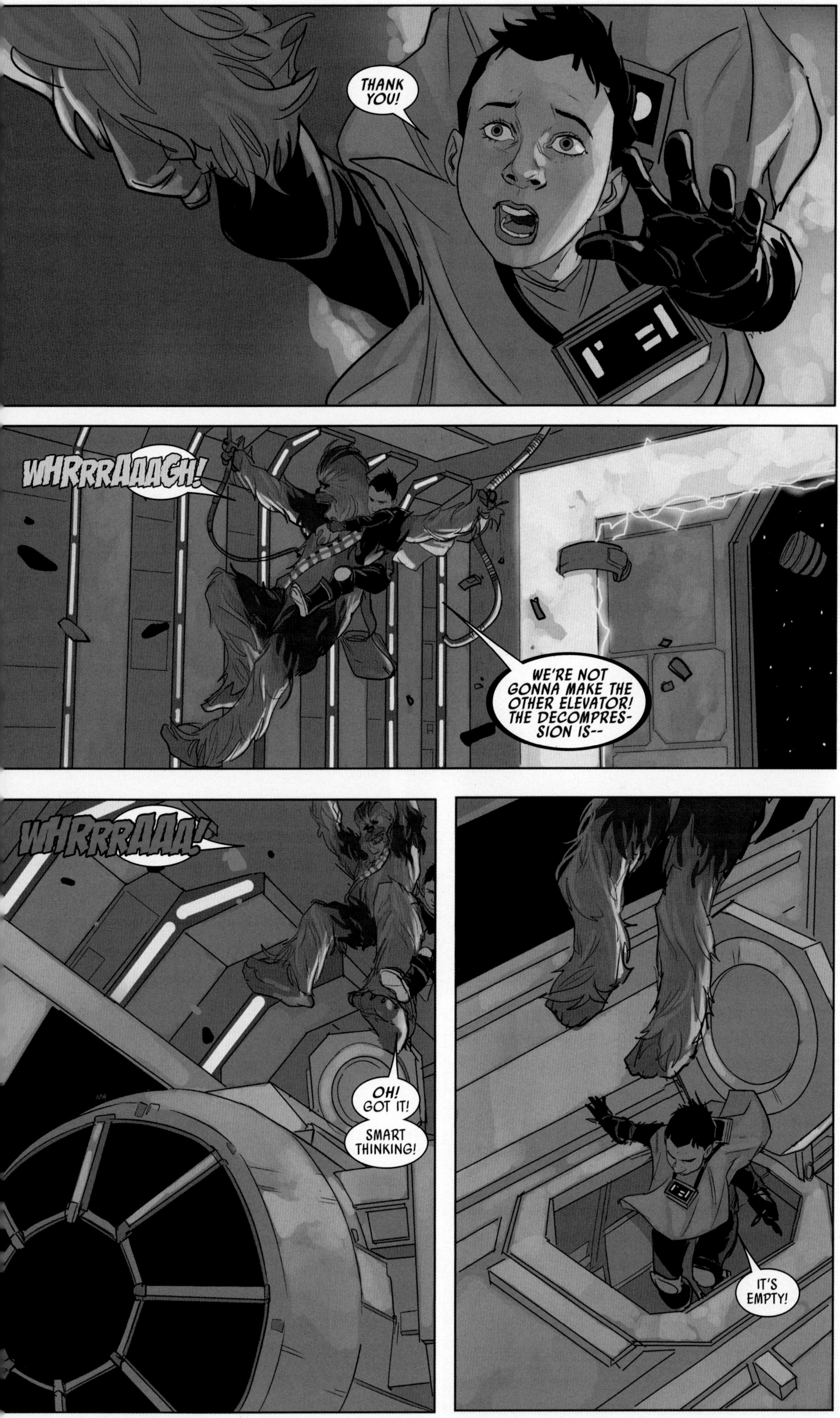
THANK YOU!
WHRRRAAAGH!
WE'RE NOT GONNA MAKE THE OTHER ELEVATOR! THE DECOMPRES-SION IS--
WHRRRAAA!
OH! GOT IT!
SMART THINKING!
IT'S EMPTY!

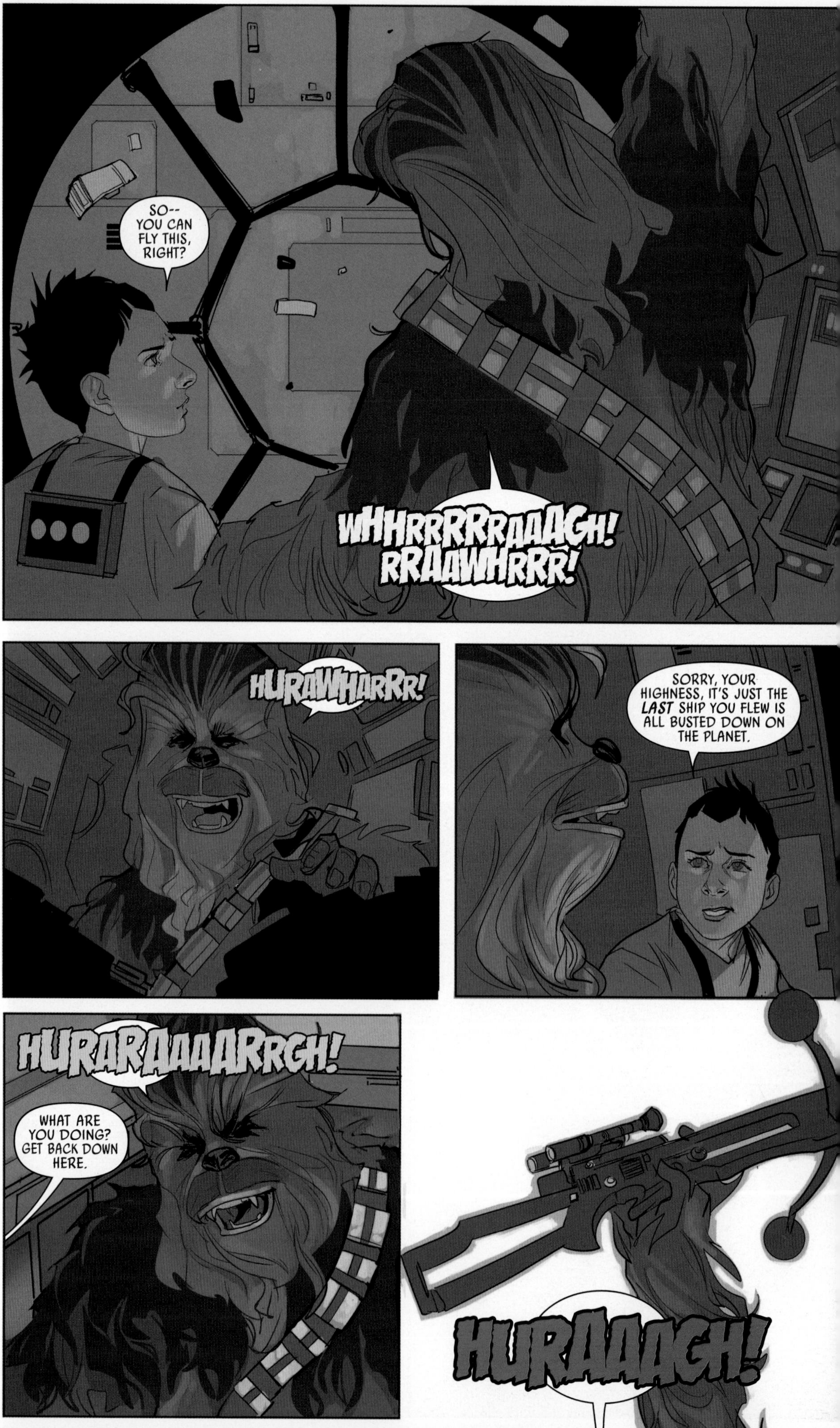
SO-- YOU CAN FLY THIS, RIGHT?
WHHRRRRRAAAGH! RRAAWHRRR!
HURAWHARRR!
SORRY, YOUR HIGHNESS, IT'S JUST THE LAST SHIP YOU FLEW IS ALL BUSTED DOWN ON THE PLANET.
HURARAAAARRGH!
WHAT ARE YOU DOING? GET BACK DOWN HERE.
HURAAACH!

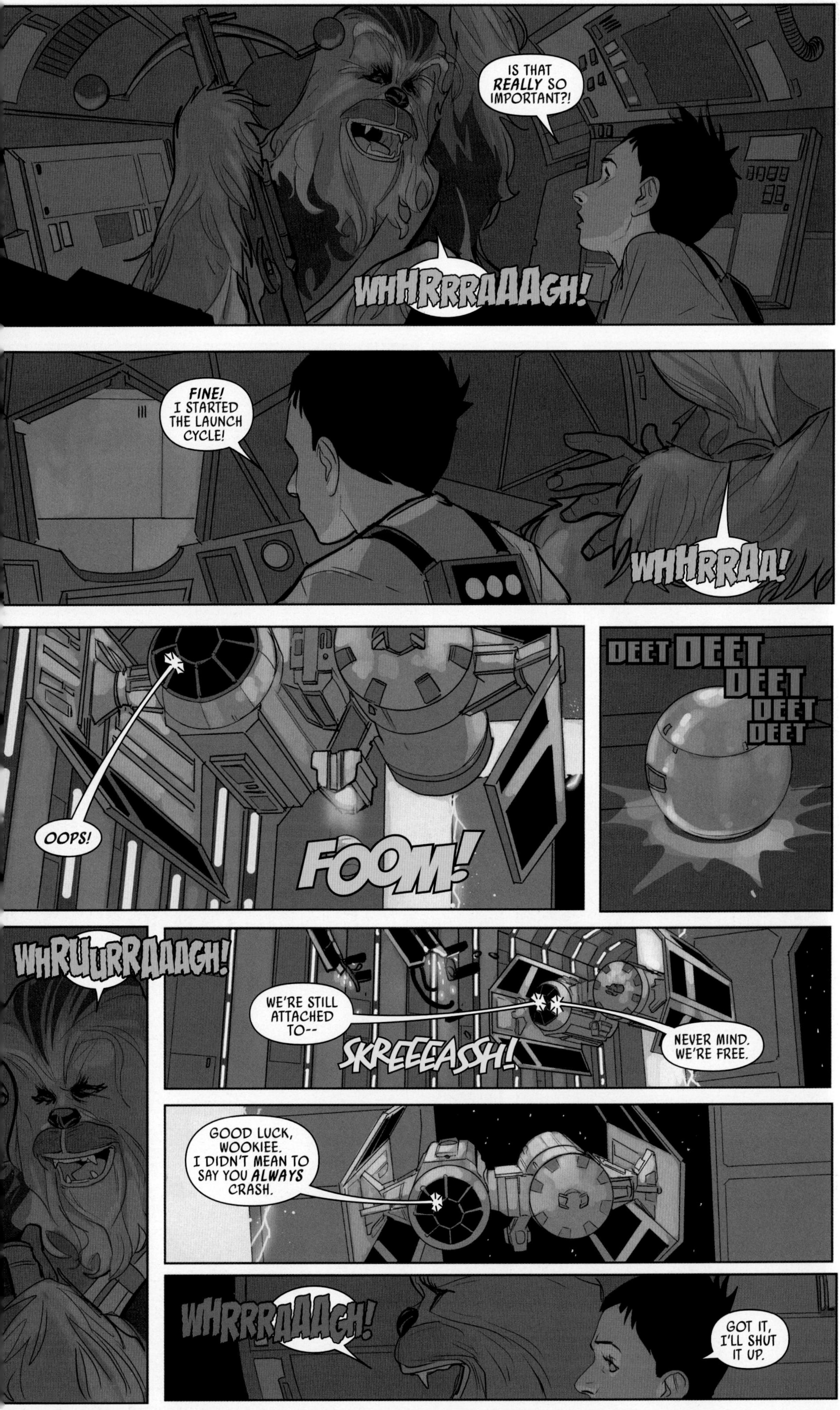
IS THAT REALLY SO IMPORTANT?!
WHHRRRRAAAGH!
FINE! I STARTED THE LAUNCH CYCLE!
WHHRRAA!
OOPS!
FOOM!
DEET DEET DEET DEET DEET
WHRUURRAAAGH!
WE'RE STILL ATTACHED TO--
SKREEEASSH!
NEVER MIND. WE'RE FREE.
GOOD LUCK, WOOKIEE. I DIDN'T MEAN TO SAY YOU ALWAYS CRASH.
WHRRRAAAGH!
GOT IT, I'LL SHUT IT UP.

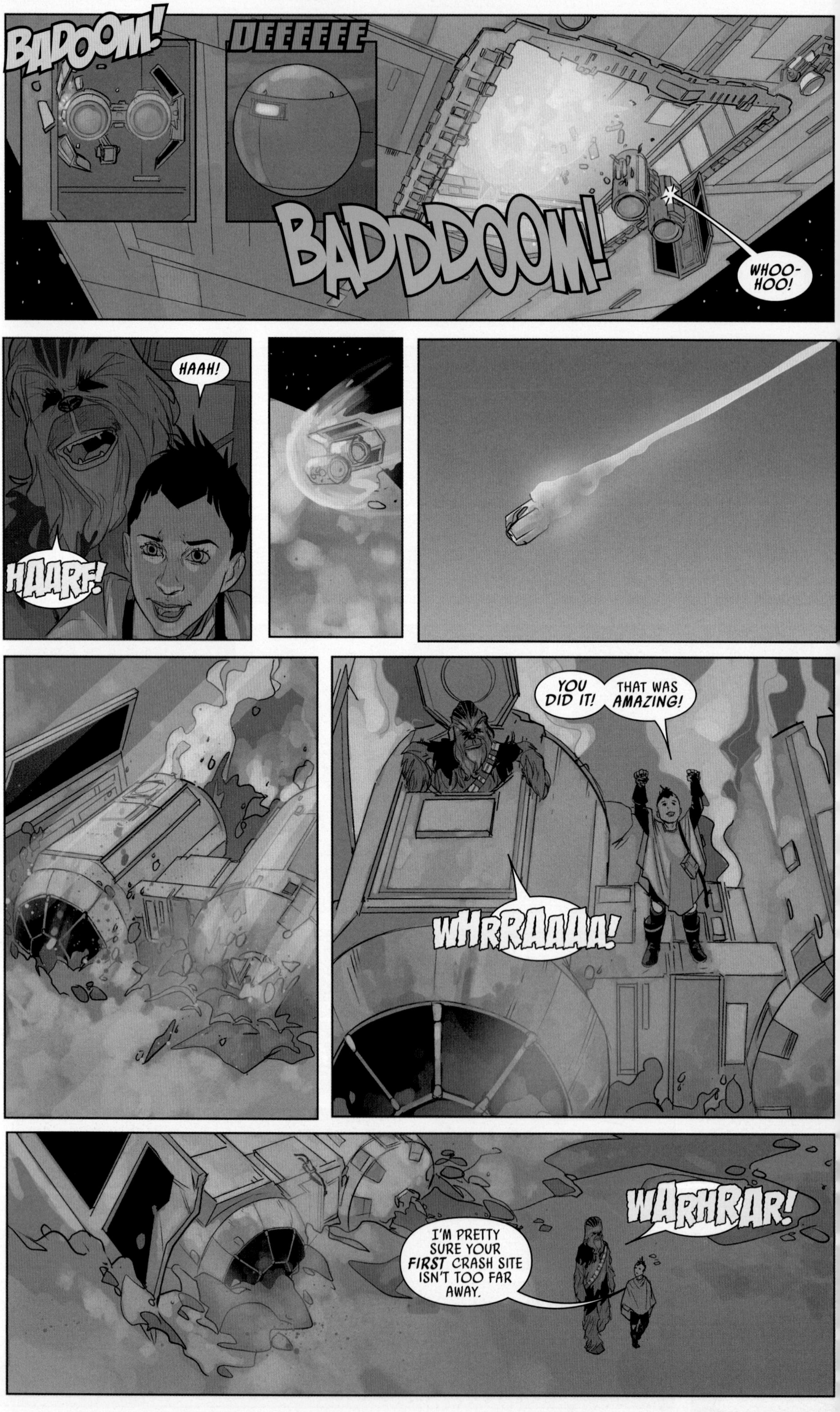
BADOOM!
DEEEEEE
BADDDOOM!
WHOO-HOO!
HAAH!
HAARF!
YOU DID IT!
THAT WAS AMAZING!
WHRRAAAA!
WARHRAR!
I'M PRETTY SURE YOUR FIRST CRASH SITE ISN'T TOO FAR AWAY.

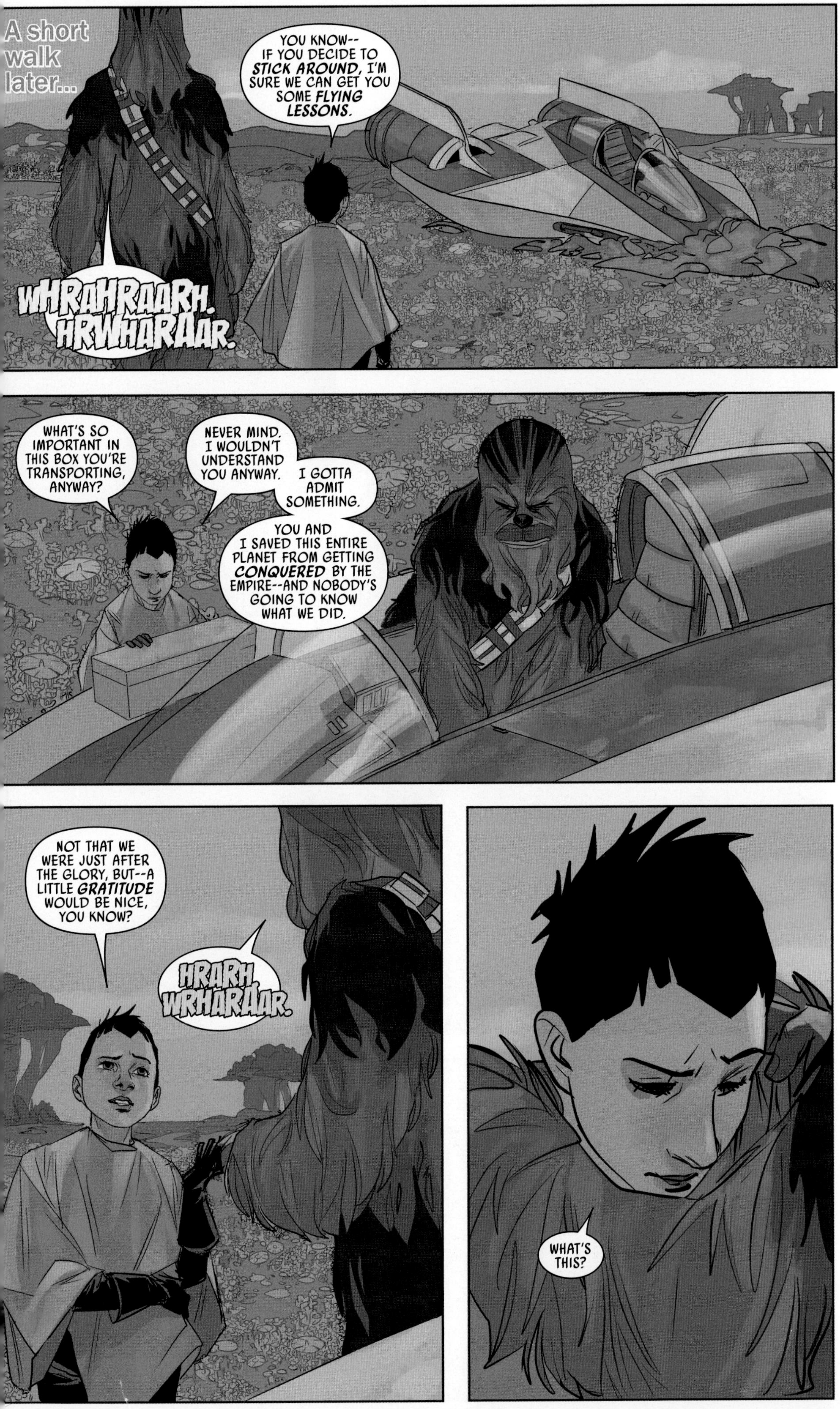
A short walk later...
YOU KNOW-- IF YOU DECIDE TO STICK AROUND, I'M SURE WE CAN GET YOU SOME FLYING LESSONS.
WHRAHRAARH. HRWHARAAR.
WHAT'S SO IMPORTANT IN THIS BOX YOU'RE TRANSPORTING, ANYWAY?
NEVER MIND. I WOULDN'T UNDERSTAND YOU ANYWAY.
I GOTTA ADMIT SOMETHING.
YOU AND I SAVED THIS ENTIRE PLANET FROM GETTING CONQUERED BY THE EMPIRE--AND NOBODY'S GOING TO KNOW WHAT WE DID.
NOT THAT WE WERE JUST AFTER THE GLORY, BUT--A LITTLE GRATITUDE WOULD BE NICE, YOU KNOW?
HRARH. WRHARAAR.
WHAT'S THIS?

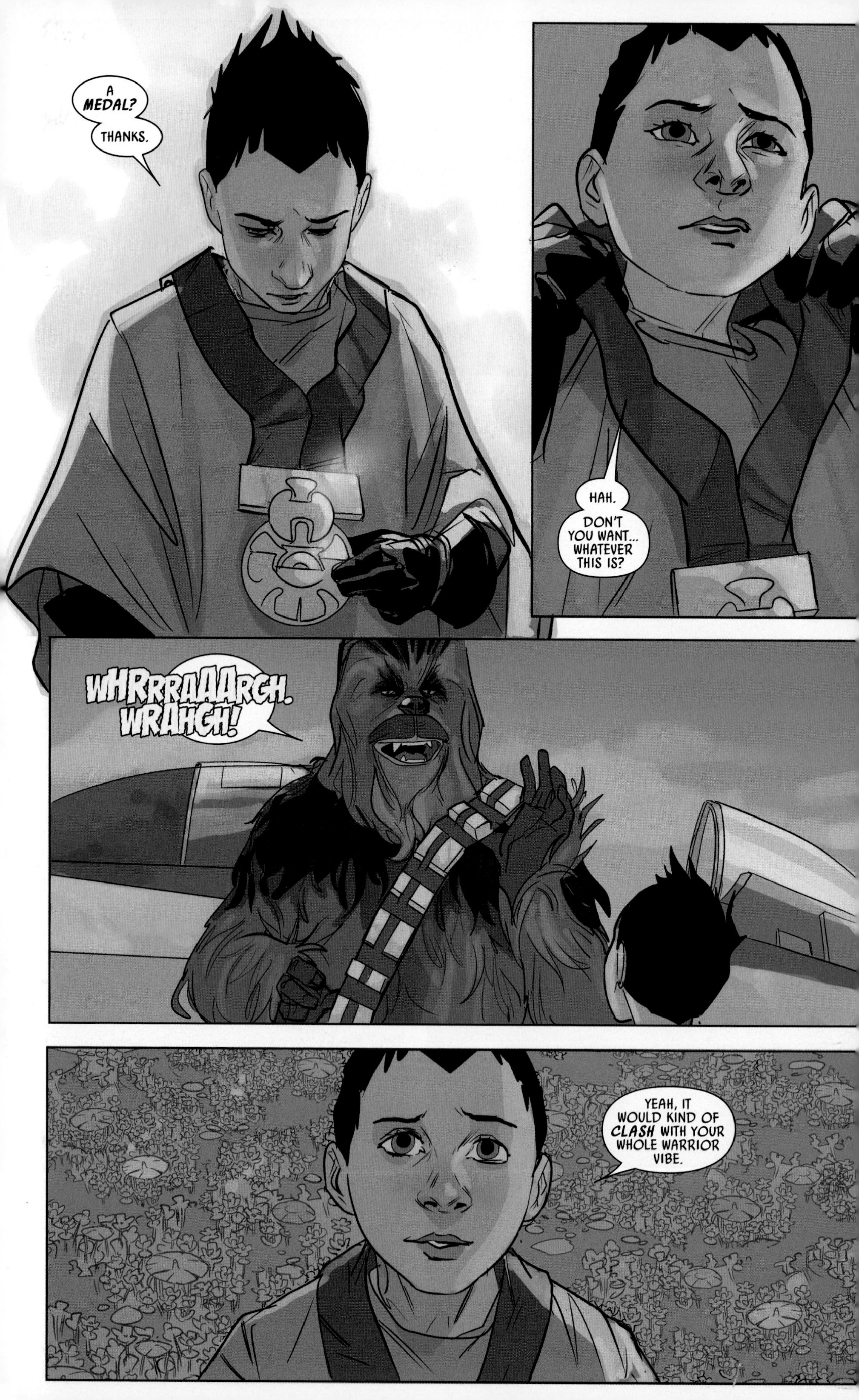
A MEDAL?
THANKS.
HAH.
DON'T YOU WANT... WHATEVER THIS IS?
WHRRRAAARGH. WRAHGH!
YEAH, IT WOULD KIND OF CLASH WITH YOUR WHOLE WARRIOR VIBE.

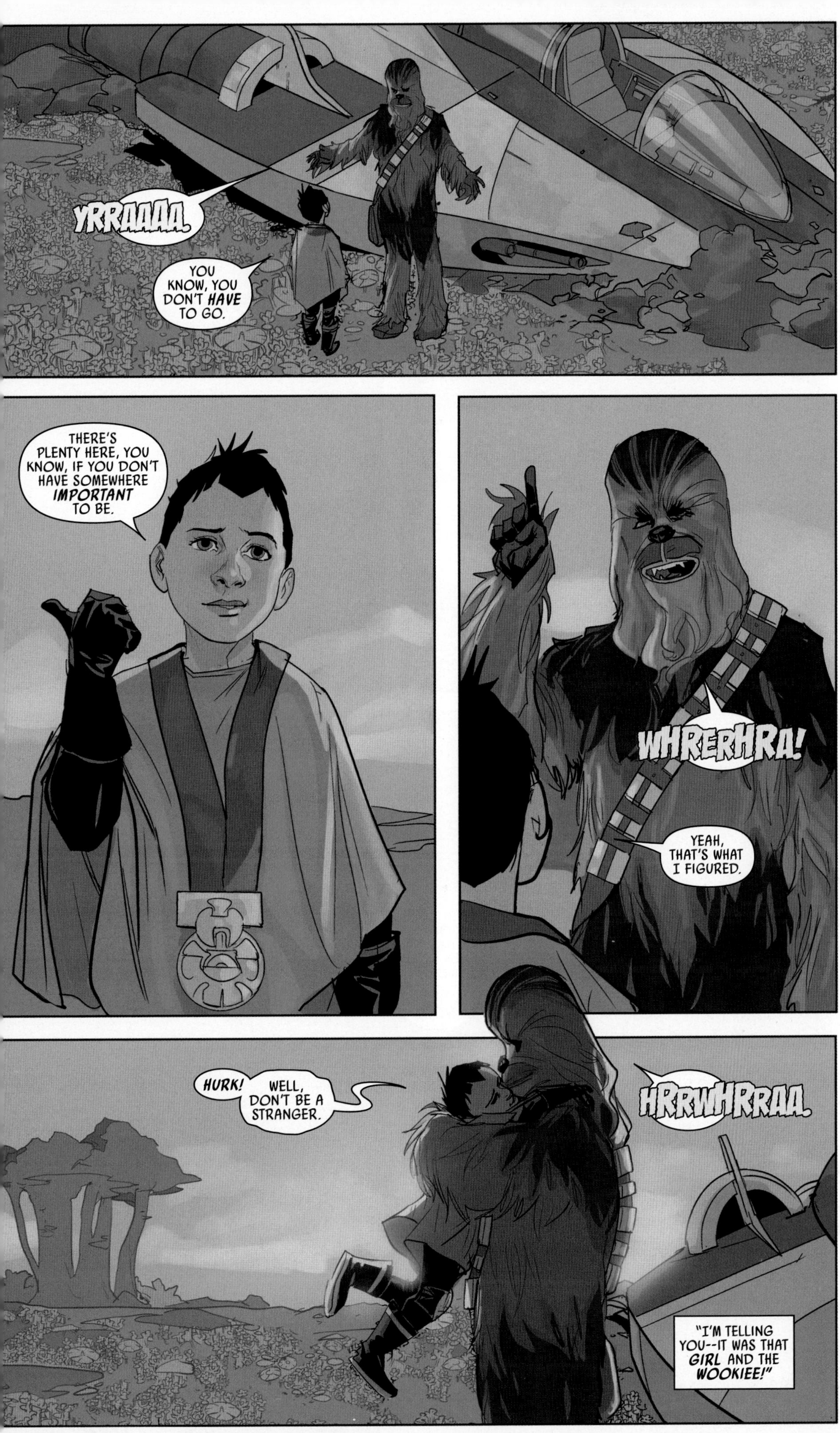
YRRAAAA.
YOU KNOW, YOU DON'T HAVE TO GO.
THERE'S PLENTY HERE, YOU KNOW, IF YOU DON'T HAVE SOMEWHERE IMPORTANT TO BE.
WHRERHRA!
YEAH, THAT'S WHAT I FIGURED.
HURK!
WELL, DON'T BE A STRANGER.
HRRWHRRAA.
"I'M TELLING YOU--IT WAS THAT GIRL AND THE WOOKIEE!"

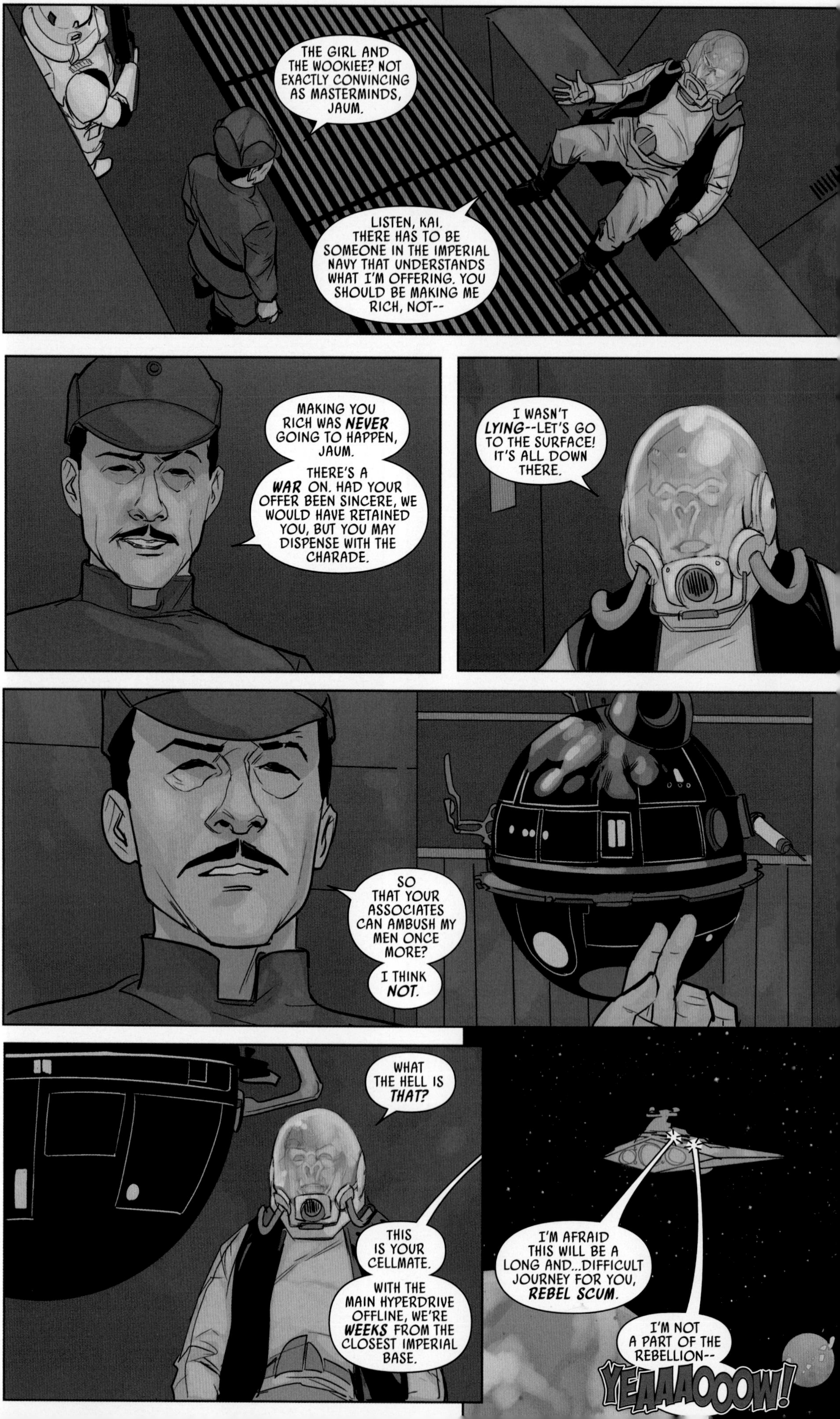
THE GIRL AND THE WOOKIEE? NOT EXACTLY CONVINCING AS MASTERMINDS, JAUM.
LISTEN, KAI. THERE HAS TO BE SOMEONE IN THE IMPERIAL NAVY THAT UNDERSTANDS WHAT I'M OFFERING. YOU SHOULD BE MAKING ME RICH, NOT--
MAKING YOU RICH WAS NEVER GOING TO HAPPEN, JAUM.
THERE'S A WAR ON. HAD YOUR OFFER BEEN SINCERE, WE WOULD HAVE RETAINED YOU, BUT YOU MAY DISPENSE WITH THE CHARADE.
I WASN'T LYING--LET'S GO TO THE SURFACE! IT'S ALL DOWN THERE.
SO THAT YOUR ASSOCIATES CAN AMBUSH MY MEN ONCE MORE?
I THINK NOT.
WHAT THE HELL IS THAT?
THIS IS YOUR CELLMATE.
WITH THE MAIN HYPERDRIVE OFFLINE, WE'RE WEEKS FROM THE CLOSEST IMPERIAL BASE.
I'M AFRAID THIS WILL BE A LONG AND...DIFFICULT JOURNEY FOR YOU, REBEL SCUM.
I'M NOT A PART OF THE REBELLION--
YEAAAOOOW!

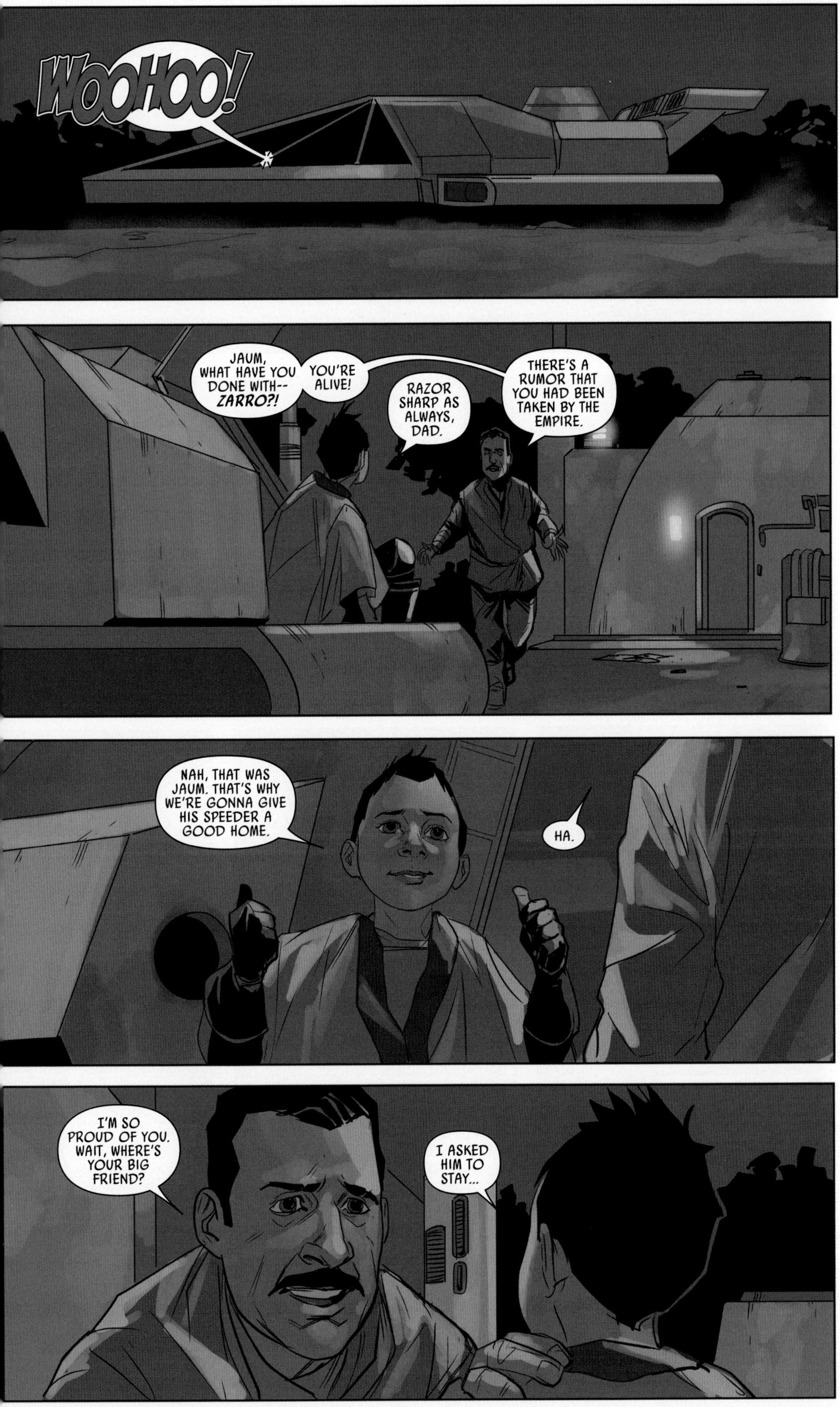
WOOHOO!
JAUM, WHAT HAVE YOU DONE WITH-- ZARRO?!
YOU'RE ALIVE!
THERE'S A RUMOR THAT YOU HAD BEEN TAKEN BY THE EMPIRE.
RAZOR SHARP AS ALWAYS, DAD.
NAH, THAT WAS JAUM. THAT'S WHY WE'RE GONNA GIVE HIS SPEEDER A GOOD HOME.
HA.
I'M SO PROUD OF YOU. WAIT, WHERE'S YOUR BIG FRIEND?
I ASKED HIM TO STAY...

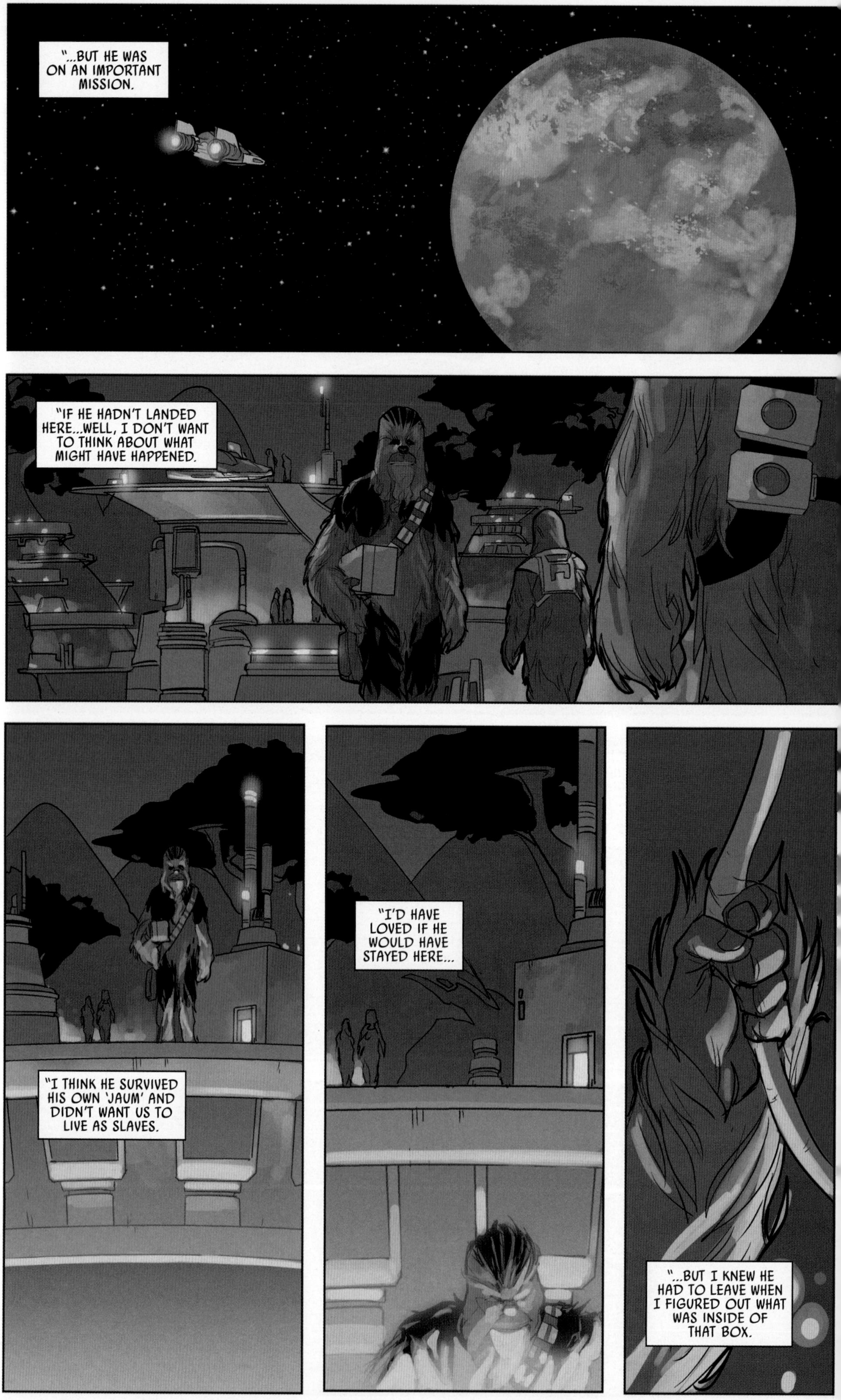
"...BUT HE WAS ON AN IMPORTANT MISSION.
"IF HE HADN'T LANDED HERE...WELL, I DON'T WANT TO THINK ABOUT WHAT MIGHT HAVE HAPPENED.
"I THINK HE SURVIVED HIS OWN 'JAUM' AND DIDN'T WANT US TO LIVE AS SLAVES.
"I'D HAVE LOVED IF HE WOULD HAVE STAYED HERE...
"...BUT I KNEW HE HAD TO LEAVE WHEN I FIGURED OUT WHAT WAS INSIDE OF THAT BOX.

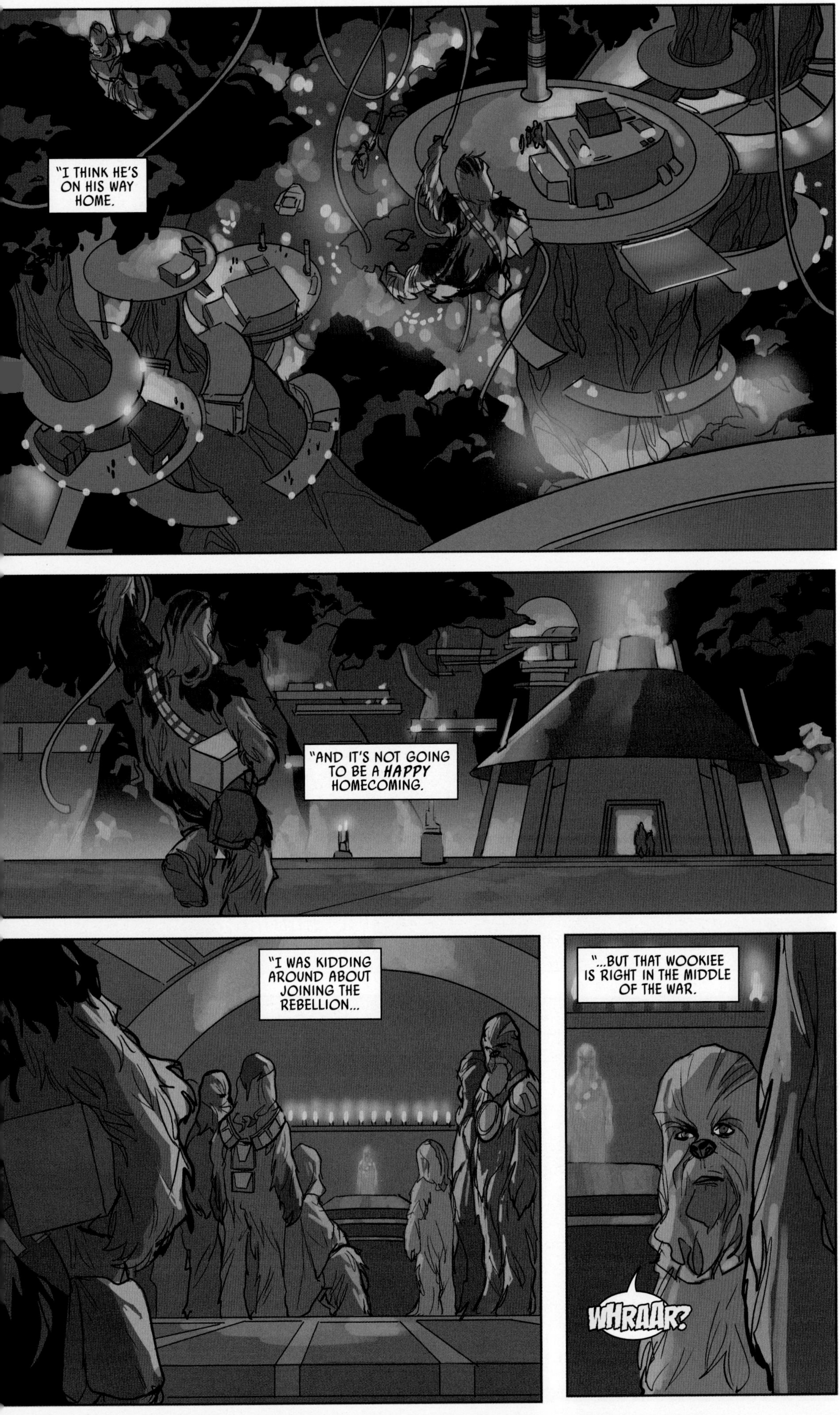
"I THINK HE'S ON HIS WAY HOME.
"AND IT'S NOT GOING TO BE A HAPPY HOMECOMING.
"I WAS KIDDING AROUND ABOUT JOINING THE REBELLION...
"...BUT THAT WOOKIEE IS RIGHT IN THE MIDDLE OF THE WAR.
WHRAAR?

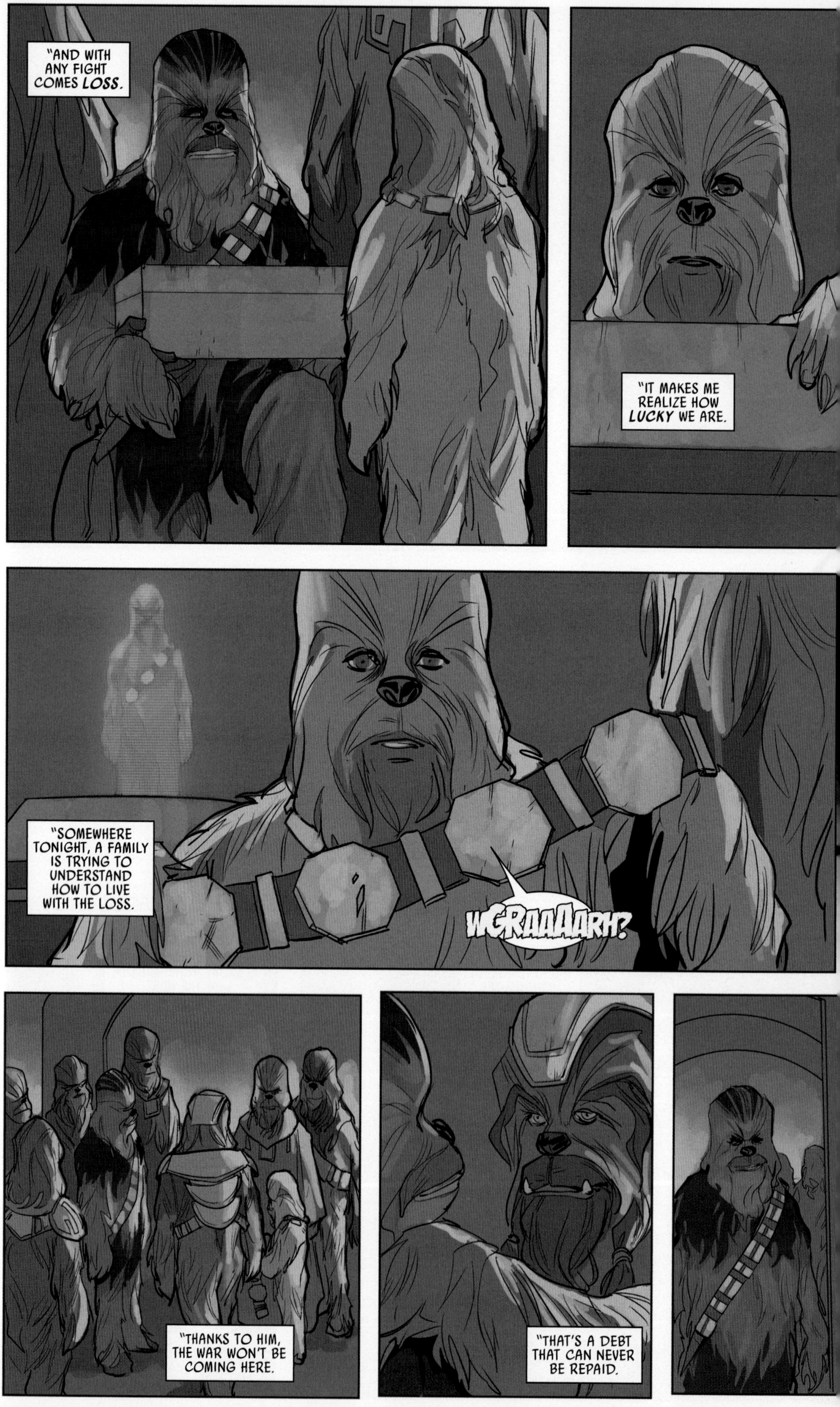
"AND WITH ANY FIGHT COMES LOSS.
"IT MAKES ME REALIZE HOW LUCKY WE ARE.
"SOMEWHERE TONIGHT, A FAMILY IS TRYING TO UNDERSTAND HOW TO LIVE WITH THE LOSS.
WGRAAAARH?
"THANKS TO HIM, THE WAR WON'T BE COMING HERE.
"THAT'S A DEBT THAT CAN NEVER BE REPAID.

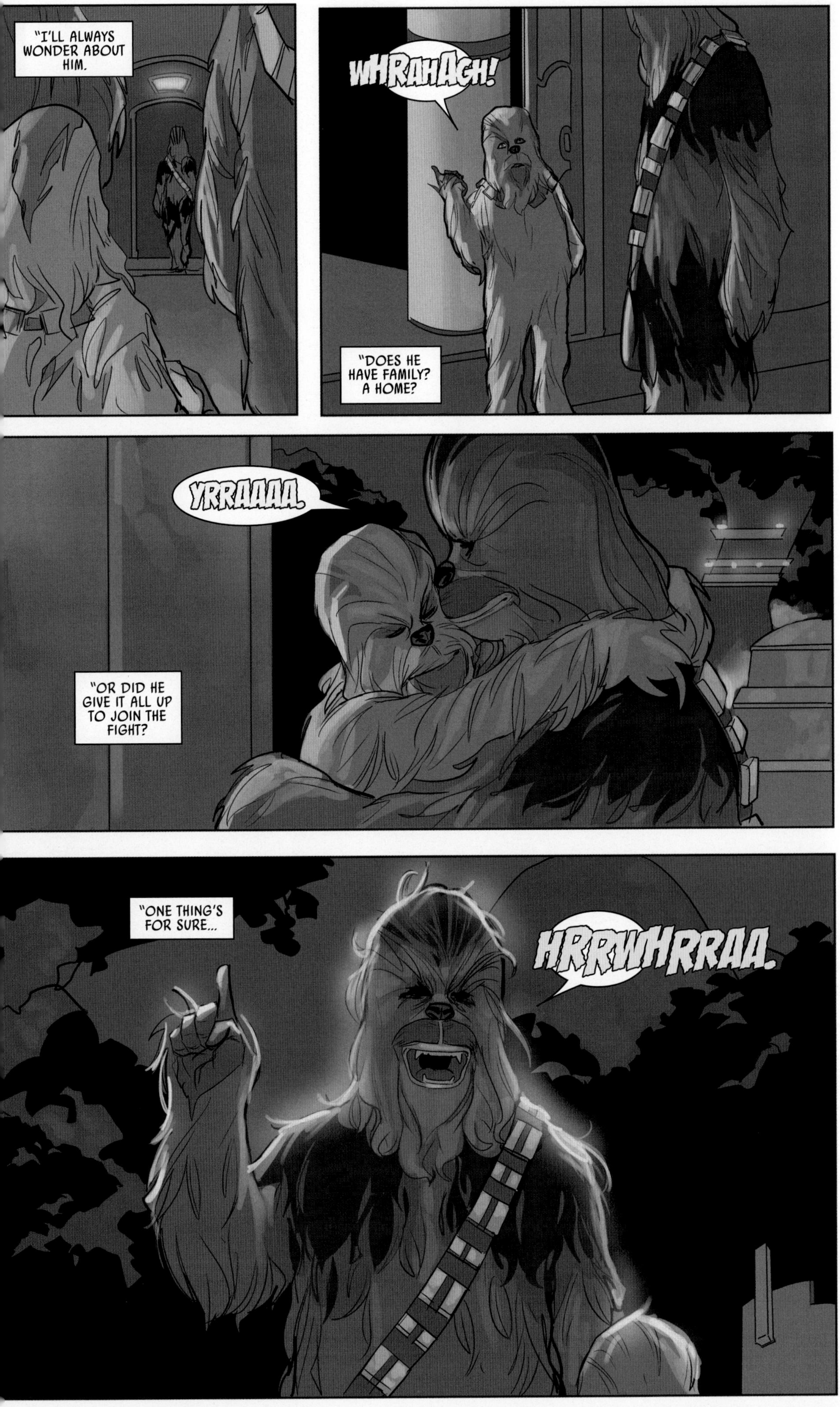
"I'LL ALWAYS WONDER ABOUT HIM.
WHRAHAGH!
"DOES HE HAVE FAMILY? A HOME?
YRRAAAA.
"OR DID HE GIVE IT ALL UP TO JOIN THE FIGHT?
"ONE THING'S FOR SURE...
HRRWHRRAA.

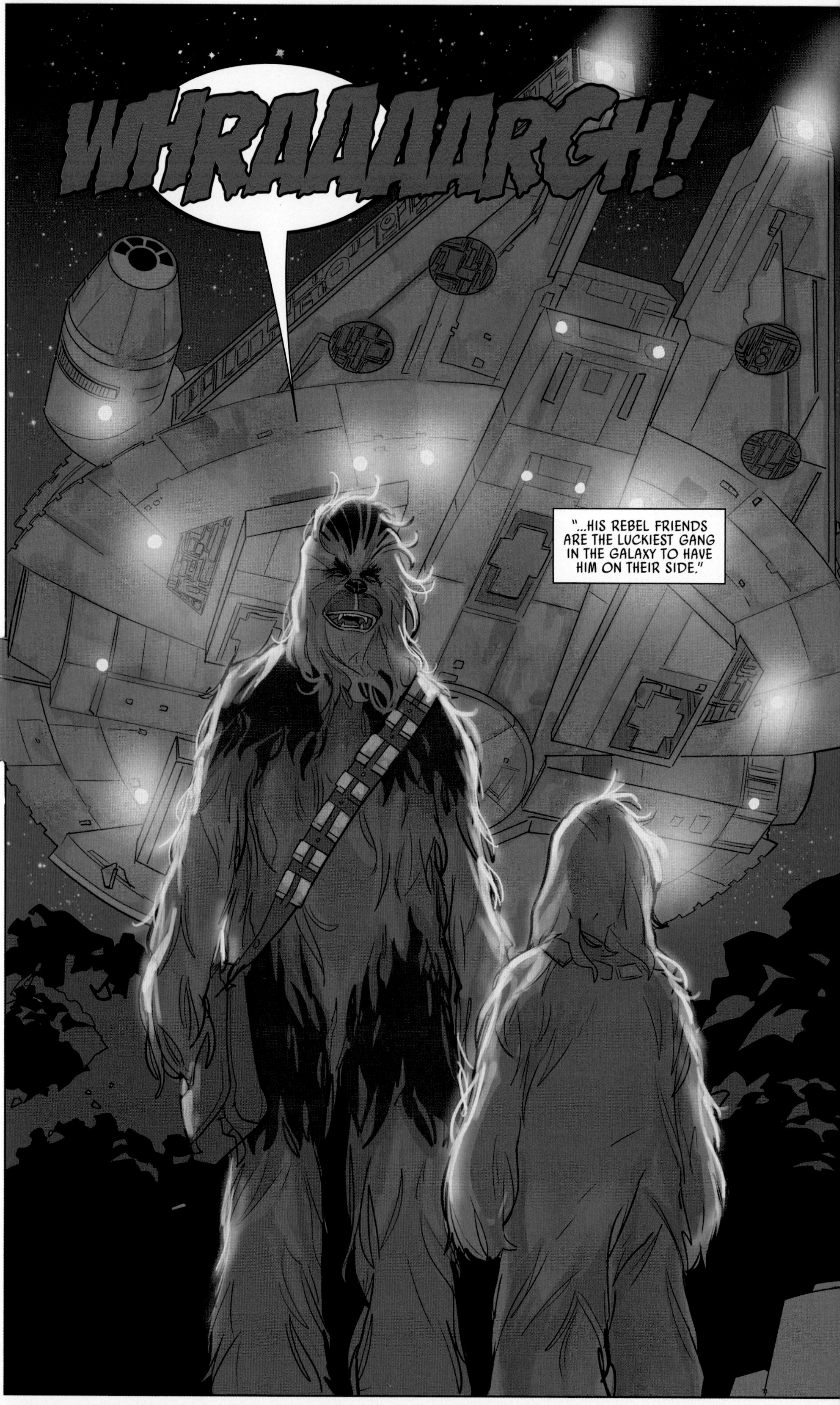
WHRAAAARCH!
"...HIS REBEL FRIENDS ARE THE LUCKIEST GANG IN THE GALAXY TO HAVE HIM ON THEIR SIDE."

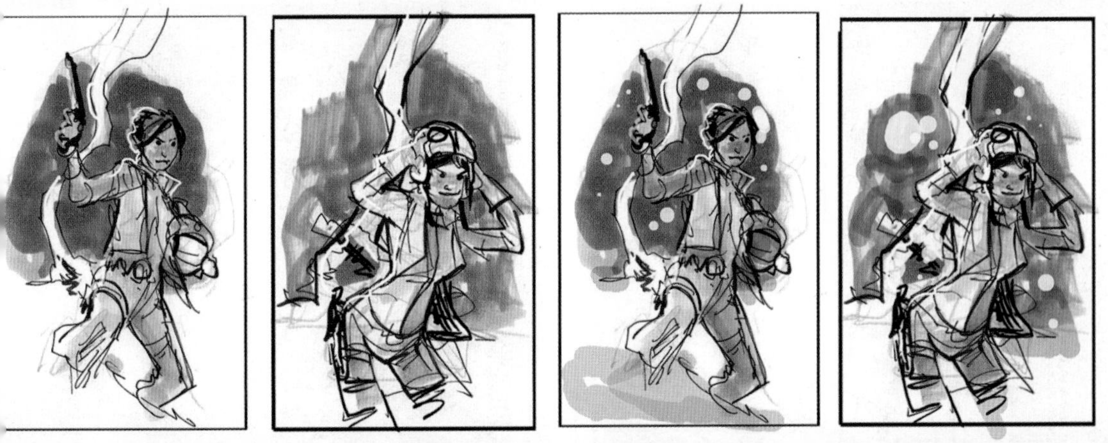

PRINCESS LEIA 1 **Cover Sketches**

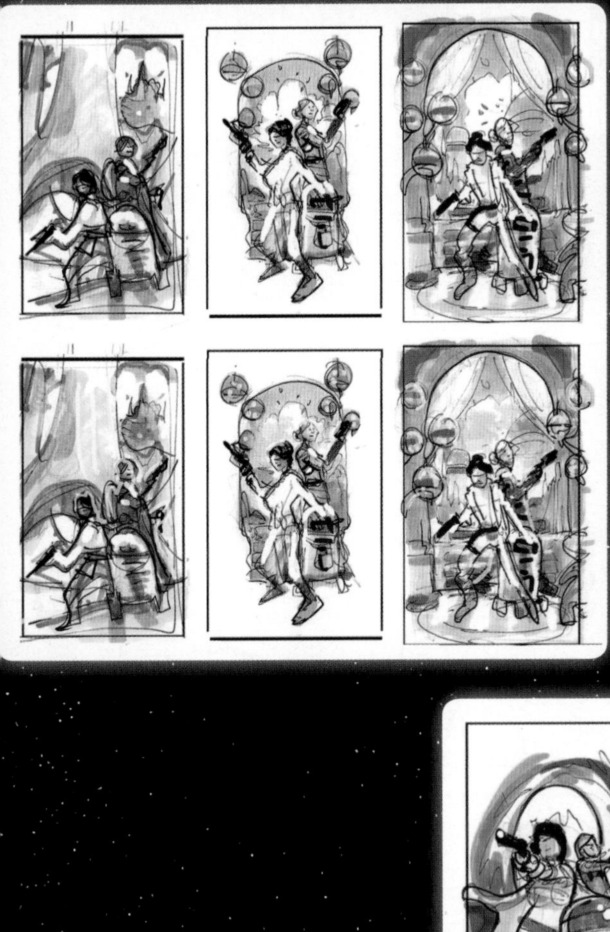

PRINCESS LEIA 2
Cover Sketches

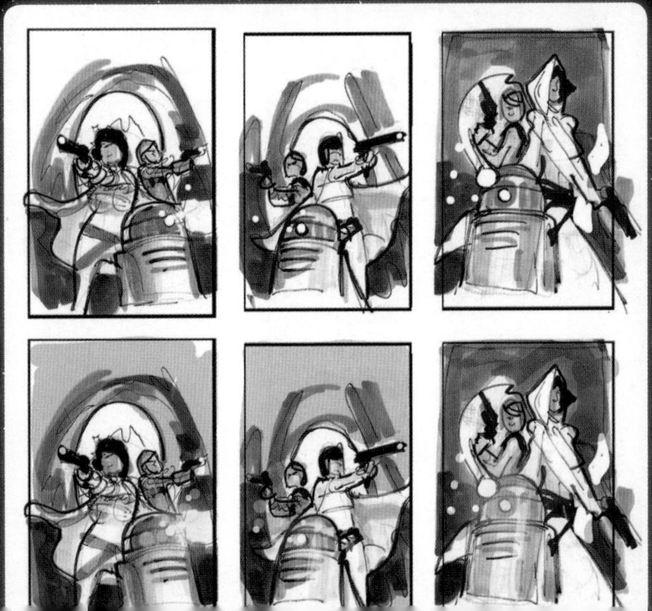

PRINCESS LEIA 3
Cover Sketches

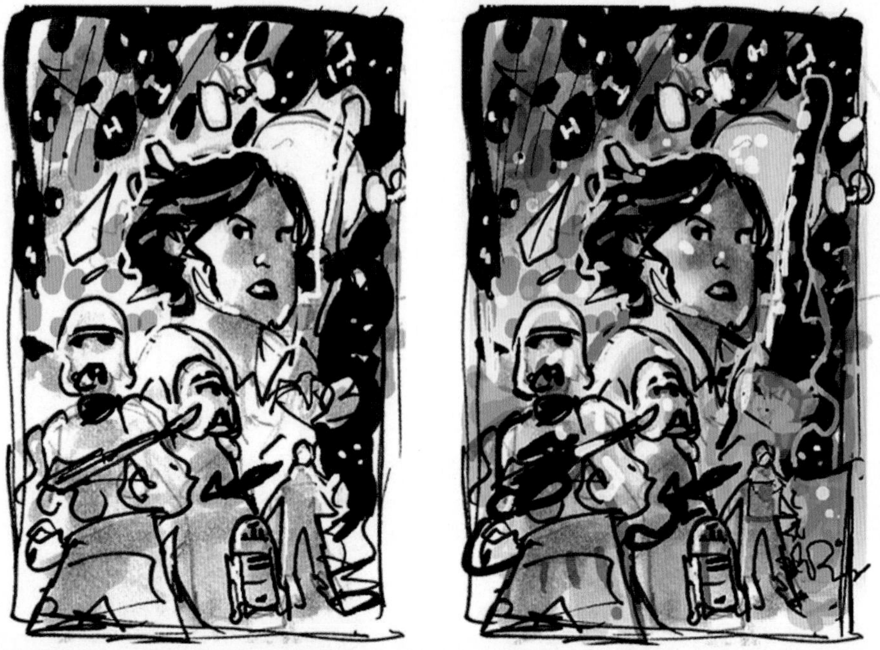

PRINCESS LEIA **4 Cover Sketches**

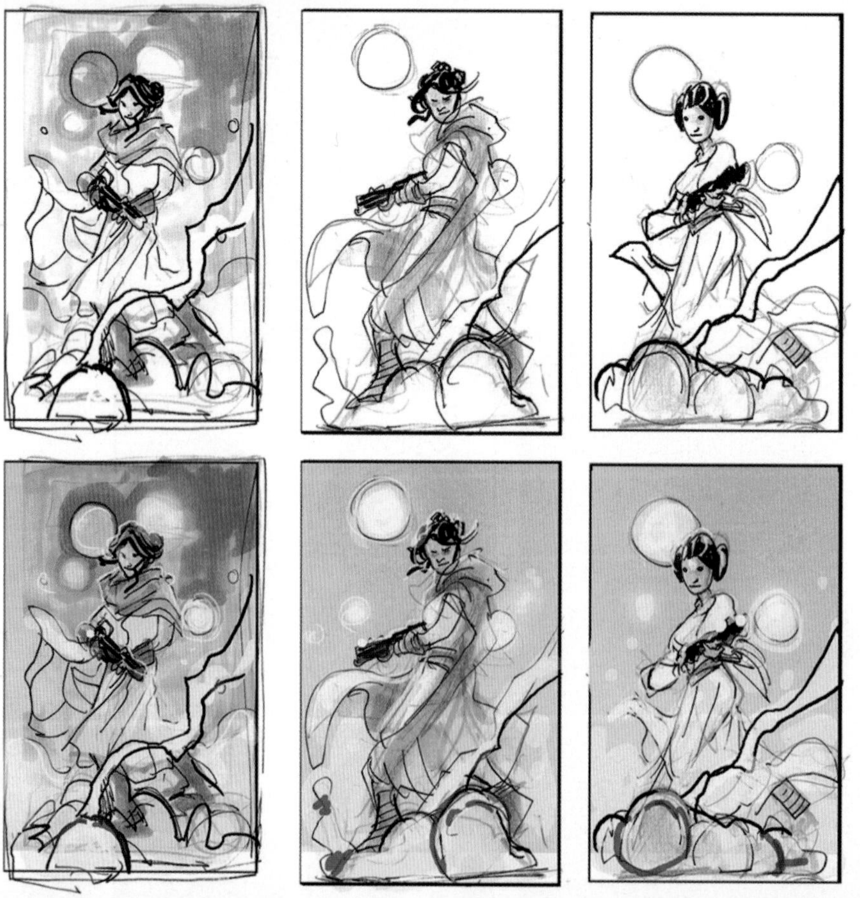

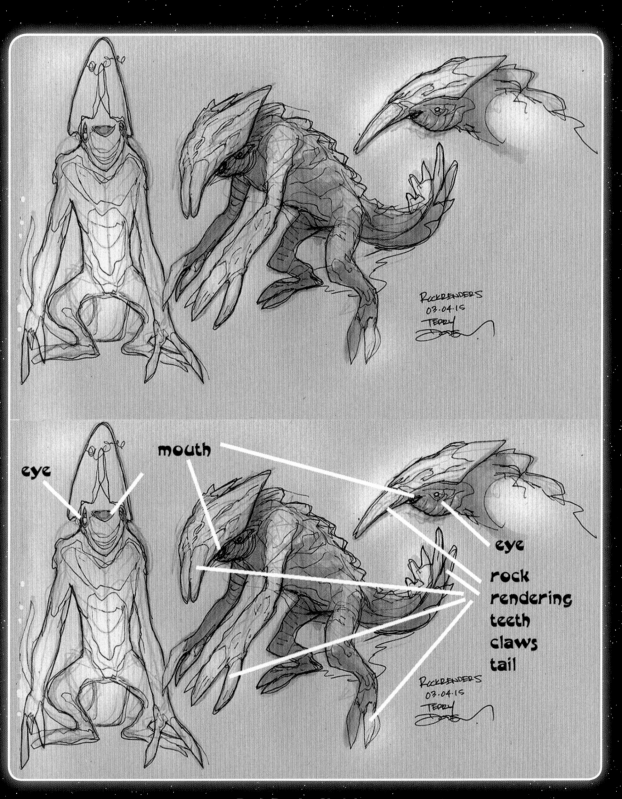

ROCKRENDERS
03.04.15
TERRY
eye
mouth
eye
rock
rendering
teeth
claws
tail
ROCKRENDERS
03.04.15
TERRY

Rock Render Sketches

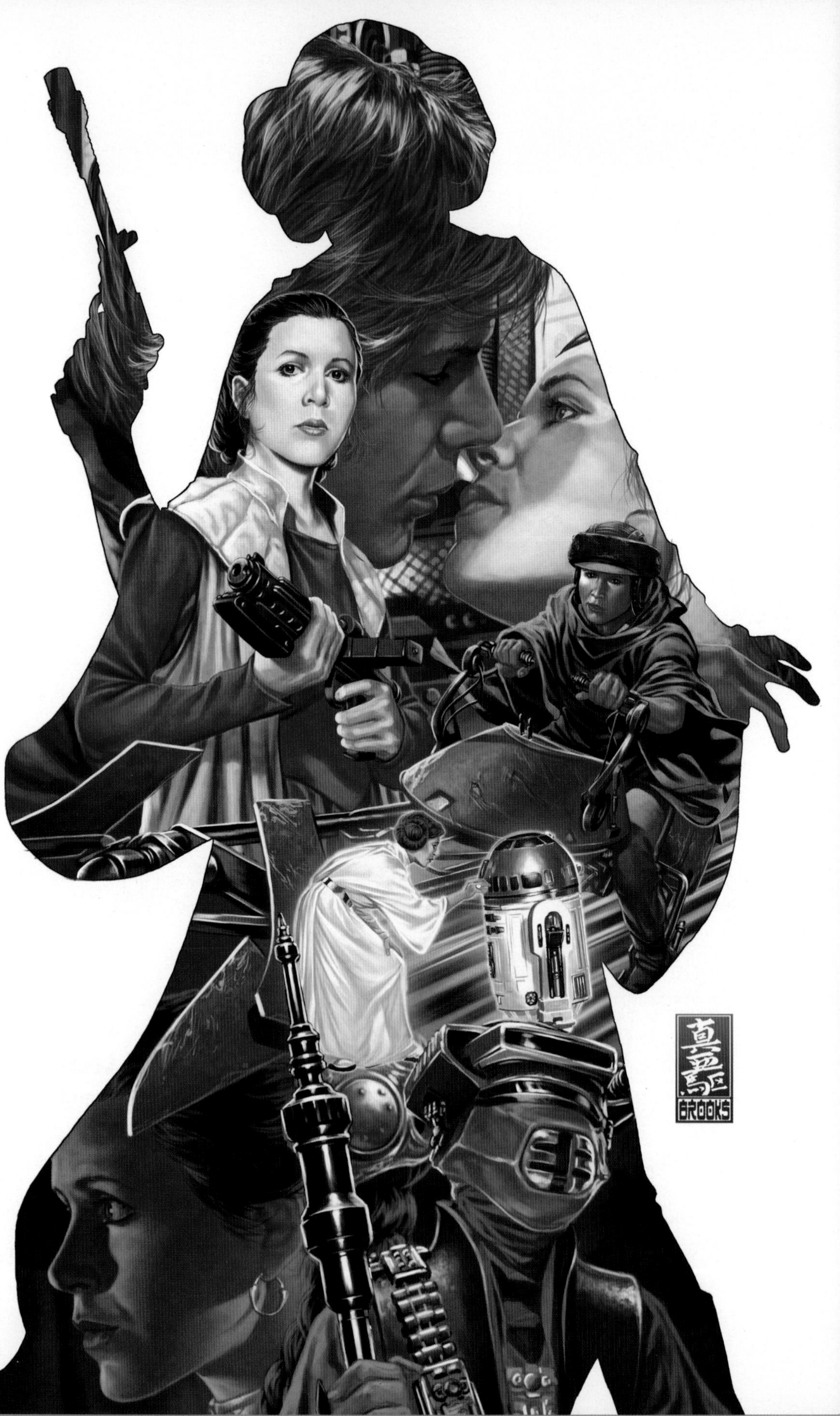
真亜駆
BROOKS

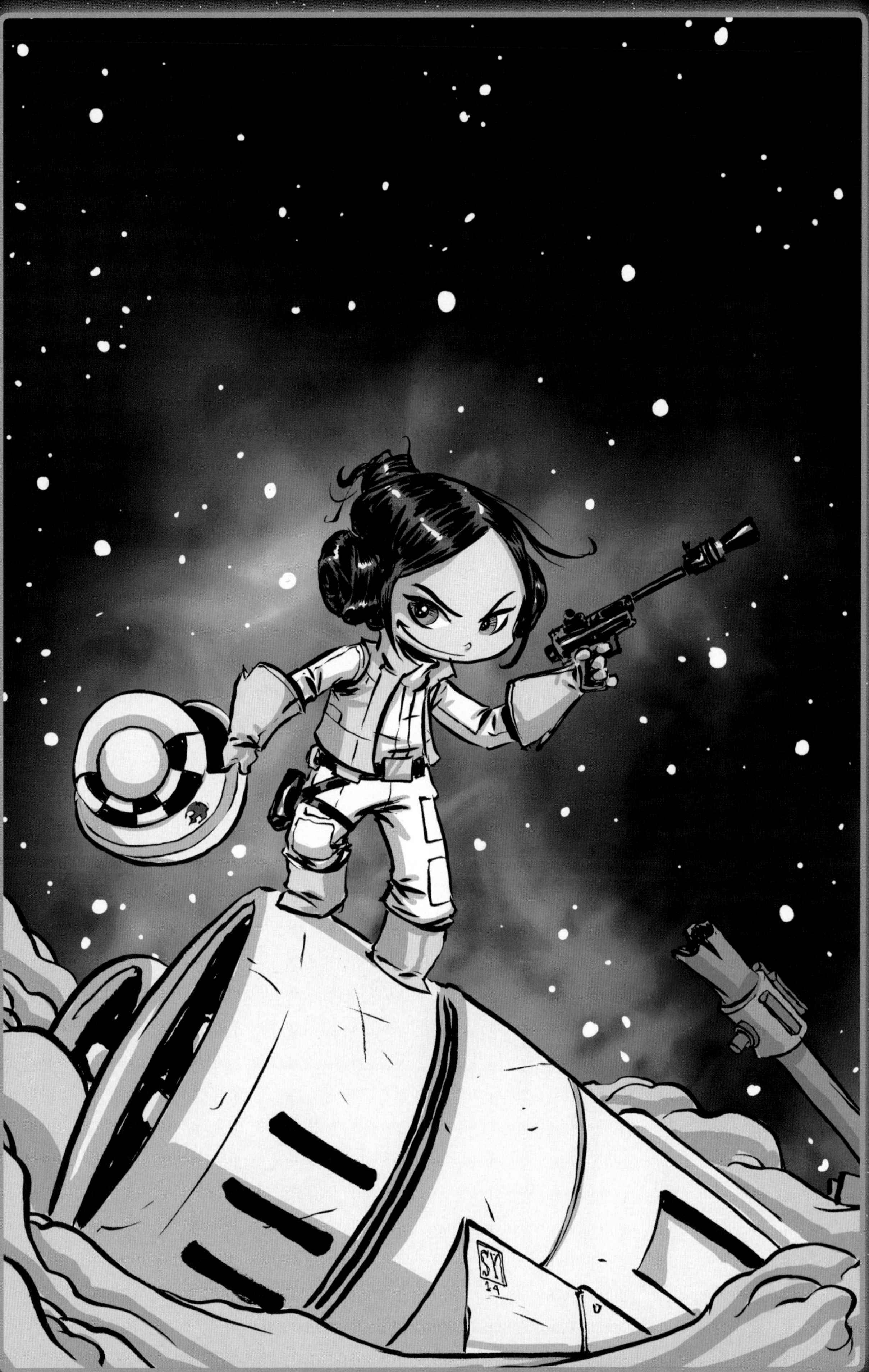

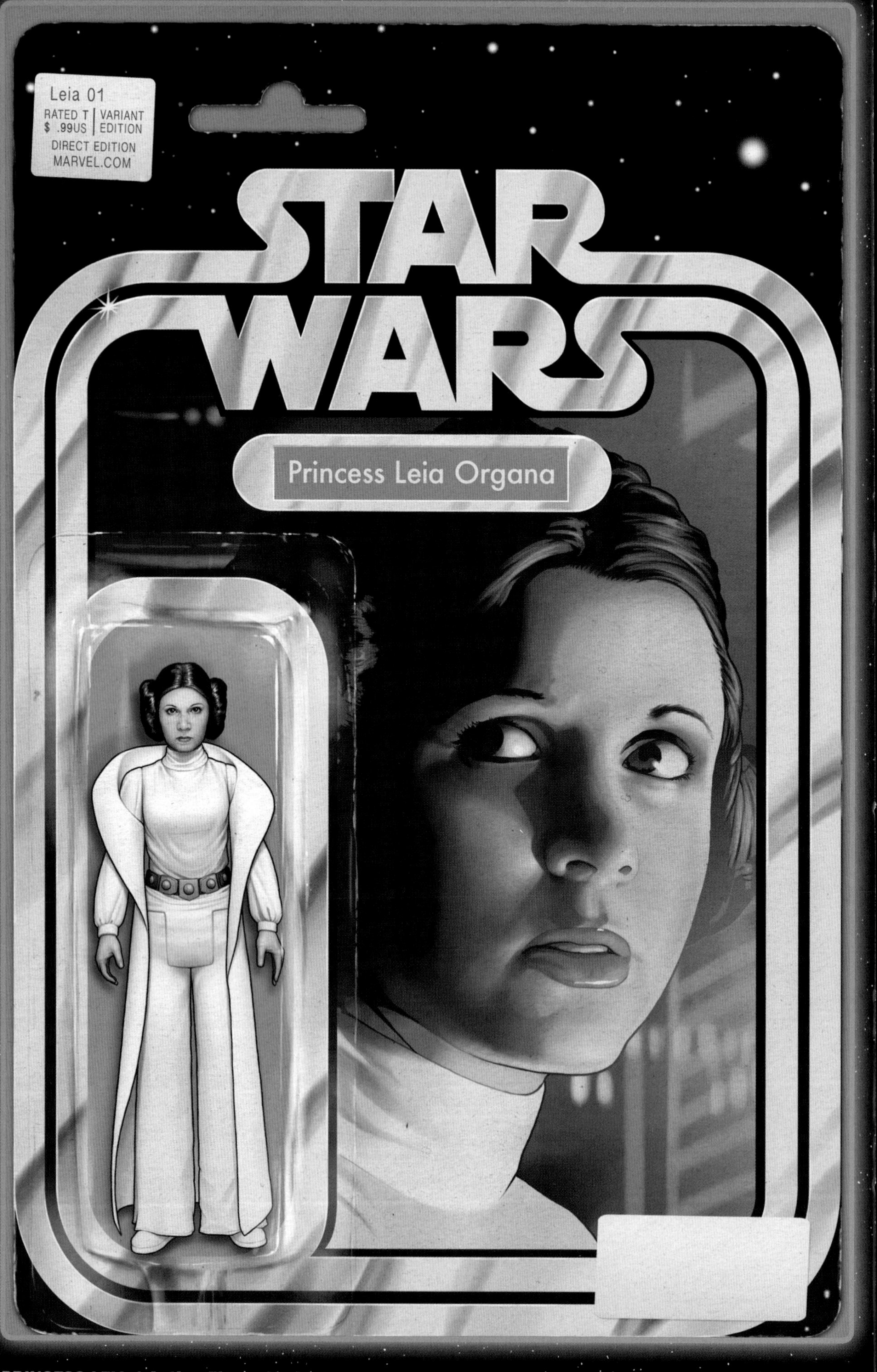
Leia 01
RATED T | VARIANT EDITION
$ .99US
DIRECT EDITION
MARVEL.COM
STAR WARS
Princess Leia Organa

PRINCESS LEIA 1 Action Figure Variant
by **JOHN TYLER CHRISTOPHER**

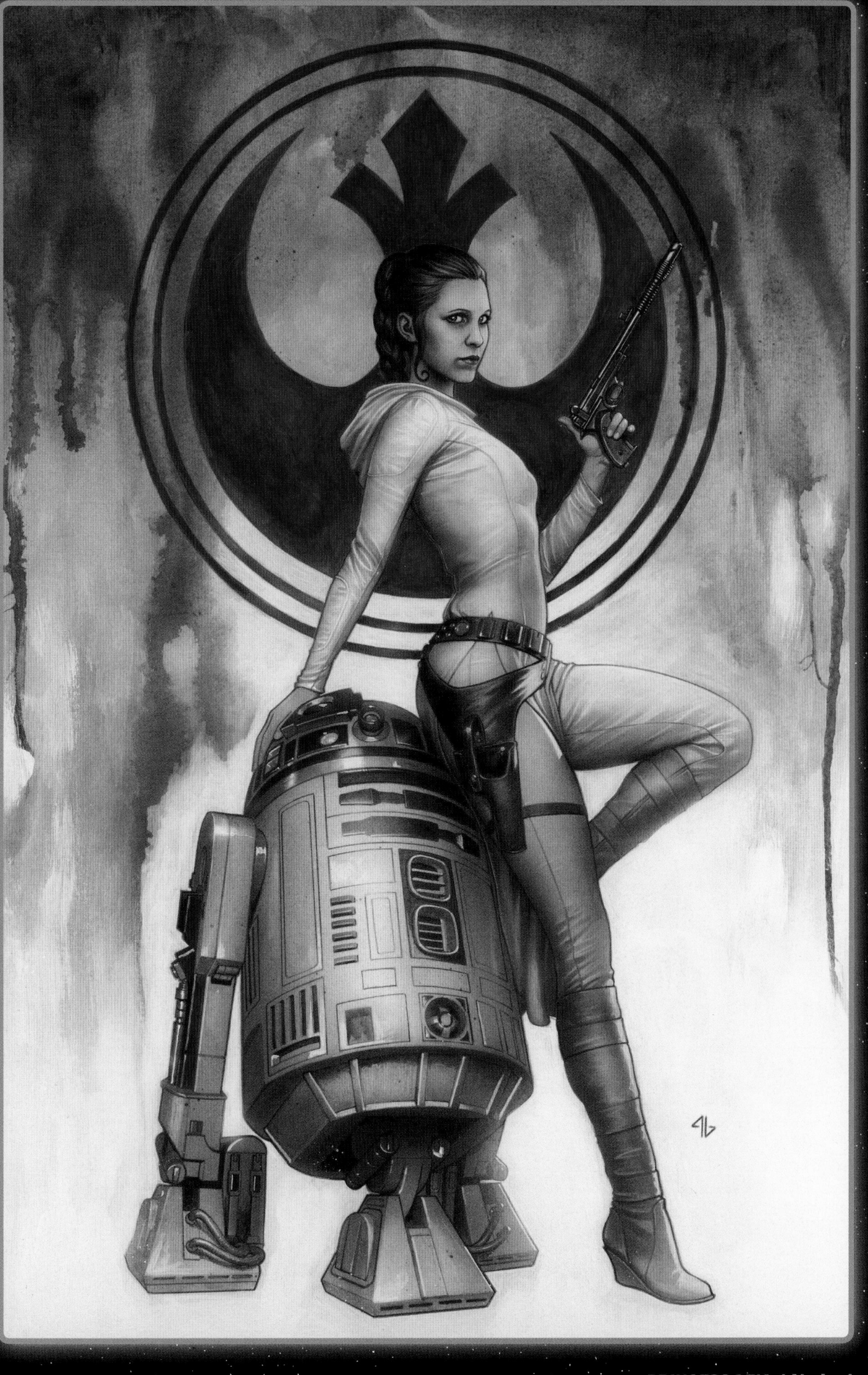

***PRINCESS LEIA* 1 Variant**
by ADI GRANOV

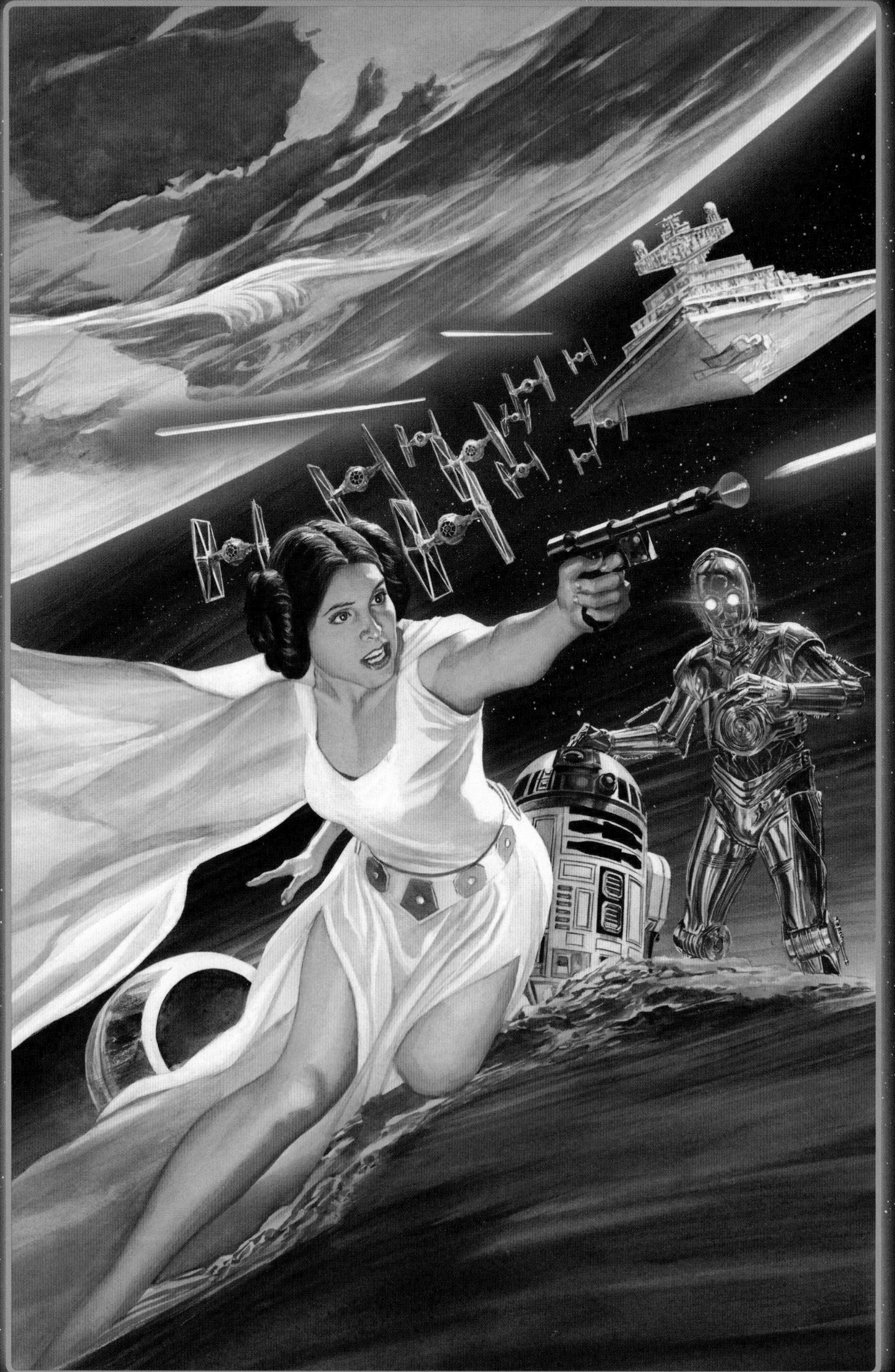

PRINCESS LEIA 1 Variant
by **ALEX ROSS**

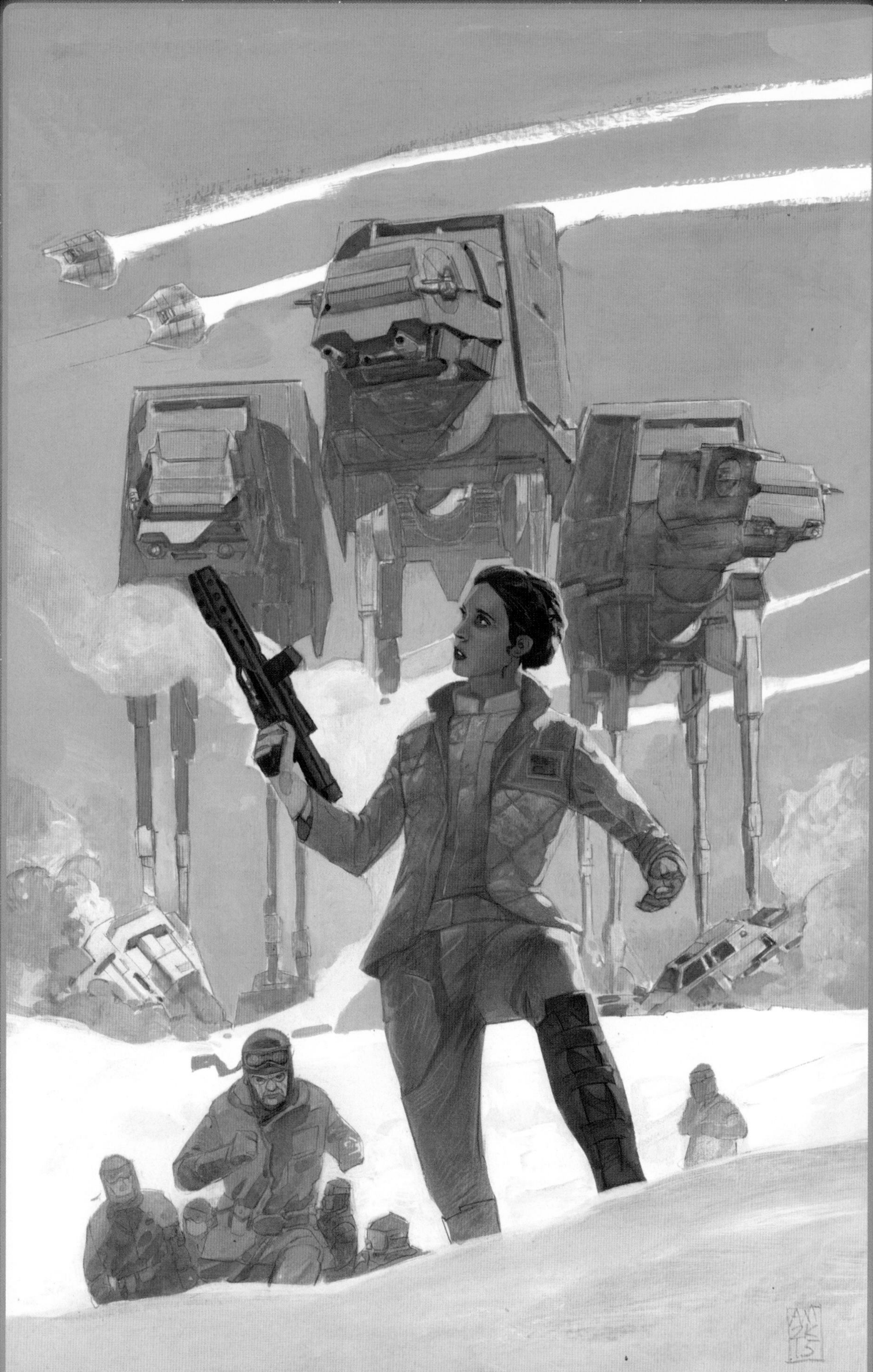

PRINCESS LEIA 2 **Variant**
by ALEX MALEEV

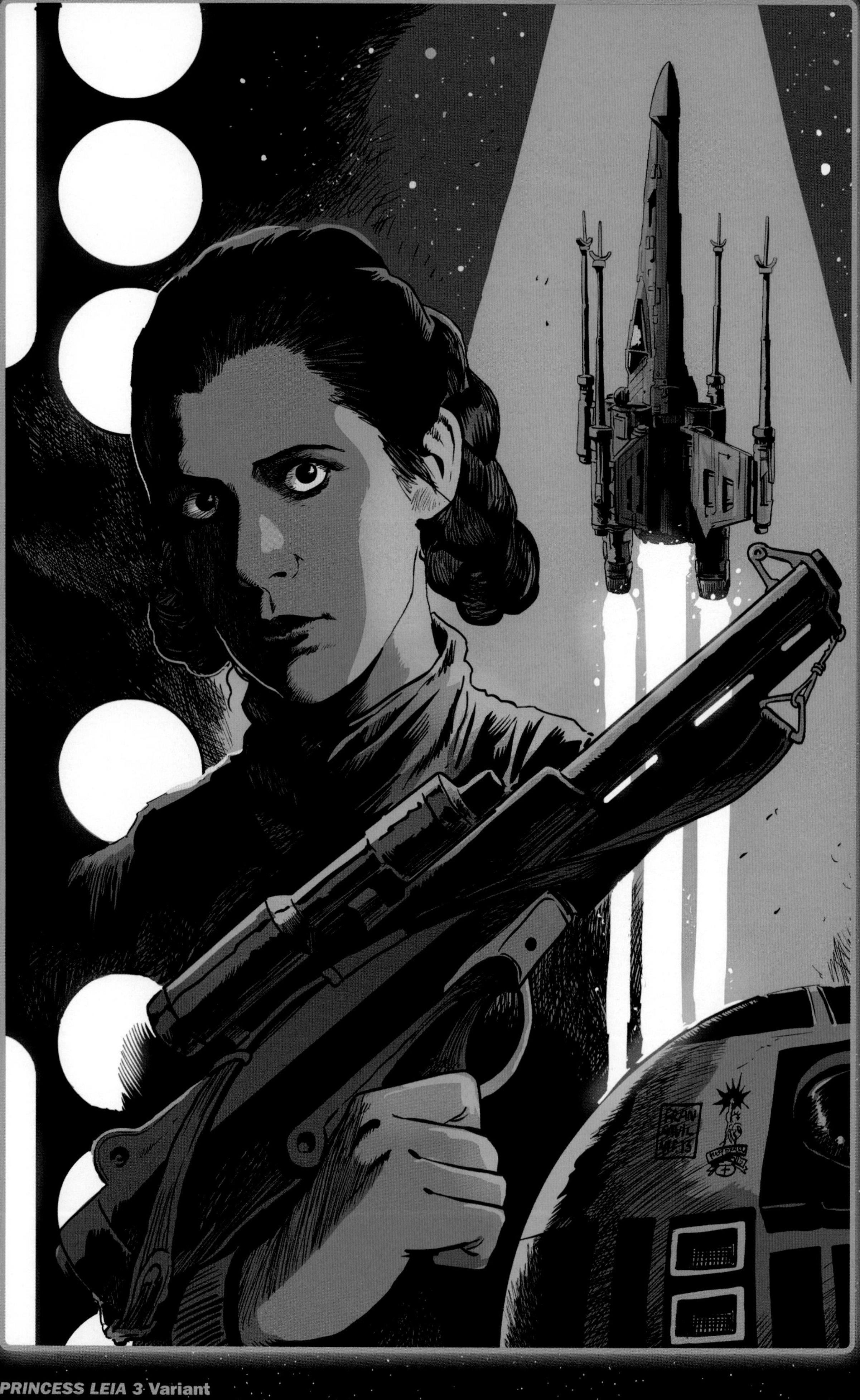

PRINCESS LEIA 3 Variant
by **FRANCESCO FRANCAVILLA**

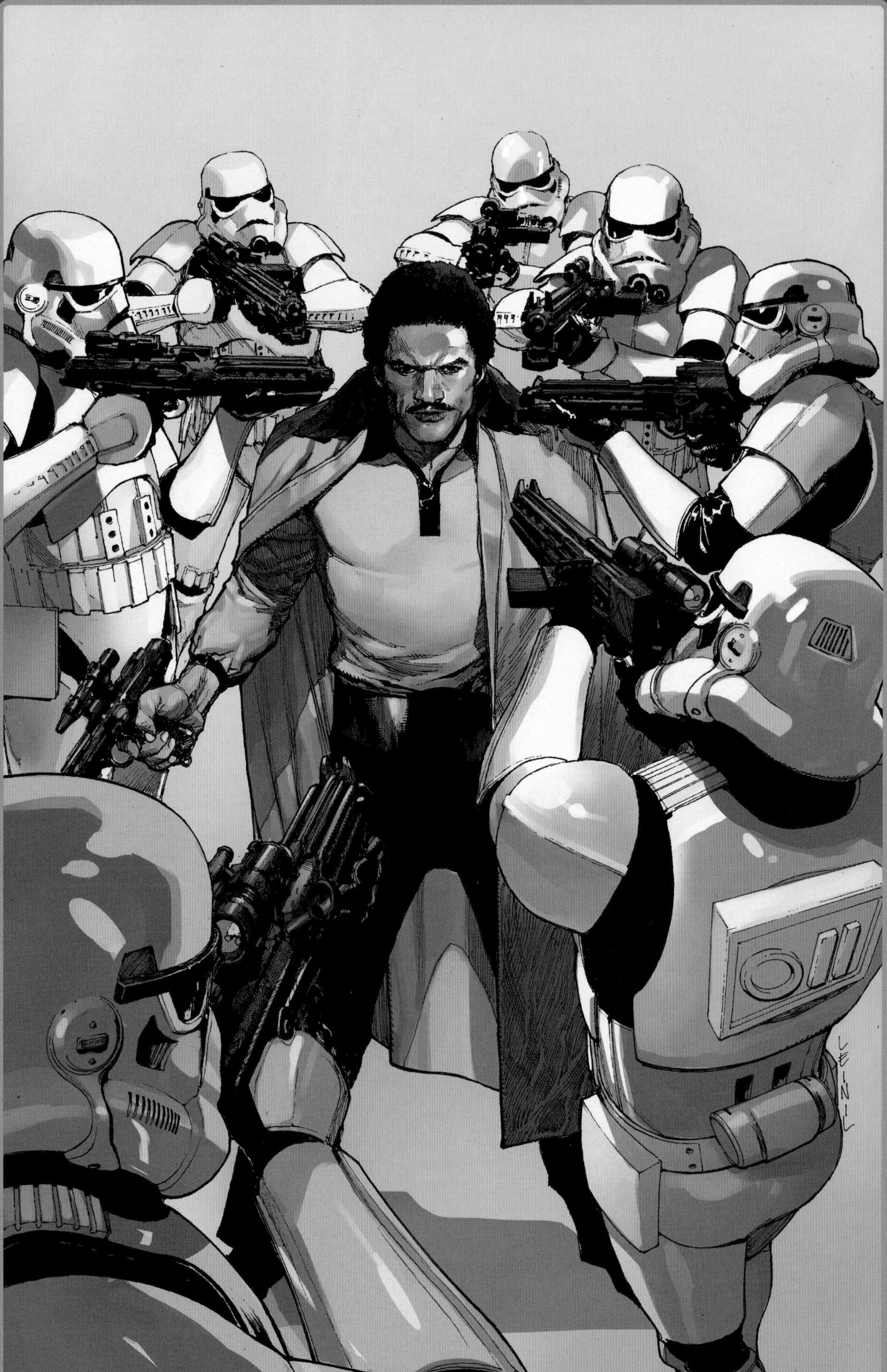
LEINIL

LANDO 1 **Variant**

by **LEINIL FRANCIS YU & SUNNY GHO**

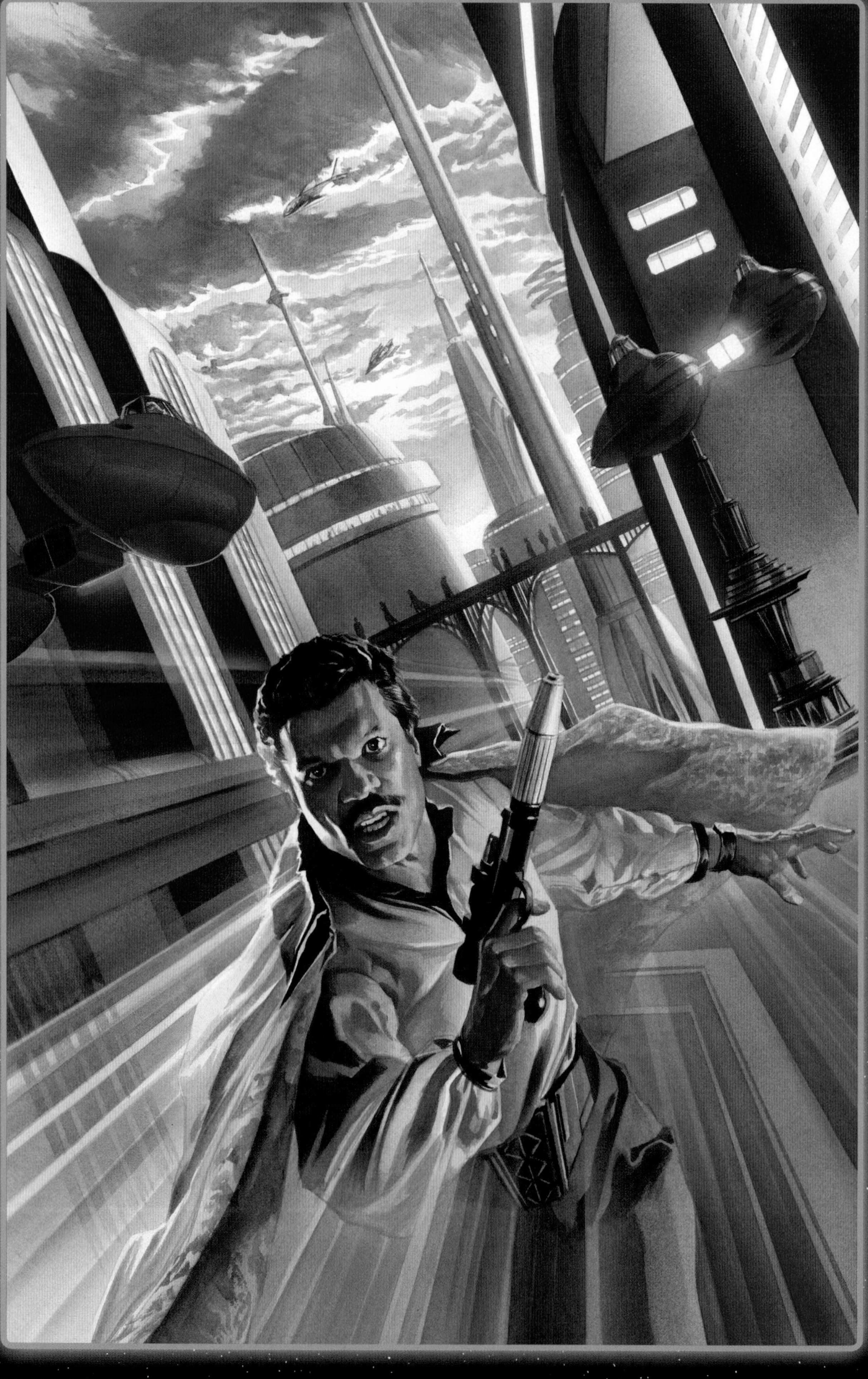

LANDO 1 Variant
by **ALEX ROSS**

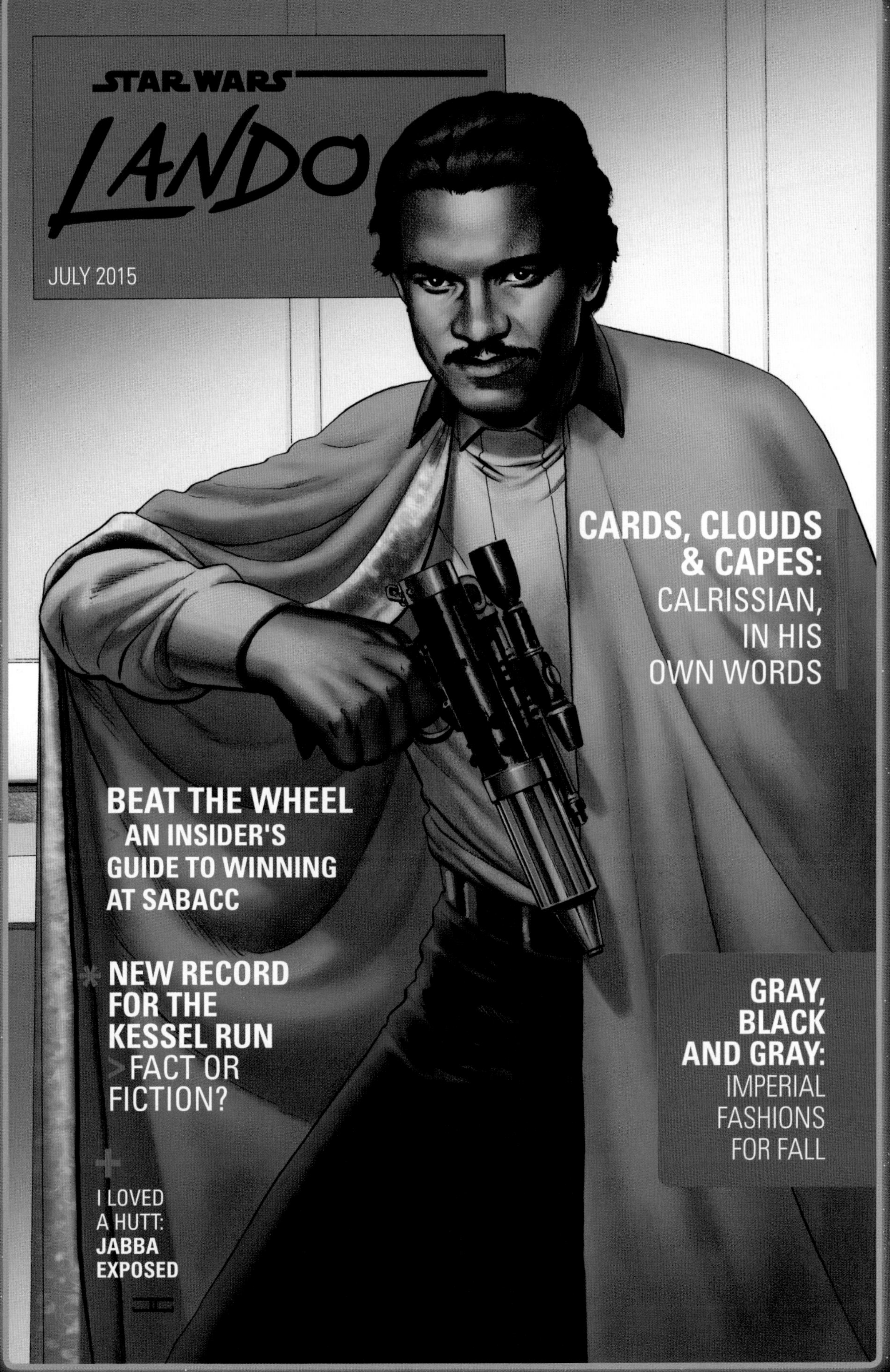
STAR WARS
LANDO
JULY 2015
CARDS, CLOUDS & CAPES: CALRISSIAN, IN HIS OWN WORDS
BEAT THE WHEEL > AN INSIDER'S GUIDE TO WINNING AT SABACC
NEW RECORD FOR THE KESSEL RUN > FACT OR FICTION?
I LOVED A HUTT: JABBA EXPOSED
GRAY, BLACK AND GRAY: IMPERIAL FASHIONS FOR FALL

LANDO 1 Variant
by JOHN CASSADAY & LAURA MARTIN

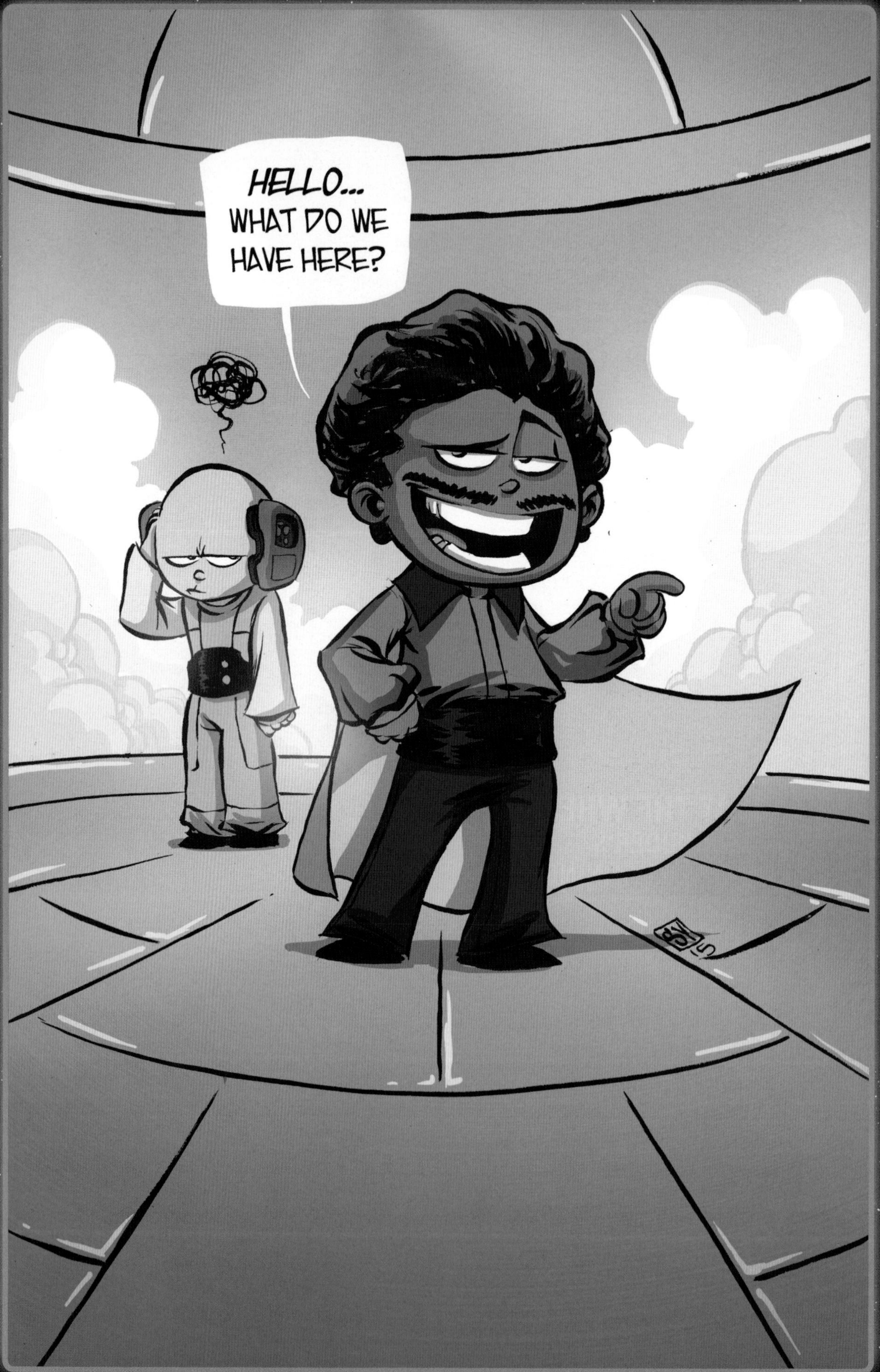
HELLO... WHAT DO WE HAVE HERE?

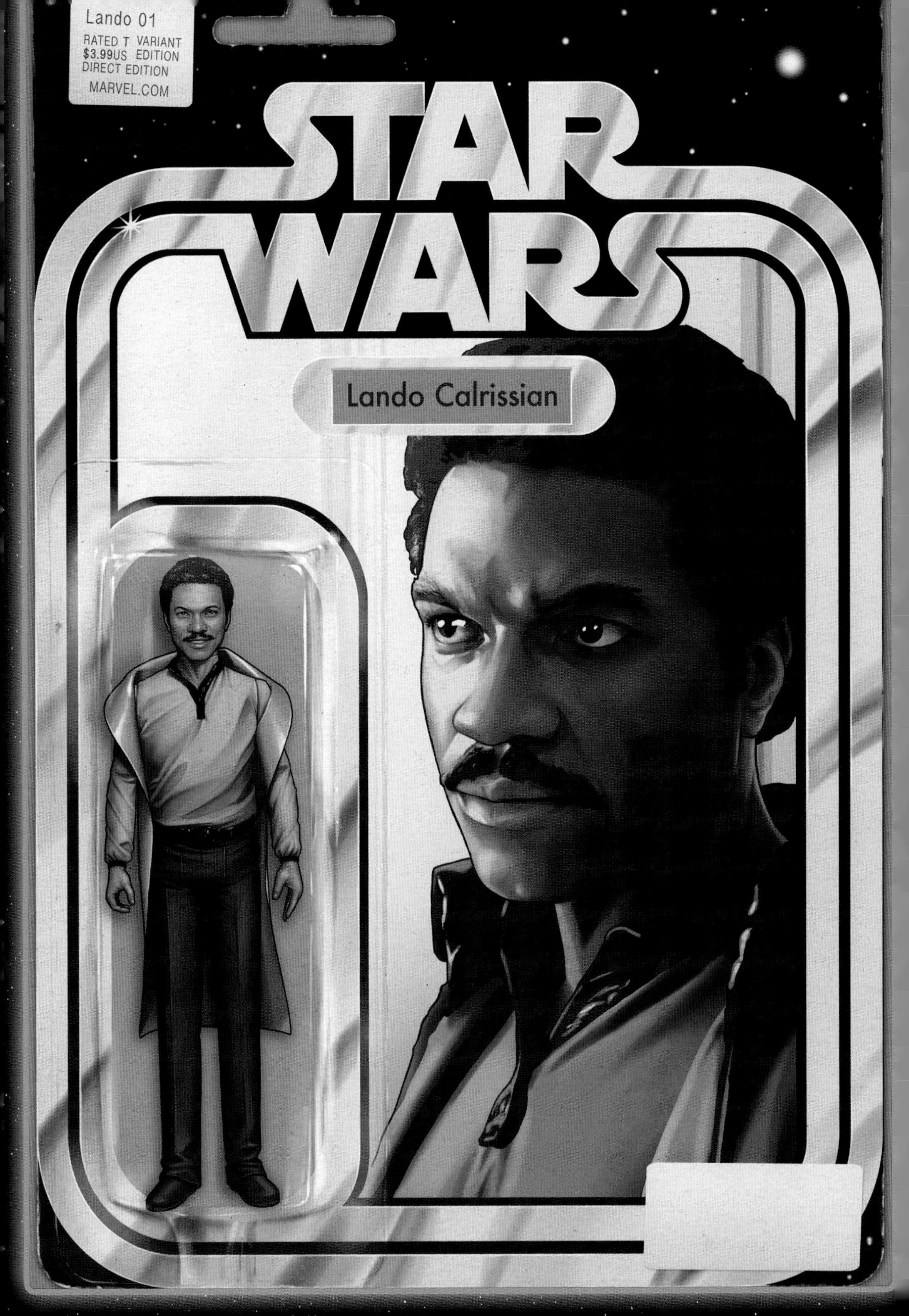
Lando 01
RATED T VARIANT
$3.99US EDITION
DIRECT EDITION
MARVEL.COM
STAR WARS
Lando Calrissian

***LANDO* 1 Action Figure Variant**

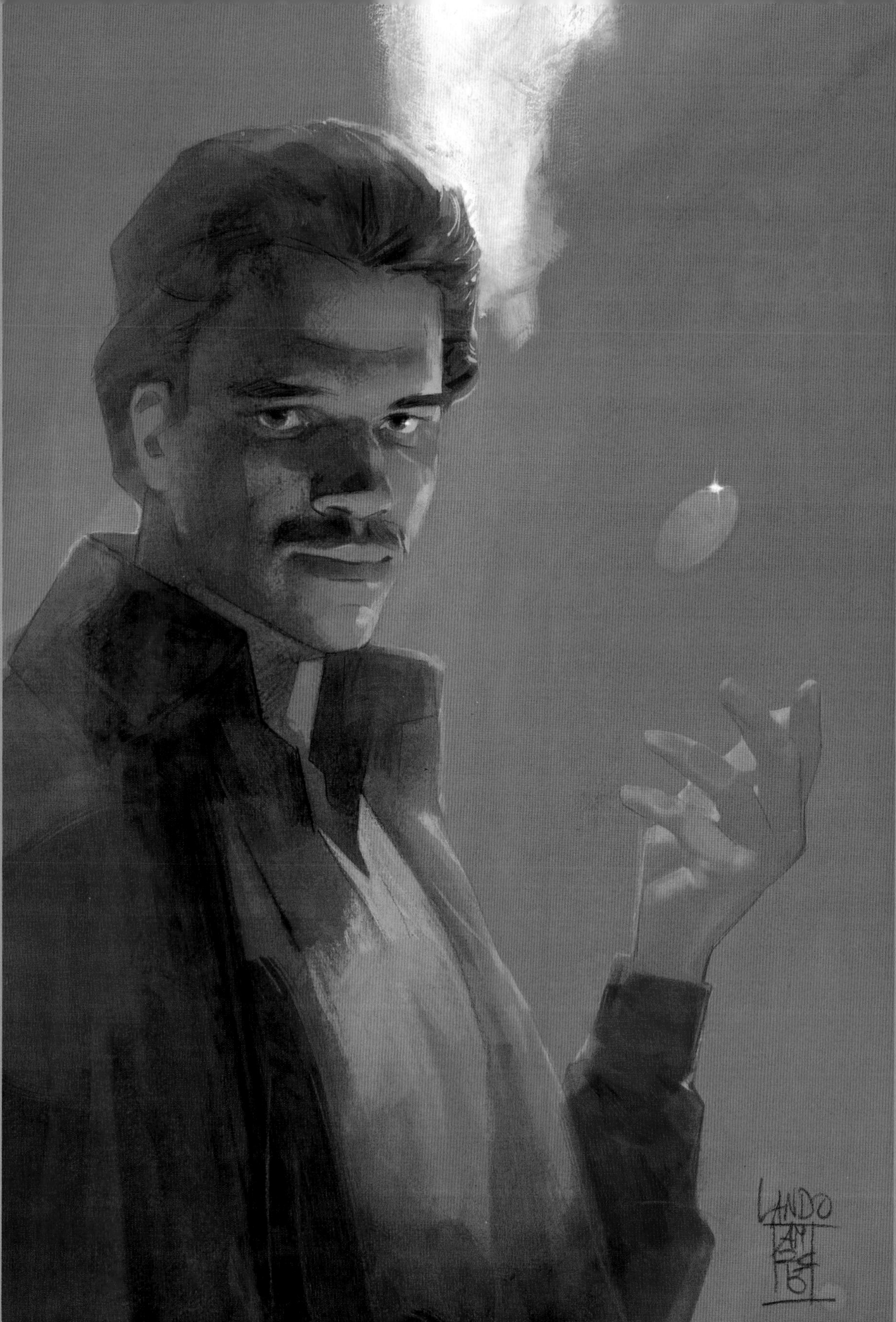
LANDO

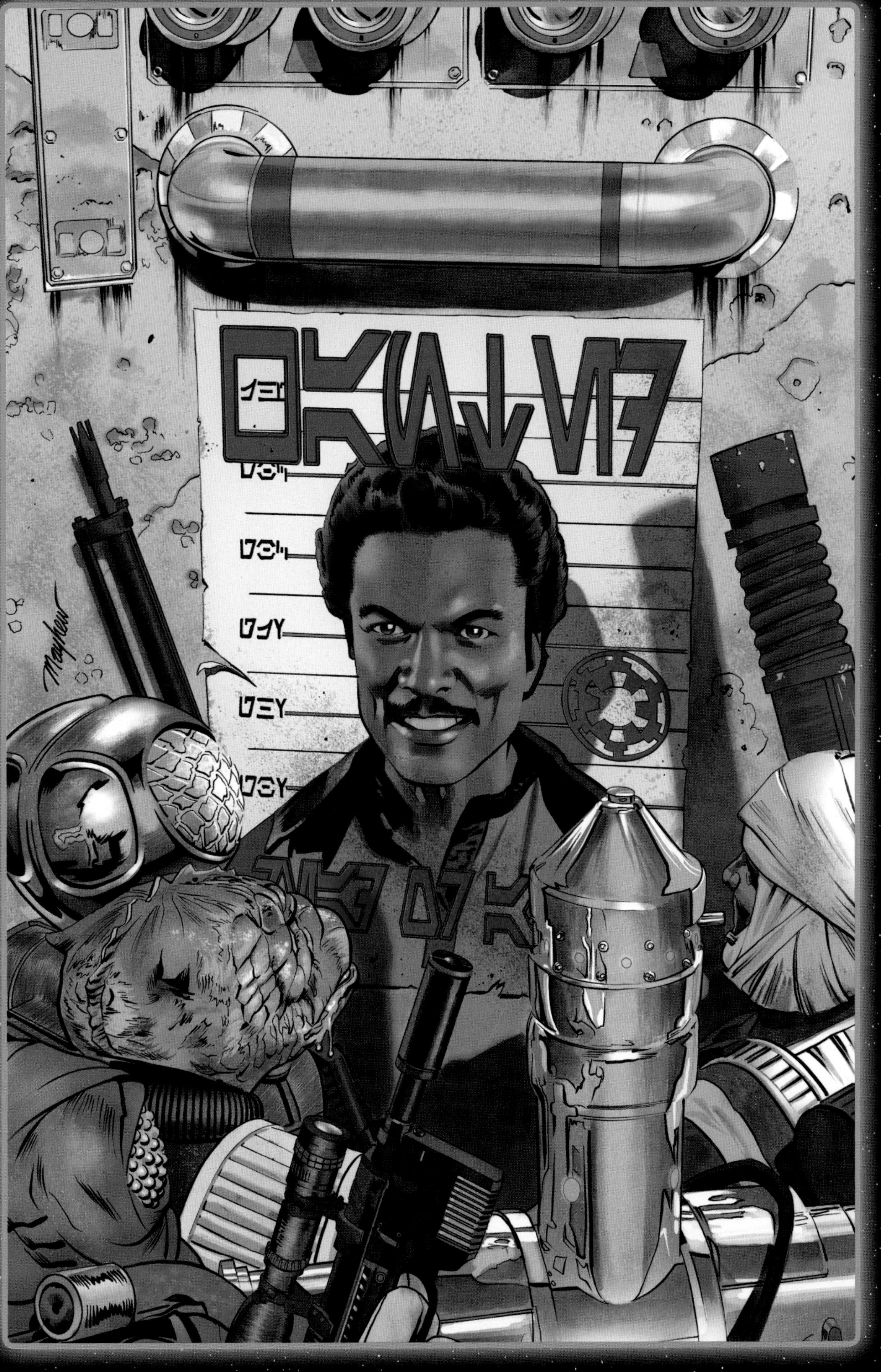

LANDO 3 Variant

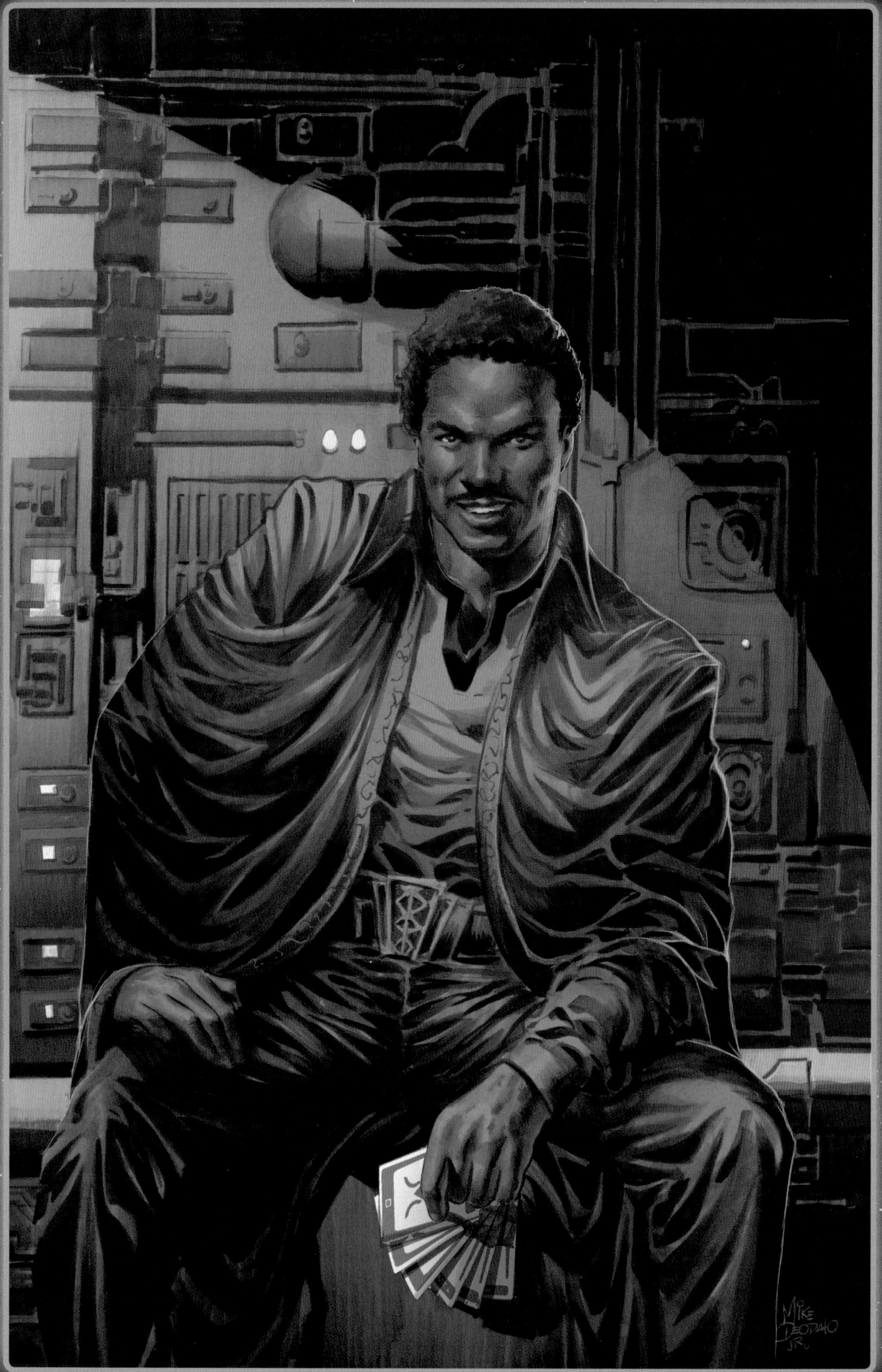

***LANDO* 5 Variant**

by MIKE DEODATO & FRANK MARTIN

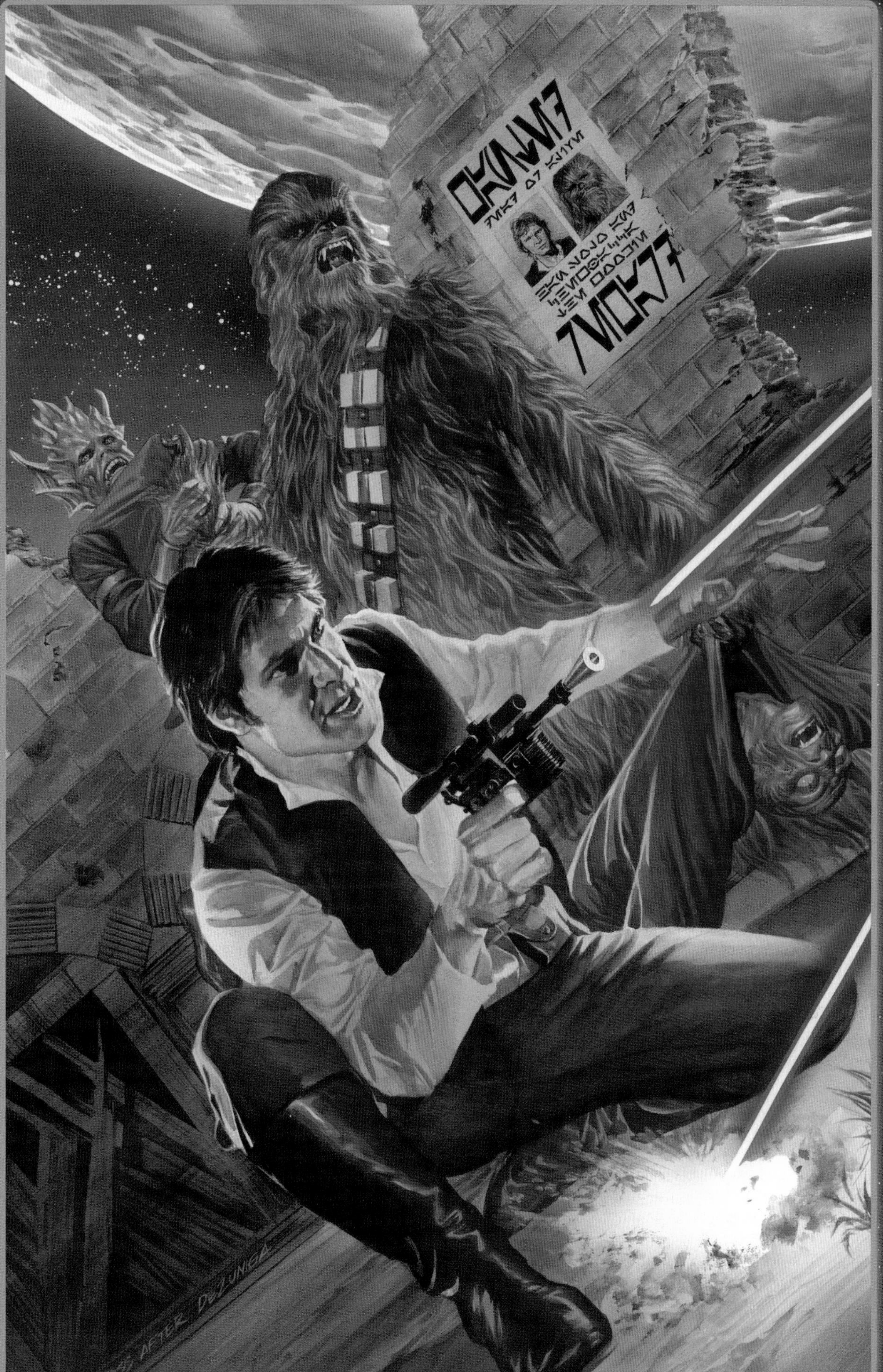
ROSS AFTER DEZUNIGA

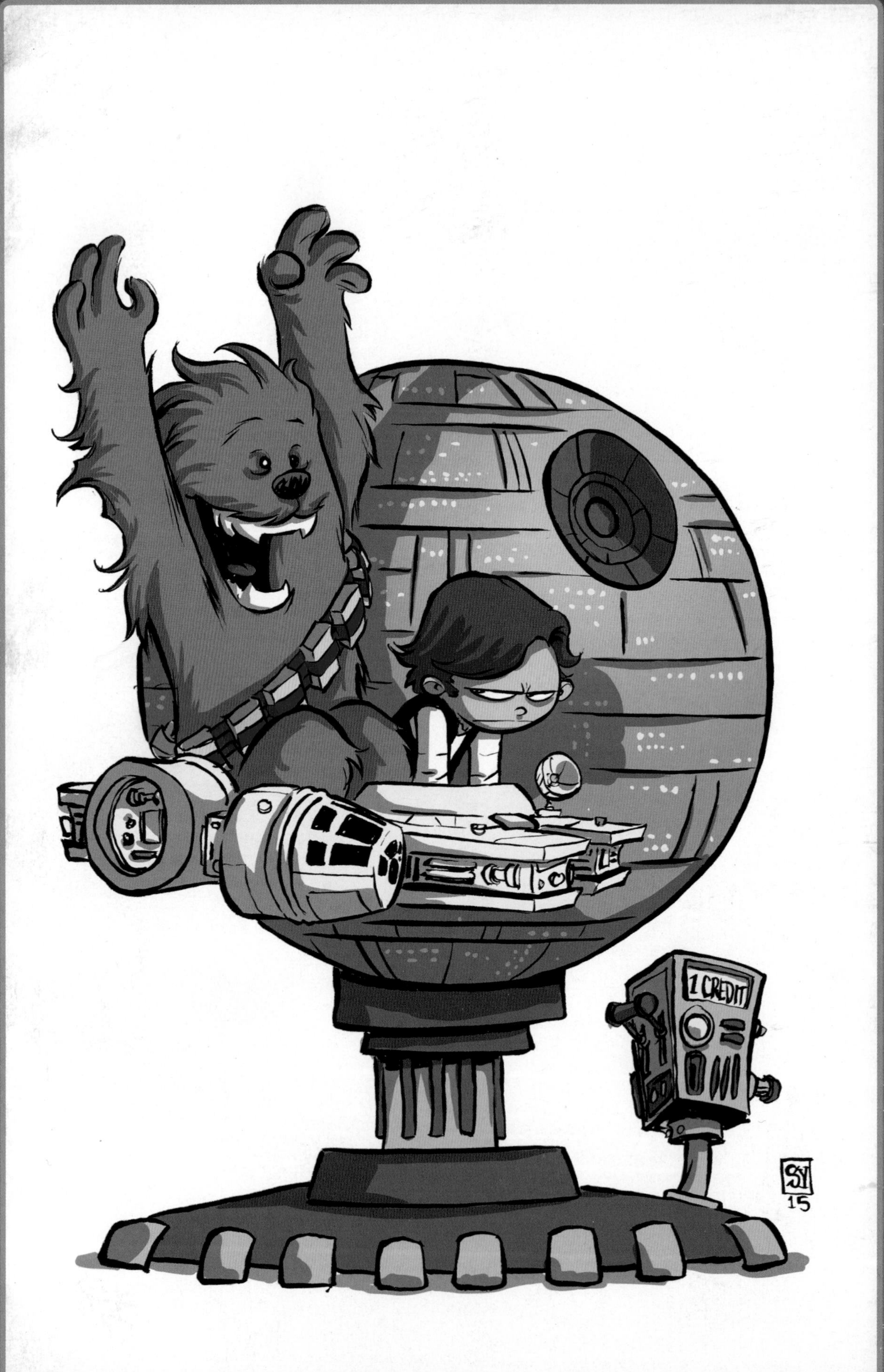
1 CREDIT
SY
15

CHEWBACCA 1 **Variant**
by **SKOTTIE YOUNG**